CORE CONCEPTS OF ACCOUNTING
Second Edition

Cecily A. Raiborn

Texas State University—San Marcos

WILEY

www.wiley.com/college/raiborn

Vice President and Publisher	*George Hoffman*
Associate Publisher	*Christopher DeJohn*
Project Editor	*Ed Brislin*
Senior Marketing Manager	*Julia Flohr*
Assistant Marketing Manager	*Diane Mars*
Production Manager	*Dorothy Sinclair*
Senior Production Editor	*Trish McFadden*
Editorial Assistant	*Kara Taylor*
Marketing Assistant	*Laura Finley*
Cover Designer	*James O'Shea*
Cover Photo	*Glowimages/Getty Images*

This book was set in Minion and printed and bound by R.R. Donnelly & Sons. The cover was printed by Phoenix Color Corp.

The book is printed on acid free paper. ∞

Copyright © 2010

This book was published by John Wiley & Sons, Inc.

ISBN-13: 978-0-470-49947-4

Printed in the United States of America

10 9 8 7 6 5 4 3 2 1

This book is dedicated to my family, friends, and students.

CONTENTS IN BRIEF

CONTENTS

PART II

ACCOUNTING FOR ASSETS   89

PART III
ACCOUNTING FOR LIABILITIES AND OWNERSHIP INTERESTS 171

7 **Liabilities 172**

PART IV
ANALYSIS OF ACCOUNTING DATA   235

PART V
MANAGERIAL ACCOUNTING   299

PREFACE

This text is designed for use in a one-semester, introductory survey of accounting class, providing the basics of both financial and managerial accounting. Financial accounting provides primarily monetary information about business activities that result in the financial statements that are published for use by people outside the business. Managerial accounting provides monetary and nonmonetary information about business activities that result in supporting details for the financial statements; it also provides information for internal organizational users to plan, control, or make decisions about operations.

The text addresses a wide variety of accounting issues and covers each in moderate depth, but the text is not intended to be a comprehensive volume in either financial or managerial accounting. Thus, supplementing the text with extended cases, online activities, and real-world discussions will provide greater breadth and depth of subject matter. To ease the inclusion of these items into course materials, the text is supported by access to a well-developed Web site.

This text is very *flexible* in its uses. It is appropriate for a one-semester course for **undergraduate nonaccounting** or **nonbusiness majors,** and with the addition of cases and current topics, it is ideal for **MBA students** who have had no prior exposure to accounting. The information contained in this text will benefit everyone going into the workforce because accounting is the language essential to economic activity worldwide. Decisions made daily use economic information and have economic consequences. Should I invest in the stock of a particular company? What will be the total cost if I take out a loan to pay for my car? How can I budget how much money I will need for the next year? All these questions can be answered using accounting information.

Although personal questions such as the preceding can be answered using accounting information, the focus of this text will be on answering questions about business. Accounting is called "the language of business" because of its usefulness in all organizational functions. The goal of this text is to present accounting as a source of information. For example, financial accounting information is commonly used when bankers are deciding whether to loan money to a company or when people are making decisions about whether to invest or disinvest in stock and bonds. Managerial accounting information is commonly used when companies are trying to determine on which products to focus their advertising budget or when sales personnel are deciding how changes in sales prices will affect organizational profitability.

Technology has made the world much smaller, and the introduction of Internet companies has created a global marketplace. Although all countries do not use the same accounting methods, basic similarities exist. Learning these basics will provide a foundation for understanding financial statements of companies, regardless of their domestic base.

The expression "Money makes the world go around" is an accurate one. And accounting essentially provides a business representation of money: where it came from and where it went; what activities occurred and how they affected profitability; what belongs to the organization and what it owes; and how changes in organizational activities could or did affect a company's performance.

ORGANIZATION AND FEATURES OF THE TEXT

This text is divided into five main parts:

I **Accounting Fundamentals** encompasses the first three chapters and presents an introduction to business organizations, defines accounting, and discusses the role of accounting in business. Concepts and principles underlying the preparation of financial statements are explained and illustrated. Double-entry bookkeeping rules, which are necessary to provide the groundwork for the preparation of financial statements, are introduced, and the activities necessary to start and complete the accounting cycle are covered.

II **Accounting for Assets**, which includes the next three chapters, discusses the majority of short-term and long-term assets (cash, accounts receivable, inventory, plant assets, and intangibles).

III **Accounting for Liabilities and Ownership Interests** contains two chapters. The first covers corporate debt, including short-term payables, contingent liabilities, bonds payable, and other long-term payables. The second addresses the corporate form of business organization and accounting for the various elements of stockholders' equity.

IV **Analysis of Accounting Data**, which includes the final two financial chapters, covers the composition of a corporate income statement, including discontinued operations, extraordinary items, and differences between accounting and taxable income. Accounting for long-term investments in stocks and bonds is also discussed. Methods of analyzing financial statement data are discussed as well as the issue of earnings quality and earnings management. This section also addresses the preparation and use of a Statement of Cash Flows.

V **Managerial Accounting** contains four chapters on information for use by internal decision makers. Differences between financial and managerial accounting are discussed, and managerial accounting terms are defined. Product costing systems and activity-based costing are introduced. Cost-volume-profit relationships, incremental costs in decision making, and the budgeting process (and its use of standard costs) are presented. The final chapter discusses how to measure and assess performance in differing organizational settings.

The text contains many features that make it friendly, flexible, and easy to understand:

Visual Recaps

Some accounting topics are more easily understood by examining them graphically rather than through reading. Thus, wherever appropriate, **Visual Recaps** are provided to illustrate significant topics in a pictorial manner or summarized in a table. These recaps are intended to capture the "one picture is worth a thousand words" adage and help students comprehend and retain concepts. For example, in Chapter 9, accounting methods for long-term investments in other companies are summarized in a simple table that recaps accounting treatment for investments, dividends, and earnings at all ownership levels. In Chapter 11, costs associated with raw material, work in process, and finished goods inventories, as well as other accounts, are depicted in a flow diagram with descriptions of each cost flow and arrows showing direction.

Accounting Information for Decision Making

Most financial chapters include a section entitled **Accounting Information for Decision Making**. This section is designed to emphasize a user (rather than preparer) perspective of accounting information. These sections will address how external parties can analyze and interpret the types of information discussed in the chapter. For example, in Chapter 4 on Cash, Short-Term Investments, and Accounts Receivable, this section addresses issues such as the decision to extend credit to customers and how to calculate and determine the meaning of the accounts receivable turnover ratio and age of accounts receivable. These chapter sections will be very beneficial for students who will not be accountants, but are taking accounting to understand financial statement amounts.

End-of-Chapter Materials and Icons

Each chapter contains a summary, key terms list, and a variety of questions, exercises, problems, and short cases for in-class discussion or homework. Some of these end-of-chapter items are marked with icons to indicate that they will address writing, ethical, and team-work skills. Other end-of-chapter items will provide faculty the option to have students use the Internet or work in groups. In addition, learning objectives are listed and numbered at the beginning of each chapter. End-of-chapter questions, exercises, problems, and cases are identified by learning objective number, making it simple to include or exclude end-of-chapter materials that pertain to topics covered or not covered in your course.

writing

ethics

Internet

group

Changes from the First Edition

- *Streamlined approach:* The second edition of *Core Concepts of Accounting* has been reformatted in a way that conveys the importance of the material to students. Real-world examples and ethical coverage are now incorporated into the main text rather than in boxed features. These changes add to the chapter's flow and readability by allowing readers to move more quickly through the chapter's substance.

- *International Financial Reporting Standards (IFRS):* Where appropriate, discussion of IFRSs is included when such standards differ from the generally accepted standards used in the United States.

- *End-of-chapter materials:* Additional questions, exercises, problems, cases, and supplementary items have been added to provide greater variety in course assignments.

- *Visual Recaps:* More Visual Recaps have been included to illustrate concepts or summarize material in a short and easily understandable format.

- *New real-world examples:* More examples of specific accounting applications are provided for companies (with their related URLs).

Supplemental Materials for Instructors and Students

This text is accompanied by several supplements for use by instructors and/or students.

Solutions Manual—The solutions manual gives solutions to all end-of-chapter questions, exercises, problems, and supplemental problems. Solutions are also given for the majority of cases, except those requiring students to select their own companies and make team analyses.

Instructors' Manual—The instructors' manual contains sample syllabi, a listing of chapter terms, chapter lecture outlines, an assignment difficulty table indicating the level of difficulty of all end-of-chapter materials, and teaching tips for each chapter.

Test Bank—The test bank provides true/false statements, multiple-choice questions, and short exercises for each chapter. There are approximately 50 questions for each chapter.

Web Site—See the comprehensive web site at www.wiley.com/college/raiborn for more information and resources.

ACKNOWLEDGMENTS

I would like to thank the many people who have helped me during the development of this text. The constructive comments and suggestions made by the following reviewers were instrumental in developing, rewriting, and improving the quality and readability of this book.

My gratitude goes out to Chris Knapp, Carol Knapp, and Stephanie Watson, who worked on prior versions of this text. Special thanks to my graduate assistant, Frank Mudzinganyama, who put in countless hours working with me on the solutions manual and to those that helped prepare the accompanying test bank and instructor's manual. In addition, Christopher DeJohn and Kara Taylor of John Wiley & Sons, Inc. who encouraged and supported me throughout the project.

ABOUT THE AUTHOR

Cecily A. Raiborn

Cecily A. Raiborn is the McCoy Endowed Chair in Accounting at Texas State University–San Marcos. She graduated from Louisiana State University with a Ph.D. in Accounting and has earned a CPA, CMA, and CrFA. She received the AICPA/Louisiana CPA Society Outstanding Educator Award in 1991. Raiborn has coauthored several textbooks and has been published in a wide variety of professional journals, including *Journal of Business Ethics, Journal of Corporate Accounting and Finance, Advances in Management Accounting, CPA Journal, Review of Business, Journal of Accounting Case Research, Business Horizons,* and *Strategic Finance.* Professional and honorary memberships include the American Accounting Association (Management Accounting section), Institute of Management Accountants, Texas Society of CPAs, Association of Certified Fraud Examiners, Beta Alpha Psi, Phi Delta Gamma, and Phi Kappa Phi. In addition to the academic setting, her work experience includes the manufacturing and not-for-profit sectors.

ACCOUNTING FUNDAMENTALS

CHAPTER 1

An Introduction to the Role of Accounting in the Business World

LEARNING OBJECTIVES

1. Identify the major types of business entities, their principal legal forms, and their key internal functions.
2. Identify the primary means by which accountants communicate financial information to decision makers.
3. Briefly describe how financial data are collected by an organization's accounting system.
4. Define the nature, structure, and major segments of the accounting profession.
5. Discuss some key changes taking place in the accounting profession.

INTRODUCTION

Well-known names in the business world include Bill Gates (Microsoft), Steve Jobs (Apple), Oprah Winfrey (Harpo, Inc.), and Sam Walton (Wal-Mart). Studying case histories of such individuals uncovers several similarities, but probably the most important trait common to these people is an ability to make wise economic decisions. Faced with limited economic resources—money, land, equipment, and so on—these business icons exhibited a knack for knowing how to wisely allocate what little they did have to maximize the profitability of their new ventures. Part of their ability to make wise choices stems from their reliance on accounting to provide the information necessary for decision making. **Accounting** provides quantitative information about economic entities that is intended to be useful in making economic decisions.

This chapter provides an introduction to the business world, including the different types of businesses, their legal forms, and their key internal functions. Next, the accounting functions of business organizations are examined more closely. Last, the ways in which accountants communicate financial data to decision makers and accounting systems collect financial data for business organizations are also discussed.

MAJOR TYPES OF BUSINESS ENTITIES

A **business** is an organization that attempts to earn a return over the cost of providing services or goods that satisfy the needs or wants of others.[1] Businesses are typically categorized into three broad groups: service, manufacturing, and merchandising companies.

Service companies do not "create" goods, but instead, provide an activity or fulfill a demand that has value to their customers. Service businesses include professional sports teams, theme parks, professional firms (legal, advertising, physicians, and the like), airlines, financial institutions, dry cleaners, day-care operators, and dating matchmaking companies.

Alternatively, manufacturing firms generate new goods by converting one or more raw materials into finished products. The finished products, whether handcrafted or high tech, are then typically sold to other manufacturers or to merchandising companies, rather than directly to customers. These firms include auto, food, airplane, computer, semiconductor, clothing, video game, CD/DVD, and steel producers. Manufacturers may be domestic or foreign based.

There are two types of merchandising companies: wholesalers and retailers. Both wholesalers and retailers purchase goods in large quantities from the producer. Rather than selling directly to consumers, a wholesaler acts as a middleman and resells goods (often in smaller lot sizes) to other wholesalers; industrial, commercial, or institutional users; or to retailers. A retailer sells products directly to end consumers; retailers are considered the "end of the supply chain." Retail merchandisers may also sell their goods by mail order, on a door-to-door basis, and/or on the Internet. As shown in Exhibit 1-1, the United States (U.S.) has more retail establishments than it has wholesalers, and retailers employ

---

[1]Some organizations exist as not-for-profit entities and, as such, provide services or goods to others but seek to do so without the underlying goal of generating profits. These organizations often focus on humanitarian, cultural, social, environmental, and religious endeavors.

Information on
Wholesalers and
Retailers in the U.S.
(for 2002)

Kind of Business	Establishments	Sales (in billions)	Paid employees
Wholesale trade	435,521	$4,635	5,878,000
Retail trade	1,114,637	$3,056	14,648,000

SOURCE   U.S. Census Bureau, 2002 Economic Census, *Wholesale Trade, Geographic Area Series, United States: 2002* (EC02–42A-1US) and *Retail Trade, Geographic Area Series, United States: 2002* (EC02–44A-1US); http://www.census.gov/compendia/statab/tables/08s1009.pdf (accessed 9/3/08)

more people than do wholesalers, but wholesalers generate approximately 50 percent more dollars of sales than retailers.

Common Legal Forms of Business Organizations

U.S. businesses operate in many different legal forms, including sole proprietorships, partnerships, and corporations. In the U.S., the most common form of business organization is the sole proprietorship. However, as indicated in Exhibit 1-2, corporations produce more goods and services than all the sole proprietorships and partnerships combined and, therefore, account for the majority of the total annual business revenues and profits. A **sole proprietorship** is a business owned by one individual. Often, sole proprietorships are service-oriented. A **partnership** is a business with two or more owners. Many large law and accounting firms are partnerships, with several hundred partners. Profits of sole proprietorships and partnerships are taxed to the owner(s) as individuals; the business organization itself pays no taxes.

A **corporation** is a legal "being" that exists separately from its owners, who are called **stockholders**. A corporation can have any number of stockholders, as long as that number is consistent with the laws of the state of incorporation. This type of business entity has some of the same rights (such as the ability to own and transfer property) and duties (such as the requirement to pay taxes) as individuals. Many corporations, such as Wal-Mart (www.walmart.com) and Ben & Jerry's (www.benjerry.com), began as either sole proprietorships or partnerships.

A corporation has several advantages over a sole proprietorship or partnership, the most important of which is limited liability. In a corporation, the stockholders have limited monetary and legal responsibility for the company's actions; that is, only a stockholder's current investment is at risk should the corporation owe more than it can pay. The same cannot be said for sole proprietorships and partnerships. In a lawsuit against a corporation, the plaintiffs can only recover any settlement or judgment from the corporation's assets, not from the personal assets of the firm's stockholders. If a sole proprietorship or partnership has debt that cannot be paid from company holdings, the owners are responsible for paying that debt,

Sole Proprietorships,
Partnerships, and
Corporations in the
U.S. (for 2004)

	Nonfarm Proprietorships	Partnerships	Corporations
Number	20,591	2,547	5,558
Sales (in billions)	$1,140	$3,142	$21,717
Net Income (in billions)	$248	$385	$1,112

SOURCE   U.S. Internal Revenue Service, *Statistics of Income*, various publications, Table 721. Number of Returns, Receipts, and Net Income by Type of Business: 1990 to 2004; http://www.census.gov/compendia/statab/tables/08s0721.pdf (accessed 9/3/08)

even if it must be paid out of the owners' personal assets. In fact, one partner could be forced to pay all of a partnership's debts if the other partners were unable to pay their "fair" share.

Three other forms of organizations are the LLP (limited liability partnership), LLC (limited liability corporation), and Subchapter S (Sub S) corporation. Each of these business forms is a hybrid between a partnership and a corporation and provides limited liability to owners. However, the owners are taxed as individuals, and the organization is not taxed as a separate legal entity.

This text concentrates on the accounting function of corporations. Most accounting issues faced by large corporations are similar, if not identical, to the accounting issues faced by smaller, unincorporated businesses. Visual Recap 1.1 summarizes the various forms of organizations.

Internal Functions of Business Organizations

Every large company has numerous internal functions that help the firm grow and succeed. Most business owners recognize that they do not have all the necessary skills to perform all these functions effectively. Therefore, owners hire individuals who have specialized skills and training. Management, marketing, finance, and accounting are among the most commonly recognized business disciplines. Within each of these disciplines is an array of "subspecialties." For example, the management function includes production management, human resource management, and strategy. Marketing functions include advertising, consumer behavior, and distribution. A person in the finance area may plan bond and stock issuances or investments in other companies. An internal accountant may be involved with the preparation of financial statements, internal cost analyses, tax return preparation, or outsourcing decisions.

This course focuses on two primary areas of the internal accounting function of business organizations: financial accounting and managerial accounting. Every working person needs to be familiar with accounting functions because he or she will probably be affected by the information they provide. Effective sales managers, personnel specialists, and chief executive officers must understand an organization's accounting functions because that understanding allows those individuals to properly interpret accounting data and recognize limitations of that data. People in the performing arts need to have a grasp of accounting information because engagements often hinge on the profitability of the performance. Advertising firms will be retained (or released) because of the sales revenues (or lack thereof) generated from commercials and media blitzes. Certainly, anyone who decides to invest money in the stock market should understand the financial statements

VISUAL RECAP 1.1

Forms and Characteristics of Business Organizations

	Sole Proprietorships	Partnerships	Corporations
Number	17,176,000	1,759,000	4,710,000
Sales (in billions)	$870	$1,297	$15,889
Profits (in billions)	$187	$1,686	$915

SOURCE   U.S. Census Bureau, *Statistical Abstract of the U.S.* (2000), p. 536

prepared by the companies in which investments are to be made. In other words, accounting is the language of business, and most people interact on a daily basis in some way with business enterprises.

THE NATURE AND ROLE OF ACCOUNTING IN BUSINESS

To make wise decisions regarding the use of money, equipment, or people, business executives must have ready access to a wide array of financial information regarding their firms. For example, in the mid-1970s, Federal Express (www.fedex.com) was almost forced to file for bankruptcy. A sudden and significant increase in fuel prices resulting from a Middle Eastern oil crisis caused Federal Express to begin losing more than $1 million per month. Based on information supplied by the firm's accounting department, FedEx was able to quickly implement cost containment measures that saved the company from financial ruin, allowing FedEx instead to become part of both the *Fortune* 500 and the Global 500 companies.[2]

In today's business world, accountants provide the majority of information needed by executives to make critical business decisions. In the current Information Age, accountants serve as information merchants for the business world. First and foremost, accounting is a service activity. Its function is "to provide quantitative information, primarily financial in nature, about economic entities that is intended to be useful in making economic decisions—in making reasoned choices among alternative courses of action."[3] Thus, accounting is a means to assist a wide variety of parties in making economic decisions. Accountants generally segregate decision makers into two groups: internal and external. Internal decision makers are executives or employees of a given entity. External decision makers, on the other hand, are third parties (such as investors, suppliers, and bank loan officers) who do not have ready access to an organization's financial records or accountants.

Internal Decision Makers

Within an organization, accounting information is used by a variety of people for a number of different purposes. CEOs use accounting information on the profitability of a division or a store to determine that manager's bonus. Sales staff members use accounting information to assess a customer's credit payment history. Purchasing agents use accounting information to determine how many parts are needed to complete production for the upcoming period. Factory shop workers use accounting information to know how long it should take to make one unit of product.

The accounting information used by internal decision makers may be either monetary or nonmonetary. Additionally, that information may be prepared in different formats to suit the needs of the individual decision maker. Some of this information may appear on the external financial statements, but much of it will not. Much accounting information is generated merely to help internal parties understand how to perform their tasks in an efficient and effective manner and how their operations generate and use money.

---

[2] In 2008, FedEx's rankings were 68 and 214, respectively, for the *Fortune* 500 and Global 500.

[3] Accounting Principles Board, *Statement Number 4: Basic Concepts and Accounting Principles Underlying Financial Statements of a Business Enterprise* (New York: AICPA, 1970), para. 40.

External Decision Makers

As indicated in Exhibit 1-3, numerous groups of people and institutions comprise the category "external decision makers." External users employ financial statements as input to a wide range of decisions, including whether to invest in a given company, whether to grant credit to a company, or, in the case of a regulatory authority, whether a company is complying with specific regulations. Financial statements are the principal means that accountants use to communicate financial information to external decision makers.

Most large companies prepare an annual financial report that is distributed to the public. This report contains a set of **financial statements** that, taken together, provide information on the financial performance of the organization over a period of time and at a specific time. Companies now commonly include their financial statements and annual reports on their Web sites, usually in the category entitled Investor Relations.

FINANCIAL STATEMENT DEFINITIONS

The form and content of financial statements are specified by formal accounting rules, concepts, and principles called **generally accepted accounting principles** (GAAP). The phrase "generally accepted" is important because most accounting principles were established from general acceptance or usage over time.[4] Presently, the **Financial Accounting Standards Board** (FASB) is the principal accounting rule-making authority within the United States.[5] The FASB (www.fasb.org) is not a government agency; it is an independent, private-sector body that receives more than half its funds from the public accounting profession and the rest from industry and the financial community.

An annual financial report is the primary communication of financial information to external users. Among other items, the annual report contains four major financial statements and their related footnotes: a balance sheet, an income statement, a statement

EXHIBIT 1-3		
External Decision Makers	**Type of Decision Maker**	**Use of Financial Statements**
	Stockholders and potential investors	Determine return on investment; estimate future returns and profitability
	Bankers and suppliers	Determine ability to repay loans and pay for purchases
	Securities and Exchange Commission and other regulatory agencies	Determine compliance with regulations
	Internal Revenue Service	Determine reliability of amounts found on tax returns

---

[4]These principles are discussed in Chapter 2.

[5]The FASB is in the process of converging its standards with the International Financial Reporting Standards (IFRSs) of the International Accounting Standards Board (IASB) (www.iasb.co.uk). The U.S. Securities and Exchange Commission (SEC) began a process to allow large U.S. multinational companies to report earnings under IFRS beginning in 2010 and, possibly, have all U.S. companies switch to IFRSs beginning in 2014. Source: Scannell and Slater, "SEC Moves to Pull Plug on U.S. Accounting Standards," *Wall Street Journal* (August 28, 2008), p. A1.

of cash flows, and a statement of stockholders' equity. Each of these statements is defined and discussed in the following sections.

Balance Sheet

A **balance sheet** is also known as a statement of financial position. This statement summarizes the assets (resources that the organization owns), liabilities (debts that the organization owes), and stockholders' equity (amounts owners have contributed and the net amount that the entity has earned for them) of an entity at a specific time. Because it is prepared for a specific moment, a balance sheet can be viewed as a financial "snapshot" of a company.

The title "balance sheet" is appropriate for this statement because the sum of an entity's assets must equal the sum of its liabilities and stockholders' (or owners') equity. Accountants refer to this equation as the **accounting equation**, or the balance sheet equation. Expressed in equation form for a corporation, this relationship appears as follows:[6]

$$\text{Assets} = \text{Liabilities} + \text{Stockholders' Equity}$$

The following simple examples illustrate this equation. Assume that a corporation's stockholders invest $100,000 in the company. The $100,000 of cash assets is equal to the $100,000 of stockholders' equity. Then the corporation decides to buy a piece of land that costs $45,000. To do so, the company pays $20,000 in cash and borrows the remaining $25,000 from the bank. After this transaction, assets of $125,000 ($100,000 + $45,000 − $20,000) equal the liabilities of $25,000 plus stockholders' equity of $100,000.

Income Statement

An **income statement** summarizes a company's revenues and expenses for a specific time period. **Revenues** generally result from selling the merchandise or providing the services that have been chosen for the company's primary business activity. More formally, revenues increase assets or decrease liabilities and result from an entity's profit-oriented activities. For instance, the primary revenue source for Ford Motor Company (www.ford.com) comes from sales of manufactured automobiles. For Enterprise Rent-A-Car (www.enterprise.com), the revenue comes from vehicle rentals. The Olive Garden's and Red Lobster's (www.darden.com) primary revenue source is food and beverage sales.

Expenses are legitimate costs of doing business. Expenses decrease assets or increase liabilities. The costs of salaries, rent, utilities, marketing, and insurance are common expenses. In addition, the cost of the products sold to customers is an extremely large expense for manufacturers and merchandisers.

Like a balance sheet, an income statement also has a basic equation:

$$\text{Revenues} − \text{Expenses} = \text{Net Income}$$

---

[6]The balance sheet equation for a sole proprietorship and partnership is essentially the same as for a corporation except that there cannot be a stockholders' equity because there are no stockholders. Thus, the equation is Assets = Liabilities + Owner's (or Owners') Equity.

People often use the phrase "the bottom line" to refer to the **net income** or profit figure reported on an income statement. If revenues exceed expenses, the business has made a profit on its business activities. Alternatively, a net loss decreases stockholders' equity because the organization's assets have been reduced. A **net loss** occurs when a company's expenses are larger than its revenues. Because the profits belong to an organization's owners, the net income for a fiscal year increases stockholders' equity (ownership interest).

An entity's **fiscal year** is the 12-month period covered by its annual income statement. The fiscal year of many companies often coincides with the calendar year (January 1 to December 31), but it may begin on any date. For instance, the fiscal year of The Walt Disney Company (corporate.disney.go.com) runs from October 1 to September 30.

Notice that the time frame of an income statement is different from that of a balance sheet. Because the income statement is prepared for a span of time, this statement can be viewed as a financial "movie" rather than a "snapshot." The income statement summarizes revenues (selling prices of goods sold) and expenses (costs of doing business) for the fiscal year only. For example, revenues generated from tickets to Disney World on October 1, 2008, will not be on the company's income statement for the fiscal year ended September 30, 2008. Instead the October 1, 2008, Disney World revenues will appear on the income statement for the year ended September 30, 2009.

Statement of Cash Flows

The **statement of cash flows** reveals how a business generated and spent cash during a given accounting period. The accounting period covered by a statement of cash flows is the same period as that covered by the income statement. The statement begins with a summary of the cash inflows and outflows from three major types of activities engaged in by business entities: operating (earning money by providing products or services), investing (buying and selling long-term assets), and financing (obtaining and repaying funds from creditors and investors). The final section of a statement of cash flows reconciles an entity's beginning and end of the period cash balances. The ending cash balance is also found on the balance sheet along with the other assets.

When decision makers review a company's statement of cash flows, the question foremost in their minds is, "How do the company's cash flows from its profit-oriented (operating) activities compare to its net income?" Successful companies should, over the long run, generate the majority of their cash from their operating activities. However, in a given accounting period, the net cash flow from operating activities may not be closely correlated with its net income. For instance, in 2007, Wachovia Corporation (www.wachovia.com) incurred a net loss of almost $9.5 million and made a net investment of almost $52 million in long-term assets; however, the cash balance only declined by $1.3 million because of the company's significant financing activities.

Even a very profitable company may not generate enough cash flows to sustain operations. Such companies may experience severe cash flow problems, including falling behind on debt payments and being unable to replace inventory as it is sold. Several factors, including slow-paying customers and rising prices for raw materials needed for the firm's day-to-day operations, could account for such circumstances.

Alternatively, a company that is experiencing losses may have positive cash flow from operations. To illustrate, for year ending March 31, 2008, Napster, Inc. (www.napster.com) reported a $16.5 million net loss on its income statement and a $4.2 million positive cash inflow from operating activities on its statement of cash flows. Time will only tell whether the net loss or the positive cash flow was more indicative of the company's actual operations.

Statement of Stockholders' Equity

The **statement of stockholders' equity** reconciles the dollar amounts of ownership equity components at the beginning and end of an accounting period. The primary question answered by this statement is, "What circumstances accounted for the changes in a company's stockholders' equity over the previous year?" In part, through its inclusion of net income as a major component of the change for the period, the statement of stockholders' equity provides a link between the income statement and the balance sheet.

Financial decision makers often disagree on which of the four primary financial statements is the most important or informative. However, most decision makers would agree that the statement of stockholders' equity is the least important financial statement.

This overview of the four primary business financial statements indicates that they are closely linked despite their differing structures, contents, and objectives. For example, many of the changes in a company's assets and liabilities (shown on the balance sheet) during a given period are a direct result of the entity's revenues and expenses (shown on the income statement) for that period. Additionally, the statement of cash flows accounts for the change in the amount of cash reported in a company's balance sheet between the beginning and end of a given period. These statements and their interrelationships are summarized in Visual Recap 1.2.

VISUAL RECAP 1.2

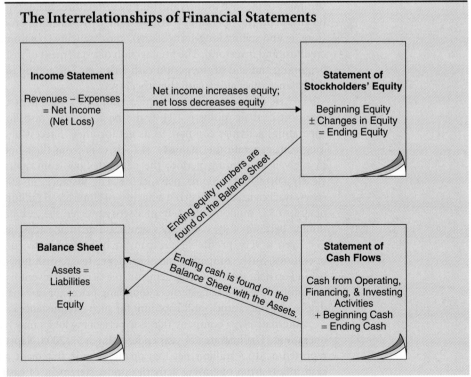

The Interrelationships of Financial Statements

Income Statement

Revenues – Expenses
= Net Income
(Net Loss)

Net income increases equity;
net loss decreases equity

Statement of Stockholders' Equity

Beginning Equity
± Changes in Equity
= Ending Equity

Ending equity numbers are found on the Balance Sheet

Balance Sheet

Assets =
Liabilities
+
Equity

Ending cash is found on the Balance Sheet with the Assets.

Statement of Cash Flows

Cash from Operating,
Financing, & Investing
Activities
+ Beginning Cash
= Ending Cash

Financial Statement Footnotes

Besides the four financial statements, the annual report contains other important information about the company. One particularly informative section of an annual report contains the **financial statement footnotes**. These footnotes assist decision makers in interpreting and drawing the proper conclusions from a business's financial statements. Footnotes to a company's financial statements identify the specific accounting methods used, significant accounting policies, assumptions that underlie key financial statement amounts, financial data regarding major business segments, and descriptions of any pending lawsuits. For instance, a footnote in the 2008 annual report of Mattel, Inc. (www.mattel.com) discusses the filing of class-action lawsuits against the company relative to voluntary product recalls. The footnote states that the lawsuits allege that the company was negligent relative to "the presence of lead in excess of applicable standards in the paint" on some toy parts and in toy design relative to the use of small magnets.[7] Results of such lawsuits could have a significant impact on Mattel's financial condition and organizational reputation. Financial statement footnotes provide crucial information about the company and should be used by current and potential investors and creditors to help them make informed decisions.

AN OVERVIEW OF THE ACCOUNTING PROFESSION

Most businesspeople think of the accounting profession as consisting of two segments: private accounting and public accounting.[8] These two sectors have completely different functions.

Private Accounting

Accountants in private accounting are employed by businesses, not-for-profit organizations, and governmental agencies. Individuals in private accounting may have job titles such as controller, internal auditor, financial accountant, cost analyst, and tax accountant. Controllers (or chief financial officers) are the top accounting executives in organizations with a primary responsibility of ensuring that an entity's periodic financial statements are prepared on a timely and accurate basis. Internal auditors monitor the compliance of an organization's employees with operating policies and procedures. Financial accountants analyze and record the transactions of an enterprise, prepare its financial statements, and perform other accounting functions such as payroll and regulatory reporting. Cost analysts may have any number of accounting-related responsibilities within an organization: maintaining production cost records for manufacturing processes, analyzing variances from budgeted expenditures, or preparing customized reports that forecast expected costs for a new operating unit. Tax accountants in the private sector collect and process the data needed to file the employing entity's periodic federal, state, and local tax returns.

---

[7]Mattel 2008 Annual Report, footnote 12, p. 95; http://files.shareholder.com/downloads/MAT/638454464x0x283677/D4E18CB7-C8B4-4A28-BCE9-C114B248A26D/MattelAnnualReport2008.pdf

[8]A third sector does exist: academic accountants who teach at colleges and universities and research the effects of accounting information on financial systems and behavior.

Public Accounting

Public accounting firms, like law firms, range in size from sole proprietorships to huge international partnerships that have hundreds of partners and thousands of employees. Among the services offered by public accounting firms are auditing, tax preparation and advice, certain types of consulting, and bookkeeping.

Auditing is the most important professional service provided by public accounting firms. An audit performed by a public accounting firm differs from the service provided by internal company auditors because the public accounting firm is independent from the company that is being audited. A business entity hires a public accounting firm that has no financial interest in, or other important ties to, the entity. The external auditors' mission is to perform a review of the company's financial statements.

The principal objective of an independent audit is to determine whether an entity's financial statements have been prepared in accordance with GAAP. That conclusion is based on an examination of the audit client's financial statements and accounting records. If the financial statements are in accordance with GAAP, those statements are presumed to fairly reflect the company's financial affairs. Business executives might have economic incentives (such as higher salaries or improved stock values) to "window dress" financial statements to make their companies appear more profitable and financially stable than they actually are. In the absence of an independent audit, external financial statement users might not believe that a company's published financial statements are honest representations of its financial affairs. The authenticity of the information contained within the financial statements is the responsibility of the organization's management (including the controller); the responsibility of the external auditor is to obtain enough assurance to attest (give an opinion) to whether the data contained in the financial statements are fairly presented.

By independently examining the financial statements and accounting records of companies, public accounting firms bolster the confidence that third parties have in the reasonableness of those statements. This higher level of confidence in financial statements increases the likelihood that individuals will invest in, or loan funds to, business entities and thus keep the economy healthy and growing. Exhibit 1-4 shows the audit report for the February 28, 2008, year-end financial statements of The Gap, Inc. (www.gapinc.com) by the public accounting firm of Deloitte & Touche LLP.

Although audits are designed to determine if financial statements have been presented fairly, on some occasions that objective fails. The most common reason for the failure of an audit to uncover financial statement errors and irregularities is management fraud. There have been several highly notable recent cases of audited financial statements consisting of "bad" figures: Enron, Adelphia Communications, and WorldCom, to name just a few. Unfortunately, the few cases that result in problems overshadow the thousands of cases in which the audited financial statements are "fairly presented" as per the attestation.

Certifications

"Accountant" is a generic term that can be applied to anyone who works in the field of accounting. However, numerous certifications may be held by accountants in the private and public sector. The three most common are certified public accountant (CPA), certified management accountant (CMA), and certified internal auditor (CIA). Becoming certified requires a candidate to pass a rigorous comprehensive examination, meet certain experience requirements, and agree to abide by continuing education and ethics rules. Obtaining any

EXHIBIT 1-4
Independent Auditors' Report

To the Board of Directors and Stockholders of The Gap, Inc.:

We have audited the accompanying consolidated balance sheets of The Gap, Inc. and subsidiaries (the "Company") as of February 2, 2008 and February 3, 2007, and the related consolidated statements of earnings, stockholders' equity, and cash flows for each of the three fiscal years in the period ended February 2, 2008. We also have audited the Company's internal control over financial reporting as of February 2, 2008, based on criteria established in *Internal Control—Integrated Framework* issued by the Committee of Sponsoring Organizations of the Treadway Commission. The Company's management is responsible for these financial statements, for maintaining effective internal control over financial reporting, and for its assessment of the effectiveness of internal control over financial reporting, included in the accompanying Management's Report on Internal Control Over Financial Reporting. Our responsibility is to express an opinion on these financial statements and an opinion on the Company's internal control over financial reporting based on our audits.

We conducted our audits in accordance with the standards of the Public Company Accounting Oversight Board (United States). Those standards require that we plan and perform the audit to obtain reasonable assurance about whether the financial statements are free of material misstatement and whether effective internal control over financial reporting was maintained in all material respects. Our audits of the financial statements included examining, on a test basis, evidence supporting the amounts and disclosures in the financial statements, assessing the accounting principles used and significant estimates made by management, and evaluating the overall financial statement presentation. Our audit of internal control over financial reporting included obtaining an understanding of internal control over financial reporting, assessing the risk that a material weakness exists, and testing and evaluating the design and operating effectiveness of internal control based on the assessed risk. Our audits also included performing such other procedures as we considered necessary in the circumstances. We believe that our audits provide a reasonable basis for our opinions.

A company's internal control over financial reporting is a process designed by, or under the supervision of, the company's principal executive and principal financial officers, or persons performing similar functions, and effected by the company's board of directors, management, and other personnel to provide reasonable assurance regarding the reliability of financial reporting and the preparation of financial statements for external purposes in accordance with generally accepted accounting principles. A company's internal control over financial reporting includes those policies and procedures that (1) pertain to the maintenance of records that, in reasonable detail, accurately and fairly reflect the transactions and dispositions of the assets of the company; (2) provide reasonable assurance that transactions are recorded as necessary to permit preparation of financial statements in accordance with generally accepted accounting principles, and that receipts and expenditures of the company are being made only in accordance with authorizations of management and directors of the company; and (3) provide reasonable assurance regarding prevention or timely detection of unauthorized acquisition, use, or disposition of the company's assets that could have a material effect on the financial statements.

Because of the inherent limitations of internal control over financial reporting, including the possibility of collusion or improper management override of controls, material misstatements due to error or fraud may not be prevented or detected on a timely basis. Also, projections of any evaluation of the effectiveness of the internal control over financial reporting to future periods are subject to the risk that the controls may become inadequate because of changes in conditions, or that the degree of compliance with the policies or procedures may deteriorate.

In our opinion, the consolidated financial statements referred to above present fairly, in all material respects, the financial position of The Gap, Inc. and subsidiaries as of February 2, 2008 and February 3, 2007, and the results of their operations and their cash flows for each of the

EXHIBIT 1-4

Continued

three fiscal years in the period ended February 2, 2008, in conformity with accounting principles generally accepted in the United States of America. Also, in our opinion, the Company maintained, in all material respects, effective internal control over financial reporting as of February 2, 2008, based on the criteria established in *Internal Control—Integrated Framework* issued by the Committee of Sponsoring Organizations of the Treadway Commission.

As discussed in Note 1 to the consolidated financial statements, the Company adopted Statement of Financial Accounting Standards No. 123(R), *Share-Based Payment*, on January 29, 2006 and Financial Accounting Standards Board Interpretation No. 48, *Accounting for Uncertainty in Income Taxes—an interpretation of FASB Statement No.109*, on February 4, 2007.

Deloitte & Touche LLP
San Francisco, California
March 28, 2008

of these certifications does not limit where an individual may work; CPAs often work in private accounting. Additionally, a CPA may also be a CMA and/or CIA.

Regulation of the Accounting Profession

In the early 1930s, Congress established the **Securities and Exchange Commission** (SEC) to deter the abusive accounting and financial reporting practices that contributed to the 1929 stock market collapse. The SEC regulates the sale and subsequent trading of stocks and bonds by companies listed on stock exchanges. Companies that market their stocks, bonds, or other securities on an interstate basis are generally referred to as publicly owned companies. The SEC does not assess the investment quality of the securities issued by the companies that it regulates nor does it prohibit the sale of highly speculative securities. Instead, the SEC ensures that publicly owned companies provide third parties with sufficient information to make informed economic decisions regarding the securities these firms sell. Thus, the SEC oversees the financial reporting and accounting practices of these companies. "Full and fair disclosure" is the SEC's motto.

The SEC closely monitors the accounting profession's rule-making processes and has the authority to override any new rules issued by the FASB to the extent that those rules apply to publicly owned companies. However, in the past, the SEC has seldom interfered with accounting rule-making bodies.

After the financial scandals at the turn of the century, the U.S. Congress passed the **Sarbanes-Oxley Act of 2002** (SOX). This Act is comprehensive legislation that was designed to enhance the accuracy and reliability of corporate financial reporting, strengthen corporate governance, and improve public accounting regulation. SOX created the **Public Company Accounting Oversight Board** (PCAOB) to regulate the accountants who audit financial statements of publicly owned companies. The PCAOB's operations are subject to the oversight of the SEC as shown in Visual Recap 1.3.

Challenges Facing the Accounting Profession

The growing trend toward multinational business enterprises and international trade promises to complicate the work roles of public and private accountants in the future.

VISUAL RECAP 1.3

Interactions in Regulation and Standard Setting

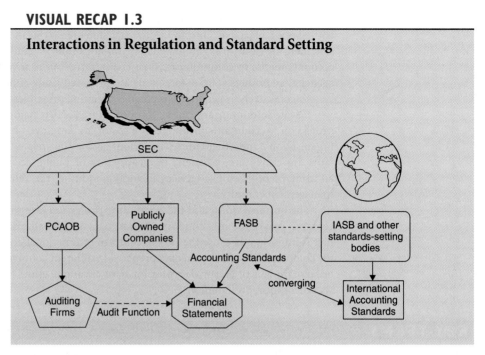

Cultural differences in business practices, varying governmental regulations, and a lack of uniform international accounting rules create "global-sized headaches" for accountants of multinational companies. The process of obtaining consistency among accounting standards around the world is a slow one, but there has been substantial progress.

Business organizations and the accounting profession face numerous challenges in the 21st century. For centuries, accountants have played an integral role in the economic success of business enterprises. Businesses that will thrive in this new century must employ accountants who understand the organization, recognize the information needs of both external and internal decision makers, and satisfy those needs on a timely basis with relevant and reliable data. Such individuals are essential in an era in which knowledge and information are key ingredients to success.

SUMMARY

The three major types of businesses are service, manufacturing, and merchandising companies. The most common legal forms of business organizations are sole proprietorships, partnerships, and corporations. The majority of U.S. businesses are sole proprietorships, although corporations account for most of the business revenues each year.

Large companies have several internal functions that are performed by individuals with specialized training and experience in a field of business. Management, marketing, finance, and accounting are the most commonly recognized specialized fields in business. The principal role of a business entity's accounting function is to provide financial information regarding that organization to internal and external decision makers.

The manner in which accountants communicate financial data depends on the type of decision maker who will use that data. Accountants communicate financial and nonfinancial data to internal decision makers using customized reports designed with specific objectives in mind. Financial statements (balance sheet, income statement, statement of cash flows, and statement of stockholders' equity) are the primary means accountants use to communicate financial information to investors, creditors, regulatory agencies, and others. These statements are prepared using concepts, guidelines, and rules known collectively as generally accepted accounting principles (GAAP).

Private accounting and public accounting are the two major segments of the accounting profession. Accountants in the private sector are employed by businesses, not-for-profit organizations, and other entities in various accounting-related work roles. Public accountants are employees, partners, or proprietors of public accounting firms that provide an array of professional services including auditing, tax return preparation, and some management consulting.

The business world and the accounting profession face several challenges in this new century. Two of the most important challenges are globalization and business ethics. The first is important because the lack of uniform international accounting standards impairs the comparability of financial data prepared in different countries. The second is important because the lack of personal, professional, or corporate ethics may be reflected in financial statement misrepresentations.

KEY TERMS

accounting
accounting equation
balance sheet
business
corporation
expense
Financial Accounting
  Standards Board (FASB)
financial statement
financial statement footnote

fiscal year
generally accepted accounting
  principles (GAAP)
income statement
net income (net loss)
partnership
Public Company Accounting
  Oversight Board (PCAOB)
revenue

Sarbanes-Oxley Act of 2002
  (SOX)
Securities and Exchange
  Commission (SEC)
sole proprietorship
statement of cash flows
statement of stockholders'
  equity
stockholder

QUESTIONS

1. Identify the three general types of businesses and provide an example of each. *(LO 1.1)*

2. Identify the three common forms of business organizations. How do these forms differ? Which form of business organization is most common in the United States? *(LO 1.1)*

3. What is the primary purpose of a business's accounting function? *(LO 1.1)*

4. Identify the four major financial statements. What information is contained on each of these statements? Why do businesses issue financial statements? *(LO 1.2)*

5. "A company's fiscal year is always the same as a calendar year." Is this statement true or false? Explain your answer. *(LO 1.3)*

6. List and define the three types of activities in which a business engages. Which financial statement uses these three activities as section headings? *(LO 1.3)*

7. Define "generally accepted accounting principles" (GAAP). What is the primary purpose of GAAP? What body is currently charged with establishing GAAP? *(LO 1.3)*

8. Distinguish between private and public accounting. Briefly describe several work roles in private accounting. *(LO 1.4)*

9. What services do public accounting firms typically offer to the public? Which of these services is the most important and why? *(LO 1.4)*

10. What prompted the formation of the Securities and Exchange Commission (SEC), and what is its primary function? *(LO 1.4)*

EXERCISES

11. **True or False** *(all LOs)*

    Following are a series of statements regarding topics discussed in this chapter.

    Required:

    Indicate whether each statement is true (T) or false (F).

    (a) Financial statements are the principal means accountants use to communicate financial information regarding business entities to external decision makers such as bank loan officers and investors.

    (b) A key advantage of the corporate form of business is that the personal assets of a corporation's owners are not at risk if the business is sued.

    (c) The Securities and Exchange Commission issues most new accounting rules in the United States.

    (d) In the U.S., sole proprietorships are the most common form of business organization and account for the majority of business revenues generated annually.

    (e) A trait common to most successful businesspeople is an ability to make wise decisions regarding the allocation of their business's economic resources.

    (f) A business's fiscal year is the 12-month period covered by its balance sheet.

    (g) A key objective of independent auditors is to provide assurance as to the integrity of a business entity's financial statements so as bolster the confidence of third parties in using those statements.

    (h) Controller, internal auditor, and cost analyst are common job titles in private accounting.

    (i) Because it is a service activity, accounting does not contribute significantly to the success of business organizations.

    (j) Reported profits of all multinational companies are not necessarily determined by the same accounting rules.

    (k) LLPs, LLCs, and Subchapter S corporations pay taxes separately from their owners.

12. **Major Types of Businesses** *(LO 1.1)*

    Businesses are often classified into three broad groups: service companies, manufacturing companies, and merchandising (retail) companies.

    Required:

    (a) Identify each of the following well-known firms as a service company (S), a manufacturing company (M), or a merchandising company (R).

    (1) General Motors

    (2) FTD

    (3) JPMorgan Chase

    (4) Toys "R" Us

    (5) Levi Strauss

    (b) For the companies listed, identify a key business decision that each firm's management likely faces on a recurring basis. What type of data might the accountants for each firm provide to management to help make the decisions identified?

13. **Common Legal Forms of Business Organizations** *(LO 1.1)*

    The text identified three common legal forms of business organizations: sole proprietorships, partnerships, and corporations.

    Required:

    (a) Compare and contrast what you believe would be key advantages and disadvantages of operating a business as a sole proprietorship versus a corporation.

    (b) Compare and contrast what you believe would be key advantages and disadvantages of operating a business as a partnership versus a corporation.

    (c) What other forms of business organizations were discussed in the chapter, and what is (are) their distinguishing characteristics?

14. **Information Needs of External and Internal Decision Makers** *(LO 1.2)*

    Each of the following items of information may be obtained from a company's accounting records:

    ■ Net income

    ■ Inventory cost per unit

    ■ Total liabilities

    ■ Total sales by geographical area of business operations

    ■ Five-year trend in total sales

    ■ Employee salaries by department

    Required:

    (a) Indicate a specific type of decision maker who would have a primary interest in each information item. The decision maker may be either an external or internal party.

    (b) Briefly explain why the decision maker identified in part (a) would have a need for the given item of information.

15. **The Need for Financial Statements** *(LO 1.2)*

    Jim's Bike Shop sells and repairs bicycles. The owner, Jim Hardy, took several accounting courses in college and has decided to maintain his business's accounting records. Although the shop has been in operation for longer than three months, Hardy has not yet prepared any financial statements for the business. Although several of Hardy's friends who are business owners prepare monthly financial statements for their businesses, Hardy has decided that it is too much of a hassle to prepare monthly financial statements for Jim's Bike Shop.

Required:

Write a memo to Hardy explaining why financial statements would help him operate his business more efficiently and effectively.

16. **Analyzing Business Transactions** *(LO 1.3)*

All business transactions affect assets (resources owned), liabilities (amounts owed), stockholders' equity (ownership interest), or some combination of these items. Following is an analysis of the equal dollar effects of two transactions.

Transaction	Assets	=	Liabilities	+	Equity
(a) Purchased $1,000 of office supplies on credit	+$1,000	=	+$1,000	+	$0
(b) Purchased a set of tires for $200 cash	+$200 − $200	=	$0	+	$0

Required:

Using the format above, analyze the effects of each of the following transactions for Fuente & Demond Realtors, Inc. on the firm's assets, liabilities, and stockholders' equity.

(a) Purchased equipment for $12,500 cash.

(b) Sold an additional $17,000 of stock in the firm to Fuente and Demond.

(c) Paid $1,500 owed to an office supply store for a purchase made the previous month.

(d) Purchased supplies for $4,000 on credit.

PROBLEMS

17. **Use of Income Statement Information** *(LO 1.2)*

The following condensed income statement is for Alana's, a fast-food restaurant chain operating in the western United States.

Alana's Fast-Food Condensed Income Statement (in 000s)

Revenues

Sales by Company-Operated Restaurants	$ 381,700
Revenues from Franchised and Licensed Restaurants	78,600
Other Income	6,100

Expenses

Operating Expenses	(449,900)
Interest Expense	(10,400)
Income Tax Expense	(1,800)
Other Expenses	(800)
Net Income	$ 3,500

Required:

(a) Describe how the following three groups of decision makers might use Alma's income statement data:

   (1) Company stockholders (its owners)

   (2) Company executives

   (3) Bankers

(b) Also identify additional information regarding this company's income statement data that each group of decision makers might request.

18. **Analyzing Financial Statement Data** *(LO 1.2)*

The following table lists the net income of three large companies from 2007 to 2009.

	2007	2008	2009
Lifestyle Magazines	$207,300,000	$246,300,000	$264,000,000
BigWin Hotel & Casino	$ 10,649,000	$ 15,966,000	$ 18,745,000
Quick & Yummy Foods, Inc.	$ 80,517,000	$ 97,432,000	$110,070,000

Required:

(a) Which of these companies was most profitable over the given three-year period?

(b) Which company's profitability improved the most over this period?

(c) What business trends, economic variables, or other factors likely influence the profitability of each of these firms? When responding to this question, consider the nature of each firm's principal line of business.

19. **Financial Statement Information** *(LO 1.2)*

The financial information of three companies is listed in the following table with some numbers omitted.

	Alpha Co.	Bravo Inc.	Charlie LLP
Assets	$510,000	(c)	$ 950,000
Liabilities	(a)	$430,000	367,000
Equity	318,000	320,000	(e)
Revenues	510,000	870,000	(f)
Expenses	320,000	(d)	678,000
Net Income	(b)	$210,000	331,000

Required:

For each of the three companies listed, find the missing numbers.

20. **Effects of Industry Accounting Practice** *(LO 1.5)*

During the 1980s, a special set of accounting rules was in effect for the savings and loan industry. These accounting rules allowed companies in that industry to record losses on sales of certain securities over a several-year period. For example, suppose that a savings and loan sold a security for $1 million that had originally cost $3 million. Rather than immediately reporting the loss on this sale, the company could spread the loss over several years in its income statement.

Required:

(a) In the example just given, how much loss would the savings and loan have reported in the year of sale had the special accounting rules not been in effect?

(b) Assume now that the savings and loan spread the loss on the sale of the security over a five-year period, recognizing an equal portion of that loss in each of those years. What portion of the loss did the savings and loan report in the year of sale?

(c) How was this special accounting treatment for losses on the sale of certain securities misleading to financial statement users?

CASES

21. **Annual Reports** *(LO 1.2, Internet)*

The annual financial report is the primary communication of financial information to external users.

Required:

Use the annual report of Carnival Corporation for the 2007 fiscal year to answer the following questions. This information can be found either on the annual report or the SEC 10-K filing at www.carnival.com by following the links to Investor Relations.

(a) On what days does Carnival Corporation's fiscal year begin and end?

(b) How many years of balance sheet information are presented?

(c) How many years of income statement information are presented?

(d) How many years of cash flow information are presented?

(e) How many years of shareholders' equity information are presented?

(f) List two places in the annual report that each of the following pieces of information can be found (list the statement and the year):

(1) 2007 ending balance of Cash

(2) 2007 beginning balance of Cash

(3) 2007 ending balance of Retained Earnings

(4) 2007 Net Income

(5) 2007 ending balance of Common Stock

(g) What public accounting firm audited the financial information of Carnival Corporation?

22. **Financial Accounting Standards Board** *(LO 1.4 and 1.5, Internet)*

Presently, the Financial Accounting Standards Board (FASB) is the principal accounting rule-making authority within the United States.

Required:

Use the FASB's Web site (www.fasb.org) to answer the following questions.

(a) What organization has statutory authority to establish financial accounting and reporting standards?

(b) How long has the FASB been the designated organization for establishing standards?

(c) What is the FASB's mission?

(d) Who is the current chairman of the FASB?

(e) List several ways that topics are added to the FASB's agenda.

(f) What is an exposure draft?

(g) Does the FASB list any exposure drafts on its homepage? What is the topic of the exposure draft(s)? (Do not read the entire draft; just look at the title.)

CHAPTER 2

Concepts and Elements Underlying Accounting

LEARNING OBJECTIVES

1. Describe the nature, purpose, and content of each of the four primary financial statements.
2. Recognize the three financial reporting objectives of business entities.
3. Discuss the key attributes or characteristics that accounting information should possess.
4. Discuss the fundamental concepts that underlie accounting and financial reporting rules and practices.
5. Define an accounting system and identify its principal elements.

INTRODUCTION

The primary objective of financial accounting and accountants is to provide useful information to external decision makers. The primary document for communicating this information, the annual report, was introduced in Chapter 1. The annual report contains four financial statements: the balance sheet, income statement, statement of cash flows, and statement of stockholders' equity. This chapter begins by expanding on the components of the financial statements. Next, the financial reporting objectives of business entities, qualitative attributes that should be possessed by financial accounting information, and fundamental concepts that underlie accounting and financial reporting practices are discussed. The last part of the chapter describes the principal elements of an accounting system.

COMPOSITION OF FINANCIAL STATEMENTS

Financial statements present monetary information by listing accounts and showing their balances. Accounts can be viewed as tabulations of one's financial interests. For example, your checking account (the money you have on deposit at the bank) is one account; your Visa account (the money you owe on your credit card) is another. Although both accounts are a summary of monetary interests, they are kept separate because they are of a different nature. Businesses use a myriad of accounts to keep track of their financial interests. As summarized in Visual Recap 2.1, there are six types of accounts:

- **Assets**—property or other things of value that belong to the business
- **Liabilities**—debts of the business
- **Stockholders' Equity**—ownership interests in the business (includes stockholder investments and profits from operations)
- **Dividends**—distributions of profits earned by the business to its stockholders
- **Revenues**—selling prices of goods or services sold by the business
- **Expenses**—costs of doing business and generating revenues

This chapter describes the content of the balance sheet and the income statement relative to the types of accounts found on each statement. Chapter 9 provides more in-depth discussion of the income statement, and Chapters 8 and 10 discuss the two other primary financial statements.

Balance Sheet

As indicated in Chapter 1, the balance sheet provides a snapshot of a corporation's assets, liabilities, and stockholders' equity at a specific time. (If a balance sheet were to be prepared for a sole proprietorship or a partnership, stockholders' equity would be renamed either *owner's equity* or *owners' equity*, as appropriate.) A balance sheet provides answers to many questions that external decision makers may have regarding a business's financial status. Examples of these questions include: "How much cash or inventory does the company have?" and "Is the cash balance large enough to allow the company to pay off the debts that are coming due in the next few months?" A simplified balance sheet is presented in Exhibit 2-1, and the key components of a balance sheet are discussed next.

VISUAL RECAP 2.1

Account Types and Their Components

Assets	Liabilities	Equity
(things of economic value)	**(debts to external parties)**	**(stockholders' interest)**
Current Assets	Current Liabilities	Paid-In Capital
Long-Term Investments	Long-Term Liabilities	Additional Paid-In Capital
Property, Plant & Equipment		Retained Earnings
Intangible Assets		

Revenues	Expenses	Dividends
(prices of goods sold)	**(costs of doing business)**	**(distributions to stockholders)**
Operating Revenues	Cost of Goods Sold	Cash Dividends
Nonoperating Revenues	Operating Expenses	Stock Dividends
	Nonoperating Expenses	

Assets

Assets are defined in accounting as items having "probable future economic benefits obtained or controlled by a particular entity as a result of past transactions or events."[1] A nonaccountant might simplify this definition to "things that a company owns." Notice that Kirtley, Inc.'s assets in Exhibit 2-1 are classified into four groups: current assets; long-term investments; property, plant and equipment; and intangible assets.

Current Assets   Current assets are typically listed first in a balance sheet. A **current asset** is cash or any other asset that will be converted into cash, sold, or used up within the next year or the normal business operating cycle, whichever is longer. A business's **operating cycle** is the average time a company takes to buy inventory, sell that inventory, and collect cash from customers. The operating cycle of a restaurant chain, such as Outback Steakhouse (www.outback.com), is usually just a few days. Outback buys unprocessed raw materials (such as flour, fruit, meats, and vegetables), converts those materials into ready-to-eat food items, and sells the food items to its customers for cash or allows them to charge their purchases on national credit cards, such as Visa, MasterCard, or American Express. Alternately, the operating cycle of a manufacturing firm such as McIlhenny Company (www.tabasco.com) can be several months or longer, in part because of the aging process of the hot sauces.

The most common current assets are cash, short-term investments, accounts receivable, inventory, and prepaid assets. Current assets are listed in descending order of liquidity or "nearness to cash." Thus, cash is the first current asset reported in a balance sheet. Short-term investments (sometimes called marketable securities) generally include investments in another company's stocks or bonds that the company expects to sell, and thereby convert into cash, within a short period of time. For example, Kirtley, Inc. might decide to invest some of its excess cash in a bond issued by Apple, Inc. (www.apple.com) so that the cash would earn interest until it is needed.

Some small retailers allow customers to only pay cash for products or services. In other instances, customers may charge their purchases on national credit cards. Retailers

---

[1] Financial Accounting Standards Board, *Statement of Financial Accounting Concepts No. 6: Elements of Financial Statements of Business Enterprises* (Stamford, CT: FASB, 1985), 25.

EXHIBIT 2-1
Balance Sheet

Kirtley, Inc.
Balance Sheet
December 31, 2009

ASSETS

Current Assets			
Cash			$ 900
Short-Term Investments			1,500
Accounts Receivable			4,800
Inventory			12,200
Prepaid Assets			100
Total Current Assets			$19,500
Long-Term Investments			15,000
Property, Plant and Equipment			
Land	$10,000		
Building	$ 50,000		
Accumulated Deprecation	(12,000)	38,000	48,000
Intangible Assets			
Patent			4,000
Total Assets			$86,500

LIABILITIES

Current Liabilities		
Notes Payable		$ 1,200
Accounts Payable		600
Accrued Wages Payable		250
Unearned Revenue		120
Total Current Liabilities		$ 2,170
Long-Term Liabilities		
Bonds Payable		20,000
Total Liabilities		$22,170

STOCKHOLDERS' EQUITY

Common Stock (20,000 shares; $1 par value)	$20,000	
Additional Paid-In Capital	15,000	
Retained Earnings	29,330	64,330
Total Liabilities and Stockholders' Equity		$86,500

allowing this type of payment usually collect the credit card charges, less a service fee, daily from the credit card companies. The customers owe the purchase price to the company that issued the national credit card, not to the merchandiser that sold the goods to the customer. Other companies, such as Dillard's, Inc. (www.dillards.com) offer "in-house" credit cards to their customers. Amounts owed to a company by its customers are referred to as **accounts receivable**. In general, accounts receivable between businesses and accounts receivable owed to a business by a customer, if paid by the first statement's due date, do not carry interest charges. To illustrate, assume you made two purchases at Dillard's, one for $150 on your Wells Fargo Visa card and one for $80 on your Dillard's card. Wells Fargo would pay Dillard's $150 less a service fee and record a $150 account receivable from you. Dillard's would also have an $80 account receivable from you.

In a retail company, **inventory** refers to the goods the company intends to sell to its customers. Manufacturing companies, such as U.S. Steel Corp. (www.ussteel.com), also have supplies, raw material, and in-process (semifinished) inventories; these items will be converted during the operating cycle into saleable goods available to wholesalers, retailers, or, in some cases, directly to customers.

Businesses often pay for costs such as rent, insurance, and advertising in advance of their due dates. For example, a company may pay for 12 months of insurance at the beginning of a year. These amounts are reported as **prepaid assets** in the current asset section of a balance sheet. These expenditures are considered assets because they still have future economic benefit.

By definition, all assets other than current assets are long-term assets. Most companies have several categories of long-term assets, including long-term investments, property, plant and equipment, and intangibles. "Other assets" may also be used as a balance sheet "catchall" classification for miscellaneous long-term assets of an insignificant amount.

Long-Term Investments In addition to short-term investments, a company may purchase the debt or ownership securities of other companies and hold these investments for an extended period. Such investments in corporate bonds and stocks are made to generate an ongoing stream of additional income (interest or dividends) for the company. Additionally, the company may want to exercise some degree of control over or form an alliance with another organization. For example, as of the end of 2007, Daimler AG (www.daimler.com) owned 85 percent of Mitsubishi Fuso Truck and Bus Corporation (www.mitsubishi-fuso.com); this investment provided the German company with access to the important Asian truck market.

Another type of long-term investment is land or any other asset that is not currently being used in business operations. For instance, assume that a company purchased land at a bankruptcy auction. If the company intended to hold the land for future resale rather than for use, the land would be considered a long-term investment.

Property, Plant and Equipment Generally, the largest category of noncurrent assets is property, plant and equipment (PP&E). This category includes land, buildings, machinery, furniture, and other such assets used in the normal operating activities of a business. To illustrate the size of this category, Aluminum Company of America (Alcoa; www.alcoa.com) had total assets of $38,803,000,000 at the end of 2007; of that, $16,879,000,000, or 43.5 percent, was included in PP&E.

Most PP&E assets have limited useful lives and are called depreciable assets. Accounting requires that the cost of depreciable assets be recorded as an expense over the time period benefited by those assets. **Depreciation** is the accounting term used to describe this write-off process. For example, assume that a company pays $25,000 for a new automobile for one of its salespeople. The salesperson is expected to use the car for three years, at which time it will have an estimated value of $13,000. The easiest way to calculate accounting depreciation is as follows:

Original cost	$25,000
Estimated value at end of use	(13,000)
Depreciable cost	$12,000
Divide by useful life	÷3
Depreciation expense per year	$ 4,000

Accumulated depreciation is the total amount of depreciation that has been recorded on a depreciable asset since its acquisition. In other words, it is the amount of the asset that has been "used up" by the company. For balance sheet purposes, the accumulated depreciation for PP&E is subtracted from the cost of the depreciable assets to obtain **book value**. For the saleperson's car, the accumulated depreciation at the end of the second year would be $8,000 (or $4,000 for each of two years), and the book value at that time would be $17,000 (or $25,000 − $8,000).

Note that the accounting and general usages of the term *depreciation* differ. Depreciation, as used in general conversation, refers to the decline in market value of an item. Continuing the preceding example, assume that the salesperson quit after one year, and the company decided to sell the car. The company might only be able to sell the car for $15,000 because it had "depreciated," or declined in market value, $10,000 in one year. In most situations, the fastest loss of market value for most assets is in the first year of use. But because accounting presumes that PP&E items were bought for long-term use rather than short-term resale, such market declines are not recorded on the financial statements.

Land is another common PP&E asset. However, land does not have a limited useful life and, therefore, is not depreciated. It is generally carried on the balance sheet at original purchase price.

Intangible Assets Intangible assets are long-term assets that do not have a physical form or substance; examples include copyrights, trademarks, and goodwill. A patent is an intangible that represents an exclusive right to manufacture a specific product or to use a specific process. Many pharmaceutical companies, such as La Jolla Pharmaceutical Company (www.ljpc.com), own important product patents that prohibit other firms from producing or selling those products or their generic substitutes. Such patents were purchased from external parties. However, other pharmaceutical companies, such as Eli Lilly (www.lilly.com), do not show any amounts for patents on the financial statements because the cost of generating those patents was incurred internally and expensed during the development period. This concept is discussed in greater depth in Chapter 6.

Liabilities

Amounts owed by businesses to third parties are called **liabilities**. These amounts represent "probable future sacrifices of economic benefits arising from present obligations of a particular entity to transfer assets or provide services to other entities in the future as a result of past transactions or events."[2] Like assets, liabilities may be current or long term.

---

[2]Financial Accounting Standards Board, *Statement of Financial Accounting Concepts No. 6: Elements of Financial Statements of Business Enterprises* (Stamford, CT: FASB, 1985), 35.

Current Liabilities A **current liability** is a debt or obligation that will be eliminated by giving up current assets or incurring another current liability. Current liabilities are listed first in the liabilities section of a balance sheet. The most common types of current liabilities are notes payable, accounts payable, accrued liabilities (such as salaries payable and interest payable), and unearned revenues.

Companies frequently borrow money from banks or other parties on a short-term basis by signing promissory notes. Such notes are legally binding commitments to repay borrowed funds with interest on the use of these funds. If the notes are due within the upcoming year or operating cycle, they are listed as current liabilities on a company's balance sheet.

Accounts payable are amounts owed by a business to its suppliers. Essentially, an account payable represents the buyer's side of a seller's account receivable. For example, if Thomasville Cabinetry (www.thomasvillecabinetry.com) sells cabinets to Home Depot (www.homedepot.com) to stock as inventory in its 1,100+ stores, Thomasville Cabinetry's balance sheet would show an account receivable from Home Depot, and Home Depot's balance sheet would show an account payable to Thomasville Cabinetry.

At the end of an accounting period, a company must determine if there are any amounts that it currently owes but has not yet recorded. These amounts typically relate to obligations incurred near the end of an accounting period and often must be estimated. For instance, a company may need to estimate its liability for electricity usage since the last electric bill was received. When such an obligation is determined, the company will record an **accrued liability** for the amount.[3] However, because of the time lag in preparing end-of-period financial statements, many of these amounts become known before the financial statements are actually issued.

Companies may also receive money in advance of selling a product or performing a service. At the time that such money is received, the company would record an account for **unearned revenue**, which is considered a company debt because a product or service must be provided to the customer or the money must be returned. For example, when Gannett Company, Inc. (www.gannett.com) receives payment from you for a one-year subscription to *USA Today*, the company owes you 12 months of papers or a refund. Only as issues are sent to you does the magazine earn revenue. Another example is Ticketmaster's (www.ticketmaster.com) sale of concert tickets. The service charge that is paid for the ticket is a nonrefundable amount that is revenue on the sale of the ticket; however, Ticketmaster does not earn the concert fee until the concert occurs.

Long-Term Liabilities Long-term liabilities are the non-current debts of a business. Examples of long-term liabilities include long-term notes payable, mortgages payable, and long-term accrued liabilities. A long-term liability that becomes due within the next year or operating cycle is reclassified from the long-term to the current liability section of the balance sheet. Thus, a five-year note payable on November 1, 2006 would be classified as long-term at the end of 2006 through 2009; for year-end 2010, that note would be reclassified as a current liability because it would be due on November 1, 2011. Quite often, a company reports the collective amount of several long-term liabilities on one balance sheet line item entitled "long-term debt" or simply "long-term liabilities."

---

[3]To *accrue* means to recognize on the financial statements before cash is paid or received.

Stockholders' Equity

Stockholders' equity represents the owners' interest in the company. The three most common components of stockholders' equity are common stock (also called paid-in capital), additional paid-in capital, and retained earnings. The total dollar amount of stockholders' equity represents the owners' claims on corporate assets.

A corporation's common stock represents that firm's ownership interest that is sold in single units, or shares. The balance sheet amount shown as **common stock** is the total par value of the number of shares of stock that the corporation has issued. **Par value** is merely the specific dollar amount per share that is printed on each stock certificate. Most companies are now establishing very small par values for common stock shares. For instance, the par value of La-Z-Boy Incorporated's (www.la-z-boy.com) common stock is $1 per share; $0.01 per share is the par value of Comcast Corporation's (www.cmcsa.com) common stock.

Generally, the par value has little, if any, relationship to the stock's initial selling price. When stock shares are first sold, the amount received by the company is more than the par value. Any amounts over par or stated value will be recorded in an account entitled Additional Paid-in Capital.[4]

The total profits generated by a company and not distributed as dividends to stockholders is accumulated in **Retained Earnings**. Profits, because they benefit stockholders, increase Retained Earnings. **Dividends**, on the other hand, are distributions of profits to stockholders and, thus, decrease Retained Earnings. It is important to realize that there is no cash in Retained Earnings: cash is a current asset on the balance sheet and not a part of stockholders' equity.

Income Statement

The two primary types of income statement accounts are revenues and expenses. Exhibit 2-2 presents an income statement for Kirtley, Inc. for the year ended December 31, 2009. The following discussion covers the primary elements that create the net income (or net loss) on an income statement.

Revenues

Revenues represent inflows of new assets into the business. Depending on how they were generated, revenues may be either operating or nonoperating. Generally, **operating revenues** reflect the sales prices of the products sold or services performed as the company's primary operations. **Nonoperating revenues** are commonly generated from "sideline" activities. For example, the interest a bank charges its customers is an operating revenue because lending money is a bank's primary operating activity. A retail store that earns interest by extending credit to customers would classify the interest as nonoperating revenue.

---

[4]There are many other acceptable titles for this account, including Paid-in Capital in Excess of Par (Stated) Value and Contributed Capital in Excess of Par.

EXHIBIT 2-2
Income Statement

Kirtley, Inc.
Income Statement
For Year Ended December 31, 2009

Sales Revenue		$190,000
Cost of Goods Sold		(75,000)
Gross Profit		$115,000
Operating Expenses		
Salaries and Wages	$52,000	
Rent	12,000	
Utilities	25,900	
Depreciation	6,000	(95,900)
Operating Income		$ 19,100
Nonoperating Revenues and Expenses		
Interest Expense		(1,800)
Income Before Income Taxes		$ 17,300
Income Tax Expense (20%)		(3,460)
Net Income		$ 13,840
Earnings Per Share (20,000 shares)		$ 0.692

Expenses

Expenses are costs of doing business. There are three basic categories of expenses: cost of goods sold, operating expenses, and nonoperating expenses. In a merchandising or manufacturing company, one of the largest expenses is Cost of Goods Sold, which reflects the price that the company paid for the inventory that is sold to customers or the total amount the company spent to produce the goods that are sold to its customers. For example, an electronics store that sells a DVD recorder/player to a customer for $150 (operating revenue) might have purchased that item for $70 (cost of goods sold).

Costs, other than cost of goods sold, that are incurred for a company's principal business operations are known as **operating expenses**. Common operating expenses include salaries and wages, sales commissions, advertising costs, rent, utilities, and depreciation. The remaining expenses listed on an income statement are nonoperating expenses that result from an entity's nonprincipal business operations. For example, interest expense that is incurred on borrowings of a retailer is a nonoperating expense.

Gross Profit

A very important and informative amount for financial statement users is **gross profit,** or the difference between sales (operating) revenue and cost of the goods sold during the period. The **gross profit percentage** (gross profit divided by sales) reflects the profit margin earned on product sales. This percentage may differ dramatically between companies or within segments of a company, depending on the type of business in which the companies or segments are engaged. Quite often, an early sign that a company's profitability is declining is a decrease in its gross profit percentage. When gross profit percentage declines, a company often has to compensate by cutting its operating expenses.

EXHIBIT 2-3		Marine		Aviation		Land	
Gross Profit Information—World Fuel Services Corp. (in Thousands)		2007	2006	2007	2006	2007	2006
	Revenue	$7,665,801	$5,785,095	$5,460,838	$4,579,337	$602,916	$420,704
	Gross Profit	$114,505	$101,177	$122,797	$106,867	$7,975	$6,025
	Gross Profit %	1.5%	1.8%	2.3%	2.3%	1.3%	1.4%
	Operating Income	$50,844	$44,225	$60,795	$56,648	$1,237	$1,138
	Operating Income %	0.7%	0.8%	1.1%	1.2%	0.2%	0.3%

Exhibit 2-3 provides a two-year comparison of the gross profits for the three primary segments of World Fuel Services Corp. (www.wfscorp.com), which is engaged in the marketing and sale of marine, aviation, and land fuel products and related services. The information shows that the aviation portion of the firm's business provides a higher gross profit percentage than the other two segments.

Operating Income

The difference between gross profit and a company's operating expenses is **operating income**, also called income from operations. This amount is an important one because a company's eventual success or failure hinges on the profitability of its principal line, or lines, of business. Exhibit 2-3 shows the operating income by segment for World Fuel Services Corp.; this information indicates that increases in the aviation segment would have the greatest positive impact on the company's net income.

Net Income

Exhibit 2-2 shows that "income before income taxes" is determined by adding (or subtracting) the net amount of other revenues and expenses to (or from) operating income. Subtracting income tax expense from income before income taxes provides the net income (or net loss) for the period. Because corporations pay taxes, an income tax expense amount is shown on Kirtley, Inc.'s income statement. Corporate income tax expense is computed using a graduated scale: Higher amounts of income are taxed at higher tax rates.

Earnings per Share

A corporation also reports an **earnings per share** (EPS) figure on its income statement. In its most simplistic form, EPS is computed as net income divided by number of shares of common stock held by stockholders. Corporations report earnings per share each period to assist stockholders in determining the profit attributable to each individual ownership interest in the firm during that period.

OBJECTIVES OF FINANCIAL REPORTING

Determining a consistent manner to present items on the balance sheet and income statement (as well as the other primary financial statements) is an important issue to the Financial Accounting Standards Board (FASB). To integrate the current, and guide the development of future, financial accounting and reporting standards, the FASB established a conceptual framework project. Some of the primary outputs of this project are discussed in the following sections.

To make sound economic decisions, external parties need a wide array of financial information about business enterprises. The starting point of the FASB's conceptual framework project was to determine the primary objectives of financial reporting by businesses. The outcome of this process was to state that businesses have the following three financial reporting objectives, each of which directly or indirectly reflects the need for a business entity's financial statements to assist external parties in making rational and informed economic decisions.[5]

1. Financial reports should provide information that is useful in making investing, lending, and other economic decisions.

2. Financial reports should provide information that is useful to decision makers in predicting the future cash flows of businesses and future cash dividends from those businesses.

3. Financial reports should provide information about the assets and liabilities of businesses and the transactions and other events that have resulted in changes in those assets and liabilities.

These three objectives assist in determining both the types of financial statements that a business should present and the types of information that should be included on those financial statements. For example, objective two focuses on the distinct need of external parties to have information about a business's cash situation—providing direct support for the Statement of Cash Flows. Objective three indicates that a business should provide information about events that caused changes in assets and liabilities; however, some items that cause such changes do not necessarily involve cash. Thus, these two objectives indicate a need for both cash-based and non-cash-based (income statement) information.

KEY ATTRIBUTES OF ACCOUNTING INFORMATION

Because of the quantitative nature of accounting, financial statement users often overlook important qualitative features of accounting information. Therefore, the FASB decided that the conceptual framework needed to define and describe the qualitative attributes that accounting information should possess.[6] If financial statement accounting data do not exhibit the following attributes, information needs of decision makers are unlikely to be satisfied, and the statements are unlikely to be useful. In fact, usefulness in the decision-making process was determined to be the most important qualitative characteristic that accounting information should possess. To qualify as useful to decision makers, accounting information should be understandable, relevant, and reliable.

Understandability

Because so many people have access to financial statements, the accounting profession has long debated the "audience" to whom the financial statements should be directed. Should

---

[5]Financial Accounting Standards Board, *Statement of Financial Accounting Concepts No. 1: Objectives of Financial Reporting by Business Enterprises* (Stamford, CT: FASB, 1978).

[6]Financial Accounting Standards Board, *Statement of Financial Accounting Concepts No. 2: Qualitative Characteristics of Accounting Information* (Stamford, CT: FASB, 1980).

EXHIBIT 2-4

Six Basic "Plain English" Principles

1. Use short sentences.
2. Use definite, concrete, everyday words.
3. Use the active voice.
4. Use tabular presentations or bullet lists for complex material whenever possible.
5. Do not use legal jargon or highly technical business terms.
6. Do not use multiple negatives.

SOURCE   Securities and Exchange Commission, Securities Act of 1933, 1998, Rule 421(b).

financial statements be understandable or comprehensible to everyone, even the most naive or unsophisticated users? Or should financial statements be principally directed toward people who have an in-depth understanding of financial reporting and accounting issues? The FASB settled this debate by stating that financial reports should be comprehensible to individuals who have a "reasonable understanding of business and economic activities and who are willing to study the information with reasonable diligence."[7]

Thus, it is not necessary that financial statements be understandable to "everyone," but they should be understandable to a broad range of users. In addition, the Securities and Exchange Commission (SEC) decided to require that companies filing certain documents with the Commission must use "plain English principles" in the writing of those documents. Although the SEC rules do not apply at this time to all financial reports or statements, plain English (rather than legalistic or overly complex wordings) is becoming more and more the norm in financial reporting. Exhibit 2-4 provides some of the plain English guidelines.

Relevance

For accounting information to be useful, it must possess a high degree of relevance by being timely and having feedback and/or predictive value. If information is provided too late to influence decisions, then it is not relevant. Feedback value enables decision makers to confirm or correct earlier expectations about, for instance, a business's operating results. Predictive value allows a user to forecast future occurrences from current information. For example, a banker considering a company's loan application should be able to use financial statements to help predict whether the company will be able to repay the loan.

Reliability

To be useful to decision makers, accounting information must also be reliable and, thus, must possess the following traits: verifiability, neutrality, and representational faithfulness. Verifiability means that multiple persons can validate the information rather than meaning that accounting data are necessarily exact or precise. The majority of financial data are not exact amounts, but rather approximations based on underlying supportable details. For example, the presentation by International Paper Company (www.internationalpaper.com) of all its financial statements in the millions of dollars could hardly be considered precise—but the information underlying those rounded amounts could be verified by different parties.

---

[7]Financial Accounting Standards Board, *Statement of Financial Accounting Concepts No. 2: Qualitative Characteristics of Accounting Information* (Stamford, CT: FASB, 1980), 22.

In certain situations, accounting data do not have to satisfy the reliability criterion. For example, accounting data do not have to be perfectly reliable if imprecision in the data would not "matter" to decision makers. **Materiality** refers to the relative importance of specific items of accounting information. An item is deemed material if it is significant enough to influence a financial statement user's decision. For example, the expensing of a $15 trash can rather than depreciating it over a useful life of five years would not create a material misstatement of any of the five years' income amounts.

To be neutral, accounting data must be presented without bias. Thus, accountants should not consciously attempt to influence the decisions of the users of accounting data. This characteristic is one reason why financial statements are said to be "general purpose" in nature.

Finally, "representational faithfulness" implies that accounting data should portray, to the greatest extent possible, the true nature of a business's economic resources, obligations, and transactions. The necessity of this characteristic can be understood in reference to a map: leaving Houston off a map showing cities in Texas would not be considered "representationally faithful" for most users; leaving off Friendswood, Texas, probably would not create difficulties—unless, of course, that was where the user was headed.

The usefulness of accounting data is enhanced by **comparability**, which refers to the ease with which the accounting information of an entity can be compared with its similar prior period information and with similar information reported by other business entities. Failure of a company to use the same accounting rules from period to period is a major threat to comparability. Therefore, if a company changes an accounting principle that will significantly affect comparability of period-to-period financial statements, the effect of that change must be highlighted in the financial statements and disclosed in the financial statement footnotes.

FUNDAMENTAL ACCOUNTING CONCEPTS

Accounting rules have evolved over several centuries on an industry-by-industry basis. At one time, one set of accounting rules was considered generally accepted by retail merchants, whereas another set of accounting rules was generally accepted within the shipbuilding industry. Eventually, accountants decided that allowing accounting rules to be validated strictly by general acceptance within an industry or economic sector was not necessarily a good idea.

Today's changing business environment continually creates new types of transactions and new variations of routine or familiar transactions. For instance, the question of whether the cost of developing a company Web site should be shown as an asset or an expense would never have been an issue in the 1980s.

Properly recording new types of transactions and analyzing financial statements require consideration of fundamental generally accepted accounting principles (GAAP). GAAP refers to the collection of concepts, guidelines, and rules that are used in recording and reporting financial information. Financial statement preparers and users can both benefit greatly from understanding the basic concepts that dictate how accounting information is recorded and reported. Such an understanding provides a grasp on both the uses and limitations of accounting data. Exhibit 2-5 provides a list of the key concepts that underlie the accounting and financial reporting rules, procedures, and practices that are important to understanding accounting information. Each of these items is discussed separately.

EXHIBIT 2-5

Key Accounting
Concepts and Principles

Accounting Period Concept

Historical Cost Principle

Unit-of-Measurement Concept

Going Concern Assumption

Entity Concept

Revenue Recognition Rules

Expense Recognition Rules

Full Disclosure Principle

Acronym: A HUGE REF

Accounting Period Concept

Determining the profitability of a business cannot be truly assessed until it ceases operations. However, decision makers demand financial information about business entities on a regular basis. The **accounting period concept** allows accountants to prepare meaningful financial reports for ongoing businesses by dividing their lives into reporting intervals of equal length. As a result, businesses typically release financial statements to external decision makers at the end of each fiscal year. Publicly owned companies regulated by the SEC must issue financial statements quarterly (the 10-Q) and annually (the 10-K). These documents can be found online at the SEC's EDGAR (Electronic Data Gathering, Analysis, and Retrieval) Web site (www.sec.gov/edgar.shtml).[8]

Historical Cost Principle

In the U.S., the **historical cost principle** dictates that most assets are shown at original cost on a company's financial statements. For instance, assume Schneider Corp. acquired a tract of land in 2000 for $500,000. That historical cost would still be reported on the 2009 balance sheet even if, by that time, nearby urban development has caused the appraised value of the land to skyrocket to $2 million.

Historical cost is used as the primary valuation basis for assets because that cost is more verifiable and less subject to estimation or opinion than current value. The cost of Schneider Corp.'s land can be found on the purchase contract. Alternatively, determining the land's current value is much more subjective and would need to be established using a real estate appraisal or market comparison. Commonly, though, appraised values differ among appraisers.

It is important to note that use of the historical cost principle can cause the values of assets that have been held for a long time to be significantly undervalued. However, liabilities are generally current amounts. This differentiation in valuations causes a "book value" that borders on meaningless. Unfortunately, an alternative would be to allow

---

[8]Changes that increase the use of XBRL (extensible business reporting language) will soon be made to the EDGAR system. Corporate financial data are put in a common format that makes company comparisons easier. More information about XBRL can be found at http://www.xbrl.org.

companies to set their own values on assets each reporting period, which would conflict with the principles of verifiability and comparability.

There are, however, several exceptions to the general accounting rule of valuing assets at historical cost. First, some investments in corporate stocks and bonds are reported in financial statements at current values rather than historical costs. Second, if an asset's value has permanently declined below its historical cost, that asset should be written down to its current value. For example, if land value were reduced because a hurricane uprooted all the trees and caused significant erosion, then the land's carrying value would be reduced. This exception is based on the **conservatism principle,** which states that when alternative valuations are possible, assets and revenues should be not be overstated, and liabilities and expenses should not be understated. This principle does *not*, however, indicate that assets and revenues should be understated, nor should liabilities and expenses be overstated. Such choices would violate the reliability characteristic discussed earlier in the chapter.

Unit of Measurement Concept

The **unit of measurement concept** mandates that businesses use a common unit of measurement in accounting for transactions. This concept allows financial data to be quantified, summarized, and reported in a uniform, timely, and consistent manner. In the U.S., the appropriate measurement unit is a "constant" dollar—that is, the dollar that is not restated for the effects of inflation or deflation.

Going Concern Assumption

Unless there is evidence to the contrary, accountants use the **going concern assumption** to reflect a belief that a business will continue to operate "long enough to use its longest-lived asset." Because businesses continuously replace old assets with new ones, this presumption often indicates that the business will continue indefinitely. The going concern concept allows firms to record PP&E assets (except land) at cost and depreciate them over their useful lives.

The going concern assumption has significant implications for the accounting and financial reporting decisions rendered by and about business enterprises. For example, a company that has severe financial problems and has filed for bankruptcy will not show its PP&E assets at book value on the balance sheet, but rather at the fair value that could be received in liquidation. When a company's status as a going concern is seriously in doubt, this fact should be disclosed in the firm's financial statements.

Entity Concept

Regardless of its legal form (sole proprietorship, partnership, or corporation), a business enterprise is treated, for accounting purposes, as a distinct and independent entity. Thus, the **entity concept** requires that the transactions of a business should be accounted for separately from its owners' personal transactions. This concept is particularly important for sole proprietorships. Financial statements would not fairly depict a sole proprietorship's financial status if the owner's personal and business assets and liabilities were commingled.

Revenue Recognition Rules

One of the most important accounting issues faced by businesses is when to record revenues and expenses. The accounting profession has established some general rules to dictate the timing of revenue recognition. These rules limit the ability of management to misrepresent a firm's operating results by being able to selectively choose the accounting periods in which to record revenues.

The FASB established a two-part **revenue recognition rule** to decide when to record revenue. Before being recorded in a business's accounting records, a revenue should be both realized and earned. Revenues are realized when assets have been exchanged for cash or a claim to cash. Revenues are earned when the company has, or has substantially, provided the product or performed the service needed for the transaction to be complete and, thus, for the company to be entitled to the revenue. For most merchandising and service companies, both of these requirements are usually satisfied at the point of service or sale. It is not necessary for cash to change hands when recognizing revenues. For example, when Macy's sells a tie and the customer uses a Macy's charge account, Macy's should recognize the revenue, even though no cash has been involved in the transaction.

In some instances the point of sale rule is improper. For example, many construction projects create economic impacts over multiple years. In such cases, revenues may need to be spread over several accounting periods rather than being recorded totally at the end of the project. For example, when Granite Construction Incorporated (www.graniteconstruction.com) is engaged in its numerous construction projects, revenues are recognized in proportion to project costs incurred to date. Thus, if Granite Construction incurs 30 percent of the total estimated cost on a project, 30 percent of the expected revenues would be recorded. This method of recognizing revenues is called the percentage-of-completion method.

Expense Recognition Rules

As discussed in the previous section, two rules exist relative to recognizing revenues in the financial statements. These rules also affect expense recognition because the costs of doing business should be recognized as expenses in the accounting period in which they provide economic benefit to the business. Typically, this rule means that the **matching principle** should apply: an expense should be recognized in the accounting period when the related revenue is recorded.

In many cases, the matching principle is simple to apply because there is a corresponding cause-and-effect relationship between a cost and the subsequent revenue that it generates. To illustrate, the cost of inventory sold should be recorded as a Cost of Goods Sold expense in the period in which the Sales Revenue is recognized. Similarly, if a commission was paid to a salesperson, that amount should be recorded as an expense in the same accounting period that the related sale was recorded as revenue.

In other situations, there is difficulty in seeing a relationship between a cost and revenue. Thus, two other possibilities exist for expense recognition. First, when a cost (such as an equipment purchase) provides an economic benefit to several accounting periods, that cost should be recorded as an asset and gradually written off to expense over the time that benefit is provided. In the case of equipment, that time would be the asset's useful life, and the write-off is called depreciation expense. Second, when no direct cause and effect can be determined and no clear expected benefit time frame can be identified, the cost should be recorded immediately as an expense. Consider the case of pharmaceutical companies that engage in long-term research programs to develop new products. Because such companies seldom know which research efforts will result in viable products, the costs are recorded when incurred as expenses.

Similar to accounting for revenues, cash need not be exchanged for an expense to be recognized. For example, a company that runs a newspaper advertisement for a back-to-school sale in August may not need to pay for that ad until September. However, advertising expense should be recognized in August.

Companies using the revenue and expense recognition rules just discussed are using the **accrual basis of accounting**. Under this accounting basis, the economic impact of a transaction is recognized whether or not the transaction involves cash. Some business entities (usually very small ones) use the **cash basis of accounting**; they record revenues when cash payments are received from customers and expenses when disbursements of cash are made to suppliers, employees, and other parties. As a result, the reported net income of a cash basis business for a given period may not be a reliable indicator of its true profitability for that period. Consider the potential manipulation that could be involved if management were able to recognize revenues and expenses only when cash was received or paid.

Full Disclosure Principle

The **full disclosure principle** requires that all information for a thorough understanding of a company's financial affairs be included in its financial statements or accompanying narrative disclosures, such as footnotes. Examples of information that users may need but that is not part of the four primary financial statements are management's plans for the future, information about employee pension plans, business risks, and details of major transactions with related parties.

Related-party transactions may be structured to economically benefit one party to the transaction at the expense of the other. Disclosure of related-party transactions allows decision makers to assess the reliability of a given firm's reported financial results. For instance, Enron was heavily involved in related-party transactions with its 3,000+ subsidiaries and partnerships. Many of these relationships were designed to allow Enron to transfer assets to those related parties at highly inflated prices and record massive amounts of profit.

AN INTRODUCTION TO THE ACCOUNTING SYSTEM

The objectives, concepts, and principles discussed in this chapter create the framework for the basic accounting system. An accounting system provides a systematic approach to collecting, processing, and communicating financial information to decision makers in an effective and efficient manner. Such systems have varying degrees of complexity and sophistication. Manual, or "pen-and-paper," accounting systems are still used by some small businesses to process financial data. However, most businesses have integrated computer accounting systems. The accounting concepts and methods in this text apply equally well to manual and computer-based accounting systems. All accounting systems use accounts, a general journal, and a general ledger.

Accounts

The basic storage units for financial data in an accounting system are called **accounts**. Financial data related to the assets, liabilities, and other financial statement items of a business are recorded and stored, either electronically or manually, in accounts. Accounts are designed to show increases, decreases, and a balance for each type financial statement element.

A **chart of accounts** is a numerical listing of all the accounts of a business and can be thought of as an address book. When recording a transaction, the chart of accounts is used to identify the proper "address" for each account affected by the transaction. Instead of being listed alphabetically, a chart of accounts is listed in financial statement order: assets, liabilities, stockholders' equity, revenues, and expenses. In this way, all similar types of accounts are grouped together. To minimize errors that might occur in the accounting process, each account is numbered based on the type of account it is.

The General Journal and General Ledger

The two principal accounting records are journals and ledgers. Each business transaction is initially recorded, or journalized, in a **general journal**. The journal is considered the book of original entry and is kept in chronological order. Essentially, a journal can be viewed as a financial diary which records the dollar amounts of transactions that affect the financial status of a business. Most transactions are recorded individually, but some might be recorded as a total amount. For instance, a small grocery store would probably record a single amount for its cash sales at the end of each day rather than individually for each customer.

The **general ledger** is the accounting record that contains all the individual accounts for a business. Although the general journal establishes a historical record of the transactions and events affecting a business, it would be very difficult to prepare financial statements directly from the hundreds, thousands, or even millions of journal entries recorded for a business during a given accounting period. Thus, the accounting data are transferred, through a process called **posting**, from the general journal to individual accounts in the general ledger. In a computerized accounting system, journalizing and posting transactions usually occur simultaneously. In a non-computerized system, posting can be performed daily, weekly, or monthly.

At the end of an accounting period, accountants prepare a listing, or **trial balance**, of the general ledger account balances. For financial statement purposes, similar account balances are often consolidated into one line item. For example, a company having ten cash accounts would add their balances together and report the total as Cash on the balance sheet. Account balances from the trial balance are eventually presented in the financial statements.

This section provides a very condensed summary of the **accounting cycle** or the set of recurring accounting procedures that must be performed in a business each accounting period. This cycle contains the following actions:

1. Financial data for transactions and other events affecting a business are journalized.
2. These data are posted to the appropriate general ledger accounts.
3. The period-ending general ledger account balances are organized into a trial balance.
4. Trial balance amounts are ultimately incorporated into the appropriate financial statements.

The next chapter discusses the activities that occur in the accounting cycle at greater length.

SUMMARY

The two financial statements discussed in this chapter are the balance sheet and income statement. A balance sheet summarizes a business's assets, liabilities, and stockholders' equity at a specific time. The asset section of the balance sheet is classified into current assets; long-term investments; property, plant and equipment; and intangibles. Liabilities can be current or long-term. The three primary components of stockholders' equity are common stock, additional paid-in capital, and retained earnings.

An income statement reports on a business's profitability for a stated period of time, usually the entity's fiscal year. Gross profit is the difference between sales revenue and cost of goods sold. Nonoperating revenues and expenses are deducted from gross profit to obtain income before income taxes. Corporate income taxes are computed on an upwardly sliding tax rate. Net income (or net loss) is the total difference between a business's revenues and expenses. Earnings per share is also shown on the face of the income statement.

The FASB developed a conceptual framework to guide the development of future accounting standards. Each of the three financial reporting objectives for business enterprises addresses the need to assist third parties in making rational and informed economic decisions. Business enterprises satisfy these reporting objectives by preparing the four primary financial statements (balance sheet, income statement, statement of cash flows, and statement of stockholders' equity) for distribution to interested third parties.

The key attribute that accounting information should possess is decision usefulness; thus, the information should be understandable, relevant, and reliable. Numerous concepts and principles underlie accounting practices. Knowledge of these items is useful both for accountants to develop proper accounting procedures for new types of transactions and for users to understand how the information on the financial statements is created. These principles include the accounting period concept, historical cost principle, unit of measurement concept, going concern assumption, entity concept, revenue recognition principles, expense recognition principles, and full disclosure principle.

The operating cycle is the time it takes for a business to make or acquire inventory, sell it, and collect cash from customers. Within the operating cycle, numerous transactions occur and are first recorded in a general journal. The information in the journal is then posted to the accounts in a general ledger for use in preparing a trial balance. From the trial balance information, the company's financial statements can be developed. A company's accounting cycle may contain multiple operating cycles; the accounting cycle encompasses the fiscal year (or other reporting period) of an entity.

KEY TERMS

account	cash basis of accounting	entity concept
accounting cycle	chart of accounts	full disclosure principle
account payable	comparability	general journal
accounting period concept	common stock	general ledger
account receivable	conservatism principle	going concern assumption
accrual basis of accounting	current asset	gross profit
accrued liability	current liability	gross profit percentage
accumulated depreciation	depreciation	historical cost principle
asset	dividend	intangible asset
book value (of a PP&E asset)	earnings per share	inventory

liability	operating expense	retained earnings
long-term liability	operating income	revenue recognition rule
matching principle	operating revenue	trial balance
materiality	par value	unearned revenue
nonoperating revenue	prepaid asset	unit of measurement concept
operating cycle	posting	

QUESTIONS

1. Financial accounting is primarily focused on serving whose information needs? Why was this group chosen? *(LO 2.1)*

2. What is the balance sheet equation? Discuss the components of a balance sheet. *(LO 2.1)*

3. What is an operating cycle, and how does it affect the classification of items on a balance sheet? *(LO 2.1)*

4. Does the Retained Earnings account contain cash? Explain your answer. *(LO 2.1)*

5. Is the income statement a "specific time" statement or a "period-of-time" statement? Discuss the difference between these two perspectives. *(LO 2.1)*

6. Briefly describe or define the following three items: revenues, gross profit, and net income. *(LO 2.1)*

7. Choose two different types of companies with which you are familiar and provide examples of an operating revenue, a nonoperating revenue, and an operating expense for that company. *(LO 2.1)*

8. What is the common theme of the three financial reporting objectives of business entities? Why is this "theme" so important? *(LO 2.2)*

9. To qualify as "reliable," accounting information should have what three traits? Provide an example of each of these traits. *(LO 2.3)*

10. What is the principal justification for using historical costs instead of current values as the primary valuation basis for assets? Could the use of historical costs create any difficulties for users? Explain the rationale for your answer. *(LO 2.4)*

11. What two conditions must be met for a company to recognize revenue from a transaction or event in its accounting records? When might these conditions differ? *(LO 2.4)*

12. What information is contained in a general journal? Why does a business need both a general journal and a general ledger? *(LO 2.5)*

EXERCISES

13. **True or False** *(all LOs)*

Following are a series of statements regarding topics discussed in this chapter.

Required:

Indicate whether each statement is true (T) or false (F).

(a) Common current assets include cash, short-term investments, prepaid expenses, and intangible assets.

(b) The revenue and expense recognition rules limit the ability of business executives to freely choose the accounting periods in which to record their firm's revenues and expenses.

(c) Operating expenses include sales commissions, advertising costs, and salaries of a firm's top executives.

(d) Revenue minus expenses is equal to gross profit.

(e) The revenue recognition principle requires that all information needed to obtain a thorough understanding of a company's financial affairs be included in its financial statements or accompanying narrative disclosures.

(f) The FASB's conceptual framework project provides a foundation for developing accounting pronouncements.

(g) The matching concept suggests that accountants can prepare meaningful financial reports for business enterprises by dividing their lives into reporting intervals of equal length.

(h) A key advantage of using historical costs for asset valuation purposes is that historical costs are more objective, or verifiable, than current values.

(i) One purpose of an income statement is to reconcile a business's cash balance at the beginning of a period to its end-of-period cash balance.

(j) To qualify as "reliable," accounting information should be timely and have feedback value and/or predictive value.

(k) Business transactions are first recorded in the general ledger and then posted to the general journal.

(l) The accounting cycle is always longer than a company's operating cycle.

14. **Balance Sheet Equation** *(LO 2.1)*

Lotterman & Son, Inc. has assets equal to twice the amount of its liabilities.

Required:

(a) Assuming Lotterman & Son's total stockholders' equity is $2,000,000, determine the company's total assets and total liabilities.

(b) Assuming $958,000 of the company's stockholders' equity consists of common stock and additional paid-in capital, determine Lotterman & Son's retained earnings.

15. **Classification of Balance Sheet Items** *(LO 2.1)*

Following are items that can be found in a balance sheet:

- Intangible assets
- Accounts payable
- Inventory
- Cash
- Notes payable (due in ten years)
- Prepaid expenses
- Property, plant & equipment
- Common stock
- Accounts receivable
- Retained earnings
- Notes payable (due in six months)
- Additional paid-in capital

Required:

Determine the correct balance sheet classification for each item listed. Choices are current assets, long-term assets, current liabilities, long-term liabilities, and stockholders' equity.

16. **Current Asset Classification** *(LO 2.1)*

Following are current assets of Solito Enterprises, Inc.:

- Accounts Receivable
- Inventory
- Cash
- Prepaid Expenses
- Short-term Investments

Required:

(a) In what order would you usually find these accounts listed in the current assets section of a balance sheet?

(b) Explain the significance of the ordering of these accounts.

17. **Liability Classification** *(LO 2.1)*

For the past several years, Farewell Distributors reported a long-term debt of $120,000 in its balance sheet. Next year,

the company will begin paying off this debt in four annual installments of $30,000 each.

Required:

(a) How should Farewell's $120,000 debt be reported in the company's balance sheet at the end of the current year?

(b) Why is the proper balance sheet classification of a company's liabilities important to the firm's creditors and potential creditors?

18. **Interpreting Gross Profit** *(LO 2.1)*

Company A and Company B operate in the wholesale shoe industry in Wisconsin. In 2009, Company A had a gross profit of $800,000, whereas Company B had a gross profit of $240,000. Both companies had approximately $2.4 million in sales.

Required:

(a) Identify at least two factors that could account for the large difference in the two companies' gross profits.

(b) If you were the president of Company B, what strategies might you implement to increase your firm's gross profit?

19. **Operating and Nonoperating Items** *(LO 2.1)*

The following items might be seen on the income statement of a large retail store.

- Sales revenue
- Revenue from cafeteria food sales to employees
- Interest revenue
- Cost of goods sold expense
- Utility expense
- Employer matched amounts for employee Social Security withholdings
- Shipping expense to obtain inventory items
- Income tax expense
- Property tax expense

Required:

Indicate whether each of the listed items would be considered an operating or a nonoperating item. Provide a brief reason for your selection.

20. **Gross Profit and Gross Profit Percentage** *(LO 2.1)*

The August 2009 income statement for Oehlke Co. contains the following items:

Wages expense	$220,000
Sales revenue	750,000
Interest expense	18,000
Cost of goods sold	480,000

Required:

(a) Determine Oehlke Co.'s gross profit for August 2009.

(b) Determine Oehlke Co.'s gross profit percentage.

(c) What are your perceptions of Oehlke Co.'s financial status based on the information given and calculated?

21. **Qualitative Characteristics of Accounting Information** (LO 2.3)

The following items refer to various qualitative characteristics of accounting information:

(a) Timeliness, predictive value, and/or feedback value

(b) The relative importance of information

(c) Continuity over time

(d) Clearness

(e) Verifiability, neutrality, and representational faithfulness

Required:

Match each narrative item with one of the following terms: understandability, relevance, reliability, materiality, comparability.

22. **Operating Cycle** (LO 2.4)

Khalid, Inc. manufactures furniture for sale to department stores. On average, 90 days elapse between Khalid's payment for raw materials and the sale of furniture produced from those raw materials. On average, the firm's customers pay for purchased goods in 45 days. All of Khalid's sales are on credit.

Required:

(a) What is the length of Khalid's operating cycle?

(b) How does the length of a company's operating cycle affect the classification of items in its balance sheet?

23. **Accrued Liabilities** (LO 2.4)

Genzyme Corp., a global biotechnology company based in Cambridge, Massachusetts (www.genzyme.com), reported accrued liabilities of $645,645,000 at the end of a recent fiscal year.

Required:

Provide two examples of transactions or events that could result in a company recording accrued liabilities in its accounting records at the end of an accounting period.

PROBLEMS

24. **Preparing an Income Statement** (LO 2.1)

Following are the line items, presented in random order, that were included in a recent income statement of Valimer Corporation:

Selling and Administrative Expenses	$ 90,050
Operating Income	?
Cost of Goods Sold	130,750
Net Income	?
Income Tax Expense	2,500
Net Sales	315,000
Income Before Income Taxes	?
Gross Profit	?
Interest Revenue	5,000

Required:

(a) Compute each missing amount.

(b) Prepare an income statement for Valimer Corporation.

25. **Computing Depreciation Expense** (LO 2.1)

Tankersley Enterprises purchased a piece of machinery for $35,000 in early January 2007. The machinery's estimated useful life is five years, and it will have no value at the end of its useful life.

Required:

(a) Using the straight-line depreciation method discussed in this chapter, compute the annual depreciation expense on this asset.

(b) At the end of 2009, what amount of accumulated deprecation will be shown for this machine on the balance sheet?

(c) What accounting principle or principles require companies to depreciate long-term assets over their useful lives instead of expensing their total cost in the year of purchase?

26. **Computing Gross Profit and Net Sales** (LO 2.1)

In 2008, Doolan Company sold 10,000 units of inventory at twice their purchase price of $27.50 each. In 2009, Doolan had a gross profit of $200,000 and cost of goods sold of $225,000.

Required:

(a) What were Doolan's sales in 2008?

(b) What was Doolan's gross profit in 2008?

(c) What were Doolan's sales in 2009?

(d) What was Doolan's gross profit percentage in 2009?

27. Statement of Stockholders' Equity *(LO 2.1)*

Following is a recent statement of stockholders' equity for Tucson Company.

	Common Stock	Paid-in Capital	Retained Earnings
Balances, January 1, 2009	$2,000,000	$400,000	$700,000
Sale of Common Stock	240,000	300,000	
Exercise of Employee Stock Options	10,000	15,000	—
Net Income	—	—	125,000
Balances, December 31, 2009	$2,250,000	$715,000	$825,000

Required:

(a) How does a company's statement of stockholders' equity relate to the firm's balance sheet?

(b) What transaction or event accounted for the largest increase in Tucson's stockholders' equity during 2009?

28. Analyzing Balance Sheet Data *(LO 2.1)*

Following is a condensed asset section of the December 31, 2009, balance sheet of Green Realty Corp., a real estate investment trust that owns and manages real estate properties. Many of the company's properties are located in New York. Amounts are expressed in thousands.

Commercial Real Estate Properties:	
Land	$ 1,436,569
Buildings and Improvements	5,919,746
Other	1,266,181
	$ 8,622,496
Less: Accumulated Depreciation	(381,510)
Total Investments in Real Estate	$ 8,240,986
Assets Held for Sale	41,568
Other Assets	
Cash	45,964
Restricted cash	105,475
Tenant receivables	49,015
Related party receivables	13,082
Other assets	2,933,988
Total Assets	$11,430,078

Required:

(a) Green Realty Corp.'s balance sheet is unusual in that it begins with Investments in Real Estate instead of Current Assets. Why do you believe the company uses this format for the asset section of its balance sheet?

(b) For what "restricted" purposes might Green Realty hold cash?

(c) If most real estate companies use this format for the asset section of their balance sheets, what accounting principle would Green Realty violate by using a different format?

29. Financial Reporting Objectives *(LO 2.2)*

Wagner Company operates a small chain of department stores. The company owner wants to open two additional stores next year, but the company does not have sufficient cash to finance this expansion project. To raise the needed funds, Wagner has asked several friends to consider investing in the firm. She has provided these individuals with audited financial statements for Wagner Company's most recent fiscal year.

Required:

(a) Besides the audited financial statements, what additional information do you believe potential investors would want to obtain before deciding whether to invest in Wagner Company? Be specific.

(b) Which financial reporting objective or objectives will Wagner Company's audited financial statements help satisfy in this context?

(c) Which of Wagner Company's financial statements do you believe the potential investors will find most useful? Defend your answer.

30. Ethics and Financial Reporting *(LO 2.4, ethics)*

Tim Michael, the chief executive officer of Kokomo Corporation, is very concerned about his company's profitability. In the next few weeks, Kokomo will apply for a large loan from a local bank. This loan is needed to replace several pieces of outdated equipment on the company's production line. Michael is worried that the loan will be rejected because Kokomo's profits have been declining over the past two years. Profits are declining because Kokomo's products cost more to produce than the comparable products of the company's primary competitor. In turn, these higher production costs are due to Kokomo's inefficient production equipment.

To ensure that Kokomo receives the loan, Michael decides to overstate the company's sales and net income for its most recent fiscal year. In his own mind, Michael believes this decision is justified because if Kokomo obtains the loan and purchases the new equipment, he is almost certain that the company will generate sufficient profits and positive cash flows to repay the bank loan. "Besides," Michael reasons, "if the loan isn't obtained, the company may go under, leaving more than 100 people without jobs."

Required:

According to Tim Michael's way of thinking, the "end justifies the means." What would you do if you found yourself in Michael's shoes? If you were almost certain that your company would be able repay the loan if granted, could you justify being dishonest to protect the jobs of the company's employees? Do you believe that any other factors have entered into Michael's decision to misrepresent Kokomo's financial data? Explain.

31. **Applying Accounting Concepts** *(LO 2.4)*

The following situations involve the application of accounting concepts or principles. In some cases, more than one concept or principle may be involved.

- Whitecotton Enterprises recently changed its method of computing depreciation for the third time in three years.

- Hethcox Distributors sold two of its five divisions immediately after the close of its most recent fiscal year. Company executives included information regarding the sale of these two divisions in the footnotes to the company's financial statements.

- Inventory is the largest asset of Still Gardening Company. Last year, Still's inventory was reported at its historical cost in the company's balance sheet. This year, the company intends to report its inventory at market value because the inventory's market value is significantly below its historical cost.

- A footnote to the recent financial statements issued by Mason, Inc. lists the cash payments that the company is required to make over the next several years under its long-term lease agreements.

Required:

(a) Identify the accounting concepts or principles involved in each of these situations.

(b) Indicate whether the given accounting concept or principle has been properly applied in each case. Explain your reasoning.

CASES

32. **Annual Reports** *(LO 2.1 and 2.3, Internet)*

Use the financial information of Carnival Corporation for the 2007 fiscal year to answer the following questions. This information can be found on either the annual report or the SEC 10-K filing at www.carnival.com by following the links to Investor Relations.

Required:

(a) Using Carnival's November 30, 2007, Income Statement (titled Consolidated Statements of Operations), answer the following questions.

    (1) Why is Interest Income separated from Revenues?

    (2) Does Carnival Corporation primarily provide a service or a product? How does this information affect the company's Cost of Goods Sold?

    (3) List several sources from which Carnival obtains its operating revenues.

(b) Using Carnival's November 30, 2007, Balance Sheet, answer the following questions.

    (1) How much does Carnival list in total assets?

    (2) What is a trademark, and why is it shown on as an asset? (Hint: Note number 2 to the financial statements may help you.)

    (3) Carnival lists its Property and Equipment as "net," which means that depreciation has been subtracted from the original cost. How much did Carnival pay for its PP&E, and how much has it been depreciated? (Hint: You will find this information in the Notes to the Financial Statements.)

    (4) Why does Carnival list its Property and Equipment at historical cost rather than fair market value?

    (5) Why are customer deposits listed as liabilities instead of revenues?

    (6) Discuss Carnival's current portion of long-term debt.

    (7) How much has Carnival generated in profits and not distributed to its stockholders?

33. **Annual Reports and the Objectives of Financial Reporting** *(LO 2.2 and 2.3, Internet)*

In its annual report for the 2007 fiscal year, Carnival Corporation lists Note 7, entitled Contingencies, in the Notes to the Financial Statements. This note explains three different situations with uncertain outcomes. Read Note 7 and answer the following questions. (This information can be found on either the annual report or the SEC 10-K filing at www.carnival.com by following the links to Investor Relations.)

Required:

(a) Is the information contained in Note 7 relevant? Why or why not?

(b) Is the information contained in Note 7 material? Why or why not?

(c) List the three objectives of financial reporting.

(d) If Carnival chose to omit Note 7, would these three objectives still be met? Why or why not?

CHAPTER **3**

The Mechanics of Double-Entry Accounting

LEARNING OBJECTIVES

1. Analyze business transactions to determine account effects.
2. Understand the rules of debit and credit.
3. Prepare general journal entries.
4. Post general journal entries to a general ledger.
5. Prepare a trial balance.
6. Develop end-of-period adjustments to general ledger account balances.
7. Prepare an income statement, a statement of stockholders' equity, and a balance sheet.
8. Perform the closing process.
9. Prepare a postclosing trial balance.

INTRODUCTION

Chapters 1 and 2 introduced the four financial statements prepared for external users. These statements present period-end account balances to users. This chapter shows how account balances are created and changed. First, an overview is provided about how an accounting system converts individual economic transactions into financial statements. Next, the chapter discusses the three basic steps in bookkeeping: record (**journalize**) transactions in a general journal, move transaction information (post) to a general ledger, and prepare a trial balance.

This chapter examines the mechanics of accounting by focusing on manual, rather than computer-based, accounting systems. The computer does not change the fundamental nature of how transaction data are collected, processed, and assimilated into a set of financial statements. The computer merely increases the speed with which transaction data are processed and enhances the reliability of accounting records.

The final section of this chapter focuses on the **accounting cycle**, or set of recurring accounting procedures, that must be completed for a business each accounting period. Understanding the process that takes place at the end of the accounting period makes it easier to obtain information from the financial statements and to perform internal managerial tasks such as budgeting.

CAPTURING ACCOUNTING DATA

Preparation of financial statements requires that information about an organization's economic events be captured and recorded in a rational and systematic manner. Financial record keeping, in one form or another, has existed for thousands of years. However, the origins of modern accounting can be traced to a mathematics book written in 1494 by Luca Pacioli, a Franciscan monk living in what is now Italy.

In his book, Pacioli discussed the mechanics of **double-entry bookkeeping**, a recordkeeping system that had been used for several decades in and around Venice. Although Pacioli did not invent the "Method of Venice," his book did formalize and document this system so that merchants could maintain financial records that summarized the operating results and financial condition of their businesses in a logical and easily understood manner. More important, double-entry bookkeeping allowed merchants to make informed and timely decisions regarding business affairs. Economic historians attribute the rapid spread of commerce across Europe during the sixteenth century in large part to the availability of this recordkeeping system.

The key premise underlying double-entry bookkeeping is that financial transactions must be recorded as consisting of two equal and opposite effects. A brief example may be helpful. Assume that Blanchard & Co. purchases $1,000 of supplies on credit from Office Depot. From the firm's perspective, this transaction can be reduced to two parts: the company obtains office supplies (assets) valued at $1,000 and assumes a debt (liability) in the same amount.

An accountant can reduce every business transaction, regardless of size, into at least two equal effects expressed in dollars. If the dual nature of each transaction is recorded properly, a company's financial records will be "in balance" at any given time. Failure to use double-entry bookkeeping results in an "unbalanced" set of financial records which, from an accounting perspective, is unacceptable.

RECORDING TRANSACTIONS: DOUBLE-ENTRY BOOKKEEPING

As stated in Chapter 1, the basic accounting equation requires that assets of a business equal the sum of liabilities and owners' equity. For a corporation, that equation is

$$Assets = Liabilities + Stockholders' Equity$$

Every transaction of a business must be recorded in such a way that the accounting equation for that business remains in balance.

The accounting cycle begins with the occurrence of an economic transaction. Most information about a business transaction is found in a **source document** that provides the underlying support for, and the key information about, the transaction. Common types of source documents include invoices, sales slips, legal contracts, checks, and purchase orders. Next, the transaction is analyzed to identify which accounts were affected by the transaction, the amount of those effects, and whether the accounts were increased or decreased.

The following discussion considers the first two transactions of Snow Mountain Retreat, a small corporation. These examples illustrate how to analyze business transactions.

1. April 1   Issued 4,000 shares of Snow Mountain Retreat's $10 par value common stock. Checks totaling $40,000 were received from stockholders.

Source documents: Checks received from investors and stock shares issued to investors.

Analysis: The corporation's cash increased by $40,000, and because 4,000 shares were issued, stockholders' equity in the form of common stock increased by $40,000.

2. April 1   Purchased furniture costing $12,000, paying $5,000 in cash and signing a 12% interest-bearing note payable for the balance. The note and interest are due in one year. The furniture is expected to have a two-year useful life with no salvage value.

Source documents: Invoice for furniture purchase; note payable to furniture seller; advertisement about furniture and its characteristics.

Analysis: The corporation had a $12,000 increase in furniture, a $5,000 decrease in cash, and a $7,000 increase in liabilities, in the form of notes payable.

As shown in Exhibit 3-1, the accounting equation format could be used to record these business transactions and their effects on Snow Mountain Retreat's assets, liabilities, and stockholders' equity. This format would contain a column for each financial statement item affected by these transactions. Think of these columns as simple accounts. After the two transactions, balances are computed to prove the equality of the balance sheet equation.

Notice that for each transaction, there is a true mathematical statement. In the first transaction, two accounts increased, but because they are on opposite sides of the equal sign, the statement $40,000 = $40,000 is true. In transaction (2), three accounts changed; two increased and one decreased. However, the mathematical statement $-$5,000 + $12,000 = $7,000 is true.

Theoretically, the process illustrated in Exhibit 3-1 could be used for an actual business. However, such a system would become extremely cumbersome as the number of transactions (rows) and their related accounts (columns) increased. Instead, as discussed

EXHIBIT 3-1

Snow Mountain Retreat
Transactions

Account Types:	Assets		=	Liabilities	+	Stockholders' Equity
Accounts	Cash	Furniture	=	Notes Payable		Common Stock
(1)	+$40,000					+$40,000
(2)	(5,000)	+$12,000		+$7,000		
	$35,000	$12,000	=	$7,000	+	$40,000

in Chapter 2, businesses enter financial data in accounting records known as journals and ledgers. However, before illustrating those records, it is important to understand debits and credits as well as the rules of double-entry bookkeeping, which dictate how financial data are recorded in the accounting records.

Debits and Credits

Debits and credits are accounting terms with specialized, but uncomplicated, meanings. Essentially, the terms debit and credit mean, respectively, left and right. A T-account is used to illustrate the use of debits and credits. A **T-account** is not really part of any formal accounting system; a T-account, whose name derived from its shape, is a device used for illustrative or analytical purposes. Following is a T-account for Snow Mountain Retreat's Cash account.

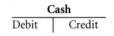

Cash	
Debit	Credit

Used as a noun, **debit** refers to an amount entered on the left-hand side of an accounting record, such as a T-account. Debit can also be used as a verb, meaning to enter a given amount on the left-hand side of an accounting record, such as a T-account. **Credit** refers to an amount entered on the right-hand side of an accounting record or to enter an amount on the right-hand side of an accounting record.

In the following T-account, cash is debited for $1,000, debited for $300, and credited for $600.

Cash	
Debit	Credit
1,000	600
300	

If the debit side of a T-account is larger than the credit side, the account has a debit balance. If the credit side is larger, the account has a credit balance. The Cash account in the preceding example has debits totaling $1,300 and a credit of $600; therefore, the account has a $700 debit balance.

Cash	
Debit	Credit
1,000	600
300	
1,300	600
700	

VISUAL RECAP 3.1

Impact of Revenues, Expenses, and Dividends on Stockholders' Equity

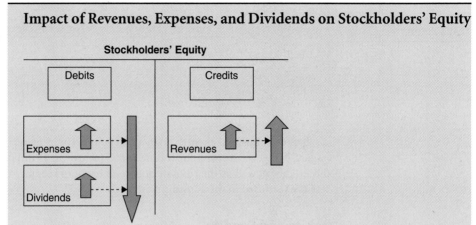

Accountants use debits and credits to define the rules of double-entry bookkeeping. The debit and credit rules can be correlated with the accounting equation. Assets are on the left-hand side of the accounting equation. To increase an asset, it must be debited, with the appropriate dollar amount being entered on the left-hand side of the account. Liabilities and stockholders' equity appear on the right-hand side of the accounting equation. An increase in one of these accounts means that the appropriate dollar amount is credited or entered on the right-hand side of the account.

When a business begins normal operations, three additional account types are used: revenues, expenses, and dividends. Revenues cause stockholders' equity to increase, and because increases in stockholders' equity are shown as credits, revenues also increase with credits. Alternatively, expenses and dividends cause stockholders' equity to decrease, and decreases in stockholders' equity are shown as debits. The more expenses a business has or the more dividends that a business distributes, the smaller stockholders' equity becomes. Thus, expenses and dividends increase with debits. These relationships are shown in Visual Recap 3.1.

The following expanded accounting equation, incorporating all six account types, is true:

$$\text{Assets} + \text{Expenses} + \text{Dividends} = \text{Liabilities} + \text{Equity} + \text{Revenue}$$

The normal balance of each account is on the side on which increases are recorded. Thus, assets, expenses, and dividends normally have debit balances; liabilities, stockholders' equity, and revenues normally have credit balances. The rules of debit and credit and for normal balances are summarized in Exhibit 3-2.

EXHIBIT 3-2		Assets	Liabilities	Stockholder's Equity	Revenues	Expenses	Dividends
Rules of Debit and Credit	Increases are	Debits	Credits	Credits	Credits	Debits	Debits
	Decreases are	Credits	Debits	Debits	Debits	Credits	Credits
	Normal balance is	Debit	Credit	Credit	Credit	Debit	Debit

VISUAL RECAP 3.2

Remembering Debits and Credits

Left-side accounts		Right-side accounts	
Assets + Expenses + Dividends	=	Liabilities + Equity + Revenues	

debit	credit	debit	credit
increase (+)	decrease (−)	decrease (−)	increase (+)
normal balance			normal balance

These rules are summarized graphically in Visual Recap 3.2, which uses the expanded accounting equation. Notice that for the left-side accounts, increases and normal balances are on the left side of the T-account (the debit side). For right-side accounts, debits and normal balances are on the credit, or right, side of the T-account.

Using Debits and Credits

The first two transactions for Snow Mountain Retreat provide simple illustrations of debit and credit rules using the company's Cash T-account. Transaction (1) increased cash (an asset) by $40,000; thus, that amount is shown as a debit. Transaction (2) decreased cash (an asset) by $5,000; thus, that amount is shown as a credit. Because the debit amount was greater than the credit amount, there is a $35,000 debit (normal) balance in the cash account after the two transactions.

Cash	
(1) 40,000	(2) 5,000
Bal. 35,000	

A fundamental rule of double-entry bookkeeping is that debits must equal credits. (This requirement is similar to the rule that states assets must always equal liabilities plus stockholders' equity.) To prove this rule, the four accounts affected by Snow Mountain Retreat's first two transactions are presented next in T-account form. Notice that for each transaction, and in total, debits are equal to credits.

	Cash		+	Furniture		=	Notes Payable		+	Common Stock	
(1)	40,000										40,000
(2)		5,000		12,000				7,000			
Bal.	35,000			12,000				7,000			40,000

When an account has a balance on the "wrong" side, it may need to be reclassified. For example, assume that Snow Mountain Retreat's next transaction was a purchase of kitchen equipment costing $38,000 for which the company wrote a check. The $38,000 would be recorded as a credit in the Cash account, resulting in a $3,000 credit balance. The company would have overdrawn its checking account and would now owe the bank the $3,000, thereby creating a liability (a credit-balanced account) for Snow Mountain Retreat.

In contrast to this situation, there are some accounts that actually have balances on what would at first glance seem to be the "wrong" side, based on their financial statement classifications. These accounts are discussed next.

Contra-Accounts

In a few circumstances, accounts are designed to show offsets to, or reductions in, other related accounts. Such accounts are called **contra-accounts**. An example of a contra-account is Accumulated Depreciation, which was discussed briefly in Chapter 2. Accumulated Depreciation is a contra-asset account because, for balance sheet purposes, its balance is subtracted from an asset account such as Equipment.

From a bookkeeping perspective, the normal account balances and bookkeeping rules for contra-accounts are exactly the reverse of those for the related type of account. For instance, contra-asset accounts have credit balances and are increased by credits and decreased by debits. Contra-liability accounts have debit balances and are increased by debits and decreased by credits. As the text continues, all contra-accounts will be distinctly noted.

THE ACCOUNTING CYCLE

Accounting is a cyclical process. When one cycle ends at the close of an operating period, another cycle begins for the next period. The four steps in the accounting cycle are as follows.

1. Collect, examine, and process transactions.
    a. Record transactions in the general journal.
    b. Post transactions to the general ledger.
    c. Prepare a trial balance.

2. Adjust account balances as necessary.
    a. Record adjustments in the general journal.
    b. Post adjustments to the general ledger.
    c. Prepare an adjusted trial balance.

3. Prepare financial statements.
    a. Income Statement
    b. Statement of Stockholders' Equity
    c. Balance Sheet
    d. Statement of Cash Flows

4. Close temporary accounts.
    a. Record closing entries in the general journal.
    b. Post closing entries to the general ledger.
    c. Prepare a postclosing trial balance.

Step 3, which was discussed in Chapters 1 and 2, is the only step that is seen by external users. Steps 1, 2, and 4 are all internal processes that create and adjust the balances of financial statement accounts. Notice that steps 1, 2, and 4 all involve journal entries. Also notice that all transactions are first recorded in a journal and then posted to the ledger accounts. After posting is completed, a trial balance is prepared.

EXHIBIT 3-3

General Journal

General Journal					
Date	Description		PR	Debit	Credit

Step 1: Collect, Examine, and Process Transactions

Step 1a: Record Transactions in the General Journal

The Snow Mountain Retreat example is continued through this chapter. As indicated earlier, business transactions must be analyzed to determine the accounts affected and the amounts of those effects. Such analyses provide the information needed to prepare a general journal entry.

The process of journalizing a transaction relies on the rules of debit and credit. A general journal has two monetary columns—one for debit amounts and one for credit amounts. Exhibit 3-3 shows a blank general journal for Snow Mountain Retreat.

Mechanically, the following steps are required to prepare a general journal entry:

1. Enter the transaction date in the general journal's Date column. Typically, the year and month are recorded only at the top of each general journal page.

2. Refer to the chart of accounts to identify the appropriate titles for the accounts affected by the transaction.

3. Enter the title(s) of the account(s) to be debited in the description column on the first line of the entry. Insert the transaction amount related to this account in the debit column.

4. On the following line, indent and enter the title(s) of the account(s) to be credited. Insert the transaction amount related to this account in the credit column.

5. Write a brief explanation of the transaction in the description column below the title of the account credited.

The following transactions for Snow Mountain Retreat took place in April 2009. The two entries provided earlier in the chapter are provided again. Each entry is first analyzed for its debit and credit effects. Next, the items are shown as they would be recorded in the general journal, using the appropriate account titles from the company's chart of accounts (Exhibit 3-4). Gaps are left in the numbering system to allow additional accounts to be inserted.

April 1   Issued 4,000 shares of Snow Mountain Retreat's $10 par value common stock. Checks totaling $40,000 were received from stockholders.

Analysis:

■ Cash, an asset account, increased by $40,000. Assets are increased with debits.

EXHIBIT 3-4
Snow Mountain Retreat
Chart of Accounts

Account Number

Assets
101   Cash
103   Accounts Receivable
120   Supplies
125   Prepaid Rent
150   Furniture
151   Accumulated Depreciation—Furniture

Liabilities
201   Notes Payable
203   Accounts Payable
206   Wages Payable
210   Interest Payable
225   Unearned Rental Revenue
280   Income Tax Payable

Stockholders' Equity
305   Common Stock
350   Retained Earnings

Dividends
400   Dividends

Revenues
510   Rental Revenue

Expenses
603   Wages Expense
605   Rent Expense
607   Supplies Expense
609   Utilities Expense
650   Depreciation Expense
670   Interest Expense
680   Income Tax Expense
700   *Income Summary (discussed later in the chapter)*

■ Common Stock, a stockholders' equity account, increased by $40,000. Stockholders' equity is increased with credits.

General Journal				
Date	**Description**	**PR**	**Debit**	**Credit**
Apr 1	Cash		40,000	
	Common Stock			40,000
	Issued stack to stockholders			
	for initial investment			

April 1   Purchased furniture costing $12,000, paying $5,000 in cash, and signing a 12% interest-bearing note payable for the balance. The note and interest are

due in one year. The furniture is expected to have a two-year useful life with no salvage value.

Analysis:

- Furniture, an asset account, increased by $12,000. Assets are increased with debits.
- Cash, an asset account, decreased by $5,000. Assets are decreased with credits.
- Notes Payable, a liability account, increased by $7,000. Liabilities are increased with credits.

General Journal					
Date		Description	PR	Debit	Credit
Apr	1	Furniture		12,000	
		Cash			5,000
		Notes Payable			7,000
		Purchased furniture by			
		giving a cash down			
		payment and signing a			
		note payable			

This type of entry is known as a **compound journal entry** because it affects more than two accounts. Compound journal entries may have several debits and one credit, several credits and a single debit, or multiple debits and multiple credits. Like all journal entries, the dollar amount of debits and the dollar amount of credits in a compound journal entry must be equal.

April 1   Signed a one-year lease on a large, partially furnished house in Castle Rock, Colorado, to be operated as a bed and breakfast establishment. Rent of $18,000 for one year was paid by check.

Analysis:

- Prepaid Rent, an asset account, increased by $18,000. Assets are increased with debits. This payment is an asset because Snow Mountain Retreat has the right to use the house for the next 12 months or to have the lease payment returned.
- Cash, an asset account, decreased by $18,000. Assets are decreased with credits.

General Journal					
Date		Description	PR	Debit	Credit
Apr	1	Prepaid Rent		18,000	
		Cash			18,000
		Signed a 12-month lease			
		for the B&B and paid			
		cash for the rental			

April 3 Purchased $500 of supplies on credit.

Analysis:

- Supplies, an asset account, increased by $500. Assets are increased with debits.

- Accounts Payable, a liability account, increased by $500. Liabilities are increased with credits.

General Journal					
Date		Description	PR	Debit	Credit
Apr	3	Supplies		500	
		Accounts Payable			500
		Bought supplies on			
		account			

April 8 Received $5,000 for two one-week rentals: April 22–28 and May 20–26. This payment is fully refundable if the reservations are canceled. Revenue received before it is earned is recorded in a liability account. In this case, an appropriate title for such a liability account is Unearned Rental Revenue.

Analysis:

- Cash, an asset account, increased by $5,000. Assets are increased with debits.

- Unearned Rent Revenue, a liability account, increased by $5,000. Liabilities are increased with credits.

General Journal					
Date		Description	PR	Debit	Credit
Apr	8	Cash		5,000	
		Unearned Rental			
		Revenue			5,000
		Received payment for			
		two weeks: one in April			
		and one in May			

As discussed in Chapter 2, when customers pay for products or services before receiving them, the company has incurred a liability—in this case, Unearned Rental Revenue. Snow Mountain Retreat owes the customers one of two things: occupancy of the rooms for the specified weeks or return of the $5,000 cash.

April 17 Rented four rooms for the weekend for $1,500 cash.

Analysis:

- Cash, an asset account, increased by $1,500. Assets are increased with debits.

- Rental Revenue, a revenue account, increased by $1,500. Revenues are increased with credits.

General Journal					
Date		**Description**	**PR**	**Debit**	**Credit**
Apr	17	Cash		1,500	
		Rental Revenue			1,500
		Earned revenue from			
		room rentals			

April 24   Rented two rooms for one week for $3,250 cash.

Analysis:

- Cash, an asset account, increased by $3,250. Assets are increased with debits.
- Rental Revenue, a revenue account, increased by $3,250. Revenues are increased with credits.

General Journal					
Date		**Description**	**PR**	**Debit**	**Credit**
Apr	24	Cash		3,250	
		Rental Revenue			3,250
		Earned revenue from			
		room rentals			

April 24   A maintenance person began working on April 6. He was paid $800 for two weeks' wages: April 6–11 and April 13–17.

Analysis:

- Wages Expense, an expense account, increased by $800. Expenses are increased with debits.
- Cash, an asset account, decreased by $800. Assets are decreased with credits.

General Journal					
Date		**Description**	**PR**	**Debit**	**Credit**
Apr	24	Wages Expense		800	
		Cash			800
		Paid maintenance			
		worker wages for two			
		weeks			

April 24   Rented two rooms for weekend for $750 to be paid by May 15. Even though the cash has not yet been received, Snow Mountain has earned the rental revenue because the rooms were provided to customers.

Analysis:

- Accounts Receivable, an asset account, increased by $750. Assets are increased with debits.

- Rental Revenue, a revenue account, increased by $750. Revenues are increased with credits.

General Journal					
Date		Description	PR	Debit	Credit
Apr	24	Accounts Receivable		750	
		Rental Revenue			750
		Earned revenue from			
		room rentals			

April 30 Paid $250 of the $500 owed on account for the supplies purchased on April 3. No new supplies are acquired on April 30; therefore, the Supplies account is not affected.

Analysis:

- Accounts Payable, a liability account, decreased by $250. Liabilities are decreased with debits.

- Cash, an asset account, decreased by $250. Assets are decreased with credits.

General Journal					
Date		Description	PR	Debit	Credit
Apr	30	Accounts Payable		250	
		Cash			250
		Paid an account payable			

April 30 Received and paid the $390 electricity bill for April.

Analysis:

- Utilities Expense, an expense account, increased by $390. Expenses are increased with debits.

- Cash, an asset account, decreased by $390. Assets are decreased with credits.

General Journal					
Date		Description	PR	Debit	Credit
Apr	30	Utilities Expense		390	
		Cash			390
		Paid the April utility bill			

April 30 Declared a dividend of $500 and paid stockholders.

Analysis:

- Dividends, a dividend account, increased by $500. Dividends are increased with debits.

- Cash, an asset account, decreased by $500. Assets are decreased with credits.

General Journal					
Date		**Description**	**PR**	**Debit**	**Credit**
Apr	30	Dividends		500	
		Cash			500
		Paid dividend to			
		company stockholders			

Remember that although a dividend account has the same debit and credit rules as an expense, dividends paid by a corporation to its stockholders are not expenses. Whereas expenses will decrease net income, dividends have no impact on net income and only affect the amount of a corporation's Retained Earnings. However, unlike this transaction, it is not common for dividends to be declared and paid at the same point in time.

Step 1b: Post Transactions to the General Ledger

After a transaction has been journalized, the information is then posted (again using the debit and credit rules) to general ledger accounts. Each ledger account has three monetary columns: one for debits, one for credits, and one for the account balance. Other information is also recorded in the general ledger, as will be discussed later. A blank general ledger is shown in Exhibit 3-5.

1. For each account listed in a general journal transaction, determine the appropriate general ledger account number in the chart of accounts. Find that account in the general ledger.

2. In the general ledger account, record the transaction date and a brief description of the transaction as provided in the general journal.

3. In the posting reference (PR) column of each affected account, indicate the journal and page number from which the amount was posted. In this example, "GJ1" is inserted in the PR column to indicate that each amount was posted from page 1 of the general journal.

4. Enter the transaction amount in the appropriate debit or credit column in the account.

5. Compute the new balance of each account and enter that amount in the balance column.

6. After posting each transaction element to the general ledger, return to the general journal and record the general ledger account number to which the debit or credit amount was posted in the PR column.

EXHIBIT 3-5

General Ledger

Account Name					Account No.	
Date		**Explanation**	**PR**	**Debit**	**Credit**	**Balance**

Posting financial data from the general journal to the general ledger summarizes the data by specific account. Journal entry data may be posted daily, weekly, or even monthly in a manual accounting system. In computer-based accounting systems, transaction data are posted to general ledger accounts simultaneously with the journalizing process. As transaction data are keyed into a computerized accounting system by a data entry clerk or captured electronically by the system, a chronological record (journal entry) of the transaction is prepared. At the same time, the dollar amounts involved in the transaction are electronically routed (posted) to the computer files (accounts) of the financial statement items affected by the transaction. Programming instructions automatically indicate whether the computer should debit or credit the dollar amounts to the individual accounts to correctly update their balances.

Exhibits 3-6 and 3-7 show, respectively, the completed general journal and general ledger accounts for the given April transactions for Snow Mountain Retreat. Note that the PR column in the general journal indicates where the information was posted; in the general ledger, this column indicates where the information came from.

Step 1c: Prepare a Trial Balance

The **trial balance** is a two-column (one debit and one credit) listing of general ledger accounts and their balances. The accounts are listed in account order, with the balance being appropriately entered in either the debit or credit column. A trial balance's purpose is to ensure that the accounting system is "in balance" (total debits and total credits are equal). Exhibit 3-8 is the trial balance for Snow Mountain Retreat.

If a trial balance does not balance, there are one or more errors in the accounting records. Those errors must be found and corrected before the accounting cycle can continue. Unfortunately, even if a trial balance has equal debits and credits, there may be errors in the accounting records. For example, if the debit or credit of a journal entry were posted to an incorrect account, the debit and credit columns of the trial balance would be equal even though at least one of the accounts would be incorrect.

Step 2: Adjust Account Balances as Necessary

As previously discussed, there are two principal accounting methods: cash basis and accrual basis. Under cash basis accounting, businesses record transactions only if they involve the payment or receipt of cash. Under accrual basis accounting, a transaction's economic impact is recorded whether or not the transaction involves cash. Most business entities use accrual accounting because it better represents the economic reality of their operations and financial condition.

When accrual accounting is used, a special category of journal entries is needed at the end of an accounting period. **Adjusting entries** are prepared to ensure that the revenue and expense recognition rules, discussed in Chapter 2, are properly applied ~h accounting period so that revenues and expenses are recorded in the accounting ~d to which they relate. For example, adjusting entries are required at the end of an ~ting period to recognize expenses that a business has incurred, but has not yet paid or

EXHIBIT 3-6

Snow Mountain Retreat
General Journal

General Journal					
Date		Description	PR	Debit	Credit
Apr	1	Cash	101	40,000	
		Common Stock	305		40,000
		Issued stock to stockholders for their initial *investmen*			
	1	Furniture	150	12,000	
		Cash	101		5,000
		Notes Payable	201		7,000
		Purchased furniture by giving a cash down *payment and signing a note payable*			
	1	Prepaid Rent	125	18,000	
		Cash	101		18,000
		Signed a 12-month lease for the B&B and paid *cash for the rental*			
	3	Supplies	120	500	
		Accounts Payable	203		500
		Bought supplies on account			
	8	Cash	101	5,000	
		Unearned Rental Revenue	225		5,000
		Received payment for two weeks: one in April *and one in May*			
	17	Cash	101	1,500	
		Rental Revenue	510		1,500
		Earned revenue from room rentals			
	24	Cash	101	3,250	
		Rental Revenue	510		3,250
		Earned revenue from room rentals			
	24	Wages Expense	603	800	
		Cash	101		800
		Paid maintenance worker wages for two weeks			
	24	Accounts Receivable	103	750	
		Rental Revenue	510		750
		Earned revenue from room rentals			
	30	Accounts Payable	203	250	
		Cash	101		250
		Paid an account payable			
	30	Utilities Expense	609	390	
		Cash	101		390
		Paid the April utility bill			
	30	Dividends	400	500	
		Cash	101		500
		Paid dividend to company stockholders			

EXHIBIT 3-7

Snow Mountain Retreat
General Ledger

Cash Account No. 101

Date		Explanation	PR	Debit	Credit	Balance
Apr	1	Sold 4,000 shares of stock	GJ1	40,000		40,000
	1	Made furniture down payment	GJ1		5,000	35,000
	1	Prepaid 12-month lease	GJ1		18,000	17,000
	8	Received rent in advance	GJ1	5,000		22,000
	17	Received & earned rental income	GJ1	1,500		23,500
	24	Received & earned rental income	GJ1	3,250		26,750
	24	Paid maintenance wages	GJ1		800	25,950
	30	Paid accounts payable	GJ1		250	25,700
	30	Paid utilities	GJ1		390	25,310
	30	Paid dividends	GJ1		500	24,810

Accounts Receivable Account No. 103

Date		Explanation	PR	Debit	Credit	Balance
Apr	24	Rental	GJ1	750		750

Supplies Account No. 120

Date		Explanation	PR	Debit	Credit	Balance
Apr	3	Bought supplies	GJ1	500		500

Prepaid Rent Account No. 125

Date		Explanation	PR	Debit	Credit	Balance
Apr	1	Prepaid 12-month lease	GJ1	18,000		18,000

Furniture Account No. 150

Date		Explanation	PR	Debit	Credit	Balance
Apr	1	Bought furniture	GJ1	12,000		12,000

Notes Payable Account No. 201

Date		Explanation	PR	Debit	Credit	Balance
Apr	1	Issued 12%, 1-year note for furniture	GJ1		7,000	7,000

Accounts Payable Account No. 203

Date		Explanation	PR	Debit	Credit	Balance
Apr	3	Bought supplies	GJ1		500	500
	30	Paid A/P	GJ1	250		250

EXHIBIT 3-7

Continued

Unearned Rental Revenue — Account No. 225

Date		Explanation	PR	Debit	Credit	Balance
Apr	8	Received 2 weeks' rent in advance	GJ1		5,000	5,000

Common Stock — Account No. 305

Date		Explanation	PR	Debit	Credit	Balance
Apr	1	Issued 4,000 shares of stock	GJ1		40,000	40,000

Dividends — Account No. 400

Date		Explanation	PR	Debit	Credit	Balance
Apr	30	Declared a cash dividend	GJ1	500		500

Rental Revenue — Account No. 510

Date		Explanation	PR	Debit	Credit	Balance
Apr	17	Earned revenue	GJ1		1,500	1,500
	24	Earned revenue	GJ1		3,250	4,750
	24	Earned revenue	GJ1		750	5,500

Wages Expense — Account No. 603

Date		Explanation	PR	Debit	Credit	Balance
Apr	24	Maintenance wages 4/6-4/11 & 4/13--4/17	GJ1	800		800

Utilities Expense — Account No. 609

Date		Explanation	PR	Debit	Credit	Balance
Apr	30	April electricity	GJ1	390		390

Step 2a. Record Adjustments in the General Journal

The specific circumstances that require adjustments to a business's general ledger account balances at the end of each accounting period must be identified. This identification process occurs through talking to management, scanning accounting records, reviewing prior periods' adjusting entries, and most important, using intuition and accounting expertise. Computerized accounting systems may automatically scan the accounting records and produce a tentative list of adjusting journal entries. However, such a list will need to be reviewed for completeness.

Deferrals and Accruals Before developing period-ending adjustments, the concepts of deferrals and accruals must first be defined and illustrated. As shown in Visual Recap 3.3, a deferred item is one for which the cash has been paid or received, but the expense or revenue

EXHIBIT 3-8

Snow Mountain Retreat
Trial Balance

Snow Mountain Retreat
Trial Balance
April 30, 2009

	Debit	Credit
Cash	$24,810	
Accounts Receivable	750	
Supplies	500	
Prepaid Rent	18,000	
Furniture	12,000	
Notes Payable		$ 7,000
Accounts Payable		250
Unearned Rental Revenue		5,000
Common Stock		40,000
Dividends	500	
Rental Revenue		5,500
Wages Expense	800	
Utilities Expense	390	
Totals	$57,750	$57,750

has not yet been recognized. An accrued item is one for which the cash has not yet been paid or received, but the expense or revenue has already been recognized. End-of-period adjusting entries may create or affect deferred and accrued items.

A **deferred expense** is an asset that represents a prepayment of an expense item. When an expense is prepaid, an asset account is debited and the Cash account credited. For example, when Snow Mountain Retreat prepaid its $18,000 12-month lease amount on

VISUAL RECAP 3.3

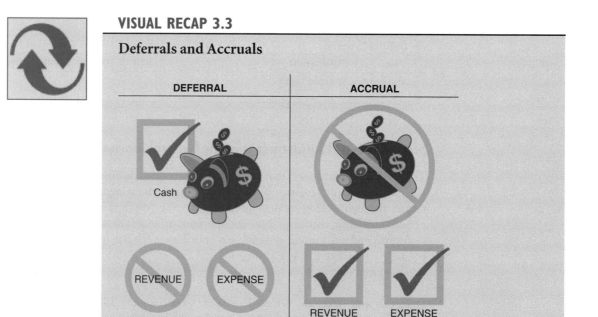

Deferrals and Accruals

April 1, the company debited Prepaid Rent, an asset account, and credited Cash. Over the lease term, the economic benefit provided by the asset will be gradually used up. As a result, by the end of the one-year lease term, the full amount of the rent prepayment will be debited to Rent Expense and credited to Prepaid Rent. Thus, a deferred expense is originally recorded as an asset, but will eventually be recognized, or written off, as an expense.

A **deferred revenue** is a liability that represents an amount received by a business for a service or product that will be provided or delivered in the future. The Unearned Rental Revenue account of Snow Mountain Retreat is a deferred revenue account. Upon receiving the funds, Snow Mountain Retreat owes its customers either room occupancy or a refund. When the customers occupy the rooms, the earnings process is completed, and the deferred revenue is debited with an offsetting credit to a revenue account. Thus, a deferred revenue is originally recorded as a liability, but will eventually be recognized as revenue.

An **accrued asset** is a receivable resulting from revenue that has been earned but has not yet been received in cash. An account receivable is the most common accrued asset. Another accrued asset is interest receivable that has been earned but not yet been collected on an amount loaned to a customer or another party.

An **accrued liability** is an expense that has been incurred but has not yet been paid in cash. A common accrued liability is salaries or wages payable. Typically, the end of a business's accounting period does not coincide with the end of a payroll period. Thus, at the end of most accounting periods, a business's employees have earned, but not been paid, some amount of salaries or wages. These amounts are recognized by debiting an expense account, such as Wages Expense, and crediting a liability account, such as Wages Payable.

Deferrals and accruals and their adjusting entries are summarized in Visual Recap 3.4. The XXX's in the graphic indicate a type of asset or liability account title. For example, if cash were paid in advance for insurance, the account titles to be used would be Prepaid Insurance and Insurance Expense. Or if cash were received in advance for rent on a building, the account titles to be used would be Unearned Rent Revenue and Rent Revenue

Adjusting Journal Entries for Snow Mountain Retreat Following are seven circumstances requiring adjustments to Snow Mountain Retreat's general ledger account balances as of April 30, 2009. An analysis of each adjustment is provided.

Adjustment A: Expiration of Prepaid Rent On April 1, 2009, Snow Mountain Retreat prepaid one year's rent on the bed and breakfast. By the end of April, one-twelfth of this deferred expense had been used. The decrease in this asset should be recognized as an expense so that the company's assets are not overstated and expenses are not understated.

Analysis:

- Rent Expense, an expense account, increased by $1,500 ($18,000 ÷ 12). Expenses are increased with debits.
- Prepaid Rent, an asset account, decreased by $1,500. Assets are decreased with credits.

Adjustment B: Depreciation of Furniture On April 1, 2009, furniture was purchased for the B&B. This asset must be systematically depreciated over the accounting periods during which the furniture provides an economic benefit to the business. Snow Mountain Retreat uses straight-line depreciation. Under this method, the asset's cost less any estimated salvage value at the end of the asset's useful life is written off in equal amounts over that useful life.

VISUAL RECAP 3.4

Adjusting Deferrals and Accruals

Deferred Expense (Asset)	**Deferred Revenue (Liability)**
Cash is paid to vendor before service is received	Cash is received before service is provided to customers

■ The cash is paid and an asset is established.
Prepaid XXX   18,000
          Cash   18,000
Prepaid one year's XXX
	■ The cash is received and a liability is recorded.
	Cash 5,000
	          Unearned XXX Revenue 5,000
	Customer paid advance

■ The expense is recorded when the asset is used up.
XXX Expense   1,500
          Prepaid XXX   1,500
Used one month of prepaid XXX
	■ The revenue is recorded when the liability is eliminated.
	Unearned XXX Revenue 2,500
	          XXX Revenue 2,500
	Earned half of customer advance

Accrued Liability (Expense)	**Accrued Asset (Revenue)**
Service is received from vendor before cash is paid	Service is provided before cash is received

■ The service is received and payable is recorded.
XXX Expense   700
          XXX Payable   700
Received XXX bill
	■ The service is rendered and a receivable is recorded.
	XXX Receivable 2,000
	          XXX Revenue 2,000
	Earned XXX revenue

■ The payable is eliminated when the cash is paid.
XXX Payable   700
          Cash   700
Paid XXX payable
	■ The receivable is eliminated when the cash is received.
	Cash 2,000
	          XXX Receivable 2,000
	Amount received on account

(Left margin labels: "Deferred" for the top row, "Accrued" for the bottom row.)

Because Snow Mountain Retreat's furniture has a zero salvage value at the end of its two-year life, the furniture's depreciation expense is computed as $12,000 divided by 24 months, or $500 per month. The decrease in this asset should be recognized as an expense so that the company's assets are not overstated and expenses are not understated.

Analysis:

■ Depreciation Expense, an expense account, increased by $500. Expenses are increased with debits.

■ Accumulated Depreciation, a contra-asset account, increased by $500. Contra-assets are increased with credits. Using the Accumulated Depreciation account to show the total amount of depreciation taken on the asset allows the furniture's $12,000 historical cost to be preserved in the general ledger asset account.

Adjustment C: Recognition of Interest Expense on Note Payable By signing the $7,000 note payable on April 1, Snow Mountain Retreat promised to pay the seller of the furniture that amount plus interest at 12% per year. However, even though the note principal and interest are not paid until April 1, 2010, Snow Mountain Retreat incurs interest expense for each day that the note is not paid. Thus, at the end of April, the company owes, but has not paid, one month's interest expense. The interest owed is calculated as

$$\text{Interest} = \text{Principal} \times \text{Rate} \times \text{Time}$$

In this case, the principal is the $7,000 original amount of the note, the rate is 12% per year, and the time is one month.[1] Snow Mountain Retreat's interest expense for April is ($7,000 \times 0.12 \times 1/12$) or $70. This expense should be recognized so that the company's expenses and liabilities are not understated.

Analysis:

- Interest Expense, an expense account, increased by $70. Expenses are increased with debits.
- Interest Payable, a liability account, increased by $70. Liabilities are increased with credits.

Adjustment D: Supplies Used At the end of April 2009, $420 of supplies remained of the $500 of supplies purchased earlier in the month. Thus, $80 of supplies had been used during April. The decrease in this asset should be recognized as an expense so that the company's assets are not overstated and expenses are not understated.

Analysis:

- Supplies Expense, an expense account, increased by $80. Expenses are increased with debits.
- Supplies, an asset account, decreased by $80. Assets are decreased with credits.

Adjustment E: Recognition of Revenue on Advance Rental Payment On April 8, 2009, a customer paid $5,000 to Snow Mountain Retreat for two rentals during the weeks of April 22–28 and May 20–26. When this amount was received, Unearned Rental Revenue (a deferred liability) was recorded. By the end of April, the customer had used her reservation for the week of April 22–28, and thus, Snow Mountain Retreat had earned $2,500 (one-half of the $5,000 advance payment). The decrease in this liability should be recognized as revenue so that the company's liabilities are not overstated and revenues are not understated.

Analysis:

- Unearned Rental Revenue, a liability account, decreased by $2,500. Liabilities are decreased with debits.
- Rental Revenue, a revenue account, increased by $2,500. Revenues are increased with credits.

---

[1]Interest rates are always stated on an annual basis unless otherwise indicated. Therefore, fractions representing the passage of time should always represent a portion of a year. For example, 5 months would be shown as 5/12.

Adjustment F: Recognition of Unpaid Salary Expense Snow Mountain Retreat's maintenance employee earns $800 every two weeks, or $80 per day for Monday through Friday. (Payroll taxes and other deductions that affect the employee's take-home pay are ignored at this point.) Payroll dates are one week after the end of the payroll period. Having started work on April 6, the employee received his first paycheck on April 24 and was scheduled to receive his second paycheck on May 1. As of April 30, the employee had worked nine days (4/20–4/24 and 4/27–4/30) for which he had not been paid. Thus, Snow Mountain Retreat owed wages of $720 to the maintenance person at the end of April. This expense should be recognized so that the company's expenses and liabilities are not understated.

Analysis:

- Wages Expense, an expense account, increased by $720. Expenses are increased with debits.
- Wages Payable, a liability account, increased by $720. Liabilities are increased with credits.

Adjustment G: Recognition of Estimated Income Tax Expense At the end of each year, Snow Mountain Retreat will be required to pay a corporate income tax on any earned profits. On April 30, 2009, Snow Mountain Retreat did not know how much would be earned for the year and, therefore, could not determine an exact amount of income tax that would need to be paid. Nevertheless, a business must estimate its income tax expense each accounting period because of the matching aspect of the expense recognition rule. After reviewing the tax rate schedule, Snow Mountain Retreat recorded a $200 accrued liability because an estimate of the corporate income tax would eventually be paid on the profit earned during April. This expense should be recognized so that the company's expenses and liabilities are not understated.

Analysis:

- Income Tax Expense, an expense account, increased by $200. Expenses are increased with debits.
- Income Tax Payable, a liability account, increased by $200. Liabilities are increased with credits.

These adjusting entries are journalized in the general journal as shown in Exhibit 3-9.

Step 2b: Post Adjustments to the General Ledger

The journal entries from Exhibit 3-9 are posted to the general ledger (Exhibit 3-10). Notice that the balances in many of the accounts previously shown in Exhibit 3-7 have not changed in Exhibit 3-10; however, some additional accounts have been added.

Step 2c: Prepare an Adjusted Trial Balance

Exhibit 3-11 presents the adjusted trial balance for Snow Mountain Retreat as of April 30, 2009. The account balances listed in the trial balance are taken from the general ledger accounts shown in Exhibit 3-10. Only general ledger accounts that have nonzero balances are included in a trial balance. The debits and credits in the trial balance are summed and found to be equal. Thus, the next step of the accounting cycle, preparing the financial statements, can be performed.

EXHIBIT 3-9

Snow Mountain Retreat
General Journal—
Adjusting Entries

General Journal					
Date		Description	PR	Debit	Credit
Apr	30	Rent Expense	605	1,500	
		Prepaid Rent	125		1,500
		One month of prepaid rent expired			
	30	Depreciation Expense	650	500	
		Accumulated Depreciation—Furniture	151		500
		Recorded one month of furniture depreciation			
	30	Interest Expense	670	70	
		Interest Payable	210		70
		Recorded one month's interest on N/P			
	30	Supplies Expense	607	80	
		Supplies	120		80
		Recorded supplies used in April			
	30	Unearned Rental Revenue	225	2,500	
		Rental Revenue	510		2,500
		Recorded the earning of revenue for the week of April 22–28			
	30	Wages Expense	603	720	
		Wages Payable	206		720
		Recorded maintenance worker wages for 9 days			
	30	Income Tax Expense	680	200	
		Income Tax Payable	280		200
		Recorded estimated income taxes for April			

Step 3: Prepare Financial Statements

After debits and credits of the adjusted trial balance are determined to be in balance, the company's financial statements can be prepared. Using the information from accounts listed in the adjusted trial balance, Snow Mountain Retreat's income statement (Exhibit 3-12), statement of stockholders' equity (Exhibit 3-13), and balance sheet (Exhibit 3-14) are developed.

Snow Mountain Retreat's statement of stockholders' equity at the end of April 2009 reconciles the beginning and end-of-period balances of the corporation's stockholders' equity accounts. Three items must be considered when computing a company's period-ending retained earnings in the statement of stockholders' equity: beginning balance, net income for the period, and dividends declared during the period.

Note that Snow Mountain Retreat's Retained Earnings account is not included in the firm's adjusted trial balance prepared on April 30, 2009. There was no balance in that account when the trial balance was prepared because the company began operations on April 1, 2009. However, all the information needed to compute the firm's Retained Earnings as of April 30, 2009, is available in the adjusted trial balance. The April 30, 2009, Retained Earnings balance is computed by subtracting the $500 of dividends for April from the April net income of $3,740. In May 2009, the $3,240 will be included in the trial balance as the beginning balance of Retained Earnings.

In most computerized accounting systems, a set of financial statements can be generated electronically after adjusting the general ledger accounts. In fact, many large public companies both prepare their financial statements electronically and deliver them

Cash   Account No. 101

Date		Explanation	PR	Debit	Credit	Balance
Apr	1	Sold 4,000 shares of stock	GJ1	40,000		40,000
	1	Made furniture down payment	GJ1		5,000	35,000
	1	Prepaid 12-month lease	GJ1		18,000	17,000
	8	Received rent in advance	GJ1	5,000		22,000
	19	Received & earned rental income	GJ1	1,500		23,500
	24	Received & earned rental income	GJ1	3,250		26,750
	24	Paid maintenance wages	GJ1		800	25,950
	30	Paid accounts payable	GJ1		250	25,700
	30	Paid utilities	GJ1		390	25,310
	30	Paid dividends	GJ1		500	24,810

Accounts Receivable   Account No. 103

Date		Explanation	PR	Debit	Credit	Balance
Apr	24	Rental	GJ1	750		750

Supplies   Account No. 120

Date		Explanation	PR	Debit	Credit	Balance
Apr	3	Bought supplies	GJ1	500		500
	30	Used supplies in April	GJ2		80	420

Prepaid Rent   Account No. 125

Date		Explanation	PR	Debit	Credit	Balance
Apr	1	Prepaid 12-month lease	GJ1	18,000		18,000
	30	One month's lease expired	GJ2		1,500	16,500

Furniture   Account No. 150

Date		Explanation	PR	Debit	Credit	Balance
Apr	1	Bought furniture	GJ1	12,000		12,000

Accumulated Depreciation—Furniture   Account No. 151

Date		Explanation	PR	Debit	Credit	Balance
Apr	30	Recorded one month's depreciation	GJ2		500	500

Notes Payable   Account No. 201

Date		Explanation	PR	Debit	Credit	Balance
Apr	1	Issued 12%, 1-year note for furniture	GJ1		7,000	7,000

EXHIBIT 3-10

Continued

Accounts Payable — Account No. 203

Date		Explanation	PR	Debit	Credit	Balance
Apr	3	Bought supplies	GJ1		500	500
	30	Paid A/P	GJ1	250		250

Wages Payable — Account No. 206

Date		Explanation	PR	Debit	Credit	Balance
Apr	30	Owe 9 days maintenance wages	GJ2		720	720

Interest Payable — Account No. 210

Date		Explanation	PR	Debit	Credit	Balance
Apr	30	Owe one month's interest on note	GJ2		70	70

Unearned Rental Revenue — Account No. 225

Date		Explanation	PR	Debit	Credit	Balance
Apr	8	Received 2 weeks' rent in advance	GJ1		5,000	5,000
	30	Earned one week rental revenue	GJ2	2,500		2,500

Income Taxes Payable — Account No. 280

Date		Explanation	PR	Debit	Credit	Balance
Apr	30	Estimate for April	GJ2		200	200

Common Stock — Account No. 305

Date		Explanation	PR	Debit	Credit	Balance
Apr	1	Issued 4,000 shares of stock	GJ1		40,000	40,000

Dividends — Account No. 400

Date		Explanation	PR	Debit	Credit	Balance
Apr	30	Declared a cash dividend	GJ1	500		500

Rental Revenue — Account No. 510

Date		Explanation	PR	Debit	Credit	Balance
Apr	17	Earned revenue	GJ1		1,500	1,500
	24	Earned revenue	GJ1		3,250	4,750
	24	Earned revenue	GJ1		750	5,500
	30	Earned revenue	GJ2		2,500	8,000

EXHIBIT 3-10

Continued

Wages Expense   Account No. 603

Date		Explanation	PR	Debit	Credit	Balance
Apr	24	Maintenance wages 4/6-10 & 4/13–4/17	GJ1	800		800
	30	Maintenance wages for 9 days	GJ2	720		1,520

Rent Expense   Account No. 605

Date		Explanation	PR	Debit	Credit	Balance
Apr	30	For April	GJ2	1,500		1,500

Supplies Expense   Account No. 607

Date		Explanation	PR	Debit	Credit	Balance
Apr	30	For April	GJ2	80		80

Utilities Expense   Account No. 609

Date		Explanation	PR	Debit	Credit	Balance
Apr	30	April electricity	GJ1	390		390

Depreciation Expense   Account No. 650

Date		Explanation	PR	Debit	Credit	Balance
Apr	30	For April on furniture	GJ2	500		500

Interest Expense   Account No. 670

Date		Explanation	PR	Debit	Credit	Balance
Apr	30	For April on N/P	GJ2	70		70

Income Tax Expense   Account No. 680

Date		Explanation	PR	Debit	Credit	Balance
Apr	30	April estimate	GJ2	200		200

electronically to external users via the Internet. The EDGAR (Electronic Data Gathering, Analysis, and Retrieval) system Internet Web site (www.sec.gov/edgar.shtml) maintained by the Securities and Exchange Commission provides investors and other interested parties timely access to hundreds of large companies' financial statements in an electronic format.

Step 4: Close Temporary Accounts

At the end of a period, a business will "close" its books so that it can start the new period with a "clean slate." Normally the closing process only takes place at the end of

EXHIBIT 3-11
Snow Mountain Retreat
Adjusted Trial Balance

Snow Mountain Retreat
Adjusted Trial Balance
April 30, 2009

	Debit	Credit
Cash	$24,810	
Accounts Receivable	750	
Supplies	420	
Prepaid Rent	16,500	
Furniture	12,000	
Accumulated Depreciation—Furniture		$ 500
Notes Payable		7,000
Accounts Payable		250
Wages Payable		720
Interest Payable		70
Unearned Rental Revenue		2,500
Income Tax Payable		200
Common Stock		40,000
Dividends	500	
Rental Revenue		8,000
Wages Expense	1,520	
Rent Expense	1,500	
Supplies Expense	80	
Utilities Expense	390	
Depreciation Expense	500	
Interest Expense	70	
Income Tax Expense	200	
Totals	$59,240	$59,240

EXHIBIT 3-12
Snow Mountain Retreat
Adjusted Trial Balance

Snow Mountain Retreat
Income Statement
For Month Ended April 30, 2009

Rental Revenue		$ 8,000
Operating Expenses		
Wages	$1,520	
Rent	1,500	
Supplies	80	
Utilities	390	
Depreciation	500	(3,990)
Operating Income		$ 4,010
Other Revenues and Expenses		
Interest Expense		(70)
Income Before Income Taxes		$ 3,940
Income Tax Expense		(200)
Net Income		$ 3,740
Earnings Per Share (4,000 shares)		$ 0.935

EXHIBIT 3-13

Snow Mountain Retreat
Statement of
Stockholders' Equity

Snow Mountain Retreat
Statement of Stockholders' Equity
For Month Ended April 30, 2009

	Common Stock	Retained Earnings
Balance, April 1, 2009	$ 0	$ 0
Sale of Common Stock	40,000	
Net Income		3,740
Dividends		(500)
Balance, April 30, 2009	$40,000	$3,240

EXHIBIT 3-14

Snow Mountain Retreat
Balance Sheet

Snow Mountain Retreat
Balance Sheet
April 30, 2009
ASSETS

Current Assets		
Cash		$24,810
Accounts Receivable		750
Supplies		420
Prepaid Rent		16,500
Total Current Assets		$42,480
Property, Plant, and Equipment		
Furniture	$12,000	
Accumulated Depreciation—Furniture	(500)	11,500
Total Assets		$53,980
LIABILITIES		
Current Liabilities		
Notes Payable		$ 7,000
Accounts Payable		250
Wages Payable		720
Interest Payable		70
Unearned Rent Revenue		2,500
Income Tax Payable		200
Total Current Liabilities		$10,740
STOCKHOLDERS' EQUITY		
Common Stock (4,000 shares; $10 par value)	$40,000	
Retained Earnings	3,240	43,240
Total Liabilities and Stockholders' Equity		$53,980

the company's fiscal year, but for illustrative purposes, it is assumed that Snow Mountain Retreat closes its books at the end of each month. Before discussing the closing process, the concept of permanent and temporary accounts must be addressed.

Every company's chart of accounts contains permanent and temporary accounts. Balance sheet accounts (assets, liabilities, and stockholders' equity) are called **permanent accounts** because their period-ending balances are carried forward to the next accounting period. Alternately, revenue, expense, and dividend accounts are referred to as **temporary accounts** because they begin each new accounting period with a zero balance. Temporary accounts all affect the balance of one permanent account: Retained Earnings. Retained Earnings is a key stockholders' equity account because, at any time, the balance of this account represents the sum of all a corporation's net income (revenues minus expenses) since its inception minus all dividends distributed to the firm's stockholders.

Step 4a: Record Closing Entries in the General Journal

The temporary accounts of a business begin each accounting period with a zero balance because the previous period balances in these accounts are transferred to Retained Earnings through the use of closing entries. An account called Income Summary is often used to help close temporary accounts into Retained Earnings each accounting period. The Income Summary account is also a temporary account.

Following are the four closing entries that businesses make at the end of an accounting period:

1. Transfer credit balances of income statement accounts to the Income Summary account.
2. Transfer debit balances of income statement accounts to the Income Summary account.
3. Transfer the balance of the Income Summary account to the Retained Earnings account.
4. Transfer the balance of the Dividends account to the Retained Earnings account.

The **closing entry** rules are depicted in Visual Recap 3.5.

VISUAL RECAP 3.5

Closing Entry Rules

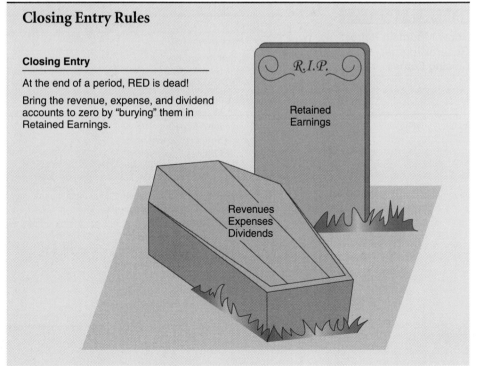

Closing Entry

At the end of a period, RED is dead!

Bring the revenue, expense, and dividend accounts to zero by "burying" them in Retained Earnings.

R.I.P.

Retained Earnings

Revenues
Expenses
Dividends

Exhibit 3-15 presents the closing entries for Snow Mountain Retreat on April 30, 2009. The first entry closes the Rental Revenue account by bringing that account balance to zero and creating a credit-balanced Income Summary account. Because the Rental Revenue account has a credit balance, debiting that account for $8,000 creates a zero balance in Rental Revenue and a total revenue amount as a credit in Income Summary. The second entry closes the debit-balanced expense accounts. Following the posting of that entry, each of Snow Mountain Retreat's expense accounts will have a zero balance, and the Income Summary account will have a net credit balance of $3,740. This amount equals the company's net income for April. By transferring the period-ending balances of all revenue and expense accounts to Income Summary, a business can confirm that the proper net income amount was calculated on the Income Statement. The third entry closes the Income Summary account by transferring its balance to Retained Earnings.

The final closing entry for Snow Mountain Retreat transfers the balance of the Dividends account to Retained Earnings. If no dividends have been paid to stockholders during a period, this entry will not be necessary. However, it is important to notice that dividends are closed separately from the company's expenses to emphasize that dividends are not expenses of the business.

Step 4b: Post Closing Entries to the General Ledger

The account numbers appearing in the post-reference column in Exhibit 3-15 indicate that the closing entries have been posted to the appropriate general ledger accounts. Only the general ledger accounts of Snow Mountain Retreat that have been affected by the closing entries are shown in Exhibit 3-16; all other account balances remain the same as they are in Exhibit 3-6.

EXHIBIT 3-15

Snow Mountain Retreat General Journal— Closing Entries

General Journal					
Date		Description	PR	Debit	Credit
Apr	30	Rental Revenue	510	8,000	
		Income Summary	700		8,000
		To close the revenue account			
	30	Income Summary	700	4,260	
		Wages Expense	603		1,520
		Rent Expense	605		1,500
		Supplies Expense	607		80
		Utilities Expense	609		390
		Depreciation Expense	650		500
		Interest Expense	670		70
		Income Tax Expense	680		200
		To close the expense accounts			
	30	Income Summary	700	3,740	
		Retained Earnings	350		3,740
		To close Income Summary and transfer net income to Retained Earnings			
	30	Retained Earnings	350	500	
		Dividends	400		500
		To close the dividends account			

EXHIBIT 3-16

Snow Mountain Retreat
General Ledger After
Closing Entries

Retained Earnings — Account No. 3

Date		Explanation	PR	Debit	Credit	Balance
Apr	30	Net income for April	GJ3		3,740	3,740
	30	Dividends declared for April	GJ3	500		3,240

Dividends — Account No. 400

Date		Explanation	PR	Debit	Credit	Balance
Apr	30	Declared a cash dividend	GJ1	500		500
	30	Closing entry	GJ3		500	0

Rental Revenue — Account No. 510

Date		Explanation	PR	Debit	Credit	Balance
Apr	17	Earned revenue	GJ1		1,500	1,500
	24	Earned revenue	GJ1		3,250	3,250
	24	Earned revenue	GJ1		750	5,500
	30	Earned revenue	GJ2		2,500	8,000
	30	Closing entry	GJ3	8,000		0

Wages Expense — Account No. 603

Date		Explanation	PR	Debit	Credit	Balance
Apr	26	Maintenance wages 4/8-4-10 & 4/13–4/17	GJ1	800		800
	30	Maintenance wages for 9 days	GJ2	720		1,520
	30	Closing entry	GJ3		1,520	0

Rent Expense — Account No. 605

Date		Explanation	PR	Debit	Credit	Balance
Apr	30	For April	GJ2	1,500		1,500
	30	Closing entry	GJ3		1,500	0

Supplies Expense — Account No. 607

Date		Explanation	PR	Debit	Credit	Balance
Apr	30	For April	GJ2	80		80
	30	Closing entry	GJ3		80	0

Utilities Expense — Account No. 609

Date		Explanation	PR	Debit	Credit	Balance
Apr	30	April electricity	GJ1	390		390
	30	Closing entry	GJ3		390	0

EXHIBIT 3-16

Continued

Depreciation Expense   Account No. 650

Date		Explanation	PR	Debit	Credit	Balance
Apr	30	For April on furniture	GJ2	500		500
	30	Closing entry	GJ3		500	0

Interest Expense   Account No. 670

Date		Explanation	PR	Debit	Credit	Balance
Apr	30	For April on N/P	GJ2	70		70
	30	Closing entry	GJ3		70	0

Income Tax Expense   Account No. 680

Date		Explanation	PR	Debit	Credit	Balance
Apr	30	April estimate	GJ2	200		200
	30	Closing entry	GJ3		200	0

Income Summary   Account No. 680

Date		Explanation	PR	Debit	Credit	Balance
Apr	30	Closing entry for revenue	GJ3		8,000	8,000
	30	Closing entry for expenses	GJ3	4,260		4,260
	30	Closing entry for net income	GJ3	3,740		0

Step 4c: Prepare a Postclosing Trial Balance

The accounting cycle concludes with the preparation of a postclosing trial balance to ensure that the general ledger is in balance. If the debit and credit column totals of this trial balance are equal, the adjusting and closing entries are assumed to have been entered correctly in the accounting records. The April 30, 2009, postclosing trial balance of Snow Mountain Retreat is shown in Exhibit 3-17. Notice that only the company's permanent, or balance sheet, accounts are listed in this trial balance. At this point, all of the temporary accounts have been closed and have zero balances. Additionally, Retained Earnings is included with the balance that was shown in the statement of stockholders' equity (Exhibit 3-13), the balance sheet (Exhibit 3-14), and the general ledger account balance in Exhibit 3-16.

In a fully computerized accounting system, a company's accounting records may be closed and a postclosing trial balance prepared in a matter of seconds by activating the appropriate computer software instructions.

SUMMARY

A system of financial record keeping known as double-entry bookkeeping has been used for centuries by businesses to capture financial data regarding transactions and related events. This system requires that at least two elements be recognized in recording each economic event.

EXHIBIT 3-17

Snow Mountain Retreat
Postclosing Trial
Balance

Snow Mountain Retreat
Postclosing Trial Balance
April 30, 2009

	Debit	Credit
Cash	$24,810	
Accounts Receivable	750	
Supplies	420	
Prepaid Rent	16,500	
Furniture	12,000	
Accumulated Depreciation—Furniture		$ 500
Notes Payable		7,000
Accounts Payable		250
Wages Payable		720
Interest Payable		70
Unearned Rental Revenue		2,500
Income Tax Payable		200
Common Stock		40,000
Retained Earnings		3,240
Totals	$54,480	$54,480

Each accounting period, a set of accounting procedures called the accounting cycle must be completed for a business. These procedures convert financial data resulting from a business's transactions during an accounting period into a set of financial statements. The accounting cycle begins with an analysis of these transactions. Key information regarding business transactions is obtained from a variety of source documents.

The next step in the accounting cycle is the preparation of journal entries. In journalizing economic transactions affecting a business, the rules of double-entry bookkeeping must be followed. The key to understanding and applying these rules is the meaning and use of the terms "debit" and "credit." Debit refers to the left-hand side of a T-account, or to the process of entering an amount on the left-hand side of an account. Credit refers to the right-hand side of a T-account, or to the process of entering an amount on the right-hand side of an account. Asset, expense, and dividend accounts normally have debit balances; increases in these accounts are recorded as debits, and decreases are recorded as credits. Liability, stockholders' equity, and revenue accounts normally have credit balances; increases in these accounts are recorded as credits, and decreases are recorded as debits.

When analyzing a transaction to prepare a journal entry, first identify the type of each account (asset, liability, and so on) affected by the transaction. Next, decide whether the account has been increased or decreased by the transaction. Then, determine whether these changes should be recorded as debits or credits. Finally, make certain that the journal entry transaction has equal debit and credit amounts.

The financial data recorded in the general journal are transferred or posted periodically to general ledger accounts. At the end of each accounting period, a trial balance of the general ledger accounts is prepared to determine whether the total debits and total credits entered in the accounting records during an accounting period are equal. Equality of the debit and credit totals in the trial balance does not, however, guarantee that transactions have been journalized and posted correctly.

Also at the end of each accounting period, general ledger accounts are adjusted for certain accrual and deferral items. After journalizing and posting the adjusting entries, the firm's financial statements are prepared. Next, closing entries to bring revenue, expense, and dividend accounts to zero are journalized and posted. A postclosing trial balance is prepared to determine that the general ledger is in balance at the end of the period.

KEY TERMS

accounting cycle	contra-account	journalize
accrued asset	credit	permanent account
accrued liability	debit	source document
adjusting entry	deferred expense	T-account
closing entry	deferred revenue	temporary account
compound journal entry	double-entry bookkeeping	trial balance

QUESTIONS

1. List two examples of each of the following components of the accounting equation: assets, liabilities, and stockholders' equity. *(LO 3.1)*

2. What types of transactions affect the stockholders' equity of a business? Provide two examples. *(LO 3.1)*

3. Identify several source documents from which accountants obtain information needed to journalize business transactions. What types of transactions would be represented by each type of source document? *(LO 3.1)*

4. Why is information posted from the general journal to the general ledger? *(LO 3.4)*

5. What is a trial balance, and what is its purpose? Does a trial balance being "in balance" mean that all transactions have been recorded correctly? Why or why not? *(LO 3.4)*

6. Define a deferred expense. Provide two examples of deferred expenses. Why are adjusting entries generally required at the end of an accounting period for deferred expenses? *(LO 3.6)*

7. Why is a deferred revenue a liability? Provide two examples of deferred revenues. Why are adjusting entries generally required at the end of an accounting period for deferred revenues? *(LO 3.6)*

8. Why is an accrued revenue an asset? Provide two examples of accrued revenues. Why are adjusting entries generally required at the end of an accounting period for accrued revenues? *(LO 3.6)*

9. How does a company's net income for a given accounting period affect its period-ending balance sheet? *(LO 3.7)*

10. Where is the Retained Earnings account presented in a set of financial statements? What is represented by this account? *(LO 3.7)*

11. What are dividends? Where are dividends shown in a set of financial statements? Are dividends considered expenses of an organization? Why or why not? *(LO 3.1 & 3.7)*

12. Define the terms *permanent* and *temporary* as related to types of accounts. Why are these terms appropriate? In which financial statement is each type of account found? *(LO 3.8)*

13. Briefly describe the nature and purpose of adjusting entries and closing entries. *(LO 3.3, 3.6, & 3.8)*

EXERCISES

14. **True & False** *(All LOs)*

Following are a series of statements regarding topics discussed in this chapter.

Required:

Indicate whether each statement is true (T) or false (F).

(a) If a journal entry affects two asset accounts and one liability account, that journal entry must be out of balance in reference to the accounting equation.

(b) If a business's trial balance is "in balance," then the entity's accounting records are free of any errors.

(c) Contra-accounts are treated as "offsets" to related accounts for financial statement purposes.

(d) If every business transaction is not recorded, the accounting equation for that business will not be in balance.

(e) A company that has consistently experienced net income throughout its existence will have a credit balance in its Retained Earnings account.

(f) The initial step of the closing process is posting journal entry data to the appropriate general ledger accounts.

(g) An Income Summary account is a temporary account that is used during the preparation of period-ending closing journal entries.

(h) A primary purpose of period-ending adjusting journal entries is to comply with the revenue and expense recognition rules.

(i) Publicly owned companies typically prepare a formal set of financial statements for external users only once per year.

(j) All accounts contained in a chart of accounts for a business begin each accounting period with a zero balance.

(k) Most of the information needed by accountants to analyze business transactions is found in source documents.

(l) Double-entry bookkeeping is a financial record keeping system used only in the United States and a few European countries.

15. **Normal Account Balances** *(LO 3.2)*

Following are account titles taken from the financial statements of three large companies. Alcoa (www.alcoa.com) is the leading worldwide producer of aluminum; Honeywell International Inc. (www.honeywell.com) produces a wide array of products including security systems; and Darden Restaurants (www.dardenrestaurants.com) is the parent company of Olive Garden, Red Lobster, and Bahama Breeze.

Alcoa	Honeywell	Darden Restaurants
Investments	Short-Term Borrowings	Cost of Sales
Accounts Payable, Trade	Insurance Recoveries	Inventories
Retained Earnings	Cash and Cash Equivalents	Unearned Revenue
Provision for Depreciation	Interest & Other Financial Charges	Preferred Stock
Sales Revenue	Property, Plant & Equipment	Trademarks

Required:

(a) For each account listed, indicate whether it is an asset (A), liability (L), equity (Q), revenue (R), expense (X), or dividend (D).

(b) For each account listed, indicate whether its normal account balance is a debit (D) or a credit (C).

16. **Analyzing General Journal Entries** *(LO 3.1 & 3.3)*

The following general journal entries (presented in a simplified format) were made recently by the bookkeeper of Morgan's Gas Emporium:

General Journal		
Description	**Debit**	**Credit**
Supplies	400	
Cash		400
Interest Expense	270	
Cash		270
Equipment	4,000	
Notes Payable		4,000

Required:

(a) Briefly describe the transaction that resulted in each of these journal entries.

(b) Suppose that the bookkeeper inadvertently recorded the third entry by debiting Notes Payable and crediting Equipment, each for $4,000. How would this error have affected the assets and liabilities of Morgan's Gas Emporium?

(c) How would the error in part (b) affect the trial balance prepared at the end of the period for Morgan's Gas Emporium?

17. **General Journal Entries** *(LO 3.3)*

Following are two recent transactions of Larson Realty:

■ Received $24,000 advance payment for one year's rent on an office building being leased to an accounting firm by Larson.

■ Paid $6,000 in advance for six months of newspaper advertising.

Required:

(a) Prepare a general journal entry to record each of these transactions in Larson's accounting records.

(b) Prepare a general journal entry for each transaction from the point of view of the other party (company) to the transaction.

(c) Were Larson's total assets increased, decreased, or unchanged as a result of each of these transactions?

18. **Analyzing T-accounts** (*LO 3.4*)

Consider the following Cash and Accounts Payable T-accounts:

Cash		Accounts Payable	
14,000	10,000	4,000	6,000
9,000	600	5,000	8,200
8,000	2,000	1,000	1,000

Required:

(a) How would each of these accounts be classified in a balance sheet?

(b) What type of balance should each T-account normally have?

(c) Compute the balance of each of these accounts.

(d) Identify two possible, different types of transactions that would have resulted in the $8,000 posting to the Cash account.

(e) Identify two possible, different types of transactions that would have resulted in the $5,000 posting to the Accounts Payable account.

19. **Posting General Journal Entries** (*LO 3.4*)

Following are several general journal entries of the House Corporation during a recent month. Journal entry descriptions have been omitted:

General Journal				
Date		Description	PR	Debit	Credit
Jan	1	Office Supplies		420	
		Cash			420
	5	Inventory		7,560	
		Accounts Payable			7,560
	7	Cash		6,750	
		Accounts Receivable			6,750
	9	Accounts Payable		6,350	
		Cash			6,350
	12	Utilities Expense		2,658	
		Cash			2.658

Following are the account numbers and Januarary 1 balances of the accounts affected by the listed journal entries:

	Account Number	January 1 Balance
Cash	101	$12,400
Accounts Receivable	111	9,300
Inventory	115	6,100
Office Supplies	121	840
Accounts Payable	201	14,200
Utilities Expense	505	0

Required:

(a) Prepare a T-account for each of the accounts affected by the general journal entries listed for the House Corporation. Enter the January 1 balance in each of these accounts.

(b) Post the journal entries to the appropriate accounts.

(c) Determine the balance of each of the accounts after the transactions have been posted.

(d) What is the purpose of posting general journal entries to general ledger accounts?

20. **Adjusting Journal Entries for Balance Sheet Accounts** (*LO 3.6*)

Following are selected December 31 account balances of Kosciusko, Inc. prior to the preparation of year-end adjusting journal entries:

Property, Plant & Equipment	$2,530,200
Cash	90,850
Unearned Rental Revenue	79,000
Common Stock	250,000
Prepaid Rent	15,400
Land	440,500
Note Payable	150,000
Retained Earnings	3,770,100

Required:

(a) Of the listed accounts, which ones will likely necessitate year-end adjusting journal entries?

(b) Briefly describe the nature of the adjusting journal entries for the accounts identified.

(c) Why would adjusting entries not be needed for each of the nonaffected accounts?

21. **Adjusting Journal Entries for Liability Accounts** (*LO 3.6*)

Following is the liabilities section of a recent balance sheet of Alliant Techsystems, Inc. (www.atk.com), a commercial ammunitions and defense and aerospace company. Amounts are expressed in millions.

CURRENT LIABILITIES:

Accounts payable	$ 215,755
Contract advances and allowances	81,624
Accrued compensation	147,287
Accrued income taxes	41,681
Other accrued liabilities	144,540
Total current liabilities	$ 630,887
Long-term debt	1,455,000
Deferred income tax liabilities	38,316
Postretirement and postemployment benefits liabilities	138,378

Accrued pension liability	84,267
Other long-term liabilities	108,238
Total liabilities	$2,455,086

Required:

(a)   Identify the current liabilities in Alliant Techsystems' balance sheet that may have been recorded or affected by period-ending adjusting entries.

(b)   If $200,000,000 of long-term debt had become due in the year after the balance sheet date, what adjusting entry related to Long-term Debt may have been required in Alliant Techsystems' accounting records? Why would this entry have been necessary?

(c)   Assume that the Accrued Compensation liability was recorded in a period-ending adjusting entry. Prepare that entry.

22.   **Adjusting Journal Entries** *(LO 3.6)*

Contemporary Designs, Inc. is an interior-decorating firm. Customers must pay 50 percent of their estimated bill before any work is performed. On November 20 of the current year, Contemporary Designs received and recorded a $5,000 advance payment from a customer on a new job that was scheduled to begin on December 1. As of December 31, the job has been completed. No further payments have been received by December 31 from the customer, nor have any additional entries relating to this job been recorded in the accounting records of Contemporary Designs.

Required:

(a)   Prepare the entry to record the November 20 advance payment.

(b)   Prepare any necessary adjusting journal entries in Contemporary Designs' accounting records as of December 31.

23.   **Failure to Record Year-End Adjusting Journal Entry** *(LO 3.6, ethics)*

Consider the following two situations:

■   On December 1, 2009, Harsha's Cleaning Service, a new business, bought $6,500 of cleaning supplies. At the end of December, the business had $3,400 of supplies on hand.

■   Silverman & Sachs is a large investment-banking firm. In December 2009, the firm earned fees of $4.1 million for investment banking services provided to three large clients. As of December 31, 2009, the firm had not been paid for these services.

Required:

(a)   Record the December 1, 2009, entry for the purchase made by Harsha's Cleaning Service.

(b)   Given the facts provided in each situation, prepare an appropriate adjusting journal entry as of December 31, 2009 for each company.

(c)   Suppose the adjusting journal entries from part (b) were not recorded. Which accounting principles or concepts would be violated by these oversights? Why are these violations important?

(d)   As an investor in these companies, would you be concerned to find that the adjusting entries had been omitted? Why or why not?

24.   **The Accounting Equation** *(LO 3.7)*

Following are the balance sheet accounts of a small business:

Cash	$ 5,000
Accounts Payable	?
Equipment	10,400
Supplies	?
Land	16,400
Owner's Equity	18,000
Notes Payable	10,800

Required:

(a)   Fill in the missing amounts, assuming that the business has total assets of $36,000.

(b)   Fill in the missing amounts, assuming that the business has total liabilities and owner's equity of $39,800.

(c)   Prepare a trial balance assuming the information in part (a).

25.   **Closing Entries** *(LO 3.8)*

Following are selected account balances from the December 31, 2009, adjusted trial balance of Hershel Supply Company:

Cash	$ 4,000
Accounts Receivable	5,000
Unearned Rental Revenue	12,200
Utilities Expense	6,000
Income Taxes Expense	8,000
Accounts Payable	3,000
Sales Revenue	50,000
Selling Expenses	12,000
Prepaid Rent	9,000

Required:

(a)   Assuming that all the corporation's temporary accounts are included in the listed accounts, prepare the appropriate December 31 closing entries for Hershel Supply.

(b)   How much net income did Hershel Supply earn during the period?

(c)   For any item not used in part (a), indicate where that item would appear on the financial statements.

26. **Need for Adjusting and Closing Entries** (LO 3.6 & 3.8, writing)

Geoff's Tailor is a small business operated by Geoffrey Restin. The accounting records for this business are maintained by Markey & Michaels, CPAs. Recently, Restin questioned the monthly accounting bill submitted to him by the CPA firm. Included in the bill were the following line items, among others:

Adjustment of year-end account balances:	
5 hours @ $80 per hour	$400
Year-end closing of revenue and expense	
accounts: 2 hours @ $80 per hour	160

Restin does not understand why his accounting records must be adjusted at year-end. In a recent telephone conversation, he complained to a partner of Markey & Michaels, "If you guys did my accounting records right the first time, you wouldn't have to adjust them at year-end." Restin went on to protest the $160 charge for closing his business's revenue and expense accounts. "Why do you close those accounts every December 31? Don't you always use them again the next year? I think you're closing them just to run up my bill."

Required:

Write a memo to Geoffrey Restin explaining the purpose of, and need for, period-ending adjusting and closing entries.

PROBLEMS

27. **Correction of Accounting Errors** (LO 3.3)

Krug Company's inexperienced bookkeeper places a question mark next to a journal entry if she is uncertain the entry is correct. Question marks appear next to each of the following entries in Krug's accounting records.

(a) Accounts Receivable	4,000	
Cash		4,000
To record collection of accounts receivable		
(b) Office Equipment	900	
Cash		900
To record purchase of office supplies for cash		
(c) Cleaning Supplies	300	
Accounts Payable		300
To record purchase of cleaning supplies on credit		

Required:

(a)   Given each journal entry and its accompanying explanation, identify the nature of the error in the entry, if any, and how the entry should have been prepared.

(b)   Given your responses in part (a), prepare any necessary correcting entries.

(c)   Analyze each of the errors you identified in part (a) in reference to the accounting equation. How would

these errors have affected the accounting equation of Krug Company, if at all?

28. **General Journal Entries** (LO 3.3)

Following are the December transactions of Cerullo Electrical Contractors.

Dec. 1	Purchased supplies for $300.
Dec. 3	Paid $250 electricity bill for November that had been properly recorded with an adjusting entry on November 30.
Dec. 9	Paid employee salaries for first week of December, $1,200. No salaries had been previously accrued.
Dec. 16	Received $600 for interest that had been earned in November on a bank account. An appropriate adjusting journal entry had been recorded for this item on November 30.
Dec. 22	Received $1,700 from customer in payment of account receivable.
Dec. 26	Paid January rent on leased office space, $400.
Dec. 30	Received $2,500 advance payment from a customer for work to be performed in January.
Dec. 31	Purchased equipment on credit for $3,000.

Required:

(a) Prepare general journal entries for these transactions.

(b) Identify which accounts affected by the journal entries prepared in part (a) are deferred expenses, deferred revenues, accrued assets, or accrued liabilities.

29. **Journalizing and Posting Transactions** *(LO 3.3 & 3.4, writing)*

Tamara Zeevah opened a hair salon recently, but did not maintain a formal set of accounting records during the first week of her business's operations. Instead, she simply maintained a checkbook for the business. Following are the entries included in Zeevah's checkbook for the period January 6–January 10, 2009:

Date	Transaction	Deposits	Withdrawals
Jan. 6	Bank loan	$40,000	
Jan. 7	Rent to landlord for January		$1,000
Jan. 7	Bought hair care products		4,000
Jan. 7	Bought equipment		650
Jan. 8	Hairstyling revenues earned	350	
Jan. 10	Paid shampoo person		360
Jan. 10	Hairstyling revenues earned	800	

Required:

(a) Prepare the necessary general journal entries for Zeevah's Hair Salon for the period January 6–January 10.

(b) Prepare T-accounts for Zeevah's Hair Salon and post the journal entries for the period January 6–January 10 to these accounts. Determine the account balances as of January 8.

(c) Verify that the general ledger accounts are in balance.

(d) In a short memo to Zeevah, explain why her current method of record keeping does not provide her with the information she needs to monitor and evaluate the financial status of her business. Be sure to indicate whether her checkbook will record all transactions that affect her business in any given period.

30. **Trial Balance** *(LO 3.5, writing)*

Following are the general ledger account balances of Balcones Company, Inc. (BCI), as of September 30, 2009:

Cash	$ 50,000
Accounts Receivable	300,000
Inventory	250,000
Equipment	450,000
Accumulated Depreciation-Equipment	110,000
Accounts Payable	350,000
Income Taxes Payable	50,000
Common Stock	95,000
Retained Earnings	100,000
Sales Revenue	600,000
Operating Expenses	255,000

Required:

(a) Prepare a trial balance for BCI as of September 30, 2009.

(b) Even if a trial balance is in balance, one or more general ledger accounts of a business may contain errors. Provide three examples of accounting errors that would not cause a business's trial balance to be out-of-balance.

(c) What steps could the management of BCI take to help ensure that its accounts are error free? Write a brief memo to the company's management listing your recommendations.

31. **Adjusting Journal Entries** *(LO 3.6, writing)*

The following information pertains to the operations of Wilke Investigating, a private detective agency, for December 2009.

■ Wilke's employees earn $420 of salary collectively each day. The employees work Monday through Friday and are paid each Friday for the week just worked. December 31 falls on a Tuesday.

■ On December 31, the owner estimates that December's electricity bill will be $240.

■ The owner also estimates that the firm will have income tax expense of $800 for December. This amount will be paid in March 2010.

■ On December 1, Wilke received and recorded a $300 payment from a customer for services to be rendered by Wilke evenly during December, January, and February. Wilke's principal revenue account is Fees Revenue.

■ Wilke received $680 cash from a new client on December 28; this amount was properly recorded. No services had been provided to this client as of December 31.

- Bonocher, Inc. owes Wilke $1,400 for services provided during December. No entry pertaining to these services has been recorded in Wilke's accounting records.

Required:

(a) For each bulleted item, prepare any necessary adjusting journal entry as of December 31 in Wilke's accounting records.

(b) Suppose that Wilke Investigating uses the cash basis of accounting instead of the accrual basis. Analyze each bulleted item and determine how Wilke's revenues and expenses for December would be affected by using the cash rather than accrual basis of accounting.

(c) Write a brief memo indicating whether the cash basis or accrual basis of accounting provides a more appropriate measure of Wilke's net income each accounting period.

32. **"Window-Dressing" Financial Statements** (LO 3.7, ethics) You are an accountant for Kelberg, Inc., an advertising agency, and you are preparing to close Kelberg's accounting records for the current year because December 31 is only a few days away. The business owner is planning to apply for a loan from a local bank in early January. To make the financial statements more acceptable to the bank, the owner instructs you to credit a $31,000 advance payment received from a customer on December 27 to a revenue account. Kelberg will not provide the services paid for by this customer until March of next year. The owner also instructs you not to record a year-end adjusting entry for $7,500 of December rent owed to the real estate firm that leases office space to Kelberg.

Required:

(a) If you comply with the owner's instructions, how will Kelberg's December 31 balance sheet for the current year be affected? How will the company's income statement for the current year be affected?

(b) What accounting principles will be violated if you comply with the owner's instructions?

(c) What will you do in this situation? Identify the parties likely to be affected by your decision to comply or not comply with the owner's requests. Indicate how each of these parties may be affected by your decision.

33. **Preparation of Financial Statements** (LO 3.7)

The following adjusted trial balance of Schneider Consulting, Inc. was prepared for the year ended December 31, 2009.

	Debit	Credit
Cash	$ 24,000	
Accounts Receivable	71,000	
Interest Receivable	1,000	
Inventory	125,000	
Prepaid Insurance	6,000	
Equipment	252,000	
Accumulated Depreciation—Equipment		$ 41,000
Accounts Payable		27,000
Interest Payable		4,000
Income Tax Payable		57,000
Notes Payable (long-term)		90,000
Common Stock		35,000
Retained Earnings		71,000
Dividends	10,000	
Consulting Fees Revenue		460,000
Interest Revenue		3,000
Salaries Expense	176,000	
Rent Expense	23,000	
Advertising Expense	22,000	
Utilities Expense	6,000	
Interest Expense	5,000	
Depreciation Expense—Equipment	10,000	
Income Tax Expense	57,000	
Totals	$788,000	$788,000

Required:

(a) Prepare an income statement for the year ended December 31, 2009.

(b) Prepare a Statement of Stockholders' Equity for the year ended December 31, 2009, assuming Schneider Consulting did not issue any new stock in 2009.

(c) Prepare a classified balance sheet as of December 31, 2009.

34. **Closing Entries** (LO 3.8)

Random Access, Inc. is a small business that leases computer equipment. Following are several account balances that were included in the company's year-end adjusted trial balance:

Cash	$200,000
Interest Revenue	5,000
Accounts Payable	60,000
Accumulated Depreciation—Equipment	46,000
Rental Revenue	252,000
Dividends	11,000
Salaries Expense	95,000
Depreciation Expense	8,000

Required:

(a) Indicate which of the listed accounts are permanent accounts and which are temporary accounts.

(b) Given the information provided, prepare all appropriate closing entries for Random Access.

(c) Assume that all the necessary accounts to compute net income are included in the list provided. What is net income for Random Access for the year?

(d) If the Retained Earnings account contained a balance of $47,000 prior to closing, what is the balance of this account after closing entries are prepared and posted?

CASES

35. Recording and Posting Transactions *(LO 3.3 & 3.4)*

The following transactions took place during the first two weeks of operations of Not So Taxing, Inc., a walk-in tax preparation service.

Mar. 2	Issued common stock of the corporation in exchange for $200,000 cash.
Mar. 3	Purchased $4,000 of supplies on account from Kidd Supply Company.
Mar. 4	Paid $3,000 of office rent for March.
Mar. 5	Completed tax work for Mr. East and billed him $650.
Mar. 6	Received a total of $7,400 from customers for services provided during the week.
Mar. 9	Received a $1,000 advance from Mr. West for tax services that have not yet been provided.
Mar. 10	Placed a telephone order for a $550 laser printer.
Mar. 11	Paid $1,200 to Kidd Supply Company.
Mar. 12	Received $450 from Mr. East.
Mar. 13	Paid an employee $790 for two weeks work.
Mar. 13	Received $3,700 cash from customers for services provided during the week.

Required:

(a) Enter the transactions into the general journal.

(b) Post the transactions to the general ledger and calculate balances for each account. Verify that the ledger is in balance.

36. Annual Reports *(LO 3.7, Internet)*

The financial statements of a company are prepared before the closing entries.

Required:

Use the annual report of Carnival Corporation for the 2007 fiscal year to answer the following questions. Specifically, look at the Income Statement (Consolidated Statement of Operations) and the Statement of Stockholders' Equity for the fiscal year ended November 30, 2007. This information can be found in either the annual report or the SEC 10-K filing at www.carnival.com by following the links to Investor Relations.

(a) Prepare Carnival's four closing entries for 2007.

(b) What was the balance of Retained Earnings at the beginning of the fiscal year (December 1, 2007)?

(c) Prepare the T-account for Retained Earnings (start with the balance on December 1, 2006) and post the closing entries you prepared in part (a).

(d) Verify that the ending balance of the Retained Earnings T-account equals the ending balance of Retained Earnings shown on Carnival's Statement of Stockholders' Equity for 1999.

(e) Prepare the T-account for Income Summary to verify that its ending balance is zero.

37. Comprehensive Accounting Cycle Problem *(LO 3.3, 3.4, 3.5, 3.6, 3.7, 3.8, & 3.9)*

During the summer of 2009, Theresa Babineaux began and incorporated a small lawn mowing service. The following information relates to the first two months of business.

Required:

(a) (1) Record the following transactions in Babineaux's General Journal.

6/1	Babineaux invested $1,200 and a lawn mower worth $300 in the business.
6/1	Babineaux borrowed $400 on a 7-month, 6% (annual rate) note payable. Principal and interest are due on January 2, 2010.
6/2	Jones paid Babineaux $150. This amount was for Babineaux to mow Jones's yard once a month for 3 months.
6/3	Babineaux placed a telephone order for $100 office supplies.
6/3	Babineaux bought $20 of gasoline.
6/5	The supplies ordered on 6/3 were received with an invoice for $100.

6/15 As of 6/15, Babineaux had mowed 30 lawns at $50 each. Twenty customers paid in cash, and the rest were billed for their balances.

6/18 Babineaux bought $20 of gasoline.

6/25 Babineaux paid $100 to a ministorage facility to store the lawnmower for the month of July.

6/30 For the second half of June, Babineaux mowed 25 lawns at $50 each. Twenty customers paid in cash, and the rest were billed for their balances.

6/30 Babineaux received $300 from customers who had been billed.

6/30 Babineaux took $500 in salary from the business.

7/2 Babineaux had to have the lawnmower repaired and received a bill for $60.

7/3 Babineaux bought $40 of gasoline.

7/10 Babineaux paid for half of the supplies received on 6/3.

7/30 During July, Babineaux mowed 65 more lawns at $50 each. Forty customers paid in cash, and the rest were billed for their balances.

7/31 Babineaux took $800 in salary from the business.

7/31 Babineaux paid the $200 lawnmower repair bill.

(2) Create a General Ledger and post the entries to it. Calculate ledger account balances.

(3) Prepare a trial balance. (Checkpoint: Trial Balance totals = $7,800)

(b) (1) Make the appropriate adjusting entries for the following information.

7/31 Babineaux has $60 of supplies remaining.

7/31 Babineaux has $6 of gas remaining.

7/31 Babineaux has mowed Jones's yard twice.

7/31 Other necessary adjustments were made. The lawnmower depreciates at $25 per month.

(2) Post the adjusting entries to the General Ledger and calculate account balances.

(3) Prepare an adjusted trial balance. (Checkpoint: Trial Balance totals = $8,104)

(c) (1) Prepare an Income Statement. (Checkpoint: Net Income = $4,472)

(2) Prepare a Statement of Stockholders' Equity.

(3) Prepare a Balance Sheet. (Checkpoint: Total Assets = $6,426)

(d) (1) Prepare the closing entries in the General Journal.

(2) Post the closing entries to the General Ledger and calculate account balances.

(3) Prepare a postclosing trial balance. (Checkpoint: Trial Balance totals = $6,476)

SUPPLEMENTAL PROBLEMS

38. Journalizing Transactions (LO 3.3, writing; Compare to Problem 28)

Felix's Gardening Supply had the following transactions involving cash during early August:

August 1 Purchased four lawnmowers for $300 each.

August 2 Purchased $320 of office supplies for cash.

August 4 Paid $400 of income taxes that had been accrued two months ago.

August 4 Received $450 for lawn care services provided.

August 5 Paid $500 of salaries that had not been accrued.

August 7 Accrued $100 of interest on a bank loan.

Required:

(a) Prepare general journal entries for the transactions.

(b) After reviewing the journal entries prepared in part (a), the owner of Felix's Gardening Supply is

convinced that each transaction has been "double-counted." Write a short memo to the owner explaining why each entry requires at least one debit and one credit and why this procedure does not double-count the transactions.

39. Journalizing, Posting, and Preparing a Trial Balance (LO 3.3, 3.4, & 3.5; Compare to Problems 28, 29, and 30.)

Jersey Enterprises uses the following general ledger accounts in its accounting system. Listed for each account is its account number and balance as of January 1, 2009.

	Account Number	Balance
Cash	101	$ 80,000
Accounts Receivable	103	85,000
Supplies	121	30,000
Office Equipment	151	325,000

Accumulated		
Depreciation—Office		
Equipment	152	135,000
Accounts Payable	201	70,000
Common Stock	301	90,000
Retained Earnings	350	225,000
Fee Revenue	401	0
Selling Expense	511	0
Salary Expense	511	0
Supplies Expense	531	0

In early January 2009, Jersey Enterprises engaged in the following transactions:

January 2   Paid $30,000 on accounts payable.

January 5   Purchased $2,100 of supplies for cash.

January 5   Purchased office equipment for $4,700 cash.

January 6   Earned and received fees (revenues) from customers of $16,400.

January 7   Paid selling expenses of $7,100.

January 8   Received $25,000 from customers who owed money at the beginning of the year.

January 9   Paid employee salaries of $15,200.

Required:

(a)   Why do some of Jersey's accounts have zero balances at the beginning of January?

(b)   Prepare a journal entry for each of the transactions listed.

(c)   Prepare general ledger accounts for Jersey Enterprises as of January 1, 2009. Post the January 2009 journal entries to these accounts.

(d)   Prepare a trial balance for Jersey Enterprises as of January 9, 2009.

40. **Preparation of Financial Statements** *(LO 3.7; Compare to Problem 33.)*

Following is an adjusted trial balance for LC & Associates for the year ended December 31, 2009.

	Debit	Credit
Cash	$112,500	
Accounts Receivable	95,000	
Supplies	12,000	
Prepaid Advertising	18,000	
Prepaid Rent	40,000	
Equipment	90,500	
Accumulated		
Depreciation—Equipment		$ 71,000
Accounts Payable		38,000
Salaries Payable		2,400
Interest Payable		70
Unearned Fee Revenue		19,930
Common Stock		75,000
Retained Earnings		34,000
Fee Revenue		315,000
Interest Revenue		9,100
Rent Expense	69,500	
Income Tax Expense	35,000	
Salaries Expense	75,000	
Depreciation		
Expense—Equipment	17,000	
Totals	$564,500	$564,500

Required:

(a)   Prepare an income statement for LC & Associates for the year ended December 31, 2009.

(b)   Prepare a classified balance sheet for LC & Associates as of December 31, 2009.

(c)   Identify three general classes of financial statement users who might make economic decisions based on the financial statements of LC & Associates. How might errors in the financial statements affect such decisions?

41. **Closing Entries** *(LO 3.8; Compare to Problem 34.)*

Following is a list of certain account balances included in the adjusted trial balance of Larry's Shoe Repair Shop as of December 31, 2009. This list includes all the business's revenue and expense accounts as well as selected additional accounts.

Prepaid Rent	$ 9,000
Accounts Payable	16,400
Utilities Expense	2,000
Cash	24,000
Accounts Receivable	6,000
Shoe Repair Revenue	70,000
Prepaid Insurance	11,000
Unearned Repair Revenue	1,400
Dividends	2,700
Salaries Expense	24,000
Salaries Payable	1,800
Bonds Payable	3,000
Income Taxes Expense	16,000

Required:

(a)   Prepare all appropriate closing entries for Larry's Shoe Repair Shop on December 31, 2009. The shop is a corporation.

(b)   What was the company's net income (loss) for 2009?

PART II

ACCOUNTING FOR ASSETS

Cash, Short-Term Investments, and Accounts Receivable

LEARNING OBJECTIVES

1. Account for the major types of transactions involving cash, accounts receivable, and notes receivable.
2. Prepare a bank reconciliation and related entries.
3. Estimate and record bad debts for accounts receivable.
4. Use ratios and other analysis techniques to make decisions about cash, short-term investments, and accounts receivable.

INTRODUCTION

This chapter focuses on accounting issues for four important, and closely related, current assets: cash, short-term investments, accounts receivable, and notes receivable. Cash is essential for an organization to pay its bills. However, companies do not want to have "too much" cash and may use some of the excess to make short-term investments. (Each organization's management makes its own determination of how much is "too much.") One factor that significantly influences a company's cash needs is the length of its operating cycle or the time between using cash for normal operating activities and collecting cash from customers. For instance, grocery stores have short operating cycles because inventory turns over quickly, and most sales are for cash or bank credit cards. Alternately, beef producers and shipbuilders have much longer operating cycles. Accounts receivable are amounts that customers owe to the organization; these amounts are usually collected in cash within the company's established credit period.

CASH AND CASH EQUIVALENTS

Current assets are listed in order of decreasing liquidity on a balance sheet. **Liquidity** refers to how readily the asset can be converted into cash; therefore, cash or "cash and cash equivalents" is generally listed as the first line item. For example, at year-end 2008, Microsoft (www.microsoft.com) had approximately $10.3 billion in cash and cash equivalents on its balance sheet. This amount is significantly larger than the $3 million for The Walt Disney Company (www.disney.go.com) or $2.1 billion by PepsiCo (www.pepsico.com) at the same time.

Cash equivalents are highly liquid amounts such as certificates of deposit (CDs), money market funds, and U.S. treasury bills. To qualify as a cash equivalent, an item must be readily convertible into a specific amount of cash and have very little risk of a change in value from the time it is acquired to the time it is changed back into cash. Given these criteria, investments in the stocks or bonds of another company do not qualify as cash equivalents because there is always risk relative to such an investment's value. This risk was exceptionally obvious in the financial market's downturn in 2008.

To illustrate the difference between a cash equivalent and a short-term investment, consider the following. **Treasury bills** (T-bills) are short-term U.S. government obligations with a term of one year or less. These debt items are sold for less than their face value and do not pay interest before maturity. The difference between the purchase price of the bill and the amount that is paid at maturity is the interest earned on the bill. For instance, on September 26, 2008, interest yields on T-bills for specific time periods were as follows:

4 weeks	13 weeks	26 weeks	52 weeks
0.17%	0.87%	1.54%	1.81%

Although the rates are quite low, T-bills are backed by the U.S. government, and thus, there is little fear of not getting the money and interest at maturity.[1] Alternatively, the

---

[1] For more information about T-bills and other U.S. government securities, go to www.publicdebt.treas.gov.

common stock of Washington Mutual (WaMu) Inc. was trading at $36.47 per share on October 5, 2007; on September 26, 2008, the stock price had plummeted to $0.16 per share because of the corporation's financial collapse and takeover by JP Morgan. An investment in WaMu shares would have resulted in a vast difference in the amount of cash received from sale of the shares, depending on the date of the sale.

Cash is considered one of the most important business assets because of its use in paying current debts. The sale of goods or services for cash and the collection of accounts receivable are probably the two most common cash transactions. Each of these transactions was illustrated in Chapter 3. The other two most common accounting issues relative to cash are petty cash and bank reconciliations. The next two sections discuss these topics.

Petty Cash

Most organizations keep a limited amount of **petty cash** on hand (in a petty cash lockbox, for example). The petty cash fund's size depends on business needs, but it is usually small enough that loss of the fund's money would be insignificant to the organization's operations. The fund is established with a debit to an account called Petty Cash and a credit to Cash:

General Journal				
Date	Description		Debit	Credit
XXX	Petty Cash		50	
	Cash			
	To establish a petty cash fund			50

One employee is designated as the custodian of the petty cash. The petty cash custodian uses the money to pay for small, but necessary, business expenses and should obtain a receipt for each expenditure. At any time, the cash plus the receipts in the petty cash box should total the fund's original amount.

Journal entries are not made when funds are expended. When the fund is low, the receipts are used as source documents to make the necessary journal entry. The expenses that created the distributions from the petty cash fund are recorded and a check is written to obtain additional cash to replenish the petty cash fund. The resulting journal entry is a debit to several expenses and a credit to cash.

Assume that, over two weeks, $45 of petty cash was spent on the following items: overnight mail charges for a package, $16; a 1G flash drive for a manager's presentation, $12; cab fare for an employee who worked overtime one evening, $13; and coffee creamer for the office coffee room, $4. At this time, there would be $5 left in the fund and $45 in receipts, totaling the original $50. The custodian would make the following entry:

General Journal				
Date	Description		Debit	Credit
XXX	Postage Expense		16	
	Office Supplies Expense		12	
	Transportation Expense		13	
	Miscellaneous Expense		4	
	Cash			45
	To replenish the petty cash fund			

The $45 check would be cashed, and the money would be returned to the petty cash fund—resulting in the original $50 fund amount.

Bank Reconciliations

A business's petty cash can be compared to the money that individuals have in their wallet. Most businesses, like most individuals, do not have a significant amount of cash on hand. Companies normally use checking accounts to pay the majority of large expenditures. A checking account provides a company a safe place to store money, some control over who has access to those funds, and source documentation (sequentially numbered checks, return of cancelled checks, and bank statements) of cash transactions. A company may have multiple bank (or other financial institution) accounts for its cash balances; for instance, one account may be used for general business expenses and one for payroll. Although each cash account is contained in a separate general ledger account, all the cash accounts will be added together to produce the "cash" line item that appears on the balance sheet.

Each month, depositors receive statements that summarize the activities that have occurred in the cash accounts for the period. Such activities include information about physical and direct deposits, checks that have cleared, ATM transactions, direct withdrawals, payments made using debit cards, and (possibly) service charges for or interest earned on the account. By properly adding and subtracting the monetary effects of these activities to and from the beginning account balance, an ending balance in the depositor's account is determined. However, the bank's information is not normally in absolute agreement with the cash account contained in the depositor's general ledger because of one or more of the following items:

- *Deposits Not Yet Recorded by Depositor*—The bank may have deposited an amount to an account without the depositor's knowledge of the amount. For example, a depositor's checking account may earn interest monthly, and that interest is deposited directly into that account. Thus, the bank records have included the addition of the amount, but the depositor's records have not. No adjustment needs to be made to the bank balance, but the general ledger cash account needs to be increased.

- *Deposits in Transit*—A depositor may have made a checking account deposit, but the bank has not yet been recorded that deposit. For example, if a deposit is made at 4:45 p.m. on a Friday afternoon, the bank will not record it until Monday morning. Thus, the book records have included this deposit as an addition to cash, but the bank records have not. No adjustment needs to be made to the general ledger cash account, but the bank balance needs to be increased.

- *Outstanding Checks*—A depositor may have written a check that has not yet cleared the checking account. Thus, the book records have included this reduction to cash, but the bank records have not. No adjustment needs to be made to the general ledger cash account, but the bank balance needs to be decreased.

- *Direct Bank Charges*—The bank may deduct amounts (such as check printing charges, service fees, and stop payment orders) from a depositor's account without the depositor knowing the amount. Thus, the bank records have included this reduction, but the book records have not. No adjustment needs to be made to the bank balance, but the general ledger cash account needs to be decreased.

■ *NSF (Not Sufficient Funds) Checks*—When a check is received from a customer, the company debits Cash for the check amount. If, however, the customer's checking account does not have the funds to cover that check, the company's bank will not record the increase to the company's checking account. Thus, the bank records will not include an increase, but the book records already recorded the addition. No adjustment needs to be made to the bank balance, but the general ledger cash account needs to be decreased for funds that did not really exist.

■ *Errors*—Despite the best efforts of the depositor and bank, errors will occasionally occur. For a depositor, the most common mistakes are that amounts are added or subtracted incorrectly or not at all (such as ATM withdrawals or debit card payments). The bank may make a deposit to, or withdraw a check from, the wrong customer's account or record an amount in error. The necessary adjustment on the reconciliation depends on which party (depositor or bank) made the error and what the erroneous transaction was. If the depositor made the error, the adjustment will be made to the general ledger cash account. If the bank made the error, its records need to be adjusted accordingly. It is important to note that depositors are more likely to make errors than banks. Bank errors (both positive and negative) should be communicated to the bank as soon as they are found.

Because of these items, neither the bank nor the depositor may know the actual cash balance at any particular moment. These differences can be explained by timing. Consider the following example. Assume you write a $100 check and mail it to the electric company. You will deduct $100 from your checking account. However, your bank has no knowledge of that check until the utility company presents it for payment. A week or more could pass, depending on the promptness of the mail service and the utility company's accounting department, before your bank receives the $100 check. If the bank prepared your month-end bank statement after you wrote the check but before the check was cashed, there would be a $100 difference between the bank's determination of your cash balance and your determination of your cash balance. However, given enough time, both sets of records would be the same (at least relative to that check).

Because of the differences that exist between the bank's and depositor's cash records, a **bank reconciliation** should be prepared whenever a bank statement is received. This reconciliation presents the differences between the bank statement and the cash account, so that an accurate balance of cash on hand can be determined for a specific time.

When preparing a bank reconciliation, the first step is to compare the bank's statement with the company's cash or bank account. The items that need to be included in the reconciliation are those that appear only on one record (either the bank statement or the company cash account). Each difference should be examined in two ways: whether it will increase or decrease the company's cash account and whether it was found on the bank statement or in the cash ledger. Items that appear on the bank statement require an adjustment to the cash ledger account. Items that appear in the cash ledger account require an adjustment to the bank balance. Company errors and bank errors should be categorized as either an increase or decrease, depending on the effect of correcting the error. Visual Recap 4.1 indicates how to categorize common reconciliation items.

The following example discusses the process of preparing a bank reconciliation for the Lily Corporation for the month ending on March 31, 2009. At this date, the company's general ledger cash account showed a balance of $6,450; the bank statement for this date showed a balance of $4,343. An analysis of the bank statement and Lily's cash account

VISUAL RECAP 4.1

Categorizing Items for the Bank Reconciliation

	Found on Bank Statement **(Adjust Cash Ledger)**	**Found in Cash Account** **(Adjust Bank Balance)**
Increase	Interest Earned Direct Deposits Company Errors	Deposits in Transit Bank Errors

Decrease	Service Charges
	NSF Charges
	Drafts
	Company Errors
	    (including unrecorded ATM or
	    debit card amounts)
		Outstanding Checks
		Bank Errors

provided the following information; explanations on the reconciliation effects are shown in italics.

Bank Statement Information:

- The bank deposited $33 to Lily's account for interest on company accounts.[2] *Lily Corporation has earned the interest (a revenue) on company accounts. The bank has added those funds to Lily's account, but Lily did not know the interest amount until receiving the bank statement. Therefore, Lily needs to increase the general ledger cash account by $33. The bank has already included the $33 as an increase in Lily's checking account balance.*

- The bank charged Lily Corporation $20 for printing checks. *Lily Corporation has incurred a cost of doing business (an expense). Even though the company ordered the checks, Lily did not know the amount of the charge until receiving the bank statement. Lily needs to decrease the general ledger cash account by $20. The bank has already included the $20 as a decrease in Lily's checking account balance.*

- The bank returned Henry Dow's check for $360 marked NSF. *When Lily Corporation received the check, Cash was debited (increased) and Accounts Receivable was credited (decreased) by $360. However, Dow did not actually make a payment because his bank account had insufficient funds to cover the check; thus, Dow still owes Lily the $360. Lily was made aware of the NSF check upon receiving the bank statement. Lily needs to decrease the general ledger cash account by $360. The bank never added the funds to Lily's account; therefore, the bank balance is correct. (NOTE: If the bank charged Lily a service fee for the NSF check, Lily's bank account would have been reduced, and Lily would have had an additional deduction to its general*

---

[2]When a bank deposits funds to a customer's account, the bank will prepare a credit memo; a reduction in a customer's account is shown on a debit memo. This situation seems odd because deposits to a customer's account increase that account and, therefore, should be debits. However, remember that on the bank records, a customer's checking account is an Account Payable of the bank to the depositor, and increases in liabilities are shown as credits; decreases are shown as debits. Thus, from the perspective of the memo preparer (the bank), the debit and credit notations are appropriate.

ledger cash account. Lily would then try to obtain that fee amount from Dow in addition to the $360 still owed.)

- The bank reduced Lily's checking account by $250 for a check from Lali Corporation that had been charged in error. *The bank incorrectly removed funds from Lily Corporation's account, thereby making Lily's checking account balance too small. Lily needs to inform the bank of the error so that a correction can be made to Lily's (and Lali's) account. Lily's bank account is too small and needs to be increased on the reconciliation. Lily's general ledger cash account balance was never affected, so that amount is correct.*

Cash Account Information:

- The company had deposited $3,000 in the bank that did not appear on the current bank statement. *Lily's book balance is correct, but the bank balance needs to be increased by $3,000. When the bank statement was printed, the bank was unaware of the $3,000. No call to the bank is necessary because deposits in transit tend to clear very quickly.*

- The company had written four checks for a total of $1,580 that were outstanding at the end of the month. *Lily's book balance is correct, but the bank balance needs to be decreased by $1,580. At the time the bank statement was printed, these checks had not been presented to the bank.*

- The company had written a check for $320 to pay an account payable; however, the amount posted from the journal entry to both Cash and Accounts Payable was $230. *Lily's general ledger cash account is overstated by $90 because too little was deducted when the check was recorded. Thus, the general ledger cash account balance needs to be decreased by $90. Lily's check cleared the bank at the proper amount of $320, so the bank account balance was not affected. Lily did not know there was an error until the bank statement arrived.*

Given the preceding explanations, Lily Corporation categorized the items for which the bank and cash accounts differed (Exhibit 4-1). Then Lily prepared the bank reconciliation shown in Exhibit 4-2. After the reconciliation is completed, the book and bank balances should agree. The reconciled amount is the actual cash that Lily Corporation has available at the end of March.

The entries needed to adjust Lily Corporation's cash account balance are shown in Exhibit 4-3. Notice that no entries are made for anything on the "bank balance" side of the reconciliation. Lily Corporation cannot make journal entries to change another entity's accounting records. Lily does need to call and inform the bank of the error related to Lali's check and have the $250 redeposited to Lily's checking account.

EXHIBIT 4-1

Categorization of Lily's Items for the Bank Reconciliation

	Found on Bank Statement (Adjust Book Balance)	**Found in Cash Account (Adjust Bank Balance)**
Increase:	Interest earned, $33	Deposits in transit, $3,000
		Error—Lali check, $250
Decrease:	Check printing, $20	Outstanding checks, $1,580
	NSF—Dow, $360	
	Error in A/P, $90	

EXHIBIT 4-2

Bank Reconciliation

Book Balance			Bank Balance		
As stated, 3/31		$6,450	As stated, 3/31		$4,343
Add:	Interest earned	33	Add:	Deposit in Transit	3,000
				Error—Lali	250
Deduct:	Printing charge	(20)	Deduct:	Outstanding checks	(1,580)
	NSF check—Dow	(360)			
	Error—A/P amount	(90)			
Correct balance, 3/31		$6,013	Correct balance, 3/31		$6,013

EXHIBIT 4-3

Journal Entries from the Bank Reconciliation

General Journal				Debit	Credit
Date		Description			
Mar	31	Cash		33	
		Interest Revenue			33
		To record March interest on company accounts			
	31	Miscellaneous Expense		20	
		Cash			20
		To record bank charges for printing checks			
	31	Accounts Receivable—Dow		360	
		Cash			360
		To record Dow's NSF check			
	31	Accounts Payable		90	
		Cash			90
		To correct error in previously recording			
		A/P payment amount			

One additional item needs to be mentioned in relation to the coverage of NSF checks. As discussed earlier, NSF refers to a check that has been given to a company by someone who does not have sufficient funds to cover it. If Lily Corporation writes a "bad" check, the cash account would have a credit balance and would be classified as a current liability. Additionally, the bank (as well as the company to whom the check was written) will charge Lily an NSF service fee for the "bounced" check. Nationally, the average fee for such checks is approximately $25.

SHORT-TERM INVESTMENTS

Companies need to hold an adequate amount of cash to meet current obligations, but do not generally want to hold significantly more cash than will be needed. Cash should be put to productive use; even cash that is deposited in an interest-bearing checking account is still generally to be considered "idle." Therefore, companies often make short-term investments of excess cash in the stocks and bonds of other companies or **available-for-sale securities**. These investments are usually sold quickly and are held only to generate a return on the investment greater than what could be earned on an interest-bearing checking account.

When preparing a balance sheet, short-term investments are shown at fair market value (FMV) rather than cost. Such an adjustment requires an end-of-period adjusting journal entry to record a loss or a gain relative to the investment cost. Although violating the historical cost principle, such accounting provides users with better information because the investments will generally be sold soon after the balance sheet date.

To illustrate the period-end adjusting entry for short-term investments, assume that Caliope Co. purchased $2,500 of stock in Orleans Corp. stock in November 2009. At December 31, 2009, Caliope still owned the stock but it was worth $2,200. The following adjusting entry would be made:

General Journal				
Date		Description	Debit	Credit
Dec	31	Loss on S-T Investment	300	
		S-T Investment in		
		Orleans Corp.		300
		To record FMV of Orleans		
		investment at year-end		

ACCOUNTS RECEIVABLE

Accounts receivable reflect amounts owed to a business by customers for their purchases of goods or services on credit. This section addresses credit specifically granted by a business to its customers (such as Sears, Neiman Marcus, and Home Depot) rather than national or bank credit cards (such as Visa, MasterCard, and American Express).

The nature of a company's operations significantly influences the proportion of total assets that is typically comprised by accounts receivable. Some companies, such as small service businesses, have relatively small amounts of accounts receivable on their balance sheets. Alternatively, manufacturers and department stores often make extensive use of in-house credit. In these industries, a company that does not allow its customers to purchase merchandise on credit finds itself at a significant competitive disadvantage.

Accounting for Accounts Receivable

A company that has decided to allow in-house credit purchases by customers will screen applicants for creditworthiness. Different types of customers are commonly given different **credit terms**. Such terms express the agreement between buyer and seller regarding the timing of payment and any discount available to the buyer for early payment.

A credit term of "net 30" (expressed as n/30) requires the buyer to pay the full invoice amount within 30 days of the invoice date. This 30-day period is known as the credit period and does not include the invoice date. For example, a customer who buys goods on May 1 with credit terms of n/30 would have until May 31 to pay for the goods.

Sales Discounts

To speed up the cash collection on credit sales, many companies offer **sales discounts** to customers so that they will pay their account balances prior to the end of the credit period. One of the most common credit terms allows a customer to subtract 2 percent from the invoice price if the bill is paid within ten days (expressed as 2/10). If payment is not made within the ten-day discount period, the full invoice amount is due 30 days following the invoice date. Thus, this credit term is expressed as 2/10, n/30.

To illustrate accounting for sales discounts, assume that Payne Company sells $400 of merchandise with credit terms of 2/10, n/30 to Brenda Joyner on March 1. At the time the sale is made, Payne Company does not know whether Joyner will take advantage of the discount. Consequently, the sales transaction is recorded in the general journal at the $400 shown on the sales invoice:

General Journal				
Date		**Description**	**Debit**	**Credit**
Mar	1	Accounts Receivable—B. Joyner	400	
		Sales		400
		To record credit sale; terms 2/10, n/30		

Assume that Joyner chooses to take advantage of the available discount and pays her account receivable on March 11, the last day of the discount period. The following entry is made:

General Journal				
Date		**Description**	**Debit**	**Credit**
Mar	11	Cash	392	
		Sales Discounts	8	
		Accounts Receivable—B. Joyner		400
		To record payment on account within		
		discount period		

The Sales Discounts account reflects the reduction in selling price granted for prompt payment. Sales Discounts is a contra-revenue account and directly reduces the balance in the Sales account. As all contra-accounts do, Sales Discounts has the opposite balance of its related account. Sales has a credit balance, so Sales Discounts has a debit balance. The use of this account allows the full amount of the sale to remain in the revenue account (Sales) in the accounting records. Sales Discounts is shown on the income statement as a reduction of Sales.

If Joyner does not take advantage of the sales discount and pays her account receivable on March 31, the following entry is required:

General Journal				
Date		**Description**	**Debit**	**Credit**
Mar	31	Cash	400	
		Accounts Receivable—B. Joyner		400
		To record payment on account		

Customers should almost always take advantage of any prompt payment discounts that are offered—even if it means having to go to the bank and borrow the money to do so. Consider the preceding example. Joyner can either pay on the 10th day of the discount period (saving $8) or on the 30th day after the invoice. The 2 percent rate is essentially an interest charge for a 20-day period. There are approximately 18 20-day periods in a year (360 days ÷ 20 days). Thus, a 2 percent rate for 20 days translates into approximately a 36 percent annual rate of interest. Assume that Joyner can borrow money from the bank at 9 percent per year. She borrows $320 on March 11 and remits those funds to Payne Company. Twenty days later (when she would have had to pay Payne Company), Joyner repays the bank; her interest charge on the $320 she borrowed for 20 days is $1.60 ($320 × 0.09 × 20/360)—a savings of $6.40.

Sales Returns and Allowances

Most merchandising companies grant cash or credit customers a full refund, or **sales return**, if they need or want to return merchandise. Additionally, customers also may be granted a price reduction, called a **sales allowance**, to persuade them to keep damaged, defective, or out-of-season merchandise. Because these items may be fairly small in amount individually, such refunds and price reductions are recorded together in another contra-revenue account entitled Sales Returns and Allowances.

The Sales Returns and Allowances account, like Sales Discounts, has a debit balance and is subtracted from Sales on the income statement. Reducing the Sales account by these two contra-accounts results in an amount called Net Sales, which is typically the first line item on a merchandising or manufacturing company's income statement. Exhibit 4-4 illustrates the use of the Sales Returns and Allowances account as well as the Sales Discount account.

Uncollectible Accounts

Two key activities are associated with a credit sale: making the sale and collecting the resulting receivable. Occasionally, the latter task is the more challenging of the two. Whenever a business decides to extend credit to customers, there is the potential for bad debts. When it becomes apparent that a receivable will not be collected, businesses should eliminate, or write off, that receivable. Such a write-off is a legitimate cost of doing business and, as such, is an expense. The two ways to account for bad debt write-offs are the direct write-off method and the allowance (or estimation) method.

Under the **direct write-off method**, a company simply waits until a particular account has been determined to be uncollectible and, at that time, writes off the account. For example, assume that in November 2009, Dozier Company sold $300 of merchandise on credit to D. Ronaho. On September 18, 2010, after vigorous collection efforts had failed, Dozier decided to write off the $300 receivable using the direct write-off method. The following entry would be made:

General Journal				
Date		Description	Debit	Credit
Sept	18	Uncollectible Accounts Expense	300	
		Accounts Receivable—Ronaho		300
		To write off A/R as a bad debt		

Under these circumstances, the write-off entry is made in September 2010, whereas the related credit sale was recorded in November 2009. The matching principle states that a company should attempt to match expenses with their corresponding revenues. Businesses will almost certainly have some bad debts when credit sales are made, and in general, a reasonable estimate of such write-offs can be made. In most cases, businesses will spend many months trying to collect from customers; therefore, the write-off often does not

EXHIBIT 4-4

Use of Contra-Revenue
Accounts

Information: On March 10, Dinah Company sold Glover's Shirt Shop 20 specially mono-grammed shirts at $35 each. Dinah grants Glover credit terms of 2/10, n/30. On March 12, Glover returns 1 shirt to Dinah because of a tear in the fabric. On March 14, Glover calls Dinah and asks for a price reduction on the remaining shirts because the logo was slightly smaller than ordered. Dinah agrees to a $38 price reduction. On March 21, Glover remits half of the amount owed and remits the remaining amount owed on April 9.

General Journal				Debit	Credit
Date		Description			
Mar	10	Accounts Receivable—Glover		700.00	
		Sales			700.00
		To record sale on account			
	12	Sales Returns and Allowances		35.00	
		Accounts Receivable—Glover			35.00
		To record return of one shirt for full credit			
	14	Sales Returns and Allowances		38.00	
		Accounts Receivable—Glover			38.00
		To record an allowance given for monogramming error			
	21	Cash		307.23	
		Sales Discount		6.27	
		Accounts Receivable—Glover			313.50
		To record partial payment on A/R within discount period			
		$700 − $35 − $38 = $627			
		$627 ÷ 2 = 313.50; $313.50 × .02 = $6.27			
Apr	9	Cash		313.50	
		Accounts Receivable—Glover			313.50
		To record payment for remaining A/R			

The revenue section of an income statement prepared using only the information about this transaction would appear as follows:

Sales			$700.00
Less:	Sales Returns and Allowances	$73.00	
	Sales Discounts	6.27	(79.27)
Net Sales			$620.73

occur until an accounting period after the credit sale. The direct write-off method violates the matching principle by ignoring the relationship between credit sales and the possibility of bad debts. Therefore, this method is not considered a generally accepted accounting principle and should *not* typically be used for financial reporting purposes.

To satisfy the matching principle, an estimate of future uncollectible accounts should be recorded as an expense in the period that credit sales are generated. Under the **allowance method**, a business estimates the uncollectible accounts expense at the end of each accounting period. This estimate is recorded through an adjusting entry that includes a debit to Uncollectible Accounts Expense and a credit to a contra-asset account called Allowance for Uncollectible Accounts. The Allowance for Uncollectible Accounts is a credit-balanced, contra-asset account; thus, increases are recorded as credits and decreases are recorded as debits. For balance sheet purposes, this account is subtracted from Accounts

Receivable to reduce that asset to its approximate net realizable value.[3] Note that, at the time that the estimate is made, no specific customers' receivables have been identified as uncollectible, and Accounts Receivable cannot be affected.

Numerous methods exist to estimate bad debts; one of the easiest is to use a percentage of credit sales, using historical or industry data. For example, assume that Onken Furniture Company had total sales in 2009 of $2,500,000. Of that amount, $1,800,000 was on credit. Onken's manager researched industry data and found that, given the company's business, customer profiles, and location, a reasonable estimate of bad debts is 1.5 percent ($1,800,000 × 0.015 = $27,000). The estimate is applied only to credit sales because the cash sales have already been collected. When adjusting entries are made on December 31, 2009, the company records the following entry:

General Journal				
Date		**Description**	**Debit**	**Credit**
Dec	31	Uncollectible Accounts Expense	27,000	
		Allowance for Uncollectible Accounts		27,000
		To record an estimate for bad debts related		
		to 2009 credit sales		

When an actual account is determined to be uncollectible, the Allowance for Uncollectible Accounts will be reduced (debited), and the customer's Account Receivable will be written off (credited). Suppose that Dan Quinn, a customer owing Onken Furniture Company $2,300, filed for personal bankruptcy in February 2010. Upon learning of this information on February 18, the company did not expect to collect Quinn's account. Under such circumstances, the following entry would have been appropriate to write off the receivable from Dan Quinn.

General Journal				
Date		**Description**	**Debit**	**Credit**
Feb	18	Allowance for Uncollectible Accounts	2,300	
		Accounts Receivable—Quinn		2,300
		To write off an A/R as a bad debt		

Note that the write-off entry does not include a debit to Uncollectible Accounts Expense. The December 31, 2009, adjusting entry for the estimated uncollectible accounts expense provided recognition that a certain percentage of the company's year-end receivables would not be collected. That adjusting entry properly matched the bad debt expense associated with such receivables to Onken's 2009 fiscal year. When specific receivables from 2009 later prove to be uncollectible, they are debited to the allowance account.

If a previously written-off account is later collected, the account must be reestablished, but only for the amount collected. The reestablishment is accomplished by reversing

---

[3] In a recession, companies often notice an increase in customers who cannot or will not pay their bills. In early 2009, online merchants noticed that "friendly" fraud was increasing. Friendly fraud is used to indicate customers who dispute an online charge but do not return (or have already used) the product. Customers may falsely claim the product was never received, the wrong product was received, or the product was never ordered. In such cases, write-offs of accounts receivable are more common occurrences. [Pui-Wing Tam, "Businesses Get Tougher on 'Friendly' Fraud," *Wall Street Journal* (May 26, 2009), p. B1.]

the write-off entry. The entry immediately following will depict the cash collection. For example, if Quinn makes restitution of $0.40 on the dollar on May 15, he would pay Onken $920 ($2,300 × $0.40). The entries to record his payment are shown below.

General Journal				
Date		Description	Debit	Credit
May	15	Accounts Receivable—Quinn	920	
		Allowance for Uncollectible Accounts		920
		To reestablish a previous bad debt write-off		
		Cash	920	
		Accounts Receivable—Quinn		920
		To collect an A/R		

Credit Card Receivables

Increased sales and larger market shares await companies that allow customers to charge purchases of goods and services. Credit cards, such as Visa, MasterCard, and American Express, have become important fixtures in the national economy. Retailers realize several important benefits by having their customers make purchases with these types of credit cards. One benefit is that credit card companies (rather than the retailers) absorb bad debt losses resulting from credit card sales. Credit card companies also relieve retail businesses of the need to check credit references of prospective customers. Finally, credit card companies pay amounts owed to retailers more quickly than do individual customers.

A company that accepts credit cards is called a merchant. Merchants typically receive payment immediately on deposit of the credit card slips but are charged a 1 to 5 percent service fee. Size of the fee commonly depends on the quantity of business that the merchant does with the credit card company. Assume that Langer Company makes $6,000 in Visa sales on February 18, 2009. Visa charges Langer a 2.5 percent service fee. The following journal entry is made for the day's Visa sales:

General Journal				
Date		Description	Debit	Credit
Feb	18	Cash	5,850	
		Credit Card Expense	150	
		Sales		6,000
		To record Visa sales and credit card fee		

The process of credit card authorization and payment is shown in Exhibit 4-5.

Notes Receivable

When unable to pay an account receivable by the due date, a customer may be asked to sign a promissory note, which is a legal document that formally recognizes a debt owed by one party to another. When such a note is signed, a customer's receivable balance is transferred from Accounts Receivable to Notes Receivable. Besides more formally documenting a customer's receivable account, a promissory note typically requires the customer to begin paying interest on the unpaid receivable balance.

EXHIBIT 4-5

Authorization and
Collection Process for
National Credit Cards

Authorization

1. Cardholder
presents a credit card
to pay for purchases.
For card-not-pres-
ent transactions, the
cardholder provides
the merchant with the
account number,
expiration date,
billing address,
and CVV2.

2. Merchant swipes the card, enters
the dollar amount, and transmits
an authorization request to the
merchant bank. For card-not-present
transactions, the account number and
other information may be digitally or
key-entered.

3. Merchant bank
electronically sends
the authorization
request to the credit
card company.

4. Credit card network
passes on the request to
the card issuer.

5. Card issuer
approves or
declines the
transaction.

8. Merchant receives the
authorization response and
completes the transaction
accordingly.

7. Merchant bank
forwards the response to
the merchant.

6. Credit card network forwards the
card issuer's authorization response
to the merchant bank.

Clearing and Settlement

10. Merchant bank credits
the merchant's account
and electronically submits
the transaction to the credit
card company for settlement.

9. Merchant
deposits the
transaction receipt
with merchant
bank.*

**11. Credit card
network:**
• facilitates
  settlement.
• pays the merchant
  bank and debits the
  card issuer account,*
  then sends the
  transaction to the
  card issuer.

12. Card issuer:
• posts the
  transaction to the
  cardholder account.
• sends the monthly
  statement to the
  cardholder.

13. Cardholder
receives the
statement.

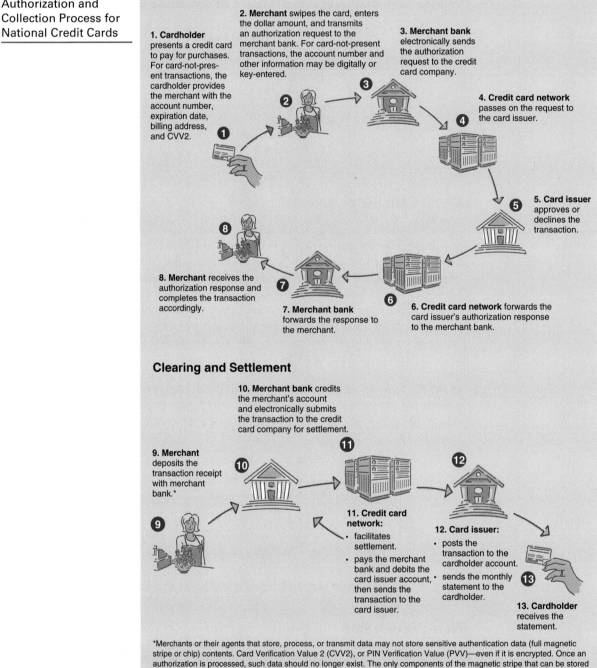

*Merchants or their agents that store, process, or transmit data may not store sensitive authentication data (full magnetic
stripe or chip) contents. Card Verification Value 2 (CVV2), or PIN Verification Value (PVV)—even if it is encrypted. Once an
authorization is processed, such data should no longer exist. The only components of the magnetic stripe that can be stored
are name, account number, and expiration date.

SOURCE   Adapted from http://usa.visa.com/download/merchants/rules_for_visa_merchants.pdf.

Assume that Guzzardi Corp. sells $2,500 worth of merchandise to Dauterive Co. on July 1, 2009; credit terms are 2/10, n/30. On July 31, Dauterive Co. informs Guzzardi that the bill cannot be paid and requests that the account be transferred to a note. A $2,500, 8%, 3-month note receivable is prepared and exchanged. The note and the $50 ($2,500 × 0.08 × 3/12) of interest are paid on the due date. Exhibit 4-6 provides the journal entries for these transactions.

The maturity point of a note depends on how the note is dated. If the note is dated in months or years, the maturity date occurs on the same day of the month that the note is dated. If the note is dated in days, each day of the month must be counted. For example, a four-month note dated March 8, 2009, matures on July 8, 2009. However, a 120-day note dated March 8, 2009, matures on July 6, 2009 (23 remaining days in March, 30 days in April, 31 days in May, 30 days in June, and 6 days in July). The date the note is signed is not counted as part of the note period.

ACCOUNTING INFORMATION FOR DECISION MAKING

Cash and accounts receivable are particularly important assets because they provide the primary means by which a business can pay its debts as they come due. Declining cash or slow accounts receivable collections can leave a business searching for other ways to raise the funds needed to finance its day-to-day operations.

Decision makers need to be informed of any unusual characteristics or conditions associated with a company's accounts or notes receivable. For example, a company that has a significant amount of receivables from related parties, such as company executives, should disclose that fact in the firm's financial statements. One reason such information is important is that management may not vigorously pursue collection efforts on such receivables or may "forgive" the loans, even if the company is in poor financial condition.

A company can also use its accounts receivable as collateral against which to borrow money. If the company "pledges" its accounts receivable for the loan and then defaults on that loan, the lender can recover the amount owed from the subsequent cash collections on the receivables pledged in support of the loan. Pledged accounts receivable should be disclosed in the firm's financial statement footnotes. Such disclosure alerts decision makers that the company has one less financing alternative available in the future.

EXHIBIT 4-6

Notes Receivable

General Journal				
Date		Description	Debit	Credit
July	1	Accounts Receivable—Dauterive	2,500	
		Sales		2,500
		To record sale on account		
	31	Notes Receivable—Dauterive	2,500	
		Accounts Receivable—Dauterive		2,500
		To record exchange of open A/R for an 8%, 90-day N/R		
Oct.	31	Cash	2,550	
		Notes Receivable—Dauterive		2,500
		Interest Revenue		50
		To record collection of N/R and interest		

Quick Ratio

Financial ratios are measures that express the relationship (or interrelationships) between (or among) two or more financial statement items. One key financial ratio involving cash is the quick ratio. The **quick ratio** is computed by dividing an entity's quick assets by its current liabilities. **Quick assets** include cash and cash equivalents, short-term investments, and the net amount of current notes and accounts receivable (receivables less any related allowance accounts).

$$\text{Quick ratio} = \text{Quick assets} \div \text{Current liabilities}$$

If the firm has more quick assets than current liabilities, the quick ratio indicates the number of times a company can pay its current liabilities. For example, if Abbott Company has a quick ratio of 1.25 (or 125%), Abbott can pay all its current liabilities and still have quick assets left. If quick assets are less than current liabilities, the quick ratio indicates the percent of current liabilities the company can pay. For example, if Babbin Company has a quick ratio of 0.92 (or 92%), the company can only pay 92% of its current liabilities with its existing quick assets.

The quick ratio is used to evaluate a business's ability to finance its day-to-day operations and to pay its liabilities as they mature. Such ability is heavily influenced by the amounts of cash that a business has on hand and can raise quickly, such as by selling short-term investments. As the quick ratio decreases, so does organizational liquidity. Insight on a company's liquidity can be gained by comparing the firm's quick ratios to key industry benchmarks. For example, one source suggests that the "average" quick ratio for the agriculture industry is 0.39, for leather/textiles/apparel manufacturers it is 0.62, and for restaurants it is 0.18.[4]

However, many companies have a strong cash position because they have recently obtained long-term loans from banks or sold stock. To determine the source of a company's cash, the firm's recent cash flow data must be examined on the statement of cash flows.

Age of Accounts Receivable

Financial analysts often consider the "quality" of a company's accounts receivable as a function of their age. Determining the age of a company's receivables is a two-step process. First, the **accounts receivable turnover ratio** is computed as follows:

$$\text{A/R turnover ratio} = \text{Net credit sales} \div \text{Average A/R}$$

The average accounts receivable is equal to the beginning plus the ending balances of accounts receivable divided by two. A/R turnover measures the number of times that a company "turns over" or collects its receivables each year. Companies want to convert their receivables into cash as quickly as possible. Consequently, a general rule is that high accounts receivable turnover ratios are better than low ratios.

The **age of receivables** is computed by dividing 360 (the approximate number of days in a year) by the accounts receivable turnover ratio:

$$\text{Age of receivables} = 360 \text{ days} \div \text{A/R turnover ratio}$$

This measurement indicates the average number of days that a company's receivables have been outstanding. Viewed another way, the age of receivables indicates the average period required for a company to collect a receivable resulting from a credit sale. This age can be

---

[4]CreditGuru.com, Key Business Ratios; http://www.creditguru.com/ratios/inr.htm (accessed 9/29/08).

compared to the standard credit terms allowed to determine if the company is collecting its receivables in accordance with its credit policies. Exhibit 4-7 provides an illustration of the computation of the accounts receivable turnover ratio and the age of receivables.

Many financial ratios, including age of receivables, vary significantly from company to company and industry to industry. For example, at the end of its fiscal year, Starbucks' (www.starbucks.com) age of receivables was only about 10 days, whereas Pfizer's (a pharmaceutical company; www.pfizer.com) age of receivables was almost seven times "older."

Starbucks (as of 9/28/08):

$$\text{Average A/R} = (\$287,900,000 + \$329,500,000) \div 2$$
$$= \$617,400,000 \div 2 = \$308,700,000$$
$$\text{A/R turnover} = \$10,383,000,000 \div \$308,700,000 = 33.6$$
$$\text{Age of receivables} = 360 \div 33.6 = 10.7 \text{ days}$$

Pfizer (as of 12/31/08):

$$\text{Average A/R} = (\$9,843,000,000 + \$8,958,000,000) \div 2$$
$$= \$18,801,000 \div 2 = \$9,400,500,000$$
$$\text{A/R turnover} = \$48,296,000,000 \div \$9,400,500,000 = 5.1$$
$$\text{Age of receivables} = 360 \div 5.1 = 71 \text{ days}$$

This comparison does not necessarily mean that Pfizer's receivables are of lower quality than those of Starbucks. Among other factors, differing credit terms offered by the two companies and varying economic conditions affecting each firm's industry may account for the large disparity in their age of receivables. The normal for the age of receivables in Starbucks' industry is about 21 days, whereas the corresponding norm for Pfizer's industry is 28 days. These industry data suggest that Starbucks collects its receivables a little more quickly than the typical company in its industry, whereas Pfizer's receivables could be considered "elderly" compared to the industry norm. This indicator might suggest that Pfizer faces a higher risk of bad debt losses than most firms in its industry.

SUMMARY

Cash typically does not pose complex accounting issues. Critical elements for cash are safekeeping and control over access. Companies handle such control, in part, by using financial institutions to store cash and by dispersing most large cash payments by check rather than using petty cash. Preparing monthly bank reconciliations allows for a formalized review of cash transactions and helps determine the actual amount of cash on hand at the

---

EXHIBIT 4-7

Accounts Receivable Turnover Ratios and Age of Receivables

Net credit sales for 2009	$704,250
Accounts Receivable, 1/1/09	$82,000
Accounts Receivable, 12/31/09	$74,500

Average Accounts Receivable = ($82,000 + $74,500) ÷ 2 = 156,500 ÷ 2 = 78,250
Accounts Receivable Turnover Ratio = $704,250 ÷ $78,250 = 9
Age of Receivables = 360 days ÷ 9 = 40 days

If normal credit terms are 2/10, n/30, the company is not doing a very good job of collecting its Accounts Receivable in the 30 days expected. On average, the A/R are 10 days overdue.

end of the bank statement period. Once that amount is found, journal entries are needed to correct the general ledger account balance.

Cash that is not needed immediately should be invested in short-term investments to earn a reasonable rate of return. Investments in government securities provide a safer, but lower, rate of return than stock investments.

Accounts receivable are recorded at the sales prices of the items sold. Companies may provide credit terms, such as 2/10, n/30, to customers to entice them to pay earlier than the end of the credit period. Such prompt payment discounts are recorded in a contra-revenue account entitled Sales Discounts. The cost of returned goods from customers and price reductions offered to entice customers to keep defective or undesired merchandise are recorded in another contra-revenue account called Sales Returns and Allowances.

The key accounting issue for accounts receivable is arriving at a reliable estimate of uncollectible accounts expense. Businesses are generally required to use the allowance method to estimate the uncollectible accounts expense for financial reporting purposes. A common approach to estimating the amount of expected uncollectible accounts at the end of an accounting period is to take a percentage of credit sales for the period. The estimate is recorded as an expense of the period and in a contra-asset account until the actual uncollectible accounts are known. Actual uncollectible accounts are written off against the allowance account.

Notes receivable may be used when a company sells goods (or loans funds) for payment terms of longer than the normal 30-day credit period. Notes receivable typically require interest to be paid on the amount of the principal of the sale (or the loan).

Decision makers need information regarding a company's ability to pay its debts as they mature and collectibility of accounts receivable. Financial ratios can be used to assess the financial health of a business. The quick ratio measures short-term debt-paying ability and the age of receivables can be used to monitor the A/R collectibility. As the average age of a company's accounts receivable increases, the percentage of those receivables that must be written off as uncollectible generally increases as well.

KEY TERMS

accounts receivable turnover ratio	cash equivalent	quick asset
	credit term	quick ratio
age of receivables	direct write-off method	sales allowance
allowance method	financial ratio	sales discount
available-for-sale securities	liquidity	sales return
bank reconciliation	petty cash	treasury bill

QUESTIONS

1. What is a "cash equivalent"? Why are cash equivalents combined with cash on a balance sheet? (LO 4.1)

2. What is the purpose of a bank reconciliation? Why should it be prepared in a timely manner? Are bank reconciliations still important when using online banking? (LO 4.2)

3. What are the most common situations that require adjustments on your personal bank reconciliation? Why do these items occur? (LO 4.2)

4. What accounting concept requires businesses to estimate their uncollectible accounts expense each accounting period? Why will such estimations provide better information to decision makers than would the direct write-off method? (LO 4.3)

5. Why might the length of a company's operating cycle affect its cash needs? (LO 4.4)

6. Why would a company choose to sell on credit rather than strictly on a cash basis? What problems would the decision

to sell on credit create for a business? How would these problems differ if the business issued its own credit cards versus allowed the use of national credit cards? *(LO 4.4)*

7. Define "liquidity." Why is liquidity important in preparing a balance sheet? *(LO 4.4)*

8. What types of decision makers are most interested in a company's liquidity and why? *(LO 4.4)*

9. How is the quick ratio computed? How do decision makers use a company's quick ratio? *(LO 4.4)*

10. How are the accounts receivable turnover ratio and age of receivables helpful in analyzing the collectibility of a company's accounts receivable? *(LO 4.4)*

EXERCISES

11. **True or False** *(All LOs)*

Following are a series of statements regarding topics discussed in this chapter.

Required:

Indicate whether each statement is true (T) or false (F).

(a) Cash equivalents are funds that companies have invested in short-term securities that mature six months or less from the date of purchase.

(b) Short-term investments and inventory are quick assets.

(c) The direct write-off method results in an appropriate matching of sales revenue with bad debts expense.

(d) The risk of third-party (national) credit cards is greater than the risk of in-house credit.

(e) Sales Discounts is a contra-revenue account.

(f) Bank errors require an adjustment to the company's general ledger cash account.

(g) Collecting a business's accounts receivable may be more difficult than selling a business's products.

(h) The credit terms for a sales transaction express the agreement between the buyer and seller regarding the timing of payment and any discount available to the buyer for early payment.

(i) On a bank reconciliation, outstanding checks decrease the bank account balance.

(j) Notes receivable are always dated in one-year increments.

12. **Journal Entries for Accounts Receivable** *(LO 4.1)*

Following are recent transactions and other events involving Tremendous Tresses, a company that markets hair-care products.

June 1   Customer purchased $400 of merchandise on credit with terms of n/60.

June 5   Wrote off an uncollectible account receivable of $350.

June 15   Customer purchased $1,200 of merchandise on credit with terms of 2/10, n/30.

June 17   Customer who purchased merchandise on June 1 returned $60 of that merchandise because it was defective.

June 25   Received amount due from customer who purchased merchandise on June 15.

June 29   Received payment in full from customer whose account balance was written off on June 5.

June 30   Received amount due from customer who purchased merchandise on June 1.

Required:

Prepare journal entries to record each of these transactions or events.

13. **Credit Card Sales** *(LO 4.1)*

The Magic Shoppe sells games, books, and party favors. Most customers charge their purchases to national credit cards. Following is a summary of The Magic Shoppe's total credit card sales for July and the service fee of each credit card honored by the business.

	PlasticCard	BanCard	BigCard
July credit card sales	$21,000	$44,000	$74,500
Service fee	3%	2%	5%

Required:

(a) Record these July credit card sales and the collection entries from the credit card companies in The Magic Shoppe's accounting records.

(b) Why do retail stores honor bank credit cards? Does allowing customers to pay for their purchases with credit cards effectively reduce a business's profit because of the fees that these cards charge? Explain your answer.

(c) Given the relatively high service fee charged by Big-Card, why might The Magic Shoppe choose to honor that card?

14. **Recording Notes Receivable** *(LO 4.1)*

On November 1, 2009, Davidson Co. received a $5,000, 10%, 4-month note from Chris Spent in exchange for his open account receivable. Davidson's fiscal year ends on December 31.

Required:

(a) Prepare the entry to record the receipt of this note receivable for Davidson.

(b) Prepare the necessary year-end adjusting entry related to this note receivable. Why is this entry needed?

(c) Assume that Davidson repaid the note and interest on the due date. Prepare and date the entry needed to record the funds received by Davidson.

15. **Estimating Uncollectible Accounts Expense** (LO 4.3)

Lernig Company had total sales of $1,350,000 for the year ended December 31, 2009; of that amount, $1,000,000 was on credit. The company had a balance of $16,300 in the Allowance for Uncollectible Accounts on January 1, 2009. During the year, bad debts totaling $12,500 were written off. On December 31, 2009, Lernig made an adjusting entry to record estimated uncollectible accounts at 2.5 percent of credit sales.

Required:

(a) Prepare the appropriate year-end adjusting entry to record the uncollectible accounts expense for this company at the end of 2009.

(b) What was the balance in Allowance for Uncollectible Accounts after making the entry in part (a)?

(c) What was the balance in Uncollectible Accounts Expense after making the entry in part (a)?

(d) Why are the answers to parts (b) and (c) different?

16. **Computing the Quick Ratio** (LO 4.4)

Macromedia, Inc. designs and markets computer software products. Following are the company's year-end current assets and current liabilities (in alphabetical order) for two recent years.

	Year 1	Year 2
Accounts payable	$ 6,007	$11,364
Accounts receivable (net)	8,040	19,601
Accrued liabilities	3,492	8,956
Cash and cash equivalents	4,230	7,829
Inventory	7,601	18,568
Other current liabilities	347	331
Prepaid expenses	1,264	4,115
Short-term investments	29,751	90,833
Unearned revenue	2,767	1,235

Required:

(a) Compute Macromedia's quick ratios for Years 1 and 2. Did this ratio improve or weaken between the end of Year 1 and the end of Year 2? Explain your answer.

(b) Briefly discuss factors that might have accounted for the change in Macromedia's liquidity position between the end of Year 1 and the end of Year 2.

17. **Analyzing Accounts Receivable** (LO 4.4)

Consider the following financial information for a recent year for two fairly similar companies:

	Aliza Corp.	Breta Corp.
Cash sales	$ 20,000	$ 40,000
Net credit sales	80,000	60,000
Total sales	$100,000	$100,000
Average accounts receivable during the year	$ 20,000	$ 5,000

Required:

(a) Compute each company's accounts receivable turnover ratio and age of receivables.

(b) Which of these companies is better at managing its accounts receivable? Explain.

PROBLEMS

18. **Petty Cash** (LO 4.1)

Maitland & Murphy, an advertising agency, established a petty cash fund to reduce the number of small checks that were written. On April 1, 2009, the fund was established for $400. On May 1, the petty cash envelope contained $187.23 in cash and coins and the following receipts:

Vendor	Amount	For
Dan's Doughnuts	$18.21	Staff meeting doughnuts
The Hardware Depot	27.54	Repairs
Jamie's Art Supply	82.54	Art supplies
U-Move Vanlines	30.75	Delivery truck rental
TexaGas	43.23	Gas for delivery truck
U.S. Post Office	10.50	Stamps

Required:

(a) Record the April 1 journal entry to establish the petty cash fund.

(b) Record the entry to replenish petty cash on May 1.

(c)   Assume that instead of $187.23, the amount of cash in the petty cash envelope was $185.02 on May 1 before replenishment. Provide two reasons why this situation could occur.

19. **Credit Card Sales** *(LO 4.1)*

Andee's Restaurant accepts three credit cards: Verra Express, United Card, and MacCard. Sales information for Andee's first three days in business is given below.

	Customer Paid With			
	Verra Express	**United Card**	**MacCard**	**Cash**
Sept. 2	$173	$181	$149	$778
Sept. 3	552	87	107	821
Sept. 4	128	344	60	668

The following payments were directly deposited into Andee's bank account on Sept. 8:

- $710.50 from Verra Express for the sales on September 2 and 3.

- $257.28 from United Card for the sales on September 2 and 3.

- $143.49 from MacCard for the sales on September 2.

Required:

(a) Record the journal entries for the sales on September 2, 3, and 4. Because of the delay in processing caused by the long weekend, Andee's Restaurant uses an Account Receivable for each credit card company to record the sales until deposits are received.

(b) Record the journal entries for the direct deposits on September 8.

(c) What percent fee does each credit card company charge?

(d) How might Andee's employees encourage customers to use the credit card with the lowest service fee?

20. **Sales of Merchandise** *(LO 4.1)*

Cousins, Inc. sells ladies clothing. Customers may pay with (1) cash or check, (2) national credit card (which charges a 1% service fee), or (3) in-house credit with terms 2/10, n/30. The following are selected transactions from Cousins.

March 1	Ms. Leonard charged $450 to her in-house account.
March 4	Cash sales were $1,124, and sales on national credit cards were $1,643.
March 6	The credit card company deposited the appropriate amount to Cousins, Inc.'s bank account.

March 8	Ms. Leonard returned $50 of her March 1 purchases.
March 15	Ms. Adams charged $800 to her in-house account.
March 22	A customer returned merchandise and was given a $120 cash refund.
March 24	Ms. Adams paid her balance in full.
March 25	Ms. Leonard paid her balance in full.

Required:

Journalize the preceding transactions.

21. **Notes Receivable** *(LO 4.1)*

All sales for Ronnie Co. are made with credit terms of 2/10, n/30. If a customer is unable to pay by the end of the credit period, Ronnie Co. will exchange the account receivable for a 12%, 90-day note receivable. On September 12, 2009, Chandra Co. purchased $5,500 of merchandise from Ronnie Co. However, Chandra Co. could not pay for the merchandise on the due date.

Required:

(a) What was Chandra Co.'s original due date for payment for the merchandise?

(b) If Chandra Co. had been able to pay for the merchandise within the discount period, on what date and how much would Chandra Co. have paid?

(c) On what date is the note receivable due? What is the total amount that will need to be paid at that time?

(d) Prepare all necessary journal entries for Ronnie Co.'s transactions with Chandra Co., assuming that payment is made for the note on its due date.

(e) Given its terms of business, do you think that Ronnie Co. should make an estimate for uncollectible notes receivable? Provide rationale for your answer.

22. **Bank Reconciliation** *(LO 4.2)*

Xenon, Inc.'s August 31 bank statement had an ending cash balance of $2,567. On August 31, Xenon's general ledger showed a balance of $860. After comparing the general ledger to the bank statement, the following items were noted:

- Outstanding checks, $2,250

- Interest paid by the bank, $12

- An NSF check from one of Xenon's customers, $32

- Deposits in transit, $1,900

- Service fee charged by the bank, $8

- A direct deposit from a customer, $1,400

- Check #345 was written to Acme Insurance; the amount of the check was $615. It was recorded in the general ledger for $600.

Required:

(a)   Prepare a bank reconciliation for Xenon, Inc.

(b)   Make the required journal entries associated with the bank reconciliation.

(c)   Discuss the benefits and drawbacks of maintaining a checking account at a financial institution rather than paying all bills in cash.

23.   **Journal Entries for a Merchandising Company** *(LO 4.1 & 4.3)*

Jenkins, Inc., which sells household appliances, begins its fiscal year on June 1. A partial balance sheet for Jenkins is given next.

Jenkins, Inc.
Partial Balance Sheet
May 31, 2009

Accounts Receivable	$35,000
Allowance for Uncollectible Accounts	(3,500)
Net Realizable Value	$31,500

The following transactions took place during June 2009.

June 1	Cash sales for the day totaled $5,100.
June 4	Sold $2,000 of merchandise to another appliance retailer, JLK Company, with terms of 2/10, n/30.
June 6	Sold $300 of merchandise to Jae Lee, terms n/20.
June 8	Wrote off an uncollectible account receivable from W5 Corp. of $450.
June 12	JLK Company returned $500 of the merchandise purchased on June 4 because the merchandise was defective.
June 14	JLK Company paid Jenkins the amount due for the June 4 transaction.
June 20	Sold $950 of merchandise to Larissa Rodriguez with terms of n/20.
June 26	Received payment from Jae Lee for merchandise sold to him on June 6.
June 29	Received a check for $450 from W5 Corp. whose account balance had been written off on June 8.

Required:

(a)   Prepare general journal entries for the June transactions.

(b)   Calculate Jenkins's net sales for June.

(c)   Calculate Jenkins's balance in Accounts Receivable and Allowance for Uncollectible Accounts.

(d)   Prepare a partial balance sheet as of June 30, 2009.

24.   **Uncollectible Accounts Expense** *(LO 4.3, ethics)*

Following are the December 31, 2008, balances of Accounts Receivable and Allowance for Uncollectible Accounts for Easton Hammer Corporation (EHC).

Accounts Receivable	$6,400,000
Allowance for Uncollectible Accounts (credit balance)	225,000

During 2009, EHC wrote off the following accounts:

May 15	Jim Cantole	$2,425
July 6	Myka Bono	730

Required:

(a)   Prepare the journal entries that were made to record the write-offs of the Cantole and Bono accounts.

(b)   At year-end 2009, the company's accountant estimates that EHC should record an estimate of $327,000 for uncollectible accounts receivable. Prepare the appropriate adjusting journal entry to record uncollectible accounts expense at year-end.

(c)   Suppose that the accountant in part (b) was too conservative in his estimate. Instead of uncollectible accounts receivable of $327,000, the company actually has uncollectible accounts of $218,000. How will the accountant's overstatement of year-end estimated uncollectible accounts receivables affect EHC's income statement and balance sheet for the year in question? How may this overstatement affect the decisions of third parties, such as bankers and investors, who rely on those financial statements?

(d)   Will the assumed overstatement referred to in part (c) affect EHC's financial statements for the following year? If so, explain how. If not, explain why not.

(e)   Is it ever permissible to intentionally overstate expenses in a company's financial statements? Defend your answer and refer to related accounting concepts or principles from Chapter 2.

(f)   Assume Myka Bono paid EHC $730 on August 14, 2010. How would this receipt be journalized by EHC?

25.   **Analyzing Liquidity** *(LO 4.4)*

Year-end balance sheet data (shown in thousands of dollars) for MamaMia Soup Company follow.

	Year 1	Year 2
Cash and cash equivalents	$ 94	$ 63
Short-term investments	2	7
Accounts receivable (net)	578	646
Inventory	786	904
Property, plant & equipment (net)	2,401	2,265
Current liabilities	1,465	1,851
Long-term liabilities	1,338	1,343

Required:

(a)   Explain the significance of the quick ratio. How do decision makers use this ratio when interpreting a company's financial statements?

(b)   Compute MamaMia's quick ratio for both years. Based strictly on these ratios, in which year was the company's liquidity position stronger?

(c)   If the average quick ratio in MamaMia's industry is 1.2, is the company's quick ratio better or worse than the industry norm?

(d)   Identify at least three factors that could account for MamaMia's quick ratio being significantly different from the industry norm.

26.   **Analyzing Accounts Receivable** *(LO 4.4)*

QL Corporation sells computer peripherals, primarily on a credit basis. Following are selected financial data, expressed in thousands, for this firm for a recent three-year period. QL had net sales of $26,128,500 in the year 2006 and accounts receivable of $3,023,000 on January 1, 2007.

	2007	2008	2009
Net sales	$22,456,000	$28,837,500	$26,889,500
A/R (year-end)	3,003,500	4,679,000	3,501,500

Required:

(a)   Compute QL's accounts receivable turnover ratio and age of receivables for years 2007 through 2009.

(b)   Did these ratios improve or weaken over this three-year period? Explain.

CASES

27.   **Establishing a Credit Policy** *(LO 4.1, writing)*

Recently, Erica Lovell, owner of Erica's Electronics, decided to allow customers to purchase merchandise on credit. Credit customers will be given 60 days to pay for their purchases. No discounts will be granted for early payment. Erica believes this new policy will increase her store's sales because her principal competitor in town has a strict cash-only sales policy.

Required:

Write a brief memo to Erica describing some of the business benefits of, and problems with, the new credit policy. Include in your memo the nonaccounting issues that Erica will confront following this policy's implementation.

28.   **Annual Reports** *(LO 4.4, Internet)*

Use the annual report of Carnival Corporation for the 2007 fiscal year to answer the following questions. This information can be found on either the annual report or the SEC 10-K filing at www.carnival.com by following the links to Investor Relations.

Required:

(a)   Calculate Carnival's quick ratios for 2006 and 2007.

(b)   What do the quick ratios calculated in part (a) indicate about Carnival's liquidity?

(c)   All else being equal, what effects would each of the following have on the quick ratio?

   (1)   An increase in cash and cash equivalents

   (2)   A decrease in short-term investments

   (3)   An increase in current liabilities

   (4)   An increase in inventory

   (5)   An increase in sales revenue

(d)   Comment on the change in the quick ratio from 2006 to 2007. What account(s) is (are) primarily responsible for this change?

(e)   Does anything in Carnival's Notes to the Financial Statements help explain the change in the accounts comprising the calculation of the quick ratio? If so, what information is provided?

29.   **Annual Reports** *(LO 4.4, Internet)*

Macy's Inc. is the parent company of Macy's and Bloomingdale's department stores. Use Macy's annual report with a year-end of February 2, 2008, to answer the following questions. The annual report can be found at www.macys.com; follow the links to investor relations.

Required:

Answer each of the following questions for the fiscal year ended February 2, 2008.

(a)   Does Macy's still have an in-house (proprietary) credit card? Explain.

(b)   What is the balance on February 2, 2008, in accounts receivable?

(c)   What amount of uncollectible accounts (related to in-house credit cards) were written off during 2005 and 2006?

(d)   What was the company's previous policy about writing off uncollectible accounts?

(e)   What is the average balance in accounts receivable?

(f) What is the total of Macy's net sales for 2007?

(g) Assume that net sales is equivalent to net credit sales. Calculate the accounts receivable turnover ratio and the age of receivables ratio. Comment on the results.

(h) What is the amount of Macy's cash and cash equivalents at February 2, 2008? How does Macy's determine what to classify within this account?

30. **Comparing Companies** (LO 4.4, group, Internet)

Identifying the similarities and differences between companies is as crucial to making investment decisions as understanding a single company's financial statements. Form groups of at least four students. Each group should select a single industry. Each group member should locate a different annual report within that industry. (The industry and individual company may be assigned by your instructor.)

Required—individual group members:

(a) Calculate the following ratios for the company you selected for the two most recent fiscal years.

   (1) Quick ratio

   (2) Accounts receivable turnover

   (3) Age of receivables

(b) Does the company you chose have any short-term investments? What percentage of current assets does the short-term investment represent? What percentage of total assets does the short-term investments represent? Why might a company have short-term investments?

Required—groups:

(c) Compile the ratio calculations for each company prepared by the individual group members into one table.

(d) Compare the results from company to company in the same fiscal year. Include in your comparison a graphical analysis. Discuss reasons why these ratios might be similar or different within an industry.

(e) Compare the occurrence and percentage of short-term investments within your industry.

Required—class:

(f) Compare the ratios from each industry. Discuss reasons why these ratios might be similar or different between industries.

(g) Does one industry seem to be a better investment than another? Do you think this is constant over time?

SUPPLEMENTAL PROBLEMS

31. **Petty Cash** (LO 4.1; Compare to Problem 18)

Theodore Bear, Inc. established a $200 petty cash account on January 2, 2009. On October 5, 2009, the account was increased to $500. On December 3, 2009, the petty cash drawer contained $219.04 in cash and coins and the following receipts:

Vendor	Amount	For
United Express Service	$79.42	Overnight shipping
Danielle's Restaurant	124.30	Client entertainment
Quick Print	46.49	Advertising brochures
Office Mart	30.75	Whiteboard markers for meeting

Required:

(a) Record the January 1 journal entry to establish the petty cash fund.

(b) Record the October 5 journal entry to increase the amount of the petty cash fund.

(c) Record the entry to replenish petty cash on December 3.

(d) Assume that instead of $219.04, the amount of cash in the petty cash envelope was $120.75. Provide two possible situations that might cause the petty cash

difference. What actions might you take to correct future instances of the two situations just discussed?

32. **Credit Card Sales** (LO 4.1; Compare to Problem 19)

Credit card sales for TentRent, a party rental company, are given for a one-week period in July. All payments from the credit card company are directly deposited into TentRent's bank account less a service fee. There is often a delay in processing the credit card company receipts, so TentRent uses an Account Receivable—Credit Card account to record all sales on credit cards. When payments are received, this account receivable is reduced.

Sale Date	Credit Card Sale Amount	Payment Date	Payment Amount
6th	$520	6th	$509.60
7th	452	8th	442.96
8th	745	9th	730.10
10th	623	13th	610.54
11th	512	13th	501.76
12th	477	13th	467.46

Required:

(a) Record the July 6th sales entry.

(b) Record the July 13th entry for the three receipts from the credit card company.

(c) What percent fee does the credit card company charge?

(d) What are the benefits and costs to TentRent for accepting third-party (national) credit cards?

(e) What would be the benefits and costs to TentRent if it were offer in-house credit cards instead rather than accepting third-party cards?

33. Bank Reconciliation (LO 4.2; Compare to Problem 22)

Radon, Inc.'s February 28th bank statement showed an ending cash balance of $10,640. On February 28, Radon's general ledger cash account showed a balance of $10,869. After comparing the general ledger to the bank statement, the following items were noted:

- Interest paid by the bank $ 129
- Deposits in transit 760
- Draft of electric bill 620
- Outstanding checks 1,227
- Service fee charged by the bank 25
- Check #657 was written to Apple Long Distance for $796; this was the amount that was also recorded in the General Journal for $796. The check was processed through the bank for $976.

Required:

(a) Prepare a bank reconciliation for Radon, Inc.

(b) Make the required journal entries associated with the bank reconciliation.

(c) It would be possible (though not probable) for a small company do business without a checking account. Discuss the problems that attempting to operate in such a manner would create for the business.

34. Uncollectible Accounts Expense (LO 4.3; Compare to Problem 23)

A partial balance sheet of Rocky Mount Wholesale Florist is provided following.

Rocky Mount Wholesale Florist
Partial Balance Sheet
December 31, 2008

Accounts Receivable	$105,000
Allowance for Uncollectible Accounts	(3,150)
Net Realizable Value	$101,850

During 2009, $2,450,000 was charged to accounts receivable, and $2,175,000 was paid on the account by customers. Also during 2009, Rocky Mount Wholesale Florist wrote off the following uncollectible accounts:

March 18	Pick-a-Daisy	$1,200
June 22	A Touch of Style	1,060
November 28	Dryer's Artistic Flowers	680

Required:

(a) Record the journal entries to write off the three uncollectible accounts.

(b) Prepare a T-account for the Allowance account and calculate the balance on December 31, 2009. How should that balance be interpreted?

(c) Prepare a T-account for Accounts Receivable and calculate the balance on December 31, 2009.

(d) Rocky Mount Wholesale Florist estimates that 4 percent of the accounts receivable balance will be uncollectible. What amount is estimated to be uncollectible at the end of 2009? What amount would be considered the net realizable value of the receivables?

(e) Rocky Mount Wholesale Florist wants to prepare an adjusting entry for uncollectible accounts that will make the net realizable value equal to the amount calculated in part (d). Prepare the journal entry to record the estimated uncollectible accounts. (Hint: The amount calculated as uncollectible will not be the amount used in the journal entry.)

35. Ratio Analysis (LO 4.4; Compare to Problems 25 and 26)

Selected financial information for Harrison, Inc. is shown next (in thousands).

	Year 1	Year 2
Cash and cash equivalents	$ 104	$ 108
Short-term investments	10	18
Accounts receivable (gross)	654	611
Accounts receivable (net)	622	580
Inventory	988	1,022
Prepaid expenses	111	92
Current liabilities	840	866
Long-term liabilities	1,181	1,304
Net credit sales	7,914	7,889

Required:

(a) What account creates the difference between gross and net accounts receivable? What does this account represent?

(b) Calculate the quick ratios for years 1 and 2.

(c) Calculate the accounts receivable turnover ratio and age of receivables for year 2.

(d) Why can the accounts receivable turnover ratio not be calculated for year 1?

(e) Assume that, in year 3, the economy took a downturn, and interest rates rose substantially. What would you expect to happen to the accounts receivable turnover ratio and the age of receivables relative to those calculated in part (c)? Explain the rationale for your answers.

CHAPTER 5

Inventory

LEARNING OBJECTIVES

1. Account for common inventory transactions.
2. Use the four major inventory cost flow methods to calculate ending inventory and cost of goods sold.
3. Use the retail inventory method to calculate ending inventory and cost of goods sold.
4. Apply the lower-of-cost-or-market rule to inventory.
5. Determine the effects of inventory errors on financial statements.
6. Use ratios and other analysis techniques to make decisions about inventory.

INTRODUCTION

Inventory consists of all goods that merchandising businesses intend to sell to their customers as well as the raw materials and in-process items that will be converted into saleable, finished goods by manufacturers. Inventory is classified as a current asset on the balance sheet. This chapter introduces the two primary inventory systems, some ordinary inventory transactions, inventory cost flow methods, and how inventory errors can affect the financial statements. Because of the proportional size of inventory to other assets and of cost of goods sold (CGS) to other expenses, financial statement users commonly analyze inventory and CGS accounts in making decisions about a company's short- and long-term prospects; such analyses are discussed at the end of the chapter.

PERPETUAL AND PERIODIC INVENTORY SYSTEMS

There are two general types of inventory accounting systems: perpetual and periodic. The primary differences between these two systems are in the accounts used to record transactions and the timing and manner in which cost of goods sold is determined. The choice to use either a perpetual or periodic inventory system is often associated with the nature of the inventory and the level of computerization of the business.

In a **perpetual inventory system**, a continuous record of inventory acquired and sold is maintained in the inventory asset account. When inventory is purchased, the inventory account is increased (debited) and either cash or accounts payable is credited. When inventory is sold, two things occur. First, the business records the inflow of cash or accounts receivable (through a debit) and an increase in revenue (through a credit to sales). In addition, the cost of the merchandise that was sold is removed from (credited to) the Inventory account and an expense account is increased (debited). Thus, at any time (assuming away losses due to theft, breakage, or spoilage), the Inventory account shows the actual quantity and cost of the inventory on hand, and the Cost of Goods Sold account shows the total cost of the merchandise sold to customers during the period. Having this information is a key advantage of using a perpetual inventory system.

In the past, perpetual inventory systems were typically used only when inventory items were unique or specifically identifiable. For example, an exclusive jewelry store can identify each Rolex watch sold by its serial number, and antique dealers can identify pieces by style and period. The perpetual inventory system was more difficult to use in businesses with many identical items. Until the widespread usage of computers and bar coding technology, perpetual inventory systems were difficult and expensive to maintain; the cost and time of record keeping was not often worth the information provided.

As companies began selling a wider variety of products and a greater emphasis was placed on cost and inventory control, the information provided by a perpetual inventory system took on greater importance. Now, bar coding of sales tags lets most retail businesses use perpetual inventory systems. Information on a product's cost (as well as size, color, and brand) can be included in the bar code, and scanning the tag not only updates inventory records, but also results in automatic indications of the need to reorder products.

Some companies, such as smaller firms and those that sell nondistinguishable or inexpensive items, still cannot or do not use perpetual inventory systems. For example, a bakery may not want to determine the cost of each doughnut sold, a florist may not care about the cost of each piece of flower wire included in a bouquet, and a hardware store may not wish to count and track every nut, bolt, or nail.

A **periodic inventory system** updates the inventory and cost of goods sold accounts only once a period rather than continuously. Instead of debiting and crediting inventory to reflect acquisitions and sales of merchandise, temporary accounts are used to record the transactions associated with acquiring inventory. The temporary accounts used in a periodic inventory system are as follows:

- Purchases, a debit-balanced account used for inventory purchases;
- Purchases Discounts, a credit-balanced contra-purchases account used for prompt payment discounts;
- Purchases Returns and Allowances, a credit-balanced contra-purchases account used for the return of merchandise to suppliers or price reductions given by suppliers; and
- Freight In, a debit-balanced account for shipping charges paid by purchaser; these charges will cause the cost of goods purchased to increase.

These accounts are all closed at the end of the accounting period.

In a periodic inventory system, no entry is made for cost of goods sold expense when a sale is made, although the revenue portion of the transaction is recorded. In these systems, the quantity of inventory on hand is determined at the end of each accounting period, and that quantity is multiplied by the appropriate per unit cost to arrive at the dollar value of ending inventory. Subtracting that figure from the total cost of goods that the company had available for sale during the period provides the cost of goods sold expense for the period. Thus, no information is available on an ongoing basis regarding the quantity or cost of inventory on hand or sold. In addition, because no information is recorded as goods are sold, the periodic inventory system provides little internal control; at the end of a period, goods that are not on hand are assumed to have been sold.

Visual Recap 5.1 compares the perpetual and periodic inventory systems. Because of its common usage, however, this chapter focuses on the use of a perpetual inventory system.

ACCOUNTING FOR COMMON INVENTORY TRANSACTIONS

Six common transactions are related to accounting for inventory: purchasing inventory from a supplier, paying for freight on purchases, returning inventory to a supplier, selling inventory to a customer, accepting returns of inventory from a customer, and paying on

VISUAL RECAP 5.1

Comparison of Perpetual and Periodic Inventory Systems

	Perpetual	Periodic
Provides good internal control	yes	no
Records Cost of Goods Sold at selling point	yes	no
Uses temporary accounts to record inventory transactions	no	yes
Information in Inventory account during the year is	current	beginning of the year balance
Information in Cost of Goods Sold account during the year is	current	nonexistent

account for purchases of inventory. Marcia's Boutique, a small retail store with a perpetual inventory system, is used to illustrate these transactions.

Purchasing Inventory from a Supplier

On August 1, Marcia's purchased 12 dresses at $50 each from a supplier, Kwon, Inc. The purchase had credit terms of 2/10, n/30 and shipping terms of FOB shipping point. The credit terms indicate that Marcia's Boutique is entitled to a 2 percent discount if the invoice is paid within ten days of the invoice date. If payment is not made by August 11, Marcia's must pay the full amount of the invoice by August 31, the last day of the 30-day credit period. As noted in the previous chapter, from the supplier's viewpoint, the credit terms reflect sales discounts; from the buyer's viewpoint, these prompt payment credit terms are called **purchase discounts**. The shipping terms for a transaction indicate whether the seller or buyer is responsible for paying the delivery cost of the goods. This topic is discussed relative to the entry on August 3.

To account for this transaction, Marcia's must increase its inventory (debit) and increase its accounts payable (credit) for the cost of the dress.

General Journal				
Date		Description	Debit	Credit
Aug	1	Inventory	600	
		Accounts Payable—Kwon		600
		Purchased inventory		
		on account		

Paying for Freight-In on Purchases

When one business purchases goods from another, the two companies must agree on which party will be responsible for paying the delivery costs for the goods. The point at which legal title to goods transfers from seller to buyer dictates the party responsible for paying delivery charges. The two most common shipping terms are FOB shipping point and FOB destination.

Under terms of **FOB shipping point,** the seller delivers the goods free on board (FOB) to the shipping point, such as the seller's loading dock. There, a freight company usually takes possession of the goods and delivers them to the buyer. With these shipping terms, the buyer pays delivery charges because title to the goods transfers to the buyer at the shipping point. When goods are shipped **FOB destination**, the seller retains legal title to the goods until they reach the destination point. As a result, the seller is responsible for paying the transportation charges.

The dresses purchased by Marcia's Boutique on August 1 were to be shipped FOB shipping point. Thus, the delivery charges increase the cost of the dresses to Marcia's Boutique. When Marcia's receives and pays the $22 freight bill on August 3, the cost of inventory is increased (debited). Had the goods been shipped FOB destination, the seller would have recorded the shipping charges (Freight Out, a selling expense), and Marcia's Boutique would have no entry.

General Journal				
Date		**Description**	**Debit**	**Credit**
Aug	3	Inventory	22	
		Cash		22
		Paid FOB charges on inventory		

Returning Inventory to a Supplier

On August 5, Marcia's Boutique returned a dress to Kwon because the dress had a fabric flaw. Merchandising companies, like their customers, are sometimes dissatisfied with goods purchased. Merchandise is occasionally received that was not ordered, was defective, or was damaged when packaged. Reductions in amounts owed to suppliers resulting from returned goods (**purchase returns**) or price concessions granted for defective or damaged goods (**purchase allowances**) are referred to collectively as purchase returns and allowances. Marcia's journalizes the return of inventory with a credit and debits Accounts Payable to decrease the amount owed to Kwon.

General Journal				
Date		**Description**	**Debit**	**Credit**
Aug	5	Accounts Payable—Kwon	50	
		Inventory		50
		Returned inventory for credit on account		

Selling Inventory to a Customer

Marcia's Boutique sells three dresses for cash ($110 per dress) on August 7. Because the company uses a perpetual inventory system, two journal entries are required. The first entry records the revenue resulting from the transaction, whereas the second entry records the related amount paid for the inventory. Cost of Goods Sold is an expense account that accumulates, through debits, the cost of inventory sold to customers during an accounting period. The second journal entry also accounts for the reduction (credit) of store inventory at the original cost of $50 per dress.

General Journal				
Date		**Description**	**Debit**	**Credit**
Aug	7	Cash	330	
		Sales		330
		Cost of Goods Sold	150	
		Inventory		150
		Sold merchandise on account		
		and recorded related CGS		

Accepting Returns of Inventory from a Customer

On August 8, one customer who bought a dress on August 7 decided to return it. The previous chapter indicated that companies establish a Sales Returns and Allowances account to record merchandise refunds and price concessions granted to customers. In a perpetual inventory system, a sales return requires two entries. The first entry records the return and the customer's cash refund (or Accounts Receivable reduction), and the second entry makes the necessary corrections to return the merchandise into inventory (debit) and reduce Cost of Goods Sold (credit).

General Journal				
Date		Description	Debit	Credit
Aug	8	Sales Returns and Allowances	110	
		Cash		110
		Inventory	50	
		Cost of Goods Sold		50
		Recorded cash remittance to customer returning merchandise		

Paying on Account for Purchases of Inventory

On August 11, Marcia's paid for the dresses purchased from Kwon. The credit terms from Kwon, Inc. allow Marcia's Boutique to deduct 2 percent from the total amount owed if payment is made by August 11. Following the August 5 purchase return, the total amount owed to Kwon is $550 ($600 − $50). Thus, Marcia's Boutique is entitled to an $11 discount ($550 × 0.02) when the company pays for the goods within the discount period. This purchase discount is credited to the Inventory account to reduce the cost of the goods acquired for sale.

General Journal				
Date		Description	Debit	Credit
Aug	11	Accounts Payable—Kwon	550	
		Cash		539
		Inventory		11
		Paid for inventory within the discount period		

The Marcia's Boutique example is simplistic first because it focused only on a single purchase of goods and the related sales of those goods. Businesses will generally have goods from many different vendors on hand and available for sale simultaneously. Second, all the dresses purchased in the example had the same acquisition cost. In most companies, purchases will be made throughout the period at various cost amounts. In such situations, a determination must be made of the inventory cost flow method to be used to record cost of goods sold. Third, the example did not attempt to attach the freight charges for the dresses to them at point of sale. Realistically, because Marcia's paid $22 for freight and had 11 dresses to sell (because one was returned), the actual cost of each dress sold was $52 (the $50 purchase price plus $2 freight) rather than $50.

The six primary transactions used in a perpetual inventory system are summarized in Visual Recap 5.2.

INVENTORY COSTING METHODS

"Inventory cost flow" is a common business expression. A merchandiser begins an accounting period with a certain amount of inventory. During the period, additional purchases of inventory are made, and shipping charges may be paid on those goods. Some inventory may be returned to the supplier or some price allowances may be granted. Adding beginning inventory and net merchandise purchases (purchases minus purchase returns) gives the **cost of goods available for sale** for that period:

Beginning inventory		BI
+ Purchases of merchandise for sale	P	
+ Freight paid by purchaser (FOB shipping point)	FI	
− Returns of merchandise to supplier	(PR)	
− Price allowances granted by vendor	(PA)	
Net purchases		NP
= Cost of goods available for sale		CGA

The cost of merchandise sold during an accounting period flows out of inventory and into cost of goods sold, which is shown on the income statement. At the end of a period, the cost of unsold merchandise is shown as ending inventory on the balance sheet. This cost flow cycle is repeated each accounting period.

VISUAL RECAP 5.2

Summary of Perpetual Inventory Transactions

Increases to Cost of Inventory			Decreases to Cost of Inventory		
Purchase			**Return of Purchase**		
Inventory	X		A/P (or Cash)	X	
A/P (or Cash)		X	Inventory		X
Freight In (FOB Shipping Point)			**Discount on Credit Purchase**		
Inventory	X		A/P	X	
Cash		X	Cash		X
			Inventory		X
Customer Return			**Sale to Customer**		
Sales R&A	X		A/R (or Cash)	X	
A/R (or Cash)		X	Sales		X
Inventory	X		Cost of Goods Sold	X	
Cost of Goods Sold		X	Inventory		X

Cost of goods available for sale   CGA
– Ending inventory   (EI)
= Cost of goods sold   CGS

For inventory, as for most assets, cost is the primary valuation basis. Two important accounting issues faced by businesses are how to determine the cost of the goods that are sold and, as a result, the cost of ending inventory. At first, these calculations may not seem to be particularly challenging—and they would not be if all similar inventory units were purchased at the same price every time a purchase was made.

Some businesses can specifically identify which goods are being sold when sales take place. For example, an automobile dealership knows which car a customer has purchased because of the VIN; the exact invoice cost to the dealer of that automobile can be determined and moved from the inventory to Cost of Goods Sold. Other businesses have fairly readily identifiable physical flows of inventory. The three most common types of physical flow are **FIFO** (first-in, first-out), **LIFO** (last-in, first-out), and average.

When a grocery dairy case is restocked, the "old" milk is moved to the front, and the "new" milk is placed in the back of the case. The intention is to create a first-in, first-out physical inventory flow. Items that are stacked (such as firewood) would typically be associated with a last-in, first-out physical flow. Under an average physical flow, all goods are mixed together and cannot be identified as to date of purchase; an example is gasoline in a storage tank.

The operations of University Bookstore are used to explore the topic of inventory costing. Exhibit 5-1 depicts inventory data for January for a *Principles of Marketing* textbook. The text is a paperback version, and thus, there are no used copies of the text available for sale. To simplify the example, it is assumed that University Bookstore only had sales on two days. Given the exhibit information, the cost of goods available for sale in January is $19,730 (or $3,000 + $14,000 + $2,730). Additionally, the bookstore has 30(100 + 400 − 360 + 70 − 180) texts on hand at the end of January. Some very important information is, however, unknown at this time. First, what amounts should be recorded as Cost of Goods Sold (and a reduction in inventory) on January 14 and 22? Second, what amount should be shown for the ending inventory on the January 31 balance sheet? The Inventory and Cost of Goods Sold accounts are directly related to each other because, only after the cost of goods sold amounts are identified, can the cost of unsold items that comprise ending inventory be computed. The following sections illustrate four different inventory costing methods that can be used to assign the cost of goods available for sale amount to cost of goods sold and ending inventory.

EXHIBIT 5-1

University Bookstore Inventory Data

1/1	Beginning inventory	100 copies @ $30	$ 3,000
1/8	Purchased	400 copies @ $35	14,000
1/14	Sold	360 copies	
1/18	Purchased	70 copies @ $39	2,730
1/22	Sold	180 copies	

Specific Identification Method

One costing method is called **specific identification**. To use this method, a business must be able to identify the actual cost of each unit of inventory sold during an accounting period and the actual cost of each unsold unit at the end of an accounting period. Assume that University Bookstore electronically bar codes each inventory item with the date and price of purchase; these codes are scanned at point of sale to have access to the data needed to apply the specific identification method.

In a perpetual inventory system, a business maintains an inventory ledger that contains an account for each inventory item. Exhibit 5-2 provides the inventory record for the marketing text.

The perpetual inventory record reveals the cost of each textbook purchased or sold during the month as well as the cost of each book on hand during the month. For example, 70 of the books sold on January 14 had a per-unit cost of $30 (these books were from the beginning inventory), whereas the remaining 290 books cost $35 each (these were from the purchase on January 8). Following the initial one-day opening, the University Bookstore had 140 copies of the marketing text on hand at a total cost of $4,750. These 140 copies were distributed across two layers: 30 books with a per-unit cost of $30 and 110 books with a per-unit cost of $35. As indicated in Exhibit 5-2, additional books were purchased on January 18 and sold on January 22.

University Bookstore's January specific identification inventory information is summarized as follows:

Ending Inventory:	30 copies:	10 @ $30	$ 300	
		10 @ $35	350	
		10 @ $39	390	$ 1,040
Cost of Goods Sold:	360 copies on 1/14		$12,250	
	180 copies on 1/22		6,440	18,690
Total cost of goods available for sale				$19,730

EXHIBIT 5-2

Perpetual Inventory Record — Specific Identification Method

Item: *Principles of Marketing*

Date	Purchases #	Unit Cost	Total	Sales #	Unit Cost	Total	Balance #	Unit Cost	Total
Jan. 1							100	$30	$ 3,000
Jan. 8	400	$35	$14,000				100	$30	$ 3,000
							400	35	14,000
							500		$17,000
Jan. 14				70	$30	$ 2,100	30	$30	$ 900
				290	35	10,150	110	35	3,850
				360		$12,250	140		$ 4,750
Jan. 18	70	$39	$ 2,730				30	$30	$ 900
							110	35	3,850
'							70	39	2,730
							210		$ 7,480
Jan. 22				20	$30	$ 600	10	$30	$ 300
				100	35	3,500	10	35	350
				60	39	2,340	10	39	390
				180		$ 6,440	30		$ 1,040

Companies that do not have the information technology to allow them to use specific identification or those that choose not to use specific identification may select a cost flow assumption (FIFO, LIFO, or average) to calculate cost of goods sold and ending inventory. Cost flow assumptions are used when the business does not actually know which goods are sold when. Visual Recap 5.3 depicts the cost flow assumptions. The calculations associated with these assumptions are discussed in detail in the following sections.

FIFO Method

The FIFO (first-in, first-out) method of inventory costing assumes that the goods acquired first (the oldest, or first in, goods) are the first ones sold (first out), and thus, their costs are the first ones to be sent to Cost of Goods Sold. In turn, the per-unit cost of the most recently acquired goods (last in) are used to determine the cost of ending inventory under the FIFO method.

Exhibit 5-3 provides the inventory record for the *Principles of Marketing* text assuming that University Bookstore applies the FIFO method. On January 8, after the purchase of 400 books at a per-unit cost of $35, there were two layers of inventory: 100 books at $30 and 400 books at $35. Applying the first-in, first-out concept to the 360 books sold on January 14, the bookstore assumed that all 100 of the oldest (first-in) books were sold. The remaining 260 books sold were assumed to have been purchased on January 8 at a cost of $35 per unit.

Following the January 18 purchase, there again were two layers of inventory: 140 books with a per-unit cost of $35 and 70 books with a per-unit cost of $39. For the sales made on January 22, the 140 $35 books were assumed to have been sold first. Additionally, 40 books from the $39 per-unit layer were also assumed to have been sold, leaving 30 of the $39 books in ending inventory. University Bookstore's January FIFO inventory information is summarized as follows:

Ending Inventory:	30 copies:	30 @ $39		$ 1,170
Cost of Goods Sold:	360 copies on 1/14		$12,100	
	180 copies on 1/22		6,460	18,560
Total cost of goods available for sale				$19,730

VISUAL RECAP 5.3

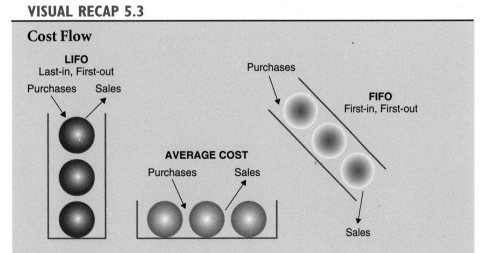

EXHIBIT 5-3

Perpetual Inventory
Record—FIFO Method

Item: *Principles of Marketing*

		Purchases			Sales			Balance	
Date	#	Unit Cost	Total	#	Unit Cost	Total	#	Unit Cost	Total
Jan. 1							100	$30	$ 3,000
Jan. 8	400	$35	$14,000				100	$30	$ 3,000
							400	35	14,000
							500		$17,000
Jan. 14				100	$30	$ 3,000			
				260	35	9,100	140	$35	$ 4,900
				360		$12,100			
Jan. 18	70	$39	$2,730				140	$35	$ 4,900
							70	39	2,730
							210		$ 7,630
Jan. 22				140	$35	$ 4,900			
				40	39	1,560	30	$39	$ 1,170
				180		$ 6,460			

LIFO Method

The LIFO (last-in, first-out) method of inventory costing assumes that the most recently acquired goods (last in) are sold first (first out), whereas the oldest acquired goods (first in) remain in inventory. Exhibit 5-4 provides the inventory record for the *Principles of Marketing* text assuming that University Bookstore applies the LIFO inventory costing method.

Similar to the FIFO example just discussed, the LIFO schedule indicates that there were two layers of books following the January 8 purchase: 100 books that cost $30 per unit and 400 books that cost $35 per unit. On January 14, the bookstore assumed that all 360 books sold cost $35 each. This assumption left intact the original layer of 100 books, as well as a layer of 40 books at a cost of $35 each.

Following the January 18 purchase, there were three layers of books: 100 books costing $30 each, 40 books costing $35 each, and the newest layer of 70 books costing $39 each. Applying the last-in, first-out concept, the January 22 sale of 180 books eliminated the layers of 70 books costing $39 and 40 books costing $35 as well as reducing the original layer to only 30 books. University Bookstore's January LIFO inventory information is summarized as follows:

Ending Inventory:	30 copies:	30 @ $30		$ 900
Cost of Goods Sold:	360 copies on 1/14		$12,600	
	180 copies on 1/22		6,230	18,830
Total cost of goods available for sale				$19,730

EXHIBIT 5-4

Perpetual Inventory
Record—LIFO Method

Item: *Principles of Marketing*

	Purchases			Sales			Balance		
Date	#	Unit Cost	Total	#	Unit Cost	Total	#	Unit Cost	Total
Jan. 1							100	$30	$ 3,000
Jan. 8	400	$35	$14,000				100	$30	$ 3,000
							400	35	14,000
							500		$17,000
Jan. 14				360	$35	$12,600	100	$30	$ 3,000
							40	35	1,400
							140		$ 4,400
Jan. 18	70	$39	$2,730				100	$30	$ 3,000
							40	35	1,400
							70	39	2,730
							210		$ 7,130
Jan. 22				70	$39	$ 2,730			
				40	35	1,400			
				70	30	2,100	30	$30	$ 900
				180		$ 6,230			

Moving-Average Method

Under the **moving-average method** of inventory costing, an average per unit cost is computed before each sale of inventory. The cost basis of ending inventory is determined by multiplying the number of unsold units of that item by its moving-average per-unit cost at the end of the accounting period. University Bookstore would make the following moving average computations for the *Principles of Marketing* text. Before the January 14 sale of 360 books, the average per-unit cost of the 500 books on hand was $34:

$$\text{Average price} = [(100 \times \$30) + (400 \times \$35)] \div 500$$
$$= (\$3,000 + \$14,000) \div 500$$
$$= \$17,000 \div 500$$
$$= \$34$$

The 360 books sold on January 14 are expensed at $34 per unit.

Before the January 22 sale, the new moving-average cost was $35.67 per unit, computed as follows:

$$\text{Average price} = [(140 \times \$34) + (70 \times \$39)] \div 210$$
$$= (\$4,760 + \$2,730) \div 210$$
$$= \$7,490 \div 210$$
$$= \$35.67 \text{ (rounded)}$$

EXHIBIT 5-5

Perpetual Inventory
Record—Moving
Average Method

Item: *Principles of Marketing*

Date	Purchases			Sales			Balance		
	#	Unit Cost	Total	#	Unit Cost	Total	#	Unit Cost	Total
Jan. 1							100	$30	$ 3,000
Jan. 8	400	$35	$14,000				100	$30	$ 3,000
							400	35	14,000
							500		$17,000
Jan. 14				360	$34	$12,240	140		$ 4,760
Jan. 18	70	$39	$ 2,730				140	$30	$ 4,760
							70	39	2,730
							210		$ 7,490
Jan. 22				180	$35.67	$ 6,421	30		$ 1,069

Thus, the total cost assigned to the 180 books sold on January 22 was $6,421 (180 × $35.67).

The moving-average inventory card is shown in Exhibit 5-5. Notice that no average cost is shown in the Balance column after each new purchase. There is no need to calculate such an average because, should another purchase take place before a sale, the average cost would change.

University Bookstore's January moving-average inventory information is summarized as follows:

Ending Inventory:	30 copies:	30 @ $35.67	$ 1,069
Cost of Goods Sold:	360 copies on 1/14	$12,240	
	180 copies on 1/22	6,421	18,661
Total cost of goods available for sale			$19,730

Generally accepted accounting principles (GAAP) allow a business to use any rational and systematic method to assign costs to the inventory sold during an accounting period. Thus, a business may use an inventory cost flow assumption that is at variance with the actual physical flow of its goods. For example, although a company sells goods in a FIFO pattern, that company may choose to use the LIFO inventory costing method. A business whose inventory flows in a LIFO pattern may elect to use the FIFO inventory costing method. Similarly, a merchandiser that can identify the actual per-unit costs of the items in ending inventory may still use the FIFO, LIFO, or the moving-average inventory costing method.

Comparison of Income Statements Effects of Inventory Costing Methods

Exhibit 5-6 shows the gross profit amounts for the *Principles of Marketing* text under each of the four inventory costing methods. This schedule assumes that the bookstore sold the marketing text for $60 per unit throughout January. These gross profit figures range from $13,570 for the LIFO method to $13,840 for the FIFO method. In absolute terms, this $270 difference seems quite small; however, in a company that engages in hundreds of thousands

EXHIBIT 5-6		Specific Identification	FIFO	LIFO	Moving Average
CGS, Gross Profit, and Inventory Amounts	Sales (540 × $60)	$32,400	$32,400	$32,400	$32,400
	Cost of Goods Sold	18,690	18,560	18,830	18,661
	Gross Profit	$13,710	$13,840	$13,570	$13,739
	Inventory (1/31)	$ 1,040	$ 1,170	$ 900	$ 1,069

of inventory transactions in a single year, the differences in total gross profit would be much more substantial.

Balance Sheet Valuation versus Income Determination

In an inflationary economic environment (that is, when the cost of purchases is rising), the FIFO method yields a higher net income (or lower net loss) than the LIFO method when these methods are applied to the same financial data.[1] The question of whether FIFO or LIFO is the most informative (or better) method of accounting for inventory has been debated for years. The problem in resolving this debate is that two important but conflicting questions must be considered. Which method results in the more appropriate balance sheet valuation for ending inventory; and which method does a better job of matching a business's expenses with its revenues? The following discussion assumes inflation; thus, the effects would be reversed when prices are falling (deflation).

FIFO yields a higher net income because the more expensive goods (those purchased later in the period) are assumed to be in ending inventory, with the "cheaper" goods (beginning inventory or early purchases) expensed to Cost of Goods Sold. Under LIFO, the reverse is true: the goods assumed to be in ending inventory are the relatively low-cost goods on hand at the beginning of, or acquired early in, the period, whereas the costs of higher-priced goods purchased later in the period are assigned to Cost of Goods Sold. For balance sheet purposes, FIFO and LIFO assign, respectively, the newest and the oldest per unit costs of goods to ending inventory. For this reason, FIFO provides a more appropriate balance sheet valuation for ending inventory. For income statement purposes, FIFO and LIFO assign, respectively, the oldest and the newest per unit costs of goods to cost of goods sold. For this reason, LIFO is generally perceived to better match current dollars of business revenues and expenses and, thereby, produces a profit figure that better reflects a business's economic reality.

Consider an extreme example. A company purchased one unit of inventory last year for $10 and one unit yesterday for $50. A sale of one unit is made today for $57. The company would need to spend $50 to replace the unit sold. Thus, after selling and replacing one unit of inventory, the company would be "better off" by $7 on the transaction, before considering other expenses such as income taxes. For accounting purposes, gross profit would be $7 on the transaction if the LIFO method were used. However, if FIFO is used for accounting purposes, the gross profit entered in the accounting records would be $47 ($57 − $10).

---

[1] The moving-average method typically yields a net income between the net income figures produced by the FIFO and LIFO methods. The specific identification method usually results in a net income figure that approximates the net income produced by applying the moving-average method.

In summary, many businesspeople maintain that LIFO does a better job of matching revenues and expenses than does FIFO. Consequently, when income determination is considered a more important issue than balance sheet valuation, LIFO is preferred over FIFO. Because most decision makers consider income determination a more critical issue than balance sheet valuation, they often prefer that businesses use the LIFO method.

FIFO versus LIFO: Tax Consequences

Tax consequences are important when choosing an inventory costing method. One of the few areas in which the U.S. tax code requires consistency between tax reporting and financial accounting relates to the use of LIFO inventory valuation. If a company uses LIFO for federal tax purposes, LIFO must also be used for financial reporting. Because LIFO yields lower profits than FIFO in a period of steadily rising prices, the LIFO method translates into lower income tax payments. Thus, from a taxation standpoint, LIFO is generally preferred by businesses over FIFO in periods of rising prices—but FIFO is still the most widely used inventory method.

International Financial Reporting Standards (IFRSs) do not allow the use of LIFO inventory in the preparation of financial statements, which has created one difficulty (of several) in moving toward the agreement between U.S. accounting standards and IFRSs. Therefore, as of 2008, Congress was discussing the possibility of eliminating the use of LIFO in the United States. Not only would LIFO elimination remove a conflict between U.S. accounting and IFRS, but it would also create a large increase in governmental tax revenues—approximately $107 billion over a ten-year period.[2]

VALUING INVENTORY AT OTHER THAN COST

Although cost is the primary valuation basis for inventory, businesses must occasionally depart from that basis to prevent financial statements from being misleading to decision makers. Two common departures from cost are the retail inventory method and the lower-of-cost-or-market rule.

Retail Inventory

The **retail inventory method** is often used in small businesses to estimate the amount of inventory on hand. To use this method, there should be a consistent relationship between the costs and selling prices of a company's products. Information on individual purchases and sales do not need to be maintained because the retail method is a type of periodic inventory system. Retail inventory, however, does allow a level of internal control not commonly provided by a periodic inventory system. This method can be used with a FIFO, LIFO, or average cost flow assumption; the average cost flow assumption is illustrated in this text, and all price changes after products are originally priced are ignored for simplicity.

Under the retail inventory method, as goods are received, information on both purchase cost and retail price is gathered. Sales are recorded at retail prices without a

---

[2]David Katz, "How LIFO Could Stall Global Accounting," CFO.com (December 3, 2007); http://www.cfo.com/article.cfm/10239047?f = bestof (accessed 10/4/08).

separate entry for Cost of Goods Sold. At period-end, retail prices of the goods on hand are added, and the cost of ending inventory is determined. The retail prices of the goods that should be on hand can be compared with the retail prices of the goods that are actually on hand to determine whether theft or breakage occurred.

Kristi's Kollections, which sells small china boxes, is used to illustrate the retail inventory method. The company began 2009 with inventory costing $100,000 on hand; these goods had selling prices totaling $145,000. During the year, Kristi's purchased $219,600 of goods and marked them to sell for $325,000. A close-of-business physical inventory was taken on December 31, 2009, with information gathered on the selling (retail) prices of inventory on hand. Because selling prices cannot be shown on the balance sheet, this information needs to be converted to a cost amount through the use of a cost-to-retail percentage. Sales for the year totaled $385,000. Exhibit 5-7 shows the calculations related to this retail inventory example.

No matter what amount of physical inventory exists at year-end, cost of goods sold for 2009 would be calculated as $261,800 ($385,000 × 0.68). If the December 31, 2009, inventory showed goods on hand marked at $85,000, the cost of inventory for balance sheet purposes would be $57,800. In this case, the amount of goods that should have been on hand was actually there: the $470,000 of goods available to sell at retail prices minus the $385,000 of goods that were actually sold at retail prices. However, if the inventory showed only $75,000 of goods on hand, Kristi's managers could conclude that $10,000 of inventory in retail prices (or $6,800 in cost amounts) had either been broken or stolen during the period. The $6,800 would be shown as a loss for the year on the income statement; the balance sheet would show a year-end inventory of $51,000 ($75,000 × 0.68).[3]

Lower-of-Cost-or-Market

The **lower-of-cost-or-market** (LCM) rule requires businesses to value ending inventories at the lower of cost (as computed using a generally accepted costing method) and current market value. For purposes of this text, market value is assumed to be the **current**

EXHIBIT 5-7

Retail Inventory Method

	Cost	Retail
Beginning inventory, 1/1/09	$100,000	$ 145,000
Purchases during 2009	219,600	325,000
Cost of goods available for sale*	$319,600	$ 470,000
Sales (at retail amounts)		(385,000)
Ending inventory at retail		$ 85,000
Times cost-to-retail %		× 0.68
Ending inventory at cost	$ 57,800	

*Cost-to-retail % = $319,600 ÷ $ 470, 000 = 68%

---

[3] A loss account is a debit balanced income statement account. However, unlike an expense, which represents a normal cost of doing business, a loss is a revenue reduction that was caused by an "unnecessary" transaction. In this case, breakage or theft is not a "necessary" cost of doing business.

replacement cost or the per unit amount that would have to be paid to buy additional inventory items. As shown in Exhibit 5-8, the LCM rule can be applied on an item-by-item basis or a total inventory basis. An inventory write-down resulting from application of the LCM rule is typically debited to Cost of Goods Sold and credited to Inventory.

To apply the LCM rule on a total inventory basis, the total cost and total market value of a firm's inventory is computed, and the lower figure is selected. For the information in Exhibit 5-8, the lower of total inventory cost and total inventory market value is $2,370. To apply the LCM rule on an item-by-item basis, the lower of cost or market value is identified for each inventory item. Then, these amounts are added to determine the dollar amount of ending inventory for financial reporting purposes. Using the item-by-item version of the LCM rule, the year-end inventory would be valued at $2,070, as shown in Exhibit 5-8.

INVENTORY ERRORS

In most merchandising businesses, inventory is one of the largest current asset accounts. Improper inventory calculations can significantly distort a company's balance sheet and income statement. Errors can be caused by miscounting or mispricing.

Because the sum of ending inventory and cost of goods sold needs to equal the cost of goods available for sale, a misstatement of one amount creates a misstatement of the other. For example, assume that University Bookstore took a physical inventory of its marketing text at the end of January and counted only 29 books on hand rather than the 30 that had been calculated using perpetual inventory. Using the LIFO information in Exhibit 5-4, one text at $30 needs to be removed from the ending inventory cost to make that amount $870 (29 books at $30 each). The easiest way to adjust the inventory balance is for University Bookstore to add that $30 to Cost of Goods Sold. If the "missing" marketing text were later found in a stack of mathematics texts, it is clear that the ending inventory of marketing texts was understated and the Cost of Goods Sold for marketing texts was overstated for January.

Additionally, a misstatement in inventory at the end of one accounting period will automatically affect the next period's beginning inventory. Thus, an inventory error affects financial statement data for at least two consecutive accounting periods. The effects of inventory errors are shown in Visual Recap 5.4.

EXHIBIT 5-8						
Lower of Cost or Market Inventory	**Item**	**Quantity**	**Unit Cost**	**Replacement* Cost**	**Total Cost**	**Total Market**	**Item-by-Item LCM**
	727 jeans	30	$14	$18	$ 420	$ 540	$ 420
	757 jeans	20	24	17	480	340	340
	Tank tops	50	15	20	750	1,000	750
	Pullovers	40	18	14	720	560	560
					$2,370	$2,440	$2,070

*Replacement cost is determined at the fiscal year end.

VISUAL RECAP 5.4

Effects of Overstating and Understating Ending Inventory

Current Year

BI (okay)
+ Net Purchases (okay)
= CGA for sale (okay)
− EI (overstated)
= CGS (understated)

Net Income (overstated)

Retained Earnings (overstated)

Next Year

BI (overstated)
+ Net Purchases (okay)
= CGA for sale (overstated)
− EI (okay)
= CGS (overstated)

Net Income (understated)

Retained Earnings (okay)

Current Year

BI (okay)
+ Net Purchases (okay)
= CGA for sale (okay)
− EI (understated)
= CGS (overstated)

Net Income (understated)

Retained Earnings (understated)

Next Year

BI (understated)
+ Net Purchases (okay)
= CGA for sale (understated)
− EI (okay)
= CGS (understated)

Net Income (overstated)

Retained Earnings (okay)

Note that ending inventory and CGS have an inverse relationship; that is, as more goods are sold, fewer goods are left in ending inventory. Therefore, an understatement of ending inventory creates an overstatement of cost of goods sold. However, beginning inventory and CGS have a direct relationship. Therefore, any effect on beginning inventory will have the same effect on cost of goods sold.

Cost of goods sold and net income also have an inverse relationship. In calculating net income, the CGS is subtracted from sales revenue; therefore, if CGS increases, net income decreases. Any effect on CGS resulting from a misstatement of beginning or ending inventory will have the opposite effect on net income.

Assuming that only one error is made during a two-year period, that error will "wash out" at the end of the second year. The income statement accounts are closed at the end of each year, and thus, only balance sheet accounts contain the errors after closing. Thus, the over- or understatement of Retained Earnings in the current year is offset by the same amount of an under- or overstatement of Retained Earnings in the next year.

Sometimes inventory errors are unintentional, but sometimes they are intentional—better known as fraud. Numerous cases of fraud involving inventory have existed over the past half-century including Phar-Mor and Leslie Faye. One 1999 study found that asset misstatements comprised nearly half of the cases of fraudulent financial statements, and the majority of those misstatements involved inventory.[4]

---

[4]Joseph T. Wells, "Ghost Goods: How to Spot Phantom Inventory," *Journal of Accountancy* (June 2001), pp. 33–36.

ACCOUNTING INFORMATION FOR DECISION MAKING

On the balance sheets of merchandising and manufacturing companies, inventory is the asset most likely to attract the attention of decision makers. Investors and other decision makers monitor business inventory levels, changes in inventory and cost of goods sold between periods, and related financial disclosures to evaluate the changing financial fortunes of those businesses.

Companies include a summary of the accounting methods used for inventory, and other major accounts, in financial statement footnotes. Decision makers should be aware of and understand the inventory accounting methods that a company uses because the choice of inventory method can dramatically affect a firm's reported inventory value and periodic earnings.

An unusual or unanticipated change in inventory often provides definite clues regarding a company's future prospects. For example, Semitool, Inc. (www.semitool.com), a maker of wafer processing equipment used to make semiconductors, took a $3 million inventory write-off in 2007 because product enhancements made some of the company's inventory obsolete.[5] M/I Homes Inc. (www.mihomes.com) took a $22.3 million write-down of its land inventory in early 2008; the builder's house inventory was down 55 percent from one year earlier, a reflection of significant economic turmoil in the housing industry.[6] The company reported a net loss of $116.3 million for the first half of 2008 and did not expect conditions to improve for the remainder of 2008 and into 2009.[7]

Inventory affects several key financial ratios. Decision makers closely monitor the age of a business's inventory similar to their monitoring of the age of accounts receivable. As a company's inventory "ages," it becomes more subject to valuation problems that can be created by spoilage, obsolescence, or related problems.

Determining the age of inventory is a two-step process. First, the inventory turnover ratio must be computed. The **inventory turnover ratio** indicates the number of times that a company sells or "turns over" its inventory each year. A business attempts to turn over its inventory as quickly as possible without running out of items to sell. A high rate of inventory turnover not only reduces the risk of inventory spoilage and obsolescence but also minimizes carrying costs for items such as insurance and handling. This ratio is computed as follows:

$$\text{Inventory Turnover Ratio} = \text{Cost of Goods Sold} \div \text{Average Inventory}$$

Average inventory refers to the beginning inventory plus the ending inventory divided by two.

The **age of inventory** is computed by dividing 360 days by the inventory turnover ratio.

$$\text{Age of Inventory} = 360 \text{ days} \div \text{Inventory Turnover Ratio}$$

---

[5]Associated Press, "Semitool Posts Loss in 4Q on Write-Off," Boston.com (November 9, 2007); http://www.boston.com/business/technology/articles/2007/11/09/semitool_posts_loss_in_4q_on_write_off/ (accessed 10/4/08).

[6]"M/I Ends 1Q in Red on Land Inventory Write-Off," *Columbus Business First* (April 30, 2008); http://columbus.bizjournals.com/columbus/stories/2008/04/28/daily16.html (accessed 10/4/08).

[7]M/I Homes, Inc., "M/I Homes Reports Second Quarter Results," Press Release (July 31, 2008); http://www.snl.com/Cache/1001142350.PDF?D=&O=PDF&IID=4006323&Y=&T=&FID=1001142350 (accessed 10/4/08).

Inventory age indicates the average period required to sell an item of inventory. As the inventory turnover ratio increases, the age of inventory is shortened. Lower is better when it comes to the age of inventory.

Data for the Shapiro Clothing Company are given in Exhibit 5-9 to illustrate the computation of inventory turnover and the age of inventory.

If Shapiro primarily restocks its inventory with every new season (four times a year, or every 90 days), the company has an extremely good turnover ratio and age of inventory.

SUMMARY

Inventory is a focal point for decision makers analyzing a company's financial statements. Perpetual and periodic are two major types of inventory accounting systems. Perpetual inventory systems provide a continually updated record of inventory quantities and cost of goods sold. In recent years, two factors have caused many firms to switch from periodic to perpetual inventory systems: declining technology cost of employing the system and increasing importance of the information advantage.

Important accounting tasks facing merchandising and manufacturing firms each accounting period are determining the ending inventory cost and cost of goods sold. Cost is the principal valuation basis used for inventory, and four primary inventory costing methods can be used by a business: specific identification, FIFO (first-in, first-out), LIFO (last-in, first-out), and moving-average. Some small businesses may use the retail inventory method, which focuses on the selling prices of goods and is a type of periodic inventory system. When inventory cost exceeds market value, the lower-of-cost-or-market (LCM) rule requires inventory to be written down to market value. Generally, current replacement cost is defined as market value for purposes of the LCM rule.

Numerous issues are important to decision makers relative to inventory. The specific method or methods used to account for this asset can significantly affect the appearance of a business's financial condition and reported operating results. Also helpful to decision makers are disclosures indicating how a company's financial data would have been affected had a different inventory accounting method been used. Information on any significant changes in inventory levels can also be important in analyzing inventory. Decision makers closely monitor a business's age of inventory because, as inventory ages, it becomes more subject to spoilage, obsolescence, or related problems. Inventory age is calculated as 360 divided by the inventory turnover ratio (computed as cost of goods sold divided by average inventory).

EXHIBIT 5-9

Inventory Turnover Ratio and Age of Inventory

Inventory, 1/1/09	$232,000
Cost of Goods Sold for 2009	791,920
Inventory, 12/31/09	184,600

Average inventory = ($232,000 + $184,600) ÷ 2 = 416,600 ÷ 2 = 208,300

Inventory turnover ratio = $791,920 ÷ $208,300 = 3.8

Age of inventory = 360 days ÷ 3.8 = 95 days

KEY TERMS

age of inventory	inventory	periodic inventory system
cost of goods available for sale	inventory turnover ratio	perpetual inventory system
current replacement cost	LIFO (last-in, first-out)	purchase allowance
FIFO (first-in, first-out)	method	purchase discount
method	lower-of-cost-or-market	purchase return
FOB destination	(LCM) rule	retail inventory method
FOB shipping point	moving-average method	specific identification method

QUESTIONS

1. Identify the key differences between a perpetual and a periodic inventory system. *(LO 5.1)*

2. Why is inventory always considered a current asset? *(LO 5.1)*

3. What is meant by the phrase "inventory cost flow"? How does physical flow differ from cost flow? *(LO 5.2)*

4. How is cost of goods available for sale determined for a merchandising company? *(LO 5.2)*

5. Identify and briefly describe the four most common inventory costing methods. *(LO 5.2)*

6. In a period of rising prices for a specific product, does the FIFO or LIFO inventory costing method yield the higher ending inventory value? Why? *(LO 5.2)*

7. Does the FIFO or LIFO inventory costing method generally provide the more appropriate method for balance sheet valuation purposes? Which method provides a more appropriate valuation for income statement purposes? Provide your rationale for each answer. *(LO 5.2)*

8. How does the choice to use FIFO or LIFO affect income taxes in the U.S.? *(LO 5.2)*

9. Explain how the retail inventory method helps managers know if goods have been broken or stolen during the year. *(LO 5.3)*

10. Is the retail inventory method a perpetual or periodic inventory system? Explain. *(LO 5.1 and 5.3)*

11. Briefly describe the lower-of-cost-or-market (LCM) rule. Which accounting principle provides the justification for use of LCM? *(LO 5.4)*

12. What effect does an overstatement of ending inventory in 2009 have on the (a) 2009 year-end balance sheet, (b) 2009 income statement, (c) 2010 year-end balance sheet, and (d) 2010 income statement? *(LO 5.5)*

13. How do decision makers use the inventory turnover ratio and age of inventory when analyzing a company's financial data? *(LO 5.6)*

EXERCISES

14. **True or False** *(All LOs)*

Following are a series of statements regarding topics discussed in this chapter.

Required:

Indicate whether each statement is true (T) or false (F).

(a) Companies may value inventory at current replacement cost if the historical cost of inventory is lower than current replacement cost.

(b) When goods are shipped FOB destination, the seller is responsible for paying the transportation charges.

(c) An error in a company's ending inventory balance automatically causes the following period's beginning inventory balance to be misstated.

(d) Under the LIFO method of inventory, the costs of the most recently acquired goods are sent to Cost of Goods Sold first, whereas the costs of the oldest goods remain in inventory.

(e) Merchandising companies want to maintain as low an inventory turnover ratio as possible.

(f) If a company uses the FIFO method of inventory costing for federal tax purposes, it must also use FIFO for financial reporting purposes.

(g) In an inflationary economic environment, the FIFO inventory costing method typically yields a higher net income than the LIFO method when these methods are applied to the same financial data.

(h) Generally accepted accounting principles require that a company select the inventory cost flow assumption that most closely matches the physical flow of its goods.

(i) Because cost of goods sold is not tracked during a period, periodic inventory systems cannot provide information to managers about theft losses during a period.

(j) As the inventory turnover gets smaller, the age of inventory gets larger.

(k) U.S. financial accounting standards allow the use of FIFO, LIFO, and average inventory costing methods, but international accounting standards only allow the use of FIFO.

15. **Shipping Terms** *(LO 5.1)*

The following items were in transit to or from Power Corp. on December 31, 2009.

- Goods costing $4,000 were sent FOB shipping point from Power Corp. to a customer.
- Goods costing $2,580 were sent FOB destination to Power Corp. from a vendor.
- Goods costing $2,960 were sent FOB destination from Power Corp. to a customer.
- Goods costing $1,957 were sent FOB shipping point to Power Corp. from a vendor.

Required:

(a) Which of these items should Power Corp. include in its December 31, 2009, inventory?

(b) Explain the rationale for either including or excluding the items.

16. **Perpetual Inventory Accounting** *(LO 5.1)*

Several transactions from Gallino Corp. are listed.

- Gallino Corp. purchased inventory from Wilen, Inc. on account.
- Gallino paid shipping for the merchandise to be shipped from Wilen, Inc. to Gallino.
- Gallino Corp. returned one defective item of inventory to Wilen, Inc.
- Gallino Corp. purchased inventory from Anderson Wholesalers on account.
- Gallino Corp. sold merchandise to Renauld Adams on account.
- Gallino paid shipping for the merchandise to be shipped from Gallino to Adams.

- Gallino Corp. paid Wilen, Inc. for the inventory purchase in time to earn a discount.
- Gallino Corp. paid Anderson Wholesalers, but did not receive a discount.
- Adams returned merchandise to Gallino Corp.
- Adams paid for the balance of the merchandise he purchased within the discount period.

Required:

(a) Assuming a perpetual inventory system, indicate for each transaction whether the Inventory account is increased or decreased.

(b) Would your answers to part (a) change if Gallino Corp. used a periodic inventory system? If so, how and why? If not, why not?

17. **Cost of Goods Available for Sale and Cost of Goods Sold** *(LO 5.2)*

Edinbrough Enterprises uses a perpetual inventory system. At year-end, Edinbrough takes a physical inventory and adjusts its records to agree with the physical inventory results. Following is selected financial information for 2009 for Edinbrough.

January 1 inventory	$ 50,000
Merchandise purchases	695,000
December 31 inventory	25,400

Required:

(a) Compute Edinbrough's cost of goods available for sale and Cost of Goods Sold for 2009.

(b) Assume that Edinbrough took a physical count of inventory at the end of 2009 and found only $21,850 of goods in inventory. What factors may be responsible for the $3,550 difference between Edinbrough's perpetual inventory records and the dollar amount of inventory determined by the year-end physical count? How would Edinbrough treat the $3,550 for financial statement purposes?

(c) List four ways that a company could help prevent inventory shrinkage from theft by employees and customers. Indicate whether your prevention method would relate to employees, customers, or both.

18. **Valuing Inventory** *(LO 5.2)*

On August 4, Big Luggage Super Store (BLSS) had eight identical black briefcases in stock. The cost of each briefcase is given in the following list in the order that the briefcases were purchased. On August 4, BLSS sold three black briefcases for $200 each.

1st briefcase	$87	5th briefcase	$ 95
2nd briefcase	89	6th briefcase	99
3rd briefcase	90	7th briefcase	101
4th briefcase	93	8th briefcase	104

Required:

Complete the following table. For the specific identification method, assume that the three briefcases sold were the 3rd, 5th, and 8th ones purchased.

	Specific ID	FIFO	LIFO
Cost of Goods Available for Sale			
− Ending Inventory			
= Cost of Goods Sold			
Revenues			
− Cost of Goods Sold			
= Gross Profit			

19. Inventory Costing Methods *(LO 5.2)*

The following schedule summarizes the inventory purchases and sales of Gregory, Inc. during February 2009:

	# of Units	Per Unit Cost
Beginning inventory	300	$4.00
February 1 purchase	325	4.50
February 5 sale	250	
February 8 purchase	375	5.00
February 12 sale	400	
February 15 purchase	420	5.40
February 19 sale	397	
February 22 purchase	375	5.75
February 28 sale	425	

Required:

(a) What is Gregory's cost of goods available for sale for February 2009?

(b) If Gregory uses the FIFO cost flow, what is cost of goods sold for February 28? Show calculations.

(c) If Gregory uses the LIFO cost flow, what is cost of goods sold for February 19? Show calculations.

(d) If Gregory uses the moving-average cost flow, what is cost of goods sold for February 12? Show calculations.

(e) Assume that Gregory sells its product for $10.50 each. Calculate Gregory's gross profit for each cost flow method.

20. Retail Inventory *(LO 5.3)*

Brendon Co. sells a variety of souvenir products on Emerald Isle, North Carolina. The company began 2009 with inventory having a cost of $136,000 and a retail value of $241,000. During 2009, Brendon purchased a total of $662,200 of goods; upon receipt of the goods, they were marked to sell at retail prices totaling $987,000. The company uses the retail inventory method, and sales for 2009 were $1,040,000.

Required:

(a) What is Brendon's actual cost of goods available for sale during 2009?

(b) What is the cost-to-retail percentage for 2009?

(c) What is the estimated ending inventory at retail?

(d) What is the estimated ending inventory at cost?

(e) Will the actual ending inventory be equal to the estimates? Why or why not?

21. Lower-of-Cost-or-Market *(LO 5.4)*

Hullabaloo sells four styles of children's canvas tennis shoes. Information about Hullabaloo's May 31 ending inventory of these four styles is given in the following table.

	Units in Ending Inventory	Per Unit Cost	Current Replacement Cost
Style 456	63	$20	$23
Style 489	40	25	22
Style 391	25	28	24
Style 599	47	32	31

Required:

(a) How much did Hullabaloo pay for the shoes that are in its May 31 inventory?

(b) If Hullabaloo had to replace its ending inventory of tennis shoes, what would it cost?

(c) What entry should be made to adjust Hullabaloo's inventory to the lower-of-cost-or-market amount if LCM is applied on a total inventory basis? On an item-by-item basis?

(d) Explain the effect the adjustment has on the income statement and balance sheet.

22. Income Statement Impact of Inventory Errors *(LO 5.5, ethics)*

Following is the income statement of Jericho Co. for its most recent fiscal year.

Sales	$267,000
Cost of Goods Sold	(93,000)
Gross Profit	$174,000
Operating Expenses	(30,000)
Operating Income	$144,000
Income Taxes Expense (30%)	(43,200)
Net Income	$100,800

Shortly after the company's financial statements were issued, Jericho's accountant discovered that the company's ending inventory had been inadvertently overstated by $12,000. This error stemmed from an error on the part of the accountant, who double counted some items of ending inventory. The inventory balance was shown at $39,000, whereas the true inventory value was $27,000.

Required:

(a) Prepare a corrected income statement for Jericho Co.

(b) Suppose Jericho's owner told her accountant to ignore the inventory error, saying, "Why bother? The financial statements have already been issued, and besides it was an honest mistake." Evaluate the owner's decision. Has she behaved unethically? Why

or why not? What parties may be affected by the owner's decision? Explain.

23. **Inventory Analysis** *(LO 5.6)*

Claremont Corp. has the following inventory balances for 2009: beginning, $468,000; ending, $444,000. The company's Cost of Goods Sold for the year was $4,370,400.

Required:

(a) What is Claremont Corp.'s average inventory for 2009?

(b) What is the company's inventory turnover ratio?

(c) Calculate the average age of inventory for Claremont Corp.

(d) Assume that Claremont Corp. is a retail toy company, and its fiscal year-end is December 31. Would Claremont's inventory be at an annual high or low at the end of the year? In this situation, would the inventory turnover ratio provide valid information to a decision maker? Why or why not?

(e) Given the information in part (d), how might you obtain a better indication of the average amount of inventory that Claremont Corp. had on hand during the year?

PROBLEMS

24. **Journalizing Transactions in a Perpetual Inventory System** *(LO 5.1)*

One Price Is Nice sells various types of jeans and uses a perpetual inventory system. All jeans, regardless of style, are sold for $35 per pair. Following are selected transactions of the One Price Is Nice for April 2009.

April 6   Purchased 30 pairs of style #256 jeans with terms of 2/10, n/30; the per-unit cost was $22.

April 9   Returned ten pairs of the #256 jeans purchased on April 6 due to fabric flaws.

April 13 Sold two pairs of style #321 jeans for cash; the per-unit cost of these jeans was $21.

April 16 Paid amount due to the supplier for jeans purchased on April 6.

April 17 Purchased 12 pairs of style #157 jeans with terms of 2/10, n/30; the per-unit cost was $18.

April 20 Sold one pair of #155 jeans on credit; the cost of this pair was $24.

April 21 A customer returned a pair of style #808 jeans because it was the wrong size; the jeans, which cost $20, were returned to inventory.

April 27 Sold two pairs of style &101 jeans on credit; the per-unit cost of these jeans was $17.

April 27 Paid amount due to the supplier for jeans purchased on April 17.

Required:

Prepare the journal entries necessary to record these transactions for One Price Is Nice.

25. **Inventory Costing Methods** *(LO 5.2)*

The following schedule summarizes the inventory purchases and sales of Brooks Street Enterprises during January 2009:

	# of Units	Per Unit Cost	Per Unit Selling Price
BI	400	$40	
Jan. 2 purchase	200	44	
Jan. 5 sale	300		$ 80
Jan. 9 purchase	200	48	
Jan. 14 sale	350		90
Jan. 18 purchase	200	50	
Jan. 21 sale	150		90
Jan. 25 purchase	500	52	
Jan. 31 sale	450		100

Required:

(a) Determine Brooks Street's ending inventory, cost of goods sold, and gross profit for January 2009, assuming the company uses a perpetual inventory system and the following inventory costing methods: (1) FIFO, (2) LIFO, and (3) moving-average.

(b) Which of the three inventory costing methods yields the most impressive financial results for Brooks Street? Explain.

(c) What factors should a company consider when choosing an inventory costing method? Should one of these factors be the inventory costing method preferred by the decision makers who will be using the company's financial statements?

26. **Retail Inventory** *(LO 5.3)*

Mount Holly, Inc. uses the retail inventory method. The company's beginning inventory for 2009 had a cost of $250,600 and a selling price of $658,000. During the year, $1,242,320 of purchases was made; these goods were marked up for sale at $1,916,000. Actual 2009 retail sales for the company were $1,752,000.

Required:

(a) What was cost of goods available for sale at cost? At retail?

(b) What was the cost-to-retail percentage for 2009?

(c) Assume that the physical ending inventory showed goods on hand that would retail for $790,000. What is the cost of the ending inventory for balance sheet purposes?

(d) How much inventory loss should be shown on the income statement for 2009?

(e) Assume that Mount Holly, Inc. is an art gallery, selling primarily paintings and sculptures. What is the most likely source of the inventory loss? Explain.

(f) What is meant by the term *bonded* when discussing employees? Is bonding an effective deterrent to employee theft? What other methods of preventing employee theft might be more effective than bonding?

27. **Lower-of-Cost-or-Market Rule** *(LO 5.4)*

Pauline's Plumbing sells kitchen sinks. The company had the following inventory quantities, per unit costs, and per unit market values (current replacement costs) at the end of a recent fiscal year.

	# of Units	Per Unit Cost	Per Unit Market Value
Industrial			
Item A	100	$160	$150
Item B	150	200	205
Household			
Item C	75	120	125
Item D	110	140	125
Utility			
Item E	80	80	80
Item F	130	75	70

Required:

(a) Compute Pauline's Plumbing's ending inventory by applying the lower-of-cost-or-market rule on an item-by-item basis.

(b) Briefly describe how the application of the LCM rule will affect the financial statement data of Pauline's Plumbing.

(c) In your view, which of the following inventory valuation methods would provide the most relevant and reliable accounting data for external decision makers: (1) valuing inventories strictly on a cost basis, (2) valuing inventories strictly on a market basis, or (3) valuing inventories on a lower-of-cost-or-market basis? Defend your choice.

28. **Analyzing Inventory** *(LO 5.6)*

Outer Reaches, Inc. is a leading firm in the aerospace and defense industries. The following selected financial data (in millions) are for three years. The company's fiscal year-end is September 30.

	2007	2008	2009
Net Sales	$1,311.7	$1,201.7	$1,643.9
Cost of Goods Sold	1,122.4	996.4	1,137.9
Net Income	63.0	63.8	72.0
Ending Inventory	146.0	118.4	169.9

Required:

(a) Compute the inventory turnover ratio and age of inventory for Outer Reaches, Inc. for each of the years listed. The company's inventory balance at the beginning of 2007 was $153 million.

(b) Would you expect companies in the aerospace and defense industries to normally have high or low inventory turnover ratios? Explain the rationale for your answer.

(c) Did Outer Reaches, Inc.'s inventory ratios improve or deteriorate between 2007 and 2009? Explain.

CASES

29. Accounting for Inventory *(LO 5.1, 5.2, and 5.4)*

Omega Sales uses the Internet to sell high-quality cookware for $350 per set. All cookware sets are purchased from Galaxy Wares for cash. On March 1, Omega had 20 sets of cookware in inventory that cost $110 each. The following transactions occurred in March 2009.

Mar. 1   Purchased 15 sets of cookware at a cost of $105 each.

Mar. 8   Sold 13 sets of cookware.

Mar. 9   Purchased 10 sets of cookware at a cost of $103.

Mar. 13   Sold 16 sets of cookware.

Mar. 16   Purchased 10 sets of cookware at a cost of $102.

Mar. 21   Sold 19 sets of cookware.

Mar. 23   Purchased 15 sets of cookware at a cost of $95.

Mar. 31   Sold 14 sets of cookware.

Required:

(a) Record the March journal entries for Omega Sales, assuming the company uses LIFO.

(b) Prepare a partial income statement (through gross profit) for Omega Sales for March.

(c) What ending inventory balance would Omega show on its balance sheet?

(d) What would be the balances of Cost of Goods Sold and ending inventory if Omega used FIFO?

(e) Assuming LIFO, apply the lower-of-cost-or-market rule on March 31st and make the appropriate journal entry. How does the fact that cookware prices are declining affect your answer? Would your answer change (and, if so, by how much?) if Omega used FIFO?

(f) Explain why Omega might choose to omit the LCM adjustment.

30. Inventory Systems *(LO 5.5, writing, ethics)*

Rosa Langley Fashions tags its inventory with retail prices, but does not keep thorough inventory records. The lax system makes it very costly for the company to determine the cost of store inventory. The cost of Rosa Langley Fashions' merchandise is typically 40% to 60% of retail price, so the company determines cost of ending inventory by calculating retail price of ending inventory and dividing by 2 (to get 50%).

Required:

Write the CEO of Rosa Langley Fashions a letter explaining the errors that might be created by the company's inventory system.

31. Analyzing Inventory *(LO 5.6)*

It's Good, Y'All! is a Texas-based company that operates a large chain of restaurants. The following information is available for the company (in thousands).

	2007	2008	2009
Net Sales	$400,577	$517,616	$640,898
Cost of Goods Sold	130,885	171,708	215,071
Net Income	33,943	46,652	57,497
Ending Inventory	23,192	28,426	41,989

Required:

(a) Compute the company's inventory turnover ratio and age of inventory for 2007 through 2009. Beginning inventory for 2007 was $15,746,000.

(b) Comment on the ratios computed in part (a). Are there any definite trends in these ratios? If so, are these trends favorable or unfavorable? Explain.

(c) Why do decision makers pay close attention to the age of inventory statistic for companies in the restaurant industry?

32. Annual Reports *(LO 5.6, Internet)*

Macy's Inc. is the parent company of Macy's and Bloomingdale's department stores. Use Macy's annual report with a year-end of February 2, 2008, to answer the following questions. The annual report can be found at www.macys.com; follow the links to investor relations.

Required:

(a) What is Macy's cost of sales?

(b) What is the average balance in inventory for the year?

(c) Calculate the inventory turnover ratio and the age of inventory. Comment on the results.

(d) What is the main method of cost flow valuation used by Macy's?

(e) Does the company write its inventory down to lower-of-cost-or-market?

(f) From February 2007 to February 2008, what was the percent increase or decrease in (1) net sales, (2) cost of sales, and (3) ending inventory? Comment on the relationship among these percentages.

33. Comparing Companies *(LO 5.6, group, Internet)*

Identifying the similarities and differences between companies is as crucial to making investment decisions as understanding a single company's financial statements. Form groups of at least four students. Each group should select a single industry. Each group member should locate a different annual report within that industry. (The industry and individual company may be assigned by your instructor.)

Required—individual group members:

(a) If you obtained the annual report of a company of which you had no previous knowledge, how would you determine whether the company sold a product as a primary means of generating income?

(b) Does the company you chose generate income primarily by selling a product?

(c) If you answered yes to part (b), calculate the following ratios for the company you selected for the two most recent fiscal years.
   (1) Inventory turnover ratio
   (2) Days in inventory

(d) If you answered yes to part (b), scan the notes to the financial statements and determine what cost flow assumption (LIFO, FIFO, or moving-average) the company uses and whether the cost of inventory is adjusted for lower-of-cost or market.

Required—groups:

(e) Compile the ratio calculations for each company prepared by the individual group members into one table. Compare the results from company to company in the same fiscal year. Include in your comparison a graphical analysis. Discuss reasons why these ratios might be similar or different within an industry. Why did some companies not have ratio calculations for part (c)?

(f) What are the differences in the financial statements between a company that sells inventory and one that does not? Is it possible to compare these two types of companies? If so, how? If not, why not?

Required—class:

(g) Compare the ratios from each industry. Discuss reasons why these ratios might be similar or different between industries. Does one industry seem to be a better investment than another? Explain. Do you think this situation is constant over time? Why or why not?

(h) Discuss the differences and similarities in the decision to invest in a company between a company that sells inventory and one that does not.

SUPPLEMENTAL PROBLEMS

34. Perpetual Inventory Systems *(LO 5.1; Compare to Problem 24)*

During July of the current year, Bobby's Auto Repair engaged in the following transactions involving car mirrors purchased from Prisms, Inc.:

July 1   Purchased ten car mirrors from Prisms, Inc., for $25 each; terms 2/10, n/30.

July 5   Sold six car mirrors on credit for $40 each; terms 1/10, n/30.

July 7   Two car mirrors sold on July 5 were returned by the customers because the mirrors were flawed.

July 9   Returned the two flawed mirrors to Prisms, Inc. for credit.

July 11   Paid the amount due Prisms, Inc. for the car mirrors purchased on July 1.

July 15   Received the amount due from customers who purchased car mirrors on July 5.

Required:

Prepare the journal entry for each transaction listed, assuming that Bobby's Auto Repair uses a perpetual inventory system.

35. Inventory Costing Methods *(LO 5.2; Compare to Problem 25)*

Heads Up is a retail store that sells baseball caps. Heads Up had the following inventory purchases and sales during May 2009:

	# of Units	Per Unit Cost	Per Unit Selling Price
BI	120	$5	
May 3 purchase	300	6	
May 7 sale	400		$11
May 9 purchase	675	7	
May 14 sale	350		12
May 16 purchase	410	8	
May 22 sale	500		14
May 25 purchase	620	9	
May 31 sale	730		14

Required:

Determine Heads Up's ending inventory, cost of goods sold, and gross profit for May 2009, assuming Heads Up uses a perpetual inventory system and the following inventory costing methods:

(a) FIFO

(b) LIFO

(c) Moving-average

36. **Lower-of-Cost-or-Market Rule** (LO 5.4; Compare to Problem 27)

Following is information regarding the year-end inventory of Bastion County Steelworks.

Item	Quantity	Original Per-Unit Cost	Replacement Cost Per Unit
Exgots	125	$17	$14
Ingots	100	12	13
Ongots	200	15	13
Ungots	50	20	19

Required:

(a) Apply the lower-of-cost-or-market (LCM) rule to Bastion County's ending inventory, assuming that the company applies the rule on (1) an item-by-item basis and (2) a total inventory basis.

(b) What accounting concept or concepts dictate that businesses apply the LCM rule? Does this rule seem reasonable to you? Why or why not?

37. **Analyzing Inventory** (LO 5.6; Compare to Prou

Fred Koontz owns and operates a sporting goc Following are selected financial data regarding Kc business over the past three years.

	2007	2008	2009
Net Sales	$840,000	$900,000	$990,000
Cost of Goods Sold	504,000	585,000	673,200
Net Income	111,300	115,500	118,800
Ending Inventory	80,000	103,000	118,000

Required:

(a) Compute the inventory turnover ratio and age of inventory for Koontz's store for each year listed. On January 1, 2007, the store's inventory was $60,000.

(b) Given the data provided and the ratios you computed in part (1), evaluate Koontz's management of inventory over this three-year period.

(c) Koontz is concerned by the slow growth in his company's net income in recent years. Given the data provided, identify factors that may be adversely affecting the business's profitability.

6

erm Assets:
operty, Plant and
Equipment, and Intangibles

LEARNING OBJECTIVES

1. Determine the acquisition cost of property, plant and equipment assets.
2. Compute depreciation expense using three depreciation methods.
3. Account for disposals of property, plant and equipment.
4. Identify major types of intangible assets and the key accounting issues related to these assets.
5. Determine the treatment of costs made for property, plant and equipment assets after acquisition.
6. Identify the key information needs of decision makers regarding long-term assets.

INTRODUCTION

Chapters 4 and 5 discussed accounting for current assets, which are the items that provide the primary economic benefits to a business over a 12-month period or a business operating cycle, whichever is longer. In comparison, long-term assets provide benefits to a business for several years, if not several decades. This chapter addresses three specific types of long-term assets: property, plant and equipment (PP&E), natural resources, and intangibles.

PROPERTY, PLANT AND EQUIPMENT

The most common types of PP&E assets are land, buildings, machinery and equipment, furniture and fixtures, automobiles, and land improvements (such as parking lots and driveways). Generally accepted accounting principles require businesses to depreciate long-term assets, with the exception of land, over their useful lives. Because land improvements are depreciated, they must be recorded separately from land.

PP&E assets pose four general accounting issues. First, the asset acquisition cost must be determined. Second, depreciation expense must be computed for each accounting period. Third, after PP&E assets are acquired, all additional related expenditures must be analyzed and recorded either as an asset or an expense. Finally, disposals of PP&E assets must be accounted for. Each of these topics is discussed in the following sections.

Acquisition of PP&E

The acquisition cost of a PP&E asset includes all reasonable and necessary expenditures incurred in obtaining the asset and preparing it for use. Elmer Co. purchases a large pneumatic heat transfer press machine with a retail price of $40,000. Because Elmer Co. has worked with the vendor many times in the past, the vendor gives Elmer Co. a 10 percent discount off the retail price. Freight charges to deliver the heat press are $550, and installation expenses total $320. During installation, an employee at Elmer's accidentally damages one of the legs on the press, resulting in a repair cost of $410. The total acquisition cost of the press is

Net invoice cost ($40,000 − $4,000 discount)	$36,000
Freight charges	550
Installation cost	320
Total cost	$36,870

Note that the $410 repair cost is not considered part of the acquisition cost because that amount was not necessary to obtain the press nor get it ready for use. The repair cost is treated as an expense in the period incurred.

The following entries would be made to record the purchase of the press. For control purposes, an identification number is generally assigned to each major PP&E asset of a business.

General Journal					
Date		Description		Debit	Credit
Apr	1	Heat Press		36,870	
		Accounts Payable			36,000
		Cash			870
		Purchased heat press (asset #231-7) on account;			
		paid charges for freight and installation			
		Repair Expense		410	
		Cash			410
		Paid cash to repair heat press			

Businesses often acquire several long-term assets in a single transaction. For example, a company may buy a production facility that includes land, land improvements, buildings, and equipment. The purchase price must be allocated, usually based on the assets' relative market values, to the individual assets. Suppose that Hodnett Company purchases land, a building, and a piece of equipment for $600,000 from a company that was going out of business. Exhibit 6-1 shows the allocation of the $600,000 to the assets and the journal entry to record the acquisition.

Depreciation of PP&E

Depreciation is the process of rationally and systematically allocating the cost of a long-term asset over its useful life. Useful life reflects the expected time that the asset will provide economic benefits to the business. Depreciating long-term assets is one method businesses use to match an accounting period's revenues with the expenses incurred to generate those revenues.

Three factors must be considered when computing depreciation expense: asset cost, useful life, and salvage (or residual) value. **Salvage value** is the estimated value of an asset at the end of its useful life. **Depreciable cost** refers to the acquisition cost of an asset less its salvage value. Thus, depreciable cost is the amount of asset cost that is expected to be consumed or "used up" over its useful life.

EXHIBIT 6-1

Allocation of
Acquisition Cost to
Multiple Assets

	Market Value	Proportion of Total Market Value	Total Cost	Allocated Cost
Land	$160,000	160 ÷ 800 = 20%	$600,000	$120,000
Building	400,000	400 ÷ 800 = 50%	$600,000	300,000
Equipment	240,000	240 ÷ 800 = 30%	$600,000	180,000
	$800,000			$600,000

May 10	Land		120,000	
	Building		300,000	
	Equipment		180,000	
	Cash			600,000
	Purchased PP&E and allocated purchase price			

Chapter 5 illustrated that a variety of methods can be used to calculate cost of goods sold and ending inventory balance. A similar situation exists for calculating depreciation expense on PP&E. Three commonly used methods are straight-line, units-of-production, and double-declining balance. A company can select different methods for different PP&E assets or use the same method for all assets. Each method results in a different amount of depreciation expense for an accounting period and, therefore, a different amount of net income.

Assume that Movie Mogul acquired a motor home on January 1, 2009. The motor home is needed as a "home away from home" for cast members during film production. The following data are used to illustrate the three depreciation methods.

Equipment:	Motor home (Asset #1427B)
Acquisition Date:	January 1, 2009
Acquisition Cost:	$168,000
Useful Life:	5 years or 100,000 miles
Salvage Value:	$48,000
Depreciable Cost:	$168,000 − $48,000 = $120,000

Straight-Line Method

Under the **straight-line (S-L) method**, a business allocates an equal amount of depreciation expense to each full year of an asset's estimated useful life. The premise underlying this method is that an asset is equally productive each year that it is in service. The annual depreciation expense under the S-L method is computed as:

$$\text{Depreciation Expense} = \text{Depreciable Cost} \div \text{Useful Life in Years}$$

Substituting the information on Movie Mogul's motor home in this formula yields an annual depreciation expense of ($120,000 ÷ 5) or $24,000. The following adjusting journal entry is required to record depreciation expense at the end of the motor home's first year of service.

General Journal				
Date		**Description**	**Debit**	**Credit**
Dec.	31	Depreciation Expense	24,000	
		Accumulated Depreciation—#1427B		24,000
		Recorded annual depreciation on motor home		

For each of the next five years, Movie Mogul will record the same depreciation amount for the motor home. As discussed in Chapter 3, accumulated depreciation is a contra-asset account and reflects the total amount of the asset's original cost that has been depreciated or charged off as an expense since the asset was acquired. The difference between an asset's cost and the balance of its related accumulated depreciation account is referred to as the asset's book value.

After five years, the asset's depreciable cost will have been completely written off to depreciation expense. The book value at that time will be equal to the asset's salvage value. The motor home will not necessarily be taken out of service at the end of five years unless it is unreliable or should be replaced for other reasons. If the asset continues to be used, additional depreciation may be taken, but only to the extent of the salvage value. An asset cannot be depreciated below its original cost.

If the motor home had been acquired during the year, rather than on January 1, Movie Mogul would compute depreciation expense for 2009 by multiplying $24,000 by the fraction of the year the motor home was owned that year. For example, if the motor home were purchased on March 1, the appropriate depreciation expense for 2009 would be $20,000 ($24,000 × 10/12). A full year's depreciation would be taken in 2010, 2011, 2012, and 2013. In 2014, only two months' depreciation, or $4,000 ($24,000 × 2/12), would be taken. Thus, the total depreciation taken ($120,000) would still equal the depreciable cost of the motor home.

Units-of-Production Method

Under the **units-of-production method**, an asset's useful life is expressed in a number of units of production or use. Depreciation expense for any given period is a function of the asset's usage during that period. This depreciation method is well suited for assets for which wear-and-tear is a predominant cause of declining usefulness. For example, vehicles are often used by an organization only for a specific number of miles before being traded-in or some industrial equipment may only be used to manufacture a given number of units of product.

Suppose that Movie Mogul applies the units-of-production method to its motor home. When the motor home was acquired, Movie Mogul estimated that the motor home would be able to be used for 100,000 miles. The per-unit depreciation expense is computed as follows:

$$\text{Per-Unit Depreciation Expense} = \text{Depreciable Cost} \div \text{Useful Life in Units}$$

Substituting the information on Movie Mogul's motor home in this formula yields a per-unit annual depreciation expense of $120,000 ÷100,000 units or $1.20. For any given period, the asset's depreciation expense under the units-of-production method is determined by multiplying the per-unit depreciation cost by the number of units produced (or, in this case, miles driven) that period:

$$\text{Depreciation Expense} = \text{Per-Unit Expense} \times \text{Total Units Produced}$$

The following adjusted journal entry would be required to record depreciation expense at the end of the motor home's first year of service, assuming that 18,900 miles were driven.

General Journal				
Date		Description	Debit	Credit
Dec.	31	Depreciation Expense	22,680	
		Accumulated Depreciation—#1427B		22,680
		Recorded annual depreciation on motor		
		home		

Each year, the amount of depreciation expense will vary depending on the miles the motor home is driven. Depreciation would no longer be taken after the total estimated miles were driven unless the overuse would cause salvage value to decline.

Unlike under the straight-line method, the units-of-production method is not affected by when during the year the asset was purchased. Depreciation is taken based on how much was produced or used, not how long the asset was in service during the period.

Double-Declining-Balance Method

Some companies use a depreciation method that allows larger amounts of depreciation to be taken in the early years of an asset's life compared to later years. In the United States, this method is called "accelerated" depreciation; under international rules, this method is called "diminishing value" depreciation. Regardless of the term used, the premise underlying this method is that proportionately more of a depreciable asset's economic benefit is consumed during the early years of the asset's useful life than in later years. Machinery, for example, generally becomes less productive over time due to increasing breakdowns and more extensive maintenance requirements. High-tech equipment loses substantial value early in its life because of new developments in the field.

Under the **double-declining-balance (DDB) method** of depreciation, annual depreciation expense is computed by multiplying an asset's book value at the beginning of a year by twice the straight-line rate of depreciation. For example, the annual straight-line depreciation rate for an asset with a ten-year useful life is 10 percent (100% ÷ 10); under DDB, the annual depreciation rate would be 20 percent (2 × 10%). Thus, the DDB depreciation calculation is as follows:

DDB Depreciation Expense = (2 × S-L rate)(Beginning of Year Book Value)

Note that book value, not depreciable cost, is used in this formula. Both the straight-line and units-of-production methods subtract salvage value from an asset's original cost to determine its depreciable cost, which is then expensed over the asset's useful life. Under the double-declining-balance method, an asset's salvage value is initially ignored when computing periodic depreciation expense. However, once the asset's book value is equal to its salvage value, no further depreciation is recorded.

For Movie Mogul's motor home, the straight-line rate of depreciation is 20 percent (100% ÷ 5 years); thus, the double-declining balance depreciation rate under the DDB method is 40 percent. Depreciation for 2009 and 2010 is calculated as follows:

Year	Book Value at Beginning of Year		DDB Rate	Depreciation Expense	Accumulated Depreciation
2009		$168,000	0.40	$67,200	$ 67,200
2010	($168,000 − $67,200)	= $100,800	0.40	$40,320	$107,520
2011	($168,000 − $107,520) =	$60,480			

Depreciation expense for 2011 would be calculated as $24,192 (40% × $60,480) under DDB. However, taking that amount of depreciation would make the motor home's book value $36,288 at the end of the year: $60,480 − $24,192 = $36,288. That amount is $11,712 below the $48,000 salvage value. Therefore, only $12,480 of depreciation expense can be taken in 2011: $60,480 − $48,000 = $12,480. No depreciation expense can be taken on the motor home for the remaining two years of the asset's useful life under the DDB method.

Like the straight-line method, the DDB method of depreciation requires an adjustment to the depreciation calculation for the purchase of an asset during, rather than at the beginning of, the year. However, the partial-period adjustment is made only in the first year of the asset's life (rather than the first and last, as under the straight-line method). If Movie Mogul had acquired the motor home on October 1, 2009, depreciation for 2009 would have been calculated as follows: (40% × $168,000) × 3/12 = $16,800. In 2010, depreciation expense would have been $60,480, computed as follows: [40% × ($168,000 − $16,800)] or (40% × $151,200). The asset would continue to be depreciated until book value was equal to salvage value.

Exhibit 6-2 provides a comparison of the full depreciation schedules for Movie Mogul's motor home, using the original assumption of a January 1 date of acquisition.

Disposal of PP&E

When PP&E assets are no longer needed or no longer provide benefits, a company will remove those assets from service and either junk them, sell them, or exchange them for other assets. A gain or loss on a sale is calculated as the cash received minus the asset's ending book value. When an asset is junked or given away, no cash is received; if the asset has a remaining book value, a loss will be recorded at the time of disposition.

If a depreciable asset is disposed at any point other than year-end, an adjusting entry must first be made to record depreciation for the period since the last entry for depreciation expense was journalized. The depreciation entry must be recorded to determine the actual book value at the date of disposal. Only after the depreciation entry is recorded can the disposal journal entry be prepared.

Movie Mogul's motor home will be used to illustrate the disposition of a plant asset.[1] These examples assume that Movie Mogul calculated depreciation on this asset using the straight-line method.

At a Loss

On January 2, 2012, the motor home was wrecked and was deemed completely destroyed by the insurance company. The insurance company determines the value of the motor home to be $60,000, immediately writes Movie Mogul a check for that amount, and removes the motor home. No additional depreciation expense needs to be recorded on this item because Movie Mogul made an adjusting entry to record depreciation on December 31, 2011. The disposition of the motor home results in a loss of $36,000 or the difference between the asset's $96,000 book value and the insurance payment of $60,000. The following entry records the disposal of the motor home.

General Journal				
Date		**Description**	**Debit**	**Credit**
Jan.	2	Cash	60,000	
		Accumulated Depreciation—#1427B	72,000	
		Loss on Disposal of Asset	36,000	
		Motor Home—#1427B		168,000
		Recorded disposal of motor home and		
		receipt of insurance proceeds		

---

[1] Asset exchange entries are not included because they are beyond the scope of this text.

EXHIBIT 6-2

Depreciation Schedules under Three Methods

Asset cost	$168,000
Salvage value	(48,000)
Depreciable cost	$120,000

Life: 5 years or 100,000 miles

Actual miles driven:	2009	18,900 miles
	2010	29,000 miles
	2011	24,500 miles
	2012	17,700 miles
	2013	9,900 miles

Straight-line

Year	Computation	Depr. Exp.	Year End Balance of Acc. Depr.	Year End Book Value*
2009	$120,000 ÷ 5	$24,000	$ 24,000	$144,000
2010	$120,000 ÷ 5	$24,000	$ 48,000	$120,000
2011	$120,000 ÷ 5	$24,000	$ 72,000	$ 96,000
2012	$120,000 ÷ 5	$24,000	$ 96,000	$ 72,000
2013	$120,000 ÷ 5	$24,000	$120,000	$ 48,000

Units-of-Production

Per unit depreciation expense = $120,000 ÷ 100,000 units = $1.20

Year	Computation	Depr. Exp.	Year End Balance of Acc. Depr.	Year End Book Value*
2009	18,900 × $1.20	$22,680	$ 22,680	$145,320
2010	29,000 × $1.20	$34,800	$ 57,480	$110,520
2011	24,500 × $1.20	$29,400	$ 86,880	$ 81,120
2012	17,700 × $1.20	$21,240	$108,120	$ 59,880
2013	9,900 × $1.20	$11,880	$120,000	$ 48,000

Double-Declining Balance

S-L rate = 100% ÷ Life in years = 100% ÷ 5 = 20%; DDB rate = 20% × 2 = 40%

Year	Computation	Depr. Exp.	Year End Balance of Acc. Depr.	Year End Book Value*
2009	$168,000 × 40%	$67,200	$ 67,200	$100,800
2010	$100,800 × 40%	$40,320	$107,520	$ 60,480
2011	$ 60,480 × 40%	$12,480**	$120,000	$ 48,000

*Computed as original asset cost ($168,000) less year-end balance of accumulated depreciation
**Cannot take the $24,192 as calculated because that amount would bring the book value to less than the salvage value of the asset

This entry removes both the cost of the motor home and its accumulated depreciation from Movie Mogul's accounting records. Gains and losses on the disposal of long-term assets are generally classified as "other items" on an income statement.

At a Gain

When the disposal of a PP&E asset generates an amount greater than its book value, a gain is recorded. Assume that Movie Mogul's motor home was not wrecked on January 1, 2012, but that the company used the motor home until March 31, 2012, and then sold it for $98,600.

On the date that the motor home is sold, three months have passed since the previous adjusting entry (December 31, 2011) for depreciation. Before recording the sale, Movie Mogul would record depreciation expense of $6,000 (or $24,000 × 3/12) to recognize use of the motor home for the first three months of 2012.

General Journal				
Date		**Description**	**Debit**	**Credit**
Mar.	31	Depreciation Expense	6,000	
		Accumulated Depreciation—#1427B		6,000
		Recorded depreciation on motor home for		
		three months		

After this entry is made, the book value of the asset is calculated as follows:

Original cost		$168,000
Less: Accumulated Depreciation as of 12/31/11	$72,000	
Adjusting entry 3/31/12	6,000	(78,000)
Book value as of 3/31/12		$ 90,000

Given the selling price of $98,600 and the book value of $90,000, Movie Mogul would record a gain of $8,600 on the sale of the motor home as reflected by the following entry.

General Journal				
Date		**Description**	**Debit**	**Credit**
Mar	31	Cash	98,600	
		Accumulated Depreciation—#1427B	78,000	
		Motor Home—#1427B		168,000
		Gain on Disposal of Asset		8,600
		Sold motor home at a gain for cash		

NATURAL RESOURCES

The most important PP&E assets of forestry, mining, and petroleum companies are natural resource properties. **Natural resources** are long-term assets that are harvested or extracted from or beneath the earth's surface; such assets would include standing timber, minerals, coal, oil, and natural gas.

Natural resources are often referred to as wasting assets because the quantity of resource declines as harvest or extraction occurs. The term **depletion** (rather than depreciation) is used to describe the allocation of natural resource cost to periods of the economic benefit. Firms in the extractive industries apply the units-of-production concept to record depletion expense on natural resource properties. To compute annual depletion, the following adaptation of the units-of-production depreciation equation is used.

$$\text{Per-Unit Depletion Expense} = \text{Depletable Cost} \div \text{Units of Resource}$$

$$\text{Annual Depletion} = \text{Per-Unit Depletion} \times \text{Total Units Recovered During Period}$$

Assume that Joyner Oil pays $20 million for oil rights on a property that has an estimated two million barrels of oil. The cost of the oil rights is debited to an account called Natural Resource. The depletion cost per barrel of oil recovered is calculated as $20,000,000 ÷ 2,000,000 barrels, or $10 per barrel. Joyner Oil sells all extracted barrels of oil without any additional processing. Because the company is in the business of selling oil, the oil is its inventory, and, as such, the cost of this product is sent to Cost of Goods Sold when the oil is sold. If Joyner Oil extracts 300,000 barrels and sells 200,000 barrels of oil during 2009, the following entries would be made at, respectively, the point of extraction and sale.

General Journal				
Date		**Description**	**Debit**	**Credit**
2009		Inventory—Oil	3,000,000	
		Accumulated Depletion—Natural Resource		3,000,000
		Recorded recovery of 300,000 barrels of oil		
		Cost of Goods Sold	2,000,000	
		Inventory—Oil		2,000,000
		Recorded cost of sale		

Note that the cost of the oil is not, in this circumstance, charged to an account called Depletion Expense. The oil is still an asset until it is sold. Use of an Accumulated Depletion contra-asset account allows Joyner Oil to have an estimate of the percentage of oil that has been recovered from the oil field. The balance sheet at the end of 2009 would show the historical cost of the oil at $20 million and an accumulated depletion of $3 million.

Intangible Assets

Long-term assets that do not have a physical form or substance are called **intangible assets**. These assets pose the same general types of accounting issues as long-term depreciable assets. For example, a cost must be assigned to an intangible asset, and then this cost must be systematically allocated to the accounting periods to which the asset provides economic benefits to the business. This intangible asset allocation process is referred to as **amortization** instead of depreciation (property, plant and equipment) or depletion (natural resources).

The general rule is that an intangible asset should be amortized over the shorter of its legal life, its useful life, or 40 years (an arbitrary period established for financial accounting purposes). Because their costs are generally not extremely significant on the balance sheet, intangibles typically do not have related Accumulated Amortization accounts, and the write-off of intangibles is made directly to the asset account. Amortization is commonly on a straight-line basis and salvage value is almost always zero.

Identifiable Intangibles

Patents, copyrights, trademarks, and leasehold improvements are the common types of identifiable intangible assets found on business balance sheets. Some intangibles have useful lives that are limited by federal statute or by a contractual agreement; other intangibles have indefinite useful lives.

Many companies engage in research and development (R&D) activities that hopefully produce patentable new products. U.S. GAAP and international financial reporting basically agree on the difference between research and development (see Exhibit 6-3), but do not completely agree on the treatment of the underlying costs. U.S. GAAP takes the most conservative approach in that all internally incurred R&D costs are expensed immediately because it is generally unknown whether R&D activities will result in a technologically feasible, marketable, or useful product. In contrast, international accounting standards require that research costs be expensed as incurred but allow development costs to be capitalized if technical and commercial feasibility for the sale or use of the asset has been established, and the company can demonstrate

(a) intention and ability to complete, use, or sell the intangible asset;
(b) availability of adequate to complete development and to use or sell the intangible asset;
(c) how the intangible asset will generate probable future economic benefits; and
(d) ability to reliably measure development costs of the intangible asset.[2]

A **patent** grants the holder an exclusive right to manufacture a specific product or to use a specific process. In most countries, new patents are granted for 20 years. Given the pace at which knowledge is expanding, however, many patents will never be useful for their entire legal lives.

EXHIBIT 6-3 Difference between Research and Development	**Research**	**Development**
	An attempt to discover new knowledge or understanding that will help in generating a new product, service, or process or in significantly improving an existing product, service, or process	The translation of research into an applied plan or design for the production of a new product or improvement of an existing product or process, whether intended for sale or internal use; occurs before the start of commercial production activities or internal use
	Examples: Laboratory research to obtain new knowledge; conceptual attempts to evaluate and select applications for research findings; product or process design on a scale that is not feasible for commercial production	Examples: Preproduction prototypes, design of production equipment using new technology; design, construction, and operation of a pilot plant appropriate to meeting practical requirements and ready for manufacture

---

[2]International Accounting Standards Board, *IAS 38 Intangible Assets* (1998).

The only patent costs that many companies will have on their accounting records will be for patents that were purchased externally. Consider that Johnson & Johnson (www.jnj.com), a global leader in the health-care industry, had only $3.299 million in amortized patents (and trademarks) on its annual report for 2008; during that year, the company expensed $7.58 million in research costs.

Assume, however, that a company purchased a patent that had an expected useful life of 10 years for $1,000,000. At the end of each full year, the company would make the following adjusting entry to record the patent amortization.

General Journal			
Date	Description	Debit	Credit
XXX	Amortization Expense	100,000	
	Patent		100,000
	Recorded amortization on patent		

Creators of songs, books, films, and other works of art may be granted a **copyright**, or the exclusive right to produce and sell those items. In the United States, the legal life of a copyright is 70 years after the death of the creator. This time frame was decided in 2000 after the Walt Disney Corporation (www.disney.go.com) spent millions of dollars to lobby Congress to extend copyright life when "Steamboat Willie" (the first Mickey Mouse cartoon) was about to be released from copyright protection. Generally, however, copyrights have a useful life of no more than a few years.

Many copyrighted items have been internally developed, and therefore, all costs related to those items are expensed as incurred. A copyright only has a cost on a financial statement if it has been purchased from an external party. Purchased copyrights may be amortized using a method similar to "units of production" depreciation; for example, estimating the number of copies of a copyrighted book that will be sold and amortizing the cost on a per-unit basis.

A **trademark** is a distinctive name, symbol, or logo used to identify a specific business entity or one of its products. One of the world's most familiar trademarks is Coca-Cola, which should always be written with the hyphen and was registered in the United States on January 31, 1893. The company's "Dynamic Ribbon" trademark has been included on products since 1969.

Trademarks can be registered with the U.S. Patent and Trademark Office, and unlike patents and copyrights, these rights can be renewed indefinitely. Companies must be extremely diligent about protecting their trademarks and trade names. Not adequately protecting these intangibles may allow them to fall into generic, or everyday, usage. For example, aspirin and escalator were once specific product names, but now anyone is able to use these terms.

Many businesses lease rather than purchase long-term assets. The lessee (the party that leases an asset) acquires the legal right to use that asset for a specified period subject to lease agreement restrictions. Companies that lease office buildings, retail stores, and production facilities often modify the leased properties to accommodate their operations. Expenditures for such modifications are referred to as **leasehold improvements**. Leasehold improvements revert to the property owner (the lessor) at the end of the lease term. The cost of leasehold improvements should be amortized over their useful life or the term of the lease, whichever is shorter.

Because of their nature, intangible assets are prone to rapidly losing their value. For instance, a patent held by a company may become worthless because a competitor develops a technologically advanced product. In such a case, the unamortized cost of the patent should be immediately written off as a loss.

Goodwill

To most individuals, goodwill represents that "warm, fuzzy feeling" that makes them shop at Grandma's Corner Grocery instead of Discount MegaMarkets USA. Superior service, excellent location, family ties to the community, and many other factors go into determining the goodwill associated with a business. However, just because Grandma's Corner Grocery has accumulated a considerable amount of goodwill with its customers does not mean that goodwill can be recorded for accounting purposes.

Goodwill can only be recorded when one business entity (or a large segment of a business) is acquired by another. In this context, **goodwill** is defined as the excess of the total fair market value of a group of net assets (assets minus liabilities) over the total book value. Suppose that Valdez Petroleum Corporation pays $15 million for a chain of service stations. If the collective market value of the chain's net assets is only $11 million, the remaining $4 million of the purchase price would be attributed to goodwill.

Until 2001, goodwill was amortized as an expense over a period not to exceed 40 years. The Financial Accounting Standards Board then required that goodwill not be amortized. Instead, a company's goodwill amount would remain in the accounting records until it was determined that the goodwill had been impaired. **Impairment** of an asset exists when its carrying value exceeds its fair market value. Since the issuance of the new rule, many companies have reviewed their goodwill accounts for possible impairment. In 2002, AOL Time Warner (www.timewarner.com) wrote off $54 billion in goodwill; in 2006, Vodafone Group (www.vodafone.com) took an approximate $45 billion goodwill write-off; and in 2008, the Tribune Co. (newspapers; www.tribune.com) wrote off $3.8 billion of goodwill.[3] According to SNL Financial, the banking industry took $4.2 billion in goodwill impairment charges in the fourth quarter of 2007, which was more than had been taken by that industry in all of the 27 previous quarters.[4] The mortgage and credit crisis of 2008 created tremendous impairment charges to be taken on the financial statements. Goodwill impairment write-offs are shown on the income statement as a separate line item before the Income from Continuing Operations subtotal, unless that loss is related to discontinued operations (discussed in Chapter 9).

Disposal of Intangibles

Disposals of intangible assets are accounted for much like the disposals of depreciable assets. If an intangible asset is sold, the gain or loss on the asset is computed by subtracting the asset's book value from the selling price.

---

[3]Various annual reports and news articles.

[4]David Milstead, "Centennial Goodwill Writedown Part of Trend," *Rocky Mountain News* (Feb. 8, 2008); http://blogs.rockymountainnews.com/material_disclosures/archives/2008/02/centennial_good.html (accessed 10/18/08).

ACCOUNTING INFORMATION FOR DECISION MAKING

Of all the items appearing in financial statements, long-term assets may be responsible for the most misconceptions in the minds of financial statement users. For this reason, it is very important that "user-friendly" information concerning long-term assets and related accounting decisions be included in a business's annual report. This section identifies several important items of information that decision makers need regarding a business's long-term assets.

Valuation

Nearly all businesses in the United States report long-term assets at historical cost less accumulated depreciation, depletion, or amortization because of the historical cost principle. However, as mentioned earlier, land is not depreciated. A key advantage of historical cost is objectivity: the historical cost of an asset is a "matter of record," whereas the current value of that same asset is a "matter of opinion."

Businesses occasionally must depart from historical cost in valuing long-term assets. The conservatism principle requires businesses to write down any long-term asset, not only goodwill, when the value has been permanently impaired. An asset is considered to be impaired when its book value is greater than the expected benefits (in terms of future cash flows) to be generated by the asset.

Many companies have reported asset write-downs in recent years. For example, for its March 31, 2008, year-end, Centex Corporation (www.centex.com) took almost $1.8 billion in land-related impairments for housing projects and land held for development and sale. U.S. GAAP does not allow companies to write up assets that were previously written down as impaired. International financial standards, however, allow the reversal of write-downs in some instances.[5]

Increases in long-term asset values are not considered in preparation of U.S. financial statements. International financial standards allow the use of either a cost or "revaluation model" that allows the write-up of PP&E if the fair value of the asset can be reliably measured and revaluation is performed regularly.[6]

Capitalization versus Expensing

When a company makes an expenditure related to a long-term asset, the amount may be capitalized or expensed depending on the circumstances. Visual Recap 6.1 provides general rules for deciding which expenditures to capitalize (or include in the asset cost) and which to expense. An example of an after-acquisition expenditure that should be capitalized because it has a life longer than one year is a building roof. A necessary after-acquisition expenditure that would be expensed (rather than capitalized) because of its short life span and insignificant cost would be a multiple-year automobile license plate.

PP&E, natural resources, and intangible assets are shown on the balance sheet; however, the related depreciation, depletion, and amortization affect both the balance sheet and

---

[5]International Accounting Standards Board, *IAS 39 Financial Instruments: Recognition and Measurement* (1998).

[6]International Accounting Standards Board, *IAS 16 Property, Plant and Equipment* (1982).

VISUAL RECAP 6.1

PP&E Expenditures: Capitalization Rules

When?	Needed?	How Often?	Accounting Treatment
Before acquisition or beginning use	Yes	Once	Capitalize
	No	Once	Expense
After acquisition or beginning use	Yes	Once or life is greater than one year and cost is large	Capitalize
	Yes	Periodically or life is one year or less	Expense
	No	Once or periodically	Expense

income statement. When an asset is sold at a gain or loss, the transaction affects both statements. The balance sheet is affected through the removal of the long-term asset and its related depreciation (or depletion), as well as the recognition of cash received (if any). The income statement records the gain or loss as part of income for the period. If an item is capitalized when it should be expensed or expensed when it should be capitalized, the balance sheet and income statements will be affected for every fiscal period of the asset's life—potentially creating extreme material distortions.

To illustrate the problems that the misrecording of transactions can create, consider the following. In mid-2002, WorldCom (at that time the largest communications company in the United States) announced that it had capitalized, rather than properly expensing, almost $4 billion of costs during 2001 and 2002. The improper accounting and the telecommunications industry downturn caused the company to file for bankruptcy in 2002.[7]

Disclosures

Decision makers demand, and generally accepted accounting principles require, businesses to disclose major classes of depreciable assets by nature or function in their financial statements. Disclosure of PP&E assets by major categories provides decision makers with insights on a company's operating policies and strategies. These disclosures also allow decision makers to draw more meaningful comparisons of different companies' financial data, particularly companies in the same industry.

Similar to the choice of an inventory accounting method, the choice of a depreciation method can significantly influence a company's apparent financial condition and reported profits. To enhance the comparability of financial statement data, disclosure in the financial statement footnotes is required for the depreciation method or methods used. A company does not, however, have to use the same depreciation method for accounting and taxation purposes. Companies often choose to use straight-line depreciation for their income statements and an accelerated method for tax returns. In the early years of asset life, such a choice provides the lowest depreciation and highest income for financial reporting and the highest depreciation and lowest taxable income (and, therefore, lowest taxes payable) for tax preparation.

---

[7]In 2003, WorldCom changed its name to MCI, which was then acquired by Verizon (www.verizon.com) in 2005.

Given their nature, intangible assets are sometimes discounted in importance by decision makers. However, the financial success of many corporations, especially those in the high-tech and medical fields, stems largely from the intangible assets those companies have developed or purchased. For example, drug companies often sell a new drug for a very high price because a patent prohibits other drug companies from producing that drug. However, when the patent expires, generic equivalents of the drug can be produced and sold for significantly less than the original. Investors should pay close attention to the age of patents, as a patent that is near the end of its useful life might signal a reduction in future product revenues.

Businesses should disclose in their financial statements any restrictions on the use of long-term assets. For example, the pledging of long-term assets as loan collateral needs to be disclosed in the financial statements because the assets cannot be disposed of without the prior approval of the lender.

Ratio Analysis

Two ratios can be used to assess the age and useful life of PP&E assets. The average useful life of PP&E assets is calculated in the following manner.

$$\text{Average Useful life} = \text{Average Investment in PP\&E} \div \text{Depreciation Expense}$$

This ratio estimates the useful life by assuming that this year's depreciation expense is a consistent proportion of the asset's cost. The useful life provided by this ratio should be used with care, however, because different deprecation methods can have different effects on the result.

The average age of plant assets can be estimated as:

$$\text{Average Asset Age} = \text{Accumulated Depreciation} \div \text{Depreciation Expense}$$

This ratio estimates how many years of depreciation have been accumulated for a particular class of assets. As with the average useful life ratio, average asset age is affected differently by the different depreciation methods. Another drawback to this ratio is its inability to account for assets that continue to be used but that have been completely depreciated (and, thus, no additional depreciation is being taken).

Alaska Air Group (www.alaskaair.com) reported aircraft and other equipment costing $4,039.6 million in 2008 and $3,556 million in 2007. The 2008 accumulated depreciation was $1,182 million, and the 2007 depreciation expense on that equipment was $205 million.[8] Using the ratio calculation, the average useful life of Alaska Air Group's PP&E (excluding equipment deposits) is approximately 18.5 years {[($4,040 + $3,556) ÷ 2] ÷ $205}, whereas the average age of PP&E is 5.8 years ($1,182 ÷ $205). Alaska Air lists the average life of each type of plane (approximately 15–20 years) in the footnotes to the financial statements, but buildings have an average life ranging from 25 to 30 years. Thus, using an "average" age of 18 years might be too long for some aircraft and too short for some buildings. The company also indicates that the average age of its aircraft is 7.3 years, which is slightly older than indicated by the ratio.

The ratio of capital spending to depreciation provides an indicator of whether a company is making sufficient capital expenditures in its business. This ratio is computed

---

[8]The depreciation amount includes amortization.

as capital expenditures (found on the statement of cash flows under investing activities) divided by depreciation expense. A rule-of-thumb for the ratio is approximately 1:1; a lower ratio could indicate that a company is reducing expenditures, perhaps to cut costs, which might indicate the potential for future financial difficulties.

SUMMARY

Major points from the chapter are summarized in Visual Recap 6.2. The starting point in accounting for long-term assets is determining their acquisition costs. Only costs that are reasonable and necessary to acquire the assets and ready them for use should be capitalized. The depreciable cost (cost minus salvage value) of most long-term assets (except land) should be allocated to the accounting periods to which those assets provide economic benefits to a business. Three major depreciation methods are straight-line

VISUAL RECAP 6.2

Long-Term Assets: Acquisition and Use under U.S. GAAP

	Property, Plant & Equipment	Natural Resources	Intangible Assets
Cost	Reasonable and necessary costs to acquire the asset	Cost of land and resources minus value of land after natural resources removed	Reasonable and necessary costs to acquire the asset; will not include any research and development costs because these are expensed when incurred
Salvage Value	Estimated value of the asset at the end of its useful life		Usually zero
Useful Life	Expected years of service or units of activity	Units of extractable resources	Shortest of legal life, useful life, or 40 years except for goodwill which is assumed to have an indefinite life
Cost Allocation Method	*Depreciation* 3 Common Methods ■ Straight-Line ■ Double-Declining-Balance ■ Units-of-Production (except for land which is not depreciated)	*Depletion* (Similar to units-of-production depreciation)	*Amortization* Often use straight-line method, although some intangibles may be amortized on a per-unit basis; goodwill is not amorized
Impairment (or loss of value)	Immediate write down in year of impairment		

method, units-of-production (or use), and double-declining-balance. Natural resources are depleted, and intangibles are amortized.

When long-term assets are retired or sold, depreciation, depletion, or amortization must be taken through the date of the disposal. The disposal of a long-term asset usually results in a gain or loss being recorded.

PP&E (except land) and natural resources are generally reported at original purchase amounts less, respectively, accumulated depreciation and depletion. Intangibles are normally shown on the balance sheet at original cost less all amortization taken to date. Two exceptions exist. First, if an asset significantly declines in value and is considered "impaired," a write-off of the difference between the asset's unamortized cost and its fair value is recorded. Second, goodwill (an intangible asset) is not amortized and is only written off when it is impaired.

Besides valuation issues related to a business's PP&E assets, decision makers should be informed of the specific types of these assets that a business owns, depreciation/depletion/amortization methods applied to these assets, and any restrictions on the use of the assets.

KEY TERMS

amortization	goodwill	patent
copyright	impairment	salvage value
depletion	intangible asset	straight-line method
depreciable cost	leasehold improvement	trademark
double-declining-balance method	natural resource	units-of-production method

QUESTIONS

1. Identify the major types of long-term assets. Provide at least two examples of each type. *(LO 6.1 & 6.4)*

2. Why is depreciation expense recorded each accounting period on depreciable assets? *(LO 6.2)*

3. Discuss how depreciation is calculated under the straight-line, units-of-production, and double-declining-balance methods. Provide a brief numerical example that would indicate why a company might use straight-line depreciation for income statement purposes and double-declining-balance depreciation for tax purposes. *(LO 6.2)*

4. How is the book value of a depreciable asset computed? How does a depreciable asset's book value change from one accounting period to the next? Discuss the difference between the terms *book value* and *fair value*. *(LO 6.2)*

5. Explain how a gain or loss on the disposal of a long-term asset is calculated. How do gains and losses differ, respectively, from revenues and expenses? *(LO 6.2 & 6.4)*

6. On January 1, 2009, Straud Co. sold a piece of equipment with a book value of $29,000 for $24,600. The equipment had cost $89,000 when it was purchased. Explain why the following journal entry is incorrect. *(LO 6.3)*

Cash	24,600	
Loss on Sale of Equipment	4,400	
Equipment		29,000

7. Explain the difference between depreciation, depletion, and amortization. What general rules dictate how long an item is depreciated, depleted, or amortized? *(LO 6.3)*

8. Explain why you think goodwill is referred to as an "unidentifiable intangible asset." What types of items would be considered "identifiable intangible assets"? Is there any difference in the annual treatment of identifiable and unidentifiable intangible assets? *(LO 6.4)*

9. Why would the FASB require that all research and development costs be expensed? What reasons might be given

to support the international accounting principle allowing the capitalization of development costs? *(LO 6.4)*

10. Identify advantages and disadvantages of using historical costs as the primary valuation basis for PP&E. *(LO 6.5)*

11. Under what circumstances can businesses depart from the historical cost principle for PP&E assets? Why might the use of the IFRS's "revaluation method" for PP&E be difficult? *(LO 6.5)*

12. What types of expenditures are included in the acquisition cost of a PP&E asset? What types of expenditures are excluded from the acquisition cost of a PP&E asset? *(LO 6.5)*

13. Identify key information needs of financial decision makers regarding a business's long-term assets. How would you prioritize these needs? Explain why you chose your priorities. *(LO 6.6)*

EXERCISES

14. **True or False** *(All LOs)*

Following are a series of statements regarding topics discussed in this chapter.

Required:

Indicate whether each statement is true (T) or false (F).

(a) The terms *depreciable cost* and *acquisition cost* for a PP&E asset are interchangeable.

(b) The salvage value of a PP&E asset is not relevant when a company applies the double-declining-balance depreciation method.

(c) If the market value of a long-term asset increased during a given accounting period, no depreciation expense should be recorded for the asset during that period.

(d) Land is not depreciated because it never declines in value.

(e) Depreciation expense is an operating expense.

(f) When PP&E assets are sold, a company generally records a gain or loss on disposal.

(g) Most intangible assets should be amortized over their legal life, their useful life, or 40 years, whichever is longer.

(h) Intangible assets are presented on the balance sheet at historical cost.

(i) Goodwill is not amortized but must be written down when it has been impaired.

(j) Expenditures that are made to a PP&E asset after it has been in service for a number of years are always capitalized.

(k) The calculation of average asset age is generally only useful if it is calculated for each specific type of PP&E assets.

15. **Acquisition Cost of PP&E Assets** *(LO 6.1)*

Li Enterprises recently purchased new computer equipment for its company headquarters. Following is information regarding the various cash expenditures related to the acquisition of this equipment.

■ The invoice price of the equipment was $300,000; however, Li's owner negotiated a 15 percent price reduction.

■ The equipment was shipped to Li's headquarters FOB shipping point. The delivery cost was $2,750.

■ Li paid $1,870 to hire a computer consultant to install and test the new equipment.

■ Supplies costing $135 were used in installing and testing the equipment.

■ The day following the installation of the equipment, one of Li's employees broke a USB port on the computer equipment. The company paid $265 to have the port replaced.

Required:

(a) Determine the acquisition cost of the computer equipment for accounting purposes.

(b) Prepare an appropriate journal entry to record the acquisition of the computer equipment and the incurrence of the related costs.

(c) A computer purchased for several thousand dollars may have little resale value one year later because of technological changes in the computer industry. Given that the resale value of computers and computer equipment can decline rapidly, is historical cost the proper valuation basis to use for such assets? Defend your answer.

16. **Depreciation Methods** *(LO 6.2)*

Ohio Box Co. purchased a bundling machine on January 1, 2009, for a cost of $22,800. The machine is expected to last 5 years, or bundle 660,000 items, at which time it should have a salvage value of $3,000. A counter on the machine revealed that the machine was used at the following levels: 2009, 110,000 bundles; 2010, 140,000 bundles; 2011, 150,000 bundles; 2012, 141,800 bundles; and 2013, 152,000 bundles.

Required:

(a) How much depreciation will be taken each year if the straight-line method of depreciation is used? Show calculations.

(b) What depreciation method is Ohio Box using if the depreciation expense in 2010 is $4,200? Show calculations.

(c) What depreciation method is Ohio Box using if the depreciation expense in 2010 is $5,472? Show calculations.

(d) At the end of the five-year useful life, what will be the (1) ending book value and (2) the balance of accumulated depreciation?

(e) Assume that Ohio Box uses the double-declining-balance method of depreciation. What is the depreciation expense in year 5?

(f) Assume that Ohio Box uses the units-of-production method of depreciation. What is the depreciation expense in year 5?

17. Computing Depreciation Expense *(LO 6.2)*

Ludmila Manufacturing purchased a piece of production equipment on January 1, 2009. The equipment cost $6,500 and was estimated to have a salvage value of $500 at the end of its six-year life or 12,000 hours of use.

Required:

(a) Compute depreciation expense on the production equipment for 2009 and 2010 and prepare the appropriate journal entries using the:

(1) straight-line depreciation method

(2) double-declining-balance depreciation method

(b) Assume that Ludmila uses the units-of-production method. Compute depreciation expense for 2009 and 2010 and prepare the appropriate journal entries, if the equipment were used 2,500 hours in 2009 and 1,900 hours in 2010.

18. Computing Depreciation Expense *(LO 6.2)*

Use the information from Exercise 17, except assume that the production equipment was purchased on October 1, 2009.

Required:

(a) Compute depreciation expense on the production equipment for 2009, 2010, and 2011 using the

(1) straight-line depreciation method

(2) double-declining-balance depreciation method

(b) Prepare the journal entries to record the acquisition of the equipment and the first year's depreciation using the straight-line depreciation method.

19. Sale of a PP&E Asset *(LO 6.3)*

On June 30, 2009, Newsom Company sold equipment for $7,250 that had been acquired for $14,500 on January 1, 2007. Newsom originally estimated that the computer would have a five-year useful life and a $500 salvage value. Newsom uses straight-line depreciation. The company's fiscal year ends on December 31 and records depreciation expense at the end of each fiscal year.

Required:

(a) Determine the book value of the computer on December 31, 2008.

(b) Prepare all entries needed on June 30, 2009, to properly account for the disposal of the computer.

20. Disposal of PP&E Assets *(LO 6.3)*

On January 1, 2006, Landers Company purchased ten washing machines to be used in its coin-operated laundry. Each washer cost $800 and was expected to have an $80 salvage value at the end of its four-year useful life. On September 30, 2009, Landers decided to purchase more efficient machines and sold the ten washers for $1,630. Landers uses straight-line depreciation for PP&E assets and records depreciation expense at the end of each year.

Required:

(a) Prepare the appropriate journal entry to record depreciation expense on the washers prior to their disposal. What is the book value of each washer following the posting of this journal entry?

(b) Determine the gain or loss on the sale of the washers. Prepare the journal entry to record the sale of the washers.

(c) Suppose that, rather than being sold, the washers were simply hauled to the junkyard. Prepare the journal entry to record the disposal of the washers.

21. Natural Resources *(LO 6.4)*

Pappas Corp. paid $5,250,000 for 1,500 acres of land. The company plans to sell the trees on the land to a lumber company. After the land is cleared, Webster believes the land will have a value of $600,000.

Required:

(a) Prepare the journal entry for the acquisition of the land and the trees.

(b) What average cost should Pappas assign to an acre of lumber? Are there any conditions that you believe would make an average cost per acre an unacceptable cost method?

(c)   Assume that Pappas sells the trees immediately after clearing the land. What journal entry would Pappas make to account for the clearing of 100 acres?

(d)   After the land is cleared, Pappas receives an offer of $4,000 per acre for the land. Should Pappas change the historical cost of the land?

(e)   Prepare the journal entry if Pappas sells 300 acres of cleared land for $3,300 per acre.

22.   **Intangibles** *(LO 6.4)*

On March 31, 2009, Lincoln MedCo acquired an existing patent to produce a pain reliever from Jefferson Pharmaceuticals for $1,871,800. The patent offers exclusive rights to produce this medication for another seven years. Lincoln's fiscal year ends on December 31.

Required:

(a)   What journal entry is made on March 31, 2009, to record the purchase of the patent?

(b)   What will be the salvage value of this patent after seven years? Explain the rationale for your answer.

(c)   What amount of amortization should be taken in 2009, 2010, and 2016?

(d)   Prepare the December 31, 2009, journal entry related to this patent.

23.   **PP&E Expenditures** *(LO 6.2 and 6.5)*

Enid Inc. purchased a piece of equipment for $144,000 on June 1, 2007. The equipment had an $18,000 salvage value and a six-year useful life. At the end of 2008 and 2009, Enid paid $350 to have the equipment cleaned. During 2008 and 2009, respectively, Enid spent $145 and $198 on lubricating oil for the equipment. On June 2, 2010, Enid spent $7,000

on a new motor for the equipment. The motor should extend the life of the equipment for two years beyond the original estimated life; the equipment's salvage value will not be affected.

(a)   If Enid Inc. uses straight-line depreciation, how much depreciation is taken on the equipment in 2007?

(b)   How should the (1) cleaning, (2) lubricating, and (3) engine replacement be treated for accounting purposes?

(c)   How much depreciation should Enid Inc. take on the equipment for the calendar years 2010 and 2011?

24.   **Long-Term Asset Analysis** *(LO 6.6)*

The following information is available from the 2009 financial statements of Boonrawd Corp.:

Income statement:	Depreciation Expense	$ 250,000
Statement of cash flows:	Equipment investment	978,000
Balance sheet:	Year-end balance of	
	Equipment	3,670,000
	Year-end balance	
	of Acc. Depr.—	
	Equipment	1,058,700

Required:

(a)   What is the average age of the equipment?

(b)   What is the average useful life of the equipment?

(c)   Would your answers to parts (a) or (b) change if you knew the equipment investment had been made on December 1, 2009? If so, why? What would your answers now be to those parts?

PROBLEMS

25.   **Acquisition of PP&E Assets** *(LO 6.1)*

In 2009, Nicola Corporation acquired several PP&E assets for its manufacturing operations. Following are descriptions of costs incurred by Nicola during 2009 related to these assets. All amounts were paid in cash.

■   On January 2, Nicola purchased land with a warehouse for $2,600,000. The land's appraised value was $700,000, whereas the warehouse had an appraised value of $2,100,000. The warehouse has an estimated useful life of 20 years and estimated salvage value of $200,000.

■   On January 3, Nicola purchased production equipment for $1,000,000 that had an estimated useful life of five years and an estimated

salvage value of $60,000. The equipment was shipped FOB destination by the seller to Nicola's place of business at a cost of $4,200.

■   The equipment purchased on January 3 was damaged during installation. The total repair cost was $2,700.

■   On April 2, Nicola purchased office furniture and fixtures for $400,000. These assets have an estimated useful life of ten years and an estimated salvage value of $30,000.

■   On July 1, Nicola purchased four delivery trucks at a cost of $12,000 each. Each truck had an estimated useful life of four years and an estimated salvage value of $2,400. Expenses paid to deliver the trucks to Nicola's business location totaled $900, and insurance paid on the trucks while they were in transit amounted to $300. Nicola immediately installed an alarm system on each truck at a cost of $600 per truck.

Required:

(a)   Prepare the journal entries to record the acquisitions of PP&E assets by Nicola Corporation during 2009.

(b)   Nicola records straight-line depreciation on its PP&E assets each December 31. Prepare the December 31, 2009, adjusting entries for depreciation expense on the assets acquired during 2009.

26.   Alternative Depreciation Methods *(LO 6.2, ethics)*

Brad Jolie recently decided to open a restaurant specializing in New Orleans cuisine. He purchased a restaurant building on January 2, 2009, at a cost of $650,000, paying 10 percent of the purchase price in cash and signing a note for the balance. The building has an estimated useful life of 25 years and an estimated salvage value of $150,000. Also on January 2, 2009, Jolie paid cash of $80,000 for used kitchen equipment with an estimated four-year useful life and $8,000 salvage value.

Required:

(a)   Prepare the journal entries to record the purchase of the building and the kitchen equipment.

(b)   Compute depreciation expense for 2009 and 2010 on the restaurant using the following methods:

(1)   Straight-line

(2)   Double-declining-balance

(c)   Prepare the year-end adjusting journal entries to record the depreciation expense amounts computed in part (a).

(d)   Compute depreciation expense on the kitchen equipment for year 2009 through 2012, assuming that the following depreciation methods are used:

(1)   Straight-line

(2)   Double-declining-balance

(e)   Suppose that Jolie believes that the double-declining-balance method most accurately reflects the true depreciation pattern of his firm's depreciable assets. Would it be unethical for the owner to apply the straight-line depreciation method to these assets? Why or why not?

(f)   Provide at least two positive and negative financial implications of buying used kitchen equipment.

27.   Alternative Depreciation Methods *(LO 6.2)*

CALAir is a small charter airline company that operates between San Francisco and Los Angeles. On January 2,

2009, CALAir purchased a jet costing $2,600,000 with an estimated salvage value of $700,000 at the end of its five-year (or 500,000 mile) life. CALAir expects that the jet will be flown the following number of miles over its life:

2009	100,000 miles
2010	120,000 miles
2011	130,000 miles
2012	90,000 miles
2013	60,000 miles

Required:

(a)   Prepare a depreciation schedule for the jet under each of the following methods:

(1)   Straight-line

(2)   Double-declining-balance

(3)   Units-of-production (use)

(b)   In your opinion, which of these three depreciation methods is most consistent with the matching principle? Defend your answer.

(c)   Shortly after the jet was purchased, CALAir wanted to borrow a large sum of money from a local bank. Which of the three depreciation methods might CALAir want to use to prepare the financial statements needed by the bank loan officer? Defend your answer.

(d)   Suppose that, at the time the jet was purchased, CALAir had a large loan outstanding from a local bank. How, if at all, would the choice of a depreciation method affect CALAir's ability to repay the bank loan? Discuss the rationale for your answer.

28.   Disposal of PP&E Assets *(LO 6.3)*

On January 2, 2009, SoCo Vending purchased five vending machines to place in a high school. Each vending machine cost $3,100 and had an estimated six-year useful life and $400 salvage value. SoCo uses the straight-line depreciation method. On April 1, 2012, the company decided to replace the vending machines and sold all of them to a single buyer.

Required:

(a)   Prepare the journal entry to record the depreciation expense on the vending machines for the first three months of 2012.

(b)   Determine the book value of the vending machines following the posting of the journal entry prepared in part (a).

(c)   Prepare the journal entry to record the sale of the vending machines for $8,000.

(d)   Prepare the journal entry to record the sale of the vending machines for $9,300.

29. **Accounting for Intangible Assets** *(LO 6.4)*

Gharigh, Inc. is a leading manufacturer of pharmaceutical products. Following are transactions or events involving Gharigh's intangible assets during 2009.

January 4	Purchased a patent on the drug Zorcerin for $1,500,000. The patent had a legal life of 12 years; Gharigh estimated the patent's useful life at five years.
February 9	Sold a patent with a book value of $753,000 to a competitor for $800,000.
June 30	A competitor introduced a new drug that made a patent on Phanesopan held by Gharigh obsolete. The patent was being amortized at $100,000 per year and the last time amortization occurred was on December 31, 2008. After that adjusting entry, the patent's book value was $607,000.
December 31	Recorded amortization expense on the Zorcerin patent.
December 31	During the year, Gharigh incurred $876,800 in research and development costs.

Required:

(a) Prepare the appropriate journal entries for Gharigh, Inc.'s 2009 transactions, assuming that the company uses U.S. accounting principles.

(b) Prepare the December 31 journal entry for R&D costs assuming that Gharigh, Inc. uses U.S. generally accepted accounting principles.

(c) Prepare the December 31 journal entry for R&D costs assuming that Gharigh, Inc., uses international accounting principles. Of the $876,800 in R&D, $336,100 was for development costs.

(d) Would the treatment in part (b) or (c) be preferable to an investor who was most concerned about a company's short-term profitability? Could there be a problem with the treatment selected?

30. **Reporting and Analysis of PP&E Assets** *(LO 6.6)*

Kosciusko Corporation is a manufacturing firm that has $3,600,000 of long-term assets that are used in operations. Following is the acquisition cost, accumulated depreciation, and depreciation expense for each asset through the end of 2009.

Description	Acquisition Cost	Accumulated Depreciation through 2009	Depreciation Expense for 2009
Office building	$ 748,000	$230,000	$34,000
Production equipment	1,072,800	112,000	89,400
Office furniture	131,500	61,000	26,300
Land	350,000	0	0
Delivery trucks	320,000	125,000	40,000

Required:

(a) Prepare the PP&E section of Kosciusko Corporation's balance sheet at the end of 2009.

(b) Why has no depreciation expense been recorded on the land owned by Kosciusko?

(c) Assuming that no PP&E assets have been acquired by Kosciusko during the year, what is the average useful life of each category of assets other than land?

(d) Assume that Kosciusko had acquired $60,000 of office furniture and $5,000 of delivery trucks during 2009. What is the capital spending to depreciation ratio for each of these two categories of assets? Discuss your assessment of this ratio.

(e) Besides the information you developed in parts (a) through (d), what other information regarding Kosciusko's PP&E assets is needed by decision makers who use the company's financial statements?

31. **Comprehensive Problem** *(LOs 6.1–6.6)*

A partial balance sheet is presented for Withers Industries.

Withers Industries
Partial Balance Sheet
December 31, 2008

Property, Plant & Equipment		
Delivery Truck	$ 35,000	
Less Accumulated Depreciation	(18,750)	$16,250
Office Equipment	$ 45,000	
Less Accumulated Depreciation	(35,280)	9,720
Factory Machinery	$100,000	
Less Accumulated Depreciation	(36,800)	63,200
Total Property, Plant & Equipment		$89,170
Intangible Assets		
Patents		$ 7,000

Notes:

■ The delivery truck was purchased on June 30, 2006, and is being depreciated over four years using the straight-line method. Salvage value was estimated at $5,000.

■ The office equipment was purchased on January 2, 2006, and is being depreciated over five years using the double-declining-balance method. Salvage value was estimated at $4,000.

■ The factory machinery was purchased on January 2, 2005, and is being depreciated over ten years using the straight-line method. Salvage value was estimated at $8,000.

■ The remaining useful life on the patent is seven years.

Required:

(a) On July 31, 2009, Withers sold the delivery truck for $9,000 cash. Prepare any necessary journal entries to record this sale.

(b) On December 1, 2009, Withers purchased land and a building for a combined cost of $400,000 by paying $100,000 cash and signing a note for the balance. An appraiser estimates the values of the building and land are, respectively, $302,500 and $247,500. Withers plans to use the building for ten years, at which time the building will probably be worth $50,000. Withers plans to use straight-line depreciation on the building. Journalize this purchase.

(c) Record all necessary depreciation and amortization entries on December 31, 2009.

(d) Prepare a partial balance sheet for Withers on December 31, 2009.

(e) How did the 2009 transactions affect Withers's Income Statement?

(f) What are the average useful life and the average age of each category of long-term asset, with the exception of land?

CASES

32.   Choosing a Depreciation Method *(LO 6.2)*

Colorado Climber, which manufactures stairway railings, purchased a $15,000 lathe on January 2, 2009. The lathe was estimated to have a salvage value of $1,000 at the end of its five-year useful life. The company's owner is trying to decide on a depreciation method to use for this new asset.

Required:

(a) Compute depreciation expense on the new lathe for 2009 and 2010 assuming that Colorado Climber uses the:

(1) Straight-line method

(2) Double-declining-balance method

(b) Suppose that the company decides to apply the units-of-production depreciation method to the new lathe. The lathe will be used to produce approximately 3,500 units of product over its useful life. Compute the depreciation expense on the lathe for 2009 and 2010 if 550 and 670 units of product are made, respectively, in 2009 and 2010.

(c) Which of the three major depreciation methods best satisfies the matching principle? Defend your choice.

(d) Under which of the three depreciation methods will Colorado Climber have the highest net income for 2009? For 2010? Show your calculations.

(e) If Colorado Climber wants to minimize its tax liability, which depreciation method should the company use for 2009 and 2010? Explain your answer.

(f) Why do you think the government allows a company to use different depreciation methods for accounting and tax purposes? Do you think that using different methods for accounting and tax purposes is ethical? Explain your answer.

33.   Accounting for Fully Depreciated Assets *(LO 6.3, writing, ethics)*

Jim's Bike Shop purchased a $2,400 air compressor four years ago. The compressor was estimated to have a four-year useful life and no salvage value. The compressor is now fully depreciated with a zero book value. Surprisingly to the business's owner, the air compressor "works like new," and he has no plans to replace it.

Required:

(a) Should this business continue to record depreciation expense on the air compressor each year? Why or why not?

(b) Should a business keep a fully depreciated asset on its books indefinitely as long as the asset is being used in the business? Why or why not?

(c) Explain how the matching principle was violated by Jim's Bike Shop and how this violation affected the financial statements of the business. Was this violation intentional? How might a company use depreciation to mislead users of the financial statements?

(d) Write a memo to Jim explaining the importance of the assumptions made at the asset's acquisition (useful life and salvage value). Include in your memo at least one suggestion of how to estimate each number.

34. **Goodwill Impairment** *(LO 6.5, Internet)*

Use the Internet or library resources to find four examples of companies that wrote off impaired goodwill within the past year.

Required:

(a) What companies did you find, and how much goodwill did each write off?

(b) How did the write-offs affect each company's financial statements?

(c) What do you think that a write-off of goodwill indicates about company management? Provide at least one positive indicator and one negative. Assume that the same managers were at the company when the goodwill was created. (Hint: Remember what needs to occur for a company to record goodwill.)

35. **Analysis of PP&E** *(LO 6.6, Internet)*

Use the annual report of Carnival Corporation for the 2007 fiscal year to answer the following questions. This information can be found on either the annual report or the SEC 10-K filing at www.carnival.com by following the links to Investor Relations.

Required:

(a) Calculate and interpret the following ratios for Carnival for the fiscal year ending November 30, 2007.

(1) Average age of assets

(2) Average useful life of assets

(b) What is the capital spending to depreciation ratio? Given the information provided (and not provided) in the annual report, what types of questions might you have about the calculation of this ratio?

(c) Does Carnival discuss the age of its assets? Is that age similar to the numbers you calculated? List some possible reasons for any differences.

(d) What depreciation method does Carnival use?

36. **Comparing Companies** *(LO 6.6, group, Internet)*

Identifying the similarities and differences between companies is as crucial to making investment decisions as understanding a single company's financial statements. Form groups of at least four students. Each group should select a single industry. Each group member should locate a different annual report within that industry. (The industry and individual company may be assigned by your instructor.)

Required—individual group members:

(a) Did your company acquire any new property, plant and equipment assets in the most recent fiscal year? If yes, is there a discussion in the financial statements about what was acquired, and where is this discussion included?

(b) Do the financial statements or notes indicate that any PPE assets were sold? Where did you find this information?

(c) Calculate the following ratios for the company you selected for the two most recent fiscal years.

(1) Average age of PPE assets

(2) Average useful life of PPE assets

(d) What depreciation method (or methods) does your company use?

(e) What is the depreciation expense for the most recent three years?

Required—groups:

(f) Compile the ratio calculations for each company prepared by the individual group members into one table. Compare the results from company to company in the same fiscal year. Include in your comparison a graphical analysis.

(g) Compile the depreciation information for each company into one table. Compare the results from company to company in the same fiscal year and across fiscal years. Include in your comparison a graphical analysis.

(h) Discuss reasons why the results from parts (f) and (g) might be similar or different within an industry.

Required—class:

(i) Compare the ratios from each industry. Discuss reasons why these ratios might be similar or different between industries.

(j) Compare the depreciation methods and trends between industries. Discuss reasons for similarities and differences between industries.

SUPPLEMENTAL PROBLEMS

37. **Acquisition of PP&E Assets** *(LO 6.1; Compare to Problem 25)*

In 2009, Giganto, Corp. acquired the following PP&E assets. All amounts were paid in cash.

■ On January 2, Giganto acquired a supercomputer for $49,000. Delivery and insurance during shipping was $1,200. Giganto had to install, at a cost of $3,000, an antistatic raised floor in the computer room before the computer could be used. Testing the computer cost $1,800, and the insurance was $900 for the first year. Giganto expects to use the computer for ten years. The expected salvage value of the computer is $1,000.

■ On March 30, Giganto bought a $25,000 delivery van. Sales tax was $1,500. Annual license and registration fees totaled $340. Giganto's logo was painted on the van at a cost of $1,300. Giganto expects to use the van for five years. The expected salvage value of the van is $1,800.

■ On August 8, Giganto bought land on which it intends to build an office building. The land cost was $80,000, which included an $8,000 real estate commission fee. Property taxes paid by Giganto included $2,200 of delinquent taxes from the prior owner and $950 for 2009. Giganto paid $5,000 to raze a building on the property and to grade the land. Giganto expects to begin construction next year and use the building for the next 20 years.

Required:
(a) Prepare the journal entries to record the acquisitions of PP&E assets by Giganto, Inc. during 2009.
(b) Giganto records straight-line depreciation on its PP&E assets each December 31. Prepare the December 31, 2009, adjusting entries for depreciation expense on the assets acquired in 2009.

38. **Depreciation Methods and Disposal of Assets** *(LO 6.2; Compare to Problems 27 & 28)*

In Style Arrival (ISA) operates a limousine and car service. On March 31, 2009, ISA purchased a car costing $52,000 with an estimated salvage value of $7,000 at the end of its life of 144,000 miles. ISA expects that the car will be driven the following number of miles each year:

2009	30,000 miles
2010	32,000 miles
2011	36,000 miles
2012	40,000 miles
2013	6,000 miles

Required:
(a) Prepare a depreciation schedule for ISA using the following depreciation methods:
(1) Straight-line
(2) Double-declining-balance
(3) Units-of-production.
(b) On October 31, 2011, ISA stopped using the car. Prepare journal entries to record the sale or disposal under each of the following four assumptions. Assume that ISA used the double-declining-balance method of depreciation.
(1) Sold the car for $15,000
(2) Sold the car for $9,479
(3) Sold the car for $9,000
(4) Junked the car because it was totaled by a company employee. No other cars were involved, and ISA carried no collision insurance. Had to pay the junk yard $150 to haul the car away from the accident site.

PART III

ACCOUNTING FOR LIABILITIES AND OWNERSHIP INTERESTS

CHAPTER 7

Liabilities

LEARNING OBJECTIVES

1. Account for the major types of transactions and events affecting current liabilities.
2. Define the key characteristics of, and account for, contingent liabilities.
3. Account for the major types of transactions and events affecting bonds payable.
4. Distinguish between operating leases and capital leases.
5. Discuss accounting issues for long-term liabilities stemming from pension and other postretirement employee benefit plans.
6. Define the key information needs of decision makers regarding liabilities.
7. Compute and interpret the current, long-term debt to equity, and times interest earned ratios as well as the amount of working capital.
8. (Appendix) Compute the issue price of bonds and prepare journal entries related to discount and premium amortization.

INTRODUCTION

This chapter focuses on current and long-term liabilities. Liabilities are debts that a company owes and may either be known or estimated amounts. Contingent liabilities are debts that may become due in the future if certain conditions arise. These liabilities pose unique accounting issues and, as such, are considered independent from other liabilities. Key information needs of decision makers regarding current and long-term liabilities are identified as well as some ratios that reflect a company's debt status.

CURRENT LIABILITIES

As discussed in Chapter 2, liabilities are amounts owed by a company to other parties. Such amounts require a company to transfer assets or provide services to another party because of either a past or present transaction. Liabilities that must be paid by a business within one year or operating cycle, whichever is longer, are classified as current liabilities.

Although specific current liabilities vary from company to company, there are two general types of current liabilities: (1) those whose dollar amounts are defined by a contractual agreement and (2) those whose dollar amounts must be estimated. An example of the first type is an account payable. When an account payable is recorded, the actual dollar amount due is known. An example of the second type is a quarterly estimate of the income tax payable that will be due at the end of the company's fiscal year.

Accounts Payable

A common current liability is an account payable, which is an amount owed by a business to its suppliers for purchases of inventory. In a business-to-business relationship, accounts payable typically do not require the payment of interest, and, as discussed in Chapter 4, sellers will often grant discount terms to encourage the prompt payment of these debts.

Current liabilities that are due to parties other than suppliers of inventory are generally recorded in accounts other than accounts payable. For instance, if a company owes a utility payment, that current liability would have recorded in Utilities Payable. Taxes owed would be recorded in Taxes Payable.

Notes Payable

Notes payable are debts that are documented by a legally binding written commitment known as a promissory note. Notes payable can be either current or long-term, depending on their maturity date. Accounting for both types of notes is the same; only the balance sheet classification differs.

No standard format exists for promissory notes. Occasionally, a promissory note is literally nothing more than a scribbled "IOU" on a piece of paper. The person signing the note and promising to pay the **principal** (or face) amount is called the **maker**. The **payee** is the party to whom payment will be made. The **maturity value** of a note is the total amount the maker must give the payee on the **maturity date** (on which payment is due) and is equal to the principal plus any interest that accrues or accumulates on the note over its term.[1]

A note's term reflects it duration. It is the number of days, months, or years from the date a note is signed until the maturity date. As discussed in Chapter 4, the maturity point of a note depends on how the note is dated. Notes dated in months or years mature on the same day of the month as the note is dated. Notes dated in days require each day of the month to be counted to find the maturity date.

The computation for interest expense on an interest-bearing promissory note (or any other interest-bearing financial instrument) is as follows:

$$\text{Interest} = \text{Principal} \times \text{Rate} \times \text{Time}$$

The principal is the amount for which the note was originally drawn. The rate refers to the **stated interest rate** in the note; interest rates are always annual unless otherwise specifically noted. The time component is expressed as a fraction, with the **term of the note** as the numerator and 360 days as the denominator.[2]

To illustrate the accounting for notes payable, suppose that Bonney's Dress Shop borrows $5,000 from a local bank on October 2, 2009, and signs a 120-day, 12% note payable. The note's maturity date is January 30, 2010: 29 days in October ($31 - 2$), 30 days in November, 31 days in December, and 30 days in January. Bonney's Dress Shop records the $5,000 loan as follows.

General Journal				
Date		**Description**	**Debit**	**Credit**
Oct	2	Cash	5,000	
		Notes Payable		5,000
		Borrowed $5,000 on a 120-day,		
		12% note		

If Bonney's has a calendar year-end, the company must record an adjusting entry for the interest expense owed on December 31, 2009, but the interest will not be paid until the following year when the note matures. The note payable will have been outstanding for 90 days by December 31 (October 2 through December 31); therefore, $150 of interest will have accrued on the note by that date ($5,000 \times 0.12 \times 90/360$). The adjusting entry to record this accrual on December 31 follows.

General Journal				
Date		**Description**	**Debit**	**Credit**
Dec	31	Interest Expense	150	
		Interest Payable		150
		Accrued interest on the		
		120-day, 12% note dated 10/2		

---

[1]There are "non-interest-bearing notes"; however, this term is slightly misleading. When a non-interest-bearing note is issued, the maker receives the principal amount of the note *less* interest at the beginning of the note term. Thus, at the maturity date, the total payment for a non-interest-bearing note is the face amount of the note; no additional interest is paid at maturity.

[2]The 360-day year is used here for simplicity of computations. Interest is actually calculated in the business world on the basis of a 365- (or 366-) day year.

On January 30, Bonney's Dress Shop will repay the bank the $5,000 principal amount plus 12% interest for the note's 120-day term. The total interest due the bank will be $200 (or $5,000 × 12% × 120/360). However, only $50 of interest expense will be recorded on the note's maturity date. This $50 reflects interest for the 30-day period January 1 through January 30. The remaining $150 of interest was recorded as an expense in the previous year. Payment of the note and interest is recorded as follows:

General Journal					
Date		Description		Debit	Credit
Jan	30	Notes Payable		5,000	
		Interest Payable		150	
		Interest Expense		50	
		Cash			5,200
		Recorded interest for January on the 120-day,			
		12% note dated 10/2 and repaid the note and			
		all interest			

Installment Notes Payable

Many notes, like bank loans for automobiles and mortgages, are due in installments, in which each periodic payment includes some interest and some principal. The amount of interest included in each payment modifies the formula shown previously as follows.

$$\text{Interest Expense} = \text{Remaining Principal} \times \text{Rate} \times \text{Time}$$

Assume that Ryan Co. purchases a $25,000 truck on January 31, 2009. The company signs a five-year note payable, and payments of $483 are to be made at the end of each month at an annual interest rate of 6 percent. Exhibit 7-1 shows the computations for the first six months of principal and interest payments (rounded to the nearest dollar), as well as the journal entries for the first two months. Note that the interest amounts are calculated as 6 percent times the outstanding time period times the remaining principal balance on the previous line. As each payment is made, the principal is reduced, and, therefore, the interest expense on the outstanding debt is also reduced in the following payment.

In this example, the amount of the monthly truck payment was given. A variety of Web sites are available that can calculate such payments, given changes in principal amounts, interest rates, and length of borrowing time. Some of these sites provide several different calculators, even those that graph interest expense reductions over the life of the loan.[3]

If an installment loan matures over multiple accounting periods, the total amount of the note payable will not be shown as a current liability. Only the amount that comes due in the next year or operating cycle, whichever is longer, is shown as the "current portion of long-term debt"; the remainder is shown as a long-term liability.

---

[3]Three calculator Web sites are www.bankrate.com/brm/auto-loan-calculator.asp, http://www.sitewidgets .com/calculator_l_withgraph.phtml, and http://www.ncfbins.com/auto_loan.html.

Date	Payment	Time	6% Interest	Principal	Remaining Principal
January 31					$25,000
February 28	$483	28/365	$115	$368	24,632
March 31	483	31/365	126	357	24,275
April 30	483	30/365	120	363	23,912
May 31	483	31/365	122	361	23,551
June 30	483	30/365	116	367	23,184
July 31	483	31/365	118	365	22,819

General Journal				
Date		Description	Debit	Credit
Feb	28	Notes Payable	368	
		Interest Expense	115	
		Cash		483
		Recorded interest expense and principal reduction on the $25,000, 5-year, 6% truck note payable		
Mar	31	Notes Payable	357	
		Interest Expense	126	
		Cash		483
		Recorded interest expense and principal reduction on the $25,000, 5-year, 6% truck note payable		

Accrued Liabilities

As illustrated by the interest accrual on the Bonney's Dress Shop note payable example and as discussed in Chapter 3, a business must record its expenses in the appropriate accounting periods. Expenses such as interest may be accrued at the end of an accounting period because of the passage of time; other expenses (such as sales commissions) may be accrued because the related revenue is recognized. When a liability accrual is recorded, an expense account is debited, and a liability account is credited. Recall that an accrued liability is a liability created by recording an expense that has been incurred but not yet paid.

Some accrued liabilities, such as wages payable, interest payable, and income taxes payable, have been discussed previously. Several additional accrued liabilities are considered in the following discussion.

Product Warranty Liability

Many companies provide a product or service warranty. Because warranties help sell products, the company must match warranty costs with sales revenue each accounting period. However, warranty work is oftentimes performed in a period (or periods) after the sale. To properly match the sales revenue with the related warranty expense, businesses estimate total expected warranty costs for products sold during one accounting period and record that amount as an expense in the same period as the sale. The offsetting credit to this expense is typically entered in the Warranty Liability account.

Suppose a high-quality ballpoint pen manufacturer has a "repair or replace forever" product warranty. The company expects that 2 percent of the pens sold will need to be repaired or replaced at an average cost of $15 per pen. If 200,000 pens are sold in 2009, the firm expects to eventually repair or replace 4,000 (200,000 × 0.02) pens at a cost of $60,000 (4,000 × $15). Given these facts, the adjusting entry to record warranty expense for 2009 is

General Journal				
Date		Description	Debit	Credit
Dec	31	Warranty Expense	60,000	
		Warranty Liability		60,000
		Recorded estimated warranty expense for year		

During 2010, the company incurs $15,100 of warranty costs. Of these costs, $10,000 was for parts, and $5,100 was a labor cost for repair personnel. The following entry would be made to recognize these costs.

General Journal				
Date		Description	Debit	Credit
XXX		Warranty Liability	15,100	
		Parts Inventory		10,000
		Cash (or Wages Payable)		5,100
		Recorded actual warranty costs as incurred		

A similar expense and liability estimation takes place for certain other types of business activities. For example, when restaurants issue "free meal" coupons that extend over the end of an accounting period, the number of coupons that will be redeemed needs to be estimated. Likewise, estimates of potential liabilities must be made when a hotel offers clients a "free stay" after a certain number of check-ins or when an airline offers free trips after a given number of flight segments. The 2007 10-K of Southwest Airlines (www.southwest.com) indicates that the "estimated incremental cost of providing free travel awards is accrued when such award levels are reached" and that, at December 31, 2007, approximately 2.2 million fully earning reward tickets were outstanding.[4]

Vacation Pay Liability

Besides earning their base salary or wages, most employees also accumulate vacation pay each payroll period. Assume that an employee who is paid $400 each week for 52 weeks is entitled to two weeks per year paid vacation. Of her annual $20,800 annual salary, $800 ($400 × 2 weeks) qualifies as vacation pay. Expressed another way, this employee accumulates $16 of vacation pay ($800 ÷ 50 weeks) for each week worked. Because of the matching principle, a business should recognize the vacation pay earned by employees each payroll period as a current liability. However, because some vacation pay accumulated by a company's workforce is usually forfeited because of employee turnover, a company usually does not record the entire estimated vacation pay amount.

Assume that Linton & Co. provides each employee an annual two-week paid vacation. Each payroll period, vacation pay accumulated by Linton employees equals 4 percent

[4]Southwest Airlines Co., *2007 10-K*, pp. 42 and 45.

(2 weeks ÷ 50 weeks) of that week's payroll. If the two-week payroll is $350,000, vacation pay earned by employees is $14,000 (0.04 × $350,000). In a typical year, 10 percent of all vacation pay accumulated by Linton employees is forfeited. Given this fact, Linton & Co. would make the following entry for each payroll period.

General Journal				
Date		Description	Debit	Credit
XXX		Vacation Pay Expense	12,600	
		Vacation Pay Liability		12,600
		Recorded estimated vacation pay for payroll period		

The $12,600 represents 90 percent of the expected $14,000 of vacation pay expense for its most recent payroll period. When Linton & Co.'s employees take their vacations, Vacation Pay Liability will be debited for the vacation pay cost, and Cash will be credited.

Accrued Payroll Liabilities

Typically, the end of a business's accounting period does not coincide with the end of a payroll period. Therefore, as discussed in Chapter 3, a company will generally have to accrue employee wages at the end of the month or year.

Although it was ignored to this point, there is often a significant difference between workers' gross pay and their net (or take-home) pay because of various payroll deductions such as employees' portion of Social Security tax,[5] federal and state income tax withholdings, union dues, and health insurance premiums. When accruing payroll expenses at the end of an accounting period, a business must also consider these employee payroll deductions.

Suppose that as of December 31, employees of Rachael's Restaurant have worked one week for which they have not been paid. The gross pay earned by these employees for this week is $4,240, of which only $2,720 is payable to the employees. The remainder, as shown in Exhibit 7-2, is payable to government tax agencies and the insurance company.

In addition to paying employee wages and salaries, employers must contribute an amount equal to the FICA taxes paid by their employees to the Social Security program. Employers must also generally pay state and federal unemployment taxes on employees' earnings. A final component of payroll-related expenses is employee fringe benefits. Fringe benefits include items such as employer contributions to an employee pension fund and payments toward employee health or other insurance premiums. At the end of each accounting period, businesses will generally need to accrue these additional payroll-related expenses in an adjusting entry.

Deferred Liabilities

Deferred liabilities are obligations to provide a product, service, or cash at a later date. A business may receive payments from customers prior to providing them products or services. For example, magazine subscriptions are paid before individual issues are sent.

---

[5] Social Security is officially known as the Federal Insurance Contributions Act (FICA) tax.

EXHIBIT 7-2

Computation of Net Pay
and Payroll Accrual

Gross Pay		$4,240
Less Payroll Deductions		
FICA Taxes	$325	
Federal Income Tax Withholdings	810	
State Income Tax Withholdings	205	
Health Insurance Premiums	180	(1,520)
Net Pay		$2,720

General Journal					
Date		Description		Debit	Credit
Dec	31	Wages Expense		4,240	
		FICA Tax Liability			325
		Federal Income Tax Withholdings Liability			810
		State Income Tax Withholdings Liability			205
		Health Insurance Premium Liability			180
		Cash			2,720
		Recorded accrued wages and payroll deductions			

Such amounts have not been earned when they are received; thus they are initially recorded as liabilities. Typically, these deferral amounts are debited to Cash and credited to a deferred revenue account such as Deferred Subscription Revenue or Unearned Rental Revenue. These advance payments are usually classified as current liabilities because the products or services will be delivered to customers within 12 months. For example, when airlines sell mileage credits to customers participating in their frequent flyer programs, the airline records a deferred liability and recognizes the revenue only in the period in which the mileage credits are used.

Contingent Liabilities

Companies face a variety of **contingent** (or potential) **liabilities** that may become actual liabilities if a specific event occurs or fails to occur. For example, when a product with a warranty is sold, a company may have to incur repair costs if the product breaks. Such a potential cost is recognized as an estimated expense and estimated liability. Other types of contingencies, such as lawsuits or environmental problems, will result in losses rather than expenses because payments related to such situations are not considered normal costs of doing business.

Large corporations regularly face nuisance lawsuits that pose no more than a minimal likelihood of resulting in actual losses. If a contingent liability has only a remote chance of resulting in an actual loss, that liability is ignored for accounting and financial reporting purposes. However, almost all legitimate loss contingencies are, at a minimum, disclosed in the footnotes to the financial statements. A journal entry must be recorded when a loss contingency meets two specified criteria: (1) it is probable that a loss will result from the contingency and (2) the amount of the potential loss can be reasonably estimated. When a loss contingency is recorded, an appropriate expense or loss account is debited with an offsetting credit to a liability account. Visual Recap 7.1 summarizes the alternative accounting treatments for loss contingencies and the related contingent liabilities.

VISUAL RECAP 7.1

Contingent Losses and Related Contingent Liabilities

Likelihood of Actual Loss	Potential Loss Subject to Reasonable Estimation	Accounting Treatment
Probable	Yes	Recorded by debiting an expense or loss account and crediting a liability account. Also disclosed in financial statement footnotes.
Probable	No	Disclosed in financial statement footnotes.
Reasonably Possible	Yes or No	Disclosed in financial statement footnotes.
Remote	Yes or No	Ignored.

Interpreting the meanings of the terms *probable, reasonably possible, remote*, and *subject to reasonable estimation* is the key to accounting properly for loss contingencies. Accounting standards do not provide definitive guidelines regarding how those expressions should be interpreted, and, thus, personal expertise and judgment as well as the opinion of legal counsel must be used in deciding the applicability of those terms.

Contingent liabilities, if shown on the balance sheet, may be current or long term. For example, if a lawsuit contingency has been recorded and settlement is to be made soon, the liability is current. If settlement on the lawsuit is not expected for several years, the amount is shown as a long-term liability.

LONG-TERM LIABILITIES

Long-term liabilities of a business include debts and obligations other than those classified as current. Common long-term debt items include bonds payable, notes payable due more than one year from a firm's balance sheet date, mortgages payable, and many leases. Long-term accrued liabilities include obligations created by pension and other postretirement benefit plans that many companies have established for their employees.

The types and dollar amounts of long-term liabilities reported by large corporations vary considerably from firm to firm. For example, as of August 3, 2008, Campbell Soup Company (www.campbellsoup.com) had $6.5 billion of assets and $1.6 billion of long-term liabilities. Alternatively, as of June 30, 2008, Microsoft Corporation (www.microsoft.com) had $72.8 billion of assets and $6.6 million of long-term liabilities, none of which was related to borrowings. Microsoft's long-term liabilities reflected unearned revenue, contingencies, and product warranty amounts.

Bonds Payable

A **bond** is a long-term, interest-bearing loan between parties. Bonds payable represents the total amount owed to parties who have purchased a company's bonds. Bonds are often identified by one or more distinctive features or characteristics. **Secured** (or mortgage) **bonds** are collateralized by specific assets, such as a building, of the issuing company.

Unsecured bonds, or **debentures**, are backed only by the issuing firm's legal commitment to make all required principal and interest payments.

Bonds payable are among the most common long-term liabilities of many large public companies. Bonds may be sold to finance construction of new production facilities, purchase other companies, or retire existing debt. In mid-November 2008, the dollar volume of bonds traded issues in the U.S. bond market totaled $16.9 trillion.[6] The sale of bonds by corporations is often a popular way to obtain long-term funds when interest rates are low.

Prior to selling a bond, a company prepares a **bond indenture** or legal contract that identifies the buyer's and seller's rights and obligations. A bond indenture identifies the following terms:

- The maturity date at which the bond will be repaid. The bond term reflects the time between when the bonds are first available for sale and when they mature.
- The face value or the amount the bondholder will receive when the bond matures.
- The stated (or contract) interest rate that will be paid in cash to bondholders based on the bond's face value. A $1,000 bond with a stated interest rate of 8 percent pays $80 of interest each year ($1,000 × 0.08 × 12/12). However, if the bond pays interest semiannually, the holder of a $1,000, 8% bond will receive $40 of interest (or 4%) every six months.

Bond indentures also generally include a call option and may occasionally include a convertibility option. **Callable bonds** can be retired or redeemed by the issuing company when one or more conditions are met, the most common of which is simply the passage of time. For instance, a bond issue may be callable by the issuing company at any point after the bonds have been outstanding for five years. If a bond issue is called, the bond indenture usually requires that the bondholders be paid a call premium (or an amount over face value). Bondholders may also be able to exchange **convertible bonds** for stock in the issuing company. For example, a convertible option may let bondholders exchange each $1,000 bond for 25 shares of the issuing company's common stock.

Bond Trading

A bond's initial sale is in the primary market, generally between the corporation and its investment banker or underwriting firm, such as Morgan Stanley (www.morganstanley.com) and Goldman Sachs (www2.goldmansachs.com). At this time, the corporation determines the bond's issue price and prepares journal entries related to the issuance. After the initial sale, corporate bonds trade on major securities exchanges, such as the New York Stock Exchange Euronext (www.nyse.com) and London Stock Exchange (www.londonstockexchange.com), known as secondary markets (or after markets). In the secondary market, transactions occur between the original purchaser and a new buyer. Unless repurchasing its bonds, the issuing corporation has no involvement in trading on a secondary market and therefore makes no journal entries for such trades.

---

[6]Using information from the Bond Market Association, *FINRA (Financial Industry Regulatory Authority) TRACE (Trade Reporting and Compliance Engine) Market Aggregate Information*; www.investinginbonds.com (accessed November 14, 2008).

Corporations typically issue bonds in $1,000 face value (or principal) denominations, and selling prices are quoted as a percentage of face value. For example, a $1,000 bond that is quoted at 102 is selling for 102 percent of face value, or $1,020. Most corporate bonds sell for slightly more or less than their face value; that is, the bonds generally sell at a premium or a discount from face value. Numerous factors influence the market price of a company's bonds, including the firm's financial condition, level of interest rates in the economy, length of time to maturity date, and investor preferences. Several investment advisory firms, including Moody's Investors Service (www.moodys.com) and Standard & Poor's (www.standardandpoors.com), monitor a range of bond issues and assign each a risk assessment rating.[7] Risk refers to the likelihood that a company will eventually default, or fail to make required interest or principal payments, on its bonds. As the factors affecting the default risk associated with individual bond issues change, investment advisory firms update their risk assessment ratings. A bond's market price fluctuates as investors react to changes in these factors; however, day-to-day changes in the market price of a company's bonds do not have accounting implications for that firm after the bond is initially sold.

Determining the Issue Price of Bonds

A bond's original issue price reflects a combination of all the factors mentioned previously. The relationship of the bond's stated interest rate to interest rates being paid in the market is a primary determinant of issue price. Hardin Manufacturing Company's five-year bonds with a face value of $1,000 and a stated interest rate of 10% are used as an example. If 100 bonds were sold at $1,000 each (or face value), Hardin would make the following journal entry:

General Journal				
Date	Description		Debit	Credit
XXX	Cash		100,000	
	Bonds Payable			100,000
	Recorded sale of 100, $1,000 bonds at face value			

Investors who consider buying Hardin's bonds will also consider other market investments. Suppose another five-year bond, paying an 11 percent interest rate, was available from Grosthe Company. Potential investors might consider this bond to be the better investment because the interest payment would be higher. If Hardin wants to attract investors, it could lower the bond's selling price to less than face value and, thus, sell the bond at a discount. Hardin would still have to pay 10 percent interest on each bond's $1,000 face value and pay the investor $1,000 at maturity. Hardin's entry to record the sale of all the bonds at 95 (or $950) each follows:

General Journal				
Date	Description		Debit	Credit
XXX	Cash		95,000	
	Discount on Bonds Payable		5,000	
	Bonds Payable			100,000
	Recorded sale of 100, $1,000 bonds at a $50 discount per bond			

---

[7]Moody's ratings and analysis track debt covering more than 12,000 corporate issuers. S&P provides credit ratings on approximately US$32 trillion of debt in more than 100 countries.

Alternatively, suppose the only alternative to Hardin's bonds were 9 percent bonds being issued by Trevor Inc. In this case, investors might be anxious to purchase Hardin's bonds. Because there is only a limited supply ($100,000) of Hardin's bonds, investors will attempt to acquire Hardin's bonds by bidding up the price to 104. Thus, Hardin is able to sell the bonds for a premium or more than face value. Hardin would only have to pay the stated 10 percent interest on the each $1,000 bond's face value and pay the investor $1,000 at maturity. Hardin's entry to record the sale of all of the bonds for $1,040 each is as follows.

General Journal				
Date	Description		Debit	Credit
XXX	Cash		104,000	
	Bonds Payable			100,000
	Premium on Bonds Payable			4,000
	Recorded sale of 100, $1,000 bonds at $40			
	premium per bond			

The actual issue price of a bond is a complex determination. A detailed discussion of this process is given in the chapter appendix. The appendix also includes a discussion of accounting for interest payments and how to amortize (write off) bond discounts and premiums. Discounts and premiums must be amortized over the life of the bonds to properly reflect the true interest rate that the company pays on the bonds. If a bond sells at a discount, the true (or effective) rate of interest is more than the stated rate; if a bond sells at a premium, the true rate of interest is less than the stated rate.

A company may decide to retire bonds before the maturity date. In doing so, the company will generally experience a gain or loss on the retirement. Assume that Hardin Manufacturing decided to retire its $100,000 bonds three years after issuance. At that time, because of amortization, the remaining premium related to these bonds was $1,600 in the accounting records. Hardin paid $100,700 to buy the bonds in the market and makes the following entry:

General Journal				
Date	Description		Debit	Credit
XXX	Bonds Payable		100,000	
	Premium on Bonds Payable		1,600	
	Cash			100,700
	Gain on Bond Retirement			900
	Recorded retirement of bonds payable and the			
	related gain			

Long-Term Liabilities Other Than Bonds

Many accounting issues presented by bonds payable are relevant to other long-term liabilities. Thus, long-term liabilities such as long-term mortgages payable, long-term lease obligations, pension liabilities, and other postretirement benefit liabilities are only briefly addressed.

Long-Term Mortgages Payable

Many long-term notes payable are actually mortgage notes payable, also commonly referred to as "mortgages payable." A company borrowing $10 million to purchase a new building may be required by the lender to sign a mortgage note that pledges the building as collateral, or security, for the loan. If the company defaults on the mortgage note, the lender can obtain legal title to the building or force the sale of the building to satisfy the unpaid balance of the mortgage. Mortgages payable usually require equal monthly payments consisting of both principal and interest. The portion of any mortgage payable that becomes due in the upcoming year is shown as a current liability in the balance sheet.

Long-Term Lease Obligations

A **leasehold** is a legal right to use a leased asset for a specified period, subject to any restrictions in the lease agreement. The two parties to a lease agreement are the lessor (the owner of the asset being leased) and the lessee (the party leasing the asset).

Accounting standards distinguish between operating leases and capital leases. An **operating lease** is cancelable by the lessee, has a relatively short term, and does not transfer ownership rights or risks to the lessee. A **capital lease** is noncancelable, is long term, and transfers at least some ownership rights or risks to the lessee. Capital leases are a very popular method for businesses to finance the acquisition of a wide range of assets, including buildings, equipment, and automobile or airplane fleets. For instance, United Air Lines Inc. (www.ual.com) reported $1.2 billion of capital lease obligations on its December 31, 2008, balance sheet.

In the United States, noncancelable leases that meet at least *one* of the following criteria qualify as capital leases, whereas all other leases are classified as operating leases.

1. The lease agreement transfers legal title of the leased asset to the lessee at the end of the lease term.

2. The lease agreement includes a "bargain purchase option" that allows the lessee to buy the asset for significantly less than fair market value.

3. The lease term is 75 percent or more of the economic life of the leased asset.

4. The present value of the lease payments equals 90 percent or more of the market value of the leased asset or, put more simply, the total lease payments approximate the purchase cost.

Under International Financial Reporting Standards, determination of whether a lease is an operating or a capital lease depends on the "substance" of the transaction. Examples are provided under IFRS, but no specific criteria are given.

When a company engages in a capital lease, both the leased asset and long-term lease liability are reported in the company's balance sheet. This accounting treatment is justified because the lease, in essence, is equivalent to an asset purchase using debt funds. Like other liabilities, a long-term capital lease obligation must be separated into its current and long-term portions for balance sheet purposes. Additionally, for both operating and capital leases, lessees must disclose in their financial statements future minimum lease payments over the next five years.

Postretirement Benefit Liabilities

Many companies have established pension plans to provide retirement income for their employees, and most of these plans require joint periodic contributions by both the employer and the employee. Under the most common type of pension plan, the contri- butions are some stated percentage of each employee's gross earnings. For the employer's contribution, the journal entry is a debit to Pension Expense and a credit to Cash or to a payable account when the full amounts owed are not funded immediately. Employees' contributions reduce their net pay and are placed in a liability account until deposited with the pension fund manager.

An individual pension account is established for each employee. Following retirement, employees receive a monthly, quarterly, or annual benefit based on the size of their individual pension accounts. In this situation, the input (contribution) to the plan is known, but the output (benefit) to the employee depends on how well the contributions are managed and on general economic conditions. By November 2008, the economic crisis had made a severe impact on the average worker's retirement accounts, dropping them between 21 and 27 percent, depending on the how old the workers were and how long they had been with their employers.[8] Worldwide, the crisis reduced retirement funds by $4 trillion, according to an estimate from the Organization for Economic Co-operation and Development.[9]

Assume that Paulette Dierk will retire at the end of 2015, at which time she will have been with RightWay Corp. for 10 years. At the end of each year, Dierk and RightWay each make a $1,000 deposit to her pension plan. These funds are generally invested in stocks or bonds of RightWay or other companies. There is no way to know how much of the $20,000 pension deposits will be in Dierk's account when she retires. If the investment does well, Dierk's pension fund will increase. If the investment does poorly, the fund could decline dramatically.

The actual computations for necessary pension contributions are extremely complex, in part because of the large number of years and employees involved. The calculations require use of time value of money concepts, which are discussed in the appendix to this chapter. Additionally, companies generally employ an actuary, who specializes in the mathematics of risk, especially as it relates to insurance and pension calculations, to help determine pension plan benefit estimates.[10]

Many businesses also provide employees with postretirement benefits other than pensions. The most common type of such benefits is health care. Similar to pension benefits, these benefits generally create long-term liabilities. Postretirement benefit liabilities are often enormous and have dramatically affected the reported financial condition of many large companies. For example, General Motors' (www.gm.com) 2008 10-K showed a $28.9 billion expense for other postretirement employee benefits—a significant decrease from the $47 billion in 2007 because of negotiations with unions and employees.[11]

ACCOUNTING INFORMATION FOR DECISION MAKING

Decision makers need information concerning all of an entity's long-term obligations and valuation methods as well as disclosure of any unusual and material circumstances involving long-term liabilities.

---

[8] Jim Puzzanghera, "Calls Grow to Overhaul 401(k) Retirement Plans," *LA Times* (November 16, 2008); http://www.latimes.com/business/la-fi-retire16-2008nov16,0,2937536.story (accessed November 16, 2008).

[9] Drew Carter, "OECD: $4 Trillion Lost by Pension Funds," *Pension and Investments Online* (November 13, 2008); http://www.pionline.com/apps/pbcs.dll/article?AID = /20081113/DAILY/811139993 (accessed November 16, 2008).

[10] Additional information on the term *actuary* and other terms can be found at www.investorwords.com.

[11] General Motors, *2008 10-K*, pp. 140 and 183.

Completeness

Investors, creditors, and other decision makers rely on businesses to provide comprehensive disclosure of their liabilities. Decision makers must have confidence that a company's balance sheet reflects all the firm's outstanding, or unpaid, liabilities. To illustrate, in 2000, Hilton Hotels Corporation (www.hilton.com) borrowed $500 million for ten years at 7.95 percent; five of the company's hotels were used as collateral for that agreement, and that information was disclosed in the company's 10-K. This information was significant because in 2003, a diminished cash flow from the properties created restrictions on the company's ability to use cash.

However, some businesses do not include certain long-term obligations in their periodic financial statements. Such "**off-balance sheet financing**" involves obtaining assets or services by incurring long-term obligations that are not reported in an entity's balance sheet. For example, certain long-term leases qualify as off-balance sheet financing arrangements. Fortunately, the accounting profession has taken steps in recent years to reduce the number of off-balance sheet long-term obligations, and the disclosures related to these items have increased.

Valuation Methods

Financial statement users need to be aware of the methods businesses use to assign dollar amounts to individual current liabilities. The reported values of most current liabilities, such as accounts payable, are equal to the amount of cash that must be paid when those liabilities become due. Occasionally, however, businesses eliminate their current liabilities (often unearned revenue items) through the delivery of goods or services. In regard to estimated liabilities, adequate disclosures should be provided in financial statement footnotes to help decision makers assess whether the estimates are valid.

Proper valuation is a concern to decision makers for most financial statement items. Valuation issues are particularly important for long-term liabilities that must be estimated using time value of money concepts. For example, companies with certain types of retirement plans annually face complex computations in determining long-term obligations. Projections must be made about employees' future salaries and rates of return on investments. A company wanting to minimize its obligations might intentionally underestimate future employee pay raises or overestimate the rate of return expected from investments. To guard against these possibilities, businesses must disclose key assumptions underlying their pension or other postretirement benefit expense and liability computations. Comparable financial statement disclosures are required for other estimated, long-term liabilities.

Unusual Circumstances

Unusual and significant circumstances that affect a major account balance should be disclosed in a firm's financial statements. An example of such a circumstance is an inability, or potential inability, by a company to pay its current liabilities as they become due. To illustrate, the 2007 10-K of Linens 'N Things Inc. indicated that if the company defaulted on its credit agreements, there was no assurance that they would have "sufficient assets to pay the amounts due."[12] This warning was extremely important, as LNT filed for bankruptcy in May 2008.

Long-term debt agreements often include restrictive debt covenants or conditions. Violations of these covenants may cause the entire amount of the long-term debt to become immediately due. Any covenants affecting a company's future operations should be disclosed in the financial statement footnotes. Two of the most common debt covenants are a limitation on the payment of dividends and the maintenance of certain financial statement ratios. For instance, Host Hotels & Resorts, Inc. (www.hostmarriott.com) is restricted in the payment of dividends only if the company meets specified ratios relative to debt (less than 65 percent of total assets) and to interest coverage.[13] When a company violates a restrictive debt covenant, or faces a high risk of doing so, external decision makers should be informed.

Analyzing Liabilities

Liquidity refers to a business's ability to finance its day-to-day operations and to pay its liabilities as they become due. One measure of liquidity, the quick ratio, was discussed in Chapter 4. Another widely used measure of liquidity is the **current ratio**, which expresses the relationship between a business's current assets and current liabilities at a given time.

$$\text{Current Ratio} = \text{Current Assets} \div \text{Current Liabilities}$$

Because a company should have more current assets than current liabilities, the current ratio should be greater than one. Although current ratios vary considerably from industry to industry, a common current ratio benchmark is at least 2:1.

Another financial measure of liquidity in which current liabilities are a prominent component is **working capital**, which is the difference between an entity's current assets and current liabilities.

$$\text{Working Capital} = \text{Current Assets} - \text{Current Liabilities}$$

A company that has a minimal amount of working capital or, worse yet, a negative working capital generally faces a high risk of defaulting on its current liabilities as they come due. Larger current ratios, quick ratios, and amounts of working capital are generally better than small ones. However, when current assets far exceed current liabilities, the company may have missed an opportunity for investments or may be experiencing other asset-management problems.

External decision makers also monitor a firm's long-term liabilities and related financial data to gain insight on whether the firm can pay off those liabilities as they become due, a condition known as solvency. The most basic solvency ratio is the **debt to total asset ratio**, which is computed by the following formula.

$$\text{Debt to Total Asset Ratio} = \text{Total Liabilities} \div \text{Total Assets}$$

Smaller values of this ratio indicate that a company is better able to meet its obligations in the long-term.

---

[12]Linens 'N Things, *2007 10-K*, p. 21.
[13]Host Hotels & Resorts, *2007 10-K*, p. 57.

A company that makes extensive use of long-term debt to meet its financing needs is said to be highly leveraged. Such companies generally face more risk of financially failing than firms that have little or no long-term debt on their balance sheets. Decision makers commonly use the **long-term debt to equity ratio** to measure financial leverage:

$$\text{Long-term Debt to Equity Ratio} = \text{Long-term Debt} \div \text{Stockholders' Equity}$$

As this ratio increases, a company is perceived as being more risky, and it will probably have to pay higher interest rates for borrowings. Exhibit 7-3 shows the current and long-term debt to equity ratios for several companies in different industries and the related industry averages.

The **times interest earned ratio** helps decision makers evaluate the ability of companies, particularly highly leveraged companies, to make interest payments on long-term debt as they become due. This ratio is calculated as:

$$\text{Times Interest Earned Ratio} = (\text{Net Income} + \text{Interest Expense} + \text{Income Tax Expense}) \div \text{Interest Expense}$$

This ratio indicates the number of times that profits earned before deducting interest expense and income tax expense "cover" a company's interest expense during a given period. The lower this ratio, the more risk a company generally faces of defaulting on interest payments on its long-term debt. As is true for most financial ratios, there is not complete agreement on what represents a reasonable level for the times interest earned ratio. Typically, this ratio is considered "comfortable" when it is 4.0 and higher.

SUMMARY

Current liabilities are obligations that must be paid, or otherwise extinguished, by a business within one year or its operating cycle, whichever is longer. The most common types of current liabilities are accounts and notes payable, accrued liabilities, deferred revenues, and the current portion of long-term debt.

A contingent liability has the potential to become an actual liability if a particular event occurs or fails to occur. Contingent liabilities that are probable and subject to reasonable estimation must be recorded by journal entries. Contingent liabilities not meeting these two criteria are generally disclosed in a firm's financial statement footnotes.

Long-term liabilities are debts and obligations other than those classified as current. The more common long-term liabilities are bonds payable, capital lease obligations, and

EXHIBIT 7-3

Some Current Ratios and LT Debt to Equity Ratios

	Best Buy	**RadioShack**	**Industry Average**
Current Ratio	1.44	2.09	1.45
LT Debt to SE	8.64	45.24	22.79

	Blockbuster	**Netflix**	**Industry Average**
Current Ratio	1.02	1.96	1.77
LT Debt to SE	51.74	0.00	6.40

	Verizon Communications	**AT&T**	**Industry Average**
Current Ratio	0.76	0.63	0.75
LT Debt to SE	25.39	33.17	47.60

debts associated with employee pension or health benefit plans. Newly issued bonds payable usually sell for more or less than their face value because their stated interest rate is either higher or lower than the market interest rate on the date they are sold. A capital lease (as compared to an operating lease) is noncancelable and meets one of four established criteria. Such leases and the assets to which they relate are recorded, respectively, as long-term debt and property, plant, and equipment.

Decision makers need to be assured that a business has recorded and, when necessary, made reasonable estimates of all liabilities in its financial statements. Any unusual and material circumstances related to a firm's liabilities, such as potential violations of restrictive debt covenants, also need to be disclosed.

Decision makers use the current ratio (current assets divided by current liabilities) to evaluate a business's liquidity. Working capital (current assets minus current liabilities) is also a good measure of liquidity. When analyzing long-term liabilities, decision makers typically focus on the firm's degree of financial leverage and its ability to make periodic interest payments on long-term debt. A common measure of financial leverage is the long-term debt to equity ratio. A firm's ability to make periodic interest payments on long-term debt is commonly evaluated by referring to its times interest earned ratio.

APPENDIX: ACCOUNTING FOR BONDS

As mentioned in the chapter, the relationship between stated and market interest rates is a major determinant of bond issue price. The following example illustrates the accounting for $100,000 of Hardin Company bonds. The bonds have a 10 percent stated interest rate, with interest being paid semiannually on September 30 and March 31. On each interest payment date, Hardin will pay $5,000 ($100,000 × 0.10 × 6/12) of interest to bondholders. The bonds have a five-year term that runs from April 1, 2009, through April 1, 2014. Hardin has a calendar year-end.

On April 1, 2009, when the market interest rate is 11 percent, Hardin sells its bonds. The market interest rate is also known as the **effective interest rate** and refers to the annual rate of return that investors can earn by purchasing any of a number of different corporate bonds that pose the same general level of default risk. The market interest rate represents the "yield to maturity" for a given bond. That yield reflects the actual interest rate that will be earned after considering both the bond interest paid in cash each year and the impact of any bond discount or premium over the bond's life.

Companies try to set a stated bond interest rate that approximates the market interest rate. However, several weeks or months may pass from the time a decision to issue a bond is made until the actual sale of the bond. Thus, the stated interest rate can be quite different from the market interest rate when the bonds are actually sold. If, at the date of the sale, the stated interest rate is equal to the market interest rate, the bonds would sell at face value.[14]

---

[14]This statement is proved as follows, using present value amounts for a 10% in the appendix at the end of the text, semiannual interest payments for five years (or factors in the present value tables for 5% and 10 periods):

PV of principal	($100,000 × 0.6139)	$61,390
PV of interest	($5,000 × 7.7217)	38,609
PV of bond (off due to rounding of the PV factors)		$99,999

If a bond is sold at face value, interest expense each period will be equal to the cash interest paid.

In the case of Hardin's bonds, however, the market interest rate is 12 percent at the issue date, and Hardin's bonds only pay 10 percent. Therefore, the bonds will sell for less than their face value, or at a discount that will be sufficiently large to allow the purchasers of Hardin's bonds to effectively earn a 12 percent yield to maturity on their investment.

To determine the selling price of Hardin's bonds, the **time value of money concept** must be applied. The concept reflects the fact that a dollar received (or paid) currently is worth more than dollar received (or paid) in the future because the current dollar can be invested to earn interest and, thus, will be larger in the future than it is now. The two key variables in a time value of money problem are the number of time periods and the effective interest rate. Because bonds will pay periodic interest in the future and their principal will be repaid in the future, these two future cash amounts can be discounted to their **present value** (worth at the current time) using the market interest rate. **Discounting** refers to the process of removing interest from future receipts (payments).

The bonds' selling price will be the present value of Hardin's future cash payments over the bonds' five-year term. The cash payments consist of ten $5,000 semiannual interest payments and a $100,000 principal payment at the end of the bond term. There are ten time periods because there are two semiannual interest periods in each year of the bond's five-year life. The 12 percent market interest rate is divided by two to reflect the two semiannual interest periods; thus, the effective interest rate is 6 percent. The key point to remember is that the market interest rate, not the stated interest rate, determines the present value of the future cash outflows related to a bond issue.

Using the present value of $1 table in the appendix at the end of the text, the factor for ten periods and a 6 percent interest rate is found to be 0.5684. Using the present value of an annuity of 1, the factor for ten periods and a 6 percent interest rate is 7.3601. (An **annuity** is a series of payments of a specified size and frequency.) These factors are multiplied, respectively, by the bond principal and interest amounts as follows.

PV of principal	($100,000 × 0.5684)	$56,840
PV of interest	($5,000 × 7.3601)	36,801
PV of principal and interest		$93,641

This computation indicates that, if $56,840 were put in a bank that paid 12 percent interest compounded semiannually, at the end of five years (ten interest periods), the balance in the bank would be $100,000. Thus, the present value of the principal amount is $56,840. If $36,801 were put in a bank that paid 12 percent interest semiannually, one could withdraw $5,000 every six months for five years, and at the end of that period, the balance in the bank would be zero. Thus, the present value of the $5,000 of semiannual interest payments for five years is $36,801. The total of the two cash flows from the bonds is $93,641, which reflects the bonds' selling price. Regardless of the selling price, Hardin must pay the bondholders $100,000 at the bonds' maturity date. In essence, Hardin is being penalized for selling bonds with a stated interest rate that is less than the market interest rate. The discount on the bonds allows the initial purchasers to earn a yield to maturity of exactly 12 percent, the market interest rate on the date the bonds are sold.

Accounting for Bonds Issued at a Discount

Hardin's $100,000 bond issue is used to illustrate the accounting for bonds that are issued at a discount. Journal entries related to the transaction are shown in Exhibit 7A-1 and are discussed in the following information.

EXHIBIT 7A-1

Journal Entries for a
Bond Issued at a
Discount

		General Journal		
Date		Description	Debit	Credit
2009				
Apr	1	Cash	93,641	
		Discount on Bonds Payable	6,359	
		Bonds Payable		100,000
		To record issuance of $100,000, 10%, 5-year		
		bonds at a market rate of 12%		
Sept	30	Interest Expense	5,636	
		Cash		5,000
		Discount on Bonds Payable		636
		To record payment of semiannual interest and		
		amortization of bond discount		
Dec	31	Interest Expense	2,818	
		Interest Payable		2,500
		Discount on Bonds Payable		318
		To record accrual of 3 months of interest and		
		amortization of bond discount		
2010				
Mar	31	Interest Expense	2,818	
		Interest Payable	2,500	
		Cash		5,000
		Discount on Bonds Payable		318
		To record payment of semiannual interest and		
		amortization of bond discount		

On April 1, 2009, the bonds are sold for $93,641. The bond liability is recorded at the principal amount of $100,000, but only $93,641 is received in cash. The $6,359 difference is recorded in a discount on the bonds payable account, which is a contra-liability account. If a balance sheet were prepared at this time, Hardin Company would report the bonds payable at a net carrying value of $93,641, or the difference between their $100,000 face value and the $6,359 balance of the bond discount account.

The semiannual interest payment dates for Hardin's bonds are March 31 and September 30. On September 30, 2009, cash interest of $5,000 is paid to bondholders. However, when bonds are sold at a discount, the interest expense recorded each interest payment date is greater than the amount of cash interest that is paid. The $6,359 discount is essentially additional interest expense on the bonds over their five-year term. The matching principle requires this additional interest expense to be recognized over the bonds' life, rather than when the principal is repaid. The Discount on Bonds Payable will be amortized, or written off, each interest period as an adjustment to interest expense using the straight-line method of amortization.[15]

Under the straight-line method, an equal amount of bond discount is amortized each interest payment period. The $6,359 discount is divided by the ten semiannual interest periods, resulting in an amortization amount of $636 each period. (The small rounding

[15] An alternative method, the effective interest method, should be used to amortize discounts (and premiums) when principal amounts are large and time to maturity is long.

error would be corrected during the final interest payment period.) Thus, total interest expense for the first interest period is the $5,000 cash payment plus the $636 discount amortization.

On December 31, an adjusting entry is necessary to recognize interest expense for the three-month period October 1 through December 31. The accrued interest amount is $2,500 ($100,000 × 0.10 × 3/12). The discount must also be amortized at this time. The six-month amortization was $636; thus, three months of amortization would be half that amount, or $318. Interest expense for the three months is $2,818, or the sum of interest payable and discount amortization.

The next interest payment date is March 31, 2010. At that time, cash interest of $5,000 is paid to the bondholders. The discount on bonds payable is amortized at $318 for the other half of the six-month period. Interest expense is $2,818 ($2,500 + $318). The interest payable accrued at December 31, 2009, is paid on March 31, 2010.

As the bond discount is amortized, the bonds' carrying value gradually increases. After the last interest payment on March 31, 2014, Hardin's bond discount account would be zero, and the carrying value of the bonds would be $100,000. The journal entry on April 1, 2014, would include a debit of $100,000 to Bonds Payable with an offsetting credit in the same amount to Cash.

Accounting for Bonds Issued at a Premium

To illustrate the journal entries for a bond selling at a premium, assume that on April 1, 2009, when Hardin sold its bonds, the market rate of interest was 8 percent. When the stated interest rate is higher than the market interest rate on the date the bonds are sold, bonds will sell at a premium. To determine the selling price, the semiannual market interest rate of 4 percent is used to discount the bond principal and interest to their present values, given ten interest periods as follows.

PV of principal	($100,000 × 0.6756)	$ 67,560
PV of interest	($5,000 × 8.1109)	40,555
PV of principal and interest		$108,115

Although Hardin sells the bonds for $108,115, the company will be required to pay its bondholders only $100,000 at maturity. A bond premium compensates the company for paying a higher interest rate on its bonds than is available in the market. Bonds sold at a premium are reported on a company's balance sheet at their net carrying value, which is the face value plus the credit balance of Premium on Bonds Payable. Premium on Bonds Payable is not a contra-liability because it has the same type of balance as its related account, Bonds Payable.

Like bond discounts, bond premiums are amortized over the bond term. Premium amortization reduces the interest expense recorded each accounting period. Using straight-line amortization, $812 ($8,115 ÷ 10) of premium is amortized each semiannual interest period.

As the bond premium is amortized, the carrying value gradually decreases. After the interest payment on March 31, 2014, the bond premium account will have a zero balance, and the carrying value of the bonds payable will be $100,000. The journal entry to record the payment to the bondholders on April 1, 2014, will include a debit of $100,000 to Bonds Payable and a credit to Cash. Exhibit 7A-2 provides the entries from the date of sale through the second interest period for Hardin's bonds when issued at a premium.

EXHIBIT 7A-2

Journal Entries for a
Bond Issued at a
Premium

General Journal				
Date		Description	Debit	Credit
2009 Apr	1	Cash	108,115	
		Bonds Payable		100,000
		Premium on Bonds Payable		8,115
		To record issuance of $100,000, 10%, 5-year bonds at a market rate of 9%		
Sept	30	Interest Expense	4,188	
		Premium on Bonds Payable	812	
		Cash		5,000
		To record payment of semiannual interest and amortization of bond premium		
Dec	31	Interest Expense	2,094	
		Premium on Bonds Payable	406	
		Interest Payable		2,500
		To record accrual of 3 months of interest and amortization of bond premium		
2010 Mar	31	Interest Expense	2,094	
		Interest Payable	2,500	
		Premium on Bonds Payable	406	
		Cash		5,000
		To record payment of semiannual interest and amortization of bond premium		

Visual Recap 7.2 provides a summary of the relationships involved in accounting for bonds payable.

VISUAL RECAP 7.2

Effect of Market Interest Rate on Bond Accounting

	Stated Rate = Market Rate	Stated Rate < Market Rate	Stated Rate > Market Rate
Bond Selling Price	Face Value	Discount (<Face Value)	Premium (>Face Value)
Interest Expense	= Interest Paid	> Interest Paid (Difference equal to amortization of bond discount)	< Interest Paid (Difference equal to amortization of bond premium)
Carrying Value of Bond	= Face Value	Carrying value increases to face value over time as discount is amortized	Carrying value decreases to face value over time as premium is amortized

KEY TERMS

annuity	discounting	payee
bond	effective interest rate	present value
bond indenture	leasehold	principal
callable bond	long-term debt to equity ratio	secured bond
capital lease	maker	stated interest rate
contingent liability	maturity date	term of a note
convertible bond	maturity value	times interest earned ratio
current ratio	note payable	time value of money concept
debenture	off-balance sheet financing	working capital
debt to total asset ratio	operating lease	

QUESTIONS

1. Define (a) liabilities, (b) current liabilities, and (c) long-term liabilities. List several examples of (b) and (c). *(LO 7.1 and 7.5)*

2. What is the difference between an account payable and a note payable? When is a note payable more likely to be used than an account payable? *(LO 7.1)*

3. Define "accrued liability" and list four examples. *(LO 7.1)*

4. Select two large companies that are likely to have product warranty liability included in their balance sheets. Go to their Web sites and access their financial statements and related footnotes. Does the expected liability appear? Is it disclosed in the footnotes? If nothing about the liability is provided, discuss your thoughts on why such a presentation is, or is not, appropriate. *(LO 7.1)*

5. What amounts do employers commonly deduct from employees' paychecks? To whom are these deductions remitted? *(LO 7.1)*

6. What is meant by the term *contingent liability*? What conditions must exist for a contingent liability to be journalized by a company? If you were an attorney asked to advise a client company about whether to journalize the potential financial implications of a lawsuit filed in a class action suit, what would your advice be? *(LO 7.2)*

7. What is a bond issue? What is the advantage to a corporation of including a call option in a bond indenture? *(LO 7.3)*

8. What are the advantages of leasing rather than purchasing an asset? What are the advantages of purchasing rather than leasing an asset? *(LO 7.4)*

9. List the distinguishing characteristics of a capital lease. What is the difference between the accounting procedures for operating and capital leases? *(LO 7.4)*

10. In contrast to the defined contribution plans discussed in the chapter, some companies had offered defined benefit pension plans. Use the Web to determine what is meant by a defined benefit plan. Why would a company prefer to offer a defined contribution plan rather than a defined benefit plan? Which type of plan would an employee prefer to have and why? *(LO 7.5)*

11. What key information needs do decision makers have regarding current liabilities and long-term liabilities? *(LO 7.6)*

12. How are the current ratio and working capital calculated? What information is provided by, and how do decision makers typically use, these ratios? *(LO 7.7)*

13. (Appendix) How does the amortization of a bond discount or premium affect bond interest expense but not the amount of bond interest paid by the issuing company? *(LO 7.8)*

EXERCISES

14. **True or False** *(all LOs)*

    Following are a series of statements regarding topics discussed in this chapter.

    Required:
    Indicate whether each statement is true (T) or false (F).

    (a) Current liabilities must be paid by a business within one year or its operating cycle, whichever is shorter.

    (b) A note payable is an obligation documented by a legally binding written commitment.

(c) A deferred liability is created when a customer requests a product or service but will not pay for it until the product or service is complete.

(d) Product warranty liability and vacation pay liability are examples of accrued liabilities.

(e) A loss contingency that has a possible chance of resulting in an actual loss and that can be reasonably estimated in amount should be accrued in a company's financial statement footnotes.

(f) Because the liability is already recorded, no journal entries are needed when a long-term debt becomes due within one year.

(g) Specific assets of the issuing company are used as collateral for secured bonds.

(h) When a business leases an asset under conditions that are comparable to purchasing that asset with borrowed funds, both the leased asset and the long-term lease obligation must be reported on the firm's balance sheet.

(i) A common restrictive debt covenant is a limitation on the payment of dividends.

(j) Financial decision makers are unconcerned about operating leases because those leases will not affect the company's ability to pay its debts.

(k) A common measure of financial leverage is the current ratio.

(l) Defined contribution pension plans specify the amounts to be paid to employees after retirement.

(m) A bond indenture is an unsecured liability of a company.

15. Liability Classification *(LO 7.1 and 7.6)*

Hamilton's Bakery borrowed $50,000 on January 1, 2009. The bakery is required to repay $5,000 of the loan principal on December 31 of each year beginning in 2009 plus an amount equal to 10 percent interest rate on the unpaid principal.

Required:

(a) How will this debt be reported in Hamilton's December 31, 2010, balance sheet? How much interest expense related to this debt will be reported in Hamilton's income statement for the year ended December 31, 2010?

(b) How will this debt be reported in Hamilton's December 31, 2011, balance sheet?

(c) If Hamilton's fails to classify any portion of the loan as a current liability in its December 31, 2011, balance sheet, how might decision makers' analysis of the company's financial statements be affected? Explain.

16. Liabilities n the Balance Sheet *(LO 7.1)*

The liabilities of Weist Co. are listed.

- Accounts Payable, $586,000
- Accrued Expenses, $178,000
- Bonds Payable (due in six years), $800,000
- Income Taxes Payable, $132,000
- Notes Payable: $78,000 is due within 12 months; $80,000 is due $10,000 per year for the next eight years.
- Salaries Payable, $195,000
- Accrued Vacation Pay, $208,000
- Employee Federal Income Tax Withholdings, $42,000

Required:

Prepare the liabilities section of the balance sheet for Weist Co.

17. Accounting for Current Liabilities *(LO 7.1, writing)*

FreeWheelers is a bike shop located near the campus of Alabama State University. The shop rents bikes on a nine-month basis. When a bike is rented, the student pays a security deposit equal to 50 percent of the bike's value. Typically, a bike is returned damaged in some way, causing some portion of the security deposit to be forfeited. Should damage to the bike be so excessive as to eliminate the security deposit, students are required to pay the difference in cash. When a security deposit is received, the company's bookkeeper debits Cash and credits Miscellaneous Revenue. If a bike is returned damaged, the bookkeeper debits Repairs Expense and credits Cash (or Inventory, if parts are used to repair the bike). Any portion of the deposit that is not required to repair the bike is returned to the student. Deposit amounts returned to students are recorded with a debit to Miscellaneous Expense and a credit to Cash.

Required:

Write a brief memo to FreeWheelers' bookkeeper regarding the accounting treatment given security deposits on bike rentals. Explain why the current accounting treatment is incorrect and how it may introduce errors into the business's financial statements. Also recommend a more appropriate method of accounting for security deposits.

18. Notes Payable *(LO 7.1)*

Three notes payable are listed. Each note requires that the principal and all the interest will be repaid on the maturity date. All companies have a December 31 fiscal year end.

- On January 1, 2009, Alpha, Inc. borrowed $3,600 on a six-month, 10% note.

■ On March 31, 2009, Beta Co. borrowed $12,000 on a one-year, 12% note.

■ On August 1, 2009, Gamma Industries borrowed $3,000 on a two-year, 9% note.

■ On November 30, 2009, Sigma, Inc. borrowed $2,000 on a 90-day note, 7% note.

Required:

(a) For each note, determine the following:

(1) Maturity date

(2) Maturity value

(3) Interest accrued on December 31, 2009

(4) Interest accrued on December 31, 2010

(b) Which notes will be listed on the 2009 balance sheet as

(1) current liabilities?

(2) long-term liabilities?

19. **Installment Notes Payable** *(LO 7.1)*

You are planning to purchase a new car as your graduation present to yourself. The car you want can be purchased for $26,500 plus tax, title, and license, which will total $2,500. You plan to finance the car over five years. Use a loan calculator to determine your car payments under the following assumptions.

Required:

(a) You make a $2,500 down payment and can obtain a loan rate for the balance at

(1) 4.5 percent.

(2) 5.0 percent.

(3) 6.0 percent.

(b) You make a $5,000 down payment and can obtain a loan rate for the balance at

(1) 4.5 percent.

(2) 5.0 percent.

(3) 6.0 percent.

20. **Payroll Accounting** *(LO 7.1)*

McGlaun Company pays its employees every two weeks. The firm last paid its employees on September 20. For the last ten days of the fiscal year ending September 30, company employees earned gross salaries of $16,400. Following is a list of employee payroll deductions for the period September 21 to 30:

Employee Payroll Deductions	
FICA Taxes	$ 827
Federal Income Taxes	2,910
State Income Taxes	416
Health Insurance Premiums	485

Required:

(a) Prepare the adjusting journal entry required on September 30 related to employee salaries and payroll deductions.

(b) What payroll-related expenses do businesses incur besides employee wages and salaries?

(c) If a person works as an "independent contractor," employers are not required to deduct income taxes from wages. If you had your choice, would you prefer to work for a company that did or did not deduct income taxes from periodic paychecks? Explain the reasons for your answer.

21. **Recording Warranty Expense** *(LO 7.1)*

Vacuum cleaners sold by Orackle carry a one-year warranty on parts and labor. However, the company expects very few warranty claims. Last year, the company sold 500 vacuum cleaners and made warranty repairs on ten vacuums at a total cost of approximately $300.

Required:

(a) If Orackle does not record a product warranty liability at the end of each fiscal year, how will the business's financial statements be affected? What accounting concepts or principles will be violated?

(b) Under what condition or conditions could Orackle reasonably argue that no product warranty liability needs to be recorded at year-end?

(c) Would the argument you made in part (b) be appropriate for General Motors? Why or why not?

22. **Accounting for Contingent Liabilities** *(LO 7.2)*

Cruisin', Inc. manufactures and sells two-person snow tubes. Periodically, the company is sued because someone using this product is injured. Cruisin' is currently the defendant in one such lawsuit. Damages requested by the plaintiff in this lawsuit total $2,400,000. The company's net income for its fiscal year just ended was $460,000, and year-end total assets were $1,232,000.

Required:

(a) What factors should Cruisin' consider in determining the accounting and financial statement treatment of this lawsuit?

(b) In reference to the pending lawsuit against Cruisin', identify the conditions under which:

(1) Cruisin' would record an expense and a liability in its accounting records.

(2) Cruisin' would disclose the lawsuit in the footnotes to its financial statements.

(3) Cruisin' would ignore the lawsuit for accounting and financial reporting purposes.

23. **Accounting for Contingent Liabilities** *(LO 7.2)*

    In 2007, there were a number of product recalls related to toys and pet foods. Some of these recalls resulted in lawsuits being filed against the companies involved. Use the Web to find three companies that have been sued over either toy recalls or pet food recalls. Go to the 10-K of those companies to find any information contained therein about the product recall lawsuits. Were the lawsuits recorded or merely disclosed? Indicate why the accounting treatment was used by the company.

24. **Bond Terminology** *(LO 7.3)*

    Following are definitions or descriptions of terms relating to corporate bonds.

    (1) The legal contract between a bond purchaser and the issuing company.

    (2) A bond backed only by the legal commitment of the issuing company to make all required principal and interest payments.

    (3) The repayment point for the bond principal.

    (4) A bond collateralized by specific assets of the issuing company.

    (5) A bond that may be exchanged for stock in the issuing company.

    (6) The typical amount for corporate bonds is $1,000.

    (7) The period between the date bonds are first available for sale and the date they must be paid.

    (8) A long-term loan made by one party to another.

    (9) The rate of interest to be paid to bondholders based on the bonds' legal agreement.

    (10) A bond that can be retired at the company's option.

    Required:

    Match each definition or description listed with the appropriate term from the following list.

    (a) Bond

    (b) Face value

    (c) Maturity date

    (d) Bond indenture

    (e) Stated interest rate

    (f) Bond term

    (g) Callable bond

    (h) Secured bond

    (i) Convertible bond

    (j) Debenture

25. **Stated Interest Rate and the Market Interest Rate** *(LO 7.3)*

    A $1,000 corporate bond has a stated interest rate of 8 percent. Interest on the bond is paid semiannually.

    Required:

    (a) How much interest will be paid on each interest payment date?

    (b) Suppose this bond was sold when the quoted market price was 98. How much did the company receive for the bond? If a bond is sold for more or less than its face value of a bond, will the amount of interest the company must pay each semiannual period be affected? Explain.

    (c) If this bond was sold at a quoted market price of 98, was the market interest rate on the purchase date higher or lower than the bond's stated interest rate? Explain.

    (d) How much will the purchaser of this bond receive on the maturity day as repayment of his or her principal? Is the amount of repayment affected by the selling price of the bond? Why or why not?

26. **Lease vs. Purchase** *(LO 7.4)*

    You are considering buying an automobile for $20,000, and you have a $2,000 down payment. The sales tax rate is 7 percent, and the interest rate to borrow the remaining funds for five years is 6 percent. Other fees involved in the purchase are $200. The market rate for current investments is 4 percent. The automobile is expected to be worth $5,000 at the end of the five years, with an annual rate of fair market value reduction of 15 percent.

    You also have the option of leasing the same vehicle for three years at an 8 percent interest rate. The dealer requires a security deposit of $500, and other front-end fees total $750. At the end of the lease term, the vehicle is expected to have a fair market value of $12,000.

    Required:

    Go to http://www.lendingtree.com/partners/autotrader/AutoLeaseBuyCalc.asp and determine the net costs of buying and leasing. Are there any other items that you would want to consider in choosing the buy or lease alternative? *(LO 7.3)*

27. **Selected Long-Term Liabilities in Corporate Balance Sheets** *(LO 7.5, writing)*

    You have been asked to write a term paper on the nature of large corporations. One aspect you are supposed to cover is how corporations finance their operations. You have found the following long-term liabilities, and related information, in recent corporate balance sheets.

    (a) Quixote Corporation (www.quixote.com), a firm in the transportation safety industry: 7% Convertible Debt Due February 15, 2025—$40,000,000

(b)   Hormel Foods Corporation (www.hormelfoods .com), a firm that manufactures and markets prepared food products: Pension and Post-Retirement Benefits Liability—$440,810,000

(c)   Time Warner (www.timewarner.com), a firm that (among other lines of business) publishes *Time*, *People*, and *Sports Illustrated*: Deferred Revenue (current)—$1,178,000,000, and Deferred Revenue (long-term)—$522,000,000

(d)   Target Corporation (www.target.com), a general merchandise and food discount retailer: Capital Lease Obligations—$147,000,000

Required:

Begin your report with a brief overview of the nature of liabilities and the general types of long-term liabilities. Next, provide a brief description of the nature and source of each of the long-term liabilities identified. Include in these descriptions how each liability is related, or likely related if you are unsure, to the given company's profit-oriented activities.

28. **Defined Contribution Pension Plan** *(LO 7.5)*

Your parents will be retiring in three years and want to have $1,000,000 in pension assets. At the beginning of 2009, they have accumulated $700,000. Because of their long history with the company, it has agreed to contribute $36,500 equally at the end of 2009, 2010, and 2011. The company's rationale was that, at an interest rate of 8%, your parents would have slightly more than the desired $1,000,000 when they retire on January 1, 2012.

Required:

(a)   Prove that the company's calculations are correct.

(b)   Assume that the retirement account for the next three years did not perform at the level company management had predicted. Actual returns for each of the years were as follows: 2009, 2%; 2010, 3%; and 2011, 5%. How much will your parents have when they retire on January 1, 2012?

29. **Analyzing Corporate Liabilities** *(LO 7.7)*

Listed in the following schedule are the current assets and current liabilities of the Laoretti Company for the firm's fiscal years ending December 31, 2008 and 2009.

	December 31	
	2008	**2009**
Cash and Cash Equivalents	$ 54,817	$ 48,902
Accounts Receivable	63,295	59,748
Inventories	116,528	121,277
Other Current Assets	18,605	15,691
Total Current Assets	$253,245	$245,618
Accounts Payable	$ 71,430	$ 73,819
Accrued Payroll Liabilities	26,608	28,456
Income Taxes Payable	12,089	11,572
Total Current Liabilities	$110,127	$113,847

Required:

(a)   Determine this company's working capital and current ratio as of December 31, 2008 and 2009.

(b)   Did the company's liquidity improve or weaken between the end of 2008 and the end of 2009? Explain.

30. **(Appendix) Accounting for Bonds** *(LO 7.8)*

Ratioli Inc. is planning a $5,000,000 bond issue. The bonds will carry an 8 percent interest rate, pay interest semiannually, and mature in 10 years.

Required:

(a)   If the market rate of interest at the date of issue is 6 percent, what will be the bond issue price? Does the bond sell at a premium or a discount?

(b)   If the market rate of interest at the date of issue is 10 percent, what will be the bond issue price? Does the bond sell at a premium or a discount?

(c)   Using your answer from part (b), how much premium or discount will be amortized each interest period?

PROBLEMS

31. **Accounting for an Interest-Bearing Note Payable** *(LO 7.1)*

On April 1, the Snake River Racing Club (SRRC) purchased ten white-water rafts with a cash price of $3,000 each. SRRC offered to pay for the rafts by making a $5,000 down payment and by signing a $25,000, 8 percent interest-bearing note. The interest and principal on this note would be due in one year.

Required:

(a)   Prepare the appropriate journal entries in the accounting records of SRRC on the following dates:

(1)   April 1, the date the sales agreement is finalized

(2)   December 31, the final day of SRRC's fiscal year

(3) April 1 of the following year, when the note matures

(b) Suppose that SRRC does not make an entry pertaining to this note payable in its accounting records on December 31. How will this oversight affect SRRC's financial statements for the year ending December 31? For the following year?

32. Accounting for a Product Warranty Liability *(LO 7.1)*

Cool Air, Inc. sells products with a one-year warranty covering parts and labor. The following table lists the company's three major product lines, the percentage of the products sold in each product line that are returned while under warranty, and the average warranty-related cost incurred on each returned item.

Product Line	Air Conditioners	Air Compressors	Fans
% of products returned while under warranty	7%	9%	6%
Warranty cost per returned item	$150	$40	$12
Unit sales during April	2,000	1,350	1,700

Required:

(a) Compute the estimated product warranty expense that should be recorded by Cool Air at the end of April and prepare the appropriate adjusting entry.

(b) During the first week in May, Cool Air paid warranty-related costs of $6,800. Prepare the entry to record these payments.

33. Payroll Liabilities *(LO 7.1)*

Tobago Inc.'s hourly employees normally work eight hours a day, five days a week. Employees who work this schedule every week for 50 weeks earn two weeks of paid vacation. The company's four hourly employees are listed along with information about the two-week pay period that ended on Friday, April 30. Employees will be paid on the following Monday. April 30 is Tobago's fiscal year end.

Employee	Hours Worked	Hourly Wage	Gross Pay	Federal Income Tax	State Income Tax	FICA	Insurance Premium
Addel	80	$10.00	$ 800	$216	$66	$61.20	$ 0
Blatty	72	12.00	864	158	52	66.10	62
Charles	80	11.50	920	248	75	6.50	115
Douglas	80	12.85	1,028	201	84	78.03	58

Required:

(a) Calculate net pay for each employee.

(b) Prepare the journal entry to record this payroll.

(c) Regarding Tobago's vacation plan,

(1) How many hours do Tobago's employees work during a year?

(2) How many hours of vacation do the employees earn if they work the full 50 weeks?

(3) How many hours does an employee have to work to earn one hour of vacation?

(4) What is the value of the vacation earned during the pay period ending April 30?

(5) Prepare the journal entry to record the accrual of the vacation pay.

34. Deferred Liabilities *(LO 7.1)*

It's Bead-i-ful is a magazine for creators of bead jewelry. The magazine currently has 6,900 subscribers who have paid $48 per year for the publication. During the week ending July 3, the magazine sold 120 annual subscriptions. The magazine is mailed on the first of each month.

Required:

(a) Prepare the journal entry to record the subscriptions for the week of July 3.

(b) What journal entry should the magazine make on August 1?

(c) On December 31, *It's Bead-i-ful* went out of business. At that time, the magazine owed 4,100 magazines to its customers. Prepare the journal entry necessary to refund the subscriber's payments.

35. Bonds *(LO 7.3)*

Brian Wood Production Company is issuing $250,000 of ten-year, $1,000-face value bonds. The bonds carry a 9.5 percent interest rate, paid annually.

Required:

(a) How much total cash interest will investors receive each year?

(b) Prepare the journal entry to issue the bonds if they are sold at

(1) 100.

(2) 97.

(3) 102.

(c) For items (1), (2), and (3) in part (b), indicate whether the bonds were sold at a premium, discount, or face value and what that means about the relationship between the stated rate of interest and the market rate of interest.

(d) For items (1), (2), and (3) in part (b), how much will the investors receive at maturity?

36. **Mortgage Payable** (*LO 7.4, Internet*)

Portland College is planning to purchase a home for its president in downtown Albuquerque. One property, with a selling price of $780,000, has been found, and the college treasurer is debating on the following purchase options:

Option A: Make a 20 percent down payment and finance the balance over 15 years at 8 percent.

Option B: Make a 20 percent down payment and finance the balance over 30 years at 8 percent.

Option C: Make a 30 percent down payment and finance the balance over 15 years at 6.5 percent.

Option D: Make a 30 percent down payment and finance the balance over 30 years at 6.5 percent.

Required:

(a) Use a mortgage calculator (such as the one at www.mortgage-calc.com) to find the monthly payments for each option.

(b) What is the total interest paid for the mortgage under each of the options?

(c) If either of the 20 percent down options is chosen, the college can invest the other 10 percent ($78,000) in a certificate of deposit for either 15 or 30 years at an annual rate of 5 percent. Which of the options should the college choose to minimize the total cost of the house?

37. **Analyzing Current Liabilities** (*LO 7.7*)

The following schedule lists the current assets and current liabilities of Iago Department Stores for the firm's fiscal years ending in February for two recent years. Dollars are presented in millions.

	December 1	
	Year 1	Year 2
Cash	$ 210	$ 34
Cash equivalent	64	278
Accounts receivable	3,876	4,162
Merchandise inventory	120	190
Total Current Assets	$4,270	$4,664
Short-term debt	$ 156	$ 0
Current maturities of long-term debt	510	170
Accounts payable	1,046	1,930
Accrued expenses	1,820	1,542
Income tax payable	238	186
Total Current Liabilities	$3,770	$3,828

Required:

(a) Determine Iago's working capital and current ratio at year-end of Year 1 and Year 2.

(b) Did Iago's liquidity improve or weaken between the end of Year 1 and the end of Year 2? Explain.

38. **Analyzing Long-Term Liabilities** (*LO 7.7*)

Following are selected financial data (expressed in millions) for Blaske Company for 2008 and 2009.

	2008	2009
Total Assets	$4,781	$5,052
Current Assets	1,606	1,709
Current Liabilities	1,483	1,279
Long-Term Debt	1,090	1,490
Stockholders' Equity	1,365	1,461
Interest Expense	99	149
Income Taxes Expense	56	25
Net Income	31	75

Required:

(a) Compute Blaske's long-term debt to equity and times-interest earned ratios for 2008 and 2009.

(b) How did Blaske's interest coverage change over this two-year period?

39. **Analyzing Long-Term Liabilities** (*LO 7.7*)

Zammillo Corp. owns and operates a variety of resorts in the United States and Canada. The following financial information was obtained from the company's 2008 and 2009 financial statements. Amounts are expressed in thousands.

	2008	2009
Total Assets	$185,110	$301,486
Long-Term Debt	121,792	161,302
Stockholders' Equity	37,153	95,791
Interest Expense	8,949	9,179
Income Taxes Expense	4,806	6,100
Net Income	9,417	11,840

In the company's annual report, executives discussed aggressive future expansion plans. Following are specific comments addressing the issue of how and whether the company would be able to finance these plans.

The company's plans to develop new resort opportunities and expand existing operations will require substantial amounts of additional capital. There is no assurance at this time that such financing is or will be available to the company or, if available, that the financing would be on favorable payment terms.

Required:

(a) Compute Zammillo Corp.'s long-term debt to equity and times interest earned ratios for 2008 and 2009. Did these ratios improve or weaken between the end of 2008 and the end of 2009?

(b) Considering the financial data presented for the company, what factor was apparently most responsible for the significant change in Zammillo's long-term debt to equity ratio between the end of 2008 and the end of 2009? Explain.

(c) Suppose that the average long-term debt to equity ratio for the resort industry is 65 percent and that the average times interest earned ratio is 4.5. Evaluate Zammillo Corp.'s ratios in reference to these industry norms.

(d) What purpose is served by the narrative disclosures in the company's annual report regarding the potential need for additional capital and related information?

40. **(Appendix) Accounting for Bonds Payable** *(LO 7.8)*

Vancouver Corporation issued $20,000,000 of five-year, 8 percent bonds on May 1, 2009. Interest payment dates are May 1 and November 1 of each year. Vancouver uses straight-line amortization for any bond premium or discount and has a December 31 fiscal year-end.

Required:

(a) Determine the total proceeds Vancouver received from the sale of these bonds, assuming that the market interest rate for similar bonds on May 1, 2009, was

(1) 7%.

(2) 11%.

(b) Prepare the appropriate journal entries on the following dates: May 1, 2009; November 1, 2009; December 31, 2009; and May 1, 2010 assuming

(1) a 7% market rate upon issuance

(2) an 11% market rate upon issuance

(c) For each assumption listed in part (a), determine the carrying value of the bonds as of December 31, 2009.

CASES

41. **Recognizing Warranty Expense** *(LO 7.1, ethics, writing)*

Warsaw Technologies, Inc. manufactures modems and disk drives. Warsaw's current year's revenues are nearly 20 percent below those of last year. As year-end approaches, the company president has instructed the accounting department not to record a December 31 adjusting entry for warranty expense on products sold during the year. "We can recognize that expense next year when we actually pay those costs. That makes more sense anyway. Why go to the trouble of estimating additional expenses at year-end? We have more than enough of the real thing."

Required:

Write a memo to Warsaw's president explaining why it is necessary to recognize estimated warranty expense at the end of an accounting period. In your memo, point out how the company's financial statements will be misleading if this expense is not recorded.

42. **Accounting for Contingent Liabilities** *(LO 7.2)*

Consider the following three scenarios involving publicly owned companies in the United States.

- One of the four wholly owned subsidiaries of Option Plastics, Inc., is located in a small South American country. Recent elections in the country have brought to power a political party that intends to nationalize all major businesses. The new president has indicated that the government will pay a "reasonable price" for these businesses. The manager of the South American subsidiary estimates that Option Plastics will suffer a loss of between $4 million and $6 million when the government buys out the subsidiary sometime in the next two years.

- Charles Ironworks has just been slapped with a $5.5 million fine by the Environmental Protection Agency (EPA). The company's legal counsel intends to contest the fine. When asked to evaluate the likelihood of overturning the EPA fine, the company's chief legal counsel responded, "I think there's a 50-50 chance that we can get the fine reduced. But I have no idea if we can reduce the fine by $2 or by $2 million."

- Joy's Toys manufactures a wide range of toys designed for children one to four years of age. This past week, a competitor, Gaver Corporation, sued Joy's Toys for $17.2 million. The suit alleges that Joy's Toys infringed on a patent that Gaver holds on a popular toy. In a press release, the chief executive of Joy's Toys observed, "This suit is complete nonsense. Gaver knows that we haven't infringed on its patent. All this company is trying to do is harass us and damage our reputation."

Required:

(a)   Evaluate each of the three scenarios in reference to the accounting and financial reporting guidelines for contingent liabilities. How would you recommend that these items be accounted for and/or reported in each firm's financial statements? Support your recommendation for each scenario.

(b)   Do companies have an incentive to intentionally downplay the significance of contingent liabilities and thus exclude them from their financial statements? Explain. If such an exclusion occurs, how are decision makers who rely on financial statement data affected?

43.   **Retirement of Bonds Payable** *(LO 7.3, writing)*

Wimberly Industries has a $10 million bond payable outstanding. The bonds were sold on February 1, 2005, with a ten-year term and a stated interest rate of 12 percent. Bond interest is paid semiannually on February 1 and August 1. The bonds have a current carrying value of $9,877,000.

If Wimberly sold bonds in today's market, the company would be required to pay annual interest of only 9 percent. Consequently, the company's management wants to retire its outstanding bonds and sell new bonds. The current market price of Wimberly's bonds is 122 1/4.

Required:

(a)   At the present market price, how much will it cost Wimberly to purchase all of its outstanding bonds? What factor or factors may account for the difference between the collective market price and carrying value of Wimberly's bonds?

(b)   Suppose that Wimberly purchases and immediately retires the bonds. Prepare the appropriate journal entry to record this transaction.

(c)   What stipulation could have been included in the bond indenture that would have allowed the company to retire the bonds without being forced to purchase them in the open market?

44.   **Current Ratio and Working Capital** *(LO 7.7)*

Charlotte Foods Corporation manufactures and distributes prepared foods. Slidell, Inc. operates more than 300 restaurants located in 19 states. The following schedule lists the year-end current assets and current liabilities of these two firms for 2008 and 2009. Dollars are presented in thousands.

Charlotte Foods Corporation	2008	2009
Cash and Cash Equivalents	$157,558	$248,599
Short-term Marketable Securities	14,862	11,360
Accounts Receivable	218,487	228,369
Inventories	220,494	213,456
Prepaid Expenses	8,503	6,431
Total Current Assets	$619,904	$708,215
Accounts Payable	$ 98,357	$112,851
Accrued Liabilities	30,212	29,320
Accrued Advertising	24,587	31,863
Employee Compensation	40,195	41,989
State and Local Taxes	14,011	17,606
Dividends Payable	8,434	9,585
Federal Income Taxes	11,262	21,303
Current Portion of Long-Term Debt	0	400
Total Current Liabilities	$227,058	$264,917

Slidell Inc.	2008	2009
Cash	$ 8,241	$ 6,699
Investments	1,947	1,399
Accounts Receivable	12,545	15,445
Inventories	19,063	20,384
Prepaid Expenses	3,371	3,514
Total Current Assets	$45,167	$47,441
Line of Credit	$ 0	$ 9,500
Accounts Payable	9,530	12,200
Dividends Payable	2,618	2,839
Federal and State Taxes	7,597	6,160
Accrued Wages & Fringe Benefits	10,163	10,830
Other Accrued Liabilities	17,185	18,023
Total Current Liabilities	$47,093	$59,552

Required:

(a)   Compute the following items for both companies for 2008 and 2009:

   (1)   Working capital

   (2)   Current ratio

   (3)   Quick ratio

(b)   Given the data computed in part (a), which of these two companies had the stronger liquidity at the end of 2008 and at the end of 2009? Why?

(c)   In your opinion, which of the three measures that you computed in part (a) is the best measure of liquidity? Explain.

(d)   Review the data presented for each company. Are there any unusual items or unusual relationships in either company's data that a decision maker might want to investigate further? If so, identify these items and the issues or questions that decision makers would likely raise.

45.   Analyzing Liabilities (LO 7.7, Internet)

Use the annual report of Carnival Corporation for the 2007 fiscal year to answer the following questions. This information can be found on either the annual report or the SEC 10-K filing at www.carnival.com by following the links to Investor Relations.

Required:

(a)   Calculate the following ratios and measurements for Carnival for the years 2006 and 2007. Comment on changes from year to year and what each ratio means for Carnival.

   (1)   Current ratio

   (2)   Working capital

   (3)   Debt to total assets

   (4)   Long-term debt to equity

   (5)   Times interest earned

(b)   Does Carnival have any contingent liabilities? If so, how does the company handle the accounting of such liabilities? Where did you find this information?

(c)   What kind of retirement plan does Carnival have for its employees?

(d)   What portion of Carnival's long-term debt is due in the next fiscal year?

(e)   Does Carnival lease any assets? If so, how does the company account for such leases?

(f)   Is Carnival currently financing its operations through the use of bonds? If so, to what extent? If not, what other methods might the company use to finance operations?

46.   Comparing Companies (LO 7.7, group, Internet)

Identifying the similarities and differences between companies is as crucial to making investment decisions as understanding a single company's financial statements. Form groups of at least four students. Each group should select a single industry. Each group member should locate a different annual report within that industry. (The industry and individual company may be assigned by your instructor.)

Required—individual group members:

(a)   Calculate the following ratios/measures for the company you selected for the two most recent fiscal years.

   (1)   Current ratio

   (2)   Working capital

   (3)   Debt to total assets

   (4)   Long-term debt to equity

   (5)   Times interest earned

(b)   What percentage of total assets is accounted for by each of the following accounts:

   (1)   Current liabilities

   (2)   Long-term liabilities

   (3)   Stockholders' equity (not including retained earnings)

   (4)   Retained earnings

Create a pie chart to depict these proportions (should total 100%). In one or two sentences, explain what is meant by each portion of the pie.

Required—groups:

(c)   Compile the ratio calculations from part (a) for each company prepared by the individual group members into one table. Compare the results from company to company in the same fiscal year. Include in your comparison a graphical analysis. Discuss reasons why these ratios might be similar or different within an industry.

(d)   Calculate an average for the five ratios that depicts the industry you are examining.

(e)   Compare your pie charts from part (b) and develop a pie chart for the industry average. How do the industry average ratios calculated in part (d) compare to the industry average pie chart?

Required—class:

(f)   Compare the ratios from each industry. Discuss reasons why these ratios might be similar or different between industries.

(g)   Does one industry seem to be a better investment than another? Do you think this situation is constant over time? Why or why not?

SUPPLEMENTAL PROBLEMS

47.   Accounting for Interest-Bearing Note Payable *(LO 7.1; Compare to Problem 31)*

Regier Homebuilders, which has a calendar year-end, borrowed $10,000 from a local bank on October 2, 2009. On that date, Regier's chief executive signed a 9 percent, 150-day interest-bearing promissory note.

Required:

Prepare the appropriate journal entries in Regier's accounting records on the following dates:

(a)   October 2

(b)   December 31

(c)   the maturity date (indicate that date in the journal entry)

48.   Accounting for a Product Warranty Liability *(LO 7.1; Compare to Problem 32)*

Lawn Ranger Manufacturing makes lawn care products that are sold with a one-year warranty covering parts and labor. The following table lists the percentage of products that are returned while under warranty, average warranty-related cost incurred on each returned item, and sales per product line for March.

Product Line	Edgers	Push Mowers	Riding Mowers
% of products returned while under warranty	1%	4%	3%
Warranty cost per returned item	$40	$90	$170
Unit sales during March	3,400	2,820	1,900

Required:

(a)   Compute the estimated product warranty expense that should be recorded by Lawn Ranger at the end of March and prepare the appropriate March 31 adjusting entry.

(b)   Suppose that during the first week of June, the company incurs warranty-related costs of $1,800 in inventory parts and $400 for labor. The labor costs will be paid on June 15. Prepare the entry to record the warranty costs.

49.   Payroll and Vacation Pay *(LO 7.1; Compare to Problem 33)*

McDeal Corporation has six salaried employees who are paid every two weeks and are given two weeks of paid vacation per year. The following payroll information is available for the two-week period ended October 31, 2009:

Gross Pay	$30,000
FICA Taxes	2,295
Federal Income Taxes	7,353
State Income Taxes	1,138
Health Insurance Premiums	1,000

Required:

(a)   Prepare the October 31 journal entry to record this payroll.

(b)   Prepare the October 31 journal entry to record the accrual of vacation pay.

(c)   Prepare the journal entry to pay the employees on November 3.

50.   Deferred Liabilities *(LO 7.1; Compare to Problem 34)*

During May 2009, its first month of operation, Pizza Palace sold 200 coupon books for $20 each. The books contain four coupons, each of which can be exchanged for a large pizza.

Required:

(a)   What journal entry would Pizza Palace make for the sale of the 200 coupon books?

(b)   During the week of June 8, 27 coupons were redeemed. Prepare the journal entry to account for the exchange of the coupons for pizzas.

(c)   Pizza Palace prepares quarterly financial statements. At the end of the third quarter on January 31, 2010, 67 coupons remained unredeemed. How should these coupon books be presented on Pizza Palace's financial statements?

51.   Analyzing Long-Term Liabilities *(LO 7.7; Compare to Problem 38)*

The following information for Kirsten Corp. has been obtained from the company's 2008 and 2009 financial statements.

	2008	2009
Total Assets	$1,218,302	$1,328,496
Current Assets	666,135	753,580
Total Stockholders' Equity	604,215	675,322
Long-Term Debt	226,279	287,837
Net Income	81,584	99,586
Interest Expense	10,203	13,985
Income Taxes Expense	28,578	42,680

Required:

(a) Kirsten Corp. has applied for a $50 million long-term loan from Prosperous Bank. Cornell Manufacturing is considering purchasing 10,000 shares of Kirsten's common stock. Would Prosperous Bank or Cornell Manufacturing be more likely to be interested in evaluating Kirsten's financial leverage? Explain your choice.

(b) Compute Kirsten's long-term debt to equity ratio in 2008 and 2009. Did the company become more or less leveraged between the end of 2008 and the end of 2009?

(c) Compute Kirsten's times interest earned ratio in both 2008 and 2009. Did this ratio improve or deteriorate between the end of 2008 and the end of 2009? Explain.

52. (Appendix) **Accounting for Bonds Payable** *(LO 7.8; Compare to Problem 40)*

When Parisian Globe issued $4,000,000 of ten-year, 11 percent bonds on September 1, 2009, the market interest rate was 9 percent. The bonds pay interest semiannually on March 1 and September 1. Parisian Globe has a calendar year-end and amortizes bond discounts or premiums using the straight-line method.

Required:

(a) Determine the present value (or issue price) of these bonds.

(b) Prepare the journal entries related to the bonds on the following dates:

(1) September 1, 2009

(2) December 31, 2009

(3) March 1, 2010

(4) September 1, 2010

(c) What is the carrying value of the bonds as of September 2, 2010?

(d) Gary Schorg had originally purchased $1,200,000 of the Parisian Globe bonds on September 1, 2009. Use present value calculations to determine what Schorg paid for his portion of the bonds. If Schorg sells his bonds to Lilly Puchiane on February 16, 2013, what journal entry will Parisian Globe make at that time? Explain your answer.

(e) Assume the market rate of interest at the date of issue had been 14 percent. What would the bond-selling price have been?

CHAPTER **8**

Stockholders' Equity

LEARNING OBJECTIVES

1. Describe the important characteristics, advantages, and disadvantages of a corporation.
2. Identify the key rights and privileges of common and preferred stockholders.
3. Account for the issuance of corporate stock.
4. Account for treasury stock transactions, cash and stock dividends, and stock splits.
5. Understand how Retained Earnings is affected by net income (loss), dividends, and prior period adjustments.
6. Prepare a statement of stockholders' equity.
7. Define the key information needs of decision makers regarding stockholders' equity, including dividend yield and return on equity.

INTRODUCTION

Businesses needing to raise substantial funds to build a factory, buy another company, or establish a foreign subsidiary have two principal financing alternatives. The companies can raise debt capital by borrowing funds (resulting in increased liabilities) or can raise equity capital by selling ownership interest to outside parties (resulting in increased stockholders' equity). Corporations raise equity capital by selling common or preferred stock.

This chapter focuses on the accounting issues related to corporate stockholders' equity and begins with an overview of the corporate form of business organization. Next, the accounting procedures for common stockholders' equity transactions are provided along with a discussion of the Retained Earnings account. The final chapter topic addresses the information needs of decision makers regarding stockholders' equity and three key financial ratios related to stockholders' equity.

THE CORPORATION

Some corporations are small and closely held, with the ownership often retained by members of the same family and with the stock not traded on a public exchange. However, it is common for corporations, after reaching a certain size or needing additional investment funds, to decide to "go public" and list the stock on a stock exchange. Listing tends to provide several benefits (Visual Recap 8.1) to the issuer. Companies may also "cross list" their stock, meaning that their stocks can be sold on several different stock exchanges, including both domestic and foreign.

Chapter 1 defined a corporation as an association of individuals that is created by law and has an existence apart from its owners. In the United States, business owners wanting to incorporate should first investigate the specific corporate laws and taxes in the various states. Once a state of incorporation is selected, the company files articles of incorporation that identify, among other things, the business's purpose, its principal operating units, and the type and quantity of stock to be issued. If all legal requirements are met, the state grants the business a **corporate charter** or contract between the corporation and its state of domicile that identifies the corporation's principal rights and obligations.

Some corporations choose not to incorporate in their domestic nation or decide to reincorporate out of the domestic nation. For example, some U.S. corporations have decided to reincorporate after years of being in business for the primary reason of minimizing income tax liabilities. Reincorporation is oftentimes in "tax havens" or locations with minimal or no taxes.[1] In 1997, Tyco International (www.tyco.com) incorporated in Bermuda, saving an estimated $280 million a year in taxes. However, even though slightly more than 26 percent of the company's shareholders voted in 2003 to have the company's incorporation be returned to the United States, as of the end of 2008, Tyco is still incorporated in Bermuda and headquartered in Connecticut.[2]

---

[1] The process of reincorporating in a tax haven is called inversion.

[2] A variety of legislation has been introduced in the U.S. Congress to eliminate the ability of companies to benefit from "sham" relocations, but none has been successful as of December 2008.

VISUAL RECAP 8.1

Benefits of Listing on a Stock Exchange

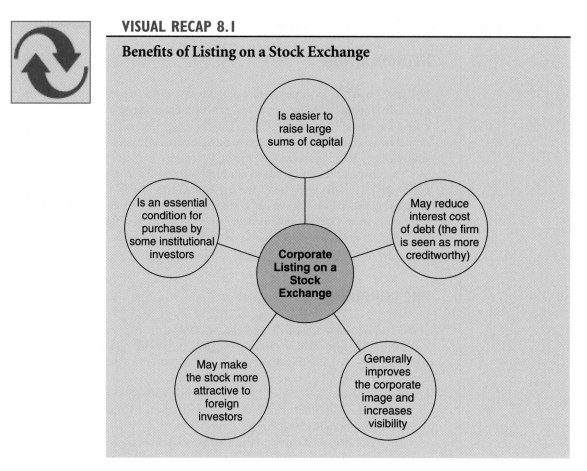

Key Advantages of the Corporation

Corporations have several advantages over sole proprietorships and partnerships. One important advantage is the limited liability of corporate stockholders. In practically all cases, the maximum amount a stockholder may lose if a corporation becomes bankrupt is his or her original investment amount. The firm's unpaid debts cannot be recovered from stockholders' personal assets. In contrast, if a sole proprietorship or partnership goes out of business without paying all its debts, the owner or each partner is individually responsible for those debts.

Unlike sole proprietorships and partnerships, a corporation's legal existence is unaffected by the death or withdrawal of individual owners. A partnership must be dissolved when one partner leaves the firm—although the remaining partners have the option of immediately forming a new partnership without any cessation of business. However, ownership interests of corporate stockholders who die pass directly to their estates or heirs.

Transferring ownership interest in a publicly held corporation is easy because shares can be sold to anyone without the prior approval of the other owners. In a partnership, the other firm members must approve of ownership transfers.

Corporations can usually raise debt and equity capital more readily and in larger amounts than unincorporated businesses. Even small corporations can raise large amounts of capital very quickly by selling stock on a nationwide basis through an IPO (initial public offering).

Key Disadvantages of the Corporation

There are also disadvantages to incorporating a business. The key disadvantage posed by the corporate form of business is the double taxation of corporate profits. Corporations are considered taxable entities, meaning that income taxes must be paid on annual earnings. When corporations distribute **cash dividends** to stockholders, stockholders must report those dividends as income on personal tax returns and pay taxes on those dividends. Incomes of sole proprietorships, partnerships, and closely held corporations are not taxed; instead, owners report their firm's profits, or their proportionate share of their firm's profits, in their individual tax returns, regardless of whether the profits have been distributed.

All businesses are subject to some degree of local, state, and federal oversight. However, corporations are generally subject to more regulations than other businesses. For example, corporations that publicly sell their stock in the United States must comply with the extensive accounting and financial reporting requirements of the Securities and Exchange Commission (SEC). Firms listing their stock on a securities exchange, such as the New York Stock Exchange Euronext (www.nyse.com), are also subject to that organization's rules and regulations.

Occasionally, some items listed earlier as advantages of corporations can become disadvantages. For example, a small corporation may be rejected for a bank loan because of the limited liability feature. Bank loan officers realize that only corporate assets, not stockholders' personal assets, can be seized to satisfy unpaid principal or interest payments if a corporation defaults on a loan. As a result, small corporations pose a higher level of credit risk than sole proprietorships and partnerships of comparable size. To gain approval of a loan application, one or more individual stockholders of a small corporation may agree to personally guarantee the loan.

CORPORATE STOCK

The charter indicates the amount of **authorized stock** or the maximum number of shares of each designated class of stock that the corporation may issue. If the charter identifies only one class of stock, that stock is automatically considered the corporation's **common stock** or the residual ownership interest. If a corporate charter identifies a second class of stock, it is usually **preferred stock**, which has certain preferences or privileges compared to common stock.

Issued stock refers to the number of shares that have been sold or otherwise distributed to organization owners, whereas **outstanding stock** is the number of shares currently owned by a company's stockholders. Differing quantities of issued and outstanding stock means that treasury stock exists. **Treasury stock** refers to the shares that the company has reacquired from owners; such stock is still counted in issued shares but is not currently outstanding. When no treasury stock exists, issued stock equals outstanding stock. For example, assume that Multimart, Inc. has one million shares of authorized stock. Of these shares, 400,000 shares have been sold to investors. Of the 400,000 issued shares, 30,000 shares have been reacquired by Multimart over the last year. Visual Recap 8.2 depicts the stock quantities associated with Multimart.

Right and Privileges of Common Stockholders

The most important legal privilege of common stockholders is the right to vote on key corporate matters, including the election of a board of directors. The board of directors establishes a corporation's long-range objectives and operating policies. A corporation's officers, who are selected by the board of directors (BOD), have the responsibility for carrying out the board's policies. Typically, the top corporate executives, such as the chief executive officer (CEO) and one or more senior vice presidents, serve on the firm's board of directors. It is fairly commonplace in U.S. companies for the CEO to also hold the position of chairman of the BOD; as of 2007, only 35 percent of S&P 500 companies had split the roles of CEO and Chairman of the BOD.[3] However, there is movement by shareholders to have companies divide those two positions, in part because of the inherent conflict of

VISUAL RECAP 8.2

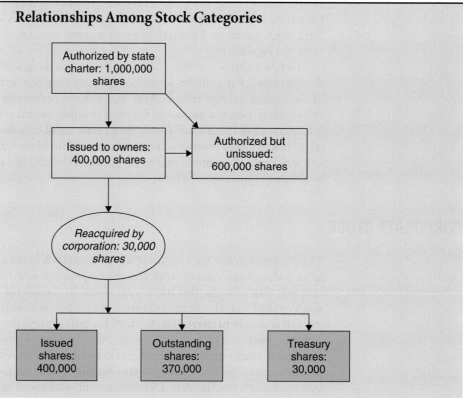

Relationships Among Stock Categories

Authorized by state charter: 1,000,000 shares

Issued to owners: 400,000 shares

Authorized but unissued: 600,000 shares

Reacquired by corporation: 30,000 shares

| Issued shares: 400,000 | Outstanding shares: 370,000 | Treasury shares: 30,000 |

---

[3] Bart Friedman and Ted B. Lacey, "An Independent Voice on the Board," *Cahill Publications* (November 17, 2008); http://www.cahill.com/news/publications/000060 (accessed 12/5/08)

interest caused by the BOD determining the CEO's salary. In most European, British, and Canadian businesses, the two roles are usually split, in an effort to promote better corporate governance.

In most states, common stockholders have a **preemptive right** to purchase enough shares to retain their proportional ownership interest when the corporation issues additional common stock. For example, assume that you own 1,000 of 10,000 shares (or 10%) of issued and outstanding common stock in Sleepy Time Hotels Incorporated. If Sleepy Time issues 2,000 additional shares, the preemptive right allows you the first option to purchase 200 of those shares to retain your 10% ownership interest (1,200 of 12,000 shares). Stockholders may decide to either exercise or forfeit their preemptive right.

Common stockholders also have the right to share proportionately in any dividends or distribution of earnings. For example, assume the BOD of Sleepy Time decides to distribute a cash dividend of $50,000 to common stockholders. If there were 10,000 shares of outstanding common stock, each common stockholder would be entitled to a $5 dividend ($50,000 ÷ 10,000 shares) for each share he or she owns. The dividend could not be allocated exclusively to a few stockholders.

Finally, if a corporation goes out of business and its assets are sold, common stockholders are entitled to share proportionately in the assets that remain after all other obligations have been satisfied. These obligations include current and long-term liabilities and any amounts that must be paid to other preferred classes of stockholders. In corporate bankruptcy, stockholders may not receive anything or may only receive a nominal amount.

Rights and Privileges of Preferred Stockholders

Preferred stockholders have some preferences relative to a corporation's common stockholders, the most important of which involves dividend payments. Preferred stockholders are usually entitled to receive a specified annual rate or amount of cash dividend per share each year. If a rate of dividend is specified, the annual dividend is that rate multiplied by the par value of the preferred stock. The corporation is not obligated to pay these dividends, but must do so before common stockholders can receive a dividend. In addition, a common feature of preferred stock is that dividends are cumulative. If a corporation fails to pay a dividend in a given year on a **cumulative preferred stock**, that dividend accumulates and must be paid in future years before common stockholders can receive a dividend.

Additionally, if a corporation is liquidated, creditors are paid, and if funds are still available, preferred stockholders are paid the par value of their stock (or another specified amount) before common stockholders receive any distribution of cash or other assets. Although the liquidation preference is considered an advantage, preferred shareholders are only entitled to a specific amount, whereas common shareholders divide the remaining assets on a per share basis. If the remaining assets are significant, the common shareholders may have a final monetary advantage over preferred shareholders.

Most preferred stocks are also **callable**, which means they can be reacquired at the corporation's option. Some preferred stock is **convertible** and may be exchanged by the stockholder for the corporation's common stock. Besides dividend preference, and unless stated otherwise in the corporate charter, preferred stockholders have almost the same rights as those identified for common stockholders. However, one important stockholder right that corporate charters typically withhold from preferred stockholders is the voting privilege.

Par Value and No-Par Value Stock

Most corporate charters designate par values for the different classes of stock that a company is permitted to issue. Par value represents a nominal dollar value assigned to each share of a given class of stock and is typically set at a very low amount. For example, the par value of UPS's (www.ups.com) common stock is $0.01 per share; par value is $0.50 per common share for Corning, Inc. (www.corning.com). Some corporations, such as Darden Restaurants (parent company of Red Lobster and Olive Garden, among others; www.darden.com), do not designate a par value for a company's stock, which is then referred to as no-par stock. Although the par value has limited, if any, economic significance relative to the selling price of the stock, this value does influence how the sale of the stock is recorded.

STOCK ISSUANCES

Corporations issue stock in many different transactions and for many different amounts per share. However, if the stock has a par value, the balance of the stock account (either common or preferred) is only the total par value of the number of shares issued. Because corporations cannot recognize gains or losses on the sale of their own stock, any proceeds above par value are credited to Additional Paid-In Capital (PIC) on Common Stock, which is a stockholders' equity account.[4] For example, Moonbeam Corporation's issuance of 100 shares of $10 par-value common stock for $18 per share follows:

General Journal		
Description	**Debit**	**Credit**
Cash	1,800	
Common Stock		1,000
Add'l PIC on Common Stock		800
Issued 100 shares of $10 par value CS		
for $18 per share		

If Moonbeam's stock had been no-par value, all proceeds from the issuance would have been credited to the Common Stock account.

If common stock is issued in exchange for equipment, buildings, or other assets, the issuance is recorded at either the fair market value of the stock issued or the asset acquired, whichever value is more evident. If the company stock is regularly traded on a stock exchange, the stock's fair market value is readily determinable. However, if the stock is not often traded, is a new issue that has never been traded, or is closely held, then the received asset's fair market value will probably be used to record the transaction.

Exhibit 8-1 provides a variety of stock issuance transactions and their respective journal entries. Assume that the company's stock trades on the NYSE.

---

[4]Companies cannot generally sell stock at an original issue price below par value.

EXHIBIT 8-1

Stock Issuance
Transactions

Prior to the following transactions, Catlin Corp.'s stock information is:

- Preferred stock (PS), no par value; authorized, 10,000 shares; no shares have ever been issued
- Common stock (CS): $1 par value; authorized 350,000 shares; 145,000 shares issued and outstanding
- Additional Paid-In Capital on CS has an assumed balance (from the issuances of the 145,000 shares) of $1,468,000.

General Journal				
Date		Description	Debit	Credit
Apr	1	Cash	27,000	
		Common Stock		1,000
		Additional PIC on CS		26,000
		Issued 1,000 shares of $1 par value CS for $27,000		
	4	Equipment	4,700	
		Preferred Stock		4,700
		Issued 200 shares of PS for equipment with a fair value of $4,700. (Because this is the first issuance of the PS, use the equipment's FMV to record.)		
	12	Building	224,000	
		Common Stock		8,000
		Additional PIC on CS		216,000
		Issued 8,000 shares of $1 par value CS for a building with a list price of $229,600. (Assume the CS traded on 4/11 for $28 per share; use the stock's FMV to record. List prices are not necessarily what an asset is worth or will sell for.)		
	19	Cash	12,500	
		Preferred Stock		12,500
		Issued 500 shares of no-par PS for $25 per share		
	20	Automobile	30,000	
		Preferred Stock		30,000
		Issued 1,200 shares of no-par PS for an automobile with a list price of $34,600. (Because the PS sold on 4/19 for $25 per share, the stock's FMV should be used to record the acquisition.)		

After these transactions, the company has

- Preferred stock (PS), no par value; authorized, 10,000 shares; 1,900 shares issued and outstanding. Preferred Stock has a credit balance of $47,200.
- Common stock (CS): $1 par value; authorized 350,000 shares; 154,000 shares issued and outstanding. Common Stock has a credit balance of $154,000.
- Additional Paid-In Capital on CS has a credit balance of ($1,468,000 + $26,000 + $216,000) or $1,710,000.

TREASURY STOCK

Stock buyback plans are not unusual for large public corporations. If corporate executives believe their company's common stock is selling for less than its actual value, the firm may purchase large blocks of the stock. Corporations typically resell such shares at a later date when the stock's market price has risen. For instance, in July 2007, Kroger Company (www.Kroger.com) announced plans to repurchase $1 billion of its shares to "lift the value of the company and improve shareholder returns."[5] Another reason for companies to buy back their own shares is to sell them to company employees as part of stock option or incentive compensation plans. A company does not have to be concerned with the preemptive right of existing shareholders when treasury stock is distributed because new shares of stock are not being issued.

The simplest way to account for treasury stock transactions is to use the cost method. When the company purchases the stock, the price paid is debited to the Treasury Stock account and credited to Cash. Treasury stock is not an asset because a company cannot be an owner of itself; Treasury Stock is a debit-balanced, contra-stockholders' equity account. When the treasury shares are sold, Cash is debited for the increase, and the cost of the shares is removed from the Treasury Stock account. Remember that a company cannot recognize gains or losses on the sale of its own stock, including treasury stock. Thus, if the cash received is greater than the original cost of the shares, Additional Paid-In Capital on Treasury Stock is also credited. If the cash received is less than the original cost of the shares, Additional Paid-In Capital on Treasury Stock is debited. If no, or an insufficient amount of, Additional Paid-In Capital-Treasury Stock exists, the debit to balance the journal entry is made to Retained Earnings.

Exhibit 8-2 continues the Catlin Corp. example and provides the journal entries for several treasury stock transactions. Notice that treasury stock transactions do *not* affect the Common Stock or Preferred Stock accounts. The balances in those accounts reflect the total amount of shares originally issued rather than those outstanding.

The account Additional Paid-In Capital on Treasury Stock is usually an insignificant amount. For reporting purposes, it is often combined with Additional Paid-In Capital on Common or Preferred Stock, as appropriate. The transactions associated with issuing common stock and repurchasing common treasury stock are summarized in Visual Recap 8.3. Preferred treasury stock transactions are handled in a manner similar to those of common stock.

DIVIDENDS

Most companies share their profits with shareholders in the form of dividends. Dividends may be distributed as cash or additional shares of stock. A cash dividend is a monetary, proportionate distribution of a company's earnings to its stockholders. Companies that pay cash dividends typically do so on a regular basis. Although some companies pay semiannual

---

[5]Press Room, "Kroger $1 Billion Stock Repurchase Program Leaves Workers Behind," *UFCW* (July 2, 2007); http://www.groceryworkersunited.org/Kroger_stock_repurchase_program.htm (accessed 6/10/09).

EXHIBIT 8-2

Treasury Stock
Transactions

General Journal				Debit	Credit
Date		**Description**			
Apr	21	Treasury Stock—Common		2,800	
		Cash			2,800
		Purchased 100 shares of own $1 par value common stock in the market for $28 per share			
May	14	Cash		930	
		Treasury Stock—Common			840
		Additional PIC on TS—Common			90
		Sold 30 shares of TS for $31 per share (selling price was $3 per share above original cost)			
	20	Cash		240	
		Additional PIC on TS—Common		40	
		Treasury Stock—Common			280
		Sold 10 shares of TS to employees for $24 per share (selling price was $4 per share less than original cost)			

After these transactions, the company has

- Preferred stock (PS), no par value; authorized, 10,000 shares; 1,900 shares issued and outstanding. Preferred Stock has a credit balance of $47,200.

- Common stock (CS): $1 par value; authorized 350,000 shares; 154,000 shares issued; 153,940 shares outstanding (154,000 − 100 + 30 + 10). Common Stock has a credit balance of $154,000 (or $1 par value for each of the 154,000 shares issued).

- Additional Paid-In Capital on CS has a credit balance of $1,710,000.

- Treasury Stock: There are 60 shares of treasury stock (100 purchased − 40 resold). Treasury Stock has a debit balance of (60 shares × $28) or $1,680.

- Additional Paid-In Capital on TS − Common Stock has a credit balance of ($90 − $40) or $50.

or quarterly dividends, many companies are beginning to only grant annual dividends because of the savings in mailing and paperwork costs.[6]

There has been a decrease in the number of companies paying cash dividends. In 1980 approximately 94 percent of the S&P 500 stocks paid dividends; in 2007, only 75% did.[7] Many high-tech companies have never paid dividends and have no plans to do so in the future. Microsoft did not pay its first dividend until 2003; that dividend amount was approximately $860 million. Other companies have a reliable history of dividend payments. Branch Banking and Trust (www.bbt.com) of North Carolina has one of the

---

[6]Katheen Pender, "Microsoft Delights Investors with First Dividend of $860 Million," *San Francisco Chronicle* (January 17, 2003); http://www.sfgate.com/cgi-bin/article.cgi?file=/c/a/2003/01/17/MN89371.DTL (accessed 12/5/08).

[7]Edward von der Linde, "The Return on Investment You Deserve," *Christian Science Monitor* (December 12, 2007); http://www.csmonitor.com/2007/1212/p09s01-coop.htm (accessed 12/5/08).

VISUAL RECAP 8.3

Stock Transactions

Common stock transactions are shown.
Preferred stock transactions are similar.
Calculations are shown in parentheses.

Abbreviations:

#S =	Number of Shares (purchased or sold)
PV =	Par Value per Share
SP =	Selling Price or Reissue Price
PP =	Purchase Price
APIC =	Additional Paid-In Capital

	Selling Price = Par Value	**Selling Price < Par Value**	**Selling Price > Par Value**

Issuing Common Stock	Cash (#S × SP)
	    CS (#S × PV)
		Cannot occur in most states	Cash (#S × SP)
			    CS (#S × PV)
			    APIC [(SP − PV) × #S]

	For any Purchase Price
Repurchasing Common Stock	TS (#S × PP) Cash (#S × PP)

	Reissue (Selling) Price = Purchase Price	**Reissue (Selling) Price < Purchase Price**	**Reissue (Selling) Price > Purchase Price**

Reissuing Treasury Stock	Cash (#S × SP)
	    TS (#S × PP)
		Cash (#S × SP)
		APIC [(PP − SP) × #S]*
		    TS (#S × PP)
			Cash (#S × SP)
			    TS (#S × PP)
			    APIC [(SP − PP) × #S]

*To the extent available; debit Retained Earnings for any additional needs.

nation's longest records of continuous dividend payments; as of the second quarter of 2009, it had a cash dividend to shareholders every year since 1903.[8]

A **stock dividend** is a proportionate distribution of a corporation's own stock to its stockholders. Stock dividends are often given so that the company can conserve its cash but, at the same time, remit something to its stockholders.

Generally, before a company can distribute a dividend to its stockholders, two requirements must be met. First, there must be a credit balance in the Retained Earnings account. Second, there must be a formal dividend declaration, or authorization, by a company's board of directors. If a cash dividend is declared, there is a third requirement: the company must have sufficient cash available to pay the dividend. Remember that having Retained Earnings is not the same thing as having cash. Retained Earnings is a stockholders' equity account that represents the total of profits earned by the business, less the dividends distributed, since incorporation. Cash is an asset that represents actual funds available for use by the company. However, regardless of the amount of Retained Earnings or Cash available, a company may be prohibited from declaring dividends due to a restrictive covenant in a bond indenture.

Three dates are important relative to dividend transactions. In chronological order, these dates are the declaration date, date of record, and payment (or distribution) date. On the dividend declaration date, a company's board of directors authorizes the dividend. On the date of record, a list of individuals who own the company's stock is prepared as

---

[8]BB&T, "BB&T Corporation Declares Increase in Dividend," *News Release* (February 24, 2009); http://www.bbt.com/bbt/about/investorrelations/newsreleasedetail.asp?date=2%2F24%2F2009+4%3A23%3A52+PM (accessed 6/10/09).

the official record of stockholders entitled to receive the dividend.[9] The dividend is paid (distributed) on the payment (distribution) date.

When dividends are declared, a debit-balanced account called Dividends is created. This temporary account is closed to Retained Earnings at the end of the accounting period. The Dividends account does not appear on the balance sheet or income statement, but is shown on the Statement of Stockholders' Equity.

Cash Dividends

When declared, a cash dividend becomes a legal liability of the corporation. The distribution amount is determined as the dividend amount per share multiplied by the number of shares outstanding (rather than issued). Dividends are not paid on treasury stock because the owner of those shares is the corporation. The company would not pay dividends to itself.

Assume that the board of directors of Catlin Corp. (from the previous examples) decided to declare an annual dividend on May 31. Given the information in Exhibits 8-1 and 8-2, and assuming no additional issuances of stock, the company had 1,900 shares of preferred and 153,940 shares of common stock outstanding on May 31. The preferred stock had a $2 per share designated annual dividend amount; the board decided to declare a $0.25 per share dividend on the common stock. The dividend is to be paid on June 25 to stockholders of record on June 10. The date of declaration is May 31; the date of record is June 10; and the date of payment is June 25. The entries shown in Exhibit 8-3 would be made on May 31 and June 25; no entry is required on the date of record.

Stock Dividends

Generally accepted accounting principles classify stock dividends as either small or large based on the percentage of the dividend declaration. When a company declares a stock

EXHIBIT 8-3

Cash Dividend Transaction

General Journal				
Date		Description	Debit	Credit
May	31	Dividends—PS	3,800	
		Dividends—CS	38,485	
		Dividends Payable		42,285
		Declared the annual dividend on PS and a $0.25 per		
		share dividend on CS		
		PS: $2 × 1,900 = $3,800		
		CS: $0.25 × 153,940 = $38,485		
June	25	Dividends Payable	42,285	
		Cash		42,285
		Paid the dividend declared on 3/31 to stockholders of		
		record on 6/10		

---

[9]There is actually a fourth date called the ex-dividend date. This date, which is filed by the stock exchange on which the stock is listed, precedes (for cash dividends) the date of record normally by two days to allow time for processing. A stock that has gone ex-dividend is marked with an "x" in newspapers on that day, and purchasers after that time will not receive the declared dividend. The ex-dividend date for stock dividends is usually set the first business day after the stock dividend is paid (and is also after the record date). U.S. SEC, *Ex-Dividend Dates: When Are You Entitled to Stock and Cash Dividends* (http://www.sec.gov/answers/dividen.htm (accessed 12/5/08).

dividend, the percentage specified reflects the percentage increase in the number of shares that will be outstanding. A small stock dividend generally involves a distribution of up to 20 percent additional stock to existing stockholders. All other stock dividends qualify as large stock dividends. Because most stock dividends are small, only the accounting treatment for these dividends is discussed in this text.

Assume that on October 5, 2009, the board of directors of Melbourne, Inc. declares a 10 percent stock dividend. The company has 1,000,000 shares of $3 par value common stock outstanding. Thus, the company will issue 100,000 additional shares (0.10 × 1,000,000) and have 1,100,000 shares outstanding after the dividend. Market value per share of the Melbourne, Inc. stock at the date of declaration is $16. The date of record is October 25 and the distribution date is November 21.

On the stock dividend declaration date, the collective market value of the shares to be issued is debited to the Stock Dividends account, a temporary account similar to Dividends. The offsetting credit in this entry consists of two amounts. First, the total par value of the shares to be issued is credited to Common Stock Dividends Distributable. Common Stock Dividends Distributable is a credit-balanced stockholders' equity account and *not* a liability because no cash or other current assets will have to be used to satisfy it. Second, the difference between the market value of the stock to be distributed and its total par value is credited to Additional Paid-In Capital—Common Stock. The journal entry for Melbourne, Inc.'s common stock dividend declaration is shown in the following entry.

General Journal				
Date		**Description**	**Debit**	**Credit**
Oct	5	Stock Dividends—CS	1,600,000	
		CS Dividends Distributable		300,000
		Additional PIC on CS		1,300,000
		Declared a 10% stock dividend on the $3 par		
		value CS. At this date, there were 1,000,000		
		shares of CS outstanding; per share market		
		value was $16.		
		1,000,000 × 0.10 = 100,000 additional shares;		
		100,000 × $16 = $1,600,000		

On the October 25 record date, a list of stockholders entitled to receive the dividend would be prepared. No accounting entry is necessary on the record date. On the stock distribution date of November 21, Stock Dividend Distributable—CS would be debited and Common Stock would be credited, as follows.

General Journal				
Date		**Description**	**Debit**	**Credit**
Nov	21	CS Dividends Distributable	300,000	
		Common Stock		300,000
		Issued the 10% stock dividend to		
		stockholders of record on 10/25		

On December 31, the $1,600,000 balance of Melbourne, Inc.'s Stock Dividends account would be closed to Retained Earnings.

Oftentimes when a stock dividend is declared, an even number of shares cannot be distributed. For example, if you owned 155 shares of Melbourne when the 10 percent stock dividend was declared, you should receive 15.5 additional shares (155 × 0.10). However, Melbourne cannot send you half a share of stock. In this case, Melbourne would send you 15 new Visual Recap 8.4 shares and the cash equivalent of one-half share.

The entries for cash and stock dividends are summarized in Visual Recap 8.4.

STOCK SPLITS

A **stock split** increases the number of shares of a company's stock through a proportionate reduction in the stock's par value. Splits typically have a similar (though not necessarily equal) effect on the stock's market value. After a stock split, the company issues new shares to stockholders and cancels the old shares. Assume that the board of directors of Melbourne, Inc. declares a 2-for-1 stock split on December 5, after the 10 percent stock dividend had been issued. Prior to the stock split, 1,100,000 shares are outstanding, each with a par value of $3. Thus, the balance in the Common Stock account is $3,300,000 (1,100,000 × $3). After the 2-for-1 split, Melbourne would have 2,200,000 shares of common stock outstanding, and each share would have a $1.50 par value. The balance in Common Stock is still $3,300,000 (2,200,000 shares × $1.50 par value). The quantity of shares authorized, issued, outstanding, never issued, and in the treasury all double as a result of the 2-for-1 split.

A **reverse stock split** reduces the number of shares through a proportionate increase in the stock's par value. Reverse stock splits are often declared specifically to affect the stock price. For example, Time Warner Inc. (www.timewarner.com) did a 1-for-3 reverse split in 2009 to "improve the marketability and liquidity of Time Warner common stock."[10]

VISUAL RECAP 8.4

Dividends

Abbreviations: Number of Shares Outstanding (#SO)
Dividend Amount per Share ($D)
Number of Shares to be Issued (#SI)
Market Price per Share ($MP)
Par Value per Share ($PV)
Additional Paid-In Capital (APIC)

Date	Cash Dividend	Stock Dividend
Date of Declaration	Dividends (#SO × $D) Dividends Payable (#SO × $D)	Dividends (#SI × $MP) Stock Dividends Distributable (#SI × $PV) APIC [(#SI × $MP) − (#SI × $PV)]
Date of Record	no entry	no entry
Date of Payment/ Distribution	Dividends Payable (#SO × $D) Cash (#SO × $D)	Stock Dividends Distributable (#SI × $PV) Common Stock (#SI × $PV)

[10]Time Warner Investor Relations, "Reverse Stock Split"; (Feb, 26, 2009); http://ir.timewarner.com/reversestocksplit.cfm (accessed 6/10/09).

Because a stock split does not affect the balance of any account, a formal journal entry is not necessary to record the announcement of a stock split. The effects of dividends and splits on the stockholders' equity accounts and share data are summarized in Visual Recap 8.5.

RETAINED EARNINGS

Financial statement users often erroneously assume that the Retained Earnings figure reported in a corporate balance sheet represents a cash fund accumulated by a company over its existence. Retained Earnings is simply a general ledger account in which certain types of entries, predominantly those related to profits and dividends, are made each accounting period. Retained Earnings is increased for net income and is decreased for a net loss and for cash or stock dividends declared.

If a significant error were made in accounting for a transaction in a prior period, another type of entry will be made to Retained Earnings. A **prior period adjustment** is a restatement of the balance of Retained Earnings to correct for a past error. For example, assume that in 2007, a company purchased a piece of land for $125,000. The land was incorrectly recorded as a debit to Land Expense (instead of Land, an asset) and a credit to Cash. After the "Land Expense" account was closed at the end of 2007, it caused Retained Earnings to be too small by $125,000. In 2009, when this error is found, a correction must be made to put the land on the books as an asset and to increase Retained Earnings. This entry is:

VISUAL RECAP 8.5

Effects of Dividends and Splits

ACCOUNTS:	Cash Dividends	Stock Dividends	Stock Splits
Stock account—total $ amount	no effect	increase	no effect
Stock account—of shares	no effect	increase	increase or decrease[1]
Additional Paid-In Capital	no effect	increase, if small dividend	no effect
Dividends (or Stock Dividends)	increase	increase	no effect
Retained Earnings[2]	decrease	decrease	no effect
Total Stockholders' Equity	decrease	no effect[3]	no effect
SHARES:			
Authorized	no effect	no effect	increase or decrease[1]
Issued	no effect	increase	increase or decrease[1]
Outstanding	no effect	increase	increase or decrease[1]
Treasury Stock	no effect	no effect	increase or decrease[1]
Par Value	no effect	no effect	decrease or increase[1]

[1] The increase or decrease depends on the type of split occurring. For example, a 2-for-1 split increases the number of shares and decreases par value; a 1-for-2 split decreases the number of shares and increases par value.
[2] When Dividends (or Stock Dividends) is closed, Retained Earnings is decreased.
[3] The increase to the Stock and APIC-CS accounts offset the decrease to Retained Earnings.

General Journal				
Date	Description		Debit	Credit
XXX	Land		125,000	
	Retained Earnings			125,000
	Correct the RE balance because of a prior period			
	error that recorded land purchase as an expense			

At the end of each period, a Statement of Retained Earnings may be prepared to show the beginning balance of RE, any prior period adjustments for the period, the net income (or loss) for the period, and the dividends declared during the period. More often, however, the Statement of RE is prepared as part of a Statement of Changes in Stockholders' Equity. An example of a Statement of Changes in Stockholders' Equity is shown in Exhibit 8-4 using assumed amounts and in which the Statement of Retained Earnings is the fourth labeled column. The Additional PIC for Common and Treasury stock accounts have been combined.

ACCOUNTING INFORMATION FOR DECISION MAKING

Together, stockholders and potential stockholders represent a large and important class of financial decision makers. These parties need a wide range of financial information to make wise investment decisions regarding corporate equity securities.

Dividend Payouts

One principal concern of most investors is the amount of cash that an investment will produce in the future. To predict future cash flows from corporate investments, investors

EXHIBIT 8-4

Statement of Changes in Stockholders' Equity (amounts in thousands)

	Preferred Stock (no par)	Common Stock ($1 par)	Additional PIC (Common)	Retained Earnings	Treasury Stock (Common)
Balances, 1/1/09	$1,200	$5,400	$10,690	$14,350	$146
Prior period adjustment				125	
Issuance of stock					
2,000 shares of PS	270				
10,000 shares of CS		10	117		
Net income				5,210	
Cash dividend				(112)	
CS stock dividend (10%)		541	6,491	(7,032)	
Purchase of common TS					42
Sale of common TS			1		(14)
Balances, 12/31/09	$1,470	$5,951	$17,299	$12,541	$174

need information concerning dividend policies and the factors that may affect those policies. Retirees, for example, often rely heavily on dividend income.

Changes in dividend amounts or rates may also influence a company's stock price. Announcements of dividend increases often result in an increase in the market price of a stock, whereas dividend reductions generally result in a market price decline. An exception to this general rule may occur when a firm is in financial difficulty. For instance, in July 2008, when Cherokee, Inc. (www.cherokeegroup.com), a leading licensor and global brand management company, cut its annual dividend rate from $3 to $2, the company's stock price increased for a period of time.

The SEC recognizes the importance of dividend information for decision makers. Companies subject to SEC regulations must disclose the cash dividends paid over the five most recent fiscal years as well as any significant restrictions on dividend payments, such as those that might be included in a bond indenture. The SEC also encourages companies to discuss their dividend policies in their annual reports.

Preferred stocks typically have a predetermined annual dividend rate or amount. However, most corporate charters do not require preferred stock dividends to be paid in any given year. When a dividend is not paid on a cumulative preferred stock, a corporation must maintain a record of these **dividends in arrears**. As indicated earlier, before a company can pay a common stock dividend, any dividends in arrears as well as current year dividends on cumulative preferred stock must be paid.

Dividends in arrears are not liabilities of the corporation because the board of directors has not formally declared the dividend. However, dividends in arrears affect a company's ability to pay future dividends, particularly to common stockholders, and therefore such dividends should be disclosed in the financial statement footnotes.

Ratios

Many companies disclose **book value per share** for their common stock. This ratio is computed as follows:

$$\text{BV per share} = \text{Total Common Stockholders' Equity} \div \text{Total Shares of Common Stock Outstanding}$$

Using the fiscal 2008 year-end information for American Eagle Outfitters (www.aeo.com), the company's book value per share is $1,340,464,000 ÷ 204,408,000, or $6.56. Although book value per share is often widely quoted, it is not very useful in determining a company's value because the majority of assets are carried in the accounting records at historical, or depreciated historical, cost. Thus, even in the event of a company's liquidation, selling assets and paying off liabilities will not generate the amount of stockholders' equity shown in the balance sheet. However, the book value per share is often considered a measure of the lowest a company's market price per share could fall without significant investor concern about the company's financial stability. For American Eagle Outfitters, the stock price for 2008 fell substantially, with a 52-week low of $6.98 per share.

Investors may also want to compute a stock's **dividend yield**, which is calculated as the annual dividend divided by the current market price of the stock. Although preferred stock has a stated dividend rate, the price of the shares will vary depending on actual events in the stock and economic markets. Thus, the actual yield will not generally be the dividend rate stated on the preferred stock. Preferred stocks typically have a dividend yield comparable to the current yield on high-quality corporate bonds.

Investors also continually monitor and assess the corporate profitability of their investments or potential investments. A key financial measure used to evaluate corporate profitability is **return on equity**. This ratio measures the rate of return earned on the capital invested in a firm by its common stockholders. Return on equity is computed as:

Return on Equity = (Net Income − Preferred Stock Dividends) ÷ Average Common Stockholders' Equity

Preferred stock dividends are subtracted from net income when computing return on equity because those dividends reduce a corporation's earnings available to common stockholders.

Using the fiscal 2008 information for PepsiCo, Inc. (www.pepsico.com), an example of ROE follows.

ROE = $5,142,000,000 − $2,000,000 ÷ [($17,325,000,000 + $12,203,000,000) ÷ 2]

= $5,140,000,000 ÷ $14,764,000,000

= 34.8%

This return on equity indicates that the company is generating an impressive rate of return on the funds that stockholders have invested and on the profits that the company has retained.

SUMMARY

Corporations have several advantages over sole proprietorships and partnerships. One primary advantage is limited liability for corporate stockholders so that the maximum financial loss stockholders face is the amount of their investment. The key disadvantage of corporations is the double taxation of profits; corporate profits are taxed by the federal, and possibly state, government and then taxed again when those earnings are distributed as cash dividends to stockholders.

When business owners decide to incorporate, articles of incorporation are filed in the locale in which the company selects to be domiciled. The company is granted a corporate charter that authorizes the issuance of a maximum number of shares of one or more classes of stock. Common stock represents the residual ownership interests in a corporation. If a corporation is liquidated, its common stockholders are entitled to share proportionately in the firm's remaining assets after all other claims have been satisfied.

Preferred stockholders are granted certain preferences relative to the firm's common stockholders. For example, preferred stockholders must receive all the dividends to which they are entitled (which would include any dividends in arrears) before common stockholders can be paid any dividends in a given year. Preferred stock often has one or more distinctive features, such as a cumulative dividend or convertibility into common stock.

Major types of stockholders' equity transactions include stock issuance, cash or stock dividend declaration and payment/distribution, and stock splits. When stock is sold for more than its par value, the difference between the proceeds and the total par value should be credited to an Additional Paid-In Capital account. To account properly for a dividend, accountants must be aware of three relevant dates: declaration, record, and payment/distribution. A stock split merely changes the number of shares and par value of a company's stock, but not the total amount contained in the Common or Preferred Stock account.

Stockholders and potential stockholders must have access to key information regarding the stockholders' equity of individual corporations, including data on organizational dividend policies and dividend yield. Return on equity is a key measure of a corporation's profitability and is computed by dividing net income, less any preferred stock dividends, by a corporation's average common stockholders' equity for a given period.

KEY TERMS

authorized stock	cumulative preferred stock	prior period adjustment
book value per share	dividend in arrears	return on equity
callable preferred stock	dividend yield	reverse stock split
cash dividend	issued stock	stock dividend
common stock	outstanding stock	stock split
convertible preferred stock	preemptive right	treasury stock
corporate charter	preferred stock	

QUESTIONS

1. Define a "corporation" and a "closely held corporation." Why would owners choose one of these forms of business over the other? *(LO 8.1)*

2. Identify the significance of the (a) articles of incorporation and (b) corporate charter to a corporate entity. Which would be more important to a stockholder and why? *(LO 8.1)*

3. Identify key advantages and disadvantages of the corporate form of business organization. *(LO 8.1)*

4. What is meant by "double taxation" of a corporation's income? Why does this double taxation not occur in sole proprietorships or partnerships? *(LO 8.1)*

5. What are the similarities of common stock and preferred stock? How do these types of stock differ? *(LO 8.2)*

6. What are the primary rights and privileges of (a) common stockholders and (b) preferred stockholders? Would you prefer to be a common stockholder or a preferred stockholder? Why? In your explanation, be certain to address

the issue of age and how that might affect your answer. *(LO 8.2)*

7. Why might a corporation decide to repurchase some of its outstanding common stock? Provide three recent examples of companies that have repurchased their own shares of stock. *(LO 8.4)*

8. How do a cash dividend and a stock dividend differ? How does each type of dividend affect stockholders' equity? *(LO 8.4)*

9. What is a stock split and how does it affect stockholders' equity? *(LO 8.4)*

10. Does a corporation with a positive balance in Retained Earnings have an equivalent amount of cash on hand? Explain. *(LO 8.5)*

11. What is a prior period adjustment, and where would it be presented in the financial statements? *(LO 8.6)*

12. How is the return on equity ratio computed? Why is this ratio important? *(LO 8.8)*

EXERCISES

13. **True or False** *(All LOs)*

Following are a series of statements regarding topics discussed in this chapter.

Required:

Indicate whether each statement is true (T) or false (F).

(a) The stock of closely held corporations is owned by a few individuals, often members of the same family, and is not publicly traded on a securities exchange.

(b) Among other items, the articles of incorporation identify a business's purpose, its principal operating units, and the type and quantity of stock that it plans to issue.

(c)   An important legal privilege of common stockholders is the right to vote on key corporate matters.

(d)   If a corporate charter identifies only one class of stock, that stock is automatically considered the corporation's preferred stock.

(e)   If common shares issued are less than common shares authorized, the company must have treasury stock.

(f)   "Authorized stock" refers to the number of shares of a corporate stock that have been sold or otherwise distributed.

(g)   Once a company begins paying a dividend on common stock, the same or a higher amount of dividend must be paid annually unless the company is losing money.

(h)   Companies subject to the regulations of the Securities and Exchange Commission must disclose the cash dividends they have paid over their five most recent fiscal years.

(i)   Book value per share is computed by dividing Retained Earnings by the number of common shares outstanding.

(j)   Return on equity is computed by dividing a corporation's net income, less preferred stock dividends, by average common stockholders' equity for a given period.

(k)   The dividend yield on preferred stock is the stated rate of dividend divided by the par value of the preferred stock.

(l)   All stock splits cause the number of shares to decrease and the par value per share to increase.

14. **Terms** *(LO 8.1 and 8.2)*

Following are definitions or descriptions of terms relating to corporations and corporate stockholders' equity.

(1)   The first-time sale of a corporation's stock to the general public

(2)   A dollar value that has been assigned to each share of stock

(3)   A "legal" being

(4)   The maximum number of shares of stock that a corporation is permitted to sell

(5)   The class of stock that normally has voting rights

(6)   A document describing the basic nature of the corporate entity

(7)   The number of shares of stock that has been sold by a corporation

(8)   The ability of stockholders to maintain their proportionate ownership interest in a company when new issues of stock are made

(9)   The number of shares of stock currently held by company's shareholders

(10)   The stock that has been issued and reacquired by a corporation

(11)   Corporate shares that are typically cumulative

Required:

Match each definition or description with the appropriate term from the following list.

(a)   Corporation

(b)   Corporate charter

(c)   Initial public offering

(d)   Authorized stock

(e)   Issued stock

(f)   Outstanding stock

(g)   Treasury stock

(h)   Preferred stock

(i)   Common stock

(j)   Preemptive right

(k)   Par value

15. **Corporate Form of Business Organization** *(LO 8.1, writing)*

Your friends, Stephanie Anderson and Jason Martinkus, are partners in Videos Unlimited, a small but rapidly growing business. Anderson and Martinkus have been told by their attorney that they should consider incorporating their business.

Required:

Anderson and Martinkus have asked your advice about incorporating their business. To help them put things in perspective, write a memo that summarizes the key advantages and disadvantages of the corporate form of business. Be sure to discuss future implications if the business is extremely successful and if the business is extremely unsuccessful.

16. **Common Stock Issuances** *(LO 8.3)*

On January 15, 2009, Tallyho Corp. incorporated in Georgia and was authorized to issue 3,000,000 shares of common stock. In an initial public offering, Tallyho sold 1,350,000 shares of common stock for $18 per share.

Required:

(a)   Prepare the journal entry to record the sale of the stock if Tallyho's common stock

(1)   has a $0.50 par value.

(2)   has a $3.00 par value.

(3)   is no-par value.

(b)   Explain why selling common stock at more than par value does not increase net income for the period.

17.   **Number of Shares** *(LO 8.3)*

The number of shares of common stock for three companies is given in the following table.

Company	Number of Shares			
	Authorized	Issued	Outstanding	Treasury
Adams Corp.	5,000,000	3,790,000	(a)	0
Brady, Inc.	2,000,000	1,600,000	1,530,000	(b)
Costanza Corp.	1,500,000	(c)	1,210,000	50,000

Required:

(a)   What is the distinction between issued and outstanding shares of stock?

(b)   Determine the number of shares that corresponds to each omitted value.

(c)   If Adams Corp. sells 10,000 more shares of stock, how many shares will be authorized, issued, outstanding, and in treasury?

18.   **Common Stockholders' Rights** *(LO 8.2, 8.4, and 8.7)*

You own 5,000 shares of $4 par value common stock of Cohen & Cohen Hardware Corp. The company has 50,000 shares of common stock outstanding. Cohen & Cohen does not have any other classes of stock outstanding.

Required:

(a)   If Cohen & Cohen declares a cash dividend of $30,000, how much of this dividend can you expect to receive? What is the amount of dividend per share?

(b)   If Cohen & Cohen decides to sell an additional 14,000 shares of common stock, how many of these shares will you be entitled to purchase? Explain.

(c)   Presently, Cohen & Cohen's total stockholders' equity is $3,200,000, and the company's common stock is trading for $71 per share on a major stock exchange. What is the total "value" of the Cohen & Cohen shares that you own? What is the book value of each of your shares? Is either of these amounts equal to the amount you paid for the shares? Explain.

19.   **Stock Split and Stock Dividend** *(LO 8.3 and 8.4)*

Marigold Enterprises is authorized to issue 1,000,000 shares of $6 par value common stock. Since incorporation, 550,000 shares have been issued. Currently, Marigold holds 40,000 of its own shares in treasury and has $3,500,000 in Retained

Earnings. Marigold is considering the following three options:

(1)   Declaring a 2:1 stock split

(2)   Declaring a 15 percent stock dividend (current market price is $15 per share)

(3)   Declaring a 1:2 stock split

Required:

(a)   What is the current balance in the Common Stock account?

(b)   How many shares of common stock are currently outstanding?

(c)   For each of the three options Marigold is considering, determine the number of shares authorized, issued, outstanding, and in treasury after the declaration. Each option should be executed on the original information.

(d)   What would be the balance in Retained Earnings if the (a) split and (b) dividend were chosen?

(e)   Determine the par value per share and the balance in the Common Stock account under each of the options.

(f)   What would you expect to happen to the market price per share of Marigold common stock if each of the three options were chosen? Explain the rationale for your answer.

20.   **Stock Dividends** *(LO 8.4)*

Denim Industries has 1,000,000 shares of $10 par value common stock authorized, of which 400,000 shares have been issued and 380,000 are currently outstanding. On November 30, 2009, when the stock is trading at $40 per share, Denim declares a 10 percent stock dividend of stockholders of record on December 24, 2009. The stock dividend will be distributed on January 10, 2010.

Required:

(a)   How many shares are in treasury on November 30?

(b)   How many shares will be distributed on January 10, 2010?

(c)   Prepare any necessary journal entries related to this stock dividend on the following dates:

    (1)   Date of declaration

    (2)   Date of record

    (3)   Date of distribution

(d)   On Denim's December 31, 2009, balance sheet, will Denim show a liability for the value of the undistributed stock divided? Why or why not?

21. **Cumulative Dividends** (LO 8.4, ethics)

Easy Automotive Manufacturers (EAM) has two classes of stock: common stock with a par value of $2 (500,000 shares authorized; 300,000 shares outstanding) and preferred stock with a par value of $100 (25,000 shares authorized; 10,000 shares outstanding). The preferred stock has an annual stated dividend rate of $5 per share. EAM declared the following dividends over a five-year period, during which no additional shares of stock are issued.

Year	Dividend Amount
2005	$170,000
2006	0
2007	110,000
2008	30,000
2009	200,000

Required:

(a) What is the total dollar amount of cash dividend to which preferred stockholders are entitled to in one year?

(b) Assume that EAM's preferred stock is noncumulative. Determine the amount of dividends for preferred and common shareholders in each of the five years.

(c) Assume that EAM's preferred stock is cumulative.

   (1) Determine the amount of dividends for preferred and common shareholders in each of the five years.

   (2) Explain how dividends in arrears, if they exist, should be noted in the financial statements.

   (3) At the end of 2006, EAM's management does not want to list the dividends in arrears in the financial statements as required because there is no legal liability to pay that amount as of December 31, 2006. Is EAM's management right about there being no legal obligation? Explain. Discuss why this omission might mislead investors.

22. **Retained Earnings** (LO 8.5 and 8.6)

Following are several items that may have an effect on the Retained Earnings account.

- Issuing common stock
- Cash dividend
- Stock dividend
- Stock split
- Purchasing treasury stock
- Selling treasury stock
- Net income
- Net loss
- Prior period error that overstated revenues
- Prior period error that overstated expenses

Required:

(a) For each item, indicate whether it increases, decreases, or has no effect on Retained Earnings.

(b) For each item, indicate whether the effect on Retained Earnings is immediate (that is, initial recording of the item would include a debit or credit to Retained Earnings in the journal entry) or occurs during closing entries.

(c) For each item, indicate whether it increases, decreases, or has no effect on total stockholders' equity.

23. **Statement of Stockholders' Equity** (LO 8.4., 8.5, and 8.6)

Biyama Corp. has two classes of stock: 5%, $100 par value preferred (authorized 10,000 shares) and $0.50 par value common (authorized 700,000 shares). At the beginning of 2009, the company had issued and outstanding 6,500 share of preferred and 360,000 shares of common. The preferred stock had all been issued at par value and the common stock had been issued at an average price of $7.80 per share. The company's Retained Earnings on January 1, 2009 was $738,400. During 2009, Biyama had the following transactions:

- Issued 4,000 shares of common stock in exchange for a building with a list price of $80,000. The common stock had sold on the NYSE the previous day for $18 per share.
- Bought 300 shares of common stock for $21 per share.
- Sold 100 shares of the previously purchased common stock for $23 per share.
- Declared a total cash dividend of $53,800.
- Had net income for 2009 of $121,650.

Required:

(a) Prepare a statement of stockholders' equity for Biyama Corp. for 2009. The additional paid-in capital for common and treasury stock may be combined.

(b) Determine the amount of cash dividend paid to preferred stockholders and to common stockholders in 2009.

24. **Book Value per Share and Return on Equity** (LO 8.7 and 8.8)

TransAmerica is an interstate railroad cargo transportation company. The following table presents key financial data for TransAmerica over a recent five-year period. Amounts are expressed in millions of dollars.

	2005	2006	2007	2008	2009
Revenues	$549.7	$587.4	$601.7	$593.0	$543.8
Net income	55.4	75.9	88.2	73.9	55.4
Common stockholders' equity (year-end)	262.3	337.8	337.4	454.1	456.1
Common shares outstanding (year-end)	59.7	63.9	64.0	64.1	62.9

Note: At the beginning of 2005, TransAmerica had $228.7 million of common stockholders' equity. Annual preferred stock dividends are $1.5 million.

Required:

(a) Compute TransAmerica's book value per share at the end of each year listed.

(b) Compute the company's return on equity for each year.

(c) Is there a definite trend apparent in either book value per share or ROE? If so, indicate whether that trend is favorable or unfavorable.

(d) Suppose that you are a potential investor in TransAmerica common stock. Identify three questions related to the company's financial data that you would want to ask the company's top executives.

PROBLEMS

25. Issuance of Common Stock (LO 8.3)

On April 21, Killarny Enterprises acquired a large tract of land from McSwain Corporation. Killarny issued 1,400 shares of its $1 par value common stock to McSwain in exchange for the land.

Required:

(a) Prepare the journal entry to record this transaction by Killarny Enterprises, if the company's stock is not publicly traded and the land has an appraised value of $110,000.

(b) Assume that on April 20, the Killarny stock traded on the New York Stock Exchange for $75 per share. The land has an appraised value of $110,000. Prepare the appropriate journal entry to record this exchange transaction by Killarny Enterprises.

(c) Suppose, instead, that Killarny sold 1,400 shares of stock on April 20 for $80 cash per share. The company then acquired the land from McSwain Corporation on April 21 for its appraised value. Prepare the journal entries for these two transactions by Killarny Enterprises.

(d) Determine the differences between the financial statement results in parts (a), (b), and (c). Explain why these differences occurred.

26. Accounting for Treasury Stock Transactions (LO 8.4)

Morris & Butler is a large discount brokerage firm. On December 31, 2008, the stockholders' equity section of the company's balance sheet indicated that 65,000 shares of the company's common stock were being held as treasury stock. This treasury stock had been acquired for $1,950,000 in a single transaction. The company's common stock has a par value of $0.10 per share.

Required:

(a) Why do companies sometimes reacquire stock that they have previously issued?

(b) Prepare the journal entry to record the purchase of the treasury stock.

(c) Assume that Morris & Butler sold 2,000 shares of its treasury stock on April 3, 2009, for $35 per share. Prepare the journal entry to record the sale of the treasury stock.

(d) Assume that on May 31, 2009, Morris & Butler sold another 3,000 shares of its treasury stock for $27 per share. Prepare the journal entry to record the sale of the treasury stock.

(e) Why is treasury stock not classified as an asset?

27. Accounting for Cash Dividends (LO 8.1 and 8.4)

Lupinski Distributors has 1,000,000 shares of common stock outstanding. On January 11 of the current year, Lupinski declared a cash dividend of $0.20 per share, payable on March 9 to stockholders of record on February 12.

Required:

(a) When did this dividend become a liability to Lupinski?

(b) Prepare any journal entries required in Lupinski's accounting records relating to this cash dividend on the following dates in the current year:

(1) January 11

(2) February 12

(3) March 9

(4) December 31

(c) What group of individuals authorized the declaration of this dividend?

(d) What general types of information must public companies regulated by the SEC disclose in their annual reports regarding their dividend policies? Why is this information important to potential investors?

28. **Dividends to Preferred Shareholders** *(LO 8.4, 8.6, and 8.7)*

As of December 31, 2008, Biloxi Corporation has 10,000 shares of 8%, $100 par value cumulative preferred stock outstanding. Biloxi has not paid any dividends to its stockholders during the past three years.

Required:

(a) What disclosure must Biloxi make in its annual report regarding the unpaid dividends on its preferred stock? What amount will be included in the disclosure, and how was that amount calculated?

(b) Where in Biloxi's financial statements will this disclosure be found?

(c) Why is this disclosure of interest to Biloxi's preferred and common stockholders?

(d) Assume that in February 2009 Biloxi declares a $500,000 cash dividend. How much will be received by Biloxi's common stockholders? If Biloxi has 250,000 shares of common stock outstanding, what is the dividend amount per common share?

(e) Use the information in part (d). If the market price per common share is $18, what is the dividend yield per common share? How would an investor determine if this yield is "good" or "bad"?

29. **Stock Dividends** *(LO 8.4 and 8.5)*

Hodges, Inc. has ten million shares of $5 par value common stock authorized. Of that amount, 4.6 million have been issued and 4.2 million are outstanding. On July 2, Hodges declared a 5 percent stock dividend to shareholders of record on July 31, distributable on August 8. On July 2, Hodges stock was trading at $18 per share.

Required:

(a) Related to this stock dividend, will the balance in any of the following accounts be affected? Explain.

(1) Cash

(2) Retained Earnings

(3) Treasury Stock

(b) How many shares are held by Hodges in the treasury? Will those shares receive the dividend? Why or why not?

(c) How many shares will be distributed in the stock dividend?

(d) Record the journal entries related to this stock dividend on the following dates:

(1) July 2

(2) July 31

(3) August 8

30. **Accounting for Stockholders' Equity Transactions** *(LO 8.3, 8.4, and 8.6)*

Dozier Manufacturing was granted a corporate charter on January 3, 2009, and began operations shortly thereafter. Dozier's charter authorizes the firm to issue up to 800,000 shares of $3 par value common stock and 50,000 shares of $100 par value preferred stock. The preferred stock carries an annual dividend rate of $5, is cumulative, and can be converted into Dozier common stock through December 31, 2018. Each share of preferred stock can be converted into two shares of Dozier common stock. During 2009, the following events or transactions affected the stockholders' equity of Dozier.

January 10	Sold 22,000 shares of common stock for $18 per share.
March 30	Sold 5,000 shares of preferred stock for $145 per share.
June 12	Exchanged 3,000 shares of common stock for a building with an appraised value of $71,000. On this date, Dozier's common stock was trading at $22 per share on a regional stock exchange.
October 3	Sold 7,000 shares of common stock for $27 per share.
November 4	Declared the annual cash dividend on outstanding preferred stock, payable on December 6, to stockholders of record on November 21.
December 6	Paid the preferred stock dividend.

Required:

(a) Prepare the journal entries for the events listed.

(b) Net income for 2009 was $734,000. Prepare all year-end closing entries for which data are available.

(c) Prepare the stockholders' equity section of Dozier's balance sheet as of December 31, 2009.

(d) Assume instead that Dozier's common stock has no par value. Prepare the journal entries for the January 10, June 12, and October 3 transactions.

(e) Refer to the transaction on June 12. Assume that Dozier's common stock is not publicly traded.

Prepare the appropriate journal entry for this transaction given this assumption.

(f)   What accounting principle dictates that Dozier include information in its financial statement footnotes regarding the specific features or stipulations attached to its preferred stock?

31.   **Analyzing Stockholders' Equity** *(LO 8.6, 8.7, and 8.8)*

Ariat Productions produces and distributes several popular television shows. Following is information about stockholders' equity for the company's 2008 and 2009 balance sheets.

■   *Preferred Stock:* $10 par value; 5,000,000 shares authorized; 1,200,000 shares were issued at par in 2008 and were outstanding all of 2009; each share of preferred has a $0.60 per share annual dividend amount.

■   *Common Stock:* $0.10 par value; 7,500,000 shares authorized; a total of 4,925,000 shares and 4,983,000 shares were issued by end of 2008 and 2009, respectively.

■   *Additional Paid-In Capital on Common Stock:* The 4,925,000 common shares were sold for $15.50 each; the common shares sold during 2009 were sold for $19.40 each.

■   *Treasury Stock:* Accounted for at cost; 120,800 shares were held in the treasury at the end of 2008, each having been purchased for $16 per share; during 2009, 20,000 shares of treasury stock were sold for $18 per share and an additional 3,500 shares were purchased for $21 per share.

■   *Retained Earnings:* Ariat had $1,819,360 and $1,083,700 of net income for 2008 and 2009. The annual dividend was paid each year on preferred stock but no dividends were paid in either year on common stock.

■   *Net Income:* respectively.

Required:

(a)   Prepare a Statement of Stockholders' Equity for Ariat Productions at the end of 2008 and at the end of 2009.

(b)   Compute the book value per share of Ariat's common stock at the end of 2008 and 2009.

(c)   Compute Ariat's return on equity for 2008 and 2009. Did this ratio improve or deteriorate in 2009 compared with the previous year?

(d)   For this requirement, assume that Ariat does not have any preferred stock and that the amount previously computed for preferred stock dividends was paid instead to common stockholders at year-end. If the average market price per common share in 2009 were $20, what would be the dividend yield on common stock in 2009?

(e)   Identify one reason that may explain why Ariat's common stock has such a low par value.

CASES

32.   **Investor Interpretations** *(LO 8.4 and 8.7, writing)*

Dee Publications has been in operation for more than 30 years and went public in the early1980s. The company has had net income in every year except one since it went public. The majority of Dee's cash flows are generated from its operations, and Dee only resorted to significant borrowing when it expanded operations.

Since it became a publicly traded company, Dee Publications has tried to declare a cash dividend every fiscal year, but always declares a cash dividend at least every other year. Last year Dee did not declare a dividend. This year, a significant portion of Dee's long-term debt is maturing, and declaring a cash dividend this year could lead to a cash flow problem. Dee Publications is gaining market share and sales are up, so management believes that this problem is unique to this operating year.

To satisfy its shareholders without declaring a cash dividend this year, Dee is considering the following options:

■   A stock dividend

■   A stock split

■   No dividend this year, but a mid-year dividend next year

Required:

Discuss how an investor would interpret each of the three options. Include in your discussion the benefits and drawbacks to each choice both from Dee's standpoint and the investor's standpoint.

33.   **Annual Reports** *(LO 8.8, Internet)*

Use the annual report of Carnival Corporation for the 2007 fiscal year to answer the following questions. This information can be found on either the annual report or the SEC 10-K filing at www.carnival.com by following the links to Investor Relations.

Required:

(a) How many shares of common stock does Carnival have authorized, issued, outstanding, and in treasury for 2006 and 2007?

(b) Has Carnival authorized the issue of preferred stock? If so, why is it not listed on the balance sheet?

(c) What kinds of dividends has Carnival declared, if any, in 2006 and 2007?

(d) Calculate the following ratios for Carnival for the years 2007. (Hint: Use the weighted average number of shares given in the footnotes for each year's calculations.)

   (1) Book value per share

   (2) Dividend yield assuming a market value per share of $25

   (3) Return on equity

(e) Comment on how an investor would interpret each of the measurements calculated in part (d). Based on the results, would you invest in Carnival? Explain the rationale of your answer.

34. **Comparing Companies** (LO 8.7 and 8.8, group, Internet)

Identifying the similarities and differences in companies is as crucial to making investment decisions as understanding a single company's financial statements. Form groups of at least four students. Each group should select a single industry. Each group member should locate a different annual report within that industry. (The industry and individual company may be assigned by your instructor.)

Required—individual group members:

(a) Calculate the following ratios for the company you selected for the two most recent fiscal years.

   (1) Book value per share

   (2) Dividend yield

   (3) Return on equity

(b) Comment on the changes from year to year.

(c) Does this company seem to be a good investment based on these four ratios? Explain your answer.

Required—groups:

(d) Compile the ratio calculations for each company prepared by the individual group members into one table.

(e) Compare the results from company to company in the same fiscal years. Include in your comparison, a graphical analysis. Discuss reasons why these ratios might be similar or different within an industry.

(f) Based on these four ratios across companies, which company is the best investment in the industry you have chosen? Explain your answer.

Required—class:

(g) Compare the ratios from each industry. Discuss reasons why these ratios might be similar or different between industries.

(h) Does one industry seem to be a better investment than another? Do you think this is constant over time? Explain your answers.

SUPPLEMENTAL PROBLEMS

35. **Issuing Stock** (LO 8.3; Compare to Problem 25)

Spader, Inc. was established in 2007 and is authorized to issue 1,000,000 shares of common stock with a par value of $1. On August 27, 2007, before the stock was publicly traded, the founders were given stock in exchange for investments in the company.

   ■ Crane invested $200,000 in exchange for 100,000 shares of stock.

   ■ Schmidt donated a piece of land and a building with appraised values, respectively, of $50,000 and $175,000 in exchange for 100,000 shares of stock.

On February 4, 2009, Spader issued 10,000 shares at $10 per share in an initial public offering. On February 7, 2009, Schmidt sold 20,000 of her shares to another investor for $12 per share.

Required:

Prepare all necessary journal entries for Spader, Inc. on the following dates:

(a) August 27, 2007

(b) February 4, 2009

(c) February 7, 2009

36. Accounting for Treasury Stock Transactions *(LO 8.2 and 8.4; Compare to Problem 26)*

Refer to the information regarding Spader, Inc. in problem 35. By December 2009, Spader had 380,000 shares of issued and outstanding common stock. As a year-end bonus for Spader's CEO, the company will give him 10,000 shares of Spader stock, which will be reacquired from the shares that are currently outstanding.

Required:

(a) Spader has one million shares authorized and only 380,000 issued. Provide an explanation why Spader cannot give its CEO 10,000 shares from the shares that have not been issued.

(b) Suppose that Spader reacquires 12,000 shares of its own stock on December 3, 2009, when the stock is trading at $40 per share. Prepare the journal entry to record this repurchase.

(c) Prepare the journal entry to give the reacquired shares to the CEO on December 31, 2009. Explain the effect of this transaction on the Common Stock account.

37. Accounting for Dividends and Splits *(LO 8.4; Compare to Problems 27 and 28)*

Gibbs Corp. has 1,000,000 authorized shares of $1 par value common stock, of which 475,000 are currently issued and 425,000 are outstanding. The following events are related to Gibbs Corp.'s common stock.

■ On November 1, 2007, Gibbs Corp. declared a 10 percent stock dividend to all shareholders of record on November 30, distributable on December 30. At the time of the declaration, the stock was trading at $50 per share.

■ On October 8, 2008, Gibbs Corp. declared a 4:1 stock split. At the time of the split, the stock was trading at $90 per share.

■ On November 5, 2009, Gibbs Corp. declared a $1 per share cash dividend to all shareholders of record on November 30, payable on December 30. At the time of the declaration, the stock was trading at $25 per share.

Required:

(a) Calculate the following amounts after each event took place:

(1) Number of shares authorized

(2) Number of shares issued

(3) Number of shares outstanding

(4) Number of shares in treasury

(5) Par value per share

(6) Balance in the common stock account

(b) Prepare the journal entries associated with each event.

(c) Why might Gibbs Corp. have declared a stock dividend in 2007 rather than a cash dividend?

(d) Why might Gibbs Corp. have split its stock in 2008?

(e) Use library and Internet resources to find three companies that have recently declared a stock dividend or a stock split. How have these declarations affected the companies' stock prices?

38. Dividends to Preferred Shareholders *(LO 8.4 and 8.6; Compare to Problem 28)*

McBain Industries, started in 2008, has both common and preferred stock. Information about each class of stock is given next.

■ The $50 par value preferred stock is cumulative and pays an annual dividend of $2.50 per share. During 2008 and 2009, 10,000 shares were outstanding.

■ The common stock has a par value of $0.01. During 2008 and 2009, 450,000 shares were outstanding.

■ In 2008, no dividends were paid by McBain. On August 8, 2009, McBain declared a $0.50 per share cash dividend for common shareholders of record September 8, payable on September 15.

Required:

(a) What type of disclosure should McBain have had in its 2008 annual report regarding dividends?

(b) Given the information on the common stock dividend, what total amount of cash dividends must have been declared by McBain in 2009? Explain.

(c) How would your answer to part (b) have differed if the preferred stock had been noncumulative?

(d) Record the journal entries related to the 2009 dividends.

(e) What type of disclosure should McBain have in its 2009 annual report regarding dividends?

39. Analyzing Stockholders' Equity *(LO 8.8, Compare to Problem 31)*

Following is the stockholders' equity information for a major restaurant corporation for 2007 through 2009. Except for the market price, which is presented in actual dollars, all information about amounts is shown in millions.

Stockholders' Equity	2009	2008	2007
Common Stock	$ 8,970	$ 9,234	$ 9,795
Retained Earnings	12,739	12,256	10,994
Treasury Stock	729	605	601
Additional Information			
Net Income	$ 1,220	$ 1,380	$ 1,830
Common stock dividends	457	0	484
Common shares outstanding at the fiscal year-end	2,068	2,071	2,070
Market price of stock at at fiscal year end	$27.95	$29.85	$32.20

Required:

(a) Calculate the following ratios for 2007, 2008, and 2009.

(1) Book value per share

(2) Dividend yield

(3) Return on equity (2008 and 2009 only)

(b) Comment on the changes from year to year.

(c) Use library or Internet resources to find averages for dividend yield and return on equity for a company in the restaurant business. How does this company compare to the industry average?

ANALYSIS OF ACCOUNTING DATA

CHAPTER 9

The Corporate Income Statement and Financial Statement Analysis

LEARNING OBJECTIVES

1. Account for investments in stocks and bonds.
2. Identify the key elements of the corporate income statement.
3. Compute earnings per share.
4. Account for corporate income taxes.
5. Discuss the objectives of, and sources for, information for financial statement analysis for different types of decision makers.
6. Prepare trend analyses of financial statement data and common-sized financial statements.
7. Compute key financial ratios including liquidity, leverage, activity, profitability, and market strength ratios.
8. Assess earnings quality.

INTRODUCTION

This chapter addresses components, other than normal operations, that affect corporate income as well as related taxation issues. The second part of the chapter considers an array of financial statement analysis techniques used to gain insights into the financial performance and financial condition of a business as reflected by its financial statements. The final part of the chapter identifies factors that influence earnings quality.

INCOME STATEMENT

An income statement may also be referred to as a "statement of earnings" or "statement of operations." Income statement components discussed to this point in the text have been the traditional revenues and expenses of most business enterprises. Income from operations represents the earnings produced by a corporation's principal profit-oriented activities. The most simplistic computation for income from operations is operating revenues minus the cost of goods sold plus other operating expenses.

Many corporations have items appearing on their income statements in addition to operating revenues and expenses. This section addresses the following items: earnings (or losses) from stock or bond investments, discontinued operations, extraordinary items, and deferred income taxes. Most corporate income statements do not contain all these elements. However, these items are common enough that each should be discussed.

Exhibit 9-1 provides three years (2005–2007) of income statements for Avon Products, Inc. (www.avoncompany.com). In 2007, the company had $9,938,700,000 in operating revenues and $9,066,000,000 in cost of goods sold, selling, and administrative expenses, resulting in operating profit of $872,700,000.

A company's expected growth rate in sales, competitive conditions in its industry, and general health of the national economy are factors that decision makers can use to project the firm's future earnings, given its current year's income from continuing operations as a base amount. Organizational risk factors are listed in Item 1A in a company's 10-K filing with the SEC. Avon, for instance, discusses the high rate of turnover of sales representatives, significant levels of competition, international market risks (political, regulatory, and foreign currency), general economic climate, and supplier relationships as factors that will affect its future business operations.

Earnings from Investments

Corporations often purchase the stocks or bonds of other entities. If such purchases are made simply to invest cash for the short run, the investments are shown as current assets. Alternatively, some investments by corporations are made for the long run, usually because the investing corporation wants to establish a working relationship with the other entity. For example, Avon has multiple investments in equity securities, of both partially owned companies and wholly owned subsidiaries (such as those in Egypt, China, and Columbia).

Avon Consolidated
Statements of Income
(in millions, except per
share amounts)

| | Years ended December 31 | | |
	2007	2006	2005
Net sales	$ 9,845.2	$ 8,677.3	$ 8,065.2
Other revenue	93.5	86.6	84.4
Total revenue	$ 9,938.7	$ 8,763.9	$ 8,149.6
Costs, expenses, and other:			
Cost of sales	(3,941.2)	(3,416.5)	(3,113.2)
Selling and administrative expenses	(5,124.8)	(4,586.0)	(3,887.4)
Operating profit	$ 872.7	$ 761.4	$ 1,149.0
Interest expense	(112.2)	(99.6)	(54.1)
Interest income	42.2	55.3	37.3
Other expenses	(6.6)	(13.6)	(8.0)
Income before taxes and minority interest	$ 796.1	$ 703.5	$ 1,124.2
Income taxes			
Current	$ (375.2)	$ (334.1)	$ (301.4)
Deferred	112.4	110.7	31.7
Total	$ (262.8)	$ (223.4)	$ (269.7)
Income before minority interest	$ 533.3	$ 480.1	$ 854.5
Minority interest	(2.6)	(2.5)	(6.9)
Net income	$ 530.7	$ 477.6	$ 847.6
Basic earnings per share	$ 1.22	$ 1.07	$ 1.82

Source: http://www.avoncompany.com/investor/annualreport/pdf/annualreport2007.pdf

Investments in Stocks

Depending on the percentage of ownership, a company may use one of two accounting methods to account for a stock investment: cost or equity. These two methods create important differences on the income statement.

If a company owns less than 20 percent of the outstanding stock of another company, the investing company uses the cost method to account for the investment. Under the **cost method**, the investing company debits the Investment account (an asset) and credits Cash for the cost of the stock purchased. When cash dividends are received, the investing company records a debit to Cash and a credit to Dividend Revenue (or Other Revenue, a nonoperating revenue). At the end of each year, the cost and the fair market value of the investment are compared, and the investment account will be written up or down as necessary to fair market value. Such gains and losses, however, do not affect the income statement; they are included, respectively, as credits and debits to stockholders' equity.

If a company owns between 20 and 50 percent of the outstanding stock of another company, the investing company uses the equity method to account for the investment. Under the **equity method**, the investing company debits the Investment account and credits Cash for the cost of the stock purchased. When the company in which the investment was made earns profits, the investing company records its share of those profits in its Investment account and on its income statement in an account called "Income from Unconsolidated Subsidiary" or "Equity in Earnings of Unconsolidated Subsidiaries" (as shown on the 2008 income statement of Sempra Energy; www.sempra.com[1]). When cash dividends are received by the investing company, it records a debit to Cash and a credit to its Investment account.

If a company owns more than 50 percent of the outstanding shares of stock, the owning company is referred to as the **parent**, and the owned company is referred to as the **subsidiary**. When such a relationship exists, the equity method of accounting for the investment is used during the year and the financial statements of the two companies are consolidated at year-end. **Consolidation** refers to the process of combining financial statements of a parent and subsidiary. Transactions that took place between the two companies are eliminated during consolidation. However, as in the case of Avon, if the parent company does not own all the stock of the other company, a **minority interest** ownership exists.

Assume that Avon owned 80 percent of the stock of Bevy of Beauty Corp., which earned revenues of $500,000 and incurred expenses of $350,000 during the year, or a net profit of $150,000. The entire revenue and expense amounts are included in Avon's revenues and expenses. However, the minority interest ownership is entitled to its 20 percent of Bevy of Beauty's profits. Thus, on the income statement, a subtraction would be made for "Minority Interest Income." The total minority interest (stock and earnings) is shown on the balance sheet, but presentation on that statement varies by company. Until late 2008, some companies (such as Avon) showed Minority Interest (MI) as part of liabilities; others (such as Sempra Energy) showed MI as a separate section between liabilities and stockholders' equity (referred to as "the mezzanine"). However, as of the end of 2008, the FASB required companies to record MI as part of stockholders' equity.[2]

The relationships between the cost and the equity methods are shown in Visual Recap 9.1.

Investments in Bonds

Investments in another company's bonds payable are another way that corporations often generate additional revenue. If bond investments are to be held to maturity, the accounting for the investment in bonds payable is essentially the mirror image of the accounting performed by the issuer of the bonds payable.

Exhibit 7A-1 in Chapter 7 provided information on $100,000 worth of 10 percent, five-year bonds payable issued by Hardin Manufacturing Company on April 1, 2009, when the market rate of interest was 12 percent. These bonds are used to illustrate the accounting for an investment in corporate bonds. Assume that Avon purchased all of Hardin's bonds at issue date and intends to hold the bonds to maturity as a long-term investment. Exhibit 9-2 provides the journal entries for the first year relative to this investment.

One important difference in the "mirror image" accounting between the buyer and the seller is that the buyer of corporate bonds does not have a discount or premium account related to the Investment account. Discounts and premiums are amortized directly

---

[1] Sempra Energy, Form 10-K Annual Report (filed February 26, 2008); http://investor.shareholder.com/sre/secfiling.cfm?filingID=86521-08-15 (accessed 12/8/08).

[2] Financial Accounting Standards Board, *SFAS No. 160: Noncontrolling Interests in Consolidated Financial Statements* (December 2007).

VISUAL RECAP 9.1

Accounting for Long-Term Stock Investments

	Cost Method	Equity Method	
Ownership interest	*Less than 20%*	*20%–50%*	*Over 50%*
Record initial investment at cost	Investment in XYZ Cash*	Investment in XYZ Cash*	Investment in XYZ Cash*
Receive dividends	Cash Dividend Revenue	Cash Investment in XYZ	Cash Investment in XYZ
Year-end procedures: Record increase in FMV (a decrease would reverse the entry and record a loss)	Investment in XYZ Unrealized Gain**	No entry	No entry
Record proportionate share of XYZ's net income (a loss would reverse the entry)	No entry	Investment in XYZ Income from Unconsolidated Subsidiary	Investment in XYZ Income from Unconsolidated Subsidiary
Consolidate the financial statements	No entry	No entry	Combine financial statements, eliminate inter-company accounts, and record any minority interest effects on the income statement and balance sheet
Sell stock at a gain (at a loss would record a loss debit); gain or loss is shown on income statement	Cash Investment in XYZ Gain on Sale of XYZ	Cash Investment in XYZ Gain on Sale of XYZ	Cash Minority Interest Investment in XYZ Gain on Sale of XYZ

*Could be other assets or stock
**Part of Stockholders' Equity on the balance sheet.

within the Investment asset account. Interest revenue appearing on the investor's income statement (as does the related interest expense on the issuer's income statement) reflects the market rate of interest rather than the stated rate. At the bond maturity date, Avon's Investment in Bonds account will have a balance of $100,000 or the face value of the bonds.

Corporate Income Taxes

Congress historically has imposed graduated, or progressive, tax rates on corporations. As corporations earn more taxable income, the percentage of that income that must be paid to the federal government generally increases. For instance, corporate tax rates for 2008 were

EXHIBIT 9-2

Journal Entries for a
Bond Investment
Purchased at a Discount

General Journal				
Date		Description	Debit	Credit
2009 Apr.	1	Investment in Bonds	93,641	
		Cash		93,641
		Recorded purchase of $100,000, 10%, 5-year bonds at a market rate of 12%		
Sept.	30	Cash	5,000	
		Investment in Bonds	636	
		Interest Revenue		5,636
		Received semiannual interest & amortized discount to the Investment account		
Dec.	31	Interest Receivable	2,500	
		Investment in Bonds	318	
		Interest Revenue		2,818
		Accrued semiannual interest & amortized discount to the Investment account		
2010 Mar.	31	Cash	5,000	
		Investment in Bonds	318	
		Interest Revenue		2,818
		Interest Receivable		2,500
		Received semiannual interest & amortized discount to the Investment account		

Taxable income over	But not over	Tax rate
$ 0	$ 50,000	15%
50,000	75,000	25%
75,000	100,000	34%
100,000	335,000	39%
335,000	10,000,000	34%
10,000,000	15,000,000	35%
15,000,000	18,333,333	38%
18,333,333		35%

Thus, a corporation having $150,000 of taxable income would owe federal income taxes of $41,750, calculated as:

$0.15 \times (\$50,000)$	$ 7,500
$+ 0.25 \times (\$75,000 - \$50,000)$	6,250
$+ 0.34 \times (\$100,000 - \$75,000)$	8,500
$+ 0.39 \times (\$150,000 - \$100,000)$	19,500
	$41,750

Corporations compute tax expense, an accounting amount, based on "income before income taxes," as shown on the income statement. But corporations compute tax payable based on "taxable income" shown on the tax return. Typically, the amounts for "income before income taxes" and "taxable income" are not equal. The tax code allows corporations to treat certain items differently for tax purposes from the way those items are treated for accounting purposes. However, in most instances, the tax and accounting treatments will "level out" over time and equalize.

Temporary differences refer to inconsistencies that will reverse themselves over time between an entity's pretax accounting income and its taxable income.[3] Temporary differences generally work to the benefit of corporations. Corporations tend, for tax purposes, to use legally allowable ways to postpone the recognition of revenues or accelerate the recognition of expenses. For example, a company may use the double-declining balance method of depreciation on equipment for tax return purposes and the straight-line method of depreciation for financial accounting purposes. This treatment allows more depreciation to be taken on the tax return early in the asset's life than is taken on the income statement. However, over the entire asset life, the total amount of depreciation that can be taken on either the tax return or the income statement is the depreciable cost.[4]

By using temporary differences to their advantage, corporations can defer (postpone) income taxes to be paid to the government. The two-line reference to income taxes in Exhibit 9-1 indicates that Avon had some temporary differences between its taxable and accounting income amounts. Footnotes to the company's income statement indicate that the majority of those differences were created by the use of different depreciation methods for tax and financial accounting.

In making its entry for year-end tax expense and tax obligation, Avon would need to recognize that these two amounts are not equal because of the temporary differences. A balancing amount will be made to either Deferred Income Tax Liability or Deferred Income Tax Asset.[5] Using the information in Exhibit 9-1, recognition of the taxes for year-end 2008 would necessitate the following entry.

General Journal				
Date		Description	Debit	Credit
Dec.	31	Income Tax Expense	262,800,000	
		Deferred Income Tax Asset	112,400,000	
		Income Tax Payable		375,200,000
		Record federal income tax expense and		
		currently payable and deferred tax amounts		

The Deferred Income Tax Asset represents income tax payments that the firm has prepaid for a later period. This account is typically classified on the balance sheet as a long-term asset. Avon chooses to classify its deferred tax assets and liabilities as part of "Other Assets" and "Other Liabilities" on its balance sheet. Many large corporations report huge deferred tax liabilities in their balance sheets. For instance, Southwest Airlines (www.southwest.com) had a $1,904,000,000 long-term liability for deferred income taxes on its 2008 year-end balance sheet.

---

[3]There are also "permanent" differences between taxable and financial accounting income amounts. These items will not "level out" over time and are beyond the scope of this text.

[4]This statement ignores the fact that tax law generally allows a company to depreciate an asset to zero, as opposed to financial accounting, which only allows depreciation to salvage value.

[5]For purposes of simplicity, it is assumed that if Tax Expense is greater than Tax Payable, the account Deferred Tax Liability is credited. If Tax Payable is greater than Tax Expense, the account Deferred Tax Asset is debited. Such an assumption is not technically correct, but discussion of the underlying reasons is beyond the scope of this text.

Nonrecurring Items

Income from continuing operations represents the earnings produced by a corporation's principal profit-oriented activities. This figure is often considered the best indicator of how a company performed in a given period and is generally used as the starting point to predict a firm's future profits. Income from continuing operations does not include income or losses produced by other nonrecurring items, such as discontinued operations and extraordinary items. If either of these other items exists, "Income from Continuing Operations" will appear on the income statement prior to these items.

Listing the "nonrecurring operations" components of the income statement separately and at the bottom of the income statement clearly indicates that they should not be considered when making future profit projections. In 2005–2007, Avon did not have any of these income statement components. Therefore, the company's income statement is complete at "Net Income," which for this company is essentially its income from continuing operations.

Visual Recap 9.2 depicts the extended form of the corporate income statement. The various noncontinuing income statement items are discussed in the following sections.

VISUAL RECAP 9.2

Corporate Income Statement Format

Corporation Name
Income Statement
For the Year Ended XX/XX/XX

+ Operating Revenues [Net Sales]
− Cost of Goods Sold
= Gross Profit
− Operating Expenses [Selling and Administrative Expenses]
= Income from Operations

± Other Income (Expenses)
= Income from Continuing Operations before Income Taxes
− Provision for Income Taxes
= Income from Continuing Operations

  Discontinued Operations
± Income (Loss) from Operations (net of tax)
± Gain (Loss) from Disposal (net of tax)
= Income before Extraordinary Items

± Gain (Loss) on Extraordinary Items (net of tax)
= Net Income

  EARNINGS PER SHARE
      Continuing operations
  ± Discontinued operations
  ± Extraordinary items
  = Net Income

Note: Mathematical relationships are shown with +, −, ±, and =, but do not appear on an actual income statement. [Alternative names are shown in brackets.]

Discontinued Operations

Most large corporations have more than one line of business. For example, Gannett Corporation's (www.gannett.com) principal lines of business are print newspapers (including *USA Today*) and broadcasting. In 2007, Gannett sold several of its newspapers and included a section entitled "discontinued operations" in the company's income statement. Because these businesses were owned for a portion of the year, their operations affected Gannett's revenues and expenses and should have been included on the income statement. However, those revenues and expenses should not have been included with income from continuing operations because, as of the end of 2007, those businesses were no longer parts of Gannett.

A **discontinued operations** section normally contains two items: the operating income (or loss) for that business segment and the gain (or loss) resulting from the segment's disposal. In the case of Gannett, the income for the year 2007 was $6,221,000 (net of income taxes) and the gain on the disposal of these businesses was $73,814,000 (net of income taxes). In a corporate income statement, important line items after income from continuing operations are shown "net of tax" to reveal the effect of such items on an entity's net income.

When a company's income statement reports discontinued operations, an accompanying financial statement footnote typically describes the nature of those operations. That footnote provides additional details, as well as the operating results and gains or losses attributable to the discontinued business segment.

Extraordinary Items

Occasionally, companies incur large gains or losses due to rare events. These items should be shown separately in a corporate income statement because they should not be considered indicators of future profit potential. Both of the following criteria must be met before a gain or loss qualifies as an **extraordinary item**.

- *Unusual in nature:* The event should be highly abnormal, taking into account the environment in which the entity operates.
- *Infrequent in occurrence:* The event should not reasonably be expected to recur in the foreseeable future, taking into account the environment in which the entity operates.

Extraordinary items follow the discontinued operations section of an income statement.

Each year, only a small percentage of publicly owned companies report extraordinary items in income statements. In one survey of 2004 financial statements, only 27 companies (0.16 percent) of the total reported extraordinary items; of those companies, the most common item reported (by 11 companies) was negative goodwill.[6] **Negative goodwill** occurs in a business combination when the fair value of the net assets acquired exceeds the price paid for the acquired company. In 2007, for example, a net extraordinary gain of $5,680,000 was recorded by Alloy, Inc. (www.alloy.com), a media and marketing services company, when it acquired Channel One Communications Corporation (which provides news and public affairs content to secondary schools in the United States).

---

[6]Theresa F. Henry and Mark P. Holtzman, "Extraordinary Items Share Exclusive Company," *Journal of Accountancy* (May 2007), pp. 80 ff.

Businesses often incur gains or losses that meet one, but not both, of the criteria for extraordinary items. For example, a company that grows agricultural products in a flood-prone area may suffer material losses every five to ten years because of a flood. Because the floods occur periodically, the resulting losses do not meet the "infrequency of occurrence" requirement for extraordinary items. On the other hand, these losses may qualify as unusual in nature. It is important to note that the magnitude of certain events does not influence the classification of extraordinary: neither the losses resulting from September 11 nor those from Hurricane Katrina were able to be classified as extraordinary. Typically, gains or losses that meet only one of the two criteria for extraordinary items are reported as separate components of an entity's income from continuing operations. Unlike an extraordinary item, an unusual or infrequently occurring gain or loss is not presented net of taxes.

International financial reporting standards (IAS 1, *Presentation of Financial Statements*) do not allow any items to be reported as extraordinary in the income statement nor reported as such in the footnotes. Given the rarity with which the classification is used, its elimination from U.S. generally accepted accounting principles would not present accounting or reporting hardships for U.S. companies and would make convergence with, and comparisons of, international financial statements more straightforward.

Earnings per Share

Earnings per share (EPS) is probably the most closely watched financial disclosure each year for publicly owned companies. In its simplest form, **earnings per share** is computed by dividing a company's net income by the weighted-average number of shares of common stock outstanding during the year.[7] In addition, separate EPS amounts are reported for income from continuing operations, discontinued operations, extraordinary items, and net income. Presenting earnings per share by its various components allows decision makers to interpret earnings data more quickly and accurately. A lower than expected earnings per share typically causes a company's stock price to decline, whereas a positive earnings surprise may trigger an increase in stock price.

In computing EPS, common stock shares are "weighted" according to how long they have been outstanding during the year. To illustrate, suppose that a company had 80,000 shares of common stock outstanding for the first six months of 2009. On July 1, the company issued an additional 20,000 shares, resulting in 100,000 shares being outstanding during the final six months of the year. The weighted-average number of shares outstanding for 2009, using this set of assumptions, is 90,000, computed as [(80,000 shares × 6/12) + (100,000 shares × 6/12)].

Avon's income statements show EPS figures of $1.82 (2005), $1.07 (2006), and $1.22 (2007). In Avon's case, net income declined, but the number of weighted-average shares also declined (from 466.28 million in 2005 to 447.4 million in 2006 to 433.5 million in 2007). Had the decline in shares not occurred, Avon's EPS would have been lower in both 2006 and 2007.

---

[7]If a company has preferred stock outstanding, dividends on preferred stock are subtracted from net income when computing earnings per share.

MAKING INFORMED ECONOMIC DECISIONS

Accounting is principally a service activity developed to provide information useful to financial decision makers. Decision makers need both access to financial data and the skills to analyze that financial data to make informed economic decisions. This chapter section focuses on the objectives of financial statement analysis and identifies the information sources used by decision makers to obtain and analyze financial statement data.

Objectives of Financial Statement Analysis

Many types of decision makers rely on the information found in corporate income statements, and the financial statement analysis objectives of those decision makers vary. Suppliers are often concerned about liquidity and profitability so they can decide whether to continue extending credit to business customers. Prospective employees are concerned with profitability and market share to identify companies that can offer secure, long-term employment opportunities. Bank loan officers, bondholders, and other long-term creditors are concerned with a firm's ability to generate sufficient profits and cash flows to pay its debts over an extended number of years. An organization's customer base typically analyzes financial statements to determine which businesses will provide a reliable source of products or services or will be in existence in the event of the need for warranty work. Finally, executives of charitable organizations may study corporate income statements to identify companies that can afford to donate funds to good causes.

Investors are the decision makers who must take the most comprehensive approach to financial statement analysis. Investors should be concerned with liquidity because an investment made in a company encountering short-term cash-flow problems is likely to disappear. Investors also want to be reassured that a firm can retire its long-term debt at maturity. Bondholders and other long-term creditors, if not paid on a timely basis, can seize a company's assets and force the firm out of business. A business's profitability is of obvious concern to investors because they want to be assured that a company will generate sufficient profits to provide a reasonable rate of return on owners' equity.

Information Sources for Financial Statement Analysis

The corporate income statement is just one source of data regarding corporations. Decision makers must analyze each financial statement in an annual report and the accompanying footnotes and other relevant information to reliably evaluate the firm's financial status and future prospects.

Typically, a public company's annual report is a condensed version of the 10–K registration statement that must be filed each year with the Securities and Exchange Commission (SEC). Investors can request a 10-K for a public company directly from the firm or access recent 10-Ks at the SEC's EDGAR (electronic data gathering and retrieval) Web site (www.sec.gov/edgar.shtml). Most large companies now include annual reports and 10-Ks on their Web sites under the heading "Investor Relations."

Content of annual reports may vary from company to company, but most annual reports contain the following items: the management's discussion and analysis (MD&A) section, a financial highlights table, the financial statements and accompanying footnotes, and an independent auditor's report. The MD&A section contains a summary discussion of factors that have recently affected the company's financial status, as well as a general overview of management's key plans for the future. The financial highlights table tracks important financial items over multiple periods. The company's audit report expresses the opinion by an independent accounting firm as to the "fairness" of presentation of the financial statements relative to generally accepted accounting principles. The audit report is generally "unqualified," which means that there is nothing out of the ordinary to report about the financial statements or the company. However, the audit report could include qualifications or discussions of items such as departures from generally accepted accounting principles (GAAP), inconsistent application of GAAP, or conditions that may threaten the firm's survival or its ability to continue as a going concern.

In addition to information provided by the company, an assortment of reference materials are published by investment advisory firms, such as Value Line, Standard & Poor's (S&P), Moody's, and Dun & Bradstreet (D&B). The Value Line Investment Survey, for example, provides a detailed analysis of key financial statistics and the future prospects of approximately 1,700 public companies. Financial and nonfinancial information for individual companies can also be obtained from business periodicals such as *Barron's, Business Week, Forbes*, and *The Wall Street Journal*.

Industry norms for a wide range of financial ratios and other financial measures are also available. Two popular sources of such information are *Industry Norms and Key Business Ratios* published by Dun & Bradstreet and *RMA Annual Statement Studies* published by Risk Management Association. Thomson One Banker also provides information on a company's industry peers. By having access to current industry norms, decision makers can better interpret an individual company's financial statement ratios.

ANALYTICAL TECHNIQUES

This section discusses and illustrates three analytical techniques for financial statements: trend analysis, common-sized financial statements, and ratio analysis. Each of these methods can be a powerful tool for analyzing and interpreting financial statements.

Decision makers examine financial statements to identify relationships—expected and unexpected—in the firm's financial data. More detailed investigation, though, is usually required to determine whether the identified relationships indicate whether a company's financial health is improving or deteriorating. Analytical techniques can be used to make predictions about future financial performance and financial condition based on a company's past data. Analysts must realize, however, that changes in a company's operations, its industry, and the overall economic environment can cause historical data to be a less-than-reliable indicator of future prospects.

Additionally, financial statement analysis is more difficult for companies that have two or more major lines of business. For such companies, analytical techniques are most useful if they are applied independently to the financial data of each major business segment of the firm. The data in this section are for Avon, which is in one major line of business used for analysis: retail beauty and beauty-related products.

Trend Analysis

A great deal of information can be learned about a company's financial condition and financial performance by simply studying changes in key financial statement items over a set time. To track the proportionate changes in items from period to period, financial statement dollar amounts are converted into percentages, and **trend analysis** is used to analyze the percentage changes over time. These percentage trends are then used to predict future dollar amounts for given financial statement items. Trend analysis allows comparisons to be made from year to year without regard for the magnitude of the numbers. Instead, relationships between and among the numbers are observed.

To apply trend analysis, a base year is selected, and each amount on the financial statements is expressed as a percentage of the base-year figure. Typically, the first or earliest year for which data are available is selected as the base year. Using the income statement information given earlier in the chapter in Exhibit 9-1, 2005 is selected as the base year for Avon's trend analysis. Exhibit 9-3 shows each amount for 2006 and 2007 expressed as a percentage of its related 2005 amount. Thus, net sales in 2007 are 122.1 ($9,845.2 ÷ $8,065.2) percent of what they were in 2005.

Reviewing the information in Exhibit 9-3 indicates that although Avon's revenues were trending upward, so were the company's expenses; thus, profitability has declined dramatically. The amount of both cost of sales and selling and administrative expenses

EXHIBIT 9-3

Avon Trend Analysis
of Income Statements

	2007	% of Base	2006	% of Base	2005	% of Base
	Years Ended December 31					
Net sales	$ 9,845.2	122.1%	$ 8,677.3	107.6%	$ 8,065.2	100%
Other revenue	93.5	110.8%	86.6	102.6%	84.4	100%
Total revenue	$ 9,938.7	122.0%	$ 8,763.9	107.5%	$ 8,149.6	100%
Costs, expenses, and other:						
Cost of sales	(3,941.2)	126.6%	(3,416.5)	109.7%	(3,113.2)	100%
Selling and administrative expenses	(5,124.8)	131.8%	(4,586.0)	118.0%	(3,887.4)	100%
Operating profit	$ 872.7	76.0%	$ 761.4	66.3%	$ 1,149.0	100%
Interest expense	(112.2)	207.4%	(99.6)	184.1%	(54.1)	100%
Interest income	42.2	113.1%	55.3	148.3%	37.3	100%
Other expenses	(6.6)	82.5%	(13.6)	170.0%	(8.0)	100%
Income before taxes and minority interest	$ 796.1	70.8%	$ 703.5	62.6%	$ 1,124.2	100%
Income taxes						
Current	$ (375.2)	124.5%	$ (334.1)	110.8%	$ (301.4)	100%
Deferred	112.4	354.6%	110.7	349.2%	31.7	100%
Total	$ (262.8)	97.4%	$ (223.4)	82.8%	$ (269.7)	100%
Income before minority interest	$ 533.3	62.4%	$ 480.1	56.2%	$ 854.5	100%
Minority interest	(2.6)	37.7%	(2.5)	36.2%	(6.9)	100%
Net income	$ 530.7	62.6%	$ 477.6	56.3%	$ 847.6	100%
Basic earnings per share	$ 1.22	67.0%	$ 1.07	58.8%	$ 1.82	100%

increased each year. Additionally, Avon had a 107 percent increase in its interest expense over the three-year period. When Avon's balance sheets are presented, they will show a significant increase in short-term debt, which could have created the large change in the amount of interest expense. The decline in earnings per share almost followed net income, but only because Avon purchased treasury stock (thus reducing the weighted-average number of shares outstanding) during each of the years.

Trend analysis (and other analytical techniques) can be enhanced by using computer-based graphics. Computer software packages such as PowerPoint, Excel, Freelance Graphics, and Harvard Graphics allow decision makers to more easily analyze and interpret financial data.

Common-Sized Financial Statements

As opposed to trend analysis, which compares year-to-year information, decision makers use common-sized financial statements to better understand relationships among items within a financial statement or series of financial statements. The intrayear relationships are then compared across years to determine whether they are maintained. In **common-sized financial statements**, each line item is expressed as a percentage of a major financial statement component. For example, in a common-sized income statement, each line item is expressed as a percentage of revenue (or net revenue). In a common-sized balance sheet, each line item is expressed as a percentage of total assets (or total liabilities and stockholders' equity).

Exhibit 9-4 presents Avon's common-sized income statements for 2006 and 2007. Percentages were found by dividing each amount on the 2006 and 2007 income statement by the total revenues of $8,763,900,000 and 9,938,700,000, respectively. Note the consistency between the years for the percentage of the various expenses compared to revenue amounts. Each year indicates a net income figure of approximately 5.5 percent on revenues generated.

Avon's 2006 and 2007 balance sheets are presented in Exhibit 9-5 with the common-sized balance sheets. Percentages for the common-sized statement were derived by dividing each 2006 and 2007 balance sheet amount by $5,238,200,000 and $5,716,200,000, respectively, the total assets at year-end.

The common-sized balance sheets indicate that the company's largest financial asset is its buildings, followed closely by inventory. The common-sized statements also indicate that, in both years, the Common Stock account represents only slightly over 3 percent of the total amount of stockholders' equity. From this information, it is easy to tell that Avon's common stock par value is extremely small. By reviewing the actual financial statements on the company's Web site, it is found that the par value per share is $0.25. At year-end 2006 and 2007, respectively, 732,700,000 and 736,300,000 shares were issued (291,400,000 and 308,600,000 shares were held, respectively, as treasury stock in 2006 and 2007).

Any unexpected changes or unusual relationships within a single year, or between years, of a company's common-sized financial statements should be investigated to assess whether these items point to developing problems areas for the firm. There are no such apparent changes in the relationships for Avon—although financial problems are noticeable (given the large percentages for cost of goods sold and selling and administrative expenses).

Common-sized financial statements also allow decision makers to more easily compare and contrast the financial data of two or more companies. Suppose that companies A and B are the two leading firms in an industry. However, Company A is much larger than Company B. This size difference makes it difficult to compare the companies' financial data. Common-sized financial statements for the two firms can be prepared to minimize

EXHIBIT 9-4				
Avon Income Statements and Common-Sized Income Statements (in millions, except for per share amounts)	Consolidated 12/31/2007	Common-Sized 12/31/2007	Consolidated 12/31/2006	Common-Sized 12/31/2006
Net sales	$ 9,845.2	99.1%	$ 8,677.3	99.0%
Other revenue	93.5	0.9%	86.6	1.0%
Total revenue	$ 9,938.7	100.0%	$ 8,763.9	100.0%
Costs, expenses, and other:				
Cost of sales	(3,941.2)	(39.6)%	(3,416.5)	(39.0)%
Selling and administrative expenses	(5,124.8)	(51.6)%	(4,586.0)	(52.3)%
Operating profit	$ 872.7	8.8%	$ 761.4	8.7%
Interest expense	(112.2)	(1.1)%	(99.6)	(1.1)%
Interest income	42.2	.4%	55.3	0.6%
Other expenses	(6.6)	(.1)%	(13.6)	(0.2)%
Income before taxes and minority interest	$ 796.1	8.0%	$ 703.5	8.0%
Income taxes				
Current	$ (375.2)	(3.8)%	$ (334.1)	(3.8)%
Deferred	112.4	1.1%	110.7	1.3%
Total	$ (262.8)	(2.7)%	$ (223.4)	(2.5)%
Income before minority interest	$ 533.3	5.3%	$ 480.1	5.5%
Minority interest	(2.6)	(0.0)%	(2.5)	0.0%
Net income	$ 530.7	5.3%	$ 477.6	5.5%

this problem. Decision makers can also use common-sized financial statements to compare a company's financial data to industry norms. Dun & Bradstreet's annual publication *Industry Norms and Key Business Ratios* provides industry averages for common-sized balance sheets in several hundred industries. Exhibit 9-6 provides selected items from Avon's 2007 common-sized balance sheet and income statement and corresponding comparative percentages for the beauty products industry.

The statistics in Exhibit 9-6 indicate that Avon had slightly more cash and current assets and substantially more PP&E, on a proportional basis, than the average beauty products company, in addition to having significantly more long-term debt. The last factor is not a positive investment indicator for Avon's common stock. Relative to the income statement, Avon's relationships are all lower than the industry average. However, Avon's return on equity is exceptionally higher than the beauty products' (or almost any industry's) norm because of the extremely small amount of stock that is currently outstanding.

Ratio Analysis

The most widely used method to analyze financial data is **ratio analysis**, or the study of relationships between two financial statement items. Decision makers use financial ratios

EXHIBIT 9-5		Consolidated December 31		Common-Sized December 31	
EXHIBIT 9-5		**2007**	**2006**	**2007**	**2006**
Avon Balance Sheets and Common-Sized Balance Sheets (in millions, except per share amounts)	**ASSETS**				
	Current assets				
	Cash and cash equivalents	$ 963.4	$ 1,198.9	16.9%	22.9%
	Accounts receivable (net of allowance)	840.4	700.4	14.7%	13.4%
	Inventories	1,041.8	900.3	18.2%	17.2%
	Prepaid and other expenses	669.8	534.8	11.7%	10.2%
	Property, plant and equipment				
	Land, at cost	71.8	65.3	1.3%	1.2%
	Buildings, improvements, and equipment (net)	1,206.4	1,034.9	21.1%	19.8%
	Other assets	922.6	803.6	16.1%	15.3%
	Total assets	$ 5,716.2	$ 5,238.2	100.0%	100.0%
	LIABILITIES & SHAREHOLDERS' EQUITY				
	Current liabilities				
	Short-term debt	$ 929.5	$ 615.6	16.3%	11.8%
	Accounts payable	800.3	655.8	14.0%	12.5%
	Accrued compensation	285.8	266.9	5.0%	5.1%
	Other accrued liabilities	713.2	601.6	12.5%	11.5%
	Sales and taxes other than income	222.3	176.1	3.9%	3.4%
	Income taxes	102.3	209.2	1.8%	4.0%
	Long-term debt	1,167.9	1,170.7	20.4%	22.4%
	Employee benefit plans*	388.7	504.9	6.8%	9.6%
	Deferred income taxes	208.7	55.0	3.6%	1.0%
	Other liabilities	147.7	155.0	2.6%	3.0%
	Shareholders' equity				
	Common stock, par value $0.25	184.7	183.5	3.2%	3.5%
	Additional paid-in capital	1,724.6	1,549.8	30.2%	29.6%
	Retained earnings*	3,169.5	2,740.5	55.4%	52.3%
	Treasury stock, at cost	(4,367.2)	(3,683.4)	(76.4)%	(70.3)%
	Minority interest**	38.2	37.0	0.7%	0.7%
	Total liabilities and shareholders' equity	$ 5,716.2	$ 5,238.2	100.0%	100.0%

*Net of accumulated comprehensive loss
**Moved from its original placement in liabilities to conform with SFAS No. 160.

EXHIBIT 9-6

Comparison of Industry
and Avon
Common-Sized
Statements

Beauty Products	Avon (2007)	Industry
Cash as a % of total assets ($963.4 ÷ $5,716.2)	16.9%	11.2%
Total current assets as a % of total assets ($3,515.4 ÷ $5,716.2)	61.5%	41.0%
PP&E as a % of total assets ($1,278.2 ÷ $5,716.2)	22.4%	39.1%
Total L-T liabilities as a % of total assets ($1,913 ÷ $5,716.2)	33.5%	12.6%
Gross profit percentage [($9,845.2 − $3,941.2) ÷ $9,845.2]	60.0%	67.2%
Operating profit percentage	8.7%	11.8%
Net income percentage	5.4%	9.4%
Return on equity ($530.7 ÷ $751.0) (excludes MI)	70.7%	18.9%

on both a cross-sectional and longitudinal basis. **Cross-sectional ratio analysis** involves comparing a company's financial ratios with those of competing companies and/or with industry norms. **Longitudinal ratio analysis** focuses on changes in a firm's financial ratios over time, generally several years.

Exhibits 9-7 through 9-11 present equations for a variety of financial ratios (some of which were discussed in earlier chapters), along with a brief explanation of their purpose. These ratios are classified into five categories: liquidity, leverage, activity, profitability, and market strength. Ratio computations for Avon for the year 2007 are also presented in the exhibits using income statement and balance sheet data from Exhibits 9-4 and 9-5. In some cases, information for Avon's ratio computation is not available. An approximated industry norm is also included, if available.

Liquidity ratios (Exhibit 9-7) are used to evaluate whether a firm has the available current assets to pay its upcoming debts. The quick ratio is often a better indicator of liquidity because it omits inventory and other often nonliquid assets (such as supplies and prepaid items) from the calculation.

Financial leverage ratios (Exhibit 9-8) focus on the relationship between creditor and ownership equity in a firm. A company's stockholders benefit if the rate of return earned on borrowed funds exceeds the interest rate paid on those funds; stockholders are placed at a disadvantage if the opposite holds true. The long-term debt to equity ratio is a key measure of the benefit (or detriment) of a company's financial leverage. The times interest earned ratio provides a margin of safety measure that is particularly useful when analyzing highly leveraged companies. The lower this ratio, the more risk a company faces of defaulting on its periodic interest payments.

Activity ratios (Exhibit 9-9) reveal how quickly a company is converting receivables into cash and how inventory is being sold. The longer receivables go uncollected, the more susceptible they are to bad debt losses. Similarly, the longer the time required to sell inventory, the higher the risk that inventory items will become obsolete, damaged, or stolen. Total asset turnover ratio can be used to gauge success in generating revenues relative to the organization's total asset base.

The most common benchmarks against which to evaluate a firm's profitability (Exhibit 9-10) are its sales, assets, and stockholders' equity. The first of these measures can help to evaluate how effectively costs have been controlled relative to revenues; and the others provide an indication of how effectively organizational resources have been used to generate profits.

Liquidity ratios measure a firm's ability to finance its day-to-day operations and to pay its liabilities as they mature.

Current Ratio = Current Assets ÷ Current Liabilities

Measures a firm's ability to pay its current liabilities from its current assets

    Avon
$$= (\$963.4 + \$840.4 + \$1,041.8 + \$669.8) \div (\$929.5 + \$800.3 + \$285.8 + \$713.2 + \$222.3 + \$102.3)$$
$$= \$3,515.4 \div \$3,053.4$$
$$= 1.15$$
    Beauty products industry norm
$$= 0.95$$

Quick Ratio = (Cash and Cash Equivalents + Net Current Receivables + Short-Term Investments) ÷ Current Liabilities

Measures a firm's ability to pay its current liabilities without relying on the sale of inventory or other nonliquid current assets

    Avon
$$= (\$963.4 + \$840.4) \div (\$929.5 + \$800.3 + \$285.8 + \$713.2 + \$222.3 + \$102.3)$$
$$= \$1,803.8 \div \$3,053.4$$
$$= 0.59$$
    Beauty products industry norm
$$= 0.87$$

The first four categories of financial ratios focus on a company's financial condition or operating results. In contrast, market strength ratios (Exhibit 9-11) focus on market perception of the company. Market strength ratios (which are updated daily) tend to be more volatile than other financial ratios because they are influenced by investors' perceptions and expectations, both of which can change rapidly. Security analysts suggest that investors often overreact to quarterly earnings data, changes in management, and news reports regarding a company's future prospects or those of its industry. The result is volatile stock prices.

A company's P/E ratio reveals how much investors are willing to pay for each $1 of the firm's earnings. Despite impressive operating results and a strong financial condition, a company's common stock may fare poorly in the capital markets when the P/E ratio is extremely high because the market believes the company's stock is overpriced. If a common stock is selling for an abnormally low P/E ratio, investors will likely view the stock as a bargain. P/E ratios are particularly insightful when analyzed on a comparative basis.

Like most financial statistics, market strength ratios may be unreliable when used independent of other available information. For example, regardless of profitability, a company's market price changes may reflect industry conditions, personnel changes (such as the retirement of key executives), and many other factors. Likewise, a company's P/E ratio can be significantly distorted in any one year by extraordinary losses and other "special" income statement items discussed earlier in this chapter.

A company's market price to book value ratio indicates how much investors are willing to pay for each $1 of the firm's net assets. The market price of a common stock often differs considerably from its book value per share because the accounting-based book value does

EXHIBIT 9-8

Financial Leverage
Ratios

Leverage ratios measure how a firm uses debt capital relative to equity capital; also known as debt utilization ratios.

Debt to Total Assets Ratio = Total Liabilities ÷ Total Assets

Measures the proportion of total assets in a firm financed by debt rather than equity

Avon
= ($929.5 + $800.3 + $285.8 + $713.2 + $222.3 + $102.3 + $1,167.9 + $388.7 + $208.7
  + $147.7) ÷ $5,716.2
= $4,966.4 ÷ $5,716.2
= 86.9%
Beauty products industry norm
= 48.7%

Long-term Debt to Equity Ratio = Long-term Debt ÷ Total Stockholders' Equity

Measures the proportion of long-term debt in a firm relative to total firm capital

Avon
= ($1,167.9 + $388.7 + $208.7 + $147.7) ÷ $5,716.2
= $1,913.0 ÷ $5,716.2
= 33.5%
Beauty products industry norm
= 24.5%

Times Interest Earned = (Net Income + Interest Expense + Income Tax Expense)
                            ÷ Interest Expense

Measures the number of times that a firm's interest expense is covered by earnings

Avon
= ($530.7 + $112.2 + $262.8) ÷ $112.2
= $905.7 ÷ $112.2
= 8.1 times
Beauty products industry norm
= 14.7 times

not necessarily reflect the "true" economic value of a corporation's common stock. Recall that, for accounting purposes, historical cost (rather than market value) is the primary valuation basis used for most assets.

No single ratio or collection of ratios can reveal which stock's market price will definitely increase or decrease in the future. Nevertheless, these ratios may provide clues about the stock market's perception of a common stock's investment potential. Decision makers must understand how to compute financial ratios, as well as recognize that common sense must be exercised in interpreting those ratios. The final part of this chapter expands on this intuitive approach to financial statement analysis by discussing the concept of earnings quality and pro forma financial statements.

ASSESSING EARNINGS QUALITY

In recent years, financial statement users have become increasingly concerned about the concept of earnings quality. Although not rigidly defined, **earnings quality** generally refers to the degree of correlation between a firm's economic income and its reported earnings determined by generally accepted accounting principles (GAAP). Economic income is

EXHIBIT 9-9
Activity Ratios

Activity ratios measure how well a firm is managing its assets; also known as asset utilization ratios.

Accounts Receivable Turnover Ratio = Net Credit Sales ÷ Average Accounts Receivable*

Measures the number of times a firm collects its accounts receivable each year

    Avon

      = $9,845.2 ÷ [($700.4 + $840.4) ÷ 2]

      = $9,845.2 ÷ $770.4

      = 12.8 times

    Beauty products industry norm (computed on 2007 year-end A/R)

      = 64.3 times

Age of Receivables = 360 Days ÷ Accounts Receivable Turnover Ratio

Measures the length of time normally required to collect a receivable resulting from a credit sale

    Avon

      = 360 ÷ 12.8

      = 28.1 days

    Beauty products industry norm

      = 5.6 days

Inventory Turnover Ratio = Cost of Goods Sold ÷ Average Inventory*

Measures the number of times a firm sells its inventory each year

    Avon

      = $3,941.2 ÷ [($900.3 + $1,041.8) ÷ 2]

      = $3,941.2 ÷ $971.1

      = 4.1 times

    Beauty products industry norm (computed on 2007 year-end Inventory)

      = 3.3 times

Age of Inventory = 360 ÷ Inventory Turnover Ratio

Measures the length of time normally required to sell inventory

    Avon

      = 360 ÷ 4.1

      = 87.8 days

    Beauty products industry norm

      = 109.1 days

Total Asset Turnover Ratio = Net Sales ÷ Average Total Assets*

Measures a firm's ability to generate sales relative to its investment in assets

    Avon

      = $9,845.2 ÷ [($5,238.2 + $5,716.2) ÷ 2]

      = $9,845.2 ÷ $5,477.2

      = 1.8

    Beauty products industry norm (computed on 2007 year-end Total Assets)

      = 1.0

*Average = (Beginning + Ending) ÷ 2

EXHIBIT 9-10

Profitability Ratios

Profitability ratios measure a firm's earnings performance.

Profit Margin Percentage = Net Income ÷ Net Sales

Measures the percentage of each sales dollar that contributes to net income

Avon
= $530.7 ÷ $9,845.2
= 5.4%
Beauty products industry norm
= 9.4%

Gross Profit Percentage = Gross Profit ÷ Net Sales

Measures the percentage of each sales dollar not absorbed by cost of goods sold; gross profit = sales — cost of goods sold

Avon
= ($9,845.2 − $3,941.2) ÷ $9,845.2
= $5,904 ÷ $9,845.2
= 60.0%
Beauty products industry norm
= 67.2%

Return on Assets = (Net Income + Interest Expense) ÷ Average Total Assets*

Measures the rate of return a firm realizes on its investment in assets

Avon
= ($530.7 + $112.2) ÷ [($5,238.2 + $5,716.2) ÷ 2]
= $642.9 ÷ $5,477.2
= 11.7%
Beauty products industry norm (computed on 2007 year-end Total Assets)
= 8.1%

Return on Equity = (Net Income + Preferred Stock Dividends) ÷ Average Common Stockholders' Equity*

Measures the rate of return on a firm's common stockholders' equity

Avon
= ($530.7 + $0) ÷ [($183.5 + $1,549.8 + $2,740.5 − $3,683.4) + ($184.7 + $1,724.6 + $3,169.5 − $4,367.2) ÷ 2]
= $530.7 ÷ [($790.4 + $711.6) ÷ 2]
= $530.7 ÷ $751
= 70.7%
Beauty products industry norm (computed on 2007 year-end Avg. CS Equity)
= 18.9%

*Average = (Beginning + Ending) ÷ 2

traditionally defined as the change in the total value of a business between two periods. The analytical techniques illustrated in the previous section do not allow a comprehensive assessment of the quality of a firm's reported earnings for several reasons.

Analysis of earnings quality requires the exercise of considerable judgment on the part of financial decision makers. An understanding of the economic factors that influence a given company's operations, knowledge of accounting rules and concepts, simple intuition, and common sense are the principal tools used in analyzing earnings quality. Exhibit 9-12 provides a list of several ways decision makers can assess the quality of a firm's reported earnings.

EXHIBIT 9-11

Market Strength Ratios

Market strength ratios measure how the capital markets, as a whole, perceive a firm's common stock.

Price/Earnings Ratio = Current Market Price ÷ Earnings per Share

Measures the amount that investors are willing to pay for each dollar of a firm's earnings for the most recent 12-month period

Avon
   = $39.53 ÷ $1.22
   = 32.4

Market Price to Book Value Ratio = Current Market Price ÷ Book Value per Share

Measures the amount that investors are willing to pay for each dollar of a firm's net assets; book value per share = total common stockholders' equity ÷ number of common shares outstanding

Avon
   = $39.53 ÷ [$711,600,000 ÷ (736,300,000 issued − 308,600,000 in treasury)]
   = $39.53 ÷ ($711,600,000 ÷ 427,700,000 shares)
   = $39.53 ÷ $1.66
   = 23.8

Note: In the five years from 2004 to 2008, Avon's P/E ratio ranged from a high of 32.6 to a low of 11.8. For the quarter ending 9/30/08, Avon's Market Price to BV ratio was 8.9. According to the *Wall Street Journal* (http://online.wsj.com/quotes/ratios.html?symbol=AVP&type=usstock; accessed 12/10/08), Avon's P/E ratio compared to the industry norm was 76.5%.

When analyzing a firm's reported earnings, decision makers usually focus on the income generated by its continuing operations. Extraordinary gains and losses are generally not given much weight in assessing future profit potential because those items involve nonrecurring and unusual events or transactions that are unlikely to affect a company's future earnings.

Information provided by financial statement footnotes includes discussion of whether a company has recently changed accounting methods and the effect of any such changes on reported earnings. Footnotes will also identify unusual items that affected the firm's past earnings or have the potential to affect its future earnings. For example, most large companies are involved in some type of litigation that may have the potential to significantly influence the future earnings. A company's financial statement footnotes will provide a summary of the major litigation cases in which it is involved, as well as the likely financial statement effects of these cases. A review of these disclosures should help decision makers determine whether they agree with management's assessment (often included in the MD&A section) of how pending legal matters may affect a company's financial status.

Firms may attempt to "manage" earnings by forcing them to meet analysts' (or management's) projected estimates. Earnings management can run from reasonable interpretations of GAAP to fraud. For instance, several alternative methods often exist that can be used to account for a specific type of transaction or event. Depreciation expense and cost of goods sold are two examples of income statement items that may be materially affected by a firm's choice of accounting methods. Thus, a good place to gain information for analyzing the quality of a company's earnings is the initial financial statement footnote in a company's annual report. This footnote is generally called "Summary of Significant Accounting Policies" and provides information on the company's accounting methods. This footnote may reveal whether a company uses income-inflating accounting methods.

EXHIBIT 9-12

Ways to Assess the Quality of a Firm's Reported Earnings

- Compare accounting principles used by a firm to those used by competitors. Does the set of accounting principles used by the firm tend to inflate reported earnings?

- Attempt to assess whether the firm's earnings are repeatable (Are they from ongoing types of operations rather than one-time events such as a plant closure?), controllable (Are they under management's control rather than from external items, such as foreign exchange rate fluctuations?), and bankable (Are they able to be collected in cash rather than from selling to high risk, potentially nonpaying customers?).

- Analyze any recent changes in accounting principles or accounting estimates to determine whether they inflated reported earnings.

- Read the footnotes to the financial statements to identify any unusual events that may have affected reported earnings.

- Review any extraordinary items included in the income statement to determine if they are actually nonoperating items.

- Attempt to determine whether there are any significant expenses not reflected in the income statement, such as warranty expense on products sold.

- Attempt to determine whether discretionary expenditures, such as advertising and maintenance, have been reduced or delayed.

Business executives can also influence their firms' reported earnings by modifying operating decisions. Such information can often be gained by reviewing the company's financial statements over several years, especially using common-sized statements. For example, if a company is having a poor year profit-wise, management may purposefully delay expenditures for advertising or maintenance or may decline to fill job positions that have become vacant. Such tactics may improve a company's reported accounting earnings for a given year, but actually diminish the overall economic value of the business. For instance, postponing maintenance expenses could result in a higher rate of equipment breakdowns, higher repair bills, and a decline in production efficiency in future years.

Although some earnings management techniques might be consider "aggressive," other tactics are considered fraud. For example, between 1993 and 1996, AOL decided to capitalize its marketing costs rather than expensing them as required under GAAP. By June 1996, the $314 million of capitalized marketing costs represented approximately 33 percent of total assets. For 1996 alone, had AOL properly expensed the costs, its reported $63 million of net profit would have been a pretax loss of $175 million.

Financial fraud obviously diminishes the correlation between a company's economic income and its reported accounting earnings. The last few years have seen many cases of management or accounting fraud, including Enron, Waste Management, Sunbeam, WorldCom, American Italian Pasta Company, and United Rentals, among many others. The United States is not alone in cases of fraud; frauds have been uncovered at Parmalat (Italy), Ahold (Netherlands), Gazprom (Russia), Livedoor (Japan), and Aristocrat Leisure (Australia).

A company's reported profits may not be closely correlated with its economic income, even if there have been no explicit efforts to distort those profits. Many financial statement items are estimates, such as warranty and bad debts expense. These estimates may be materially in error, although they are made honestly and objectively. Additionally, GAAP do not capture, or quantify, all events that affect the change in the economic value of a business during a given period. In fact, GAAP are not intended to capture all these variables; for example, increases in the current or market value of most assets are not recorded under GAAP nor are values of intellectual capital.

SUMMARY

Corporate income statements are an important source of information for financial decision makers. Of particular interest to investors is a corporation's income from continuing operations, which represents the earnings of a company's principal profit-oriented activities. Investors often use this figure as the starting point for predicting a corporation's future profits. Discontinued operations and extraordinary items are "special" income statement items that may influence a corporation's net income for any given year but should have little, if any, impact on future years' profitability. These items are reported on the income statement net of the income taxes caused (if a gain) or saved (if a loss).

Income taxes are a large expense for most corporations and pose complex accounting issues. Corporations often use different methods of determining the items that appear on the income statement and tax return. As a result, a corporation's income tax expense and tax payable for a given year are typically not equal. The difference between these two amounts is recorded in a Deferred Income Tax account. Deferred income tax is usually a long-term liability, although occasionally it may be a current liability or even an asset.

To make informed economic decisions, financial statement users must be able to analyze financial data and draw proper conclusions from such analyses. Different types of decision makers have different financial statement analysis objectives, but investors typically must take the most comprehensive analysis approach.

Annual reports are the principal source of information used in analyzing financial statement data. Several sections of an annual report that are particularly useful are the management discussion and analysis, financial highlights table, financial statement footnotes, and the independent auditor's report. Other sources of information include the publications of investment advisory firms such as Standard & Poor's and Dun & Bradstreet.

Common approaches to analyzing financial statements include trend analysis, common-sized financial statements, and ratio analysis. Trend analysis studies percentage changes in financial statement items over time and is often used to predict the future value of a financial statement item. Common-sized financial statements illustrate the relationships among items within a financial statement or series of financial statements. Ratio analysis involves a comparison of the relationship between two (or more) financial statement items. A company's financial ratios are often compared to its historical amounts and to industry norms. The five general types of financial ratios are liquidity, leverage, activity, profitability, and market strength.

In recent years, financial statement users have focused increasing attention on assessing earnings quality, which refers to the degree of correlation between the economic income and reported accounting earnings of a business. Factors influencing earnings quality include the need to estimate many financial statement amounts, and the ability to choose alternative accounting methods, concerted efforts to manipulate or distort financial data, and financial fraud.

KEY TERMS

common-sized financial
statement
consolidation
cost method (of accounting
for a stock investment)
cross-sectional ratio analysis
discontinued operation
earnings per share

earnings quality
equity method (of accounting
for a stock investment)
extraordinary item
income from continuing
operations
longitudinal ratio analysis
minority interest

negative goodwill
parent company
ratio analysis
subsidiary
temporary difference
trend analysis

QUESTIONS

1. Explain how a long-term investment by Paolo Company in Sanri Company affects the income statement and balance sheet of Paolo Company if: (a) Paolo owns less than 20 percent of Sanri; (b) Paolo owns between 20 percent and 50 percent of Sanri; and (c) Paolo owns more than 50 percent of Sanri. *(LO 9.1)*

2. Why would one firm want to make a long-term investment in the stock of another firm? *(LO 9.1)*

3. Why is a firm's income from continuing operations of interest to decision makers? *(LO 9.2)*

4. What financial data are presented on a corporate income statement for a discontinued line of business? Why are these data reported separately in the income statement? *(LO 9.2)*

5. What is earnings per share, and how is it computed? Why is EPS presented on the income statement as opposed to all other financial statement ratios? *(LO 9.3)*

6. Distinguish between "taxable income" and "income before income taxes." How does each item affect the balance sheet and income statement? *(LO 9.4)*

7. Define the term *temporary difference* in reference to corporate income taxes. How does a temporary difference affect the balance sheet? *(LO 9.4)*

8. Is the Deferred Income Tax account typically a liability or an asset account? Is the Deferred Income Tax account typically classified as current or long term? Explain the rationale for your answers. *(LO 9.4)*

9. Briefly explain why the objectives of financial statement analysis vary among different types of financial decision makers. *(LO 9.5)*

10. Identify three analytical techniques used to analyze financial statements. Define each technique and explain how each is used by decision makers. *(LO 9.6, 9.7, 9.8)*

11. Define the following terms in relationship to ratio analysis: (a) liquidity, (b) leverage, (c) activity, (d) profitability, and (e) market strength. What ratios are used to measure each category? *(LO 9.8)*

12. Define earnings quality. Identify several factors that influence the quality of a company's reported earnings. *(LO 9.9)*

13. Many companies have been said to "manage earnings." Use library or Internet resources to find out what is meant by *earnings management* and discuss how it could affect earnings quality. *(LO 9.9)*

EXERCISES

14. **True or False** *(All LOs)*

Following are a series of statements regarding topics discussed in this chapter.

Required:

Indicate whether each statement is true (T) or false (F).

(a) Corporations pay taxes based on the amount of income before income taxes.

(b) A company that changes from one accounting principle to another generally must report an extraordinary item in its income statement in the year of the change.

(c) The market price to book value ratio indicates how much investors are willing to pay for each $1 of a company's net assets.

(d) If a corporation's common stock has a much higher price-earnings ratio than its historical norm, sophisticated investors will typically view that stock as "bargain" priced.

(e) If Company A owns 35 percent of Company B's common stock, Company A should use the equity method of accounting and consolidate both companies' financial statements at year-end.

(f) Decision makers commonly use activity ratios to evaluate a company's liquidity.

(g) Common-sized financial statements can be used to identify important structural changes in a company's operating results and financial condition over a period of time.

(h) Financial leverage works to the advantage of company owners when the interest rate paid on borrowed funds exceeds the rate of return earned on those funds.

(i) The study of percentage changes in financial statement items over a period of time is known as trend analysis.

(j) Earnings quality generally refers to the degree of correlation between a firm's economic income and its reported earnings determined by generally accepted accounting principles.

(k) In a common-sized balance sheet, each line item is expressed as a percentage of current assets.

(l) At date of original issuance, Company P buys $100,000 of Company F's long-term bonds for $97,500. Both companies will have a contra-account on their financial statements: Company P has Discount on Bond Investment and Company F has Discount on Bonds Payable.

(m) When a company sells a business segment, the company may report both an income and a loss amount in its discontinued operations section of the income statement.

15. **Elements of a Corporate Income Statement** *(LO 9.2)*

Following are some items often reported in corporate income statements.

- Operating Income
- Gross Profit
- Discontinued Operations
- Net Income
- Extraordinary Loss
- Income from Continuing Operations

Required:

(a) List these items in their proper order in a corporate income statement.

(b) Which, if any, of these items will be shown "net of tax"?

(c) Why are extraordinary items included as separate components of a corporate income statement?

(d) If you were going to make a judgment about a company's future financial performance, on which income statement line would you base that judgment? Explain the reason for your answer.

16. **Income Statement Terms** *(LO 9.2)*

Following are definitions or descriptions of terms relating to corporate income statements or income measurement.

(1) A difference between an entity's taxable income and pretax accounting income that arises from applying different accounting methods for taxation and financial reporting purposes

(2) An account in which a corporation records the difference between its income tax expense and income tax payable each year; typically a long-term liability account

(3) Generally, net income divided by the weighted-average number of shares of common stock outstanding during a given year

(4) A material gain or loss that is both unusual in nature and infrequent in occurrence

(5) The amount that represents the earnings produced by a corporation's principal profit-oriented activities

(6) A correction of a material error occurring in a previous accounting period that involves a revenue or expense

(7) A section of a corporate income statement devoted to a business segment that is not part of the company at year-end

Required:

Match each definition or description with the appropriate term from the following list.

(a) Earnings per share
(b) Discontinued operation
(c) Extraordinary item
(d) Income from continuing operations
(e) Deferred income tax
(f) Temporary difference
(g) Prior period adjustment

17. **Preparing a Corporate Income Statement** *(LO 9.2)*

Robin Mackey is a business major at Southern Missouri University. Robin is struggling with an accounting homework assignment to prepare an income statement for Wambaugh Inc., an imaginary firm. Robin has decided that the following items should be included in this income statement.

(a) Cost of Goods Sold
(b) Income Taxes Payable
(c) Accounts Receivable
(d) Income Tax Expense
(e) Earnings per Share

(f) Loss from Discontinued Operations (net of taxes)

(g) Net Sales

(h) Possible Loss from Lawsuit

(i) Accounts Payable

(j) Dividends (declared by the Board of Directors)

(k) Gain on Sale of Equipment

(l) Salaries Payable

(m) Selling and Administrative Expenses

(n) Stock Dividends Distributable

Required:

Help Robin complete her homework assignment. Which of the items listed should be included in Wambaugh Inc.'s income statement? In what order should these items appear in the income statement? Where will the remaining items appear in the financial statements? Will any of the amounts not be included in the actual financial statements? If so, explain.

18. **Computation of Earnings per Share** *(LO 9.3)*

Fazzino Corporation had 400,000 shares of common stock outstanding for the first three months of the year. The company issued 80,000 additional shares on April 1 and another 120,000 shares on September 1. Fazzino reported net income of $375,000 for the year ended December 31. Fazzino has no preferred stock.

Required:

(a) Compute Fazzino's weighted-average number of shares of common stock outstanding during the year.

(b) Compute Fazzino's earnings per share for the year.

(c) Why is the weighted-average number of shares of common stock outstanding during a year used for earnings per share rather than the number of shares outstanding at the end of the year?

19. **Analysis Terminology** *(LO 9.6, 9.7, and 9.8)*

Following are definitions or descriptions of terms relating to ratio analysis.

(1) Involves studying the relationship between two or more financial statement items

(2) Indicates the amount that investors are willing to pay for each $1 of a company's earnings over the past 12 months

(3) Involves a comparison of a company's financial ratios with those of competing companies or industry norms

(4) Measures a firm's ability to generate sales relative to its investment in assets

(5) Focuses on changes in a firm's ratios over a period of time

(6) Indicates how the capital markets as a whole perceive a company's common stock

(7) Indicates the percentage of each sales dollar that contributes to net income

(8) Measures a firm's ability to pay its current liabilities without relying on the sale of its inventory

(9) Indicates how well a company is managing its assets

(10) Indicates the number of times that a firm sells or turns over its inventory each year

(11) Measures a firm's ability to pay its current liabilities from its current assets

Required:

Match each definition or description listed with an appropriate term from the following list:

(a) Ratio analysis

(b) Inventory turnover ratio

(c) Total asset turnover ratio

(d) Cross-sectional ratio analysis

(e) Current ratio

(f) Profit margin percentage

(g) Longitudinal ratio analysis

(h) Leverage ratio

(i) Market strength ratio

(j) Quick ratio

(k) Price-earnings ratio

20. **Objectives of Financial Statement Analysis** *(LO 9.5)*

Abercrombie & Fitch (www.abercrombie.com) is a specialty retailer selling casual sportswear, personal care products, and men's and women's accessories. As of February 2, 2008, the company operated 1,035 stores in the United States, Canada, and the United Kingdom. In its 2007 10-K filing to the SEC, A&F reported net income of $475,697,000 on revenues of nearly $3,749,847,000.

Required:

(a) Indicate what objective or objectives the following decision makers would likely have in mind when reviewing the financial statements of Abercrombie & Fitch.

(1) Potential investors in the company's common stock

(2) An individual applying for a management position with the company

(3) A banker reviewing a loan application submitted by the firm

(4) Businesses that supply goods or services to the company

(b) Identify information sources that the parties listed in part (a) could use to analyze the financial statement data of Abercrombie & Fitch.

21. **Trend Analysis** *(LO 9.6)*

Access the 2007 10-K for Abercrombie & Fitch (www.abercrombie.com).

Required:

Prepare a trend analysis for 2006 and 2007, using 2006 as the base year.

22. **Common-Sized Financial Sta**tements *(LO 9.6)*

Access the 2007 10-K for Abercrombie & Fitch (www.abercrombie.com).

Required:

(a) Prepare a common-sized balance sheet for 2007 for Abercrombie & Fitch.

(b) Prepare a common-sized income statement for 2007 for Abercrombie & Fitch.

23. **Ratio Analysis** *(LO 9.8)*

Access the 2007 10-K for Abercrombie & Fitch (www.abercrombie.com).

Required:

(a) Compute the following ratios for Abercrombie & Fitch:

(1) Current ratio

(2) Quick ratio

(3) Debt to total assets

(4) Long-term debt to equity

(5) Accounts receivable turnover

(6) Inventory turnover

(7) Gross profit percentage

(8) Return on equity

(b) What are Abercrombie & Fitch's significant accounting policies?

(c) What are some of Abercrombie & Fitch's business risk factors?

24. **Earnings Quality** *(LO 9.9, writing)*

Charlie Harper wants invest in the stock market but knows very little about accounting and financial reporting practices. Recently, he read an article in *The Wall Street Journal* that focused on the subject of "earnings quality." After reading the article, Charlie was baffled and asked one of his friends, "How can there be a difference in the quality of earnings across companies? Corporate earnings are hard, cold facts, right? Accountants just add numbers here and subtract numbers there to arrive at a company's net income, right? Any way you cut it, two plus two equals four … right?"

Required:

Write a memo to Charlie that explains the concept of earnings quality and discusses several factors that influence earnings quality. Because Charlie is unfamiliar with accounting and financial reporting practices, include numerical examples in the memo to clarify how these factors influence earnings quality. Conclude your memo with a few suggestions to Charlie regarding how he can evaluate the quality of reported earnings data.

PROBLEMS

25. **Accounting for Investments in Stocks and Bonds** *(LO 9.1)*

Selected transactions for Adler Co. follow.

- On January 1, 2009, Adler Co. invested $300,000 of Walker, Inc. common stock

- On November 15, 2009, Adler Co. received a $5,000 dividend from Walker, Inc.

- Walker, Inc. earned $100,000 of net income for 2009.

- On January 1, 2009, Adler Co. invested in the bonds of McFarland Enterprises by purchasing five newly-issued, $1,000, 10 percent, 10-year bonds for $4,900.

- On June 30, 2009, McFarland Enterprises paid semiannual interest to bondholders.

Required:

(a) Record the journal entries for these transactions related to Walker, Inc., assuming that:

(1) Adler Co. owns 10 percent of Walker, Inc.

(2) Adler Co. owns 40 percent of Walker, Inc.

(3) Adler Co. owns 80 percent of Walker, Inc.

(b) Describe Adler Co.'s year-end procedures related to Walker, Inc. under each assumption from part (a).

(c) Record the entries for Adler Co.'s investment in McFarland Enterprises.

26. **Corporate Income Statement** *(LO 9.2 and 9.3)*

Following is information taken from the accounting records of Kagawa Company at the end of 2009.

- Net Sales, $660,000
- Operating Income (from discontinued operations), $64,000
- Cost of Goods Sold, $370,000
- Gain on Sale of Assets (from discontinued operations), $55,000
- Operating Expenses, $134,000
- Flood Loss, $167,000
- Kagawa had 150,000 shares of common stock issued and outstanding throughout the year.

Kagawa's effective tax rate is 40 percent and is based in an area that does not normally experience floods. Kagawa's taxable income from the tax return is $100,000.

Required:

Prepare an income statement for Kagawa Company for 2009, including an earnings-per-share section.

27. **Earnings per Share Computations** (LO 9.3)

Following are income statement data for Mylin Corporation for the company's most recent fiscal year:

Income from Continuing Operations Before Tax			$ 800,000
Income Tax Expense			(240,000)
Income from Continuing Operations			$ 560,000
Discontinued Operations			
Operating Income	$ 40,000		
Less Income Tax	(12,000)	$ 28,000	
Loss on Disposal	$(50,000)		
Less Income Tax Savings	15,000	(35,000)	(7,000)
Income before Extraordinary Item			$ 553,000
Extraordinary Loss due to Foreign Expropriation of Assets		$(100,000)	
Less Income Tax Savings		30,000	(70,000)
Net Income			$ 483,000

At the beginning of the year, Mylin had 252,000 shares of common stock outstanding. On February 1, Mylin sold an additional 48,000 shares of common stock. On October 1, Mylin sold an additional 60,000 shares of common stock. On December 1, Mylin bought 12,000 shares of common stock to hold as treasury stock; thus, these shares are no longer outstanding and will not participate in earnings per share calculations after this date.

Required:

(a) Compute the weighted-average number of shares of common stock that Mylin had outstanding during the year.

(b) Compute and clearly label the earnings per share figures for Mylin's income statement.

28. **Temporary Differences for Tax Purposes** (LO 9.4)

Over a recent three-year period, Travis Country Enterprises (TCE) had the following pretax accounting income and taxable income amounts.

	Accounting Income	Pretax Taxable Income
Year 1	$880,000	$760,000
Year 2	950,000	820,000
Year 3	740,000	980,000

For each year, the difference between TCE's pretax accounting income and its taxable income was due to its use of different depreciation methods for financial accounting and taxation purposes. Recently, a local attorney, who is a new member of TCE's board of directors, reviewed the company's financial records. At the next board meeting, this individual suggested that the use of different accounting methods for financial accounting and taxation purposes was, in her opinion, unethical.

Required:

(a) Is it unethical to use different accounting methods for financial accounting and taxation purposes? Why or why not?

(b) TCE's effective tax rate in recent years has been 40 percent for both financial accounting and taxation purposes. Compute the company's income tax expense and income taxes payable for Years 1–3. Some of the temporary differences from years 1 and 2 reversed in year 3.

(c) Prepare an appropriate journal entry to record TCE's income tax expense for Years 1–3.

29. **Trend Analysis** (LO 9.6)

Following are selected financial data for a recent five-year period for Walters & Cruz, Inc. (Amounts are expressed in thousands except for per share data.)

	Year 1	Year 2	Year 3	Year 4	Year 5
Sales	$254,882	$298,468	$392,549	$348,351	$387,430
Operating Income	6,546	9,023	9,842	7,343	10,666
Earnings per Share	0.52	0.54	0.61	0.56	0.62
Book Value per Share	1.22	1.78	2.97	2.77	3.87

Required:

(a) Prepare a trend analysis for each listed financial item of Walters & Cruz using Year 1 as the base year.

(b) How is trend analysis used by financial decision makers? What are the limitations of trend analysis?

30. **Common-Sized Financial Statements** *(LO 9.7)*

Eikner, Inc. operates two small clothing stores in southeastern Idaho. Following are this company's income statements for the years ended December 31, 2007 through 2009, and year-end balance sheets for 2007 through 2009.

Eikner, Inc.
Income Statements
For the Years Ended December 31, 2007–2009

	2007	2008	2009
Sales*	$ 641,900	$ 652,000	$ 654,500
Cost of Goods Sold	(304,500)	(323,700)	(339,200)
Gross Profit	$ 337,400	$ 328,300	$ 315,300
Operating Expenses	(154,200)	(155,800)	(161,900)
Operating Income	$ 183,200	$ 172,500	$ 153,400
Other Revenue (Expense)**	13,400	(6,400)	(1,200)
Income before Income Tax	$ 196,600	$ 166,100	$ 152,200
Income Tax Expense	(78,600)	(66,400)	(60,900)
Net Income	$ 118,000	$ 99,700	$ 91,300

*All the company's sales are on a credit basis.
**Includes interest expense of the following amounts: $8,900 (2007); $7,400 (2008); and $7,100 (2009).

Eikner, Inc.
Balance Sheets
December 31, 2007–2009

	2007	2008	2009
ASSETS			
Cash	$ 22,000	$ 9,100	$ 3,700
Accounts Receivable (net)	72,500	103,300	116,900
Inventory	109,800	102,000	89,000
Prepaid Expenses	2,500	1,400	1,700
Total Current Assets	$206,800	$215,800	$211,300
Property & Equipment (net)	212,000	201,500	189,400
Other Assets	3,200	2,600	1,500
Total Assets	$422,000	$419,900	$402,200
LIABILITIES			
Accounts Payable	$ 51,900	$ 57,200	$ 64,900
Notes Payable	25,000	15,000	12,000
Accrued Liabilities	41,100	35,800	7,400
Total Current Liabilities	$118,000	$108,000	$ 84,300
Bonds Payable	100,000	80,000	80,000
Total Liabilities	$218,000	$188,000	$164,300
STOCKHOLDERS' EQUITY			
Common Stock ($1 par value)	$ 50,000	$ 50,000	$ 50,000
Additional Paid-in Capital	130,000	130,000	130,000
Retained Earnings	24,000	51,900	57,900
Total Stockholders' Equity	$204,000	$231,900	$237,900
Total Liabilities and Stockholders' Equity	$422,000	$419,900	$402,200

Required:

(a) Prepare common-sized income statements for Eikner, Inc. for 2007 through 2009.

(b) What major structural changes occurred over this three-year period in Eikner's income statement data? Are these changes apparently favorable or unfavorable? Explain.

31. **Liquidity and Leverage Ratios** *(LO 9.8)*

Refer to the financial statements of Eikner, Inc. in Problem 30.

Required:

(a) Compute the liquidity and leverage ratios discussed in this chapter for Eikner, Inc. for 2007 through 2009.

(1) Overall, did the company's liquidity improve or deteriorate between 2007 and 2009? Explain.

(2) Did this company become more or less leveraged between 2007 and 2009?

(b) Compute the activity ratios discussed in this chapter for Eikner, Inc. for 2008 and 2009.

(1) Indicate which of these ratios improved and which deteriorated between 2007 and 2009.

(2) Overall, did the company do a better job of managing its accounts receivable, inventory, and total assets in 2009 compared with 2008? Explain.

(c) Compute the profitability and market strength ratios discussed in this chapter for Eikner, Inc. for 2007 through 2009. (Note: The company had total assets on January 1, 2007, of $425,000, whereas the company's total stockholders' equity on that date was $186,000.) Market prices for the company's stock were $8.50 (2007), $7.75 (2008), and $6.50 (2009).

(1) Evaluate the company's profitability ratios for the period 2007–2009. Did the company

become more or less profitable over this time period? Explain.

(2) Evaluate the company's market strength ratios for the period 2007–2009. What do the changes in these ratios over this period indicate?

32. **Market Price to Book Value Ratio** *(LO 9.8)*

Rent 'N Drive, Inc. is a publicly owned, truck leasing company based in Iowa. Presented in the following schedule are selected financial data for Rent 'N Drive's common stock over a recent five-year period.

	2005	2006	2007	2008	2009
Earnings per share	$ 0.10	$ 3.02	$ (1.68)	$ 3.90	$ 3.72
Dividends per share	0.60	0.60	0.60	0.60	0.60
Book value per share	35.00	36.52	25.62	28.66	31.28
Market price per share	44.26	48.95	44.12	61.05	62.78

Required:

(a) Compute Rent 'N Drive's market price to book value ratio for 2005 through 2009.

(b) Given the industry in which it operates, what factors may have contributed to the decline in Rent 'N Drive's book value per share in 2007?

(c) Would you consider investing in Rent 'N Drive? Discuss the reasons for your answer.

33. **Comparative Analysis of Financial Data** *(LO 9.5 and 9.8)*

The following schedule provides the norms for certain key financial ratios in a given industry and the ratios for three companies in that industry.

	Industry Norm	Alonso Co.	Buckley Inc.	Cosgrove Corp.
Current ratio	2.4	1.6	2.3	2.5
Quick ratio	1.0	0.4	1.3	1.2
Long-term debt to equity ratio	0.5	0.6	0.4	0.2
Times interest earned ratio	4.5	2.4	5.6	14.9
Age of receivables	89 days	101 days	77 days	80 days
Age of inventory	97 days	99 days	92 days	76 days
Profit margin percentage	3.4%	2.3%	3.6%	4.7%
Return on assets	4.9%	3.4%	5.6%	6.0%
Return on equity	7.1%	4.9%	7.1%	8.9%
Price-earnings ratio	10.2	7.5	7.7	12.7
Market price to book value	1.9	1.3	1.2	3.2

Required:

(a) Evaluate the overall financial health of these three firms. Given the information provided, which firm do you believe is in the strongest financial condition? Explain.

(b) Again, based only on the data provided, which firm's common stock do you believe would be the most attractive investment alternative? Why?

(c) List three other items of financial or nonfinancial information that you would want to review before making an investment decision regarding the common stocks of these companies.

34. **Market Price to Book Value Ratio** *(LO 9.5 and 9.8)*

The ratio of a stock's market price to its book value per share reveals how much investors are willing to pay for each $1 of a company's net assets per share. The following information is available for companies A, B, and C.

	Company A	Company B	Company C
Total assets	$3,000,000	$2,250,000	$6,000,000
Total liabilities	750,000	1,200,000	4,500,000
Number of common shares outstanding	300,000	600,000	375,000
Year-end per share stock price	$25.13	$21.07	$32.16

Required:

(a) For each of the companies listed, compute the book value per share and the market price to book value ratio. (Note: None of the companies have preferred stock outstanding.)

(b) How is it possible for a company's market price to book value ratio to differ significantly from 1.0?

35. **Price-Earnings Ratio** *(LO 9.5 and 9.8)*

Following are price-earnings (P/E) ratios on December 10, 2008, for several prominent companies:

	P/E Ratio
Pfizer Inc.	10.6
Lowe's Cos.	13.3
Sears Holdings Corp.	22.6
JPMorgan Chase & Co.	16.9
Microsoft	10.9
Berkshire Hathaway Inc. Cl A	21.3
General Motors	0.0

Required:

(a) What factors may account for the large variance in the P/E ratios of the companies listed?

(b) Why would the P/E of General Motors have been 0.0 (as was Ford Motor's P/E ratio) on that date?

(c) Explain the difference between a company's P/E ratio and its market price to book value ratio. Which of these two ratios do you believe is more relevant to potential investors? Defend your answer.

36. **Impact of Accounting Errors on Financial Ratios** *(LO 9.8)*

Following are examples of errors that can be made in processing accounting data. Listed next to each error is a financial ratio.

■ Recording a sales transaction twice (Gross profit percentage)

■ Overstating ending inventory (Quick ratio)

■ Debiting a payment of a long-term payable to a short-term payable account (Return on assets)

■ Understating the estimated useful life of a depreciable asset (Return on equity)

■ Failing to prepare a year-end adjusting entry to record interest revenue (Price-earnings ratio)

■ Failing to record the declaration of a cash dividend shortly before year-end (Profit margin percentage)

■ Recording a purchase of a long-term asset in a current asset account (Current ratio)

Required:

(a) In general, indicate the effect on any ratio when the following happens:

(1) Numerator increases

(2) Numerator decreases

(3) Denominator increases

(4) Denominator decreases

(b) Indicate whether each error listed increases (overstates), decreases (understates), or has no impact on the financial ratio with which it is coupled.

37. **Earnings Quality** *(LO 9.9)*

Benson Corporation and Stabler Company are two firms in the same industry. These two firms have approximately the same annual revenues and total assets. Following is the most recent income statement of each firm. Benson Corporation uses the LIFO inventory costing method and an accelerated depreciation method, whereas Stabler Company uses FIFO inventory costing and the straight-line depreciation method.

	Benson Corp.	Stabler Co.
Sales	$1,324,900	$1,337,300
Cost of Goods Sold	(690,200)	(640,900)
Gross Profit	$ 634,700	$ 696,400
Operating Expenses		
Selling	(90,000)	(86,400)
General & Admin.	(72,000)	(87,000)
Depreciation	(102,000)	(71,000)
Operating Income	$ 370,700	$ 452,000
Other Revenue	5,200	3,700
Income before Income Tax	$ 375,900	$ 455,700
Income Tax Expense	(150,000)	(182,300)
Net Income	$ 225,500	$ 273,400

Required:

(a) Define earnings quality.

(b) Why is earnings quality an important consideration for financial decision makers when evaluating financial statement data?

(c) Suppose that a friend of yours is considering investing in the common stock of either Benson Corporation or Stabler Company. Write a memo to your friend explaining the concept of earnings quality and comment on how the quality of these firms' reported earnings might be affected by their use of different accounting methods.

CASES

38. **Trend Analysis** *(LO 9.6, Internet)*

Use the annual reports of Carnival Corporation for the 2005–2007 fiscal years to answer the following questions. This information can be found on either the annual report or the SEC 10-K filing at www.carnival.com by following the links to Investor Relations.

Required:

(a) Prepare a trend analysis using 2004 as the base year to compare Carnival's balance sheets and income statements for 2004, 2005, 2006, and 2007. (Hint: Though no template is provided, this task is simplified by using Excel.)

(b) Interpret the trend analysis. For at least three accounts that show reasonable differences, depict the trend using a bar or line graph.

39. **Common-Size Financial Statements** (LO 9.7, Internet) Use the annual reports of Carnival Corporation for the 2005–2007 fiscal years to answer the following questions. This information can be found on either the annual report or the SEC 10-K filing at www.carnival.com by following the links to Investor Relations.

Required:

(a) Prepare a common-sized balance sheet and income statement for Carnival for 2006 and 2007. (Hint: Though no template is provided, this task is simplified by using Excel.)

(b) Were there any significant changes from 2006 to 2007? If so, discuss those changes.

(c) Were the changes noted in part (b) as obvious by examining raw numbers as they were by examining the common-sized statements? Discuss.

40. **Comparative Ratio Analysis** (LO 9.5 and 9.8, Internet, group)

Identifying the similarities and differences in companies is as crucial to making investment decisions as understanding a single company's financial statements. Form groups of at least four students. Each group should select a single industry. Each group member should locate a different annual report within that industry. (The industry and individual company may be assigned by your instructor.) Note: Additional references may be needed for some data (such as stock trading price and beginning balance of certain accounts for Year 1).

Required—individual group members:

(a) Calculate the following ratios for the company you selected for the two most recent fiscal years.

(1) Current ratio
(2) Quick ratio
(3) Debt to total asset ratio
(4) Long-term debt to equity ratio
(5) Times interest earned
(6) Accounts receivable turnover ratio
(7) Age of receivables
(8) Inventory turnover
(9) Age of inventory
(10) Total asset turnover
(11) Profit margin ratio
(12) Gross profit percentage

(13) Return on assets
(14) Return on equity

(b) Comment on the changes from year to year.

(c) Does this company seem to be a good investment based on these ratios?

Required—groups:

(d) Compile the ratio calculations for each company prepared by the individual group members into one table.

(e) Compare the results from company to company in the same fiscal years. Include in your comparison a graphical analysis. Discuss reasons why these ratios might be similar or different within an industry.

(f) Based on these four ratios across companies, which company is the best investment in the industry you have chosen? Explain the rationale for your choice.

Required—class:

(g) Compare the ratios from each industry. Discuss reasons why these ratios might be similar or different between industries.

(h) Does one industry seem to be a better investment than another? Explain. Do you think this judgment would be constant over time? Explain.

41. **Accounting Errors and the Impact on Financial Statement Data** (LO 9.2 and 9.8, ethics)

Following is a condensed version of the 2009 income statement of Petersen Company.

Sales	$ 2,176,200
Cost of Goods Sold	(1,212,900)
Gross Profit	$ 963,300
Operating Expenses	(333,900)
Operating Income	$ 629,400
Other Revenue	30,600
Income before Income Tax	$ 660,000
Income Tax Expense	(264,000)
Net Income	$ 396,000

Petersen's accountant overlooked a $9,600 utility bill at the end of 2009. This bill should have been recorded with a debit to Utilities Expense and a credit to Accrued Liabilities. The company's year-end Inventory account balance was also incorrect. Because of errors made during the counting of inventory, Petersen's year-end inventory was listed as $522,900 in its accounting records instead of the correct figure of $453,600. This overstatement of year-end inventory caused Petersen's Cost of Goods Sold for the year to be understated by an equal amount.

Following is other information regarding Petersen Company.

Average total assets during 2009	$2,461,500*
Interest expense for 2009 (included in Other Revenues and Expenses)	102,000
Average common stockholders' equity	1,140,000*
Average income tax rate	40%

*These averages were computed by adding the beginning-of-the-year and end-of-the-year amounts and dividing by two.

Required:

(a) Ignoring the two errors discovered in Petersen's accounting records, compute the company's profitability ratios for 2009.

(b) Compute Petersen's profitability ratios for 2009 after adjusting the company's financial data for the two errors.

(c) Did the two errors have a material effect on Petersen's profitability ratios? Defend your answer.

(d) Do you believe that companies manipulate numbers intentionally to mislead investors? Explain.

SUPPLEMENTAL PROBLEMS

42. Accounting for Investments in Stocks and Bonds (LO 9.1; Compare to Problem 25)

Following are selected transactions that affected NoQWERTY during 2009.

- On January 1, NoQWERTY paid $300,000 for 15,000 shares of LQTM, Inc.

- On January 1, LQTM, Inc. declared and paid a $0.32 per share dividend on its stock to all shareholders.

- On July 1, WYWH Corp. issued 300, $1,000, 5 percent, ten-year bonds for $320,000. NoQWERTY purchased 150 of the WYWH bonds on issuance.

- On December 31, WYWH paid semiannual interest to all bondholders.

- On December 31, LQTM reported a net loss of $9,000.

Required:

(a) Record the journal entries for the listed transactions related to NoQWERTY, assuming that:

   (1) NoQWERTY owns 5 percent of LQTM, Inc.

   (2) NoQWERTY owns 35 percent of LQTM, Inc.

   (3) NoQWERTY owns 90 percent of LQTM, Inc.

(b) Describe NoQWERTY's year-end procedures related to LQTM, Inc. under each assumption from part (a).

(c) Record the entry for NoQWERTY's investment in the WYWH bonds and the subsequent receipt of the annual interest.

(d) Under what circumstance(s) would NoQWERTY show minority interest on its financial statements? Explain. Is there an instance in which NoQWERTY would not show a minority interest? If so, explain.

43. Corporate Income Statement (LO 9.2 and 9.3; Compare to Problem 26)

Following are income statement data for Allaboutme Corporation for the year ended December 31, 2009. These items are presented in random order.

Cost of Goods Sold	$720,000
General Expenses	36,000
Gain on Sale of Machinery	44,000
Income Tax Expense on Income from Continuing Operations	?
Operating Income from Operations	20,000
Selling Expenses	46,000
Extraordinary Loss due to Fire	50,000
Net Sales	1,040,000
Loss on Disposal of Discontinued Operations	40,000
Administrative Expenses	38,000

Allaboutme's average income tax rate is 40 percent on all taxable income items. Throughout 2009, Allaboutme had 100,000 shares of common stock outstanding.

Required:

Prepare an income statement for Allaboutme Corporation, including an earnings per share section. (Hint: Remember that certain items on the income statement must be shown with their related tax amounts.)

44. Deferred Income Taxes (LO 9.4; Compare to Problem 28)

For the current year, Watertown Dakota Corp. (WDC) has a $20,000 difference between its pretax accounting income and its taxable income, as indicated in the following schedule.

	Pretax Accounting Income	Taxable Income
Income Before Depreciation Expense	$200,000	$200,000
Depreciation Expense	(40,000)	(60,000)

Required:

(a) Define "temporary difference" as it applies to the pretax accounting income and taxable income of a corporation. What is the dollar amount of the temporary difference in this situation?

(b) Prepare WDC's year-end adjusting entry to record income tax expense for the current year. Assume that WDC's effective income tax rate is 40 percent for both financial accounting and taxation purposes.

(c) Suppose that WDC pays the amount of tax due for the current year on January 15 of the following year. Record this payment.

(d) How much less income tax did WDC pay in the entry recorded in part (c) due to the temporary difference related to depreciation expense?

(e) Will WDC eventually pay the dollar amount you computed in part (d)? If so, what advantage does WDC realize as a result of the depreciation-related temporary difference?

45. Trend Analysis (LO 9.6; Compare to Problem 29)

Murtaugh, Inc. provides communication systems and support to large businesses. Presented in the following schedule are selected financial data reported recently by Murtaugh. Amounts are expressed in millions of dollars except dividends per share.

	Total Revenues	Dividends per Share	Total Assets
2006	$361.9	$0.252	$143.9
2007	364.0	0.252	137.8
2008	418.7	0.273	159.3
2009	455.1	0.360	167.7

Required:

(a) Prepare a trend analysis for each of the three financial statement items listed for Murtaugh using 2006 as the base year.

(b) Predict the 2010 figure for each financial statement item. In which of these predicted amounts do you have the most confidence? Why?

(c) During 2010, Murtaugh actually had total revenues of $448.3 million, paid dividends of $0.39 per share, and had total assets at year-end of $181.1 million. Compute the percentage error between each of these actual amounts and the corresponding prediction you made in part (b). Comment on any additional insight these results provide you regarding trend analysis.

46. Common-Sized Financial Statements (LO 9.7; Compare to Problem 30)

Following are balance sheets for Narragansett & Warren as of December 31, 2008 and 2009.

Narragansett & Warren
Balance Sheets
December 31, 2008 and 2009

	2008	2009
ASSETS		
Cash	$ 18,400	$ 37,400
Accounts Receivable (net)	16,600	28,800
Inventory	25,000	29,400
Prepaid Expenses	1,600	600
Total Current Assets	$ 61,600	$ 96,200
Equipment (net)	62,400	55,600
Total Assets	$124,000	$151,800
LIABILITIES		
Accounts Payable	$ 14,200	$ 5,400
Accrued Liabilities	6,600	7,200
Total Current Liabilities	$ 20,800	$ 12,600
Long-Term Note Payable	20,000	20,000
Total Liabilities	$ 40,800	$ 32,600
STOCKHOLDERS' EQUITY		
Common Stock	$ 24,000	$ 24,000
Additional Paid-in Capital	48,000	48,000
Retained Earnings	11,200	47,200
Total Stockholders' Equity	$ 83,200	$119,200
Total Liabilities and SE	$124,000	$151,800

Required:

(a) How are common-sized financial statements used by decision makers?

(b) Prepare common-sized balance sheets for Narragansett & Warren as of December 31, 2008 and 2009.

(c) What major structural changes occurred in this business's balance sheet during 2009? What factors may have accounted for these changes?

47. **Ratio Analysis** *(LO 9.8; Compare to Problem 42)*

Big Lots is the largest closeout retailer in the United States. Locate the consolidated income statements filed in the 10-K of Big Lots, Inc. for year-end February 3, 2007, and February 2, 2008 (www.biglotscorporate.com).

Required:

(a) Calculate the 14 liquidity, leverage, activity, and profitability ratios for Big Lots for 2007 and 2008.

(b) Comment on any changes from year to year.

CHAPTER 10

Statement of Cash Flows

LEARNING OBJECTIVES

1. Identify and distinguish among operating, investing, and financing activities.
2. Prepare a statement of cash flows using the indirect method.
3. Prepare a statement of cash flows using the direct method.
4. Identify the principal uses of the statement of cash flows for financial decision makers.
5. Compute and interpret cash flow ratios, cash flow per share, and free cash flow.

INTRODUCTION

Business managers must be concerned with both generating revenues and properly managing the firms' cash resources. Some companies with long histories of reporting profits eventually fail because their owners or managers did not pay sufficient attention to cash flows. Thus, businesses are required to include a **statement of cash flows** (SCF) within the annual financial report. This statement summarizes cash receipts and disbursements information and indicates causes of the net change in the cash balance for a specific time. The SCF is not intended to replace either the balance sheet or income statement. Decision makers use these three major financial statements in combination to analyze the financial condition, operating results, and future prospects of business entities.

This chapter opens with an introduction to the statement of cash flows and follows with a discussion of the preparing of an SCF on both the indirect and direct methods. The chapter concludes with a discussion of three approaches that can be used to analyze and interpret cash-flow data.

THREE PRIMARY TYPES OF BUSINESS ACTIVITIES AND CASH FLOWS

From a technical standpoint, a statement of cash flows has one primary objective: to account for the change in an organization's cash balance during a given accounting period. To achieve this objective, all transactions that affected cash during that period must be identified. For SCF purposes, "cash" includes both cash and cash equivalents. Recall from Chapter 4 that cash equivalents are investments in short-term securities that have, when purchased, 90 days or less to maturity.

As shown in Visual Recap 10.1, the SCF consists of four sections. The first three sections summarize the cash inflows (receipts) and cash outflows (disbursements) from a business's activities during the year as related to the following three categories: operating activities, investing activities, and financing activities. The final section reconciles a business's cash balance at the beginning and end of an accounting period. This reconciliation involves adding the net cash provided or used by operating, investing, and financing activities to the beginning cash balance to arrive at the period-ending cash balance.

Operating activities are those transactions and events related to the production and delivery of goods and services by businesses. In other words, operating activities reflect the day-to-day profit-oriented activities of a business. Principal cash inflows from operating activities are cash receipts from customers from both cash sales and collections of accounts receivable. Other cash inflows from operating activities include receipts of interest revenue and cash provided by the sale of investments in trading securities. Major sources of cash outflows from operating activities include payments to suppliers, employees, and taxing authorities. Financial statement users tend to focus on cash flows related to operating activities because, over the long run, a business must generate positive cash flows from its profit-oriented activities to be economically viable.

Investing activities typically involve long-term asset accounts. Thus, **investing activities** include the lending and collecting of loans receivable; acquisition and disposal of property, plant, and equipment; and purchase and sale of long-term investments in debt and equity securities.

VISUAL RECAP 10.1

The Statement of Cash Flows

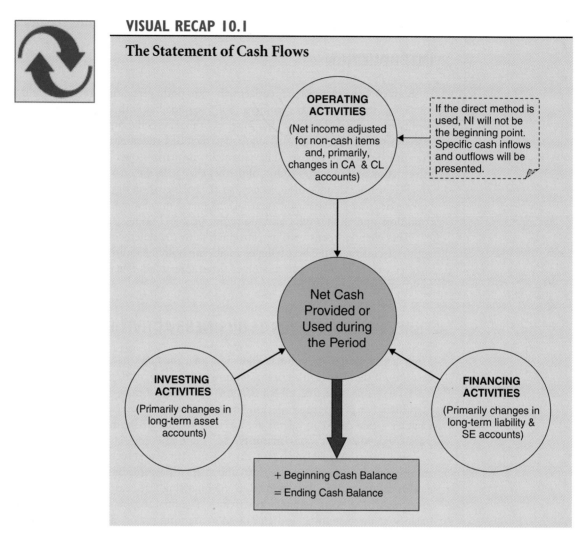

The majority of financing activities involve long-term liability and stockholders' equity contributed capital (common and preferred stock) accounts. However, short-term borrowings using notes payable are also included in financing activities. **Financing activities** involve borrowing cash through long-term notes, selling bonds, repaying debts, selling stock to investors for cash, repurchasing stock from investors (obtaining treasury stock) for cash, and providing stockholders with a return on their investments in the form of cash dividends. Although transactions related to notes and bonds are classified as financing activities, under U.S. GAAP, interest expense (as well as interest received) must be classified as an operating activity. International financial reporting standards (IFRS), however, allow interest paid (or received) to be classified as either operating or financing.

Exhibit 10-1 provides a listing of the primary cash inflows and outflows from operating, investing, and financing activities. Note that the classification of cash flows from the sale or purchase of investments in debt and equity securities depends on whether the investment is classified as short-term or long-term.

EXHIBIT 10-1

Summary of
Transaction
Classifications
for the SCF

Operating Activities

Cash Inflows	Cash Outflows
Receipts from customers	Payments to suppliers
Receipts of interest (under U.S. GAAP)*	Payments to employees
Receipts of dividends	Payments of interest (under U.S. GAAP)*
Receipts from the sale of debt and equity securities classified as short-term investments	Miscellaneous payments related to operating activities
Miscellaneous receipts related to operating activities	Payments for purchasing debt and equity securities classified as short-term investments
	Payments of taxes

Investing Activities

Cash Inflows	Cash Outflows
Receipts from the sale of property, plant and equipment (PP&E)	Payments to acquire property, plant and equipment (PP&E)
Receipts from the sale of long-term investments in debt and equity securities	Payments to acquire long-term investments in debt and equity securities
Receipts from the repayment of long-term loans receivable	Payments for long-term loans receivable made to other companies or to business officers

Financing Activities

Cash Inflows	Cash Outflows
Receipts from the issuance of common stock and preferred stock	Payments for dividends
Receipts from the issuance of bonds payable	Payments to acquire treasury stock
Receipts from short or long-term borrowings from banks and other parties	Payments to retire bonds payable and to repay short- or long-term bank loans

*May be considered a financing activity under IFRS.

DIRECT VERSUS INDIRECT METHOD OF PREPARING A STATEMENT OF CASH FLOWS

A statement of cash flows can be prepared under either the direct or indirect method. The difference between the two methods reflects the way in which net cash flow from operating activities is reported. In preparing an SCF using the **direct method**, the operating section lists specific cash inflows and outflows from operating activities, such as those indicated in Exhibit 10-1. Exhibit 10-2 shows Fierro Inc.'s statement of cash flows prepared using the direct method. Notice the use of specific cash receipt and payment terminology.

The SCF shown in Exhibit 10-3 for Fierro Inc. is prepared using the indirect method. Cash flows from investing and financing activities are determined and reported in the same manner under both the direct and indirect methods; the only difference in the statements

EXHIBIT 10-2

Fierro Inc.'s
SCF—Direct Method

Fierro Inc.
Statement of Cash Flows
For the Year Ended December 31, 2009

Cash flows from operating activities:		
Receipts from customers	$ 575,043	
Payments to suppliers	(449,245)	
Payments to employees	(79,866)	
Payments for insurance	(2,635)	
Receipt of interest on bank savings	3,454	
Payments of interest on capital leases	(7,273)	
Payments of income taxes	(21,950)	
Net cash provided by operating activities		$ 17,528
Cash flows from investing activities:		
Proceeds from sale of PP&E	$ 1,228	
Purchases of PP&E	(11,853)	
Purchases of LT equity investments	(10,009)	
Net cash used by investing activities		(20,634)
Cash flows from financing activities:		
Proceeds from long-term borrowings	$ 6,245	
Principal payments on capital leases	(4,994)	
Proceeds from issuance of common stock	4,058	
Purchases of treasury stock	(520)	
Payments of cash dividends	(1,736)	
Net cash provided by financing activities		3,053
Net decrease in cash and cash equivalents		$ (53)
Cash and cash equivalents, beginning of year		3,485
Cash and cash equivalents, end of year		$ 3,432

is in the operating section. Under the direct method, specific cash flows from operating activities are not listed in the operating section. When the **indirect method** is used to prepare an SCF, the net cash flow from operating activities is determined by making adjustments to net income. Net income is determined using the accrual basis and includes some items that are not actual cash flows. For example, sales revenue includes some credit sales that have not been collected in cash by year-end; salaries expense may include some salaries that have been accrued but not paid at year-end.

The information needed to determine the specific net income adjustments for Fierro's SCF is provided in the next section. Determining the amount of these adjustments requires information from the income statement for the year as well as the beginning and ending balance sheets.

Under U.S. GAAP (but not under IFRS), companies using the direct method of preparing a statement of cash flows must include a schedule reconciling net cash flow from operating activities with net income in their annual reports. Thus, these companies must essentially prepare the operating section of the SCF twice. This duplication feature causes the direct method of SCF preparation to be less popular than the indirect method. Although the direct method discloses specific types of operating cash flows and is thereby

EXHIBIT 10-3
Fierro Inc.'s
SCF—Indirect Method

Fierro Inc.
Statement of Cash Flows
For the Year Ended December 31, 2009

Cash flows from operating activities:		
Net Income	$ 58,601	
Adjustments to reconcile net income to net		
cash provided by operating activities:		
Depreciation expense	29,738	
Loss on sale of equipment	460	
Increase in Accounts Receivable	(24,957)	
Increase in Inventory	(12,684)	
Decrease in Prepaid Insurance	2,575	
Decrease in Accounts Payable	(38,405)	
Increase in Income Taxes Payable	2,200	
Net cash provided by operating activities		$ 17,528
Cash flows from investing activities:		
Proceeds from sale of PP&E	$ 1,228	
Purchases of PP&E	(11,853)	
Purchases of LT equity investments	(10,009)	
Net cash used by investing activities		(20,634)
Cash flows from financing activities:		
Proceeds from long-term borrowings	$ 6,245	
Principal payments on capital leases	(4,994)	
Proceeds from issuance of common stock	4,058	
Purchases of treasury stock	(520)	
Payments of cash dividends	(1,736)	
Net cash provided by financing activities		3,053
Net decrease in cash and cash equivalents		$ (53)
Cash and cash equivalents, beginning of year		3,485
Cash and cash equivalents, end of year		$ 3,432

more informative than the indirect method for financial statement users, the indirect method is more widely used by businesses.

PREPARING A STATEMENT OF CASH FLOWS: INDIRECT METHOD

The initial issues to address when preparing a statement of cash flows are where to obtain and how to organize the data needed for this financial statement. Unlike the preparation of a balance sheet and income statement, which requires general ledger account balances, few cash flow statement items are general ledger account balances. Cash flow amounts must be determined from analyzing the information contained in a business's accounting records and in other financial statements. A streamlined approach to collecting and organizing the cash flow data is used to introduce the accumulation of data for a statement of cash flows prepared on the indirect method.

Analyzing Transactions for a SCF—Operating Activities

The starting point for determining net cash flow from operating activities on an indirect basis is a business's net income. As mentioned earlier, a company's net income seldom equals the net cash flow generated by its operating activities. There are two reasons for the difference. First, certain noncash or nonoperating items are considered in computing net income. Second, the revenue and expense amounts included in net income are determined on an accrual, rather than cash, basis. The adjustments for these items are shown in Visual Recap 10.2.

Noncash Items

Depreciation and amortization are noncash expenses. The journal entry to record either of these items is a debit to an expense and a credit to a contra-asset or an asset account. Thus, neither results in cash outflows, but both decrease net income. To reconcile net income to net cash flow from operating activities, depreciation and amortization expenses must be added to net income. Depreciation is generally included first in the adjustments to net income because it is often one of the largest adjustment amounts. The depreciation and amortization amounts are generally found on the income statement, but they can also be calculated using the beginning and ending balances of related accounts on the balance sheet and other investment and disposal information.

Gains and Losses

Several examples of gains and losses have been discussed in earlier chapters, including gains and losses on the disposal of property, plant, and equipment. Losses reduce income whereas gains increase it, but neither is a cash flow (although they will affect the amount of cash received in the transaction). As shown in Visual Recap 10.2, losses are added to net income when computing net cash flow from operating activities, whereas gains are subtracted from net income. These adjustments remove the effects of the loss and gain from the net income amount and allow the cash effect to be shown separately.

To illustrate this treatment, consider the loss on equipment disposal incurred by Fierro Inc. Assume that the company sold equipment for $1,228 cash. The equipment had originally cost $35,000 and, at the time of the sale, had a book value of $1,688. Thus, Fierro had recorded $33,312 ($35,000 − $1,688) of depreciation over the equipment's useful life. The journal entry for the sale follows:

VISUAL RECAP 10.2

Net Income Adjustments for Preparing the Operating Activities Section under the Indirect Method

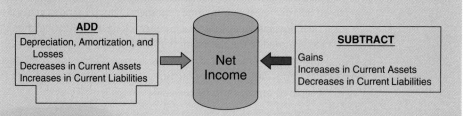

ADD		SUBTRACT
Depreciation, Amortization, and Losses	Net Income	Gains
Decreases in Current Assets		Increases in Current Assets
Increases in Current Liabilities		Decreases in Current Liabilities

General Journal			
Date	Description	Debit	Credit
Apr 9	Cash	1,228	
	Accumulated Depreciation—Equipment	33,312	
	Loss on Disposal of Asset	460	
	Equipment		35,000
	Sold equipment at less than book value		

In the SCF, transactions involving the purchase or sale of PP&E qualify as investing activities. Thus, the $1,228 actual cash inflow from Fierro's equipment sale is reported in that section of the statement of cash flows. However, the $460 loss on this transaction was included in calculating the firm's net income. Without an appropriate adjustment to net income, the total cash flow from this transaction would be reported as a net $768 in Fierro's SCF: a negative $460 in cash flows from operating activities (through inclusion of the loss in net income) and a positive $1,228 in cash flows from investing activities. To remedy this problem, the $460 loss must be added back to net income in Fierro's SCF to determine net cash flow from operating activities.

If the equipment had been sold for $2,100, a $412 gain would have been included in determining net income. On the SCF, the gain would be subtracted from net income when computing Fierro's net cash flow from operating activities, and the full $2,100 would be shown as the proceeds from sale in the investing section of the statement.

Determination of adjustments for gains and losses requires a review of the income statement for the existence of such amounts and of changes in (typically long-term) asset account balances and, if necessary, any related contra-accounts (such as Accumulated Depreciation or Accumulated Amortization).

Current Assets

Most of the adjustments required to convert net income to net cash flow from operating activities involve current asset (other than cash) and current liability accounts. As indicated in Visual Recap 10.2, changes in these accounts must be added to, or subtracted from, net income when computing net cash flow from operating activities. Determinations of these adjustments require the use of income statement revenue and expense information in conjunction with beginning and ending account balances on the balance sheet.

Accounts Receivable is used to illustrate the logic underlying the adjustments to net income for changes in current assets. For simplicity, assume that Fierro Inc. began the year 2009 with a balance of $0 in Accounts Receivable. At the end of the year, the company's income statement showed total sales (all assumed to be on account) of $600,000, and the balance sheet showed Accounts Receivable of $24,957. As a result, Fierro's sales for the year produced cash flows from operating activities of only $575,043 ($600,000 − $24,957).

$$\text{Beginning A/R} + \text{Sales} - \text{Cash collected} = \text{Ending A/R}$$
$$\$0 + \$600,000 - X = \$24,957$$
$$\$600,000 - X = \$24,957$$
$$X = \$575,043$$

When computing the firm's net cash flow from operating activities, the $24,957 not yet collected from sales must be deducted from its net income because it has not been realized in the form of cash.[1] On the SCF prepared using the direct method (Exhibit 10-2), the $575,043 is shown as cash receipts from customers.

If the balance of Accounts Receivable increases during a year, fewer dollars of sales were collected than were recorded. Thus, the increase is deducted from net income when computing net cash flow from operating activities. Conversely, if the balance of Accounts Receivable decreases during a year, the decrease is added to net income when computing net cash flow from operating activities. This adjustment gives recognition to the fact that the cash inflows from customers exceeded the sales recorded during the year.

Similar reasoning can be applied to other noncash current assets that are related to operations. Increases in such current assets are deducted from net income, and decreases in these assets are added to net income when computing net cash flow from operating activities under the indirect method.

Current Liabilities

To illustrate the rationale for the treatment of current liabilities, Income Taxes Payable is used. Remember that credits to this account would commonly reflect the accrual of income tax expense, whereas debits to this account would reflect the payment of taxes. Tax expense is shown in determining net income on the income statement, but for purposes of the SCF, the important piece of information is the amount of taxes that were paid in cash during the year. Assume that at the beginning of 2009, Fierro Inc. owed $100 of taxes payable. During 2009, Fierro showed $24,150 in tax expense on the income statement. Fierro's 2009 year-end balance in Income Taxes Payable is $2,300 (an increase of $2,200). As shown in the following calculation, the company only paid $21,950 ($100 + $24,150 − $2,300) in cash for taxes during 2009. The remaining taxes will be paid in the following year.

$$\text{Beginning Taxes Payable} + \text{Tax Expense} - \text{Taxes Paid} = \text{Ending Taxes Payable}$$
$$\$100 + \$24{,}150 - X = \$2{,}300$$
$$\$24{,}250 - X = \$2{,}300$$
$$X = \$21{,}950$$

The $2,200 difference between the beginning and ending balances of Taxes Payable represents the amount that was expensed but was not paid in cash. This increase is added to net income on the SCF prepared using the indirect basis to determine cash flow from operating activities. On the SCF prepared using the direct basis (Exhibit 10-2), the $21,950 is shown as cash payments of income taxes.

Alternatively, assume that Fierro's Income Tax Payable account had a credit balance of $3,000 at the beginning of 2009. If the company recorded $24,150 of income tax expense

---

[1]To simplify the examples in this chapter, the assumption is made that there are no uncollectible accounts receivable and, thus, no allowance for uncollectible accounts. However, the amount recorded for uncollectible accounts expense is (similar to depreciation expense) a noncash expense. That amount would need to be added back to net income. Actual cash collected would be calculated using the AR balance, adjusted for any actual write-offs of uncollectible accounts.

for 2009 and reported a balance of $800 (a decrease of $2,200) at the end of the year, the actual amount of cash payments for taxes would be $26,350.

$$\text{Beginning Taxes Payable } + \text{ Tax Expense } - \text{ Taxes Paid } = \text{ Ending Taxes Payable}$$
$$\$3,000 \ + \ \$24,150 - X = \$800$$
$$\$27,150 - X = \$800$$
$$X = \$26,350$$

Because a greater amount of taxes were paid than were expensed, the $2,200 decrease in the account would be subtracted from net income in the SCF prepared on an indirect basis to arrive at net cash flow provided by operating activities.

Other current liabilities can be analyzed in the same manner. Increases in current liabilities that are related to operations are added to net income, and decreases in such current liabilities are deducted from net income when computing net cash flow from operating activities under the indirect method.

Analyzing Transactions for a SCF—Investing and Financing Activities

Most businesses have only a few transactions or events each year that qualify as investing or financing activities. These items may be identified by reviewing the company's beginning and ending balances of short-term notes receivable and payable, long-term assets and liabilities, and stockholders' equity accounts. The statement of changes in stockholders' equity can be used to obtain necessary details about the causes of changes in stockholders' equity account balances. Income statement information relative to gains and losses may also be necessary.

Investing Activities

The most common investing activities generating cash inflows are sales of a company's PP&E items or investments. The most common cash outflow investing activities are purchases of these same items. An earlier section discussed the sale of a piece of equipment by Fierro Inc. and its impacts on the statement of cash flows. This section will discuss the purchase of another PP&E item.

Assume that Fierro had a $198,500 beginning and a $175,353 ending balance in its PP&E account. Without any other information, it could be estimated that Fierro sold PP&E costing $23,147 ($198,500 − $175,353) during the year. However, it was previously indicated that the cost of equipment sold by Fierro during the year was $35,000. If that had been the only PP&E purchase or sale transaction, the PP&E account would have had an ending balance of $163,500 ($198,500 − $35,000). Instead, the ending balance is $175,353. Thus, Fierro Inc. must have purchased $11,853 of equipment in addition to selling some equipment:

$$\text{Beginning PP\&E } + \text{ Equipment purchased } - \text{ Cost of equipment sold } = \text{ Ending PP\&E}$$
$$\$198,500 \ + \ X - \$35,000 = \$175,353$$
$$\$163,500 \ + \ X = \$175,353$$
$$X = \$11,853$$

The purchase of this equipment is shown as a cash outflow in the investing activities section of the SCF.

Financing Activities

The most common financing activities generating cash inflows are issuances of notes and bonds payable as well as sales of common, preferred, or treasury stock. The most common cash outflow financing activities are principal payments on notes, capital leases and bonds, repurchases (retirements) of bonds at a price other than book value, purchases of treasury stock, and payment of cash dividends on common and preferred stock. Transactions involving the repurchasing of bonds will likely generate a gain or loss that will need to be adjusted for in the operating section of the SCF; transactions involving stockholders' equity items will not involve gains or losses.

Completing the Analysis

Fierro's 2009 income statement and comparative balance sheets are given, respectively, in Exhibits 10-4 and 10-5. Assume the following information about the remaining amounts in Fierro's SCF.

- Inventory increased by $12,684 ($30,638 − $17,954); this amount is subtracted from net income in the operating section of the SCF prepared on an indirect basis.
  - On the SCF prepared on a direct basis, no line item is shown specifically for inventory; the cash flow amount related to inventory reflects payments made to suppliers.
- Prepaid Insurance decreased by $2,575 ($2,425 − $5,000); this amount is added to net income in the operating section of the SCF prepared on an indirect basis.

EXHIBIT 10-4

Fierro Inc.'s 2009
Income Statement

Fierro Inc.
Income Statement
For Year Ended December 31, 2009

Sales Revenue		$ 600,000
Cost of Goods Sold		(398,156)
Gross Profit		$ 201,844
Expenses:		
Depreciation	$29,738	
Wages and Salaries	79,866	
Insurance	5,210	(114,814)
Other Revenues and Expenses:		
Interest Revenue (on bank savings)	$ 3,454	
Interest Expense (on capital leases)	(7,273)	(3,819)
Loss on Sale of Equipment		(460)
Income Before Income Tax		$ 82,751
Income Tax Expense		(24,150)
Net Income		$ 58,601

EXHIBIT 10-5

Fierro Inc. Comparative
Balance Sheets

Fierro Inc.
Balance Sheets
For Years Ended December 31, 2009 and 2008

	12/31/09	12/31/08
ASSETS		
Current Assets:		
Cash and Cash Equivalents	$ 3,432	$ 3,485
Accounts Receivable	24,957	0
Inventory	30,638	17,954
Prepaid Insurance	2,425	5,000
Long-Term Investments	13,809	3,800
PP&E	175,353	198,500
Less Accumulated Depreciation	(86,113)	(89,687)
Total Assets	$164,501	$139,052
LIABILITIES		
Current Liabilities:		
Accounts Payable	$ 13,695	$ 52,100
Income Taxes Payable	2,300	100
Long-Term Liabilities:		
Capital Lease Payable	14,506	19,500
Notes Payable	7,245	1,000
Stockholders' Equity:		
Common Stock (no-par value)	64,058	60,000
Retained Earnings	63,217	6,352
Treasury Stock	(520)	(0)
Total Liabilities and Stockholders' Equity	$164,501	$139,052

- On the SCF prepared on a direct basis, $2,635 is shown as "Payments for insurance":

  Beginning balance + Payments made−Insurance Expense = Ending balance

  $$\$5,000 + X - \$5,210 = \$2,425$$
  $$X - \$210 = \$2,425$$
  $$X = \$2,635$$

- Long-Term Investments increased by $10,009 ($13,809 − $3,000); this amount represents a purchase of investments and is shown as a cash outflow in the investing section of the SCF.
- Accumulated Depreciation was accounted for in reference to depreciation expense and the sale of PP&E as follows:

  Beginning balance + Depreciation Expense − Depreciation on PP&E sold =

  Ending balance

  $$\$89,687 + \$29,738 - \$33,312 = \$86,113$$
  $$\$86,113 = \$86,113$$

■ Accounts Payable decreased by $38,405 ($13,695 − $52,100); this amount is subtracted from net income in the operating section of the SCF prepared on an indirect basis.

   • On the SCF prepared on a direct basis, the $449,245 amount of payments to suppliers results from computations related to Inventory and Accounts Payable. To make this computation, it is assumed that all inventory is purchased on account. The amount of inventory purchased must first be calculated; then the amount of payments to suppliers is calculated.

$$\text{Beginning Inventory} + \text{Purchases} - \text{CGS} = \text{Ending Inventory}$$
$$\$17,954 + X - \$398,156 = \$30,638$$
$$X - \$380,202 = \$30,638$$
$$X = \$410,840$$

$$\text{Beginning A/P} + \text{Purchases} - \text{Payments to Suppliers} = \text{Ending A/P}$$
$$\$52,100 + \$410,840 - X = \$13,695$$
$$\$462,940 - X = \$13,695$$
$$X = \$449,245$$

■ Capital Lease Payable decreased by $4,994; this amount represents a principal payment on the lease obligation and is shown as a cash outflow in the financing section of the SCF.

■ Notes Payable increased by $6,245; this amount represents borrowings and is shown as a cash inflow in the financing section of the SCF.

■ Common Stock increased by $4,058; this amount represents the issuance of stock and is shown as a cash inflow in the financing section of the SCF. If a company declared a stock dividend, there would have been implications for the stock account, a paid-in capital in excess of par account, and the Retained Earnings account. Information on stock dividends would need to be provided in addition to balance sheets and an income statement. Stock dividends are not shown on a statement of cash flows because no cash is involved.

■ Retained Earnings increased by $56,865; this change represents two items: (1) income of $58,601, which is shown as the starting point in the operating section of the SCF prepared on an indirect basis, and (2) dividends declared of $1,736, which are shown as a cash outflow in the financing section of the SCF. The dividends declared are calculated in the following manner:

$$\text{Beginning balance} + \text{NI} - \text{Dividends} = \text{Ending balance}$$
$$\$6,352 + \$58,601 - X = \$63,217$$
$$X = \$1,736$$

Had dividends been declared but not paid, the balance sheet would have contained a Dividends Payable account. Only the cash amount of dividends appears on the SCF.

■ Treasury Stock increased by $520; this amount represents stock repurchased by Fierro Inc. and is shown as a cash outflow in the financing section of the SCF.

In the SCF in which the operating section is prepared on a direct basis for Fierro Inc., the payments to employees, receipt of interest on bank savings, and payments of interest on capital leases are amounts taken directly from the income statement. There were no asset or liability accounts related to these amounts on Fierro's balance sheet; therefore, these revenues and expenses represent actual cash amounts.

Noncash Investing and Financing Activities

Companies occasionally engage in significant noncash investing or financing activities. For example, a company might acquire a building by issuing a long-term promissory note to the seller. Although these types of transactions do not involve cash, they must be disclosed by a firm. Such disclosure is required whether the indirect or direct method of preparing a statement of cash flows is used. Typically, noncash investing and financing activities are included in a schedule that follows the SCF.

ACCOUNTING INFORMATION FOR DECISION MAKING

An SCF helps decision makers evaluate a company's ability to generate positive net future cash flows. Economists define the true value of an asset, or entire business, as the present value of its future cash flows. Although an SCF reports historical cash-flow data, a strong correlation usually exists between a company's historical and future cash flows.

The second use of cash-flow data focuses on the information needs of specific types of financial statement users. For example, suppliers want to be reassured that business customers can generate sufficient cash to pay their bills as due. Stockholders, on the other hand, want to know whether a business has the ability to generate sufficient cash to periodically pay dividends. Employees are concerned with whether their employer will have sufficient cash to pay earned salaries and wages.

A statement of cash flows also allows decision makers to reconcile a business's net income with the cash receipts and disbursements produced by its principal operating activities. Profitable companies may not constantly generate sufficient cash to finance their day-to-day operations. However, if a company's net income significantly exceeds the cash generated by its principal business operations, decision makers will want to investigate this difference. Consider a company that reports a large increase in net income but a negative cash flow from its operating activities in a given year. Further investigation may reveal that the firm increased its net income by adopting a more liberal credit policy that resulted in increased sales to high-risk customers. If many of these new customers are unable to pay their bills, the company essentially inflated its reported profit over the short term by "giving away" inventory.

Finally, an SCF can help decision makers assess the effect of investing and financing transactions on a business's financial position. A large increase in cash during a recent year from profitable operations is a positive signal of a company's financial health. However, a company that finances its cost of operations—inventory purchases, payroll costs, and so forth—by selling property, plant, and equipment or by engaging in borrowings projects a substantially different image. Companies that intend to remain in business cannot continuously sell off productive assets to raise cash; such financing sources are very short-lived. Additionally, there is a limit to the amount of cash a company can raise by selling stocks or bonds or by taking out long-term loans. To be economically viable over the long term, a company must eventually generate positive net cash flows from its principal operating activities.

Much can be learned about a company's financial status and future prospects by analyzing the three components of its cash flows. For example, Fierro Inc.'s SCF indicates that the company produced a positive net cash flow from operating activities. Additionally, the SCF reveals that a large proportion of the company's investing cash outflows were for the purchase of PP&E, which is a positive indication of future prospects. Finally, dividend payments were included in Fierro's financing cash outflows for 2009, and few stockholders (or potential stockholders) will complain regarding that use of a company's cash resources.

Cash Flow Ratios

Rather than using specific balance sheet or income statement information to make solvency and liquidity ratio computations, some financial statement users prefer to partially assess corporate performance based on cash flows. For example, the operating cash flow ratio (cash flow from operating activities divided by current liabilities) can be calculated. Similar to the current or quick ratio, the operating cash flow ratio indicates a company's ability to meet short-term obligations. The cash interest coverage ratio (cash flow from operating activities plus interest and tax expense divided by interest expense) can be used rather than that times interest earned ratio. A capital expenditure ratio (cash flow from operating activities divided by capital expenditures) measures a company's ability to finance growth.

As with all ratios, "appropriate" values for cash flow ratios depend on the industry in which a company operates. Businesses in the gaming industry, for example, will generate substantially greater operating cash flows than companies in telecommunications or heavy manufacturing.

Cash Flow per Share

One financial measure often tracked by decision makers is cash flow per share. In the United States, businesses are prohibited from reporting cash flow per share in annual reports. The FASB believes that cash flow per share is not a valid alternative to net income as an indicator of a company's performance and to present such information might lead to that implication.[2] However, IFRSs do not specifically prohibit the reporting of cash flow per share. Cash flow per share information is often provided by investment advisory firms.

One problem relative to cash flow per share disclosures is a lack of consistency in how this financial measure is computed. The following equation provides one of the more widely accepted approaches to computing **cash flow per share** for an accounting period.

$$\text{Cash Flow per Share} = \frac{\text{Net Cash Flow from Operating Activities} - \text{Preferred Stock Dividends}}{\text{Weighted Average Number of Common Stock Shares Outstanding}}$$

When a company's earnings per share and cash flow per share are significantly different in a given year, decision makers may be concerned and want additional information. Quite often, a company's operating cash flows begin declining in advance of a decrease in earnings. For example, during the early stages of an economic recession, a company's sales may remain stable. However, the collection period on those sales may lengthen if the recession continues, causing cash flows from operating activities to decline. If economic conditions fail to improve, a company's earnings will likely begin to decline because of falling sales, increases in bad debt expense, and write-offs (or write-downs) of slow-moving inventory.

---

[2]Financial Accounting Standards Board, *SFAS No. 95 Statement of Cash Flows* (Norwalk, CT) (November 1987), 33.

What decision makers really want is information about a business's future, rather than historical, cash flows and earnings. The Securities and Exchange Commission (SEC) encourages public companies to release financial forecasts, but projections of cash flows, revenues, and earnings are rarely included in annual reports. To promote the issuance of forecasted financial data, the SEC established a "safe harbor" rule under which the SEC will help protect a company from lawsuits if a financial forecast prepared in good faith by the firm proves to be a poor predictor of future operating results. However, business executives are still reluctant to include financial forecasts in their companies' annual reports because of the risk of being sued if their projections are not achieved.

Free Cash Flow

One computation often made by bankers, financial analysts, and other financial statement users is **free cash flow** (FCF), which represents the amount of cash that a company can generate after funding items necessary to maintain or expand its asset base. As with other financial tools, there are a variety of definitions for FCF, but in general, it can be approximated follows:

FCF = Cash provided by operating activities − Capital investments for PP&E

Another definition of FCF also allows for the subtraction of dividends and mandatory debt interest and principal repayments. A negative amount of FCF is not necessarily bad; it could simply mean that a company is currently engaged in substantial investment projects that may produce high rates of return for the company in the future.

Although not required, some companies report FCF in press releases, along with definitions of how FCF was computed. For example, BWAY Holding Company (www.bwaycorp.com), a leading container supplier, released information that its FCF was $39.8 million for fiscal 2008 and projected FCF for fiscal 2009 of $44 to $46 million.[3]

Companies with high levels of FCF may not be engaging in a sufficient amount of capital expenditures. Market valuations of companies are also often assessed on the basis of whether those valuations can be supported by free cash flows. One estimate is that most companies should be generating approximately an equal amount of net income and free cash flow; stronger companies tend to produce about 120 percent of NI in free cash flow, and poor companies only create about 80 percent of NI in FCF.[4]

Some regulatory agencies, such as the New Jersey Gaming Commission, use FCF in assessing financial viability analysis.[5] Users may also want to use FCF to calculate some liquidity measurements: FCF to sales and FCF to total interest on debt. One analyst believes that FCF is "the most transparent metric to gauge company performance" and indicates true earnings quality.[6] However, until a consistent definition is adopted,

---

[3]BWAY Press Release, "BWAY Holding Company Announces Strong Quarter Fiscal 2009 Earnings Results and Increases Annual Guidance" (5/4/09); http://investors.bwaycorp.com/phoenix.zhtml?c=84049&p=irol-newsArticle&ID=1284020&highlight=free%20cash%20flow (accessed 6/12/09).

[4]Charles Keenan, "Behind the Numbers," *Black Enterprise* (July 2008), pp. 35 ff.

[5]John Mills, Lynn Bible, and Richard Mason, "Defining Free Cash Flow," *The CPA Journal* (January 2002), pp. 36–41.

[6]Joseph Chang, "Investors Sharpen Focus on Free Cash Flow," *Chemical Market Reporter* (July 22–29, 2002, pp. 1, 18.)

comparisons of corporate-reported FCFs will not necessarily provide consistent and reliable information for analysis.

SUMMARY

Businesses engage in three principal activities that result in cash inflows and outflows: operating, investing, and financing activities. Operating activities involve transactions and events related to the production and delivery of goods and services. Receipts from customers are the primary cash inflows from operating activities for most businesses, whereas payments to suppliers and employees are typically among the largest operating cash outflows. Acquisition and disposal of property, plant, and equipment, as well as long-term investments in debt and equity securities, are important sources of cash flows from investing activities. Finally, cash flows from financing activities include proceeds from the sale of a firm's common and preferred stock, payments of dividends, and principal payments on long-term loans.

Businesses may use either the direct or indirect method of preparing statements of cash flows. The difference between these two methods appears in the operating activities section. Under the direct method, net cash flow from operating activities is the sum of specific cash flows, such as cash received from customers and cash paid to suppliers. Under the indirect method, net cash flow from operating activities is computed by making adjustments to net income for gains and losses, noncash expenses such as depreciation and amortization, and changes in noncash current assets and liabilities. Regardless of the method used to calculate cash from operating activities, the amount is the same. The indirect method is used more often than the direct method.

One common method decision makers apply in analyzing cash-flow data is to compare the three components of a firm's cash flows over several years. Such analysis may reveal trends in those cash flows that yield insights on the company's financial condition and future prospects. Although businesses in the United States are prohibited from reporting cash flow per share, that amount may be calculated by investment analysts. A common formula for this computation is (net cash flow from operating activities minus preferred stock dividends) divided by the weighted average number of shares of common stock outstanding. Cash flow per share can be compared to the company's earnings per share, and any significant divergence from the normal relationship between these two key financial measures should be investigated.

Users may also calculate solvency and liquidity ratios using cash flow rather than net income. One measure of a company's ability to continue is its free cash flow (FCF), which can be computed as cash flow from operating activities minus expenditures for capital investments.

KEY TERMS

cash flow per share	free cash flow	operating activity
direct method (of preparing a statement of cash flows)	indirect method (of preparing a statement of cash flows)	statement of cash flows
financing activity	investing activity	

QUESTIONS

1. What is the principal use of a statement of cash flows from the perspective of financial decision makers? *(LO 10.1)*

2. Why is a statement of cash flows necessary when an income statement is provided to users? *(LO 10.1)*

3. Define and provide two examples of each of the following: (a) operating activities, (b) investing activities, and (c) financing activities. *(LO 10.1)*

4. Why do changes in most current asset and current liability accounts affect the operating activities of a firm? *(LO 10.1)*

5. What is the starting point for determining a business's net cash flow from its operating activities under the indirect method? Why is this figure used? *(LO 10.2)*

6. Under the indirect method of preparing a statement of cash flows, why is depreciation expense added to net income when determining net cash flow from operating activities? *(LO 10.2)*

7. Under the indirect method of preparing a statement of cash flows, why do gains and losses affect net income when determining net cash flow from operating activities? *(LO 10.2)*

8. Why might users prefer the direct method of preparing a statement of cash flows to the indirect method? Which method is more commonly used? Why? *(LO 10.2 and 10.3)*

9. Cost of goods sold is shown as a distinct line item on the income statement. Where is information related to cost of goods sold shown on the statement of cash flows under both the direct and indirect methods? *(LO 10.2 and 10.3)*

10. How are significant noncash investing and financing activities typically reported in a set of financial statements? Other than the example provided in the book, give two examples of significant noncash investing or financing activities. *(LO 10.2 and 10.3)*

11. What can an investor learn from looking at the relationship between operating, financing, and investing cash flows from year to year? *(LO 10.4)*

12. Why would an operating cash flow ratio be more informative than a current or quick ratio for solvency or liquidity information? *(LO 10.5)*

13. How is cash flow per share typically computed? Why would the inclusion of cash flow per share not be desirable in annual reports? *(LO 10.5)*

14. Is cash flow per share or earnings per share typically larger each year for a business? Why? *(LO 10.5)*

15. What items are needed to adjust cash flow from operating activities to free cash flow? Why are investors interested in free cash flow? *(LO 10.5)*

EXERCISES

16. **True or False** *(All LOs)*

    Following are a series of statements regarding topics discussed in this chapter.

    Required:

    Indicate whether each statement is true (T) or false (F).

    (a) Increases in noncash current liabilities are added to net income when computing net cash flow from operating activities under the indirect method.

    (b) Profitable companies do not necessarily generate sufficient cash to finance their day-to-day operations.

    (c) Operating activities are generally those transactions and events related to the production and delivery of goods and services by businesses.

    (d) Decision makers prefer companies to generate most of their cash inflows from investing and financing activities.

    (e) Cash flows from all types of activities are reported differently under the indirect and direct methods of preparing a statement of cash flows.

    (f) The acquisition and disposal of property, plant, and equipment are examples of financing activities.

    (g) Decision makers use free cash flow to evaluate a business's ability to sustain future growth.

    (h) The direct method of preparing a statement of cash flows requires that certain adjustments be made to net income to determine the net cash flow from operating activities.

    (i) Similar to the income statement, the statement of cash flows is prepared for a specific time.

    (j) International Financial Reporting Standards allow businesses to report cash flow per share in their financial statement footnotes.

(k) Free cash flow is normally calculated both in total and on a per share basis.

(l) The amount of dividends paid is computed as the beginning balance of Retained Earnings plus net income minus the ending balance of Retained Earnings.

17. **Classification of Cash Flows** *(LO 10.2 and 10.3)*

Cash flows can be categorized as one of the following:

(1) Cash inflow from operating activities

(2) Cash outflow from operating activities

(3) Cash inflow from investing activities

(4) Cash outflow from investing activities

(5) Cash inflow from financing activities

(6) Cash outflow from financing activities

Required:

Classify each of the following transactions into one of the six categories:

(a) Receipts from customers

(b) Payments to employees

(c) Loans made to other firms

(d) Payments to retire outstanding bonds

(e) Payments to acquire trading securities

(f) Receipts from the sale of property, plant, and equipment

(g) Sales of treasury stock

(h) Payments of interest

(i) Payments made to acquire controlling interests in other firms

(j) Payments to suppliers

(k) Receipts of dividends from a subsidiary

(l) Issuance of preferred stock at more than par value

18. **Completing a Statement of Cash Flows** *(LO 10.2)*

Following is a partially completed statement of cash flows for Purr N Fur Company.

Cash flow from operating activities		
Net income		$ 2,866
Adjustments to reconcile net income to net cash provided by operating activities:		
Depreciation expense		?
Gain on sale of land		(230)
Changes in current assets and liabilities:		
Increase in accounts receivable		(1,726)
Decrease in inventories		700
Decrease in prepaid expenses		1,334

Decrease in short-term notes payable		(800)
Decrease in accrued liabilities		(2,008)
Net cash provided by operating activities		$?
Cash flows from investing activities		
Sale of land	$?	
Purchase of property, plant, & equipment	(15,278)	
Net cash used by investing activities		(2,226)
Cash flows from financing activities		
Sale of common stock	$ 12,658	
Dividend payments	?	
Net cash provided by financing activities		8,144
Net increase in cash		$ 8,230
Cash balance, 12/31/07		?
Cash balance, 12/31/08		$ 22,664

Required:

(a) What method does Purr N Fur Company use to prepare its statement of cash flows? How does the method used differ from the alternative?

(b) Complete Purr N Fur's statement of cash flows.

(c) What was Purr N Fur's largest source of cash during the year in question?

(d) Based on the SCF, how would you assess Purr N Fur's performance during the year?

19. **Analyzing Cash-Flow Effects** *(LO 10.2)*

Myancor Corp. had the following balances in its Equipment and Accumulated Depreciation-Equipment accounts at the beginning and end of 2009.

	Jan. 1	Dec. 31
Equipment	$300,000	$360,000
Accumulated Depreciation-Equipment	75,000	54,000

During 2009, Myancor engaged in the following transactions involving equipment:

March 9 Purchased new equipment for $120,000.

July 16 Sold equipment that originally cost $60,000 and had a current book value of $24,000 for $49,500.

Required:

(a) How much depreciation expense did Myancor Corp. record on its equipment during 2009?

(b) Indicate how Myancor's depreciation expense and its transactions involving equipment would appear in the company's 2009 statement of cash flows, assuming the company uses the indirect method of preparing a statement of cash flows.

20. **Analyzing Cash-Flow Effects** *(LO 10.2 and 10.3)*

Saliba Corp. had beginning and ending balances in Salaries Payable of, respectively, $5,340 and $4,479. Saliba's income statement for 2009 showed Salaries Expense of $119,835.

Required:

(a) Why would Saliba Corp. have a balance in Salaries Payable at the beginning of its fiscal year?

(b) How much was paid to employees for salaries during 2009?

(c) Indicate how the information for salaries would appear in Saliba's 2009 statement of cash flows, assuming the company uses the indirect method of preparing a statement of cash flows.

(d) Indicate how the information for salaries would appear in Saliba's 2009 statement of cash flows, assuming the company uses the direct method of preparing a statement of cash flows.

21. **Analyzing Cash-Flow Effects** *(LO 10.2 and 10.3)*

Heliski Corp. had a $7,320 beginning balance in Dividends Payable and an ending balance in that account of $12,492. During 2009, Heliski's board of directors declared total cash dividends of $0.20 per share on the 649,475 shares of outstanding common stock.

Required:

(a) What was the total dividend declared by Heliski Corp. during 2009?

(b) How much was paid to stockholders for dividends during 2009? Where would this amount appear on the statement of cash flows?

(c) If Heliski Corp. had declared a 10 percent stock dividend in 2009, would that declaration have affected the balance in Dividends Payable? Explain.

22. **Preparation of the Operating Section of Statement of Cash Flows Using the Indirect Method** *(LO 10.2)*

The following information has been obtained from Sardy Corp.'s 2009 income statement and beginning and ending 2009 balance sheets.

Sales	$624,000
Cost of goods sold	235,000
Depreciation expense	43,600
Rent expense	32,000
Wages expense	165,240

Loss on sale of machine	21,000	
Tax expense	50,864	

	1/1/09	12/31/09
Accounts Receivable	$34,100	$31,800
Inventory	2,300	2,450
Prepaid Rent	850	1,400
Accounts Payable	12,040	13,295
Wages Payable	15,390	17,210
Tax Payable	10,100	0

Required:

Prepare the operating activities section of a statement of cash flows using the indirect method.

23. **Preparation of the Operating Section of Statement of Cash Flows Using the Direct Method** *(LO 10.3)*

Use the information from Exercise 22.

Required:

Prepare the operating activities section of a statement of cash flows using the direct method.

24. **Comparative Analysis of Cash Flows** *(LO 10.4)*

The following data were included in a recent annual report of YUM, a wholesaler of grocery products. Amounts are in thousands.

	Year 1	Year 2	Year 3
Net income	$ 3,716	$ 3,818	$ 8,639
Net cash flow from operating activities	7,461	12,556	15,390
Net cash flow from investing activities	(7,792)	(41,527)	(32,851)
Net cash flow from financing activities	15,113	17,479	14,983

Required:

(a) Why is a company's net income typically less than its net cash flow from operating activities?

(b) Why do most companies, including YUM, typically have negative cash flows from investing activities?

(c) Over the three-year period, what type of activities was the largest source of funds for YUM? Do business executives want these activities to be their firm's principal source of funds? Explain.

25. **Net Income and Net Cash Flow from Operating Activities** *(LO 10.4)*

Kaleidoscope Technology manufactures computer products. The company suffered a loss of nearly $450 million in 2009. However, the company's statement of cash flows for that year reported a net cash flow from operating activities of approximately $20 million.

Required:

(a) How could this company incur a large loss in a given year but still have a positive cash flow from operating activities in 2009?

(b) Do you think the loss or the positive cash flow is more important to current and future investors? Explain your answer.

26. **Cash Flow Ratios and Free Cash Flow** (LO 10.5)

The following information is available from various financial statements for Round Rock, Inc.:

Net cash inflow from operating activities	$700,000
Net cash outflow from investing activities	926,000
Cash purchases of property, plant, and equipment	580,000
Interest expense	114,000
Tax expense	256,000
Net income	468,000
Current assets	359,200
Current liabilities	184,200

Required:

(a) Compute the current ratio and the operating cash flow ratio. Discuss any significant differences between the two ratios.

(b) Calculate the times interest earned ratio and the cash interest coverage ratio. Discuss any significant differences between the two ratios.

(c) Calculate free cash flow for Round Rock, Inc. Discuss any significant differences between FCF and net income.

27. **Cash Flow Share** (LO 10.5)

The following data are available for Saffron City, a large discount retailer.

	2007	2008	2009
Net Income	$ 88,935,000	$121,392,500	$184,085,000
Net Cash Flow from Operating Activities	106,782,500	90,490,000	108,142,500
Weighted-Average Number of Common Shares Outstanding	165,765,000	168,202,500	172,522,500
Preferred Stock Dividends Paid	—	—	1,930,000

Required:

(a) Compute Saffron City's earnings per share and cash flow per share for each year.

(b) For each year, express Saffron City's earnings per share as a percentage of its cash flow per share.

(c) What factors possibly accounted for Saffron City's net cash flow from operating activities being less than the firm's net income in 2007 and 2009? Why would a potential investor in this firm want to identify these factors?

PROBLEMS

28. **Classification of Cash Flows** (LO 10.2)

Following are classifications for items that may appear on a statement of cash flows prepared on an indirect basis:

(1) Cash inflow from operating activities
(2) Cash outflow from operating activities
(3) Cash inflow from investing activities
(4) Cash outflow from investing activities
(5) Cash inflow from financing activities
(6) Cash outflow from financing activities
(7) Positive noncash adjustment to net income
(8) Negative noncash adjustment to net income
(9) Does not appear on the statement of cash flows prepared on an indirect basis

Required:

Determine how each of the following items would be shown using the classifications.

(a) Repurchase of common stock
(b) Principal payment on long-term notes payable
(c) Cash paid for taxes
(d) Interest received
(e) Refund of income taxes
(f) Purchase of property and equipment
(g) Cash paid to employees
(h) Increase in accounts payable
(i) Proceeds from issuing long-term note payable
(j) Principal payments under capital lease obligations
(k) Increase in accounts receivable
(l) Proceeds from issuing common stock
(m) Depreciation expense
(n) Payment of dividends on preferred stock
(o) Principal payments on mortgages

(p)   Gain on sale of equipment

(q)   Decrease in prepaid insurance

(r)   Decrease in wages payable

(s)   Cash paid to suppliers for inventory

(t)   Loans to corporate officers

(u)   Issuance of treasury stock for cash

(v)   Cash received from customers

(w)   Declaration of a stock dividend

(x)   Issuance of common stock for land

(y)   Proceeds from the sale of property, plant, and equipment

(z)   Declaration of a 2-for-1 stock split

29.   **Classification of Cash Flows** *(LO 10.2)*

Following are classifications for items that may appear on a statement of cash flows prepared on a direct basis:

(1)   Cash inflow from operating activities

(2)   Cash outflow from operating activities

(3)   Cash inflow from investing activities

(4)   Cash outflow from investing activities

(5)   Cash inflow from financing activities

(6)   Cash outflow from financing activities

(7)   Does not appear on the statement of cash flows prepared on a direct basis

Required:

Determine how each of the items (a) through (z) listed in Problem 28 would be shown using the classifications.

30.   **Statement of Cash Flows** *(LO 10.2)*

Following are the line items included in the 2009 statement of cash flows prepared by The Nine Muses, Inc. (amounts are in thousands):

Proceeds from sale of long-term investments	$ 14,077
Depreciation expense	8,275
Increase in accounts receivable	2,396
Increase in accounts payable	6,590
Purchase of long-term investments	29,939
Net income	22,214
Increase in accrued salaries	4,072
Proceeds from sale of property and equipment	2,468
Increase in inventories	7,320
Issuance of long-term notes	126
Reductions of long-term debt	572
Gain on disposal of long-term assets	415
Issuance of common stock	10,000
Cash and cash equivalents, beginning of the year	21,750

Increase in income taxes payable	5,608
Acquisitions of property and equipment	31,083
Net increase (decrease) in cash and cash equivalents	?
Cash and cash equivalents, end of year	?

Required:

Prepare The Nine Muses' statement of cash flows using the indirect method.

31.   **Statement of Cash Flows** *(LO 10.3)*

Use the information in Problem 30 for The Nine Muses, Inc., and assume the following 2009 account balance information is also available.

Credit sales	$3,756,000
Cost of goods sold	1,810,000
Tax expense	434,000
Salaries expense	695,000

Required:

Determine the following items that would appear on a statement of cash flows prepared on a direct basis.

(a)   Cash collected from customers

(b)   Cash paid to suppliers (assuming that all inventory purchases are made on account payable)

(c)   Cash paid for taxes

(d)   Cash paid for salaries

32.   **Determining Net Cash Flow from Operating Activities, Indirect and Direct Methods** *(LO 10.2 and 10.3)*

Following is an income statement for Wickenia Corporation for the year ended December 31, 2009, and a schedule listing the company's current assets and current liabilities at the end of 2008 and 2009. Amounts are in thousands.

Wickenia Corporation		
Income Statement		
For the Year Ended December 31, 2009		
Sales		$38,800
Cost of Goods Sold		(22,200)
Gross Profit		$16,600
Operating Expenses		
Selling and Administrative Expenses	$4,400	
Depreciation Expense	950	(5,350)
Operating Income		$11,250
Gain on Sale of Land		2,750
Income before Income Tax		$14,000
Income Tax Expense		(5,600)
Net Income		$ 8,400

	12/31/08	12/31/09
Cash	$5,850	$2,050
Accounts Receivable	2,250	4,900
Inventory	3,350	5,650
Prepaid Expenses	1,750	400
Accounts Payable	1,450	2,800
Accrued Liabilities	750	1,400

Required:

(a) Prepare a schedule documenting Wickenia Corporation's net cash flow from operating activities for the year ended December 31, 2009, using the indirect method.

(b) Prepare a schedule documenting Wickenia Corporation's net cash flow from operating activities for the year ended December 31, 2009, using the direct method.

(c) Briefly evaluate the schedule you prepared in part (a). Does this schedule provide any clues regarding the financial health of Wickenia Corporation? Explain.

33. **Interpreting Cash-Flow Data** (LO 10.4)

Over a recent three-year period, Vino Veritas' statements of cash flows revealed cumulative increases in the company's accounts receivable of $145 million.

Required:

(a) How does an increase in accounts receivable affect a company's net cash flow from operating activities?

(b) If a company's accounts receivable balance is continually increasing from one year to the next, does that indicate, necessarily, that the firm is doing a poor job of "managing" or collecting its accounts receivable? Explain.

34. **Using Cash Flow Data** (LO 10.4)

The statement of cash flows for Circuit City (www .circuitcity.com) for the fiscal years ending February 28 or 29, 2006 to 2008 follows. Dollars are in millions, and some of the line items have been aggregated for simplicity.

	2008	2007	2006
Operating Activities:			
Net (loss) earnings	$ (321.4)	$ (8.4)	$ 145.1
Adjustments for noncash items:			
Depreciation expense	183.4	177.8	160.6
Amortization expense	4.2	3.6	2.6
Write-off of goodwill	26.0	92.0	—
Loss (gain) on dispositions of PP&E	2.7	(1.4)	2.4
Provision for deferred income taxes	27.6	72.7	(14.3)
Other noncash changes	27.4	26.6	25.0
Changes in current assets and liabilities:			
Accounts receivable, net	45.8	(133.1)	16.5
Merchandise inventory	84.4	49.4	(231.1)
Prepaid expenses and other current assets	5.9	(9.6)	(17.3)
Other assets	(4.8)	.5	(3.1)
Accounts payable	(19.2)	73.3	211.4
Expenses payable	11.5	55.7	40.9
Accrued expenses & other operating liabilities	(119.1)	(82.8)	26.2
Cash Flow from Operating Activities	$ (45.6)	$ 316.3	$ 364.9
Investing Activities:			
Purchases of property and equipment	(325.4)	(285.7)	(254.5)
Proceeds from sales of property and equipment	71.5	38.6	55.4
Purchases of investment securities	(2,649.7)	(2,002.1)	(1,409.8)
Sales and maturities of investment securities	3,246.3	1,926.1	1,015.0
Other investing activities	(1.5)	(11.6)	—
Cash Flow from Investing Activities	$ 341.2	$ (334.7)	$ (593.9)
Financing Activities:			
Proceeds from short-term borrowings	276.2	35.7	74.0
Principal payments on short-term borrowings	(275.6)	(56.9)	(53.9)
Debt issuance costs	(19.8)	—	—
Proceeds from long-term debt	—	1.2	1.0
Principal payments on long-term debt	(19.1)	(6.7)	(1.8)
Repurchases of common stock	(46.8)	(237.4)	(338.5)
Issuances of common stock	4.9	89.7	38.0
Dividends paid	(26.8)	(20.1)	(12.8)
Other financing activities	(50.9)	33.7	(24.4)
Cash Flow from Financing Activities	$ (157.9)	$ (160.8)	$ (318.4)
Exchange Rate Effect on Cash & Disc. Operations	17.1	4.4	(16.3)
Increase (decrease) in cash and cash equivalents	154.9	(174.8)	(563.7)
Cash and cash equivalents at beginning of year	141.1	316.0	879.7
Cash and cash equivalents at end of year	$ 296.1	$ 141.1	$ 316.0

Required:

(a) How would a supplier interpret this data?

(b) How would a current or potential investor interpret this data?

(c) How would an employee interpret this data?

(d) Use Internet resources to determine what happened to Circuit City in 2008 and thereafter. Discuss the occurrences in relationship to the cash flows statements presented in this problem.

35. Cash Ratios, Cash Flow Share, and Free Cash Flow *(LO 10.5)*

In addition to the Circuit City information provided in Problem 34, the following information is available.

■ Weighted average common shares outstanding were:

Year	Shares
2006	165,134,000
2007	170,448,000
2008	177,456,000

■ Circuit City has no preferred stock.

■ Interest expense for each year was as follows:

Year	Amount
2006	$3,143,000,000
2007	1,519,000,000
2008	1,180,000,000

Required:

(a) Using only the information presented, calculate Circuit City's cash interest coverage.

(b) Calculate Circuit City's capital expenditure ratio.

(c) Calculate Circuit City's cash flow per share.

(d) Calculate Circuit City's basic earnings per share.

(e) Interpret your calculations from year to year. Comment on significant relationships.

(f) Calculate Circuit City's free cash flow.

CASES

36. Annual Report *(all LOs, Internet)*

Use the annual report of Carnival Corporation for the 2007 fiscal year to answer the following questions. This information can be found on either the annual report or the SEC 10-K filing at www.carnival.com by following the links to Investor Relations.

Required:

(a) Does Carnival use the direct or indirect method to prepare a statement of cash flows?

(b) List the major cash inflows from each of the three activities sections for 2007.

(c) List the major cash outflows from each of the three activities sections for 2007.

(d) Compare Carnival's net income and cash flows from operations for 2005, 2006 and 2007. Comment on the relationship each year and the change from year to year.

(e) Calculate cash flows per share for 2005, 2006, and 2007. How does cash flow per share compare to basic earnings per share?

(f) In part (d), you compare cash flows from operations and net income. In part (e), you compare cash flows per share and earnings per share. Is one of these techniques better than another?

(g) Assume the viewpoint of a supplier, an investor, and an employee. Comment on the cash flow data from each perspective.

(h) Does Carnival raise a significant portion of money through financing activities or investing activities? List any significant inflows.

(i) Does the industry in which Carnival operates and/or the economy affect how much cash is provided or used by each business activity?

(j) Calculate all cash flow ratios that are possible using the data available.

(k) What is Carnival's free cash flow? Did Carnival spend a significant amount of money on purchasing PP&E assets? What does that indicate from an investor's perspective?

37. Comparing Cash Flows *(LO 10.4 and 10.5, Internet, group)*

Identifying the similarities and differences in companies is as crucial to making investment decisions as understanding a single company's financial statements. Form groups of at least four students. Each group should select a single industry. Each group member should locate a different annual report within that industry. (The industry and individual company may be assigned by your instructor.) Note: Additional references may be needed for some data, such as stock trading price and the beginning balance of certain accounts for the first year.

Required—individual group members:

(a) Calculate cash flow per share for the most recent two years. Comment on the changes from year to year.

(b) Calculate or locate basic earnings per share for the most recent two years.

(c) Calculate free cash flow for the most recent two years. Comment on the changes from year to year.

(d) Compare net income and cash flows from operations for the most recent two years. Comment on the relationships.

(e) Does the company use the direct or indirect method to prepare their statement of cash flows? If it uses the direct method, locate the reconciliation of net income to operating cash flows.

(f) For each of the following items, indicate how they affected the cash flows of the company you selected, and interpret the effect.

   (1) Change in accounts receivable

   (2) Change in taxes payable

   (3) Change in short-term investments

   (4) Change in accounts payable

   (5) Change in accrued liabilities

Required—groups:

(g) Compare the cash flow per share, earnings per share, cash flow from operations, net income, and free cash flow from company to company in the same fiscal years. Include in your comparison a graphical analysis. Discuss reasons why these figures might be similar or different within an industry.

(h) Based on a comparison of these five items, which company is the best investment in the industry you have chosen?

Required—class:

(i) Compare the cash flow per share, earnings per share, cash flow from operations, net income, and free cash flow from each industry. Discuss reasons why these items might be similar or different between industries.

(j) Does one industry seem to be a better investment than another? Do you think this judgment would necessarily be constant over time?

SUPPLEMENTAL PROBLEMS

38. **Classification of Cash Flows** *(LO 10.1; Compare to Problem 28)*

Following are the sections of a statement of cash flows:

■   Operating activities

■   Financing activities

■   Investing activities

Required:

For each of the following line items included in recent statements of cash flows prepared on the indirect method by a national retailer, indicate in which section of the statement of cash flows it would appear, and indicate whether the item is a cash inflow, cash outflow, or noncash adjustment.

(a) Accounts receivable, increase

(b) Accounts payable, decrease

(c) Accrued expenses, decrease

(d) Capital expenditures

(e) Deferred income taxes (long-term), increase

(f) Depreciation and amortization expense

(g) Dividends paid

(h) Purchase common stock in subsidiary

(i) Income taxes payable, decrease

(j) Issuance of common stock

(k) Issuance of long-term debt

(l) Issuance of short-term debt

(m) Repayment of long-term debt

(n) Merchandise inventories, decrease

(o) Other current assets, increase

(p) Cash proceeds from disposals of property and equipment

(q) Sale of treasury stock

(r) Loss on sale of property and equipment

39. **Statement of Cash Flows on the Indirect Method** *(LO 10.2; Compare to Problem 32)*

Following is an income statement for Caliope, Inc., for the year ended December 31, 2009, and the company's balance sheets as of December 31, 2008 and 2009. The prepaid expenses and accrued liabilities included in Caliope's balance sheets involve selling or general (operating) expenses. All of Caliope's sales and merchandise purchases are made on a credit basis. Following is additional financial information that was obtained from Caliope's accounting records for 2009.

Collections of accounts receivable	$194,300
Purchases of merchandise	70,200
Prepayments of operating expenses	34,600
Payments to suppliers	74,000
Proceeds from sale of land	5,200
Sale of 600 shares of $1 par value common stock for $8 per share	4,800
Declaration and payment of cash dividends on common stock	15,000
Payments of 2009 income taxes	26,000

Caliope, Inc.
Income Statement
For the Year Ended December 31, 2009

Sales		$185,800
Cost of Goods Sold		(73,600)
Gross Profit		$112,200
Operating Expenses		
Selling & Administrative Expenses	$29,200	
Depreciation Expense	11,400	(40,600)
Operating Income		$ 71,600
Loss on Sale of Land		(5,000)
Income before Income Tax		$ 66,600
Income Tax Expense		(26,400)
Net Income		$ 40,200

Caliope, Inc.
Balance Sheets
December 31, 2008 and 2009

	2008		2009	
ASSETS				
Cash		$ 24,200		$ 78,900
Accounts Receivable		21,200		12,700
Inventory		29,400		26,000
Prepaid Expenses		2,600		8,000
Total Current Assets		$ 77,400		$125,600
Equipment	$104,000		$104,000	
Accumulated Depreciation	(32,600)	71,400	(44,000)	60,000
Investment in Land		10,200		0
Total Assets		$159,000		$185,600
LIABILITIES				
Accounts Payable	$ 14,200		$ 10,400	
Accrued Liabilities	6,600		7,000	
Total Current Liabilities		$ 20,800		$117,400
STOCKHOLDERS' EQUITY				
Common Stock	$ 9,000		$ 9,600	
Additional Paid-In Capital	36,400		40,600	
Retained Earnings	92,800		118,000	
Total SE		138,200		168,200
Total Liabilities & SE		$159,000		$185,600

Required:

Prepare a statement of cash flows for Caliope, Inc. for the year ended December 31, 2009, using the indirect method.

40. **Statement of Cash Flows on the Direct Method** *(LO 10.2; Compare to Problem 32)*

Use the information given in Problem 39 to prepare a statement of cash flows for Caliope, Inc. for the year ended December 31, 2009, using the direct method.

MANAGERIAL ACCOUNTING

CHAPTER 11

Fundamental Managerial Accounting Concepts

LEARNING OBJECTIVES

1. Differentiate between financial and managerial accounting.
2. Distinguish between product and period costs; direct and indirect costs; controllable and noncontrollable costs; and variable, fixed, and mixed costs.
3. Discuss the different costing systems and valuation methods used by organizations.
4. Calculate and use a predetermined overhead rate.
5. Classify product costs as direct material, direct labor, and overhead.
6. Record the flow of costs through the accounting system.
7. Prepare a statement of cost of goods manufactured.
8. Identify cost flows in a service company.

INTRODUCTION

All the chapters to this point concentrated on accounting information that is used in the preparation of external financial statements. However, companies also use accounting information internally, and much of this information is never disclosed in the financial statements. This chapter defines and discusses the concepts and terminology related to managerial accounting and distinguishes it from financial accounting. Different methods of accumulating and presenting costs in manufacturing and service organizations are discussed, and the preparation of a statement of cost of goods manufactured (or cost of services rendered) is illustrated.

COMPARISON OF FINANCIAL AND MANAGERIAL ACCOUNTING

Accounting exists for three primary purposes: (1) to provide information to external parties (stockholders, creditors, and various regulatory bodies) for investment and credit decisions; (2) to provide information to internal parties for planning and controlling operations; and (3) to estimate an organization's product or service cost. The financial accounting concepts presented earlier in this text are designed to meet the first purpose. **Managerial accounting** is designed to satisfy the second two purposes. In addition, the estimated product or service cost is used in the preparation of financial statements to satisfy the first purpose. The primary differences between the financial and managerial accounting disciplines are listed in Visual Recap 11.1.

Although the objectives of financial and managerial accounting differ, the information relies on the same underlying details, same recording system, and same set of accounts. Financial accounting information is generally focused on the past and specified in monetary terms. It is verifiable because of the use of generally accepted accounting principles and the need for consistency in external financial statements. Financial accounts reports are usually summarized and relate to the organization as a whole.

Alternatively, managerial accounting is not required, but should provide information for internal management needs. Thus, managerial accounting is more likely to be concerned with specific organizational units and to be less precise than financial accounting because it is generally more important for information used in internal decision making to be timely rather than extremely precise. However, managerial accounting information should still be based on factual data and valid estimates, not "wild guesses" or unsupported projections. One important use of managerial accounting information is to determine an organization's product or service cost. This cost is then used in preparation of the financial statements for inventory and cost of goods sold (or cost of services rendered). Managerial accounting information should only be developed and provided if its benefit is greater than the cost of producing it.

TYPES OF COSTS

Because the term *cost* has many meanings, an adjective is usually attached to indicate what information is being provided. For example, the term *historical cost* is used in financial accounting to indicate the amount for which an asset was purchased and first recorded

Primary Differences between Financial and Managerial Accounting

	Financial	Managerial
Primary users	External	Internal
Organizational focus	Whole	Parts
Time focus	Past	Present and future
Required	Yes, for publicly held companies	No
Frequency of reports	Monthly and annually	When necessary
Precision of information	High; use GAAP to determine requirements	Reasonable; use cost-benefit to determine usefulness

in the accounting records. However, an asset's historical cost is not very important in managerial accounting because that type of cost lacks present relevance. Thus, managerial accounting often focuses on an asset's **replacement cost,** or the amount that would need to be paid currently to buy the asset. A discussion of four distinct pairings of cost terms follows.

Product and Period Costs

Companies often distinguish between product and period costs. A **product cost** relates to items that generate organizational revenues. In a retail company, product costs are the costs of buying inventory to sell to customers; these costs reflect the inventory costs discussed in Chapter 5. Before the inventory is sold, these costs appear in the balance sheet as a current asset called Merchandise Inventory; after sale, they are transferred to the income statement as an expense called Cost of Goods Sold.

In a manufacturing organization, product costs include all the costs needed to make the goods that are sold to wholesalers or retailers. Product costs include amounts paid for direct material, direct labor, and overhead; each of these items is discussed in depth later in this chapter. Product costs of a manufacturing company appear in the balance sheet in the current asset section. Depending on the product's degree of completion, the product costs may be included in Raw Material Inventory (material purchased but not yet used in production), Work in Process Inventory (uncompleted units), or Finished Goods Inventory (products that are ready for sale). When goods are sold, product costs are transferred to the income statement's Cost of Goods Sold expense.

In a service organization, product costs also include direct material (or supplies), direct labor, and overhead. Most service companies do not have a Services in Process Inventory, although one could exist if the company's services required a long time to complete and cost a significant amount of money. For example, a dry cleaner would not have an In Process account because the time to clean clothing is short, and the cleaned clothing is usually collected by owners in a very short time. However, a hospital might have an In Process account because a patient may be in a hospital for several days or more, and the individual items related to the patient's care could become very expensive. Additionally, service companies generally do not have a Finished Services Inventory account. When service is complete, the total service cost is transferred either directly from the Raw Material (or Supplies) Inventory account or the Services in Process Inventory to the income statement as Cost of Services Rendered, an expense account.

Period costs relate to an organization's selling and administrative functions. These costs are closely associated with a specific time period or with the passage of time. Period costs that have future benefits (such as Prepaid Insurance) are classified as assets; period costs having no future benefits (such as Insurance Expense) are expensed.

Direct and Indirect Costs

Costs can also be described as being either direct or indirect. This distinction reflects whether a cost can be related to a particular **cost object**, such as an organizational product, service, department, or territory. A **direct cost** is one that is clearly and easily traceable to, and a monetarily important part of, a specified cost object. An **indirect cost** is one that is neither clearly nor easily traceable, or is not a monetarily important part of, a specified cost object. However, indirect costs may be assigned, if desired, to cost objects using a variety of techniques.

To illustrate the difference between direct and indirect costs, assume a global organization has three sales territories (West U.S., East U.S., and Europe) (see Visual Recap 11.2). The West U.S. sales territory has three salespeople; the East U.S. has four salespeople. One manager oversees both U.S. territories, and another manager oversees Europe. If a sales territory is considered the cost object, the salaries of the salespeople who work solely in one territory would be considered a direct cost of that territory. However, the U.S. manager's salary would be considered an indirect cost to both the West and East U.S. territories. One way the manager's $120,000 salary could be assigned to the two territories would be to use each territory's proportion of total sales dollars. If West U.S. territory sales were $1,500,000 and East territory sales were $2,500,000, then 37.5 percent ($1,500,000 ÷ $4,000,000), or $45,000 of the U.S. manager's salary, could be assigned to the West territory, and 62.5 percent ($2,500,000 ÷ $4,000,000), or $75,000, could be assigned to the East territory. If the U.S. and Europe were considered the cost objects, the total U.S. salespeople's and manager's salaries ($365,000) would be considered direct costs of the U.S.; the €85,000 manager's salary (plus any individual salespeople's salaries) would be a direct cost to Europe. If the company is considered the cost object, all salaries are considered direct.

Controllable and Noncontrollable Costs

Organizations may also differentiate between controllable and noncontrollable costs. Any cost that a manager can authorize or directly influence in terms of dollar size is a **controllable cost**. Costs that are not under the control of a specific manager are called **noncontrollable costs**. These cost categories may overlap with, but are not the same as, direct and indirect costs. For example, if the U.S. manager in the previous example can set salespersons' salaries within the West and East territories, then those salary costs are direct *and* controllable costs of the territory. The U.S. manager's salary is direct to the U.S. territory (although not to the separate territories), but is noncontrollable because the manager cannot set her own salary. However, the U.S. manager's salary is a controllable cost to the manager's supervisor (the Vice President of Sales). It is important to distinguish between controllable and noncontrollable costs because a manager should only be held responsible for costs that he or she can control.

VISUAL RECAP 11.2

Direct versus Indirect Costs

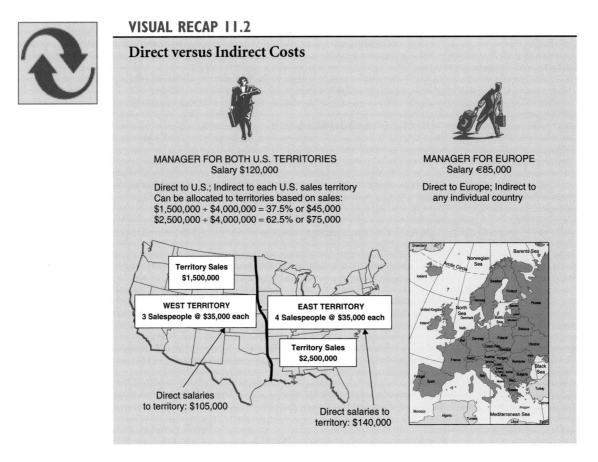

MANAGER FOR BOTH U.S. TERRITORIES
Salary $120,000

Direct to U.S.; Indirect to each U.S. sales territory
Can be allocated to territories based on sales:
$1,500,000 ÷ $4,000,000 = 37.5% or $45,000
$2,500,000 ÷ $4,000,000 = 62.5% or $75,000

MANAGER FOR EUROPE
Salary €85,000

Direct to Europe; Indirect to
any individual country

Territory Sales
$1,500,000

WEST TERRITORY
3 Salespeople @ $35,000 each

EAST TERRITORY
4 Salespeople @ $35,000 each

Territory Sales
$2,500,000

Direct salaries
to territory: $105,000

Direct salaries to
territory: $140,000

Variable and Fixed Costs

Costs can be distinguished by how they behave *in total* as activity changes. Activity can be measured in many ways, including sales, service, or production volume; machine or labor time; number of suppliers used; number of purchase orders sent; number of different products manufactured; or number of services performed.

A **variable cost** changes in total in direct proportion to changes in activity. For example, in a furniture manufacturing company, the more tables that are made, the more wood costs are incurred. In a casino, the more square footage of floor space that there is, the more security cost is necessary. In a steak restaurant, the more meals that are sold, the more pounds of beef are purchased and used. Thus, a variable cost is constant per unit of activity. Once the per-unit variable cost is known, cost estimates can be made for any expected activity.

Alternatively, a **fixed cost** remains constant in total with changes in activity. For example, the cost of annual straight-line depreciation is a fixed cost, as are the costs of monthly rent and monthly pay of salaried employees. However, on a per-unit basis, a fixed cost varies inversely with levels of activity. Thus, the higher the activity, the lower the cost per unit. For example, assume a chef is paid $200 per night, regardless of how many dinners are prepared. On a night when 20 meals are prepared, the chef is paid $10 per each meal ($200 salary ÷ 20 meals); on a night when 50 dinners are prepared, the chef is paid $4 per meal ($200 ÷ 50 meals).

EXHIBIT 11-1

High-Low Method of
Separating Mixed Costs

Electricity Cost for Six Months

kWhs	Cost		
1,478	$308.65		
2,651	438.73		
1,243	285.02 low activity		
1,584	325.34		
3,350	537.86 high activity		
1,859	356.97		
High	3,350		$537.86
Low	1,243		285.02
Changes	2,107		$252.84

$252.84 ÷ 2,107 = $0.12 per kWh

VC(activity) + FC = Total Cost

$0.12(3,350) + FC = $537.86 (can use either high or low activity level)

$402 + FC = $537.86

FC = $135.86

Cost formula for electricity: $0.12 per kWh + $135.86

Given enough time and shift in underlying activity, variable costs will change on a per-unit basis, and fixed costs will change in total. Thus, to estimate variable and fixed costs, a **relevant range** of activity must be specified. This range can be viewed as the organization's normal annual operating range. For example, assume that a theater has 250 seats, has four showings per day, and is open 360 days per year. The relevant range of activity is zero to 360,000 people (250 × 4 × 360). If the theater wants to serve more people, additional fixed costs would have to be incurred to obtain more square footage or additional variable costs would have to be incurred to hire additional workers to support additional showings.

A third category of costs, as defined by behavior, is a **mixed cost**. This type of cost has both a variable and a fixed element. The total cost changes with changes in activity, but not in direct proportion to those activity changes. One common mixed cost is electricity. An organization pays a flat rate simply to have electrical service and then pays an additional fee for usage in kilowatt-hours. For accounting purposes, mixed costs are divided into their variable and fixed components and treated separately for cost analysis.

An easy way to separate a mixed cost is the high-low method. The high and low levels of activity are selected (assuming they are within the relevant range), along with their related costs. The change in cost is attributed to the change in activity and reflects the variable cost portion. The fixed cost is then determined as shown in Exhibit 11-1. The resulting cost formula can be used to predict costs at any level within the relevant range of activity.

A summary of all costs discussed in this section is presented in Visual Recap 11.3.

COMPONENTS OF PRODUCT COST FOR MANUFACTURING COMPANIES

As discussed in the previous section, product costs are related to the items that are sold to generate an organization's primary revenues. In a manufacturing company, there are three components of product cost: material, labor, and overhead. Some material and labor costs are considered direct or specifically related to a cost object; other, material and labor costs

VISUAL RECAP 11.3

Summary of Costs

Product Cost	Period Cost
A cost associated with making a product or providing a service (such as material, labor, or overhead)	A cost associated with the sales or administrative functions of a business (such as sales commissions, headquarters insurance, or legal fees)

Direct Cost	Indirect Cost
A cost that is easily traceable and monetarily significant to a cost object (such as lumber for a table or sales salary for a sales territory)	A cost that is not easily traceable or is not monetarily significant to a cost object (such as the vice president's salary to units of production or cost of electricity to number of pizzas sold)

Controllable Cost	Noncontrollable Cost
A cost that a manager has the authority to change (such as the salary of a subordinate)	A cost that a manger cannot change (such as his/her own salary or a government mandated cost)

Variable Cost	Fixed Cost	Mixed Cost
A cost that varies in total in direct proportion to changes in activity but that is a constant amount for each unit change in activity (such as the cost of hamburger patties at a fast-food restaurant)	A cost that does not vary in total with changes in activity but that varies inversely on a per-unit basis with changes in activity (such as the monthly building rent for a restaurant)	A cost that has both a variable and fixed portion (such as a car rental agreement that has a fixed daily rate plus a specific amount for each mile driven)

are considered indirect and are included in overhead. When discussing product cost, the cost object is defined as the inventory being manufactured. Direct labor and overhead are necessary to convert raw material (or purchased parts) into a finished product and, as such, are together referred to as **conversion cost**.

Direct Material Cost

A **direct material** is any clearly identifiable and conveniently traceable item that becomes a part of a manufactured product. Also, for a material to be considered direct, its cost must be monetarily significant to total product cost. Direct material costs are variable with production volume. The cost of any product part that is not identifiable, traceable, or monetarily significant is classified and accounted for as an **indirect material** and is included in overhead.

Direct Labor Cost

The people who manufacture company products are called **direct labor**. In a factory setting, direct labor includes seamstresses, bakers, and machine operators. Direct labor cost includes the ordinary wages (usually hourly) earned by direct labor employees, as well as the taxes (such as Social Security and Medicare) that the employer pays on behalf of the employee. Direct labor costs are generally variable with production volume.

Employees who do not work directly on production but are part of the production "team" (such as custodial staff and supervisors) are considered **indirect labor**. The wages of these people are included in overhead. Costs of indirect labor outside the production area (such as company administrators) are period, rather than product, costs.

Overhead Cost

Overhead is any product cost incurred in the manufacturing area that cannot be, or is not, directly traced to the product. Overhead consists of indirect material, indirect labor, and other indirect costs. For example, the cost of electricity to run production machinery cannot be directly attributed to an individual product and, therefore, is considered overhead.

Some labor costs that would appear to be direct are treated as indirect. Two specific examples are overtime bonuses and premiums paid to late-shift workers. Generally, to treat these costs as direct to production would provide inappropriate information on product costs. Assume that day-shift workers are paid $10 per hour, late-shift workers are paid a shift premium of $2 per hour, and three hours are needed to make one unit of product. If a product were manufactured during only day-shift hours, it would have a direct labor cost of $30. If it were manufactured during the late shift, and shift premiums were included in direct labor, that same product would have a direct labor cost of $36. The same type of result would occur if the product were manufactured in "regular" time rather than overtime. Because production scheduling is random, a product's direct cost should not depend on when it was manufactured; thus, overtime and shift premiums are generally considered part of overhead.

Overhead can be thought of as a "holding bin" for indirect costs. These costs are waiting to be associated with a particular product. The method of attaching overhead to products is discussed later in this chapter.

Overhead costs may be variable or fixed. Variable overhead includes the costs of indirect material, hourly wages of indirect labor, unit-of-production depreciation, and the variable portion of any type of mixed factory charges (such as maintenance and utilities). Fixed overhead includes the monthly salaries indirect labor, straight-line depreciation, factory insurance and property taxes, and the fixed portion of mixed factory costs.

INVENTORY COSTING SYSTEMS

A manufacturing company must have a system to accumulate direct material, direct labor, and overhead costs and attach those costs to its products. Inventory costing systems (such as perpetual or periodic) for retail companies were discussed in Chapter 5. The two most common inventory costing systems in a manufacturing company are job order costing and process costing. The organization's choice of costing system depends on the type of product that is being manufactured.

Job Order Costing

Job order costing systems are used by manufacturers that produce goods in relatively small quantities, often to customer specifications. Costs are accumulated by **job**, which is a cost object related to a specific order or customer. At any time, the total cost of any job can be found in detailed information that supports the Work in Process Inventory account. An easy example of a job order costing system is airplane production. When Boeing (www.boeing.com) manufacturers airplanes, exact costs of the planes must be accumulated for each airline's order. Delta Air Lines (www.delta.com) and American Airlines (www.aa.com) will want different interior and exterior colors on the planes, as well as different cabin layouts, colors, and fabrics. Boeing will need to keep the costs for Delta's planes separate and distinct from the costs of American's planes. The flow of costs in a job order costing system is illustrated in depth later in the chapter.

Processing Costing and Equivalent Units of Production

Manufacturers that produce mass quantities of similar goods (such as breakfast cereals, gasoline, or dog food) use a **process costing system** to accumulate costs. Because the goods are all the same and may flow through many production departments, costs are accumulated by batches of goods rather than by "job." At any time, total accumulated costs relate to a large number of units, some of which may have been completed and some of which are still in production. To assign costs to each of these categories of goods requires the use of **equivalent units of production** (EUP). EUP is an estimate of the number of fully completed units that could have been made during a period if all production efforts had resulted in completed units.

To illustrate, assume that Country Home, Inc. (CHI) makes wooden picnic tables. The company began operations in January 2008. During January, CHI placed enough wood into production to make 3,000 tables, and workers began manufacturing tables. January's costs for wood and labor were $60,000 and $38,250, respectively. At the end of January, the company had completed 2,400 tables and had 600 tables that were one-fourth complete. Because 100 percent of the wood necessary for the tables was placed into production, the cost per table for wood is $60,000 ÷ 3,000 tables, or $20. All labor activity, however, did not result in completed tables. The EUP for labor would be stated as [2,400 completed tables + (600 tables × 0.25 complete)], or 2,550 EUPs; the labor cost per table is $38,250 ÷ 2,550, or $15. Additional processing activity and costs in February will complete the 600 tables in January's ending inventory.

VALUING INVENTORY

After determining the appropriate costing system to use, a manufacturing or service company needs to decide on a valuation method. The costing system (job order or process) identifies which costs to attach to the cost object and how to attach them. A valuation method determines the dollar amount of the costs to attach. Such a method is similar to the cost flow choice of FIFO or LIFO for merchandise inventory.

Inventory Valuation Methods

The three valuation methods are actual cost, normal cost, and standard cost. In an **actual cost system**, the actual costs of direct material, direct labor, and overhead are used to compute product cost. Although tracing actual direct material and direct labor costs to products can be fairly easy, tracing overhead costs to products is generally quite tedious; additionally, the information needed is often time delayed. For example, if a product is manufactured on January 3, the cost of electricity used to manufacture that product is uncertain. Although the January electric bill can be divided among all units produced, the electric bill may not arrive until January 31 or later—possibly long after the product has been sold.

In a **normal cost system**, the actual costs of direct material and direct labor, as well as an estimated cost for overhead, are used to compute product cost. Normal cost systems overcome the problems of attempting to attach actual overhead cost to products. In a **standard cost system**, estimated "norms" for materials, labor, and overhead are used to compute product costs.[1]

Predetermined Overhead Rate

The estimated overhead cost used in normal and standard cost systems to assign overhead to products or services is called a **predetermined overhead rate**. This rate is an expected cost per unit of activity. To calculate a predetermined overhead rate, the company divides estimated future overhead costs at a specified activity level by that activity level. Predetermined overhead rates are always computed in advance of the period of use and are often computed separately for variable and fixed costs.

Estimating future overhead costs requires that a measure of activity be selected. If the majority of overhead costs are created by factory machine time, machine hours (MHs) could be viewed as the "driver" or responsible cause for overhead costs. A **flexible budget** can be prepared that reflects the expected overhead costs for the upcoming period based on various activity levels.

Near the end of 2008, CHI (the picnic table manufacturer) decides to estimate predetermined production overhead rates for 2009. Using MHs as the activity measure and assumed information on various costs, a flexible budget for overhead costs is developed (Exhibit 11-2). The budget depicts all components of overhead in the left-most column and the associated costs in the next column. The other three columns show estimated overhead at three activity levels: 20,000 MHs, 30,000 MHs, and 40,000 MHs. Note that the variable cost remains constant per MH, regardless of the activity level, but the fixed cost per MH declines as the activity level increases.

If CHI expects to work 40,000 MHs in 2009, its predetermined variable and fixed overhead rates will be, respectively, $6.35 per MH and $9.85 per MH. For each hour of machine time worked in 2009, CHI will apply (add) $6.35 for variable overhead costs and $9.85 for fixed overhead costs to the actual (or standard) costs of direct material and direct labor in a normal (or standard) cost system. Assume that, by year-end 2009, 43,000 total MHs were incurred. The total overhead applied to products, based on the predetermined rates, will be $696,600: variable overhead of $273,050 ($6.35 × 43,000) and fixed overhead of $423,550 ($9.85 × 43,000). Applied overhead is added to direct material and direct labor costs in Work in Process Inventory.

Total predetermined variable and fixed overhead costs for the year are compared, respectively, to actual variable and fixed overhead costs at year-end. If the overhead added to production costs using the predetermined rates is less than the actual overhead costs incurred for a period, the difference is called **underapplied overhead**. If using the predetermined rate leads to the addition of more costs than were actually incurred, the difference is called **overapplied overhead**.

---

[1] Standard cost systems are discussed in Chapter 13.

	Variable cost per MH	Number of Machine Hours (MHs)		
		20,000	30,000	40,000
Variable costs:				
Indirect material	$1.20	$ 24,000	$ 36,000	$ 48,000
Indirect labor	5.00	100,000	150,000	200,000
Variable portion of electricity	.15	3,000	4,500	6,000
Total variable cost		$127,000	$190,500	$254,000
Variable cost per MH	$6.35	$6.35	$6.35	$6.35
	Total fixed cost per year			
Fixed costs:				
Rent	$ 60,000	$ 60,000	$ 60,000	$ 60,000
Depreciation	12,000	12,000	12,000	12,000
Manager salaries	270,000	270,000	270,000	270,000
Insurance	24,000	24,000	24,000	24,000
Taxes	26,200	26,200	26,200	26,200
Fixed portion of electricity	1,800	1,800	1,800	1,800
Total fixed cost	$394,000	$394,000	$394,000	$394,000
Fixed cost per MH		$19.70	$13.13	$9.85

EXHIBIT 11-2

CHI's Flexible Budget for Production Overhead Costs

FLOW OF PRODUCT COSTS

The production process of a job order costing manufacturer is used to illustrate the flow of product costs through the accounting system. The company uses a perpetual inventory system (as discussed in Chapter 5) with normal costs (actual direct material costs, actual direct labor costs, and a predetermined overhead rate to apply overhead costs).

In a manufacturing company, the cost of a completed unit of product (a finished good) must contain the costs of direct material, direct labor, and overhead. A manufacturer must track these costs through the production process using three inventory accounts: Raw Material (RM) Inventory, Work in Process (WIP) Inventory, and Finished Goods (FG) Inventory. The RM Inventory account may be used for both direct and indirect materials. When direct materials are issued to production, their cost is transferred from RM Inventory to WIP Inventory; indirect material costs are transferred to an overhead account.

The CHI example is continued to illustrate the flow of manufacturing costs. The January 1, 2009, inventory account balances for were as follows: Raw Material Inventory, $15,000; Work in Process Inventory, $36,200; and Finished Goods Inventory, $55,700.

CHI uses separate variable and fixed overhead accounts. Each overhead account shows actual overhead costs on the debit side and **applied overhead** (the amount added to WIP Inventory using the predetermined rates) on the credit side. Overhead accounts are closed at the end of an accounting period. The predetermined variable and fixed overhead rates, respectively, were shown in Exhibit 11-2 as $6.35 and $9.85 per machine hour at a 40,000 expected level of activity. The following transactions represent CHI's activity for the year

2009. Effects on the three inventory accounts, variable overhead, fixed overhead, and Cost of Goods Sold, are shown in parentheses.

1. During 2009, CHI bought $328,050 of raw material on account (an increase to RM Inventory).

2. Direct material costing $273,400 and indirect material costing $55,980 were transferred to the production area (a decrease to RM Inventory and increases to WIP Inventory and Variable Overhead).

3. Direct and indirect labor wages for the year totaled $643,740 and $486,480, respectively. Of the indirect wages, $211,630 was a variable cost, and the remainder was for fixed costs such as supervisory and management salaries (increases to WIP Inventory, Variable Overhead, and Fixed Overhead).

4. Electricity cost of $10,885 was paid; of this cost, $7,905 of this amount was variable and $2,980 was fixed (increases to Variable Overhead and Fixed Overhead).

5. CHI also paid $63,200 for factory rent and $29,150 for property taxes on the factory, depreciated the factory assets $16,820, and recorded the expiration of $29,085 of prepaid insurance on the factory assets (increases to Fixed Overhead).

6. During 2009, 43,000 machine hours were used; this activity level is used to assign overhead cost (based on the predetermined rates) to WIP Inventory (decreases to Variable Overhead and Fixed Overhead and an increase to WIP Inventory).

7. During 2009, $1,187,120 of goods were completed and transferred to FG Inventory (a decrease to WIP Inventory and an increase to FG Inventory).

8. Sales on account in the amount of $1,883,250 were recorded during the year; the goods that were sold had a total cost of $1,166,220 (a decrease to FG Inventory and an increase to Cost of Goods Sold).

These transactions are summarized in Exhibit 11-3. Selected T-accounts are shown in Exhibit 11-4. The flow of costs is summarized in Visual Recap 11.4.

COST OF GOODS MANUFACTURED AND SOLD

The perpetual inventory system used in Exhibits 11-3 and 11-4 provides detailed information about production costs incurred, costs transferred from work in process, and cost of goods sold (CGS). However, this detail is not readily available in a company using a periodic inventory system. A schedule of **cost of goods manufactured** (CGM) can be prepared to help determine cost of goods sold in a periodic inventory system or to confirm the CGS calculated in a perpetual inventory system. The CGM represents the total production cost of the goods that were completed and transferred to FG Inventory during the period.

The schedule of CGM starts with the beginning balance of WIP Inventory and adds all product costs (direct material, direct labor, and applied overhead) incurred for the period. The summation is called "total costs to account for" and represents all costs that were in WIP Inventory during the period. Some of these costs will remain in WIP Inventory because the goods to which those costs relate are not yet complete. The remaining costs will be transferred, as CGM, to FG Inventory along with the completed goods.[2]

---

[2] This statement assumes that no goods are lost, stolen, or spoiled during the period.

EXHIBIT 11-3

CHI 2009 Production
Journal Entries

	General Journal		
	Description	**Debit**	**Credit**
(1)	Raw Material Inventory	328,050	
	Accounts Payable		328,050
	Purchased raw materials on account		
(2)	Work in Process Inventory	273,400	
	Variable Overhead	55,980	
	Raw Material Inventory		329,380
	Transferred direct and indirect material to production		
(3)	Work in Process Inventory	643,740	
	Variable Overhead	211,630	
	Fixed Overhead	274,850	
	Salaries and Wages Payable		1,130,220
	Accrued salaries and wages for direct and indirect labor		
(4)	Variable Overhead	7,905	
	Fixed Overhead	2,980	
	Cash		10,885
	Paid electricity cost		
(5)	Fixed Overhead	138,255	
	Cash		92,350
	Accumulated Depreciation		16,820
	Prepaid Insurance		29,085
	Paid factory rent and factory property taxes; accrued depreciation; and recorded expiration of prepaid insurance on factory		
(6)	Work in Process Inventory	696,600	
	Variable Overhead		273,050
	Fixed Overhead		423,550
	Applied overhead to WIP ($6.35 × 43,000 MHs and $9.85 × 43,000 MHs)		
(7)	Finished Goods Inventory	1,187,120	
	Work in Process Inventory		1,187,120
	Transferred goods completed during the period		
(8a)	Accounts Receivable	1,883,250	
	Sales		1,883,250
	Recorded sales on account for period		
(8b)	Cost of Goods Sold	1,166,220	
	Finished Goods Inventory		1,166,220
	Recorded cost of goods sold for period		

The CGM is added to the beginning balance of FG Inventory to find the cost of goods available (CGA) for sale during the period. Ending FG Inventory is calculated by multiplying a physical unit count times a unit cost. Subtracting the cost of the ending FG Inventory from the CGA for sale provides a figure for cost of goods sold. Formal schedules of cost of goods manufactured and cost of goods sold are presented in Exhibit 11-5, using the information from Exhibits 11-3 and 11-4.

Note that CGM was calculated using normal costing: actual direct material cost, actual direct labor cost, and overhead applied using predetermined rates. As shown in Exhibit 11-4, the Variable and Fixed Overhead T-accounts have balances at the end of 2009. Debits

EXHIBIT 11-4

Selected CHI
T-accounts for 2009

Raw Material Inventory			
Beg. bal.	15,000	(2)	329,380
(1)	328,050		
End. bal.	13,670		

Variable Overhead			
(2) IM	55,980	(6)	273,050
(3) IL	211,630		
(4) Elec.	7,905		
Underapp.	2,465		

Work in Process Inventory			
Beg. bal.	36,200	(7)	1,187,120
(2) DM	273,400		
(3) DL	643,740		
(6) OH	696,600		
End. bal.	462,820		

Fixed Overhead			
(3) IL	274,850	(6)	423,550
(4) Elec.	2,980		
(5) Other	138,255		
		Overapp.	7,465

Finished Goods Inventory			
Beg. bal.	55,700	(8b)	1,166,220
(7)	1,187,120		
End. bal.	76,600		

Cost of Goods Sold			
(8b)	1,166,220		

VISUAL RECAP 11.4

Flow of Product Costs

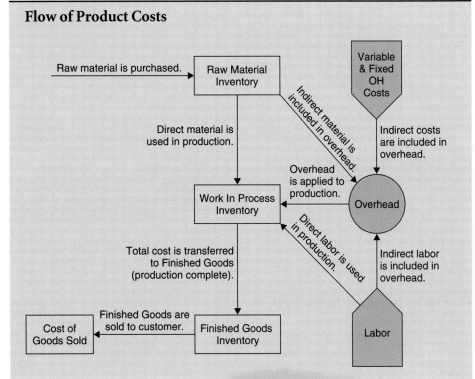

EXHIBIT 11-5

Schedules of Cost of
Goods Manufactured
and Cost of Goods Sold

Country Home, Inc.
Schedule of Cost of Goods Manufactured
For Year Ended December 31, 2009

Beginning balance of Work in Process Inventory, 1/1/09		$ 36,200
Manufacturing costs for the period:		
Raw Material Inventory (direct and indirect)		
Beginning balance, 1/1/09	$ 15,000	
Purchases of raw material	328,050	
Raw material available for use	$343,050	
Ending balance, 12/31/09	(13,670)	
Total raw material used	$329,380	
Indirect material used	(55,980)	
Direct material used	$273,400	
Direct labor	643,740	
Variable overhead applied	273,050	
Fixed overhead applied	423,550	
Total manufacturing costs		1,613,740
Total costs to account for		$1,649,940
Ending balance of Work in Process Inventory, 12/31/09		(462,820)
Cost of goods manufactured		$1,187,120

Schedule of Cost of Goods Sold
For Year Ended December 31, 2009

Beginning balance of Finished Goods Inventory, 1/1/09	$55,700
Cost of goods manufactured	1,187,120
Cost of goods available for sale	$1,242,820
Beginning balance of Finished Goods Inventory, 12/31/09	(76,600)
Cost of good sold	$1,166,220

in these overhead accounts represent actual overhead costs incurred during the period; credits represent overhead applied using the predetermined rates. The underapplied and overapplied overhead calculations for CHI are shown in Exhibit 11-6.

When the difference between actual and applied overhead is not a significant amount, underapplied or overapplied overhead is closed at the end of the period to Cost of Goods Sold. Remember that closing an account means bringing that account balance to $0. Underapplied overhead, because fewer dollars of cost were sent to WIP Inventory than actually were incurred, has a debit balance and will cause CGS to increase. Overapplied overhead, because more dollars of cost were sent to WIP Inventory than actually were incurred, has a credit balance, which will cause CGS to decrease. For CHI, the net adjustment to CGS would be a decrease of $5,000 ($2,465 − $7,465).

COSTS IN SERVICE COMPANIES

Although service companies do not manufacture a product, there is still a cost associated with the service they provide. For example, when lawyers work on a case or represent a person in court, a portion of their salary is associated with the service provided to that client. Instead of product cost, service companies track service costs.

Actual variable overhead		
Indirect material	$ 55,980	
Indirect labor	211,630	
Electricity	7,905	$ 275,515
Applied variable overhead ($6.35 VOH rate × 43,000 actual MHs)		(273,050)
Underapplied variable overhead		$ 2,465
Actual fixed overhead		
Indirect labor	$274,850	
Electricity	2,980	
Factory rent	63,200	
Factory property taxes	29,150	
Factory asset depreciation	16,820	
Factory insurance	29,085	$ 416,085
Applied variable overhead ($9.85 FOH rate × 43,000 actual MHs)		(423,550)
Overapplied variable overhead		$ (7,465)

Closing entry to CGS, assuming these amounts are immaterial:

Fixed Overhead	7,465	
Variable Overhead		2,465
Cost of Goods Sold		5,000

Variable Overhead

(2) IM	55,980	(6)	273,050
(3) IL	211,630		
(4) Elec.	7,905		
Underapp.	2,465	Closing	2,465
Ending bal.	0		

Fixed Overhead

IL	274,850	(6)	423,550
(4) Elec.	2,980		
(5) Other	138,255		
Closing	7,465	Overapp.	7,465
Ending bal.	0		

Cost of Goods Sold

(8b)	1,166,220	Closing	5,000
Ending bal.	1,161,220		

Like manufacturers, service companies use direct labor and overhead to perform a service. However, in many service companies (such as firms of professionals such as accountants or lawyers), the amount of raw or direct material used may be almost negligible and, often, may not be easily traced to a designated cost object (the service performed). Thus, most service companies will not have a Raw Material Inventory account. These companies commonly use a Supplies Inventory because the majority of materials used in performing services are indirect, rather than direct, to a job.

Service companies generally use a job order costing system to keep track of work in process (incomplete jobs). For example, job order costing is essential for patient accounts at a hospital. When a patient checks into a hospital, a separate account is created for that person. At any time during the hospital stay, the total cost associated with that patient can be obtained by adding up the accumulated costs in that patient's account. Upon discharge from the hospital, the patient will receive a bill for all costs related to the hospital stay.

Service companies are normally very labor intensive. Individuals who work specifically on performing services are called direct labor, and their pay is a direct labor cost. For instance, in a restaurant, the cooks, waitstaff, and bartenders would be classified as direct labor; shift managers, hosts/hostesses, and bus staff would be classified as indirect labor.

Overhead costs are often quite high in service organizations. Any service-related cost that is not or cannot be directly traced to performing a service for sale to others is considered overhead. These costs may be variable or fixed, depending on how they react in total to changes in some designated measure of activity.

Because most services cannot be warehoused, the costs of finished jobs are usually transferred directly from WIP Inventory to a Cost of Services Rendered (CSR) account on the income statement to be matched against job revenues. The CSR account is similar to a CGS account. There is no need for a FG Inventory account.

SUMMARY

Accounting has two primary variations: financial and managerial. Managerial accounting is designed to provide information to organizational personnel for use in planning and controlling operations and making decisions. Both financial and managerial accounting use the same accounting system and set of accounts, but may process information differently. Managerial accounting information tends to be more flexible and future oriented, as well as less aggregated, than financial accounting.

The term *cost* is generally preceded by an adjective that helps define that term. Product cost, period cost, direct cost, indirect cost, controllable cost, and noncontrollable cost are just some types of costs. Costs that are defined by their reaction in total to changes in activity are called variable, fixed, and mixed costs. Within the relevant range of activity for an organization, total variable costs change in direct proportion to activity changes, whereas total fixed costs remain constant. A mixed cost has both a variable and a fixed component.

A manufacturer will typically use either a job order or a process costing system to accumulate product costs (direct material, direct labor, and production overhead). Service companies typically use a job order system. In a job order system, costs are totaled by cost component per job and assigned to units produced (or services performed) at the end of the job. In a process costing system, products are indistinguishable from one another, and costs are accumulated and assigned to goods on leaving each department. At the end of the period in a manufacturing company, a cost of goods manufactured schedule will be prepared to support the company's cost of goods sold computation.

Companies may assign values to production units (or services) using an actual, normal, or standard costing system. Only actual costs are used in an actual costing system. In a normal costing system, actual costs are accumulated for direct material and direct labor, but a predetermined overhead rate is used to assign overhead to products (or services). A standard costing system uses expected norms (or predetermined amounts) for all types of costs.

KEY TERMS

actual cost system
applied overhead
controllable cost
conversion cost
cost object
cost of goods manufactured
direct cost
direct labor
direct material
equivalent units of production
fixed cost

flexible budget
indirect cost
indirect labor
indirect material
job
job order costing system
managerial accounting
mixed cost
noncontrollable cost
normal cost system
overapplied overhead

overhead
period cost
predetermined overhead rate
process costing system
product cost
relevant range
replacement cost
standard cost system
underapplied overhead
variable cost

QUESTIONS

1. Define each item in the following sets and discuss the primary differences between the items in each set. *(LO 11.1, 11.2, and 11.3)*

   (a) Financial and managerial accounting

   (b) Product and period costs

   (c) Direct and indirect costs

   (d) Variable, fixed, and mixed costs

   (e) Job order and process costing

   (f) Actual, normal, and standard costing

2. Describe the rationale behind using job order costing and process costing. Provide examples of three types of companies that would use each. *(LO 11.3)*

3. Why does a company need to use equivalent units of production in a process costing system? Explain the calculation for equivalent units of production. *(LO 11.3)*

4. What is a predetermined overhead rate? How is it calculated? Why is it used? *(LO 11.4)*

5. What is meant by (a) underapplied and (b) overapplied overhead? Why does underapplied or overapplied overhead exist at year-end? How are underapplied and overapplied overhead treated in the financial statements at year-end? *(LO 11.4)*

6. Could a managerial accountant have a motivation to misrepresent data such as direct or indirect material, labor,

or other overhead costs? Explain your answer with an example. Compare the motivation to misrepresent data between managerial and financial accounting. *(LO 11.5, ethics)*

7. Why might the buttons used to make a shirt not be classified as a direct material? Give an instance in which buttons would be classified as a direct material. *(LO 11.5)*

8. For each of the following companies, select one product manufactured or service provided and identify a direct material cost, a type of direct labor, a variable overhead cost, and a fixed overhead cost. *(LO 11.5)*

   (a) Toyota

   (b) Dell Computers

   (c) KPMG

   (d) Applebee's Restaurants

   (e) Kellogg Company

   (f) H&R Block

9. What is meant by the term *cost of goods manufactured* (CGM)? How is CGM calculated? *(LO 11.7)*

10. In a service company, what is the equivalent to Cost of Goods Sold on the income statement? How does the calculation of this equivalent differ from CGS? *(LO 11.8)*

EXERCISES

11. **True or False** *(All LOs)*

    Following are a series of statements regarding topics discussed in this chapter.

    Required:

    Indicate whether each statement is true (T) or false (F).

(a)   A mixed cost is part controllable and part noncontrollable.

(b)   All period costs in an organization are expensed as incurred.

(c)   Raw materials can be direct or indirect to a product being manufactured.

(d)   A cost can be direct to one cost object and indirect to another.

(e)   Job order costing is typically used in companies that manufacture products to a customer's specifications.

(f)   Managerial accounting is more future oriented than financial accounting.

(g)   All controllable costs are variable costs, but not all variable costs are controllable costs.

(h)   In normal costing, overhead is applied to Work in Process Inventory at a predetermined rate, but actual direct costs are accumulated in Work in Process Inventory.

(i)   When overhead is overapplied at year-end, the "driver" (or basis for application) chosen was inappropriate.

(j)   As the number of units manufactured increases, a fixed cost per unit decreases.

(k)   Variable and fixed costs are defined by a relevant range and may change when the business operates outside that range.

(l)   Service organizations typically have a higher portion of direct material than manufacturing companies.

(m)   A flexible budget allows the computation of predetermined overhead rates for fixed, variable, and mixed costs.

12.   Roles of Accountants (LO 11.1)

Following are several duties performed by accountants.

(a)   Valuation of investments

(b)   Cost of goods manufactured calculation

(c)   Production of intermittent reports for management

(d)   Budgeting future production costs

(e)   Income statement preparation

(f)   Reporting historical data

(g)   Valuation of work in process inventory

(h)   Preparation of a statement of cash flows

(i)   Determination of equivalent units of production

(j)   Calculation of a depreciation schedule for a plant asset

(k)   Preparation of a cost of goods sold schedule

(l)   Preparation of a flexible budget for the calculation of a predetermined overhead rate

Required:

For each duty, indicate whether it would be performed by a financial or managerial accountant. If uncertain, provide an explanation of why that function could be performed by either a financial or managerial accountant.

13.   Types of Costs (LO 11.2)

YouWin! manufactures and sells custom wooden trophies. Each of the company's two divisions, Production and Sales, has a manager, who is responsible for all costs in his/her division. Following are selected costs from YouWin!.

- Wood
- Brass ornamentation
- Engraving materials
- Adhesive for trophy production
- Salary of sales staff
- Wages of machine operators
- Wages of factory custodial staff
- Production manager's salary
- Rent and insurance on factory building
- Rent on headquarters building
- Engraving machine
- Electricity in factory building
- Depreciation of office equipment
- Maintenance on engraving machines

Required:

For each cost listed, fill in the following chart. If a definite distinction cannot be made for any category, indicate why and what additional information would be needed before classification can be made.

Item	Product or Period	Direct or Indirect	Variable, Fixed or Mixed	Controllable or Noncontrollable (from view of Production Manager)

14.   Variable, Fixed, and Mixed Costs (LO 11.2)

Letitia Corp. manufactures kitchen timers. The company incurred the following costs to produce 25,000 timers in May 2009.

Timer mechanisms	$11,250
Resin bases	8,750
Direct labor	9,000
Machinery depreciation (calculated on a straight-line basis)	3,750
Supervisory salaries	6,000
Utilities	2,000
Total	$40,750

Required:

(a) Considering behavior in relationship to activity changes, how would each of these costs be classified?

(b) What did each timer cost?

(c) If Letitia Corp. increases production in June 2009 to 30,000 units, what will be the total cost of each cost component? If you cannot determine the total cost of a cost component, discuss the reason.

15. **Variable, Fixed, and Mixed Cost** *(LO 11.2)*

The following information is available about the cost of leased copier equipment.

Month	# of Copies	Rental Fee Paid to Lessor
May	12,500	$612.50
June	18,320	752.70
July	17,195	715.20
August	20,050	801.25
September	19,350	791.50
October	13,620	618.40

The company pays the lessor a fixed amount per month plus a usage fee based on number of pages. The total fee may be adjusted for bad copies or improper usage.

Required:

(a) Determine the cost formula for this mixed cost.

(b) What is the estimated total rental fee if 15,970 copies are expected to be produced in December?

16. **Inventory Costing** *(LO 11.3)*

Following are several businesses that produce a product or provide a service.

- Manufacturer of Rolls-Royce automobiles
- Brick manufacturer
- Interior decorator
- Assisted-living facility
- Manufacturer of household cleaning products
- Producer of a weekly television drama

Required:

(a) For each of the business listed, indicate whether it probably uses job order costing or process costing.

(b) Explain how a company that uses process costing assigns a cost to the inventory that is in process.

(c) In each of the listed businesses, do you believe that cost is the primary determinant of the selling price for the product or service? Explain your answer for each business.

17. **Predetermined Overhead** *(LO 11.4)*

Intercept, Inc. estimated that, for 2009, $761,250 of overhead costs would be incurred at 175,000 machine hours. During 2009, the company incurs 182,000 machine hours and has actual overhead costs of $782,630.

Required:

(a) What is Intercept's predetermined overhead rate per machine hour for 2009?

(b) How much overhead was applied to production in 2009?

(c) Is overhead underapplied or overapplied at the end of 2009? By what amount?

(d) What is the disposition of the underapplied or overapplied overhead determined in part (c)? How, if at all, will this disposition affect the income statement?

18. **Predetermined Overhead Rate** *(LO 11.4)*

The production manager at Landis Corp. has the following information available about some of the costs in her department. Her department produces only one product, and she has determined that machine hours are the best predictor of costs.

Indirect labor wages (all variable)	$529,200 at 135,000 MHs
Rent	14,500 per month
Factory insurance	1,680 per month
Indirect material (all variable)	351,000 at 135,000 MHs
Supervisory salaries	8,260 per month
Depreciation	4,150 per month
Electricity	680 per month plus $0.42 per MH

Required:

(a) Prepare a flexible budget at the following activity levels: (1) 120,000 MHs; (2) 130,000 MHs; and (3) 150,000 MHs.

(b) What would be the variable and fixed predetermined overhead rates at each activity level in the flexible budget? Do these rates differ at different levels? Explain.

19. **Direct Labor** *(LO 11.5)*

Gladnish Manufacturing Company operates two shifts of workers. Day workers are paid $12 per hour; evening workers are paid a shift premium of 20 percent. Overtime premiums are 50 percent above day or evening wages. In August 2009, the following factory payroll information is available:

Total hours worked during the month
(70% by day; 30% by evening) 18,000
Overtime hours worked during the month
(only by day workers) 1,000

Required:

(a) What were the total wages paid to employees during the month?

(b) Of the amount in part (a), how much would be considered direct labor cost?

(c) Of the indirect labor cost, how much is for shift premiums and how much is for overtime premiums?

20. **Cost Components and Flows** (LO 11.5 and 11.6)

In a normal costing system for a furniture manufacturer, costs are accumulated in one of five categories: raw material (RM), work in process (WIP), finished goods (FG), fixed overhead (FOH), or variable overhead (VOH). During production, costs flow from one category to another.

Required:

Identify each of the following costs as direct material (DM), direct labor (DL), indirect material (IM), or indirect labor (IL) and indicate which category (RM, WIP, FG, FOH, or VOH) that cost would flow <u>from</u> and <u>to</u>. (Hint: When costs originate, they only flow into a category.)

(a) Purchased machine oil

(b) Purchased unfinished wood, nails, and stain

(c) Used stain to varnish a desk

(d) Oiled the woodworking machinery

(e) Paid insurance on the factory and equipment

(f) Paid a machine operator who oils and maintains the machinery

(g) Used machinery to cut wood to specifications for a desk

(h) Used cut wood and nails to assemble a desk

(i) Paid a woodworker to build a desk

(j) Applied overhead based on direct labor hours

(k) Completed a desk, which is ready to be sold

(l) Sold a desk

21. **Cost of Goods Manufactured** (LO 11.7)

The cost of goods manufactured schedule for Spanglish Industries is presented below with numbers omitted.

Spanglish Industries
Cost of Goods Manufactured Schedule
For the Month Ended June 30, 2009

Beginning Inventory—
Work in Process $?

Manufacturing costs for the period:

Raw Material (direct and indirect)		
Beginning balance	$180,000	
Purchases	?	
Raw Material available	$?	
Ending balance	210,000	
Total Raw Material used	$495,000	
Indirect Material	(60,000)	
Direct Material used		$?
Direct Labor used		465,000
Variable Overhead Applied		142,500
Fixed Overhead Applied		217,500
Total Manufacturing Costs		1,260,000
Total Costs to Account For		$1,860,000
Ending Balance— Work in Process		?
Cost of Goods Manufactured		$1,102,500

Additional information:

Beginning balance of Cost of Goods Sold	$ 0
Beginning balance of Finished Goods	728,625
Beginning units in Finished Goods	100,500
Units sold during June	147,000

Required:

(a) Calculate the missing numbers.

(b) If 150,000 units were produced during June, what is the cost of manufacturing per item?

(c) What is the Cost of Goods Sold during June? Spanglish uses the FIFO cost flow assumption.

(d) What is the ending balance in Finished Goods Inventory (in dollars and units) on June 30?

22. **Cost of Services Rendered** (LO 11.8)

Urdue Clinic had the following costs for October 2009.

Nurses' salaries	$ 24,900
Doctors' salaries	108,000
Electricity (75% related to patient care)	2,400
Building rental (75% related to patient care)	5,700

Depreciation on office equipment	2,010
Depreciation on medical equipment	7,200
Medical supplies purchased	17,400
Medical supplies on hand, October 1	450
Medical supplies on hand, October 1	4,350
Office salaries (35% related to patient care)	3,900

Required:

Prepare a Schedule of Cost of Services Rendered for October 2009.

PROBLEMS

23. **Determining Total Cost** *(LO 11.2)*

Green Wings, Corp. pays EH, Inc. $1,360 for an annual service contract on its kitchen equipment. In addition, Green Wings pays $35 each time a technician is called to work on any of the equipment. No other costs (material or labor) are incurred for the service calls under the service contract.

Required:

(a) Prepare a flexible budget for Green Wings's service contract costs if technicians are called 12, 18, and 24 times per year.

(b) Determine the cost per service call for each level of service listed in part (a). Why does the cost per service call change?

(c) The average price of a service call without the contract is $95. At what number of service calls is Green Wings saving money by having the service contract?

(d) Why would Green Wings enter into this service contract if the company only expects to have 15 service calls per year?

24. **Predetermined Overhead Rates** *(LO 11.4)*

Companies often set predetermined overhead rates to assign overhead costs to products and services. In such cases, a set amount is applied to product cost for each actual unit of "predictor" or "driver" activity incurred. Following are some overhead costs that would be incurred in an all-inclusive hotel (includes a restaurant, pool, spa, fitness facility, meeting rooms, ballroom, and business center).

- Salary of concierge
- City property taxes
- Wages for housekeeping staff
- Electricity
- Wages for table cleaners (bus staff)
- Internet provider cost
- Unemployment taxes
- Water bill for spa
- Cleaning supplies
- Liability insurance for fitness facility
- Liquor license fee
- Laundry services
- Food costs
- Insurance policy

Required:

(a) For each of the listed items, indicate three items that could be considered causal factors of the overhead cost. For instance, one predictor of cleaning supplies could be the number of rooms cleaned.

(b) Each hotel room has a phone. The monthly cost of phone service to the hotel is $8,400 plus long-distance charges; this rate has not changed in three years. Why might the hotel charge customers an "access" fee of $2 per call for every call made to outside the hotel? Why might this fee have increased from the $1 charged three years ago?

25. **Predetermined Overhead Rates** *(LO 11.4)*

Alanzary Co. has the following estimated 2010 information for its two departments: Production and Assembly.

	Production	Assembly
Est. overhead costs	$603,000	$66,600
Est. direct labor hours	4,500	30,000
Est. machine hours	45,000	9,000

The production department is highly automated, and the assembly department is highly labor intensive.

Product N, made by the company, requires the following quantities of machine and direct labor hours in each department.

	Production	Assembly
Direct labor hours	0.15	1.20
Machine hours	8.00	0.30

Required:

(a) Assume that Alanzary Co. chooses to use direct labor hours to apply all overhead costs to products. What is the predetermined overhead rate for 2010?

How much overhead would be assigned to each unit of Product N in 2010? (Round all calculations to the nearest penny.)

(b) Assume that Alanzary Co. chooses to use machine hours to apply all overhead costs to products. What is the predetermined overhead rate for 2010? How much overhead would be assigned to each unit of Product N in 2010? (Round all calculations to the nearest penny.)

(c) If Alanzary Co. decides to use the most appropriate base in each department to apply overhead to products, what would be the predetermined overhead rate in each department? How much overhead would be assigned to each unit of Product N in 2010? (Round all calculations to the nearest penny.)

(d) Why do the overhead amounts applied to Product N differ among parts (a), (b), and (c)?

26. Flow of Product Costs *(LO 11.6)*

Selected transactions regarding Peyvandi Corp.'s manufacturing process are listed.

(a) Purchased raw material on account, $84,000

(b) Used direct material in production, $44,000

(c) Incurred labor costs: 3,400 direct labor hours at $40,000, and 800 indirect labor hours at $12,000

(d) Recorded depreciation on factory equipment, $4,400

(e) Recorded the expiration of one month of prepaid insurance, $2,000

(f) Received but did not pay an electricity bill, $1,700

(g) Pay an external company to repair factory equipment, $500

(h) Applied overhead to goods in process at a rate of $5 per direct labor hour

(i) Transferred completed goods to finished goods, $107,200

(j) Sold goods costing $100,000 to credit customers for $178,000

Required:

Prepare journal entries to record the Peyvandi's transactions. Use a single account for both variable and fixed overhead (Overhead Control).

27. Cost of Goods Manufactured and Cost of Goods Sold *(LO 11.7)*

Lang Products had the following beginning and ending inventory balances for April 2009.

	4/1/09	4/30/09
Raw Material Inventory	$18,000	$20,800
Work in Process Inventory	85,200	50,800
Finished Goods Inventory	43,200	14,700

All raw materials are considered direct to the manufacturing process. During April, the company purchased $260,000 of raw materials. Direct labor cost for the month was $342,000; workers are paid $9.50 per hour. Overhead is applied at the rate of $12.50 for each direct labor hour.

Required:

(a) Prepare the Schedule of Cost of Goods Manufactured.

(b) Calculate Cost of Goods Sold for April 2009.

28. Cost of Services Rendered *(LO 11.3, 11.5, and 11.8)*

Schatzie's is a veterinary clinic. At the beginning of July, the clinic had $720 of veterinary supplies on hand. The following information is available for July 2009.

Salaries for veterinary staff	$32,000
Salaries for veterinary assistants	12,000
Salary for receptionist	2,500
Wages for office workers	6,000
Veterinary supplies purchased in July	9,600
Veterinary supplies on hand on July 31	1,150
Depreciation on hospital and lab equipment	8,600
Depreciation on office equipment	3,000
Building rent (60% related to treatment)	3,600
Utilities (80% related to treatment)	1,800

Required:

(a) What is the overhead amount related to the cost of services rendered?

(b) Compute Cost of Services Rendered.

(c) Schatzie's collected $88,000 in treatment fees. What was Schatzie's gross profit and net income? (Hint: Gross profit is revenues minus cost of services provided.)

CASES

29. Cost Classifications *(LO 11.2)*

Ivan Abuzi is a house painter. He incurred the following costs during August 2009, when he painted four houses. In

the first week of August, Abuzi placed a $60 classified ad for his business in the newspaper. He also bought two pairs of coveralls for $35 each to wear while working. Abuzi spent

$25 for a day-planner book in which he records hours spent at each job, mileage to and from jobs (at a rate of $0.32 per mile), information on referral work, and bids submitted for other jobs. Toll road charges for driving to various job locations were $0.75 for each section of toll road traveled. Cell phone charges for the month were $60; Abuzi has a cell phone plan that allows up to 2,000 minutes of nationwide calling, a time frame that he has never exceeded. Abuzi uses the cell phone for both business and personal calls. In August, approximately 40% of his calls were business related. Materials costs for the month were $500 for paint, $40 for mineral spirits, and $155 for brushes. Abuzi hired a helper who worked 15 hours at $18 per hour on one of Abuzi's jobs. The insurance on Abuzi's work truck is $50 per month.

Required:

Using the following headings, indicate how each of the August costs incurred by Abuzi would be classified. Assume that the cost object is a house-painting job.

Type of Cost	Variable	Fixed	Direct	Indirect	Period	Product

30. **Controllable and Noncontrollable Costs** (LO 11.2, writing, ethics)

You are Manager of Special Events at a large hotel in Great Neck. The meeting rooms and ballroom take up one floor of the 12-story building. The other managers at the hotel have responsibilities for Accommodations, Restaurant, and Guest Facilities (pool, fitness club, business center, tennis courts, parking garages, etc.). Each manager, except Guest Facilities, is evaluated on how profitable his/her area of operation was during the period. The Guest Facilities manager is evaluated on the basis of cost control because no fees are charged for many of the services under her control.

Required:

(a) How will you determine what costs incurred at the hotel are controllable or noncontrollable? Be sure to discuss the selection of a cost object.

(b) One month you notice that the Restaurant Manager had decided to charge you "fees" for the following items: laundering linens used in special events, overtime premiums for the cooking and waitstaff for special events, and hourly wages of room service personnel who helped out during special events (when not delivering room service items). The Accommodations Manager had decided to charge you "fees" for one-twelfth of the property taxes, electricity, and building depreciation. The Guest Facilities manager had decided to charge you a "fee" per parking space for every person expected at all special events held

during the month. Write a memo to the company president discussing these fees and how they could affect your performance evaluation.

31. **Cost Flow** (LO 11.6, writing)

Micro Laser Systems (MLS) produces small electronics parts for other companies. MLS uses process costing because the items manufactured by the company are produced to customer specifications. Currently, MLS is having difficulty identifying the difference between direct and indirect material and labor. As a result, MLS is adding almost all labor and a large portion of material cost to overhead. The rationale of MLS's production management is that the overhead eventually gets applied to the job anyway.

Required:

Write a memo to MLS's management to explain problems that might be encountered by misclassifying things as overhead as opposed to direct material or labor.

32. **Using Cost Information** (LO 11.7)

A massive fire began in the production building of Pflugerville Co. in the early morning of September 18, 2009. The fire destroyed all the company's work in process. To determine the amount of the loss, Pflugerville Co. has gathered the following information:

- Sales for the period September 1 through September 17 were $110,000. The gross margin on product sales has typically been 30%.

- At the beginning of September, Work in Process Inventory contained $27,000 of goods.

- The finished goods warehouse was not affected by the fire. The Finished Goods Inventory account balance was $3,600 at the beginning of the month and $2,900 after an inventory count on the day of the fire.

- Records indicated that the company used $64,000 of direct material during the first 17 days of September.

- Wages paid to direct labor employees for the first 17 days of September totaled $8,750; direct labor employees are paid $7 per hour.

- The predetermined overhead rate was set using an expected total overhead of $176,400 and expected annual direct labor hours of 18,000.

Required:

(a) Determine the value of the lost work in process inventory for Pflugerville Co.

(b) What other information might Pflugerville Co. need to submit to the insurance company to substantiate its loss claim?

33. **Comparing Costs** (LO 11.2, Internet, group)

Identifying the similarities and differences among companies is crucial to understanding the nature of operations. Form groups of at least four students. Each group should select a single industry. Each group member should locate a different annual report within that industry. (The industry and individual company may be assigned by your instructor.)

Required—individual group members:

(a) For your business, scan the annual report to gain an understanding of its primary line of business, which should relate to the industry in which the company operates.

(b) List five types (or as many as you can) of the following costs your company probably incurs.

(1) Direct material

(2) Indirect material

(3) Direct labor

(4) Indirect labor

(5) Overhead (other than indirect material and labor)

(c) For each cost you listed, indicate whether it is a product or period cost.

(d) For each cost you listed, indicate whether it is fixed, variable, or mixed.

Required—groups:

(e) Compare the costs you listed with the other members of your group.

(f) The companies you are comparing operate in the same industry. How similar were the costs you listed?

(g) Compile a list of costs in each category that represents the industry you are investigating.

Required—class:

(h) Compare the costs each group listed across industries.

(i) The industries you are comparing are varied. Does the industry in which a company operates affect the lists of costs in each category? Which categories of costs are most different, and which are most similar across industry?

SUPPLEMENTAL PROBLEMS

34. **Predetermined Overhead Rates** (LO 11.4, writing; Compare to Problem 24)

Intronin, Inc. manufactures two products, X and Y. For 2009, Intronin estimated overhead costs would be $4,800,000, direct labor will be 192,000 hours, and there would be 960,000 machine hours. At the end of October 2009, each product used the following machine and direct labor hours.

	Product X	Product Y
Direct labor hours per unit	2.0	3.2
Machine hours per unit	23	6.0
Number of units produced	6,000	9,000

Required:

(a) Assume that Intronin chooses to use direct labor hours to apply all overhead costs to products. What is the predetermined overhead rate? How much overhead would be assigned to each unit of Product X and Product Y?

(b) Using your calculations from part (a), calculate the underapplied or overapplied overhead based on October's portion of the annual estimate.

(c) Assume that Intronin chooses to use machine hours to apply all overhead costs to products. What is the predetermined overhead rate? How much overhead would be assigned to each unit of Product X and Product Y?

(d) Using your calculation from part (c), calculate the underapplied or overapplied overhead based on October's portion of the annual estimate.

(e) The manager of Product X argues that direct labor hours should be used to apply overhead, while the manager of Product Y argues that machine hours should be used. Why are they arguing?

(f) Write a memo to Intronin's management explaining some of the items that should be considered when deciding how to apply overhead.

35. **Flow of Product Costs** (LO 11.6 & 11.7; Compare to Problem 26)

Nassor, Inc. has the following balances in its inventory accounts at May 1.

Raw Material (all direct to production)	$ 5,000
Work in Process	65,080
Finished Goods	12,500

The following transactions occurred in the company for May.

- Purchased raw material on account, $205,700.
- Issued raw material to production, $190,000.
- Accrued direct labor wages for 11,000 hours, $98,240.
- Recorded depreciation on factory equipment, $9,500.
- Paid indirect labor wages, $38,565.
- Recorded the expiration of prepaid insurance on the factory building, $4,000.
- Received and paid the utility bill, $3,500.
- Paid maintenance costs of the factory and factory equipment, $6,250.
- Applied overhead to goods in process. Nassor, Inc. applies overhead to production at a rate of $4.50 per direct labor hour.
- Transferred completed goods to finished goods, $328,655.
- Sold goods costing $306,140 to credit customers for $572,320.

Required:

(a) Prepare journal entries to record the May transactions for Nassor, Inc. Use a single account for both variable and fixed overhead.

(b) Compute the balances in the three inventory accounts at May 31.

(c) Prepare a Schedule of Cost of Goods Manufactured.

(d) Is overhead underapplied or overapplied for May, and by how much? If this overhead were to be closed, would closing cause Cost of Goods Sold to increase or decrease? Explain.

(e) Prepare a Statement of Cost of Goods Sold. Because this is not the end of the year, do not include the underapplied or overapplied overhead in the statement.

CHAPTER 12

Cost-Volume-Profit Analysis

LEARNING OBJECTIVES

1. Define break-even point (BEP) and cost-volume-profit (CVP) analysis, and recognize their limiting underlying assumptions.
2. Use BEP and CVP analysis in both single-product and multiproduct companies.
3. Develop a break-even chart and profit-volume graph.
4. Calculate the margin of safety and operating leverage and use those concepts in analysis.

INTRODUCTION

Many companies and organizations use the break-even point (BEP) concept and cost-volume-profit (CVP) analysis to understand how income will be affected by changes in selling prices, sales volumes, fixed costs, or variable costs. At the break-even point, a company's total revenues are equal to its total costs. The CVP model allows managers to integrate desired profitability into the BEP model. This chapter discusses the BEP and CVP models using income statements, formulas, and graphs. The last part of the chapter addresses two other models, the margin of safety and degree of operating leverage, which are similar to BEP and CVP in the information they provide and in their use.

ASSUMPTIONS OF BREAK-EVEN AND CVP ANALYSIS

Break-even and CVP analysis are used in all organizations. The **break-even point** is the level of sales at which no profits are generated and no losses are incurred. Although companies do not want to operate at this sales level, the BEP provides a reference point so that managers can set sales targets that should generate operating income for the organization. **Cost-volume-profit analysis** expands on the break-even point by allowing managers to assess the relationships among, and the profitability impacts of, selling prices, costs, and volumes. CVP analysis is applicable to both single-product and multiproduct organizations. Before attempting to determine the BEP or use CVP analysis, the organizational cost structure must first be understood. The following important assumptions form the foundation for BEP and CVP analysis.

1. The company is operating within its relevant range of activity (as defined in Chapter 11).
2. All costs are categorized as either variable or fixed.
3. Both selling price and variable cost are constant per unit and, thus, will change in total in direct proportion to level of activity or volume.
4. Contribution margin is constant per unit. Per-unit **contribution margin** is the difference between the selling price per unit and the total variable cost per unit. Because both of those items are constant per unit, so is contribution margin. The contribution margin indicates the amount of revenue available to contribute to the coverage of fixed costs and to generate profits. (Total contribution margin is equal to total revenues minus total variable costs for all units sold.)
5. Total fixed cost is constant per period, and thus, fixed cost per unit varies inversely with changes in volume.

Because these assumptions are so strictly stated, they severely limit the model's ability to reflect business reality. Additionally, it is highly unlikely that the assumptions would hold true for any lengthy period; thus, use of the model is restricted to the short run. For example, the relevant range is likely to change as businesses expand and revenues, variable, and fixed costs change with some regularity over time. However, the model is useful in assessing the profitability effects of changes in the organization's cost structure or sales volume.

BREAK-EVEN POINT

Profit equals the excess of total revenues over total costs. A company is said to "break even" when profit is exactly equal to zero. Therefore, the starting point of CVP analysis is the break-even point, which can be expressed either in units or dollars of revenue.

Income statement information for Beattie Company (Exhibit 12-1) is used to demonstrate computations for the BEP and CVP analysis. The company produces a single product: a high-quality glass paperweight. All units produced are sold.

Break-even and CVP analysis are based on the income statement formula. Total revenues on the income statement are calculated as selling price per unit multiplied by number of units sold. Costs on the income statement are either variable or fixed expenses. Total variable expenses are equal to the variable cost per unit multiplied by the number of units sold. Total fixed expenses are a constant amount and do not depend on the number of units sold. Thus, the following equation reflects the income statement information:

$$\text{Total Revenues} - \text{Total Costs} = \text{Profit}$$
$$R(X) - [VC(X) + FC] = P$$
$$R(X) - VC(X) - FC = P$$

where

$$R = \text{revenue (selling price) per unit}$$
$$X = \text{number of units sold (volume)}$$
$$R(X) = \text{total revenues}$$
$$VC = \text{variable cost per unit}$$
$$VC(X) = \text{total variable costs}$$
$$FC = \text{total fixed costs}$$
$$P = \text{pretax profit}$$

At BEP, there is no profit, so the formula can also be expressed as Total Revenues − Total Costs = $0.

Using the known information from Exhibit 12-1, the equation can be solved for Beattie Company's break-even point as follows:

EXHIBIT 12-1			
Income Statement Information for Beattie Company	Sales (25,000 units @ $50)		$1,250,000
	Variable expenses		
	Production (25,000 units @ $9)	$225,000	
	Selling (25,000 units @ $6)	150,000	(375,000)
	Contribution margin (25,000 units @ $35)		$ 875,000
	Fixed expenses		
	Production	$495,000	
	Selling & administrative	152,500	(647,500)
	Pretax profit		$ 227,500

$$\$50X - (\$9X + \$6X) - \$647,500 = \$0$$
$$\$50X - \$15X - \$647,500 = \$0$$
$$\$35X = \$647,500$$
$$X = \$647,500 \div \$35$$
$$X = 18,500 \text{ units}$$

Beattie Company receives $50 for each paperweight, but must spend $15 per paperweight (variable cost) to produce and sell it. Thus, each paperweight provides a $35 (or $50 − $15) contribution margin toward Beattie's profits. Before Beattie can generate profits, fixed costs of $647,500 must first be covered. It takes the contribution of 18,500 units (or $647,500 ÷ $35) to cover the fixed costs. As shown in the formula, the break-even point in units (BEP_u) equals the total fixed expenses divided by the contribution margin per unit:

$$BEP_u = FC \div CM_u$$

where

$$CM_u = \text{contribution margin per unit}$$

By selling 18,500 units, Beattie earns revenues of $925,000 (18,500 × $50) and incurs variable costs of $277,500 (18,500 × $15) and fixed costs of $647,500. Revenues minus total costs ($277,500 + $647,500) equals zero.

The break-even point in units can be converted into break-even revenues ($BEP_\$$), also called break-even dollars of sales, by multiplying the units by the selling price per unit. However, the contribution margin ratio can also be used to compute the break-even point in sales dollars. The formula for the CM ratio is

$$CM \text{ ratio} = (R - VC) \div R$$
$$CM \text{ ratio} = CM \div R$$

The **contribution margin ratio** indicates the percentage of revenue that remains after variable costs are covered. This calculation can be made either on a per-unit basis when the amounts represent revenue and contribution margin for one unit or on a total dollar basis when total revenues and contribution margin are used. For Beattie Company, the CM ratio is 70 percent ($35 ÷ $50). To use the CM ratio to calculate $BEP_\$$, divide fixed costs by the CM ratio; for Beattie Company, the calculation is $647,500 ÷ 0.70, or $925,000.

Subtracting the CM ratio from 100 percent gives the **variable cost (VC) ratio**, or the variable cost percentage of each revenue dollar. For Beattie Company, the VC ratio is 30 percent (100% − 70%).

Managers want their organizations to earn profits rather than merely break even (or incur losses). Thus, a desired amount of profit can be substituted into the formula to convert break-even analysis into cost-volume-profit analysis.

CVP ANALYSIS

Because the BEP and CVP formulas reflect income statement information, managers can use that formula to analyze a variety of considerations. One common and important use is to determine the sales volume necessary to achieve a desired amount of organizational profit. Profits may be stated on either a before-tax or after-tax basis. The Beattie Company example is continued in the following situations.

Before-Tax Profit

Variable costs are incurred each time a product is made or sold. Thus, the selling price of an item should first cover the variable expenses of production and sales. After variable costs are covered, the remainder (or contribution margin) goes to cover fixed expenses and then to generate profits. After covering all fixed expenses (that is, reaching the BEP), each dollar of contribution margin is a dollar of pretax profit.

Assume that Beattie Company's managers want to generate a pretax profit of $472,500. As shown in the following calculation, substituting this amount in the CVP formula indicates that 32,000 units must be sold.

$$R(X) - VC(X) - FC = P$$
$$\$50X - \$15X - \$647,500 = \$472,500$$
$$\$35X = \$1,120,000$$
$$X = 32,000 \text{ units}$$

Beattie Company must have $1,600,000 of revenues (32,000 units × $50 selling price per unit) to generate the desired $472,500 of profit. Using an income statement format, this amount can be confirmed.

Sales (32,000 units × $50)	$1,600,000
Variable costs (32,000 × $15)	(480,000)
Contribution margin (32,000 × $35)	$1,120,000
Fixed costs	(647,500)
Pretax profit	$ 472,500

After-Tax Profit

Because income taxes represent an important element in business decision making, managers must understand that choosing a desired profit amount will cause income tax effects. Thus, earning a desired profit before income taxes will not generate a similar amount of organizational net profitability. Most managers are more concerned about the "bottom line" (income after taxes or net income) than the pretax profitability. Determining the sales volume needed to achieve a desired net income requires that managers first determine the pretax income to be earned, given the applicable tax rate.

Pretax income minus income taxes equals net income. It is assumed, for simplicity, that the income tax rate is a flat rate (rather than one that increases at various levels of pretax income). If the tax rate is 35 percent, pretax earnings of $100,000 will cause a tax expense of $35,000 (0.35 × $100,000) and result in a net income of $65,000. Therefore, to convert a net income amount to pretax amount, divide net income by (1 minus the tax rate).

$$\text{Necessary pretax income} = \text{Desired net income} \div (1 - \text{tax rate})$$

Once the pretax amount has been obtained, it can be inserted into the same formula as was used in the previous example.

Assume that Beattie Company's tax rate is 35 percent and managers want to earn $325,000 in after-tax profits. The necessary pretax profit desired is ($325,000 ÷ 0.65), or $500,000. Inserting this amount into the CVP formula gives

$$R(X) - VC(X) - FC = P$$
$$\$50X - \$15X - \$647,500 = \$500,000$$
$$\$35X = \$1,147,500$$
$$X = 32,786 \text{ units (rounded)}$$

Proof of this result is shown in the income statement shown in Exhibit 12-2.

Other Considerations

Variables other than profit may also be the focal point of CVP analysis. In some companies, selling prices are set by market competition, and each company has a fairly well defined market volume (or market share). In such cases, managers may use CVP to determine an "allowable" variable cost per unit: a variable cost amount that will allow the company to make a desired contribution margin per unit.

For example, assume that the total annual market for paperweights is 300,000 units. Beattie Company holds approximately a 9 percent market share (or 27,000 units) and cannot significantly affect the $50 market selling price. The company's fixed costs are still assumed to be $647,500, and the tax rate is 35 percent. Beattie Company management wants to earn $234,000 of after-tax net income in the upcoming year. What amount can the company incur as variable cost per unit to earn the desired net income?

First, the company's income objective must be restated as pretax profit: $234,000 ÷ 0.65 = 360,000. This amount is used in the CVP formula for profit. Note, however, that the unknown is no longer units, but variable cost per unit.

$$R(X) - VC(X) - FC = P$$
$$\$50(27,000) - VC(27,000) - \$647,500 = \$360,000$$
$$\$1,350,000 - VC(27,000) - \$647,500 = \$360,000$$
$$\$702,500 - VC(27,000) = \$360,000$$
$$VC(27,000) = \$342,500$$
$$X = \$12.69 \text{ (rounded)}$$

Given these circumstances, Beattie Company can spend a maximum of $12.69 on variable cost per unit if the company wants to achieve its desired after-tax profit. The results are shown in Exhibit 12-3.

EXHIBIT 12-2			
Proof of Beattie Company's Net Income Profitability	Sales (32,786 units @ $50)		$1,639,300
	Variable expenses		
	Production (32,786 units @ $9)	$295,074	
	Selling (32,786 units @ $6)	196,716	(491,790)
	Contribution margin (32,786 units @ $35)		$1,147,510
	Fixed expenses		
	Production	$495,000	
	Selling & administrative	152,500	(647,500)
	Pretax profit		$ 500,010
	Tax expense (35%)		(175,004)
	Net income (off due to rounding)		$ 325,006

Sales (27,000 units @ $50)		$1,350,000
Variable expenses		
Production & selling (27,000 units @ $12.69)		(342,630)
Contribution margin		$1,007,370
Fixed expenses		
Production	$495,000	
Selling & administrative	152,500	(647,500)
Pretax profit		$ 359,870
Tax expense (35%)		(125,955)
Net income (off due to rounding)		$ 233,915

Note that the answer was given in terms of total variable cost per unit. If Beattie Company cannot reduce its product cost of $9 per unit and still retain the quality of its paperweights, company management will have to concentrate on reducing the variable selling cost per unit from its current level of $6 per unit to a maximum of $3.69. If neither of these situations can occur, company management will need to raise its market share or find ways to reduce its fixed costs for the desired level of profitability to be obtained.

Companies have many ways to adjust the costs that are incurred to produce or sell a product. Variable expenses may be decreased or increased by changing product manufacturing specifications, direct material quality, direct labor inputs, or distribution costs. Fixed costs may be modified through investments in, or sales of, capital facilities or changes in managerial salaries or other contract items (such as rent or lease agreements).

The CVP formulas are summarized in Visual Recap 12.1.

USING INCREMENTAL ANALYSIS

Answers from break-even or CVP computations are valid only if the assumptions given at the beginning of the chapter are true. Any change in selling price or cost relationships will cause a change in the BEP and the sales volume needed to obtain a desired profit. All else being equal, the following mathematical relationships can be stated as follows.

- BEP_u and $BEP_\$$ increase (decrease) if total fixed expenses increase (decrease).
- BEP_u and $BEP_\$$ increase (decrease) if CM per unit or the CM ratio decreases (increases).

VISUAL RECAP 12.1

Summary of BEP and CVP Relationships

$R(X) - VC(X) - FC = P$

$R - VC = CM$

$CM(X) - FC = P$

$BEP_u = FC \div CM_u$

$BEP_\$ = FC \div CM \text{ ratio}$

After-tax profits = Pre-tax profits $\div$ (1 − tax rate)

- Contribution margin will decrease (increase) if the company has a decrease (increase) in unit selling price.
- Contribution margin will decrease (increase) if the company has an increase (decrease) in unit variable cost.

Changes in any of these revenue or cost factors will also cause changes in total profits or losses at any level of activity.

Focusing on factors that change from one course of action to another is called **incremental analysis**. Examples of some potential organizational changes and the incremental analysis that would be used to determine the BEP or profitability effects follow. For simplicity, all profits are stated on a pretax basis; after-tax analysis would apply the 1 − tax rate factor to profits. The original information (Exhibit 12-1) for Beattie Company is used in each example. Each of the following four incremental analyses is considered independently.

Increase in Fixed Cost

Beattie Company believes that 3,000 more paperweights can be sold if advertising is increased by $125,000. Before profits can be obtained from these sales, the additional fixed cost must first be covered by the increased total contribution margin. Should the company incur this additional fixed cost?

Increase in CM generated (3,000 paperweights × $35)	$ 105,000
− Increase in fixed cost	(125,000)
= Net incremental loss	$ (20,000)

The advertising campaign would increase contribution margin by $105,000 but increase costs by $125,000, generating a reduction in profits of $20,000. The campaign should not be undertaken.

Decrease in Selling Price

Beattie Company estimates that lowering the paperweight's selling price to $45 will generate additional sales of 10,000 units annually. Sales volume will increase from 25,000 units to 35,000 units, but the unit contribution margin will fall from $35 to $30. Should the company reduce the selling price?

Total CM generated (35,000 paperweights × $30)	$1,050,000
− Total fixed costs (unchanged)	(647,500)
= New pretax profit	$ 402,500
− Current pretax profit (from Exhibit 12-1)	(227,500)
= Net incremental benefit	$ 175,000

Beattie Company will increase its pretax profit and, thus, should reduce its selling price.

Increase in Sales Volume and Costs (1)

Beattie Company believes that increasing paperweight quality will cause sales volume to increase by 1,500 units. Quality could be improved by: (1) purchasing a higher grade of raw material and (2) buying an automated glass blowing machine to reduce "bubbles" in the paperweights. The higher grade of raw material would raise variable cost per unit by $1.50; the new machine will cause an increase in depreciation expense (a fixed cost) of $8,000. Should the company make these efforts to raise quality?

Variable cost will increase from $15 per unit to $16.50, reducing the contribution margin per unit from $35 to $33.50. Thus, the total CM from the sales of the original 25,000 will decrease. Fixed expenses will increase from $647,500 to $655,500.

Decrease in CM on old paperweight sales (25,000 paperweights × $1.50)	$(37,500)
+ Increase in CM from new paperweight sales (1,500 × $33.50)	50,250
– Increase in annual fixed cost	(8,000)
= Net incremental benefit	$ 4,750

There is an incremental benefit in this situation, so Beattie Company should make the quality enhancement efforts and, thereby, increase sales volume.

Increase in Sales Volume and Costs (2)

Beattie Company has been approached by a foreign company that wants to purchase, for resale, 3,000 paperweights at $24 per unit. Additional packaging and shipping will cause variable cost per unit to increase by $3 for the units produced for the foreign company. Additionally, the fixed cost will increase by $8,500 because of the depreciation on a new machine that will need to be purchased. (It is assumed that this machine can be used for other purposes and for several years.) Beattie Company's current sales will not be affected by this opportunity, and the additional units fall within the company's relevant range of activity. Should the company make this sale?

The total variable cost per "foreign" paperweight is $18 ($15 current + $3 additional shipping and packaging), creating a contribution margin for each "foreign" unit of $6 ($24 selling price – $18 total variable cost). Beattie Company is already making profits, so all current fixed costs are covered. However, the new $8,500 of fixed cost will need to be covered by the additional sales.

Total contribution margin (3,000 paperweights × $6)	$18,000
– Additional fixed cost (depreciation)	(8,500)
= Net incremental benefit	$ 9,500

Total contribution margin provided from the sale is greater than the additional fixed cost. Thus, Beattie Company's total income would increase by accepting this opportunity, and the sale should be made.

All the examples given have been evaluated solely on a monetary basis. However, managers making these types of decisions should consider both monetary *and* nonmonetary factors, as well as considering short-term and long-term implications. How close to reality are the increased sales projections? What if cost increases are greater than projected? Will increased workloads create stress for employees, who may begin to exhibit fatigue that generates quality problems? Have all future costs truly been considered? (For example, when new equipment is to be purchased, might there be additional costs for maintenance and employee training that have not been estimated?) Or might increased advertising benefit sales for years beyond the time frame? Additional considerations include future production capacity, quality control, raw material and other resource availability, and possible legal implications of different sales prices to different customers.

CVP ANALYSIS IN A MULTIPRODUCT ENVIRONMENT

All the previous situations are based on a single-product company, but most companies produce and sell a variety of items. Some companies sell related products (such as golf clubs and bags or tablecloths and napkins); other companies are quite diversified and sell completely unrelated products.

Performing CVP analysis in a multiproduct company requires an additional assumption to the ones stated at the beginning of the chapter: that of a constant product sales mix. The **constant mix** (or "basket") **assumption** reflects the notion that the company sells a consistent set of goods as a package. For example, a furniture company could assume that, for every dining room table sold, four chairs will also be sold. Without the constant sales mix assumption, a BEP could not be calculated, and CVP analysis could not be used. The constant mix assumption allows a weighted average contribution margin (or CM ratio) to be computed for the basket of products being sold. Thus, the CM (or CM ratio) is affected by the quantity of each product in the "basket."

To continue the Beattie Company example, assume that management has decided to also produce glass bookends. It is estimated that, for every five paperweights sold, the company will sell two sets of bookends. Therefore, the products have a 5:2 ratio within the "basket." Beattie Company will need to purchase additional machinery to make the bookends; this purchase will result in $34,190 of additional fixed costs for depreciation on the machine. Exhibit 12-4 provides relevant company information and shows the break-even computations.

Any difference in the product sales mix from the stated 5:2 relationship at a sales level of 3,665 "baskets" will cause Beattie Company to either incur a loss or generate a profit. If the proportion of bookends sold within the "baskets" increases, Beattie Company will incur a loss because the contribution margin of that product (18.3%) is lower than that of

EXHIBIT 12-4							
Multiple Product Cost Information for Beattie Company		Paperweights		Bookends		"Basket"	
		per Unit	per Basket	per Set	per Basket	Total	%
	Number in basket		5		2		
	Selling price	$50.00	$250.00	$30.00	$60.00	$310	100%
	Variable expenses	(15.00)	(75.00)	(24.50)	(49.00)	(124)	(40)%
	Contribution margin	$35.00	$175.00	$ 5.50	$11.00	$186	60%

New fixed costs: $647,500 + $34,190 = $681,690

$$R(X) - VC(X) - FC = P$$
$$\$310X - \$124X - \$681,690 = \$0$$
$$\$186X = \$681,690$$
$$X = 3,665 \text{ baskets}$$

Because products are sold in a 5:2 ratio, the basket result requires that Beattie Company sell 18,325 (3,665 × 5) paperweights and 7,330 (3,665 × 2) sets of bookends to break even.

the paperweights (70%). If the proportion of paperweights sold increases, Beattie Company will earn a profit.

Assume that Beattie Company sells 3,665 "baskets," but the actual sales mix is four paperweights for every three sets of bookends sold. Thus, the proportion has shifted toward the product with the lower contribution margin ratio and a loss results. The results of such a sales mix are shown in Exhibit 12-5.

GRAPHIC APPROACHES TO BEP AND CVP PROBLEMS

Solving break-even and CVP problems using the algebraic or income statement approach provides a specific numerical answer (although that answer may need to be rounded).[1] However, solutions may also be presented in a pictorial, or graphic, form. Two depictions, the break-even graph and the profit-volume graph, are provided in the following sections with a related discussion.

Break-Even Graph

The **break-even graph** plots the relationships among revenue, volume, and the various costs. The x-axis (horizontal) represents volume in units, whereas the y-axis (vertical) represents dollars earned or spent by the company. Each line on the graph represents revenues or costs. The graph is created as follows.

1. Total fixed cost is a line drawn horizontal to the x-axis. The line is parallel to the x-axis because at any volume, the total fixed costs do not change. The fixed-cost line crosses the y-axis at the dollar value of fixed costs.

2. Total cost is shown as a line that originates at the point where the total fixed cost line intersects the y-axis because when zero units are produced, no variable costs are incurred, and therefore total costs are equal to fixed costs. Per-unit variable

---

EXHIBIT 12-5

Change in Sales Mix for Beattie Company

	Paperweights per Unit	Paperweights per Basket	Bookends per Set	Bookends per Basket	"Basket" Total	%
Number in basket		4		3		
Selling price	$50.00	$200.00	$30.00	$90.00	$290.00	100%
Variable expenses	(15.00)	(60.00)	(24.50)	(73.50)	(133.50)	(46)%
Contribution margin	$35.00	$140.00	$ 5.50	$16.50	$156.50	54%

New fixed costs: $647,500 + $34,190 = $681,690

$$R(X) - VC(X) - FC = \text{Profit or Loss}$$
$$\$290(3,665) - \$133.50(3,665) - \$681,690 = \text{Profit or Loss}$$
$$\$156.50(3,665) - \$681,690 = \text{Profit or Loss}$$
$$\$573,572.50 - \$681,690 = \text{Profit or Loss}$$
$$\$(108,117.50) = \text{Loss}$$

---

[1]Rounding in BEP or CVP should always be upward, even when the decimal is less than half. Such an increase is necessary to avoid having a loss (or less than desired profit) created from the calculations.

cost is represented by the slope of the total-cost line. For every additional unit produced and sold, total costs increase by the variable cost per unit.

3. At each volume level, the distance between the fixed cost and the total cost lines represents total variable cost.

4. Total revenue is plotted from zero, using a slope that represents the selling price per unit. For each additional unit sold, revenue increases by the selling price per unit.

5. The break-even point is at the intersection of the revenue and total cost lines. At that point total revenues and total costs are equal.

6. Beyond the BEP (to the right), profit is represented as the distance between the total revenue and total cost lines for any number of units. To the left of BEP is the loss area.

Exhibit 12-6 shows the break-even graph for Beattie Company. Notice that at 18,500 units both costs and revenues are equal to $925,000, as calculated earlier in the chapter.

Profit-Volume Graph

A **profit-volume (PV) graph** provides the same information as a BEP graph, but shows profit or loss amounts at each level of volume. As in the BEP graph, volume in units is represented on the PV graph's horizontal axis, and dollars are represented on the vertical axis. However, in this graph, the dollars represent the differences between revenue and cost amounts or the profit (loss) amounts. Amounts above the horizontal axis are positive and indicate profits; amounts below the horizontal axis are negative and indicate losses.

Total fixed costs are shown on the vertical axis under the sales volume line as a negative amount. If a company were to sell no units of product, a loss in the amount of total fixed

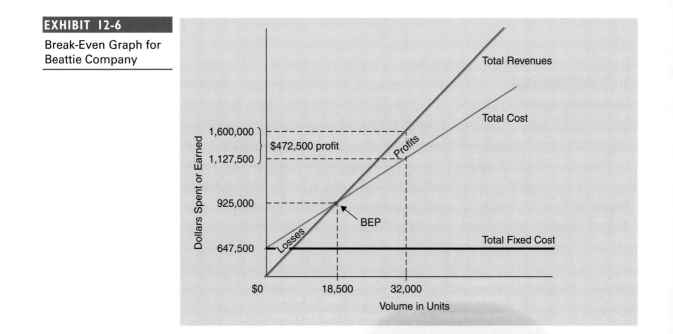

EXHIBIT 12-6

Break-Even Graph for Beattie Company

costs would occur. The horizontal axis of zero profitability is placed at the break-even point, which is determined using the algebraic formula. A profit line is drawn between the total fixed costs and the break-even point and extended at the same slope. This line allows the profit or loss amount for any sales volume to be read from the vertical axis. The PV graph for Beattie Company is shown in Exhibit 12-7.

Graphic representations of break-even are visually appealing, but they do not provide exact solutions to problems because of the inability to read precise points on a graph. Therefore, accurate computations of profit and loss figures must still be made using the algebraic formula.

OPERATING ABOVE BREAK-EVEN

Managers are often concerned with how close the current level of operations is to the break-even point. Two tools are commonly used to analyze the relationship between current operations and BEP: the margin of safety and the degree of operating leverage.

Margin of Safety

Managers presented with new opportunities often consider the organization's **margin of safety** (MS), or the excess of sales over break-even point. The MS represents the level by which sales can fall before the BEP is reached and, thus, indicates a loss "cushion" measure. The MS can be calculated in units or dollars.[2]

$$MS_u = \text{Actual units sold} - \text{Break-even units}$$

$$MS_\$ = \text{Actual sales in } \$_S - \text{Break-even sales in } \$_S$$

Beattie Company's break-even point is 18,500 units, or $925,000 of sales. Exhibit 12-1 indicates that Beattie Company is currently selling 25,000 paperweights, providing $1,250,000 of total revenue. Beattie Company's margin of safety is calculated in the following equations.

EXHIBIT 12-7

Profit-Volume Graph
for Beattie Company

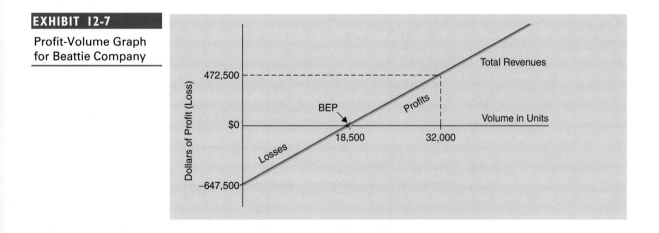

---

[2]The margin of safety can also be expressed as a percentage: (MS in units or $) ÷ (Actual sales in units or $).

$$MS_u = 25,000 - 18,500 = 6,500 \text{ paperweights}$$
$$MS_\$ = \$1,250,000 - \$925,000 = \$325,000$$

Beattie Company's margin of safety is fairly high.

The margin of safety provides an indication of organizational risk. As the MS gets smaller, managers must become more aware of sales levels and cost control so that the sales will not deteriorate, forcing the company into a loss situation.

Degree of Operating Leverage

The **degree of operating leverage** (DOL) is closely related to the margin of safety. The DOL reflects an organization's variable and fixed cost relationship and measures how a percentage change in sales from the current level will affect profits. Thus, it indicates an organization's sensitivity to sales volume changes. The formula for the degree of operating leverage factor is given below.

$$DOL = \text{Total Contribution Margin} \div \text{Pretax Profit}$$

Organizations with high variable costs (and often high direct labor costs) and low fixed costs have low contribution margins and low degrees of operating leverage. These organizations have high break-even points. Alternately, organizations (often those that are highly automated) with high fixed costs and low variable costs have high contribution margins and high degrees of operating leverage. These organizations have low break-even points. As organizations become more automated, they will need higher sales volumes to cover their fixed costs. However, once fixed costs are covered, each unit sold above the BEP provides a generous contribution to profits. Thus, a small sales volume increase can dramatically influence a company's profits.

The Beattie Company example is continued with one change from the original information. Assume that Beattie Company is currently selling only 19,000 paperweights (rather than the original 25,000). Exhibit 12-8 provides the income statement and degree of operating leverage at the 19,000 sales volume and at two other sales volumes.

When a company experiences a specified percentage increase (or decrease) in sales volume, the profit change equals the DOL times the percentage change in sales. The DOL

EXHIBIT 12-8 Degree of Operating Leverage for Beattie Company		**Current Level** **19,000 units**	**Decrease of 20%** **15,200 units**	**Increase of 30%** **24,700 units**
	Sales (@ $50)	$ 950,000	$ 760,000	$1,235,000
	Variable costs (@ $15)	(285,000)	(228,000)	(370,500)
	Contribution margin (@ $35)	$ 665,000	$ 532,000	$ 864,500
	Fixed costs	(647,500)	(647,500)	(647,500)
	Pretax profit	$ 17,500	$(115,500)	$ 217,000

DOL at 19,000 units = $665,000 ÷ $17,500 = 38

At 15,200 units, pretax profits decline by $133,000 (or $17,500 + $115,500) or 7.6 times ($133,000 ÷ $17,500), which is equal to the DOL of 38 times the 20 percent volume reduction.

At 24,700 units, pretax profits increase by $199,500 (or $217,000 − $17,500) or 11.4 times ($199.500 ÷ $17,500), which is equal to the DOL of 38 times the 30 percent volume reduction.

decreases as an organization moves away from its break-even point. For example, at 24,700 units, Beattie Company's DOL is ($864,500 ÷ $217,000), or 3.98 (rounded). An additional 30 percent increase in sales only increases pretax profits by 1.19 times (3.98 × 30%). This calculation is proved as follows:

$$24{,}700 \text{ units} \times 1.3 = 32{,}110 \text{ units of sales}$$
$$(32{,}110 \times \$35 \text{ CM}) - \$647{,}500 \text{ FC} = \text{Pretax profit}$$
$$\$1{,}123{,}850 - \$647{,}500 = \text{Pretax profit}$$
$$\$476{,}350 = \text{Pretax profit}$$
$$\$476{,}350 - \$217{,}000 = \$259{,}350 \text{ increase}$$
$$\$259{,}350 \div \$217{,}000 = 1.19 \text{ times (rounded)}$$

When an organization's sales are close to the break-even point, the margin of safety is small but the DOL is large, so that each percentage increase in sales can make a dramatic impact on net income. As the organization's sales volume increases, the margin of safety increases, but the degree of operating leverage declines. However, it is important to note that a 1,000 times increase in net income of $1 is not as significant as a 3 times increase in net income of $500,000.

SUMMARY

In contemplating future activities, management must consider selling prices, volume levels, and variable and fixed costs. These monetary elements will affect the contribution margin, break-even point (BEP), and profits (or losses). The relationships among these elements are examined in break-even and cost-volume-profit (CVP) analysis.

At BEP, total revenues are equal to total costs, and the organization neither incurs a loss nor generates a profit. The CVP model adds a desired profit to the income statement equation. An important amount in the BEP or CVP model is contribution margin, which is equal to selling price per unit minus variable cost per unit. Dividing total fixed costs by contribution margin per unit provides the BEP in units. After total fixed costs are covered, each dollar of contribution margin will generate a dollar of pretax profit.

The BEP and CVP models require that certain underlying assumptions about the income statement elements be made. These assumptions limit the ability of the models to reflect reality, but are necessary for the models to be usable. If any assumptions are violated, the information resulting from the model will be less than reasonable.

When an organization sells a variety of products, break-even and cost-volume-profit analyses must be performed using an assumed constant product sales mix (or "basket") assumption. A weighted average contribution margin (or contribution margin ratio) is computed for the organization's "basket" of products. Results of BEP or CVP computations are in "baskets" of products; the sales mix ratio is used to convert these "basket" amounts to quantities of individual products.

The margin of safety (MS) can be calculated in units or sales dollars. The MS shows how far an organization is operating from its BEP. The degree of operating leverage (DOL) shows how many times profit would change from its current level, given a specified percentage change in sales volume.

KEY TERMS

break-even graph
break-even point
constant mix assumption
contribution margin

contribution margin ratio
cost-volume-profit analysis
degree of operating
 leverage

incremental analysis
margin of safety
profit-volume graph
variable cost ratio

QUESTIONS

1. What is the break-even point? Why is calculating break-even point the starting point for cost-volume-profit analysis? *(LO 12.1)*

2. Why is the assumption that a company is operating within its relevant range necessary for break-even analysis and cost-volume-profit analysis? What will happen if the company begins operating (a) above or (b) below its relevant range? *(LO 12.1)*

3. Discuss the realism of the underlying assumptions of break-even analysis (that is, how likely it is that the assumptions will hold in reality). *(LO 12.1)*

4. In discussing BEP or CVP analysis, why is it necessary to assume that all units produced by the company are also sold? What difficulties would be caused in the BEP or CVP calculations if units were produced but not sold? *(LO 12.1)*

5. What is contribution margin, and why does it fluctuate in direct proportion with sales volume? To what does a contribution margin "contribute"? *(LO 12.2)*

6. What is the formula for the contribution margin ratio? What information does the ratio provide? *(LO 12.2)*

7. Why is the constant mix assumption necessary to use CVP in a multiproduct firm? Is this assumption realistic? Explain. *(LO 12.2)*

8. Describe the difference between the break-even graph and the profit-volume graph. Which graph do you think provides better information? Explain the reason(s) for your answer. *(LO 12.3)*

9. How do the margin of safety and degree of operating leverage apply to CVP analysis? How are these two concepts related to one another? *(LO 12.4)*

10. Explain the benefits and drawbacks of using the margin of safety and degree of operating leverage to determine how well positioned an organization is in the marketplace. *(LO 12.4)*

EXERCISES

11. **True or False** *(All LOs)*

    Following are a series of statements regarding topics discussed in this chapter.

    (a) At the break-even point, total revenue dollars equal total variable costs.

    (b) To compute a desired after-tax profit, the before-tax profit is divided by $(1 - \text{the tax rate})$.

    (c) Incremental analysis focuses on the financial implications of possible changes.

    (d) To perform CVP analysis for a multiproduct company, each product's BEP must be determined separately.

    (e) The profit-volume graph does not depict revenues separate from costs.

    (f) Fixed costs divided by the contribution margin ratio equals the break-even point in dollars.

    (g) Margin of safety and degree of operating leverage may be expressed in dollars, in units, or as a percentage.

    (h) After fixed costs are covered, contribution margin is the amount the sale of one unit contributes to net income.

    (i) The break-even graph depicts fixed costs, total costs, and revenues for any level of output.

    (j) The further away a company gets from BEP, the higher its degree of operating leverage.

    (k) When variable cost per unit decreases or fixed cost in total increases, contribution margin per unit or in total will decrease.

    Required:

    Indicate whether each statement is true (T) or false (F).

12. **Break-Even Point** *(LO 12.2)*

Selected information for five different companies is listed in the following table.

Company	Revenue per Unit	Variable Cost per Unit	Fixed Cost	Sales Volume
R	(a)	$ 8.00	$165,000	10,000
S	$40.00	(b)	360,000	20,000
T	8.00	3.50	59,994	(c)
U	59.00	40.00	(d)	42,700
V	35.00	22.00	30,745	(e)

Required:

Find the missing amounts, assuming each company is operating at the break-even point.

13. **CVP Analysis** *(LO 12.2)*

Selected information for four different companies is listed in the following table.

Company	Revenue per Unit	Variable Cost per Unit	Fixed Cost	Desired Pretax Profit
A	$75.00	$38.25	$678,037.50	$155,452.50
B	60.00	40.00	720,000.00	196,000.00
C	12.50	9.50	240,000.00	46,860.00
D	41.25	15.51	84,993.48	90,038.52

Required:

(a) Calculate the contribution margin and contribution margin ratio for each company.

(b) Determine the break-even point for each company.

(c) Determine the number of units that must be sold to earn the desired profit for each company.

14. **Pretax and After-tax Profits** *(LO 12.2)*

Selected information for three companies is provided in the following table.

Company	Pretax Profit	Tax Rate	After-Tax Profit
P	(a)	35%	$1,300,000
Q	$5,000,000	(b)	3,200,000
R	1,900,000	29%	(c)

Required:

Find the missing amounts.

15. **Break-Even Point** *(LO 12.2)*

Wasabi Corp. has a contribution margin ratio of 45 percent. Product selling price per unit is $320, and total fixed costs per year are $2,385,360.

Required:

(a) Using the contribution margin ratio, what is the break-even point for Wasabi Corp.?

(b) What is the product's variable cost ratio? What is the product's total variable cost per unit?

(c) Use two different ways to calculate how many units Wasabi Corp. needs to sell to break even.

16. **CVP Analysis** *(LO 12.2)*

Cost-volume-profit analysis is used to analyze the relationship between revenues, variable costs, fixed costs, profits, and units produced.

Required:

For each of the following situations, calculate the missing items.

(a) Acme, Inc. sells its product for $45. The variable cost per unit is $24, and fixed costs are $1,672,500. What profit will Acme make if 225,000 units are produced and sold?

(b) Beta Co. can sell 140,000 units in one year. Variable costs are $130 per unit, and fixed costs are $4,040,000. How much should Beta sell its product for per unit if the company wants to make a pretax profit of $2,260,000?

(c) Capitol Enterprises sells 85,400 units in one year. The product has a contribution margin of $44, and fixed costs are $1,907,600. What is Capitol Enterprises' pretax profit?

(d) Denson, Inc. sells its product for $135. The product has a variable cost of $105 and fixed costs of $36,000,000. How many units should the company sell if it wants to earn pretax profits of $27,000,000?

(e) Edgar Co. has a tax rate of 35 percent. The company sells a product with an $18.50 contribution margin; fixed costs of $9,000,000 are incurred by the company annually. How many units should the company sell if it wants to earn after-tax profits of $3,325,000?

17. **Incremental Analysis** *(LO 12.2)*

Use the information from Exercise 15. Wasabi Corp. is currently selling 30,000 units per year and has a 35% tax rate.

Required:

(a) What is Wasabi Corp.'s current annual income after taxes?

(b) Management believes that increasing advertising costs by $150,000 will increase unit sales by 20 percent. What will be Wasabi Corp.'s new annual income if this change is made? Should the company make the change?

(c) Management believes that increasing the quality of the material used in the production process will increase the attractiveness of the product to purchasers. The higher-quality material will cost an additional $3 per unit. Wasabi's marketing department believes that using this material will not allow an increase in unit selling price, but by spending $45,000 on advertising to inform the public of the higher quality, sales volume should increase by 5 percent. What will be Wasabi Corp.'s new annual income if this change is made? Should the company make the change?

18. **Multiproduct CVP** *(LO 12.2)*

Lizbeth's Linens sells kitchen potholders and towels. The company generally sells two potholders for every three towels. Each potholder sells for $1.00 and has a $0.50 contribution margin. Each towel sells for $2.50 has a $1.50 contribution margin. Fixed costs for the company are $8,800 per month. The company has a tax rate of 25 percent.

Required:

(a) How much revenue is needed to break even each month? How many potholders and towels would this represent?

(b) How much revenue is needed to earn an annual after-tax profit of $40,500? How many "baskets" of potholders and towels is this?

(c) If the company sells the number of "baskets" determined in part (b), but did so by selling four towels for every two potholders, what would be the company's pretax profit (or loss)? Why is this amount not the desired $40,500?

(d) If the company sells the number of "baskets" determined in part (b), but did so by selling three potholders for every two towels, what would be the company's pretax profit (or loss)? Why is this amount not the desired $40,500?

19. **Graphical Approaches** *(LO 12.3)*

The break-even graph for Zalia Corp. follows.

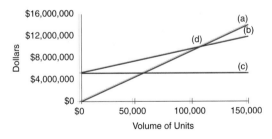

Required:

(a) What do the numbers on the *x*-axis (horizontal axis) represent?

(b) What do the lines (a), (b), and (c) represent?

(c) What is represented by point (d)?

(d) In approximate dollars, what is the value of the following?

   (1) Fixed costs

   (2) Variable cost per unit

   (3) Revenue per unit

   (4) Break-even point in units

   (5) Break-even point in dollars

   (6) Profit if 150,000 units are produced and sold

   (7) Total revenues if 50,000 units are produced and sold

   (8) Total variable costs if 100,000 units are produced and sold

20. **Margin of Safety; Degree of Operating Leverage** *(LO 12.4)*

Changing Times sells 185,000 bottles of TempeTingler nail polish each year. The product, which is very popular with teens, sells for $13 per bottle, and variable cost per unit is $5.50. Total annual fixed costs are $1,260,000.

Required:

(a) What is the margin of safety in units? In dollars?

(b) What is the degree of operating leverage?

(c) If the company can increase unit sales by 20 percent, what percentage increase will it experience in income? Prove your answer using an income statement.

(d) Use original data. If the company increases advertising by $65,000, sales in units will increase by 8 percent. What will be the new break-even point? The new degree of operating leverage?

PROBLEMS

21. **Break-Even Point** *(LO 12.2)*

Barkley, Inc. has the following revenue and cost information.

Revenue	$300 per consulting hour
Variable costs	$170 per consulting hour
Fixed costs	$93,600 per month

Required:

(a) What is the break-even point per month in consulting hours?

(b) What is the break-even point per month in revenue dollars?

(c)   If the average consulting engagement is 28 hours, how many consulting engagements per year will Barkley, Inc. need to break even?

(d)   Assume that Barkley, Inc. wants to earn $7,800 in profits each month and has a 25 percent tax rate. How many consulting hours does the company need to work each month?

(e)   How might Barkley, Inc. decrease variable costs per consulting hour? Fixed costs per month?

(f)   Assume that Barkley, Inc. has decided to limit air travel by consultants. Instead the company will invest in a state-of-the-art satellite teleconferencing system. How will these decisions affect variable and fixed costs? What are the potential drawbacks of this decision?

22. CVP Analysis *(LO 12.2)*

S'No'Kones has the following cost structure.

Selling price per unit	$1.50
Variable cost per unit	$0.45
Fixed costs per month	$1,260

Required:

(a)   What is the break-even point for S'No'Kones?

(b)   If the owner wants to earn a monthly pretax profit of $1,200, how many units would need to be sold each month?

(c)   The owner wants to earn a pretax profit of $24,360 annually. The snow cone stand is only open five months of the year (May through September) and no fixed costs are incurred when the stand is not open. How many snow cones would need to be sold in total during those five months? If three months of the five generate 75 percent of the company sales, how many snow cones would need to be sold during those three months?

(d)   Recalculate your answer to part (c) assuming a tax rate of 20 percent and a desired after-tax profit of $24,360.

(e)   S'No'Kones is located in the panhandle of Florida. Discuss circumstances that might cause the BEP and CVP assumptions to be inaccurate.

23. CVP Analysis *(LO 12.2)*

Robbie's Ribs has the following sales and cost information.

Average number of pounds sold per year	39,750
Average selling price per pound of ribs	$11.50
Variable expenses per pound:	
Raw material	$3.70
Variable labor and overhead	$3.20

Annual fixed costs:	
Production expenses	$37,300
Selling & administrative expenses	$15,186

The company's tax rate is 30 percent. The company's costs have slowly been rising and profits rapidly falling. Robbie Shaw, company president, has asked your help in answering the following questions.

Required:

(a)   What is the contribution margin per pound of ribs? The contribution margin ratio?

(b)   What is the break-even point in pounds of ribs? In dollars?

(c)   How much revenue must be generated to produce $39,974 of pretax income? How many pounds of ribs would this level of revenue represent?

(d)   How much revenue must be generated to produce $24,500 of after-tax income? How many pounds of ribs would this represent?

(e)   A restaurant has contacted Shaw about buying 15,000 pounds of ribs per year. Shaw has the capacity to do this, is interested in taking advantage of this opportunity, and wants to generate an after-tax profit on his total sales of $120,000. To make this profit, how much should he charge the restaurant per pound of ribs? (Round to the nearest penny.) Prepare an income statement proof of your answer.

(f)   Use original data. Shaw believes that he can raise the selling price per pound of ribs by $3, but he expects this would cause a 5,000-pound decline in ribs sold. Should he make this change?

(g)   Shaw wants to lease a new heavy-duty smoker; this action will cause his fixed costs to increase by $12,000 per year. If he makes this change, as well as the price change discussed in part (f), what will be his new break-even point in pounds of ribs and dollars of sales?

24. CVP and Incremental Analysis *(LO 12.2 and 12.4)*

Each unit of product made by Jeremy, Inc. sells for $120. The company has an annual production and sales volume of 35,000 units. Costs per unit are as follows:

Direct material	$27.00
Direct labor	9.00
Variable overhead	3.60
Variable selling expenses	12.60
Total variable cost	$52.20

Total fixed costs are $1,830,600 per year.

Required:

(a) Calculate the contribution margin and contribution margin ratio for the product.

(b) Determine the break-even point in units.

(c) Calculate the break-even point in dollars using the contribution margin ratio.

(d) Determine Jeremy, Inc.'s margin of safety in units and sales dollars, as well as a percentage.

(e) Compute Jeremy, Inc.'s degree of operating leverage. If sales increase by 20 percent, by what percentage would pretax income increase?

(f) Use original data. How many units would Jeremy need to sell to break even if fixed costs increase by $94,920?

(g) Use original data. How many units must be sold for Jeremy, Inc. to earn $339,000 after-tax if the company has a 25 percent tax rate?

(h) Quanta Corp. has offered to buy 15,000 units from Jeremy, Inc. The variable cost per unit in this sale would increase by $4.50 because of special shipping and packaging. Fixed costs for this sale would be $9,000. Additionally, Jeremy, Inc. will need to pay a 10 percent commission on selling price to the manager who brought in the offer. This sale would not affect other sales or their costs. If Jeremy, Inc. wants pretax income from this sale to be $11,250, at what price should the units be sold? Prove your answer using an income statement for these 15,000 units.

25. **Multiproduct CVP** (LO 12.3)

Salida LLP provides two kinds of services to clients: telephone answering and billing. Because Salida's clients for each type of service are approximately the same size, the company has standardized fees for its services: $3,600 per month for telephone answering and $5,000 per month for billing. The company has three telephone clients for every two billing clients. Variable costs of the services are $2,160 for telephone clients and $3,810 for billing clients. Fixed costs are $2,345,000 per year.

Required:

(a) How many telephone clients and billing clients are needed to break even each year?

(b) If Salida LLP has a tax rate of 35 percent, how many telephone clients and billing clients are needed to earn an after-tax income of $217,750?

(c) Salida LLP currently has 2,460 telephone answering clients and 1,640 billing clients. What is Salida's pretax income? The company is considering lowering fees for telephone answering and billing clients to $3,200 and $4,400, respectively. If this change is made and no new clients are added, how many dollars of fixed costs can the company incur and still maintain the same pretax income as is currently being generated?

(d) Use original data. Salida LLP is considering raising the fee for billing clients to $6,350. If this increase were made, the telephone answering to billing client ratio would decline to 3:1. How many telephone clients and billing clients would be needed to break even each year if fixed costs do not change?

(e) What circumstances might affect Salida's ability to use the current financial data to calculate BEP or other CVP factors over the next three years?

26. **Graphic Approaches** (LO 12.4)

The Philadelphia Phenoms is a private club. The following fee and cost information for the club is available: monthly membership fee per person, $140; monthly variable cost per person, $88; monthly fixed cost, $4,940. Members provide the majority of services and supplies for the club. The club currently has 120 members, and its cash balance has been declining for the past year.

Required:

(a) Prepare a break-even graph for Philadelphia Phenoms.

(b) Prepare a profit-volume graph for Philadelphia Phenoms.

(c) If you were giving a talk to the membership to get members to understand the need for an increase in membership fees, which of the two graphs would you want to show, and why?

CASES

27. **Relevant Range** (LO 12.1, writing)

Whitney Enterprises sells embossed cookbooks that contain not only recipes but also color photography of the food and local scenery. In 2008, Whitney sold 50,000 books for $80 per set. In 2008, the costs to manufacture those sets included the following:

Variable cost per book:	
Paper	$10
Cover and internal art	18
Direct labor	5
Variable overhead	12
Fixed overhead	$1,250,000

In 2009, Whitney received a 10 percent discount on paper, cover material, and ink because of the volume of those items that were purchased. Because of the increased use of the Internet to obtain recipes, sales are expected to decrease in future years. The decrease in sales will require a decrease in production.

Required:

(a) Calculate Whitney's pretax profit in 2008 using CVP analysis.

(b) Calculate Whitney's pretax profit for 2009 if both total variable cost increases by 15 percent and sales volume decreases by 10 percent.

(c) Calculate Whitney's pretax profit for 2009 if both total variable cost decreases by 20 percent and sales volume increases by 15 percent.

(d) Write a memo to Whitney's management discussing how variable and fixed costs might be decreased to compensate for the decrease in volume.

28. **Contribution Margin** *(LO 12.1 and 12.2, group)*
Identifying the similarities and differences in companies is crucial to understanding the nature of operations. Form groups of at least four students. Your group (or your instructor) should decide on a product that you could reasonably produce. (Don't try to be innovative; select something simple like a doghouse or bird feeder.)

Required—individual group members:

(a) Identify the costs associated with producing the product your group selected. Separate your list into variable and fixed costs.

(b) Go shopping. Try to find valid prices for the costs to manufacture one item.

(c) Can you find better prices if you produce 50 items? How about 100? Explain.

(d) Assuming that the contribution margin is $10 and labor is paid at a rate of $8 per hour, complete the following table.

	1 unit	50 units	100 units
Revenue per item			
Variable costs per unit			
List variable costs here			
Contribution margin	$10	$500	$1,000

Required—groups:

(a) Compare your results with your group members. Identify a complete list of variable costs.

(b) Prepare the table again, as in part (d), using the lowest costs found by each group member.

(c) Are there significant savings per unit if you can produce 50 or 100 as compared to one item? How would such savings affect the assumptions underlying BEP and CVP analysis?

SUPPLEMENTAL PROBLEMS

29. **CVP Analysis** *(LO 12.2; Compare to Problems 22 and 23)*
The Sleep-Over Kennel has a capacity of 50 animals and is open 360 days per year. Operating costs of the kennel are as follows:

Annual depreciation on the building	$18,000
Labor	$35,000 per year plus $2 per animal per day
Food	$3 per animal per day
Utilities	$15,000 per year plus $0.25 per animal per day
Other (including advertising)	$22,000 per year plus $0.50 per animal per day

Required:

(a) The kennel has an average annual occupancy rate of 80 percent. Determine the minimum daily charge that must be assessed per animal per day to break even.

(b) The kennel's tax rate is 25 percent. What must the charge per pet per day be to earn an after-tax income of $38,400? (Round to the nearest dollar.)

(c) The kennel typically has a 1:9 cat-to-dog proportional occupancy. If cat owners are charged $15 per day, what do dog owners need to be charged per day to earn an annual aftertax income of $42,000? (Round to the nearest dollar and show proof of your answer.)

(d) The kennel's owners are considering renovating the kennel area to provide more spacious private rooms for the dog "guests." The renovation will cost approximately $12,000 and will decrease the number of possible occupants to 30 per day. Cats will still make up 10% of the kennel's clientele and will be charged $15 per day. What will the kennel now need to charge per dog per day to cover the cost of renovations and still earn an after-tax income of $42,000? (Round to the nearest dollar. Ignore depreciation on renovations.)

(e) The kennel is considering adding a dog obedience school to the kennel services. Costs of the school have been estimated at $3,680 per year for the trainer plus $8 per dog. Kennel owners are planning to charge $40 per dog to attend obedience school, and they want to earn a pretax profit of $8,000 on the school. How many dogs need to attend the school to earn the desired profit?

30. **Multiproduct CVP** *(LO 12.2; Compare to Problem 25)*

Sandford, Inc. makes three types of products: ties, blouses, and shirts. The following selling prices and variable costs are expected for 2009.

	Ties	Blouses	Shirts
Selling price	$18.50	$43.00	$40.00
Direct material	5.30	8.95	11.80
Direct labor	2.80	5.40	7.80
Variable overhead	2.00	4.15	5.75
Variable selling expenses	1.50	3.25	5.00
Variable administrative expenses	1.20	2.10	3.30

In addition, fixed costs are as follows:

Fixed overhead	$920,000
Fixed selling expenses	150,000
Fixed administrative expenses	174,100

The company expects to have the following sales mix: two ties, three blouses, and one shirt.

Required:

(a) Which product is the most profitable? Which is the least profitable? Does this make sense to you? Explain.

(b) What is the expected break-even point for 2009?

(c) How many units of each product are expected to be sold at the break-even point?

(d) Assume that the company desires a pretax profit of $1,010,360. How many units of each product would need to be sold to generate this profit level? How much revenue in total would be required?

(e) Sandford, Inc. wants to earn $806,000 after-tax, with a tax rate of 35 percent. Use the contribution margin ratio to determine the revenue needed (round to the nearest dollar).

(f) If Sandford, Inc. earns the revenue determined in part (d), what is the company's margin of safety in dollars and as a percentage?

31. **Graphic Approaches** *(LO 12.3; Compare to Problem 26)*

Koontz, Ltd. had the following income statement for 2009:

Sales (30,000 gallons @ $14)		$420,000
Variable Costs		
Production (30,000 gallons @ $6)	$180,000	
Selling (30,000 gallons @ $0.50)	15,000	(195,000)
Contribution margin		$225,000
Fixed costs		
Production	$ 52,500	
Selling and Administrative	64,000	(116,500)
Income before Taxes		$108,500

Required:

(a) Prepare a break-even graph for Koontz, Ltd.

(b) Prepare a profit-volume graph for Koontz, Ltd.

(c) Prepare a short explanation for company management about each of the graphs.

CHAPTER 13

The Master Budget and Standard Costing

LEARNING OBJECTIVES

1. Assess the importance of budgeting.
2. Prepare a master budget.
3. Discuss the uses of a rolling budget.
4. Explain how standard costs are used in preparing budgets and assessing responsibility.
5. Calculate material and labor variances for purposes of control and performance evaluation.

INTRODUCTION

Organizations must plan for the future, and those plans should include both narrative descriptions and monetary indications of organizational goals. The process of **budgeting** is the interpretation of future plans into monetary amounts so that progress toward organizational goals can be determined. The end result of the budgeting process is a **budget** or financial plan for the future. At specified times during the budget period, budgeted and actual amounts are compared to determine differences (**variances**), which indicate a positive or negative goal achievement and can help pinpoint responsibility, relative to those goals, to organizational units and managers.

THE BUDGETING PROCESS

Budgeting is a critical activity for all organizations, but no single budgeting process is appropriate for all organizations. In small organizations, good budgeting can mean the difference between staying in business and going bankrupt. In large organizations, budgeting is important to allocate resources to the many available projects and operating activities.

The budgeting process requires that information and assumptions about the organization's operating environment be considered when planning future activities. Additionally, the budgeting process should involve people and ideas from throughout the organization. At one extreme of the budgeting process, top management prepares the budget with little or no input from subordinates. Budgets are imposed on lower-level personnel, who must perform their operating activities in conformity with the budgets. At the other extreme, there is total coordination and cooperation between top management and lower-level employees, with employees participating fully in budget development. Most commonly, the budgeting process falls somewhere between these extremes. It is common for organizational budgets to be prepared using a coordinated approach of gathering input from subordinates and having revisions made by top management.

Regardless of who is involved or to what extent, the financial budgeting process traditionally converts narrative organizational goals into monetary amounts, beginning with a revenue estimate for sales or, in a service organization, fees. In a not-for-profit entity, the starting point may be contributions or funding levels. From there, the process employs information on all organizational resources, such as materials, personnel, overhead, cash, and plant assets. The result is called a **master budget**, which is a comprehensive set of budgets, budgetary schedules, and **pro forma** (projected) **financial statements**.

THE MASTER BUDGET

The master budget is generally prepared for the company's fiscal year and is based on a single revenue level. Although budgeting software has made it easier for master budgets to be prepared at numerous revenue levels, a single level must be selected so that actual operating activities can be compared against it to assess organizational performance.

The master budget begins with annual sales estimates of the types, quantities, and timing of demand for products; this information is then subdivided into quarterly and monthly periods. The sales level chosen affects all other organizational components. For example, the number of units to be sold directly affects the number of units to be produced, which in turn directly affects the quantity of material to be purchased, labor force to be hired, and space to be acquired. Sales estimates and the expected accounts receivable collection pattern are used to determine the amounts and timing of cash receipts. Sales information also allows the types, quantities, and timing of product production to be specified.

Coordinating this information with estimated cash payment patterns for material and labor indicates the amount and timing of some large cash outflows. Thus, because of such interrelationships, all master budget components must be coordinated. As indicated in Visual Recap 13.1, one department's budget is often essential to the development of another department's budget.

Preparing a Master Budget

Preparation of a master budget is illustrated using information on Fast-Food Funthings, a small company that has been in business for one year. The company produces small plastic toys as giveaways for fast-food restaurants. It is in the process of preparing its 2010 budget

VISUAL RECAP 13.1

Flow of Budgeted Information through the Master Budget

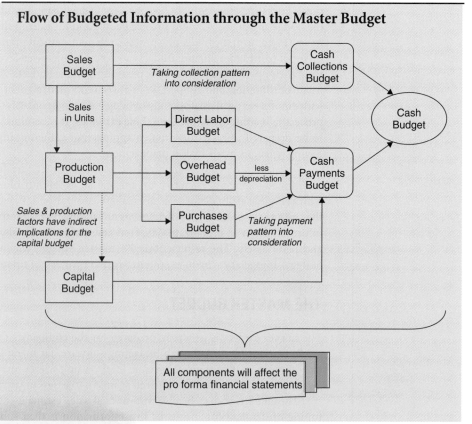

EXHIBIT 13-1

Fast-Food Funthings
Projected Balance
Sheet December 31,
2009

Fast-Food Funthings
Projected Balance Sheet
December 31, 2009

ASSETS

Cash		$ 5,000
Accounts Receivable		123,200
Inventories		
Direct Material (175,500 ounces*)	$ 8,775	
Finished Goods (40,000 units)	30,000	38,775
Property, Plant & Equipment	$200,000	
Accumulated Depreciation	(60,000)	140,000
Total Assets		$306,975

LIABILTIES & STOCKHOLDERS' EQUITY

Accounts Payable		$ 42,000
Dividends Payable (due in January 2010)		25,000
Common Stock	$160,000	
Retained Earnings	79,975	239,975
Total Liabilities & Stockholders' Equity		$306,975

*This quantity of plastic is the amount needed to produce 58,500 units (3 ounces per unit); each ounce of plastic costs $0.05.

and has estimated total annual sales for that year at 3,900,000 units. For convenience, this illustration will focus only on the budgets for the first quarter of 2010.

Exhibit 13-1 provides the company's December 31, 2009, balance sheet, which is needed to begin preparing the master budget. Projected balances are used for year-end balances because the 2010 budget process must begin significantly before December 31, 2009. The time needed by an organization to prepare a budget depends on factors such as size and level of employee participation. Larger organizations and higher employee participation translate into longer budget preparation periods.

Sales Budget

The sales budget is prepared in both units and dollars. Estimated sales in units is multiplied by the selling price per item; in the case of Fast-Food Funthings, each toy sells for $2. Exhibit 13-2 shows monthly sales for the first quarter of 2010 (each month and a quarter total); April and May data are included because some parts of the March budget require the following months' information.

EXHIBIT 13-2

Fast-Food Funthings
Sales Budget

	January	February	March	Quarter	April	May
Sales in units	400,000	300,000	180,000	880,000	100,000	140,000
Unit sales price	×$2	×$2	×$2	×$2	×$2	×$2
Total sales	$800,000	$600,000	$360,000	$1,760,000	$200,000	$280,000

Production Budget

The production budget is used to calculate how many items need to be manufactured in a particular period. Units to be sold are the starting point of the production budget. In addition, information on beginning inventory and desired ending inventory quantities is needed. Desired ending inventory generally depends on demand in the upcoming period in relation to ability to produce. Management may require that ending inventory be a specific percentage of the next period's projected sales or be a constant amount. Alternatively, inventory may be increased to compensate for future high-demand periods (such as the Christmas season in the toy industry) or be maintained at a near-zero level in a just-in-time inventory system.

Fast-Food Funthings has a policy that ending finished goods inventory will be 10 percent of the next month's sales level. Given this policy and sales information (Exhibit 13-2), the production budget shown in Exhibit 13-3 is prepared. Because the company wants to begin each month with some inventory, desired ending inventory is added to sales each month to determine the total number of units needed for the month. All these units do not, however, have to be produced during the month because some are already in beginning inventory.

Note that the estimated December 31, 2009, ending inventory balance is 40,000 units, which represents 10 percent of January 2010's estimated sales of 400,000 units. The desired ending inventory in any month is used as the beginning inventory in the following month. Desired March ending inventory is 10 percent of April sales of 100,000. For simplicity, it is assumed that Fast-Food Funthings completes all units placed into production during a month by the end of that month and, therefore, does not have any Work-In-Process inventory.

Purchases Budget

The purchases budget is prepared to determine quantities of raw material to buy to complete the budgeted production, given the quantities of material in the beginning and ending Direct Material Inventory. Fast-Food Funthings must buy enough material each period to meet production needs and be in conformity with the company's desired ending inventory policies. Company policy for direct material is that the ending inventory level be maintained at 15 percent of the quantity needed for the following month's production.

The purchases budget is first stated as units of finished product. It is then converted to direct material component requirements and dollar amounts. A Fast-Food Funthings

EXHIBIT 13-3

Fast-Food Funthings Production Budget

	January	February	March	Quarter	April	May
Sales in units	400,000	300,000	180,000	880,000	100,000	140,000
Desired EI (10%)*	30,000	18,000	10,000	10,000	14,000	20,000
Total needed	430,000	318,000	190,000	890,000	114,000	160,000
BI units	(40,000)**	(30,000)	(18,000)	(40,000)	(10,000)	(14,000)
Production in units	390,000	288,000	172,000	850,000	104,000	146,000

*Assume that June's sales are projected at 200,000 units.
**From Exhibit 13-1

Fast-Food Funthings
Purchases Budget

	January	February	March	Quarter	April
Production in units	390,000	288,000	172,000	850,000	104,000
Ounces per unit	×3	×3	×3	×3	×3
Total ounces needed	1,170,000	864,000	516,000	2,550,000	312,000
Desired EI (15%)	129,600	77,400	46,800	46,800	
BI	(175,500)*	(129,600)	(77,400)	(175,500)	
Total ounces to purchase	1,124,100	811,800	485,400	2,421,300	
Cost per ounce	×$0.05	×$0.05	×$0.05	×$0.05	
Total cost of plastic	$ 56,205	$40,590	$24,270	$ 121,065	

*From Exhibit 13-1

toy requires three ounces of plastic that costs $0.05 per ounce. Exhibit 13-4 provides the purchases budget for Fast-Food Funthings for each month of the first quarter of 2010. Note that beginning and ending inventory quantities are expressed first in terms of finished product (toys), and then converted to the appropriate quantity measure (ounces of plastic). If the product requires more than one raw material, a separate purchase budget is produced for each.

Direct Labor Budget

Given expected production, direct labor requirements are calculated on the direct labor budget. Labor needs are stated in total number of people, specific number of skilled and unskilled laborers, and labor hours needed. Total labor cost is calculated from union labor contracts, minimum wage laws, fringe benefit costs, and payroll taxes.

The direct labor budget begins by converting the number of units to produce (from the production budget) to direct labor hours (DLHs). Direct labor cost is found by multiplying DLHs by the cost per labor hour. Assuming that all direct labor workers are paid the same wage per hour, the direct labor budget is shown in Exhibit 13-5. All compensation is paid in cash in the month in which it is incurred.

Overhead Budget

The overhead budget is used to compute overhead costs for budgeted production levels. Companies typically prepare a production overhead budget and a separate selling and administrative budget; however, Fast-Food Funthings has chosen to combine these two budgets into a single overhead budget (Exhibit 13-6).

Fast-Food Funthings
Direct Labor Budget

	January	February	March	Quarter
Production in units	390,000	288,000	172,000	850,000
DL hours needed per unit	×0.01	×0.01	×0.01	×0.01
Total DL hours needed	3,900	2,880	1,720	8,500
DL wage rate per hour	×$9	×$9	×$9	×$9
Total DL cost (cash)	$35,100	$25,920	$15,480	$76,500

EXHIBIT 13-6

Fast-Food Funthings
Overhead Budget

	January	February	March	Quarter
Production in units	390,000	288,000	172,000	850,000
Total OH cost per unit (all cash)	×$0.565	×$0.565	×$0.565	×$0.565
Total production OH	$220,350	$162,720	$ 97,180	$ 480,250
Total sales (Ex. 13-2)	$800,000	$600,000	$360,000	$1,760,000
Variable commission rate	×0.05	×0.05	×0.05	×0.05
Variable commission cost	$ 40,000	$ 30,000	$ 18,000	$ 88,000
Fixed salesperson salary cost	14,000	14,000	14,000	42,000
Fixed administrative salary cost	25,000	25,000	25,000	75,000
Fixed depreciation expense	5,000	5,000	5,000	15,000
Total S&A cost	$ 84,000	$ 74,000	$ 62,000	$ 220,000
Total production OH	$220,350	$162,720	$ 97,180	$ 480,250
Total S&A cost	84,000	74,000	62,000	220,000
Total OH & S&A cost	$304,350	$236,720	$159,180	$ 700,250
Total OH & S&A cash cost	$299,350	$231,720	$154,180	$ 685,250

Assume that Fast-Food Funthings has only variable production overhead costs, which are incurred for hourly paid indirect labor personnel, electricity on a per kWh basis, and equipment lease rates paid for each hour of use. For 2010, the overhead cost is $0.565 for each unit of production.

Selling and administrative expenses are budgeted similarly to overhead costs except that the sales, rather than the production, level is the activity driver for this budget. Company salespeople are paid a total of $14,000 salary per month plus 5 percent commission on sales. Administrative salaries total $25,000 per month. Depreciation on selling and administrative equipment totals $5,000 per month. Depreciation is the only noncash cost incurred by Fast-Food Funthings.

Capital Budget

If the company plans to make any purchases of plant assets during the master budget period, those amounts are included in a **capital budget**. Exhibit 13-7 shows that Fast-Food Funthings has decided to buy $100,000 of equipment in February 2010. Eighty percent of this purchase will be paid for in February and the remainder in March. The company will not begin using the equipment until April 2010, after all workers have completed proper training. Thus, overhead will not change by any additional equipment depreciation in either February or March 2010.

EXHIBIT 13-7

Fast-Food Funthings
Overhead Capital
Budget

	January	February	March	Quarter
Purchase of PP&E	$0	$100,000	$ 0	$100,000
Cash payments for PP&E	$0	$ 80,000	$20,000	$100,000

Cash Budget

After all the preceding budgets have been developed, a cash budget can be constructed. However, the sales and purchases budgets must first be converted to a cash basis before the cash budget can be prepared.

Schedule of Cash Collections from Sales

The schedule of cash collections reflects the amount that will be collected in a month rather than the amount that was sold. The sales dollars shown in Exhibit 13-2 are stated on an accrual basis and need to be translated into cash information using an expected collection pattern. A collection pattern should be based on recent experiences with customers and, if necessary, can be adjusted for conditions that might change the current collection pattern. For example, changes that could improve current collection patterns include decreases in interest rates and stricter credit granting practices; deterioration of general economic conditions could cause customers to pay more slowly.

All Fast-Food Funthings customers buy on credit and receive no discounts for prompt payment. The company is very careful about granting customers credit and experiences no bad debt problems. Fast-Food Funthings' collection pattern stretches over three months: 30 percent of sales are collected in the month of sale, 60 percent of sales are collected in the month following the sale, and 10 percent of sales are collected in the second month following the sale. For example, Fast-Food Funthings expects to sell $800,000 in January on credit. Using the expected collection pattern, the company expects to collect cash for January sales of $240,000 (0.30 × $800,000) in January, $480,000 (0.60 × $800,000) in February, and $80,000 (0.10 × $800,000) in March.

Because cash collections extend over three months, there will be some collections in January and February 2010 from November and December 2009 sales. Using November and December 2009 sales information and the expected collection pattern, management can estimate cash receipts from sales during the first three months of 2010. November and December sales were $168,000 and $152,000, respectively. Projected monthly first quarter collections are shown in Exhibit 13-8. Note that January and February collections for the remaining balances of November and December equals the $123,200 of Accounts Receivable shown in Exhibit 13-1's December 31, 2009, balance sheet. Additionally, 10 percent of February's sales ($600,000) and 70 percent of March's sales ($360,000), or a total of $312,000, remain in Accounts Receivable to be collected in the second quarter of the year.

If appropriate, the schedule of cash collections may also include provisions for discounts extended to customers for timely payments and provisions for uncollectible accounts receivable.

Schedule of Cash Payments for Purchases

The purchases information from Exhibit 13-3 can be translated into a schedule of cash payments using a cash payments pattern. Fast-Food Funthings buys all direct material on credit and pays for 20 percent of each month's purchases in the month of purchase and the remainder in the month after purchase. The company receives no cash discounts for prompt payment. Exhibit 13-9 provides the schedule of cash payments for purchases for the first quarter 2010. Note that the payment in January for the remaining balance of December

	January	February	March	Quarter
Collection of Nov. sales				
($168,000 × 10%)	$ 16,800			$ 16,800
Collection of Dec. sales				
($152,000 × 60%)	91,200			91,200
($152,000 × 10%)		$ 15,200		15,200
Collection of Jan. sales				
($800,000 × 30%)	240,000			240,000
($800,000 × 60%)		480,000		480,000
($800,000 × 10%)			$ 80,000	80,000
Collection of Feb. sales				
($600,000 × 30%)		180,000		180,000
($600,000 × 60%)			360,000	360,000
Collections of March sales				
($360,000 × 30%)			108,000	108,000
Total cash collections	$348,000	$675,200	$548,000	$1,571,200

purchases (assumed to be $52,500) equals the Accounts Payable shown in Exhibit 13-1's December 31, 2009, balance sheet. Additionally, 80 percent of March's purchases of $24,270 (or $19,416) remains in Accounts Payable to be collected in the second quarter of the year.

Comprehensive Cash Budget

Using the information shown in Exhibits 13-5 through 13-9, Fast-Food Funthings' cash budget (Exhibit 13-10) can be prepared. This company, like most, maintains a management-specified minimum cash balance in its cash account, which provides a "cushion" to compensate for uncertainty. The budgeting process provides only estimates; actual events of the budget period are not likely to be the same as those estimated. At the end of any monthly period, if Fast-Food Funthings does not have enough cash to

	January	February	March	Quarter
Payment for Dec. purchases				
($52,500 × 80%)	$42,000			$ 42,000
Payment for Jan. purchases				
($56,205 × 20%)	11,241			11,241
($56,205 × 80%)		$44,964		44,964
Payment for Feb. purchases				
($40,590 × 20%)		8,118		8,118
($40,590 × 80%)			$32,472	32,472
Payment for March purchases				
($24,270 × 20%)			4,854	4,854
Total payments for purchases	$53,241	$53,082	$37,326	$143,649

EXHIBIT 13-10

Fast-Food Funthings
Cash Budget

	January	February	March	Quarter
Beginning cash balance	$ 5,000	$ 5,309	$ 5,137	$ 5,000
Cash collections (Ex. 13-8)	348,000	675,200	548,000	1,571,200
Cash available	$353,000	$680,509	$553,137	$1,576,200
Cash paid for				
DL (Ex. 13-5)	(35,100)	(25,920)	(15,480)	(76,500)
Cash OH & S&A (Ex. 13-6)	(299,350)	(231,720)	(154,180)	(685,250)
Plant assets (Ex. 13-7)	0	(80,000)	(20,000)	(100,000)
Purchases (Ex. 13-9)	(53,241)	(53,082)	(37,326)	(143,649)
Pay dividends	(25,000)			(25,000)
Balance	$ (59,691)	$289,787	$326,151	$ 545,801
Borrow (repay)	65,000	(65,000)		
Sell (acquire) investments		(219,000)	(323,000)	(542,000)
Interest received (paid)		(650)*	2,190**	1,540
Ending cash balance	$ 5,309	$ 5,137	$ 5,341	$ 5,341

*Interest on borrowings repaid for one month: $65,000 × 0.01 = 650
**Interest on investment for one month: $219,000 × 0.01 = 2,190

meet its minimum balance (assumed to be $5,000), the company will have to borrow the necessary funds.

If more cash is available than the minimum balance, the company will invest the excess funds to earn a reasonable rate of return. For simplicity, it is assumed that any borrowings or investments are made in end-of-month $1,000 increments. Interest on company borrowing or investments is at a simple annual rate of 12 percent, or 1 percent per month. The interest charged or received is subtracted from or added to the company's cash account at month end.

Exhibit 13-10 indicates that Fast-Food Funthings expects a $59,691 negative cash balance in January, without considering the $5,000 desired minimum balance. Thus, the company needs to borrow $65,000. However, in February, the company has significantly more cash than is necessary to meet the minimum cash balance so the $65,000 plus interest can be repaid and the remaining $219,000 of "excess" funds can be invested. In March, additional funds are available for investment, and Fast-Food Funthings receives the interest earned for one month on February's investment. The company will need to cash over half of its short-term investments to pay the projected taxes payable when they are due. If funds are needed for the long-term, companies may issue stock or sell bonds rather than signing notes payable.

Budgeted Financial Statements

The last component of the master budget is the preparation of pro forma financial statements for the period. These statements indicate the financial results that will occur if all budget estimates and assumptions are correct. If the projected results are not acceptable, management can make necessary changes prior to the start of the budget period. For instance, if pro forma net income is perceived as unacceptable, management may (if possible) raise product selling prices or find ways to decrease costs.

Cost of Goods Manufactured Schedule

In a manufacturing company, this schedule must be prepared before Cost of Goods Sold can be determined for the income statement. Using information from previous budgets, the Fast-Food Funthings' budgeted cost of goods manufactured schedule is shown in Exhibit 13-11. Note: The only reason that cost of goods manufactured equals the period's total costs to be accounted for is that this example assumed there were no beginning or ending work in process inventories. Had work in process inventory existed, the computations would be more complex and are beyond the scope of this text.

Income Statement

Exhibit 13-12 presents the pro forma income statement for Fast-Food Funthings for the first quarter of 2010.

Balance Sheet

After completing the income statement, a pro forma balance sheet for March 31, 2010, can be prepared (Exhibit 13-13).

Statement of Cash Flows

The income statement, balance sheet, and cash budget information are used to prepare a Statement of Cash Flows (SCF). This statement (Exhibit 13-14) arranges cash flows into

EXHIBIT 13-11

Pro Forma Schedule of Cost of Goods Manufactured

Fast-Food Funthings
Pro Forma Schedule of Cost of Goods Manufactured
For the Quarter Ending March 31, 2010

Beginning Work in Process Inventory, 1/1/10		$ 0
Direct material used		
Beginning balance of DM Inventory (Ex. 13-1)	$ 8,775	
Purchases (Ex. 13-4)	121,065	
Ending balance of DM Inventory (Note A)	(2,340)	
Direct material used		127,500
Direct labor (Ex. 13-5)		76,500
Production overhead (Ex. 13-6)		480,250
Total costs to be accounted for		$684,250
Ending Work in Process Inventory, 3/31/10		(0)
Cost of Goods Manufactured (Note B)		$684,250

Note A:

Ending balance of DM in ounces (Ex. 13-4)	46,800
Cost per ounce	×$0.05
Cost of ending balance of DM	$ 2,340

Note B:

CGM ÷ Number of units manufactured = Cost per unit (Ex. 13-2)
$684,250 ÷ 850,000 = $0.805

EXHIBIT 13-12

Pro Forma Income
Statement

Fast-Food Funthings
Pro Forma Income Statement
For the Quarter Ending March 31, 2010

Sales (Ex. 13-2)		$1,760,000
Cost of Goods Sold		
Beginning Finished Goods Inventory (Ex. 13-1)	$ 30,000	
Cost of Goods Manufactured (Ex. 13-11)	684,250	
Ending Finished Goods Inventory (Note A)	(8,050)	(706,200)
Gross Margin		$1,053,800
Selling and Administrative (Ex. 13-6)		(220,000)
Other Revenues and Expenses		
Interest Revenue (Ex. 13-10)	$ 2,190	
Interest Expense (Ex. 13-10)	(650)	1,540
Income before Income Taxes		$ 835,340
Income Tax (assumed rate of 30%)		(250,602)
Net Income		$ 584,738

Note A:
Units in ending FG Inventory (Ex. 13-3) × Cost per unit (Ex. 13-11, Note B)
10,000 × $0.805 = $8,050

three areas of activity (operating, investing, and financing). As discussed in Chapter 10, on a long-run basis, the majority of a company's cash flows should be provided from its operating activities.

EXHIBIT 13-13

Pro Forma Balance
Sheet

Fast-Food Funthings
Pro Forma Balance Sheet
March 31, 2010

ASSETS

Cash (Ex. 13-10)		$ 5,341
Accounts Receivable [(10% × $600,000) + (70% × $360,000)]		312,000
Short-Term Investments (Ex. 13-10)		542,000
Inventories		
Direct Material (46,800 × $0.05) (Ex. 13-4)	$ 2,340	
Finished Goods (10,000 × $0.805) (Ex. 13-3)	8,050	10,390
Property, Plant & Equipment ($200,000 + $100,000)	$300,000	
Accumulated Depreciation ($60,000 + $15,000)	(75,000)	225,000
Total Assets		$1,094,731

LIABILTIES & STOCKHOLDERS' EQUITY

Accounts Payable ($24,270 × 80%)		$ 19,416
Taxes Payable (Ex. 13-12)		250,602
Common Stock (Ex. 13-1)	$160,000	
Retained Earnings ($79,975 + $584,738)	664,713	824,713
Total Liabilities & Stockholders' Equity		$1,094,731

Pro Forma Statement
of Cash Flows

Fast-Food Funthings
Pro Forma Statement of Cash Flows
For Quarter Ended March 31, 2010

Operating Activities		
Net Income (Ex. 13-12)		$584,738
+ Depreciation Expense (Ex. 13-6)		15,000
− Increase in Accounts Receivable ($312,000 − $123,200)		(188,800)
+ Decrease in Direct Material Inventory ($2,340 − $8,775)		6,435
+ Decrease in Finished Goods Inventory ($8,050 − $30,000)		21,950
− Decrease in Accounts Payable ($19,416 − $42,000)		(22,584)
+ Increase in Taxes Payable ($250,602 − $0)		250,602
Net cash inflow from operating activities		$667,341
Investing Activities		
Purchase of short-term investments (Ex. 13-10)	$(542,000)	
Purchase of PP&E (Ex. 13-7)	(100,000)	
Net cash outflow from investing activities		(642,000)
Financing Activities		
Issued short-term note payable	$ 65,000	
Repaid short-term note payable	(65,000)	
Paid dividend	(25,000)	
Net cash outflow from financing activities		(25,000)
Net decrease in cash		$ 341
Beginning cash balance		5,000
Ending cash balance		$ 5,341

THE ROLLING BUDGET

Many companies are finding that a static 12-month budget is not truly useful in today's dynamic business environment. These companies have instituted rolling (or continuous) budgets into their planning process. In general, a **rolling budget** is maintained on a continual 12-month cycle: as one month (or quarter) passes, another month (or quarter) is added to the budget. This process allows the company to continually have a 12-month planning cycle, and budgeting becomes an ongoing process, rather than something that is performed at year-end.

A rolling budget allows a company to adjust its expectations in response to changes in the business environment. Companies often find that their budgets become out of date soon after they have been prepared because of new business opportunities or changed economic circumstances. Also, managers often become complacent or frustrated with the budget, depending on whether they have met their budget figures or feel that the budgeted figures will be impossible to obtain in the "remaining" budget period. The rolling budget eliminates the artificial "cutoff" or end of the budget period and allows people to be more focused on goal achievement rather than budget achievement.

STANDARD COSTS

After the budget is adopted, managers must begin exercising control over operations. This phase includes making budget-to-actual comparisons, investigating the causes of differences between the budget and actual figures, determining and taking corrective action in the event of poor performance, and providing feedback to individuals working under the budget figures.

Many budget computations are based on standard costs, quantities, and times. For example, the estimated per-unit quantity of material used in the production budget is a standard. A **standard** is simply a norm or average. Standards are developed for both quantities and costs. A **standard cost** is the budgeted cost to make one unit of product (or perform one unit of service). Standards are developed from historical information and adapted for changed conditions as well as internal and external benchmarks.

At the end of the period, standard and actual costs are compared, and variances are calculated to indicate how well costs and quantities were controlled during the period. **Variance analysis** is the process of determining the standard-to-actual differences and assessing whether those differences are favorable or unfavorable. Variances are generally calculated for all components of product cost: material, labor, and overhead. The following discussion focuses on material and labor variances; the overhead variances reflect the underapplied or overapplied amounts discussed in Chapter 12.

Material Variances

Material variances indicate how close actual material usage and cost were to standard (or expected) material usage and cost. To calculate material variances, three costs are needed.

■   The actual cost of material equals the actual price (AP) paid per unit of material times the actual quantity (AQ) of material used.

■   The standard cost of the actual quantity of material equals the standard price (SP) per unit of material times the actual quantity of material used.

■   The standard cost of material equals the standard price per unit of material times the standard quantity (SQ) of material needed for the production activity that actually took place.

These costs are used to compute the three common material variances illustrated in Exhibit 13-15: material price variance, material quantity variance, and total material variance.

The **material price variance** (MPV) indicates the cost difference that arose because the amount paid for material was either below or above the standard price. The MPV is the difference between actual cost at actual quantity (AP × AQ) and standard price at actual quantity (SP × AQ). If total actual cost is larger than total expected cost for the amount purchased, the variance is unfavorable. If total actual cost is less, the variance is favorable.

The **material quantity variance** (MQV) indicates the cost difference that arose because the actual quantity used was either below or above the standard quantity allowed for the actual output. The MQV is calculated as the difference between standard cost of the actual quantity (SP × AQ) and standard cost of the standard quantity (SP × SQ). If the actual quantity is larger than the standard quantity, the variance is unfavorable because more

EXHIBIT 13-15

Material Variance
Calculations

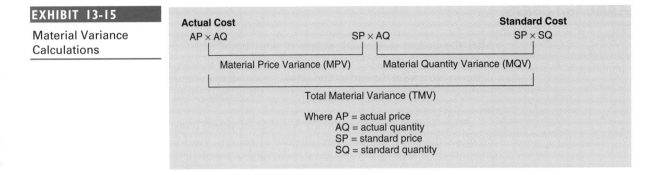

material was used than was expected to be used. If less material was used than was expected, the variance is favorable.

The total material variance (TMV) is the difference between total actual cost and total standard cost. If actual cost is lower than standard, the TMV is favorable; if actual cost is greater than standard, the TMV is unfavorable. The TMV can also be calculated as the sum of the material price and quantity variances.

Fast-Food Funthings information is used to illustrate these computations. Exhibit 13-3 indicates that January production should be 390,000 units. Each toy requires three ounces of plastic, and each ounce costs $0.05. Ignoring the purchase requirements previously stated, assume that, in January 2010, the company produces 390,000 toys, buys and uses 1,165,000 ounces of plastic, and pays $81,550 (or $0.07 per ounce) for the plastic. The standard cost of January's production is as follows: 390,000 toys × 3 ounces per toy × $0.05 per ounce = $58,500. The total material variance is $23,050 ($81,550 − $58,500). Because the actual cost is greater than the standard cost, the variance is unfavorable.

Two situations combined to cause the $23,050 unfavorable material variance. First, the company paid $0.02 per ounce more than standard for the plastic. Second, the company used less plastic than was required to produce the toys. The **standard quantity allowed** (SQA) translates the actual output of the period (390,000 toys) into the standard quantity of input that should have been needed to achieve that output. The SQA is 390,000 toys times three ounces of plastic or 1,170,000 ounces. Inserting the numbers into the model provides the following:

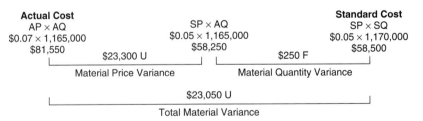

Thus, Fast-Food Funthings paid $23,300 above standard for the plastic but saved $250 because 5,000 fewer ounces of plastic were used than standard.

In most instances, a company does not purchase and use an equal quantity of material in a period. When differences in quantities occur, it is not possible to calculate a total material variance because the "actual quantity" used in the material price and in the material quantity variances are not the same as shown in Exhibit 13-16.

EXHIBIT 13-16

"Split" Material
Variance Calculations

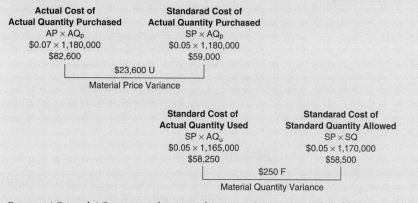

Assume that Fast-Food Funthings purchased 1,180,000 ounces of plastic in January 2010 at $0.07 per ounce, but only used 1,165,000 ounces of plastic in producing 390,000 toys. The following calculations are needed.

Because AQ_p and AQ_u are not the same, the two variances cannot be added to obtain a Total Material Variance.

Labor Variances

Labor variances are analyzed in a similar manner to material variances. The model for labor variances is shown in Exhibit 13-17.

The **labor rate variance** (LRV) shows the difference between actual wages paid and the standard wages allowed for all hours worked during the period. Multiplying the standard wage rate by the difference between the actual hours worked and the standard hours allowed for the production achieved results in the **labor efficiency variance** (LEV).

The January information from Exhibit 13-5 is used to illustrate these computations. According to this exhibit, production of 390,000 toys should require 3,900 direct labor hours; each worker is paid $9 per hour. Thus, the total standard cost for the production of 390,000 toys is $35,100. Assume that in January, 3,860 direct labor hours were worked, and because of contract renegotiations, hourly pay was raised to $9.10. Inserting these amounts into the model provides the following variance computations:

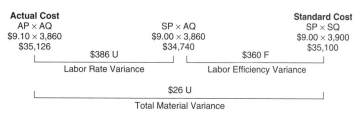

These calculations indicate that the company incurred an additional $386 above what was budgeted in direct labor cost for January because of the difference between the standard and actual pay rates. However, the direct labor workers were very efficient in the production process in January and the toys were produced in 20 hours less than what was expected, thereby saving the company $360 of budgeted cost. The total labor variance is only $26 unfavorable because the favorable and unfavorable variances were almost equal.

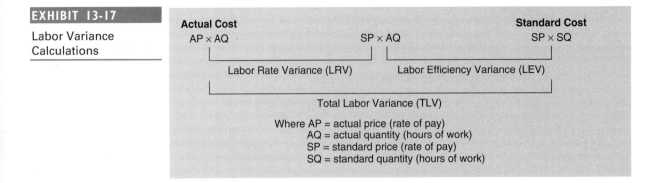

EXHIBIT 13-17

Labor Variance Calculations

Understanding Variances

It is important to note that an extremely large favorable variance is not necessarily a good variance. Such a variance could mean an error was made when the standard was set or that a related, offsetting unfavorable variance exists. For example, if low-quality material is purchased, a favorable price variance may result, but additional material may need to be used to overcome defective production. Additionally, an unfavorable labor efficiency variance could result because it took longer to complete a job because many defective units were produced using the inferior material. Another common "linked" variance situation begins with labor rather than material: the use of less-skilled, lower-paid workers will result in a favorable rate variance, but may cause excessive material usage. Managers must constantly be aware that relationships between and among variances exist and, thus, should not analyze variances in isolation.

In implementing control procedures, managers must recognize that their time is a scarce resource, so distinctions must be made between situations to ignore and those to investigate. The establishment of upper and lower limits of acceptable deviations often guides this distinction from standard. These tolerance limits for deviations allow managers to exercise **management by exception**. This technique lets managers take no action if a variance is small and within an acceptable range. However, if a variance is large, the manager responsible for the cost should determine why the variance occurred. Finding the cause(s) and taking corrective action (if possible or recommended) will allow future operations to adhere more closely to established standards.

Variances large enough to fall outside the management by exception acceptability ranges often indicate trouble. However, calculating a variance does not reveal the variance cause or the person or group responsible. To determine variance causes, managers must investigate significant variances through observation, inspection, and inquiry. Such investigations will involve the time and effort of operating and accounting personnel. Operating personnel should try to spot variances as they occur and record the reasons for the variances to the extent that they are discernible. For example, operating personnel could readily detect and report causes such as machine downtime or material spoilage.

SUMMARY

Budgeting refers to the monetary quantification of a company's plans. Managers may either impose budgets on subordinates or allow subordinate managers to participate in the budgeting process. Participation is generally useful because organizational departments interact with each other and one department's budget may be the basis of, or have an effect on, another department's budget.

A master budget is a complete set of budgetary projections that begins with a sales budget and ends with pro forma financial statements. The master budget is generally specified by months and quarters within the annual period. The primary budgets in a master budget are the sales budget, production budget (if a manufacturing company), purchases budget, direct labor budget, overhead (production and/or selling and administrative) budget, capital budget, and cash budget.

In preparing budgets, standards are used because they represent the norms for making one unit of product or performing one service activity. At the end of a period, budgeted costs (standards) are compared with actual costs to determine how well a company performed relative to cost control. A variance is any difference between an actual and a standard cost. A total variance is composed of price and quantity subvariances. For material, the subvariances are the price and quantity variances. For labor, the subvariances are the rate and efficiency variances. Variances must be designated as favorable (actual less than standard) or unfavorable (actual greater than standard).

KEY TERMS

budget	master budget	standard
budgeting	material price variance	standard cost
capital budget	material quantity variance	standard quantity allowed
labor efficiency variance	pro forma financial	variance
labor rate variance	statement	variance analysis
management by exception	rolling budget	

QUESTIONS

1. What is a budget, and why is it needed in a business? Is it more important for a large business or a small business to budget? Explain. *(LO 13.1)*

2. Who prepares a budget? Under what circumstances are lower-level employees involved in the budgetary process? What are the benefits of involving lower-level employees? *(LO 13.2)*

3. With what information does the budgeting process start? How does this information affect master budget components? *(LO 13.2)*

4. How are production and purchases budgets similar, and how do they differ? What type of organizations will use each of these budgets? *(LO 13.2)*

5. One of the younger workers in your production operations asks you, "Why do we have ending inventory at the end of the month? Why not just produce the exact quantity on the sales budget?" How do you respond to these questions?

6. Explain the purpose of adding desired ending inventory and subtracting beginning inventory to the production budget. How do the desired ending inventory and beginning inventory amounts on a production budget differ from the desired ending inventory and beginning inventory amounts on a purchases budget? *(LO 13.2)*

7. Why do production overhead and selling and administrative expenses need to be separated into their variable and fixed components for budgeting purposes? Why would production overhead costs need to be distinguished from selling and administrative expenses in the budgeting process? *(LO 13.2)*

8. Compare an organization's cash budget to your checking account. Include in your comparison a short discussion of minimum cash balances. What actions can an organization take if a cash shortage is expected to develop? What actions can you take if a cash shortage is expected to develop? What causes any differences in these actions? *(LO 13.1)*

9. Why does the master budget conclude with a presentation of pro forma financial statements? Will the amounts shown on pro forma financial statements be equal

to the amounts shown on actual financial statements at the end of the budget period? Why or why not? *(LO 13.2)*

10. What are the benefits of a rolling budget? Will the use of a rolling budget create more or less work for managers? Explain the rationale for your answer. *(LO 13.3)*

11. Why does a company use standard costs? How would standard costs be developed? *(LO 13.4)*

12. What is the difference between a material price variance and a material quantity variance? Can one occur without the other? What are some causes of material price and quantity variances? *(LO 13.5)*

13. You are the manager of a midsize restaurant. In making budget-to-actual comparisons this month, you find that there is a large favorable material price variance and a large unfavorable material quantity variance. Are you pleased with the individual who purchases your food items and disappointed with the chef? Explain. *(LO 13.5)*

14. List at least three reasons why a company might experience (1) a labor rate variance and (2) a labor efficiency variance. Will each of your explanations result in favorable or unfavorable variances? Explain. *(LO 13.5)*

15. What is management by exception? Why is this process useful? *(LO 13.5)*

EXERCISES

16. **True and False** *(All LOs)*

Following are a series of statements regarding topics discussed in this chapter.

(a) The production budget is used to determine how much raw material is needed to manufacture the units that will be sold in a month.

(b) If a company has no plans to purchase new equipment in the next year, the company should still prepare a capital budget.

(c) The cash payments budget is used only for cash disbursements related to purchases of raw material.

(d) A favorable total material variance is a positive indication that materials are being used efficiently.

(e) A flexible budget is prepared one month or one quarter at a time.

(f) A labor efficiency variance is the difference between (actual labor rate multiplied by actual labor quantity) and (actual labor rate multiplied by standard labor quantity).

(g) The direct labor budget should include the cost of all individuals working in the production area.

(h) A budget is the quantitative representation of a company's plans for the future.

(i) The order in which budgets are prepared is based on reverse chronological order.

(j) A company only produces one sales budget, production budget, and purchase budget for a product regardless of the number of units sold, units produced, or different raw materials required.

(k) If a company experiences a favorable material price variance, there will usually be a favorable material quantity variance.

(l) In preparing the production budget, beginning inventory units are added to, and desired ending inventory units are subtracted from, the units to be produced.

(m) Depreciation expense is included in the overhead budget and the pro forma income statement, but not in the cash budget.

(n) Both the cash collections and cash payments pattern for a company may include a percentage for amounts not paid.

Required:

Indicate whether each statement is true (T) or false (F).

17. **Sales Budget** *(LO 13.2)*

Warehouse Foods, Inc. expects to sell one million cases of flexible straws in 2010. Typically, Warehouse Foods has the following selling pattern: 7 percent of annual sales are made in January, February, May, and October; 11 percent in March and June; 12 percent in April and July; 8 percent in August and December, and 5 percent in September and November. In the first half of the year, a case is expected to sell for $7.50; in the last half of the year, a case is expected to sell for $7.60.

Required:

Prepare the sales budget for Warehouse Foods, Inc. for 2010. Include both a quarterly and yearly total.

18. **Production Budget** *(LO 13.2)*

The production budget for Ensinada Mfg. Co. for the second quarter of 2010 follows.

	April	May	June	Quarter
Sales in units	36,000	(1)	45,000	120,000
Desired ending inventory	(2)	6,750	6,300	(3)
Total needed	41,850	45,750	51,300	126,300
Beginning inventory	5,625	5,850	(4)	(5)
Budgeted units to produce	(6)	(7)	(8)	(9)

Required:

(a) Find the missing numbers represented by the numbers (1) through (9).

(b)   Was the ending inventory in March in conformity with company policy? Explain.

(c)   What is the budgeted amount of sales in July?

19. **Purchases Budget** *(LO 13.2)*

Ensinada Mfg. Co., from Exercise 18, produces candles that contain four raw materials: wax, dye, scented oil, and a wick. Each candle uses eight ounces of wax and one ounce of dye, which Ensinada purchases for $0.15 and $0.02 per ounce, respectively. Ensinada ends each month with enough wax to manufacture 10 percent of the following month's production needs; desired ending inventory for dye is 15 percent of the following month's production needs. Production for July is calculated at 41,775 units.

Required:

Prepare Ensinada's purchases budgets for wax and dye for each month of the second quarter and the total for the second quarter of 2010.

20. **Direct Labor Budget** *(LO 13.2)*

Ensinada Mfg. Co., from Exercises 18 and 19, estimates that an employee can make 20 candles per hour. Ensinada's employees are paid $9.50 per hour.

Required:

Prepare Ensinada's direct labor budget for each month of the second quarter and the total for the second quarter of 2010.

21. **Production and Purchases Budgets** *(LO 13.2)*

Sit Straight makes bookends. Metal is stamped and bent to form the bookend, and felt is glued to the bottom to keep the bookends from sliding on surfaces. Each set of bookends requires five ounces of metal ($0.20 per ounce) and two pieces of precut felt ($0.03 per 10 pieces). Sit Straight wants to have a desired ending inventory of 10 percent of the following month's sales needs relative to finished goods and 15 percent of the following production month's needs relative to direct materials. The company's 2010 second and third quarter sales budgets for sets of bookends follow.

April	May	June	July	August	September
25,000	20,000	38,000	35,000	40,000	21,000

Sit Straight expects to begin April with 2,400 sets of bookends, 18,500 ounces of metal, and 7,250 pieces of felt.

Required:

Prepare the production and purchases budgets for the second quarter of 2010.

22. **Cash Collections Budget** *(LO 13.2)*

Warehouse Foods, Inc. (from Exercise 17) makes 15 percent of sales for cash and the rest on credit. Of those sales made on credit, 60 percent are collected during the month of sale, 30 percent are collected during the following month, and the remaining 10 percent are collected two months after the sale.

Required:

Prepare Warehouse Foods, Inc.'s cash collections budget for the second quarter of 2010.

23. **Cash Collections Budget** *(LO 13.2)*

Management at Breaker Corp. expects an Accounts Receivable collection pattern of 80 percent in the month of sale, 15 percent in the month after sale, and 5 percent in the second month after sale. All sales are on credit and Breaker Corp. has rarely had any uncollectible Accounts Receivable. Actual sales for the last two months of 2009, and budgeted sales for the first quarter of 2010 follow:

November 2009	December 2009	January 2010	February 2010	March 2010
$680,000	$925,000	$864,000	$732,000	$788,000

Required:

Prepare Breaker Corp.'s cash collections budget for the first quarter of 2010.

24. **Cash Collections Pattern** *(LO 13.2)*

McNally Inc.'s sells 25% of its goods for cash and 75% on credit. The company's Accounts Receivable collection pattern is 70% in the month of sale, 20% in the month after sale, and 10% in the second month after sale. The Accounts Receivable balance at May 31 is $234,600, of which $170,400 represents the remainder of May's sales. There are no receivables prior to April. Total sales for June are expected to be $864,500.

Required:

(a)   What were total sales for April?

(b)   What were credit sales for May?

(c)   What are projected cash collections for June?

(d)   What is the projected Accounts Receivable balance at June 30?

25. **Material Variances** *(LO 13.4 and 13.5)*

For 2009, PMD Inc. had set the following standards for production of metal tables: 35 pounds of iron at a standard cost of $2.60 per pound. During June, the company produced 300 tables. The company bought 10,625 pounds of iron at a cost of $25,500.

Required:

(a)   What was the actual price per pound of the iron?

(b)   What is the standard quantity of material allowed for June's production?

(c)   Assume that all the iron purchased was used during June. What are the material price, quantity, and total material variances for June?

(d) Assume instead that the company purchased 12,500 pounds of iron during June at the actual price per pound computed in part (a), but only used 10,625 in the production of the 300 tables. What are the material price and quantity variances for June? Can a total material variance be computed? Explain.

(e) Who would normally be considered responsible for the material price variance? The material quantity variance? Would you assign responsibility differently if the material purchased in June were of lower-than-normal quality? Explain.

26. **Missing Information for Materials** *(LO 13.5)*

Standard and actual material information is given in the following table for four companies.

	Company A	Company B	Company C	Company D
Units produced	?	10,000	14,400	?
Standard quantity per unit	6 lbs.	24 oz.	? pts.	8 pieces
Standard quantity allowed	? lbs.	? lbs.	3,600 gals.	82,400 pieces
Standard cost per quantity	$12/lb.	$24/lb	$18/gal.	$?/piece
Actual quantity used	24,050 lbs.	15,100 lbs.	?	83,420 pieces
Actual material cost	$280,000	?	$60,000	$250,000
Material price variance	?	$3,700 F	?	?
Material quantity variance	$480 F	$2,400 U	$450 F	$3,009 U

Required:

For each company, calculate the missing figures. Assume that the quantity of material purchased is the same as the quantity of material used in each case.

27. **Labor Variances** *(LO 13.4 and 13.5)*

Imello & Havers, CPAs, set the following standards for the staff portion of an audit at a large client company: 350 hours at an average billing rate of $180 per hour. The firm's staff personnel actually worked 325 hours during the audit, and the client was billed $60,250.

Required:

(a) Compute the labor rate, efficiency, and total labor variances for the audit.

(b) What concerns might the partners at Imello & Havers, CPAs, have because fewer hours were worked than were budgeted?

28. **Missing Information for Labor** *(LO 13.4 and 13.5)*

Standard and actual labor information is given in the following table for four companies.

	Company A	Company B	Company C	Company D
Units produced	3,000	1,500	(g)	4,800
Standard hours per unit	6	(d)	10.5	5.1
Standard hours allowed	(a)	(e)	22,050	(j)
Standard rate per hour	$14	(f)	$12	$10.50
Actual hours worked	16,650	6,180	(h)	(k)
Actual labor cost	(b)	$44,499	$260,715	$257,420
Labor rate variance	$3,330 U	$1,857 U	$3,285 F	(l)
Labor efficiency variance	(c)	$828 F	(i)	$840 F

Required:

For each company, calculate the missing figures.

PROBLEMS

29. **Production Budget** *(LO 13.2)*

Projected unit sales for Astor Corp. for the last half of 2009 are

July	30,000	October	36,000
August	60,000	November	54,000
September	48,000	December	57,200

Finished goods inventory on June 30, 2009 is 7,400 units. The company tries to keep an ending inventory of 25 percent of the following month's expected sales.

Required:

Prepare a production budget for the third quarter 2009.

30. **Production and Purchases Budgets** *(LO 13.2)*

Gizzardi Company has projected the following sales of Product #431 for the first four months of 2010: January,

8,000 units; February, 7,600 units; March, 11,200 units; April, 5,800 units; and May, 6,100 units. Each unit of product requires two-and-a-half gallons of Material X and three pounds of Material Y. Expected beginning-of-the-year inventories for all items follow.

Product #431	1,680 units
Material X	5,800 gallons
Material Y	7,200 pounds

Gizzardi desires an ending inventory for Product #431 of 20 percent of the following month's sales and ending inventories for components X and Y of 30 percent of that month's production quantity needs. Material X costs $5.90 per gallon, and Material Y costs $3.75 per pound.

Required:

(a)   Prepare a production budget for Product #431.

(b)   Prepare purchases budgets for Materials X and Y.

31.   **Sales, Production, Purchases, and Direct Labor Budgets** *(LO 13.2)*

McKenzie's Complete Cook makes and sells mixers and bread makers. In November 2009, McKenzie's began the budgetary process. Project sales for 2010 are 60,000 mixers at $50 each and 40,000 bread makers at $120 each. Management gathered the following data to begin the 2010 budget process:

(a)   The following purchased components are needed to produce one unit of product:

Component	Mixer	Bread maker
Plastic housing	1 #531B @ $8	1 #648C @ $24
Motor	1 #KMU @ $15	1 #KBU @ $17.80
Beaters	2 #BU6 @ $2.20	4 #BU6 @ $2.20

(b)   Expected and desired inventories are as follows:

	Expected EI Dec. 31, 2009	Desired EI Dec. 31, 2010
Mixers	3,000	2,000
Bread makers	6,000	2,800
#531B plastic housings	500	700
#648C plastic housings	620	800
#KMU motors	1,100	2,400
#KBU motors	1,380	1,200
#BU6 beaters	5,000	4,000

(c)   Projected direct labor requirements for 2010 and rates are as follows:

Product	Class A labor ($10 per hour)	Class B labor ($12 per hour)
Mixer	1.3 hours per unit	1.5 hours per unit
Bread maker	1.6 hours per unit	2.2 hours per unit

Required:

(a)   Prepare sales budget (in dollars) for 2010.

(b)   Prepare a production budget (in units) for 2010.

(c)   Prepare a components purchases budget (in units and dollars) for 2010.

(d)   Prepare a direct labor budget (by class in hours and dollars) for 2010.

(e)   What types of items would be included in production overhead for this company?

(f)   The company is thinking of manufacturing its plastic housings rather than buying them from suppliers. What types of costs would such insourcing create? What types of costs would such insourcing eliminate? How would you suggest that company management assess such a decision?

32.   **Cash Collections** *(LO 13.2)*

Johnny Bard & Co. is developing its monthly cash budgets for the first quarter of 2010. The company has been in business since April 2008 and has experienced the following approximate cash flows: sales each month are 30 percent cash and 70 percent credit. Of the credit sales, 50 percent are paid for in the first month after the sale, 40 percent in the second month after sale, and 10 percent in the third month after sale. The company has almost no bad debts, and thus, these can be ignored. Total sales for the last three months of 2009 and expected total sales for the first three months of 2010 are as follows:

October	$720,000	January	$378,000
November	$480,000	February	$550,000
December	$1,040,000	March	$440,000

Required:

(a)   Prepare a monthly schedule of cash collections for Johnny Bard & Co. for the first quarter of 2010.

(b)   Calculate the expected Accounts Receivable balance at March 31, 2010.

(c)   In early February 2010, the company realized that cash inflows from sales and collections for the previous month were only $725,000, which was significantly less than the budgeted amount. What explanation could be offered for this situation?

33.   **Cash Collections** *(LO 13.2)* **chgd amts.**

The Accounts Receivable balance at January 1, 2010, for Formen Corp. was $512,100. Of that balance, $432,000 represents remaining Accounts Receivable from December billings. The normal collection pattern for the firm is 40 percent of billings in the month of sale, 45 percent in the month after sale, and 14 percent in the second month following sale. The remaining 1 percent of billings is uncollectible. January billings are expected to be $630,000.

Required:

(a)   What were November billings for the company?

(b)   What amount of December billings is expected to be uncollectible?

(c)   What are projected January 2010 cash collections for the company?

(d)   How can a company decrease the amount of uncollectible accounts it has? How, if at all, will these techniques impact the company's total dollars of revenue?

34. **Cash Budget** (LO 13.2)

Kalama-Rama's monthly sales are typically 20 percent for cash and 80 percent on credit. All cash sales are given a 2 percent discount. The company's credit A/R collections are in the following pattern: 80 percent in the month of sale, 18 percent in the month after sale, and 2 percent uncollectible.

Sales for December 2009 were $600,000, and projected total sales for the first four months of 2010 are January, $800,000; February, $700,000; March, $750,000; and April, $680,000. Kalama-Rama's average gross profit on sales is 30 percent.

Kalama-Rama buys inventory to meet the current month's sales demand and to meet a desired inventory policy of 25 percent of the following month's sales. All purchases are made on account, and the company pays for 60 percent of the goods purchased in the month of purchase and 40 percent in the month following the purchase.

Kalama-Rama has a monthly salary expense of $133,000, pays monthly utility bills of $78,500, pays $50,000 per month in building rent, incurs monthly depreciation charges of $3,500, and desires a $7,000 minimum cash balance. If necessary, the company can borrow funds at 12 percent per year or invest funds at 6 percent per year. Borrowings are assumed to be made on the first day of the month and investments on the last day of the month. Interest owed or earned is only accounted for when funds are paid or withdrawn. Borrowing and investments are made in even $1,000 amounts.

Required:

Prepare a cash budget for Kalama-Rama for January and February 2010, assuming that the January 1, 2010, cash balance is $7,125.

35. **Pro Forma Income Statement** (LO 13.2)

The income statement for the year ended December 31, 2009, for Chico Co. follows:

Sales (140,000 × $15)		$2,100,000
Cost of goods sold		
Direct material	$560,000	
Direct labor	350,000	
Overhead	122,500	(1,032,500)
Gross profit		$1,067,500
Expenses		
Selling	$120,000	
Administrative	150,000	(270,000)
Income before taxes		$ 797,500
Income taxes		(319,000)
Net income		$ 478,500

Sales volume in 2010 is expected to increase by 15 percent because of a 5 percent decrease in selling price. Material costs are expected to increase 7 percent, but labor costs are expected to decrease by 10 percent due to increased automation at the company. Overhead is applied to production based on a percentage of direct labor costs; this percentage will increase by 5 percent because of the newly installed automated equipment. Seventy percent of the selling expenses are variable; the remainder is fixed. All administrative costs are fixed and are expected to increase by 20 percent in 2010. The company's tax rate will not change.

Required:

(a) Prepare a pro forma income statement for the year ended December 31, 2010.

(b) If management wanted net income to be $636,000 in 2010, what would selling price per unit (rounded to the nearest cent) have to be at the new sales volume? Prepare a pro forma income statement to prove your answer.

36. **Comprehensive Master Budget** (LO 13.2)

Bobcat Paws produces maroon foam #1 hands to wave at athletic events. The company has asked you to prepare its 2010 master budget and has given you the following information.

■ Following is the company's estimated December 31, 2009 balance sheet.

Bobcat Paws
Balance Sheet
December 31, 2009

ASSETS

CURRENT ASSETS		
Cash		$ 10,200
Accounts Receivable		24,300
Raw Material Inv.		750
Finished Goods Inv.		1,460
Total Current Assets		$ 36,710
PLANT & EQUIPMENT		
Equipment	$425,000	
Acc. Depr.	(90,000)	335,000
Total Assets		$371,710

LIABILITIES & EQUITY

LIABILITIES		
Notes Payable		$ 25,000
Accounts Payable		4,200
Dividends Payable		25,000
Total Liabilities		$ 54,200

EQUITY

Common Stock	$230,000	
Paid-in Capital	20,000	
Retained Earnings	67,510	317,510
Total Liabilities & SE		$371,710

■ The selling price per "hand" is $12. Estimated sales of foam hands follow.

January	8,000
February	10,000
March	15,000
April	12,000
May	11,000

■ Seventy percent of sales are for cash. Of the remaining sales on credit, 25 percent is collected in the month of sale, and the remainder is collected in the month after the sale. Bobcat Paws expects no bad debts.

■ Each foam hand has the following direct material and direct labor standard quantities and costs:

Foam	$1.25 per sheet
1/10 hour of direct labor	$6.00 per hour

■ Variable overhead is applied to production at the rate of $12 per machine hour. It takes five minutes of machine time to make one foam hand. All variable overhead costs are paid in cash. Total annual fixed overhead of $360,000 is applied to production based on an expected annual capacity of 450,000 "hands." Fixed overhead is incurred evenly throughout the year and is paid in cash, except for $48,000 of depreciation.

■ All work in process is completed during the period.

■ Accounts Payable is only for raw material purchases. Sixty percent of purchases (rounded to the nearest dollar) are paid in the month of purchase, and the remainder are paid in the next month.

■ The dividend payable will be paid in February 2010.

■ A new piece of equipment costing $12,000 will be purchased on February 1, 2010. Eighty percent of the cost will be paid in February and 20 percent in March. The equipment will have no salvage value and has a useful life of three years. The equipment will not be put into use, and thus not be depreciated, until April 2010.

■ The note payable (due in 2011) has a 12 percent interest rate, and interest is paid at the end of each month. Because of a large prepayment penalty, the note cannot be paid early.

■ Bobcat Paws's management has set a minimum cash balance of $10,000. Investments and borrowings are made in even $1,000 amounts at the end of the month. Investments will earn one-half percent per month, deposited to the company's checking account at the end of each month.

■ The ending inventories of raw material and finished goods should be, respectively, 5 percent and 10 percent of the next month's needs. This situation is not true at the end of 2009, due to sales and production miscalculation.

■ Selling and administrative costs per month are as follows: salaries, $14,000; rent, $10,000; and utilities, $1,800. These costs are paid in cash as they are incurred.

■ The company's tax rate is 40 percent.

Required:

(a) What is the standard cost per foam hand? How many foam hands are in the beginning Finished Goods Inventory?

(b) How many sheets of foam are in the beginning Raw Material Inventory?

(c) Prepare a master budget for each month of the first quarter of 2010 and pro forma financial statements for the first quarter of 2010. Note that, in reference to fixed overhead, actual production for the quarter is not the same as expected production for the quarter.

37. **Direct Material Variances** *(LO 13.4 and 13.5)*

Conceal? Corp. makes sheer wraparound bathing suit cover-ups. During April 2009, the company purchased and used 7,560 yards of material at $7.50 per yard. Each cover-up requires 1.5 yards of material; the standard material cost is $7.30 per yard. During April, the company produced 5,000 cover-ups.

Required:

(a) What is the standard quantity of material allowed for the actual production?

(b)   Compute the material price and quantity variances.

(c)   Why might the actual price of a raw material be greater than the standard price set for the material? How might Conceal? Corp.'s management try to contain the cost of raw material?

38. **Direct Labor Variances** (LO 13.4 and 13.5)

Maison D'Orleans Department Store has two employees who wrap packages for customers. The standard time to wrap a package is five minutes. During November, the employees worked a total of 380 hours and wrapped 4,320 packages. The company's standard hourly wage rate is $9.00 per hour, but these employees were actually paid $9.10 per hour.

Required:

(a)   What are the standard hours allowed for the total packages wrapped?

(b)   Compute the labor rate and efficiency variances.

(c)   Provide some possible explanations for the variances.

39. **Direct Material and Direct Labor Variances** (LO 13.4 and 13.5)

Dauterive Co. manufactures wooden pen and pencil holders. The following material and labor standards have been set for one holder.

5 ounces of wood at $0.50 per ounce	$2.50
4 minutes of labor time at $9.00 per hour	0.60

During July, the company incurred the following costs to manufacture 46,800 holders.

14,250 pounds of wood at $8.30 per pound	$118,275
3,840 hours of labor time at $9.25 per hour	35,520

Required:

(a)   What is the standard quantity of material allowed for the actual production?

(b)   Compute the material price and quantity variances.

(c)   What are the standard hours of labor time allowed for the actual production?

(d)   Compute the labor rate and efficiency variances.

(e)   What relationship might exist between the material price variance and the material usage and labor efficiency variances?

(f)   What relationship might exist between the labor rate variance and the labor efficiency variance?

CASES

40. **Cash Budget** (LO 13.2)

Leroy Landry, the accountant for Louie's Laundry, unfortunately left the company's second quarter budget folded in his shirt pocket when his wife Lola washed his clothes. Finding bits of paper in the bottom of the washer, she tried piecing the scraps together. Some of the figures were still readable; others were blurred; and others just weren't there. All borrowings, repayments, and investments must be made in even $100 amounts and are made at the beginning of a month. Interest is paid on borrowings at 12 percent per year and earned on investments at 8 percent per year. Interest paid or received is directly taken out of, or deposited into, the company's checking account. The company has no investments at the beginning of April 2009; however, an outstanding bank loan of $200 was obtained in February 2009.

	April	May	June	Total
Beginning cash balance	$ 385	$ e	$ 346	$ r
Cash collections	2,750	f	1	s
Total cash available	$ a	$4,548	$ m	$11,065
Cash payments for				
Supplies	$ 890	$ g	$ 880	$ 2,430

Labor	b	1,525	1,550	t
Other	970	h	895	u
Total payments	$3,290	$ i	$ n	$ 9,720
Cash available (short)	$ c	$1,443	$ 741	$ v
Borrow (repay)	500	(700)	o	w
Sell (buy) investments	0	j	(400)	x
Interest received (paid)	(7)	3	p	y
Ending cash balance (minimum $300)	$ d	$ k	$ q	$ 347

Required:

Complete the missing numbers on the cash budget.

41. **Budgeted Financial Statements** (LO 13.2, writing, ethics)

Withers Breaux Corp. is a manufacturing company that produces grooming appliances such as hair dryers and curling irons. The managers of each division prepare a master budget, but Withers Breaux does not require budgeted financial statements.

Required:

Write a memo to Withers Breaux's upper management explaining why budgeted financial statements are important. Include in your memo a discussion of the potential for misleading budgets that do not contain pro forma financial statements.

42. **Budget Slack** (*LO 13.2 and 13.5, writing, ethics*)

Many times, allowing employees to participate in the budgeting process creates an unpleasant side effect: budget slack. Budget slack occurs when revenue estimates are understated and expense estimates are overstated so that, when the actual results are known, it appears that employees did a great job in generating sales or controlling costs.

You are the restaurant manager in a medium-size hotel in a city that is extremely popular with tourists. The CEO of the hotel has asked his upper-level managers to prepare budgets for their areas for the upcoming year. Your friend, the manager in charge of group sales, has decided to reduce his expected projections of events and revenues by 15 percent in preparing his budget. His reasoning is that he receives a year-end bonus of $1,000 for every one percentage point above budget that his actual revenues are.

Required:

(a) Write a memo to your friend explaining how his understatement of expected revenues will affect the budget that you will be preparing.

(b) Write a memo to the CEO addressing some of the problems with the current bonus system. Do not implicate your friend in any way or address his budget behavior in this memo.

(c) For what types of material, labor prices, and quantities would you be able to develop standards for in preparing your budget for the CEO?

43. **Starting a Business** (*LO 13.2, group*)

Part of starting a business is preparing a budget for the first quarter or year of operations. The budget should help determine if the idea is feasible, how much start-up money will be needed, and whether the effort and time is worth it. Form groups of four students and decide on a small manufacturing business you can start. Try to select a product to manufacture (such as T-shirts, buttons, or cookies) that will not require several different pieces or expensive machinery.

Required—Individuals:

(a) Research your idea. Find prices for the raw materials and determine what labor and overhead costs will be associated with manufacturing different amounts of the product.

Required—Groups:

(b) Get together as a group and combine your research. Compile an entire list of raw materials and other costs.

(c) Based on the costs, set a selling price for your product.

(d) Prepare the following budget for the first quarter of operations:

   (1) A sales budget

   (2) A production budget

   (3) A purchases budget for each raw material

   (4) A direct labor budget

   (5) An overhead budget

   (6) A capital budget if you must buy equipment

   (7) A cash collections budget

   (8) A cash payments budget

   (9) A cash budget

   (10) A budgeted cost of goods manufactured schedule

   (11) A budgeted income statement

   (12) A budgeted balance sheet

   (13) A statement of cash flows.

(e) Is this endeavor feasible? Explain.

(f) How much start-up money will be needed?

SUPPLEMENTAL PROBLEMS

44. **Production and Related Budgets** (*LO 13.2; Compare to Problems 30 and 31*)

Consolidate-It, Inc. produces and sells plastic drawers and containers. Standard quantities for one unit of each product follow.

Overhead is applied to production at the rate of $3 per direct labor hour. Consolidate-It expects to sell 42,000 drawers and 35,000 containers in 2010. Expected inventories at the beginning and end of the year follow.

	January 1, 2010	December 31, 2010
Drawers	3,500 units	4,100 units
Containers	4,900 units	3,850 units
Plastic	3,900 pounds	5,300 pounds
Dye	12,000 ounces	9,800 ounces

	Plastic ($0.75 per pound)	Dye ($0.20 per ounce)	Direct Labor ($9.50 per hour)
Drawers	0.5 pound	1 ounce	0.10 hour
Containers	1.3 pounds	3 ounces	0.20 hour

Required:

(a) Prepare the following:

  (1) The production budget for drawers and containers

  (2) The purchases budget in units and dollars for plastic and dye

  (3) The direct labor budget in hours and dollars

  (4) The schedule of overhead to be applied to production

(b) Assume that total actual overhead at the end of 2010 was $35,400. Consolidate-It actually produced 45,000 drawers and 37,000 containers, working a total of 12,200 direct labor hours. Is overhead underapplied or overapplied at the end of 2010 and by how much?

45. Production and Purchases Budgets *(LO 13.2; Compare to Problems 30 and 31)*

Maynor Ltd. makes a single type of product and carries no Work in Process Inventory. The company has prepared the following sales forecast for each half of 2010:

January through June	1,500,000 units
July through December	1,680,000 units

Estimated ending finished goods inventories are

December 31, 2009	120,000 units
June 30, 2010	104,000 units
December 31, 2010	60,000 units

Each unit of product requires 2.5 pounds of Material A (cost, $6 per pound) and 1.5 pounds of Material B (cost $11 per pound). Estimated raw material inventories are

	Material A	Material B
December 31, 2009	40,000 units	10,000 pounds
June 30, 2010	26,000 units	18,000 pounds
December 31, 2010	15,200 units	44,000 pounds

Required:

(a) Prepare a production budget for each half of 2010.

(b) Prepare purchases budgets for Materials A and B for each half of 2010 (in units and dollars).

(c) Maynor Ltd. expects to steadily decrease its ending inventory of Material A, but shows a significant increase in its holdings of Material B (the more expensive material). Why would a company want to hold such large quantities of a raw material inventory item? Give an example of an inventory item of which a company might want to increase its

holdings. What costs would a company incur for holding large quantities of an inventory item?

46. Sales, Production, Purchases, and Cash Budgets *(LO 13.2 and 13.4; Compare to Problem 31)*

HoDown Hats makes felt cowboy hats with leather trim that sell for $70 each. Each hat requires three-fourths of a yard of felt and 24 inches of leather. Felt costs $3 per yard; leather costs $15 per yard. The company's policy is to have raw materials equal to at least 10 percent of the next month's production needs. HoDown can only buy felt in 100-yard quantities and leather in 5-yard quantities. Thus, if HoDown needs 4,257 yards of felt, it must purchase 4,300 yards. This situation means that there might be more ending inventory than desired at the end of a month for felt and leather. Such a circumstance would affect the quantity of the beginning inventory for the following month.

Another company policy is to have a monthly finished goods ending inventory of 25 percent of the next month's sales.

During the first quarter of 2010, management expects no work in process inventories at the beginning or ending of any month. Additionally, the company expects April's production of hats to be exactly equal to its sales volume for that month.

Sales for the first four months of 2010 follow.

	January	February	March	April
Sales volume	13,400	9,200	10,400	12,000

The company collects 35 percent of its Accounts Receivable in the month of sale and the remainder in the month following the sale. There are no uncollectible accounts.

The December 31, 2009, balance sheet revealed the following selected balances: Cash, $3,500; Accounts Receivable, $162,500; Raw Material Inventory (450 yards of felt and 305 yards of leather), $5,925; Finished Goods Inventory (3,200 hats), $80,800; and Accounts Payable, $31,500.

The company pays for 30 percent of a month's purchases of raw material in the month of purchase (rounded to the nearest dollar). The remaining amount is paid in the month after purchase.

Direct labor cost per hat is $9 per hat produced and is paid in the month of production. Total factory overhead is $18,000 per month plus $2.50 per hat produced; of that amount, $3,000 per month is for depreciation. Total nonfactory cash costs are equal to $32,800 per month plus 10 percent of sales revenue. All factory and nonfactory cash expenses are paid in the month of incurrence. In addition, the company plans to make an estimated quarterly tax payment of $245,000 and pay executive bonuses of $435,000 in March 2010.

Required:

(a) Prepare a sales budget by month and in total for the first quarter of 2010.

(b) Prepare a schedule of cash collections from customers by month and in total for the first quarter of 2010. The Accounts Receivable balance on December 31, 2009, represents the unpaid amount of December sales.

(c) What were total sales for December 2009? What is the April 1, 2010, balance of Accounts Receivable?

(d) Prepare a production budget by month and in total for the first quarter of 2010.

(e) Prepare purchases budgets for felt and leather by month and in total for the first quarter of 2010.

(f) Prepare a schedule of cash payments for purchases by month and in total for the first quarter of 2010. The Accounts Payable balance on December 31, 2009, represents the unpaid amount of December purchases.

(g) What were total raw material purchases for December 2009? What is the April 1, 2010, balance of Accounts Payable?

(h) Prepare a combined payments schedule for factory overhead and nonfactory cash costs for each month and in total for the first quarter of 2010.

(i) Prepare a cash budget for each month and in total for the first quarter of 2010.

(j) What is the standard cost per cowboy hat? (Hint: Review the beginning balance information.) How was this cost calculated? Given the cost per hat for fixed production overhead, what is the expected quantity of production each month?

47. **Material Variances** *(LO 13.5; Compare to Problem 37)*

Leisure Wear produces caftans. Leisure Wear estimates that it will take two yards of fabric and five yards of thread to make one caftan. Typically, one yard of fabric costs $2, and one yard of thread costs $0.25.

At the end of October, Leisure Wear had produced 35,000 caftans using 68,100 yards of fabric that cost $140,200 and 140,800 yards of thread costing $34,900.

Required:

Calculate the following variances:

(a) Total material variance for fabric

(b) Material price variance for fabric

(c) Material quantity variance for fabric

(d) Total material variance for thread

(e) Material price variance for thread

(f) Material quantity variance for thread

48. **Labor Variances** *(LO 13.5; Compare to Problem 38)*

Leisure Wear, from Exercise 47, uses two types of labor to produce the caftans: workers who cut the fabric are paid $9.25 per hour and can cut five caftans per hour, and workers who sew the fabric are paid $10.50 per hour and can sew ten caftans per hour.

At the end of October, Leisure Wear had produced 35,000 caftans using 7,150 hours of cutting time at a labor cost of $66,352 and 3,400 hours of sewing time at a labor cost of $35,020.

Required:

Calculate the following variances:

(a) Total labor variance for cutting labor

(b) Labor rate variance for cutting labor

(c) Labor efficiency variance for cutting labor

(d) Total labor variance for sewing labor

(e) Labor rate variance for sewing labor

(f) Labor efficiency variance for sewing labor

49. **Material and Labor Variances** *(LO 13.5; Compare to Problem 39)*

Sail Away produces boats and uses a standard cost system for material (fiberglass and paint) and labor. Standard costs and quantities for materials and labor for one boat follow.

1,600 pounds of fiberglass @ $4.25 per pound	$6,800.00
3 quarts waterproof paint @ $25 per gallon	18.75
50 hours of labor @ $15 per hour	750.00

In June 2009, Sail Away's actual data for the production of 150 boats were as follows:

Fiberglass	245,000 pounds purchased and used @ $4.65 per pound
Paint	115 gallons @ $23.50 per gallon
Direct labor	7,250 hours @ $16 per hour

Required:

(a) Calculate the material and labor variances for Sail Away for June 2009.

(b) Provide some possible reasons for each of the variances.

CHAPTER 14

Activity-Based Management and Performance Measurement

LEARNING OBJECTIVES

1. Distinguish between value-added and non-value-added activities as part of activity-based management.
2. Identify cost drivers of activities.
3. Allocate costs using activity-based costing.
4. Identify financial and nonfinancial performance measurements for different responsibility centers.
5. Discuss the use of a balanced scorecard in performance evaluation.
6. Align the use of rewards with the performance measurement system.

INTRODUCTION

This chapter discusses activity-based management and activity-based costing as ways to develop better product or service cost information. Activity-based management identifies business activities as being value-added and non-value-added so that the non-value-added activities can be reduced or eliminated to, in turn, reduce product or service costs. Activity-based costing is used when traditional means of overhead allocation (such as direct labor hours or machine hours) do not generate reasonably accurate product or service costs.

Because control of product or service costs is often used in assessing managerial performance, the topic of performance measurement is also presented in this chapter. Performance may be judged using financial and/or nonfinancial measurements. Regardless of the type(s) of metrics used, performance rewards should be tied to the measurements selected.

ACTIVITY-BASED MANAGEMENT

Product and service costs help managers determine issues such as whether entry into a particular market is appropriate, whether a specific product or service is providing an acceptable rate of return, and which products and services require, or should receive, additional investments. Businesses generally make and sell items only if they produce a "reasonable" profit margin. Customers generally purchase items only when prices are perceived to be "reasonable" for the value received from the items. There are, however, exceptions to these rules. Businesses may sell products or provide services at less than cost if there are opportunities to "make up the difference" elsewhere, such as by selling related products or services. Customers may purchase a product or service, such as gasoline or electricity, because it is essential rather than because it is perceived as being a good value.

Activity-based management (ABM) is concerned with the activities performed during the manufacturing or service process and the related costs of those activities. The goal of ABM is to understand how a production or service process occurs and thereby be able to streamline it which, in turn, may reduce costs and increase customer value and business profitability. Major components of ABM are discussed in this section.

Analyzing Activities

An **activity** is any repetitive action performed to fulfill a business function. To begin analyzing activities, the organizational processes or functions must be identified. All activities have associated costs that can be eliminated if the activities are eliminated. However, businesses should concentrate on trying to eliminate activities that provide little or no value to the end customer purchasing the product or service.

An activity or process usually overlaps several functional areas. For example, the production process also affects engineering and design, purchasing, warehousing, accounting, personnel, and marketing. In a hotel, the service process affects (in general) reservations, the front desk, and housekeeping. Several processes should be selected for intense investigation, which begins with the preparation of a process map. A **process map** is a visual representation of all the steps, not just the obvious ones, taken in performing an activity. For example, in the process of checking e-mail, two obvious steps are turning on the computer and accessing the e-mail program. But time is also spent waiting for the computer to boot up and program to be accessed, waiting for the e-mail to be downloaded and scanned for viruses, opening the e-mail, and so forth. Some e-mails will need to be saved to a file; others may require adjustments for sound volume. A simplistic process map is illustrated in Visual Recap 14.1.

The process map for each activity will be unique to an organization and its employees. Once a process map is complete, the time necessary to complete each activity and a designation of whether each activity is value-added or non-value-added should be included.

Value-Added and Non-Value-Added Activities

If a "black-or-white" perspective is adopted, process activities are either value-added or non-value-added. **Value-added** (VA) **activities** increase a product or service's worth to a customer who is willing to pay for them. **Non-value-added** (NVA) **activities** increase the time spent making a product or performing a service, but do not increase the product's or service's worth to the customer. Thus, from the customer's perspective, NVA activities are unnecessary and create costs that could be eliminated without affecting the product's or service's market value or quality.

A simple example of value-added and non-value-added activities can be seen in a baseball game. The activities of pitching, batting, running bases, catching, and throwing would certainly be considered value-added by the fans (customers) because these are the activities that the fans came to see. However, the activities of switching teams on the field and discussions between players and coaches might be considered to be non-value-added by the fans. Other NVA activities might include waiting for the game to start or the seventh-inning stretch. Some NVA activities may be necessary for the game to run more smoothly and, as such, cannot be eliminated, but that does not necessarily make them "valuable" to the customer. The NVA activities that are necessary because of the way an organization functions, but that would not be seen as "valuable" by customers, are called **business-value-added activities**. For example, a company will usually prepare invoices as documentation for sales and collections. Preparing invoices creates a business cost that must be covered by the selling prices of the company's products or services. However, invoice preparation adds no direct value to a company's products or services, and customers would prefer not to have to pay for this activity.

VISUAL RECAP 14.1

Process Map to Check E-Mail

Turn on computer	Wait for boot-up	Click on Internet	Wait for connection	Click on e-mail server	Wait for connection	Click on Send/Receive	Wait for download	Read e-mail
1 sec.	2–10 sec.	1 sec.	2–25 sec.	1 sec.	2–30 sec.	1 sec.	2 sec.– 5 min.	10 sec.– 1 hour

Process could take from 22 seconds to 65 minutes. The only time that is "desired" in the process is whatever time it takes to read the e-mail!

All activities use up time, either productively (VA) or unproductively (NVA). Time usage can be classified in four ways: processing (or service), transfer, idle, and inspection. Activities necessary to manufacture a product or perform a service require processing or service time; these activities are, and the time taken to perform them is, value-added. Moving products or components from place to place uses transfer time; storage of parts or waiting at a production operation for processing necessitates idle time. Transfer and idle time are non-value-added.

Performing quality control creates inspection time, which is generally considered non-value-added. Customers expect that activities within a process will be performed correctly, and it should not be necessary to inspect goods while they are being made or while services are being performed. However, there are some exceptions to this attitude. Customers would generally consider quality control essential in the pharmaceutical, food-processing, and airline industries. In these settings, customers would be willing to have the time taken, and to pay, for quality inspections, making those activities value-added.

Companies should try to eliminate or minimize the activities that, from the customer's perspective, add the most time, most cost, and least value. Although few companies can eliminate all business value-added activities, understanding that these activities are, in fact, non-value-added should encourage managers to minimize such activities to the greatest extent possible.

COST DRIVERS

A cost cannot be eliminated or reduced unless the reason for its incurrence is known. A **cost driver** is the factor that has a direct cause–effect relationship on a cost. Many drivers may be identified for a business or single cost. For example, the drivers for hotel insurance cost could include number of employees, property value, number of accidents or claims during a specified time period, location of property, and coverage desired. In a restaurant, the primary cost drivers would be items such as square footage (or number of tables), hours of operation, number of employees, availability of alcohol, and meals served per month. A company should attempt to select a reasonable number of cost drivers that would affect the majority of the organization's costs.

As discussed in Chapter 11, accountants have traditionally accumulated overhead into one or two accounts (such as total or fixed and variable factory overhead) and used one or two drivers (such as direct labor hours or machine hours) to assign overhead costs to products and services. These procedures, although causing no problems for financial statement preparation, may produce inappropriate product or service costs for management's use in complex production or service environments.

LEVELS OF COST INCURRENCE

Costs are created by various drivers that reflect different groupings of activities. For example, direct material and direct labor are unit based, and the total cost of these items will increase with each increase in production or service volume. Some overhead costs, such as indirect material or indirect labor, are also unit based. In each case, the more units that are produced or the more services that are performed, the greater the total cost for the cost element. However, other costs are incurred for broader-based categories of activity such as batch, product or process, and organizational.

Costs that are caused by a group of things being made, handled, or processed at a single time are referred to as batch-level costs. The cost of setting up a machine is an example of a batch-level cost. To illustrate, assume that a company makes products A and B. Setting up a machine to make either one of these products costs $500. During one month, the machine is set up twice: once to manufacture 4,000 units of product A and once to manufacture 1,000 units of product B. Total setup cost for the month is $1,000. If setup cost is viewed as a unit-based cost, the setup cost per unit of A or B will be $0.20 per unit ($1,000 ÷ 5,000 units). However, the actual setup cost per unit of Product A is $0.125 ($500 ÷ 4,000 units) and $0.50 ($500 ÷ 1,000 units) per unit of Product B. Treating setup as a batch-level cost indicates the commonality of the cost to the units within the batch and is more indicative of the relationship between the activity (setup) and the driver (different production runs).

The development, production, or acquisition of different items causes a product-level (or process-level) cost. Assume that a travel agency has the following customers during July: a group of ten senior citizens, a group of six college students, and a family of four. The agency makes five itinerary changes during the month at a cost of $200 per change. Four of these changes related to the group of senior citizens and one change related to the group of college students; no changes were made for the family. If the cost of the changes were viewed as unit based, the overhead cost per unit for changes would be $50 ($1,000 ÷ 20 people). Use of this method inappropriately assigns $200 ($50 × 4) of the cost to the family, which had no itinerary changes. If the cost of the changes were viewed as batch based, the overhead cost per batch would be $333.33 ($1,000 ÷ 3 groups); again assigning a cost to the family that had no changes. Using a product/process-level driver (number of changes) for these costs assigns $800 ($200 × 4) of costs to the senior citizens and $200 ($200 × 1) to the college students—in other words, attaching the precise costs to the precise groups that caused the costs. These costs could then be assigned, on a per-unit basis, to the individual members of the groups at $80 and $33.33, respectively, per senior citizen and college student.

Certain overhead costs are incurred only for the purpose of supporting facility operations. These costs are common to many different activities, products, and services and can only be allocated to products and services arbitrarily. For example, the driver of building depreciation cost is the passage of time, rather than production of units or performance of services. Organizational-level costs should theoretically not be assigned to products at all, but because the amounts are insignificant relative to all other costs, most companies allocate organizational-level costs to goods produced or services rendered using some arbitrary basis such as direct labor or machine hours.

ACTIVITY-BASED COSTING

Activity-based costing (ABC) is an overhead allocation method. Costs are collected by cost driver categories and are then attached to products and services based on the activities performed to make, render, distribute, or support those products and services. Three fundamental components of ABC are (1) classifying costs into multiple levels of incurrence, (2) accumulating costs by cost drivers, and (3) using multiple cost drivers to assign costs to products and services. Activity-based costing is useful in companies that:

- Make (or render) many different kinds of products (or services) in significantly different volumes

■ Have high overhead costs, often related to automation, that can be traced to specific products using nontraditional cost drivers

■ Are showing profits for low-volume, hard-to-make (perform) products (services) and losses for high-volume, easy-to-make (perform) products (services)

In ABC, overhead costs are accumulated in the traditional manner (for instance, by variable or fixed cost behavior) in the general ledger. These costs are then regrouped based on two aspects of the cost: level of incurrence (unit, batch, or product/process) and primary underlying cost driver (such as kilowatt-hours of electricity, square feet of occupancy, or number of transactions). Organizational-level costs may or may not be regrouped by cost drivers, depending on whether those costs are to be allocated to products or services. Each group of (rather than total) costs is assigned to products and services using an overhead allocation method similar to that discussed in Chapter 11. This concept is illustrated in Visual Recap 14.2.

For example, assume that Hyde, Inc. produces two products: Product Q (which sells for $40 per unit and has direct material and direct labor costs of $27) and Product R (which sells for $150 and has direct material and labor costs of $89). In 2009, Hyde, Inc. produced and sold 70,000 units of Q and 8,000 units of R. Total overhead for the year was $579,800. Exhibit 14-1 illustrates Hyde, Inc.'s overhead allocation process using the traditional cost driver of direct labor hours (DLHs).

VISUAL RECAP 14.2

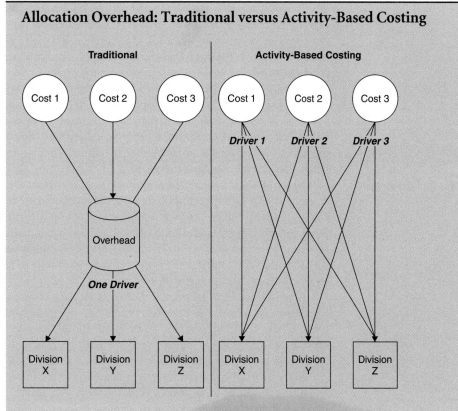

Allocation Overhead: Traditional versus Activity-Based Costing

EXHIBIT 14-1
Hyde, Inc. Overhead Allocation (Traditional)

Overhead cost = $579,800

Cost Driver: Direct Labor Hours (DLHs)

Product Q	70,000 units @ 2.5 DLHs	175,000 DLHs
Product R	8,000 units @ 6.0 DLHs	48,000 DLHs
Both products		223,000 DLHs

Overhead rate per DLH = $579,800 ÷ 223,000 = $2.60 per DLH

Overhead Assigned

Product Q	2.5 DLH × $2.60 per DLH $ 6.50 per unit
Product R	6.0 DLH × $2.60 per DLH 15.60 per unit

Profit Analysis per Unit

	Product Q	Product R
Selling price	$ 40.00	$150.00
DM & DL cost	(27.00)	(89.00)
OH cost (assigned on DLHs)	(6.50)	(15.60)
Profit margin	$ 6.50	$ 45.40
Profit as a % of selling price (rounded)	16%	30%

In this situation, total overhead is divided by total direct labor hours (the cost driver), resulting in $2.60 of overhead assigned for every DLH. Each unit of product is assigned overhead based on the number of DLHs required to produce a single unit. As a result, Product Q receives $6.50 of overhead per unit, whereas Product R receives $15.60.

If Hyde, Inc. used activity-based costing, the overhead would be divided into groups, and each group would be applied using a different driver. Assume that the $579,800 of total overhead consists of $240,000 in material movement costs, $189,000 in utilities, $126,800 in cleanup costs, and $24,000 in setup costs. Exhibit 14-2 indicates the overhead allocations to the two products if ABC were used. In this situation, there are four drivers and allocation bases, one for each overhead category.

Note the significant difference in overhead cost per unit of Product Q and Product R using activity-based costing. Using the direct labor hour method to allocate overhead cost to products makes Product R appear to be the more profitable of the two products. However, when overhead is allocated using activity-based costing, Product R is shown to be significantly less profitable than Product Q. Having this information may lead management to make a decision to promote Product Q more effectively or to raise the cost of Product R to generate a more reasonable profit margin.

Activity-based costing often indicates that a large number of costs are associated with low-volume products and complex production operations, and that these costs are not properly allocated under traditional overhead allocation systems. ABC tends to reduce the overhead cost attached to high-volume, standard products and increase the overhead costs attached to low-volume, complex specialty product costs.

Activity-based costing is not appropriate for all organizations because it is expensive and time consuming to implement. Additionally, ABC does not change the total overhead incurred; it merely distributes that overhead cost in a more appropriate manner. Overhead

EXHIBIT 14-2

Hyde, Inc. Overhead Allocation (Activity-Based Costing)

Overhead:

Material move cost (MMC)	$240,000
Utility cost (UC)	189,000
Clean-up cost (CC)	126,800
Setup cost (SC)	24,000
Total OH cost	$579,800

Cost Drivers:

Pounds of material moved	400,000
Number of kilowatt hours used	630,000
Hours of clean-up labor	31,700
Number of setups	6

Overhead Rates:

MMC	$240,000 ÷ 400,000	$0.60 per pound
UC	$189,000 ÷ 630,000	$0.30 per kWh
CC	$126,800 ÷ 31,700	$4.00 per hour
SC	$24,000 ÷ 6	$4,000 per setup

Overhead Assigned:

	Product Q			Product R		
	Driver Used	× Rate	Overhead Assigned	Driver Used	× Rate	Overhead Assigned
MMC	140,000 lbs.	× $0.60	$ 84,000	260,000 lbs.	× $0.60	$156,000
UC	175,000 kWh	× $0.30	52,500	455,000 kWh	× $0.30	136,500
CC	21,000 hrs.	× $4.00	84,000	10,700 hrs.	× $4.00	42,800
SC	2 setups	× $4,000	8,000	4 setups	× $4,000	16,000
Total OH assigned			$228,500			$351,300
Units of product			÷70,000			÷8,000
OH per unit of product (rounded)			$3.26			$43.91

Profit Analysis per Unit

	Product Q	Product R
Selling price	$ 40.00	$150.00
DM & DL cost	(27.00)	(89.00)
OH cost (using ABC)	(3.26)	(43.91)
Profit margin	$ 9.74	$ 17.09
Profit as a % of selling price (rounded)	24%	11%

cost can only be minimized by using activity-based management techniques to eliminate or reduce NVA activities and their related costs.

ABC provides two important benefits from its reallocation of overhead costs. First, decision making is improved because product and service costs are more accurate and better reflect the resources used by the production or performance process. Second, performance measurement is improved because the enhanced product or service cost information is a more appropriate way to judge how well costs were controlled and how profitable a product or organizational unit was.

MEASURING SHORT-RUN PERFORMANCE

To be successful, organizations must meet many different goals and objectives. First and foremost, a business organization must be profitable to survive. Profitability performance measures are short-run in nature and relate to the type of organizational unit being evaluated.

A **responsibility center** is an organizational unit that is under the control of a designated manager. Responsibility centers are classified based on the manager's authority and type of financial responsibility. The three most common classifications are cost, profit, and investment centers. In a **cost center**, the manager is responsible only for controlling costs in the unit. In a **profit center**, the manager is responsible for both cost control and revenue generation in the unit. In an **investment center**, the manager is responsible for cost control, revenue generation, and the unit's asset base. A manager's performance should be evaluated only on the specific areas under his or her control.

Cost Center

In a cost center, the only means to judge performance is an assessment of whether the center's costs were in line with budgeted amounts. Thus, actual costs are compared to budgeted costs at the same level of activity to determine the variance amount. Consider the following information: Lee Larkind is the manager of the Reservations Department in HLS Corp. For October, the department's budget was as follows, based on an activity level of 480 hours (three people working 40 hours per week for four weeks in the month):

Personnel costs ($12 per hour × 480 hours)	$ 5,760
Supplies ($15 per hour worked × 480 hours)	7,200
Electricity ($0.50 per hour worked × 480 hours)	240
Depreciation ($2,000 per month)	2,000
Total budgeted costs	$15,200

During October, company management gave reservations employees a $0.50 per hour wage increase. The employees worked a total of 500 hours, and the department reported the following costs:[1]

Personnel costs ($12.50 per hour × 500 hours)	$ 6,250
Supplies ($14.25 per hour worked × 500 hours)	7,125
Electricity ($0.90 per hour worked × 500 hours)	450
Depreciation ($2,000 per month)	2,000
Total budgeted costs	$15,825

At first glance, it appears that Larkind has not controlled departmental costs well during October. However, the two sets of figures should not be compared directly because they have been calculated using different levels of activity. The original budget first needs to be restated at the actual activity level of 500 hours before making the comparison.

---

[1] HLS Corp. does not pay overtime wages, but keeps track of the hours and gives those hours back, with pay, to the employees when business is slow.

	Budget at actual activity level	Actual costs	Difference
Personnel costs ($12 per hour × 500 hours)	$ 6,000	$ 6,250	$ 250
Supplies ($15 per hour worked × 500 hours)	7,500	7,125	(375)
Electricity ($0.50 per hour worked × 500 hours)	250	450	200
Depreciation ($2,000 per month)	2,000	2,000	0
Total budgeted costs	$15,750	$15,825	$ (75)

Reviewing this information indicates that the department's costs were only $75 more than what would have been budgeted if the actual activity level had been used in the original budget. Larkind controlled departmental costs fairly well, considering the increase in wage rates and hourly electricity costs—especially when it is realized that neither of those factors were under his control.

Profit Center

In a profit center, performance can be judged on both cost control and revenue generation. A profit center manager's goal is to maximize the center's net income. Profit centers are generally independent organizational units whose managers have the authority to buy goods, obtain resources, and set selling prices.

In addition to the type of cost control comparison shown in the previous section, performance evaluation in a profit center will also include revenue and profit measurements. **Sales price** (difference between total actual selling price and budgeted selling price at actual volume) and **sales volume** (difference between budgeted selling price at actual volume and total budgeted sales) **variances** are illustrated in the following revenue variance model (assuming the profit center sells only one type of product):

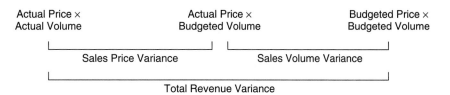

Continuing the previous example, assume that Reservations Department is a profit center, rather than a cost center, and "charges" the hotel $10 for each reservation generated by the department.[2] It was estimated that the department would make 2,000 reservations during October; thus, expected revenue for the department was $20,000. In October, the department actually generated 2,200 reservations. During that month, a new reservation system was implemented that reduced the work involved; therefore, the hotel "charge" per reservation was lowered to $9.50. The price, volume, and revenue variances for October are as follows:

---

[2]Many companies allow one unit to "charge" another unit for services rendered. These charges are referred to as **transfer prices**. The transfer amounts are generally not actually transferred in actual funds between departments.

Actual Price ×	Actual Price ×	Budgeted Price ×
Actual Volume	Budgeted Volume	Budgeted Volume
$9.50 × 2,200	$10 × 2,200	$10 × 2,000
$20,900	$22,000	$20,000

$1,100 U	$2,000 F
Sales Price Variance	Sales Volume Variance

$900 F
Total Revenue Variance

Even though the price charged per reservation was reduced, the increase in volume for the Reservation Department was sufficient to produce more than the total expected revenue for the month.

Budgeted profits for the Reservations Department should also be compared to actual profits in evaluating performance as follows:

Budgeted revenues	$20,000	Actual revenues	$20,900
Budgeted costs (at actual volume)	(15,750)	Actual costs	(15,825)
Expected profit	$ 4,250	Actual profit	$ 5,075

The Reservations Department and its manager performed exceptionally well during October by controlling costs, increasing revenues, and increasing profitability.

Investment Center

In an investment center, performance can be judged on the basis of cost control, revenue generation, and return on investment. Most investment centers are independent, free-standing divisions or subsidiaries of an organization. Center managers can acquire, use, and sell plant assets to earn the highest rate of return on the center's asset base. Thus, in addition to the measures shown previously for cost and profit centers, an investment center's performance can also be measured by calculating **return on investment** (ROI):

$$ROI = Income \div Assets$$

Assume that Larkind of the Reservations Department has control over the department's asset base of $50,000. Using the $5,075 income from above, ROI is computed as:

$$ROI = Income \div Assets$$
$$= \$5,075 \div \$50,000$$
$$= 10.2\%$$

The 10.2 percent rate would be compared to the rate desired by the corporate entity to determine whether it was reasonable and acceptable.

The **Du Pont model**, a restatement of the ROI formula, can be used to provide information about two factors that comprise the rate of return: profit margin and asset turnover. **Profit margin** is the ratio of income to sales and indicates the portion of each sales dollar that is not consumed by expenses. **Asset turnover** reflects the dollars of sales generated by each dollar of asset investment and, as such, indicates asset productivity.

$$Du\ Pont\ Model\ of\ ROI = Profit\ Margin \times Asset\ Turnover$$
$$Profit\ Margin = Income \div Revenues$$
$$Asset\ Turnover = Revenues \div Assets$$

The Du Pont model uses the product of the profit margin and asset turnover to calculate ROI. For the Reservations Department, these calculations are

$$
\begin{aligned}
\text{ROI} &= \text{Profit Margin} \times \text{Asset Turnover} \\
&= (\text{Income} \div \text{Revenues}) \times (\text{Revenues} \div \text{Assets}) \\
&= (\$5{,}075 \div \$20{,}900) \times (\$20{,}900 \div \$50{,}000) \\
&= 24.3\% \times 41.8\% \\
&= 10.2\%
\end{aligned}
$$

To determine acceptability of performance, results of these calculations should be compared to internal (other organizational units) and external (world-class companies) benchmarks.[3]

MEASURING LONG-RUN PERFORMANCE

Companies must be managed to be profitable in the short run and to exist for the long run. To this end, mission statements should be developed that reflect management's view of how the organization will uniquely and continuously meet customers' needs with its products or services. A company that makes shoddy products or does not maintain a competitive edge may be profitable this year and next, but probably will not exist in 10 years. In addition, managers who make decisions that increase this year's profits at the expense of future profits will "look good" this year, but not in the future. Thus, it is necessary for management to have both short-run and long-run objectives that are compatible with the organization's mission statement.

Balanced Scorecard

Short-run objectives generally reflect a predominantly financial focus and, as such, can be measured with the traditional monetary metrics discussed in the previous section. Alternatively, an organization's long-term objectives will involve actions and efforts that will enhance market position. Traditional financial measures cannot indicate progress toward these goals although, in the long run, these goals will definitively affect an organization's profitability. Thus, nonfinancial performance measures are instituted to indicate progress toward the success factors of a global organization. Such measures help assess performance in the areas of customer satisfaction, quality, cycle time, and organizational learning. A **balanced scorecard** is a methodology for determining measurements for both financial and nonfinancial aspects of performance. Visual Recap 14.3 illustrates the style and use of the balanced scorecard.

Each balanced scorecard section should indicate specific measurements that would help assess the organization's process toward its long-run goals and objectives. The measurements should be easy to understand and to compute. Following are some examples of nonmonetary measurements for each scorecard area other than the financial section.

---

[3] Many other short-term financial performance measurements (such as residual income and cash flows) may also be used to evaluate performance. These measurements are beyond the scope of this text.

VISUAL RECAP 14.3

Balanced Scorecard Illustration

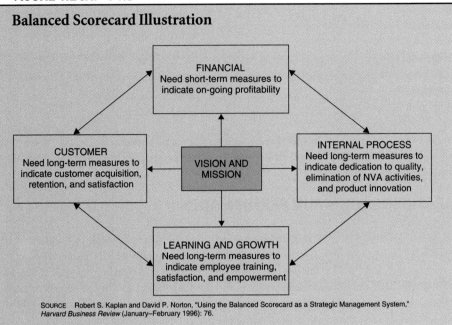

SOURCE   Robert S. Kaplan and David P. Norton, "Using the Balanced Scorecard as a Strategic Management System," *Harvard Business Review* (January–February 1996): 76.

Customer:

- Increase in market share from prior period
- Percentage of customers retained from prior period
- Percentage of new customers out of total customers this period
- Score of at least 90% on all customer satisfaction surveys

Internal Process:

- Defect rate this period vs. defect rate of industry leader
- Increase in cycle efficiency (value-added time ÷ total production or performance time) from prior period
- New product time-to-market vs. average time-to-market in industry
- Number of patents obtained this period vs. number obtained by primary competitor
- Sales dollars generated from new products vs. total sales dollars

Learning and Growth:

- Percentage of employees retained from prior period vs. goal of 95%
- Number of employee suggestions implemented vs. number submitted
- Hours of training per employee this period vs. goal of 40 hours per employee
- Percentage of employees who are cross-trained in three or more functional areas vs. goal of 100 percent
- Number of projects worked on by teams of different business units vs. total number of projects

Benchmarking

To assess the success of an activity, a measurement should compare a numerator and a denominator, make a comparison between periods, or make a comparison with an internal or external benchmark. **Benchmarking** means comparing an organization's products, processes, or services against those of organizations that have been proven to be "best in class." These "best in class" organizations may or may not be in competition with the organization doing the benchmarking. For example, if an organization wanted to judge its warehouse "picking" process (selecting goods to ship to customers), one of the best in class organizations is L.L. Bean (www.llbean.com). To judge the efficiency and effectiveness of its picking process, a company would not have to be in the catalog clothing business to compare picking processes with L.L. Bean.

Some organizations may want to use internal goals or other organizational units as benchmarks of performances. If this choice is made, the organization should be certain that those internal goals or units are set to reflect the success criteria shown by market leaders. Otherwise, the organization may find itself the best at doing something that no one wants done or performing significantly better than in the past, but not well enough to compete with the market leaders.

DECIDING ON PERFORMANCE MEASURES

Different balanced scorecards should be created for different levels of managerial responsibility. As the responsibility level goes lower in the organization, the measurements will become more job specific and, generally, more individualized. Specific responsibility for performance should be assigned for each measurement target as well as a monitoring schedule. Monitoring of performance will probably be performed more frequently at lower levels of responsibility.

Performance measurements should reflect an organization's need to concentrate on those factors that provide customer value. Probably two of the most important current performance measures of businesses are product or service quality and customer responsiveness. In committing to product or service quality, an organization must adjust how products are designed and manufactured, employees are trained and utilized, and plant assets are justified for purchase. Setting multiple financial and nonfinancial performance measures should cause organizations to implement techniques (such as total quality management) that will help improve the organization, its products, its processes, and its customer and supplier relations, as well as reduce costs to provide better value. Visual Recap 14.4 illustrates some choices of performance measures.

REWARDING PERFORMANCE

For a performance measurement system to be effective, it should be aligned with the performance reward system. The important issues in designing a performance reward system are that the system

- Reflects the performance measurements that have been set;
- Is tied to individual and, if appropriate, group performance;
- Encourages both a short-run long-run organizational perspective; and
- Is balanced between financial and nonfinancial incentives.

VISUAL RECAP 14.4

Choice of Performance Measures

	Measures of Performance	Cost Center	Revenue Center	Investment Center	Balanced Scorecard
Short-term Financial Measures	Costs in line with **budget**	✓	✓	✓	
	Ability to generate **revenues** (Revenue variance)		✓	✓	✓*
	Return on Investment (ROI and DuPont Model)			✓	
Long-term Nonfinancial Measures	**Customer:** acquisition, retention, and satisfaction	X**	X	X	✓
	Internal processes: quality, innovation, and elimination of non-value-added activities	X	X	X	✓
	Learning and growth: employee training, satisfaction, and empowerment	X	X	X	✓

*Indicates that at least one short-run financial measure should be included on a balanced scorecard
**Cost centers have "internal" customers that must be satisfied through the delievery of products and services.

Typically, rewards above basic salary and wages have been tied to performance above certain stated objectives—usually a financial accounting measure such as organizational net income or earnings per share. However, because the measurement system is changing from a focus totally on financial aspects of performance to multiple performance measurement characteristics, the compensation system also needs to be changed. New performance reward plans should be designed to encourage higher levels of employee performance and loyalty for behaviors that lead to achievement of organizational goals. Like the nonfinancial performance measures, performance rewards should encourage employees to adopt a long-run perspective. For example, some rewards now involve the issuance of common stock to employees because it is believed that employees who are partial owners of their employing company develop the same perspective as other stockholders.

A **stock option** is a right to buy a company's stock at a future date at a guaranteed price, such as the current market price. In today's business environment, any discussion of the use of stock options as performance rewards for employees has to include this reward's potential for problems. Many high-tech companies were corporate leaders in dispersing stock options to employees. Unfortunately, the downturn in the technology market left a substantial number of employee-would-be-millionaires holding options that had lost all their value.

Another consideration in performance reward systems is the use of team as well as individual rewards. In today's business environment, employees often function as teams rather than as individuals. Team incentives are necessary to encourage cooperation among employees. However, if only team incentives are offered, the reward system may be ineffective. As the team grows larger, individual employees may shirk their duties or try to "free ride" on the team. Balancing individual and team rewards requires a careful assessment of activities and a performance measurement system that can differentiate between individual and team skills and efforts.

An employee's organizational level and current compensation should also affect the performance rewards offered. Individuals at different levels in the organization typically view rewards differently because of the relationship of pay to standard of living. At lower employee levels, more incentives should be monetary and short term; at higher levels, more incentives should be nonmonetary and long term. However, the system should also include some nonmonetary and long-term incentives for lower-level employees and some monetary and short-term incentives for top management. Such a compensation system provides lower-level employees with more money to directly enhance their lifestyles, but also provides long-run rewards (such as stock options) to encourage an "ownership" view of the organization. In turn, more long-run rewards should be given to top managers so that they will be more concerned about the organization's long-run rather than their short-run personal gains.

One problem with the use of stock options is that high-level managers sometimes feel the need to make certain that their stock options will be valuable—and those managers do so by fraudulently inflating the organization's profits. In the early part of the 21st century, several major frauds caused companies to take another look at their policies of issuing stock options and, in doing so, make decisions to reduce or eliminate the use of options as performance rewards.

Another potential problem with stock options is that they can lose their value as compensation if the granting company's stock price falls. For example, assume that at December 31, 2004, Company A grants an executive 100,000 stock options that allow the purchase of the company's stock for $50 per share; the option can be exercised (or used) for 7 years. At the time of the grant, Company A's stock price on the NYSE was $50. The expectation is that the stock price will rise, and exercising the options will become valuable. The executive does not exercise the options in 2005, 2006, or 2007 as the stock price continues to rise; by the end of 2007, the stock price is $85. At that point, the executive has "received" compensation of $35 per share: the difference between the market price of the stock and the option price at which the stock can be purchased from the company. However, due to the financial crisis that took place in 2008, Company A's stock price began to rapidly fall and, by year-end 2008, the market price of Company A's stock was $15 per share. The stock options are now considered "underwater" and valueless. In fact, by the end of 2008, it was estimated that 72 percent of the *Fortune* 500 companies' stock options were underwater and that approximately 93 percent of the options held by *Fortune* 500 CEOs had no value at the then-current market prices.[4]

All employees value and require money to satisfy basic human needs, but employees also appreciate other types of "compensation" that satisfy their higher-order social needs. For example, employees are generally more productive in an environment in which their efforts are appreciated. Compliments and small awards can be used to formally recognize employee contributions. Implementing employee empowerment contributes to making a work environment more fulfilling. Other types of perquisites (or "perks") such as additional paid days off, on-site child care, free parking, and health or recreational club memberships are also frequently used as rewards for performance.

---

[4]Phred Dvorak, "Firms Jump to Salvage 'Underwater' Stock Options," *Wall Street Journal* (December 22, 2008), B1.

SUMMARY

Activity-based management stresses the (1) differentiation between value-added and non-value-added activities and (2) reduction or elimination of the non-value-added activities to the greatest extent possible. A process map can be prepared to indicate all the steps taken in performing a process. Cost drivers of the various activities and the levels (unit, batch, product/process, or organizational) at which those drivers occur should be determined.

Activity-based costing is an alternative method of allocating overhead to products and services based on the activities performed, rather than using a single allocation base such as direct labor or machine hours. ABC often shows that the traditional method of allocating overhead assigned too much overhead to high-volume, standard products and not enough to low-volume, specialty products.

Organizations have to meet many goals and objectives to achieve success. Determining progress toward those goals and objectives requires a performance measurement system that considers both the short run and long run. Financial measures of performance must reflect a manager's area of responsibility. Thus, each type of responsibility center (cost, profit, or investment) has different types of performance measures that can be used. However, all financial measures are historical in nature and, thus, are more focused on the past than on the future.

The balanced scorecard stresses the need for both financial and nonfinancial performance measures. The nonfinancial categories of the scorecard are customer, internal process, and learning and growth. Measurements should be designed that indicate an organization's ability to meet today's global success factors of customer satisfaction and responsiveness, high-quality products or services, and innovation.

The performance reward system should be directly tied to the performance measurement system and include both financial and nonfinancial rewards, as well as short-run and long-run rewards. Different levels of employees will need a different balance of these rewards, but the system should reflect the value placed on work activities and should encourage employees to adopt a long-run perspective for their organization.

KEY TERMS

activity	cost driver	responsibility center
activity-based costing	Du Pont model	return on investment
activity-based management	investment center	sales price variance
asset turnover	non-value-added activity	sales volume variance
balanced scorecard	process map	stock option
benchmarking	profit center	transfer price
business-value-added activity	profit margin	value-added activity
cost center		

QUESTIONS

1. Define and give four examples in a business organization of value-added, non-value-added, and business-value-added activities. Why, in the strictest possible definition, should business-value-added activities be classified as non-value-added activities? *(LO 14.1)*

2. Select a reasonably simple activity (similar to the checking e-mail example given in the chapter) that you perform in your daily routine. What activities would be included in a process map for your chosen activity? Classify each of the activities as value-added or non-value-added, as related to the outcome of the activity. *(LO 14.1)*

3. What is a cost driver? Provide one example (other than that given in the text) of a cost being incurred at the batch, product/process, and organizational levels. Why is it important to classify costs by their level of incurrence? *(LO 14.2)*

4. How does activity-based costing differ from traditional costing methods? On what type of cost does activity-based costing focus? *(LO 14.3)*

5. How does the use of activity-based costing generally affect product costs? Will the use of activity-based costing lower a company's total costs? Why or why not? *(LO 14.3)*

6. Differentiate among the three common classifications of responsibility centers. Choose two different kinds of organizations and provide an example (other than those given in the text) of each type of center.

7. How is the ability to measure performance affected by a responsibility center's classification? Why is it important to only evaluate managers based on the costs that they are able to control? *(LO 14.4)*

8. What two formulas can be used to calculate return on investment? What additional information is provided by the use of the Du Pont model to calculate ROI? *(LO 14.4)*

9. What is a balanced scorecard? Why is each category included in the balanced scorecard important to an organization? *(LO 14.5)*

10. Define benchmarking. Should every process at a company be benchmarked against best practices? When would it be appropriate not to benchmark? *(LO 14.5)*

11. Why does an organization not need to focus solely on industry competitors when determining a benchmark comparison? *(LO 14.5)*

12. Why should an organization select multiple metrics to measure performance? Why is there a need to measure performance using both short-run and long-run time horizons? *(LO 14.6)*

13. Why must an organization's reward system be aligned with its performance measurement system? Why should the reward system not be tied solely to monetary bonuses? *(LO 14.6)*

EXERCISES

14. **True and False** *(All LOs)*

Following are a series of statements regarding topics discussed in this chapter.

(a) To assess a firm's ability to pay an annual dividend, short-run performance measures are better than long-run performance measures.

(b) Product-level cost drivers should be used when the company manufactures products to each customer's specification.

(c) The Du Pont model is a return on investment measurement.

(d) As the level of responsibility goes lower in an organization, the measurements of a manager's job performance will become more general.

(e) Corporations should eliminate as many non-value-added activities as possible, but should not consider eliminating business-value-added activities.

(f) A manager's performance measurements should correspond to the type of responsibility center the manager heads.

(g) Activity-based costing is useful to companies that have high direct material and direct labor costs and relatively low overhead.

(h) Quality inspection is generally viewed as a non-value-added activity.

(i) Cost drivers should be chosen so that expenses are distributed evenly between divisions.

(j) Long-run performance measures are typically financial.

(k) A process map should include only those activities that can be accurately timed.

(l) Benchmarking is often useful between companies that have different products but similar processes.

(m) It is possible to engage in activity-based management techniques without using activity-based costing.

Required:

Indicate whether each statement is true (T) or false (F).

15. **Value-Added and Non-Value-Added Activities** *(LO 14.1)*

Different types of businesses engage in different types of activities. Four businesses follow.

(a) Dillard's (department store)

(b) Applebee's (restaurant)

(c) Saturn (automobile manufacturer)

(d) Comet (dry cleaner)

Required:

For each business, list two examples of

(a) A value-added activity

(b) A non-value-added activity

(c) A business-value-added activity

16. **Cost Levels and Cost Drivers** *(LO 14.2)*

    Following are ten cost activities that might be incurred in an organization.

    (a) Paying a franchise license fee

    (b) Transferring a production run to the warehouse

    (c) Setting up a printer to run 5,000 copies of a textbook

    (d) Maintaining engineering designs for company products

    (e) Using wood to manufacture a table

    (f) Depreciating a factory building

    (g) Delivering meals to hospital patients

    (h) Putting a stamp on an envelope

    (i) Developing dietary guidelines for special-need meals in a rest home

    (j) Drilling a hole in a product

    Required:

    Classify each of the costs as unit-level, batch-level, product/process level, or organizational level. Identify a cost driver for each item, and explain why that driver is appropriate.

17. **Cost, Profit, and Investment Centers** *(LO 14.4)*

    DingDong Corp., a manufacturing company, has three divisions, and each produces a different item: widgets, whatchamacallits, and whosey-whatsits. Each product is distinctly different, so the divisions do not share raw material, labor, or machinery.

    Required:

    (a) If the Widgets Division were a cost center, list several costs for which the division manager would be responsible.

    (b) How would your answer in part (a) change if the Widgets Division were a profit center?

    (c) How would your answers from parts (a) and (b) change if the Widgets Division were an investment division?

    (d) Would it be possible for the Widgets Division to be an investment center if the three divisions used similar raw material? Explain.

    (e) Would it be possible for the Widgets Division to be an investment center if the three divisions shared machinery? Explain.

    (f) Assume that the widgets, whatchamacallits, and whosey-whatsits were transferred to a fourth division that puts them together to make a final product. Would it be possible for the Widgets Division to be a profit center? Explain.

18. **Return on Investment** *(LO 14.4)*

    Alliance Division has the following information for the year ended December 31, 2009.

Assets invested	$12,800,000
Revenues	8,750,000
Expenses	5,975,000

    Required:

    (a) Calculate return on investment.

    (b) Calculate profit margin.

    (c) Calculate asset turnover.

    (d) Use the answers from parts (b) and (c) to prove the answer in part (a).

19. **Performance Measurements** *(LO 14.4)*

    Consider your enrollment in this class as your job.

    Required:

    Using each of the four balanced scorecard categories, develop two measurements that would be appropriate to judge your performance in this class.

20. **Performance Rewards** *(LO 14.6)*

    You are the new manager of a local health club. You are being paid what you perceive to be a good monthly salary with an annual three-week paid vacation and good health-care benefits. The club's owner has stated she wants the club to earn a reasonable rate of return, increase membership, and have low employee turnover.

    Required:

    (a) Provide the answers that might be given by the owner in response to your question of, "Can you be more specific about how these goals will be measured?"

    (b) What performance rewards might you request under these measurements?

PROBLEMS

21. **Process Map** *(LO 14.1)*

    You and some friends are watching a football game on television and suddenly realize that you're really hungry.

    Required:

    Prepare a process map that extends from the point of the "hungry" determination to the point of hunger satisfaction.

22.   Value-Added and Non-Value-Added Activities *(LO 14.1)*

Several activities related to different businesses follow.

(a)   Preparing a purchase order

(b)   Storing raw materials

(c)   Reworking products

(d)   Handling customer complaints

(e)   Sewing fabric to make clothing

(f)   Inspecting quality of purchased material

(g)   Matching receiving reports to purchase orders

(h)   Ringing up a customer sale on a register

(i)   Printing a customer's airline ticket

(j)   Moving products from one area to another

(k)   Copying documents in a law office

(l)   Inspecting the finished product in a pharmaceutical company

(m)   Packing men's dress shirts in cellophane bags

(n)   Designing a new product

(o)   Filing paid supplier invoices

(p)   Issuing engineering change orders for products

(q)   Mixing ingredients to make salad dressing

(r)   Assembling product parts

(s)   Cleaning up spills

(t)   Bagging a 12-pack of soda at the grocery store

Required:

Identify which of the listed items are value-added and which are non-value-added from the standpoint of the end customer for the organization performing the task.

23.   Activity-Based Costing *(LO 14.2 and 14.3)*

Kiawanee Corp. manufactures Products X, Y, and Z. These products have the following costs and production operating statistics:

	Product X	Product Y	Product Z
Direct material and labor cost	$ 360,000	$280,000	$400,000
Direct labor hours required	80,000	60,000	20,000
Machine hours required	30,000	40,000	80,000
Pounds of material required	1,200,000	600,000	200,000
Number of setups required	40	50	20
Number of units produced	160,000	80,000	20,000

The company's total overhead cost is $2,458,000, which is comprised of costs for the following activities (shown with an appropriate cost driver):

Activity	Cost	Driver
Materials handling	$1,400,000	Pounds of material used
Scheduling and setup	264,000	Number of setups
Utilities and depreciation	690,000	Machine hours incurred
Indirect materials used	104,000	Direct labor hours

The competitive market process has set the selling prices of Products X, Y, and Z at $22, $30, and $90, respectively.

Required:

(a)   Assume that the company applies overhead on a direct labor hour basis. Determine the overhead cost (round to two decimal points) per direct labor hour. Determine the total cost per unit of Products X, Y, and Z.

(b)   Using the information determined in part (a) and the sales prices given, what decision might Kiawanee management make about its products?

(c)   Calculate the overhead cost per activity if the designated cost drivers are used.

(d)   Determine the cost per unit of Products X, Y, and Z if the company applies overhead on the activity-based costing information developed in part (c).

(e)   Using the information determined in part (d) and the sales prices given, what decision might Kiawanee management make about its products? Why does this decision differ from that determined in part (b)?

(f)   Is Kiawanee using the appropriate cost drivers? Give an alternate suggestion for each cost driver and explain why that suggestion was made.

24.   Cost Center Performance Measurement *(LO 14.4)*

The following budgeted and actual costs existed for the placement office of Tempe's Community College for 2009.

	Budget	Actual
Salaries for professional staff	$459,000	$495,000
Printing and postage	1,950	2,730
Job fair events	13,800	20,400
Depreciation on computer equipment	3,600	3,600
Supplies	8,700	9,600

Required:

(a)   Determine the variances for each budget item.

(b)   Do you think that the placement director did a good job in controlling costs? Why or why not?

(c)   Would you change your answer to part (b) if you knew that the placement office had expected to place 65 percent of the college's graduates in 2009, but instead, they placed 85 percent of the graduates? Why or why not?

25.   Profit Center Performance Measurement *(LO 14.4)*

Silence is Golden is a division of Tranquility, Inc. The division produces relaxation tapes and is considered a profit center. The following budgeted and actual information is available for August 2009:

Budgeted sales   300,000 tapes at $18 per tape
Actual sales   380,000 tapes at $15 per tape

Required:

Compute the sales price, sales volume, and total revenue variances for the division.

26. **Cost and Profit Center Performance Measurement** (LO 14.4, Internet)

The El Paso Division of the Tejas Fence Co. is currently operated as a cost center. The following standard costs have been determined for the production of one metal gate at the El Paso Division.

Pipe (50 feet at $0.80 per foot)		$40.00
Direct labor (2 hours at $9.00 per hour)		18.00
Overhead:		
Indirect material	$1.20	
Indirect labor	.60	
Depreciation	3.50	
Utilities	.90	
Maintenance	.50	
Other	1.30	8.00
Total		$66.00

These costs have been determined using a normal production quantity of 55,000 gates per month. All gates are transferred to the Amarillo Division, where they are hung on posts, painted with rustproof paint, and sold to distributors.

During October 2009, El Paso Division produced 50,000 gates and incurred the following costs.

Pipe (2,590,000 feet purchased and used)	$1,813,000
Direct labor (120,000 hours)	1,086,000
Indirect material	40,000
Indirect labor	25,000
Depreciation	155,000
Utilities	52,500
Maintenance	17,500
Other	55,000

Required:

(a) What is the standard total cost for October's production? What was the total actual cost of production for October? Based on these figures, did the manager of the division do a good job in controlling costs?

(b) Prepare a line-by-line comparison of standard and actual costs for October. Based on these figures, what

concerns might be expressed about the manager's ability to control costs?

(c) Assume that top management of Tejas Fence Co. has decided to establish a "selling price" of $85 for the gates from El Paso Division to the Amarillo Division. One of the reasons for the increased usage of pipe during October was that the pipe purchased was of slightly inferior quality than the pipe normally used. Because of this, Amarillo Division refused to "pay" $85 for the gates and established a price of $80 per gate. Calculate the revenue variances for El Paso Division.

(d) A "selling price" between divisions is referred to as a transfer price. Use logic and library or Internet resources to discuss how and why such a price might be set.

27. **Return on Investment** (LO 14.4)

Gray Corp. has three divisions that are classified as investment centers. Selected financial information about the each division follows.

	Division 1	Division 2	Division 3
Net income for year	$ 900,000	$ 1,960,000	$ 2,680,000
Sales for year	3,138,000	7,972,000	16,462,000
Assets	28,700,000	58,876,000	54,518,000

Required:

(a) Calculate the return on investment for each division. How would you rank the divisions in terms of levels of performance?

(b) Calculate the profit margin and asset turnover for each division. How would you rank the divisions in terms of levels of performance?

(c) Assume that the manager of Division 1 was new to her job. She has found that the previous manager did not dispose of approximately $4,800,000 of assets that were no longer being used by the division to manufacture products. Exclude these assets from the asset base and recalculate the asset turnover and return on investment for Division 1. Does this information affect your rankings of the division's performance? Explain.

28. **Balanced Scorecard and Performance Reward** (LO 14.5 and 14.6)

You are the owner of a small movie-rental store run by a full-time manager.

Required:

(a) Develop a brief mission statement for your business.

(b) Prepare a balanced scorecard for the manager, providing at least three measurements in each balanced scorecard category. Make certain that your measurements reflect the business mission.

(c) Prepare a balanced scorecard for the four part-time employees of the business, providing at least two measurements in each balanced scorecard category.

(d) Why are there differences between the scorecards developed in parts (b) and (c)?

(e) Design a reward system that would encourage the store manager to achieve the scorecard metrics.

CASES

29. **Value-Added and Non-Value-Added Activities** (LO 14.1, writing)

There is a distinct difference in many organizations between instituting activities that enhance quality production or service and activities that would be considered quality inspection. For example, installing a machine that has an automatic cutoff when a flawed product is detected is considered quality enhancement and is value-added. Having employees inspect each product after production is completed is non-value-added.

Required:

Choose an organization with which you are familiar, such as your school or your workplace. Write a short paper on some of the quality activities that you believe are value-added and some of the quality activities that you believe are non-value-added. Explain the reasons for your classifications.

30. **Benchmarking** (LO 14.6, group, Internet)

The most successful companies often earn that distinction by having the most successful operating procedures. Companies competing in the same industry often want to mimic those procedures; however, some procedures might be successful in noncompeting companies as well. For example, excellence in customer service is good for all industries. Form groups of four students and choose an industry (manufacturing or service) to research best practices.

Required—Individuals:

(a) Use library and Internet resources to research benchmarking and "best in class" (or "world-class") companies.

(b) What organizations did you find that were mentioned as being "best in class"?

(c) What types of criteria were used to make this judgment?

Required—Groups:

(a) Get together as a group and combine your research. How was your research similar and different?

(b) Are the best practices you found specific to the industry in which the organization operates or would they be useful in other industries?

31. **Profit Center and Performance Measures** (LO 14.4 and 14.6, writing, ethics)

Icon Film Manufacturers makes film for still and motion picture cameras and other related items. Icon is divided into several divisions, each of which is treated as a profit center. Icon's upper management rewards the manager of the 35 mm film division with an annual bonus equal to a percentage of the net income of the division.

Required:

(a) Is net income the best way to evaluate the manager's performance? Explain your answer.

(b) Should net income be the only method used to evaluate the manager's performance? If not, list other measures.

(c) Can the manager of a profit center manipulate net income to increase his/her year-end bonus? Explain your answer.

(d) During a conversation with the chief executive officer (CEO) of Icon, you learn that the manager of the 35 mm film division is planning to retire in two years. Write a memo to Icon's CEO explaining the items discussed in parts (a), (b), and (c) and why these evaluation methods and concerns may be more important given the manager's impending retirement.

32. **Annual Reports** (LO 14.3 and 14.4, Internet)

Use the annual report of Carnival Corporation for the 2007 fiscal year to answer the following questions. Specifically, look at the Income Statement (Consolidated Statement of Operations) and the Statement of Stockholders' Equity for the fiscal year ended November 30, 2007. This information can be found on either the annual report or the SEC 10-K filing at www.carnival.com by following the links to Investor Relations.

Required:

(a) Assume that Carnival has two investment centers: cruise and tour. (Hint: See page F-21 of the 10-K and consider "Other" to be "Tours.")

    (1) Calculate the return on investment for 2005, 2006, and 2007 for each center using the Du Pont model.

    (2) Compare year to year for each division and comment on the trend for each division.

    (3) Compare the two divisions and comment on the relationship.

(b) Carnival lists corporate expenses that are not assigned to a particular division. If Carnival plans to treat divisions as investment centers, should the corporate expenses be divided between the divisions? If yes, what is the best method?

33. Performance Rewards *(LO 14.6; writing)*

Holland's is a small ladies' clothing store with 14 employees. On any day, eight or nine employees will be scheduled to work. More than 95 percent of Holland's revenues are from the sale of clothing, and the remainder is from the sale of accessories such as gentle fabric wash, stain remover, padded hangers, and so forth.

Employees are informed of the daily sales projection, but individual employees are not given a sales quota. March is Holland's slowest month. To encourage the salespeople to work harder in March, they are given $0.25 for every accessory item they sell, and the top salesperson gets a $10 bonus for the month.

Required:

(a) Is the $0.25 incentive a good performance reward? Can it be improved? Explain.

(b) Is the $10 bonus a good performance reward? Can it be improved? Explain.

SUPPLEMENTAL PROBLEMS

34. Value-Added and Non-Value-Added Activities *(LO 14.1; Compare to Problem 22)*

Judy Eibel is the personnel manager at Smart, Inc. She has analyzed her applicant interview process for the last two weeks and has found she consistently performs the following activities.

(a) Reads applicant's resume

(b) Straightens desk prior to interview

(c) Walks from desk to get cup of coffee

(d) Returns to desk and drinks coffee

(e) Scans applicant's resume

(f) Uses intercom to ask receptionist to send in applicant

(g) Stands to greet applicant

(h) Shakes applicant's hand

(i) Sits down

(j) Picks up resume and scans

(k) Interviews applicant

(l) Stands to say goodbye to applicant

(m) Shakes applicant's hand

(n) Sits down

(o) Scans resume

(p) Makes notes on interview

(q) Walks from desk to get cup of coffee

(r) Returns to desk and drinks coffee

(s) Makes decision about whether to hire applicant

Required:

Indicate whether each of these activities is value-added or non-value-added, as related to the outcome of the activity. Provide a brief reason for each of your determinations.

35. Activity-Based Costing *(LO 14.3; Compare to Problem 23)*

The purchasing department of Xena Co. creates $676,000 of overhead costs each year. The annual cost and quantity of activity involved in each primary task in the department follow.

Activity	Cost	Driver	Quantity of Driver
Finding suppliers	$160,000	# of Internet searches	50,000
Issuing purchase orders	380,000	# of purchase orders	10,000
Matching POs and receiving reports	136,000	# of matches	8,000

The number of purchase orders differs from the number of matches required because many suppliers ship multiple orders together. Product #548 required 25 Internet searches, 4 purchase orders, and 1 match.

Required:

(a)   Assume that Xena allocates all purchasing department costs to products using number of purchase orders issued only. Calculate the purchasing department cost that would be allocated to Product #548.

(b)   Assume that Xena allocates purchasing department costs to products using activity-based costing.

Determine the cost per type of activity in the purchasing department. Determine the purchasing department cost that would be allocated to Product #548.

(c)   Which of the two allocations do you believe to be a more accurate representation of the cost of Product #548? Explain the reasoning for your answer.

APPENDIX

Table A-1 Present Value of $1

Period	1.00%	1.50%	2.00%	2.50%	3.00%	3.50%	4.00%	4.50%	5.00%	5.50%	6.00%	6.50%
1	0.9901	0.9852	0.0980	0.9756	0.9709	0.9662	0.9615	0.9569	0.9524	0.9479	0.9434	0.9390
2	0.9803	0.9707	0.9612	0.9518	0.9426	0.9335	0.9246	0.9157	0.9070	0.8985	0.8900	0.8817
3	0.9706	0.9563	0.9423	0.9286	0.9151	0.9019	0.8890	0.8163	0.8638	0.8516	0.8396	0.8278
4	0.9610	0.9422	0.9239	0.9059	0.8885	0.8714	0.8548	0.8386	0.8227	0.8072	0.7921	0.7773
5	0.9515	0.9283	0.9057	0.8839	0.8626	0.8420	0.8219	0.8025	0.7835	0.7651	0.7473	0.7299
6	0.9421	0.9145	0.8880	0.8623	0.8375	0.8135	0.7903	0.7679	0.7462	0.7253	0.7050	0.6853
7	0.9327	0.9010	0.8706	0.8413	0.8131	0.7860	0.7599	0.7348	0.7107	0.6874	0.6651	0.6435
8	0.9235	0.8877	0.8535	0.8208	0.7894	0.7594	0.7307	0.7032	0.6768	0.6516	0.6274	0.6042
9	0.9143	0.8746	0.8368	0.8007	0.7664	0.7337	0.7026	0.6729	0.6446	0.6176	0.5919	0.5674
10	0.9053	0.8617	0.8204	0.7812	0.7441	0.7089	0.6756	0.6439	0.6139	0.5854	0.5584	0.5327
11	0.8963	0.8489	0.8043	0.7621	0.7224	0.6850	0.6496	0.6162	0.5847	0.5549	0.5268	0.5002
12	0.8875	0.8364	0.7885	0.7436	0.7014	0.6618	0.6246	0.5897	0.5568	0.5259	0.4970	0.4697
13	0.8787	0.8240	0.7730	0.7254	0.6810	0.6394	0.6006	0.5643	0.5303	0.4986	0.4688	0.4410
14	0.8700	0.8119	0.7579	0.7077	0.6611	0.6178	0.5775	0.5399	0.5051	0.4726	0.4423	0.4141
15	0.8614	0.7999	0.7430	0.6905	0.6419	0.5969	0.5553	0.5167	0.4810	0.4479	0.4173	0.3888
16	0.8528	0.7880	0.7285	0.6736	0.6232	0.5767	0.5339	0.4945	0.4581	0.4246	0.3937	0.3651
17	0.8444	0.7764	0.7142	0.6572	0.6050	0.5512	0.5134	0.4732	0.4363	0.4025	0.3714	0.3428
18	0.8360	0.7649	0.7002	0.6412	0.5874	0.5384	0.4936	0.4528	0.4155	0.3815	0.3503	0.3219
19	0.8277	0.7536	0.6864	0.6255	0.5703	0.5202	0.4746	0.4333	0.3957	0.3616	0.3305	0.3022
20	0.8195	0.7425	0.6730	0.6103	0.5537	0.5026	0.4564	0.4146	0.3769	0.3427	0.3118	0.2838
30	0.7419	0.6398	0.5521	0.4767	0.4120	0.3563	0.3083	0.2670	0.2314	0.2006	0.1741	0.1519

Period	7.00%	7.50%	8.00%	8.50%	9.00%	9.50%	10.00%	10.50%	11.00%	12.00%	20.00%
1	0.9346	0.7488	0.9259	0.9212	0.9174	0.9132	0.9091	0.9050	0.9009	0.8929	0.8333
2	0.8734	0.6966	0.8573	0.8495	0.8417	0.8340	0.8265	0.8190	0.8116	0.7972	0.6944
3	0.8163	0.6479	0.7938	0.7829	0.7722	0.7617	0.7513	0.7412	0.7312	0.7118	0.5787
4	0.7629	0.6028	0.7350	0.7216	0.7084	0.6956	0.6830	0.6707	0.6587	0.6355	0.4823
5	0.7130	0.5607	0.6806	0.6650	0.6499	0.6352	0.6209	0.6070	0.5935	0.5674	0.4019
6	0.6663	0.5216	0.6302	0.6129	0.5963	0.5801	0.5645	0.5493	0.5346	0.5066	0.3349
7	0.6228	0.4852	0.5835	0.5649	0.5470	0.5298	0.5132	0.4971	0.4817	0.4524	0.2791
8	0.5820	0.4513	0.5403	0.5207	0.5019	0.4838	0.4665	0.4499	0.4339	0.4039	0.2326
9	0.5439	0.4199	0.5003	0.4799	0.4604	0.4419	0.4241	0.4071	0.3909	0.3606	0.1938
10	0.5084	0.3906	0.4632	0.4423	0.4224	0.4035	0.3855	0.3685	0.3522	0.3220	0.1615
11	0.4751	0.3633	0.4289	0.4076	0.3875	0.3685	0.3505	0.3340	0.3173	0.2875	0.1346
12	0.4440	0.3380	0.3971	0.3757	0.3555	0.3365	0.3186	0.3018	0.2858	0.2567	0.1122
13	0.4150	0.3144	0.3677	0.3463	0.3262	0.3073	0.2897	0.2731	0.2575	0.2292	0.0935
14	0.3878	0.2925	0.3405	0.3191	0.2993	0.2807	0.2633	0.2471	0.232	0.2046	0.0779
15	0.3625	0.2720	0.3152	0.2941	0.2745	0.2563	0.2394	0.2237	0.209	0.1827	0.0649
16	0.3387	0.2531	0.2919	0.2711	0.2519	0.2341	0.2176	0.2024	0.1883	0.1631	0.0541
17	0.3166	0.2354	0.2703	0.2499	0.2311	0.2138	0.1978	0.1832	0.1696	0.1456	0.0451
18	0.2959	0.2190	0.2503	0.2303	0.2120	0.1952	0.1799	0.1658	0.1528	0.1300	0.0376
19	0.2765	0.2037	0.2317	0.2122	0.1945	0.1783	0.1635	0.1500	0.1377	0.1161	0.0313
20	0.2584	0.1895	0.2146	0.1956	0.1784	0.1628	0.1486	0.1358	0.124	0.1037	0.0261
30	0.1314	0.1142	0.0994	0.0865	0.0754	0.0657	0.0573	0.0500	0.0437	0.0334	0.0042

Table A-2   Present Value of an Ordinary Annuity of $1

Period	1.00%	1.50%	2.00%	2.50%	3.00%	3.50%	4.00%	4.50%	5.00%	5.50%	6.00%	6.50%
1	0.9901	0.9852	0.9804	0.9756	0.9709	0.9662	0.9615	0.9569	0.0524	0.9479	0.9434	0.9390
2	1.9704	1.9559	1.9416	1.9274	1.9135	1.8997	1.8861	1.8727	1.8594	1.8463	1.8334	1.8207
3	2.9410	2.9122	2.8839	2.8560	2.8286	2.8016	2.7751	2.7489	2.7233	2.6979	2.6485	1.6485
4	3.9020	3.8544	3.8077	3.7620	3.7171	3.6731	3.6299	3.5875	3.5460	3.5051	3.4651	1.4258
5	4.8534	4.7826	4.7135	4.6458	4.5797	4.5150	4.4518	4.3899	4.3295	4.2703	4.2124	1.1557
6	5.7955	5.6972	5.6014	5.5081	5.4172	5.3286	5.2421	5.1579	5.0757	4.9956	4.9173	1.8410
7	6.7282	6.5972	6.4720	6.3494	6.2303	6.1145	6.0021	5.8927	5.7864	5.6830	5.5824	1.4845
8	7.6517	7.4859	7.3255	7.1701	7.0197	6.8740	6.7327	6.5959	6.4632	6.3356	6.2098	1.0888
9	8.5660	9.2222	8.1622	7.9709	7.7861	7.6070	7.4353	7.2688	7.1078	6.9522	6.8017	1.6561
10	9.7413	10.0711	8.9826	8.7521	8.5302	8.3167	8.1109	7.9127	7.7217	7.5376	7.3601	1.1888
11	10.3676	10.9075	9.7869	9.5142	9.2526	9.0020	8.7605	8.5290	8.3064	8.0925	7.8869	1.6890
12	11.2551	11.9075	10.5753	10.2578	9.9540	9.6633	9.3851	9.1186	8.8633	8.6185	8.3838	1.1588
13	12.1337	11.7315	11.3484	10.9832	10.6350	10.3027	9.9857	10.2228	9.3936	9.1171	8.8527	1.5997
14	13.0037	12.5439	12.1063	11.6909	11.2961	10.9205	10.5631	10.7396	9.8986	9.5897	9.2950	1.0138
15	13.8651	13.3432	12.8493	12.3814	11.9379	11.5174	11.1184	11.2340	10.3797	10.0376	9.7123	1.4027
16	14.7179	14.1313	13.5777	13.0550	12.5611	12.0941	11.6523	11.7072	10.8378	10.4622	10.1059	1.7678
17	15.5623	14.9077	14.2919	13.7122	13.1661	12.6513	12.1657	12.1600	11.2741	10.8646	10.4773	10.1106
18	16.3983	15.6726	14.9920	14.3534	13.7535	13.1897	12.6593	12.5933	11.6896	11.2461	10.8276	10.4325
19	17.2260	16.4262	15.6785	14.9789	14.3238	13.7098	13.1339	13.0080	12.0853	11.6077	11.1581	10.7347
20	18.0456	17.1686	16.3514	15.5892	14.8775	14.2124	13.5903	13.4047	12.4622	11.9505	11.4699	11.0185
30	25.8077	24.0159	22.3965	20.9303	19.6004	18.3921	17.2920	16.2889	15.3725	14.5338	13.7648	13.0587

Period	7.00%	7.50%	8.00%	8.50%	9.00%	9.50%	10.00%	10.50%	11.00%	12.00%	20.00%
1	0.9346	0.9302	0.9259	0.9217	0.9174	0.9132	0.9091	0.9050	0.9009	0.0897	0.8333
2	1.8080	1.7956	1.7833	1.7711	1.7591	1.7473	1.7355	1.7240	1.7125	1.7012	1.5278
3	2.6243	2.6005	2.5771	2.5540	2.5313	2.5089	2.4869	2.4651	2.4437	2.4226	2.1065
4	3.3872	3.3493	3.3121	3.2756	3.2397	3.2045	3.1699	3.1359	3.1025	3.0696	2.5887
5	4.1002	4.0459	3.9927	3.9406	3.8897	3.8397	3.7908	3.7429	3.6959	3.6499	2.9906
6	4.7665	4.6938	4.6229	4.5536	4.4859	4.4198	4.3553	4.2922	4.2305	4.1703	3.3255
7	5.3893	5.2966	5.2064	5.1185	5.0330	4.9496	4.8684	4.7893	4.7122	4.6370	3.6046
8	5.9713	5.8573	5.7466	5.6392	5.5348	5.4334	5.3349	5.2392	5.1461	5.0556	3.8372
9	6.5152	6.3789	6.2469	6.1191	5.9953	5.8753	5.7590	5.6463	5.5371	5.4311	4.0310
10	7.0236	6.8641	6.7101	6.5613	6.4177	6.2788	6.1446	6.0148	5.8892	5.7678	4.1925
11	7.4987	7.3154	7.1390	6.9689	6.8052	6.6473	6.4951	6.3482	6.2065	6.0698	4.3271
12	7.9427	7.7353	7.5361	7.3447	7.1607	6.9838	6.8137	6.6500	6.4924	6.3406	4.4392
13	8.3577	8.1259	7.9038	7.6909	7.4869	7.2912	7.1034	6.9230	6.7499	6.5835	4.5327
14	8.7455	8.4892	8.2442	8.0101	7.7862	7.5719	7.3667	7.1702	6.9819	6.8013	4.6106
15	9.1079	8.8271	8.5595	8.3424	8.0607	7.8282	7.6061	7.3938	7.1909	6.9967	4.6755
16	9.4467	9.1415	8.8514	8.5753	8.3126	8.0623	7.8237	7.5962	7.3792	7.1719	4.7296
17	9.7632	9.4339	9.1216	8.8252	8.5436	8.2760	8.0216	7.7794	7.5488	7.3291	4.7746
18	10.0591	9.7060	9.3719	9.0555	8.7556	8.4713	8.2014	7.9452	7.7016	7.4700	4.8122
19	10.3356	9.9591	9.6036	9.2677	8.9501	8.6496	8.3649	8.0952	7.8939	7.5964	4.8435
20	10.5940	10.1945	9.8182	9.4633	9.1286	8.8124	8.5136	8.2309	7.9633	7.7098	4.8696
30	12.4090	11.8104	11.2578	10.7468	10.2737	9.8347	9.4269	9.0474	8.6938	8.0552	4.9789

GLOSSARY

A

account The basic storage unit for financial data in an accounting system; the compilation of all accounts is the general ledger

accounting cycle The set of recurring accounting procedures that must be performed for a business each accounting period

accounting equation The mathematical expression indicating that the sum of an entity's assets must equal the collective sum of its liabilities and stockholders' (or owners') equity

accounting period concept An accounting principle that allows accountants to prepare meaningful financial reports for ongoing business enterprises by dividing the lives of these entities into regular reporting intervals of equal length; also referred to as the *periodicity principle*

accounting A service activity designed to provide quantitative information about economic entities that is intended to be useful in making economic decisions

account payable A current liability that represents an amount owed by a business to a supplier (generally for inventory purchases)

account receivable A current asset owed to a business, generally used for an as-yet uncollected sale to a customer

accounts receivable turnover ratio A measure of how often a business collects or "turns over" its accounts receivable each year; calculated as net credit sales divided by average accounts receivable

accrual basis of accounting A method of accounting in which the economic impact of a transaction is recognized

(recorded), whether or not the transaction involves cash

accrued asset A receivable resulting from a revenue that has been earned but not yet received

accrued liability A debt resulting from a past transaction that was recorded at the end of an accounting period; often must be estimated

accumulated depreciation The total amount of depreciation that has been recorded on a depreciable asset or group of depreciable assets since acquisition

activity Any repetitive action performed to fulfill a business function

activity-based costing A method of allocating overhead costs to products and services that collects and allocates costs based on the underlying activities performed to make, render, distribute, or support those products and services

activity-based management The process of investigating activities performed during product manufacturing or service performance to classify those activities as value-added or non-value-added; helps management streamline the process to increase customer value and business profitability

actual cost system An inventory valuation method that uses the actual costs of material, labor, and overhead to compute product cost

adjusting entry A journal entry made at the end of an accounting period to ensure that the revenue recognition and expense recognition rules are properly applied that period

age of inventory A measure of how old inventory on hand is; calculated as 360 days divided by the inventory turnover ratio

age of receivables A measure of the collectibility of accounts receivable; calculated as 360 divided by the accounts receivable turnover ratio

allowance method An accounting method used to estimate and record the uncollectible accounts expense each accounting period

amortization The accounting process of writing off, as an expense, the cost of an intangible asset over its useful life to the business

annuity A series of payments of a specified size and frequency

applied overhead The amount of predetermined overhead that is added to the Work in Process Inventory account

asset turnover A ratio that indicates the dollars of sales generated by each dollar of asset investment; calculated as (sales divided by asset investment)

asset A probable future economic benefit obtained or controlled by a particular entity as a result of past transactions or events

authorized stock The maximum number of shares of a given class of stock a company is permitted to issue under the terms of its corporate charter

available-for-sale securities Investments in stocks or bonds that are made for the short term and to generate a rate of return that is greater than what could be earned by investing excess cash in an interest-bearing account

B

balance sheet A financial statement that summarizes the assets, liabilities, and stockholders' (owners') equity of an entity at a specific point in time

balanced scorecard A performance measurement system that provides

403

monetary and nonmonetary measurements for financial, customer, internal process, and learning/growth/innovation categories; focuses on multiple types of leading and lagging indicators

bank reconciliation A schedule that presents the differences between the bank statement and the cash account so that an accurate cash balance can be determined at a specific time

benchmarking The process of comparing an organization's products, processes, or services against those of organizations that have been proven to be ''best in class''

bond indenture The legal contract between a bond purchaser and the issuing company; identifies the rights and obligations of each party

bond A long-term loan made by one party to another that is legally documented by a bond certificate

book value (of a PP&E asset) The cost of a depreciable property, plant, and equipment asset minus its accumulated depreciation

book value per share Common stockholders' equity per share for a corporation; calculated by dividing total common stockholders' equity by the number of outstanding shares of common stock

break-even graph A visual depiction of the relationships among revenue, volume, fixed costs, and variable costs; the point at which the total revenue and total cost lines intersect is the break-even point

break-even point The level of sales at which no profits are generated and no losses are incurred

budget A financial plan for the future

budgeting Planning for the future using monetary amounts

business value-added activity An activity that is essential to operations, but for which customers would not willingly choose to pay

business An organization that attempts to earn a return over the cost of providing services or goods that satisfy the needs or wants of others

C

callable bond A bond that can be retired or redeemed by the issuing company when one or more conditions are met

callable preferred stock Preferred stock that can be reacquired, usually at a call premium, at the option of the issuing corporation

capital budget The plan for long-term expenditures for plant assets

capital lease A lease that is generally noncancelable, is long term, and transfers at least some ownership rights or risks to the lessee

cash basis of accounting A method of accounting in which revenues are recorded when cash is received and expenses are recorded when cash is disbursed

cash dividend A proportionate distribution of a company's prior earnings to its stockholders made in the form of cash

cash equivalent Any investment in a short-term security, such as a certificates of deposit (CD), money market fund, and U.S. treasury bill, that has 90 days or less to maturity when purchased

cash flow per share A measure of the net cash flow from operating activities for an accounting period, less preferred stock dividends, divided by the weighted average number of shares of common stock outstanding during that period

chart of accounts A numerical listing, by assigned account number, of a business's accounts

closing entry A journal entry made at the end of an accounting period to transfer the balance of one or more temporary accounts to the appropriate stockholders' (owners') equity account

common stock A class of stock that represents a corporation's residual ownership interests

common stock The total par or stated value of the number of shares of stock that a corporation has issued

common-sized financial statement A financial statement in which each

line item is expressed as a percentage of a major financial statement component

comparability A measure of the degree to which an entity's accounting information can be easily compared with similar information reported for the entity in prior accounting periods and with similar information reported by other entities

compound journal entry A journal entry that affects more than two accounts

conservatism principle An accounting principle dictating that uncertainty regarding an asset's or revenue's valuation should generally be resolved in favor of understating the asset or revenue; for liabilities and expenses, the uncertainty should be resolved in favor of overstatement

consolidation The process of combining the financial statements of a parent and its more-than-50-percent owned subsidiary at the end of a period

constant mix assumption An assumption made in break-even or cost-volume-profit analysis for a multiproduct firm that products will be produced and sold in a stated proportional relationship to one another

contingent liability A potential liability that may become an actual liability if one or more events occur or fail to occur

contra-account An account that is an offset to or reduction of a related account for financial statement purposes

contribution margin ratio The percentage of revenue that remains after variable costs are covered; calculated as unit contribution margin divided by unit selling price

contribution margin The difference between the selling price per unit (or in total) and the total variable cost per unit (or in total)

controllable cost A cost that a manager can authorize or directly influence in terms of dollar magnitude

conversion cost The cost of direct labor and overhead

convertible bond A bond that may be exchanged for stock in the issuing company at the option of a bondholder

convertible preferred stock Preferred stock that can be exchanged, at the option of a preferred stockholder, for common stock of the issuing corporation

copyright An exclusive right granted by the government to produce and sell "knowledge" works such as songs, books, and films

corporate charter A contract between a corporation and its state of domicile; identifies the corporation's principal rights and obligations

corporation An entity created by law and having an existence apart from that of its members as well as distinct and inherent rights and duties

cost center A responsibility center in which the manager is solely responsible for controlling costs

cost driver A factor that has a direct cause–effect relationship with a cost

cost method (of accounting for a stock investment) The method of accounting used when a company owns less than 20 percent of another company; the investing company recognizes Dividend Revenue when cash dividends are received

cost object Any item to which management wants to attach costs, such as an organizational product, service, department, or territory

cost of goods available for sale The sum of beginning inventory and merchandise purchases minus purchase returns for an accounting period or (for a manufacturing company) the sum of the cost of beginning Finished Goods Inventory and cost of goods manufactured for an accounting period

cost of goods manufactured The total cost of production for a period; calculated as the cost of beginning Work in Process Inventory plus the cost of direct material, direct labor, and overhead used during the period minus the cost of ending Work in Process Inventory

cost-volume-profit analysis A model that expands the break-even model to include the profitability effects created by the relationships among selling prices, costs, and volumes

credit term An agreement between a buyer and seller regarding the timing of payment by the buyer and any discount available to the buyer for early payment

credit The right-hand side of a T-account or an entry made on the right-hand side of a T-account (or in the credit column of an account); as a verb, to enter an amount on the right-hand side of a T-account or in the credit column of an account

cross-sectional ratio analysis A comparison of a company's financial ratios with those of competing companies and/or with the industry norms for those ratios

cumulative preferred stock Preferred stock on which dividends that are not paid in a given year accumulate and must be paid in the future before common stockholders can receive a dividend

current asset Cash or another asset that will be converted into cash, sold, or consumed during the next fiscal year or the normal operating cycle of a business, whichever is longer

current liability A debt or obligation of a business that will be eliminated by giving up current assets or incurring another current liability

current ratio A measure of liquidity calculated as current assets divided by current liabilities

current replacement cost The per unit cost that a business must pay to replace an item sold or disposed of

D

debenture A bond backed only by the issuing firm's legal commitment to make all required principal and interest payments

debit The left-hand side of a T-account or an entry made on the left-hand side of a T-account (or in the debit column of an account); as a verb, to enter an amount on the left-hand side of a T-account or in the debit column of an account

debt to total asset ratio A solvency ratio that indicates the ability of a company to meet its long-term debts; calculated as total liabilities divided by total assets

deferred expense An asset representing a prepayment of an expense item

deferred revenue A liability resulting from an amount received by a business for a service or product that will be provided or delivered in the future

degree of operating leverage A measure of the extent to which a percentage change in sales from the current level will affect profits (or losses); calculated as total contribution margin divided by pretax profit

depletion The accounting process of writing off, as an expense, the cost of a natural resource asset over its useful life to the business

depreciable cost The acquisition cost of a depreciable asset less its salvage value

depreciation The accounting process of writing off, as an expense, the cost of a property, plant or equipment asset over its useful life to the business

direct cost A cost that is clearly and conveniently traceable to, and a monetarily important part of, a specified cost object

direct labor Factory or service employees who work specifically on manufacturing a product or providing a service; the wages (or salaries) of such employees

direct material A readily clearly identifiable and conveniently traceable part of a product, the cost of which is monetarily significant to the total product; the cost of such a product part

direct method (of preparing a statement of cash flows) An approach to preparing the statement of cash flows in which specific cash inflows and outflows from a business's operating activities are specifically listed in the initial section of the financial statement

direct write-off method An accounting method in which uncollectible accounts expense is recorded when it is determined that a specific account receivable is unlikely to be collected; a non-GAAP alternative to the allowance method that may be used for tax purposes

discontinued operation A business segment that is no longer a part of the organization; information on the income and asset disposal of such a segment is shown (with related tax effects) as a separate section of the income statement

discounting The process of removing the interest portion of future cash receipts (payments) so as to obtain the present value of those future receipts (payments)

dividend in arrears The unpaid dividend amount on cumulative preferred stock; should be disclosed in a company's financial statement footnotes

dividend yield The annual dividend paid on a stock divided by its current market price

dividend A distribution of earnings by a corporation to stockholders

double-declining-balance method A depreciation method in which annual depreciation expense is calculated by multiplying an asset's book value at the beginning of the year by twice the straight-line rate of depreciation

double-entry bookkeeping A method of maintaining financial records developed more than five hundred years ago that serves as the foundation of modern accounting systems worldwide

Du Pont model A restatement of the return on investment formula to provide information about profit margin and asset turnover; calculated as (income ÷ sales) × (sales ÷ asset investment)

E

earnings per share The corporate earnings for a period that accrue to an individual share of stock; calculated as (net income minus PS dividends) divided by the weighted-average number of shares of common stock outstanding during a given year

earnings quality The degree of correlation between a firm's economic income and its reported earnings determined by generally accepted accounting principles

effective interest rate The market interest rate on the date bonds are initially sold; represents the true rate of interest incurred over a bond's life by the issuing company;

also known as the market interest rate

entity concept An accounting principle dictating that a business enterprise be treated as a distinct unit independent of its owners

equity method (of accounting for a stock investment) The method of accounting used when a company owns 20 percent or more of another company; the investing company recognizes its proportionate share of the investee's profits (or losses) for the period in income and as an increase to the Investment account; the Investment account is reduced when cash dividends are received

equivalent units of production An estimate of the number of fully completed units that could have been manufactured in a process costing production environment during a certain period if all production efforts had resulted in completed units

expense A cost of doing business; a decrease in an asset or an increase in a liability resulting from an entity's profit-oriented activities

extraordinary item A material gain or loss that is both unusual in nature and infrequent in occurrence in the environment in which the business operates; the gain or loss is shown (with related tax effects) as a separate section of the income statement

F

FIFO (first-in, first-out) method An inventory costing method in which the per unit costs of the most recently acquired goods are used to establish the cost basis of ending inventory

Financial Accounting Standards Board (FASB) The private-sector rule-making body that has the primary authority for establishing accounting standards in the United States

financial ratio A measure that express the relationship or interrelationships between, or among, two or more financial statement items

financial statement footnote An inclusion to an annual report that is intended to assist decision makers

in interpreting and drawing proper conclusions from an entity's financial statements

financial statement A report about monetary information related to a business; the most common financial statements are the income statement, balance sheet, statement of stockholders' equity, and statement of cash flows; collectively, these items are the principal means accountants use to communicate financial information regarding business entities and other organizations to investors, creditors, and other decision makers external to those entities

financing activity Any transaction or event of a business that involves obtaining cash from lenders and/or repaying those amounts as well as obtaining cash from investors and providing them with a return of and a return on their investments

fiscal year The 12-month period covered by an entity's income statement; begins on other than Jan. 1

fixed cost A cost that remains constant in total with changes in activity as long as operations are within the relevant range; varies inversely on a per-unit basis with changes in activity

flexible budget A series of expected costs for the upcoming period based on various levels of activity

FOB destination Shipping term in which the seller delivers the goods free on board (FOB) to the destination; the seller incurs the freight charge and retains legal possession of the goods until they reach the destination

FOB shipping point Shipping term in which the seller delivers the goods free on board (FOB) to the shipping point; the buyer incurs the freight charge and obtains legal possession of the goods once they reach the shipping point

free cash flow A measure of the cash generated by a company's operations in excess of that needed to maintain current organizational productivity; calculated as cash flow from operating activities minus capital investments for property, plant, and equipment

full disclosure principle An accounting principle dictating that all information needed to obtain a thorough understanding of an entity's financial affairs be included in its financial statements or accompanying narrative disclosures

G

general journal The accounting record in which amounts for transactions and other financial events are initially recorded by a business; the book of original entry for transactions

general ledger The accounting record that contains each of the individual accounts for a business's assets, liabilities, stockholders' (owners') equity, revenues, expenses, and dividends

generally accepted accounting principles (GAAP) The collection of concepts, guidelines, principles, and rules that are used in applying double-entry bookkeeping to recording and reporting financial information

going concern assumption An accounting principle dictating that an entity should be treated as if it will continue to operate long enough to use its longest-lived asset; this time frame is often assumed to be indefinite, unless there is evidence to the contrary

goodwill The excess of the cost of assets over their collective market value minus any liabilities acquired

gross profit percentage The profit margin generated by a product's sale; calculated as cost of goods sold divided by sales

gross profit The difference between net sales and cost of goods sold during an accounting period

H

historical cost principle An accounting principle dictating that the primary valuation basis for most assets is their historical or original costs

horizontal ratio analysis *See trend analysis*

I

impairment The excess of the carrying value of an asset over its current fair market value or the present value of its expected future net cash flows

income from continuing operations The earnings produced by a corporation's principal profit-oriented activities

income statement A financial statement summarizing a business's revenues and expenses (and gains and losses) for a given accounting period

incremental analysis A method of finding solutions to problems by focusing only on the factors that change from one course of action to another

indirect cost A cost that is not clearly and conveniently traceable to a cost object or is not monetarily significant to the total cost of a cost object; a cost that is assigned to a cost object using some rational allocation base

indirect labor Factory (or service) employees who do not work directly on production (or sales), but are considered part of overhead; the wages (or salaries) of such employees

indirect material A product part that is not identifiable, traceable, or monetarily significant to the product; included as part of overhead; the cost of such a product part

indirect method (of preparing a statement of cash flows) An approach to preparing the statement of cash flows in which net cash flow from operating activities is determined by making certain adjustments to a business's net income

intangible asset A long-term asset used in the business that does not have a physical form or substance

International Financial Reporting Standards (IFRS) A set of global accounding standards with which U.S. accounding standards are being converged

inventory turnover ratio A measure of how often a business sells or turns over its inventory each year; calculated as cost of goods sold divided by average inventory

inventory Any item that a business intends to sell to customers as well as, in a manufacturing company, any raw material and in-process item that will be converted into a saleable good

investing activity Any transaction or event of a business that includes the making and collecting of loans, acquiring and disposing of property, plant and equipment, and/or purchasing and selling debt and equity securities (other than trading securities and cash equivalents of another firm)

investment center A responsibility center in which the manager is responsible for controlling costs, generating revenue, and obtaining a positive return on the asset base

issued stock The number of shares of a class of stock that have been sold or otherwise distributed by a corporation; these shares may be outstanding or held as treasury stock

J

job order costing system An inventory costing system used by manufacturers producing goods in relatively small quantities, often to customer specifications, or by service companies that need to accumulate costs for individual customers

job A cost object related to a specific order or customer

journalize The process of recording financial data about a transaction of a business in a journal

L

labor efficiency variance The cost saved (favorable) or lost (unfavorable) because of the difference between the actual hours worked and the standard hours allowed for the actual production multiplied by the standard wage rate

labor rate variance The cost saved (favorable) or lost (unfavorable) because of the difference between the actual wages paid and the standard wages allowed for the actual hours worked

leasehold A right given to use property for a given period of time in exchange for rent payments; the property user is the lessee and the property owner is the lessor

leasehold improvement A betterment made to a leased property by a lessee that reverts to the lessor at the end of the lease

liability A probable future sacrifice of economic benefits; an amount owed by an entity to a nonowner

LIFO (last-in, first-out) method An inventory costing method in which the per unit costs of the earliest acquired goods are used to establish the cost basis of ending inventory

liquidity The ability to finance day-to-day operations and pay liabilities as they mature; closeness of an asset to cash

longitudinal ratio analysis A variation of ratio analysis that focuses on the changes in a business's ratios over a period of time

long-term debt to equity ratio A common measure of financial leverage; calculated by dividing long-term debt by stockholders' equity

long-term liability An organization's debt that will be paid or eliminated beyond the current year or operating cycle

lower-of-cost-or-market (LCM) rule An accounting rule that requires businesses to value their ending inventories at the lower of cost or market value, the latter typically being defined as current replacement cost

M

maker The party who has signed a promissory note and is thus obligated to pay a certain amount to another party by a certain date

management by exception A technique in which managers set upper and lower tolerance limits for deviations and investigate only deviations that fall outside these tolerance ranges

managerial accounting The function of gathering, processing, and analyzing information (both quantitative and qualitative) to (1) provide information to internal parties for planning and controlling operations and (2) develop product or service cost

margin of safety The excess of sales over break-even point; calculated in units as actual sales in units minus break-even sales in units or in dollars as actual sales dollars minus break-even sales dollars; can also be calculated as a percentage

master budget A complete set of operating budgets (sales, production, purchases, etc.) and projected (pro forma) financial statements

matching principle An accounting principle requiring that expenses be recorded (to the extent possible) in the same accounting period as the related revenues

material price variance The cost saved (favorable) or lost (unfavorable) because of the difference between the actual price paid for material and the standard price for material purchased

material quantity variance The cost saved (favorable) or lost (unfavorable) because of the difference between the actual quantity of material used and the standard quantity of material allowed for the goods produced during the period multiplied by the standard material price

materiality An accounting principle referring to the relative quantitative or qualitative importance of accounting information as to the influence that information may have on a financial statement user's decision

maturity date The date that the maker of a promissory note must pay its maturity value to the payee

maturity value The sum of the principal and interest due on a promissory note on its maturity date

minority interest The portion of ownership interest of a subsidiary not owned by the parent company

mixed cost A cost that is comprised of both a variable and a fixed element

moving-average method An inventory costing method in which an average cost of goods on hand is used to establish the cost basis of ending inventory; used with a perpetual inventory system

N

natural resource A long-term asset, such as a coal deposit, oil and gas reservoir, or tract of standing timber, that is extracted or harvested from, or from beneath, the earth's surface; a wasting asset

negative goodwill The result of purchasing a company for less than the fair market value of the acquired net assets; this amount then proportionately reduces specific asset values

net income (net loss) The positive (negative) difference between an entity's revenues and expenses during an accounting period

noncontrollable cost A cost that a manager cannot authorize or directly influence in terms of dollar magnitude

nonoperating revenue The inflow of new assets into a business from "sideline" (nonprimary) company activities

non-value-added activity An activity that increases the time spent on a product or service but does not increase its worth to the customer

normal cost system An inventory valuation method that uses actual costs of material and labor and an estimated (predetermined) cost for overhead to compute product cost

note payable An obligation that is documented by a legally binding written commitment known as a promissory note; can be either a current or long-term liability, depending on its maturity date

O

off-balance sheet financing The use of long-term obligations that are not reported in an entity's balance sheet to acquire assets or services

operating activity Any transaction or event related to the normal production and delivery of goods and services by a business

operating cycle The time elapsing from the use of cash in the normal operating activities of an entity to the collection of cash from the entity's customers

operating expense A cost that an entity incurs in its principal business operations

operating income An entity's gross profit less its operating expenses; represents the income generated by an entity's principal line or lines of business

operating lease A lease that is usually cancelable by the lessee, covers a short term, and does not transfer ownership rights or risks to the lessee

operating revenue The inflow of new assets into a business from the sale of products or services considered the company's primary operations

outstanding stock The number of shares of a given class of stock owned by a company's stockholders

overapplied overhead The result of applying more overhead (through the use of a predetermined rate) to the Work in Process Inventory than the actual amount of overhead incurred

overhead Any cost incurred in the manufacturing area that is not directly traced to the product, or any service-related cost that is not directly traced to performing a service for sale to others

P

par value The specific dollar amount per share that is printed on each stock certificate

parent company A company that owns more than 50 percent of another company (the subsidiary)

partnership An unincorporated business with two or more owners

patent An exclusive right granted by the a government to manufacture a specific product or use a specific process

payee The party to whom the maker of a promissory note must eventually pay the maturity value of that note

period cost Any cost related to the selling and administrative functions of an organization

periodic inventory system An inventory accounting system in which inventory outflows are not accounted for during the period; the dollar value of ending inventory is determined by counting the goods on hand at the end of each accounting period and then multiplying the quantity of each item by the appropriate per unit cost

permanent account An account whose period-ending balance is carried forward to the next accounting period

perpetual inventory system An inventory accounting system in which a perpetually updated record of the quantity of individual inventory items and their per unit costs is maintained

petty cash A limited amount of cash that is kept on hand by a business to pay for small items

posting The process of transferring accounting data from a journal to the appropriate general ledger accounts

predetermined overhead rate A budgeted overhead cost per unit of activity that is used to assign overhead to products or services

preemptive right The right of a stockholder to retain a proportional ownership interest in a corporation when additional stock is issued

preferred stock A class of stock that has certain preferences or advantages over a company's common stock

prepaid asset A future expense that a company has paid in advance

present value The current value of one or more future cash receipts (payments) that have been discounted at the market rate of interest rate

principal The amount initially owed by the maker of a promissory note

prior period adjustment A restatement of the balance of Retained Earnings because of a correction of an error in a past accounting period

product cost Any cost related to the manufacture of a product or performance of a service; includes direct material, direct labor, and manufacturing overhead

pro forma financial statement A projected or budgeted balance sheet, income statement, statement of cash flows or statement of changes in stockholders' equity; the end result of the master budgeting process

process costing system An inventory costing system that is used by manufacturers producing mass quantities of similar goods

process map A type of flowchart that indicates all steps taken in performing an activity

profit center A responsibility center in which the manager is responsible for controlling costs and generating revenues

profit margin A ratio that indicates the portion of each sales dollar that is left after expenses; calculated as income divided by sales

profit-volume graph A visual depiction of the relationships among revenue, volume, fixed costs, and variable costs showing the profit or loss amounts at each volume level; the point at which the total cost line insects the volume axis is the break-even point

Public Company Accounting Oversight Board (PCAOB) A five-member, private-sector, not-for-profit corporation created by the Sarbanes-Oxley Act of 2002; its purpose is to oversee the auditors and auditing firms of publicly held companies; members are appointed by the SEC

purchase allowance A price concession granted by a supplier in exchange for keeping damaged or defective goods

purchase discount A discount offered by a supplier to encourage prompt payment of credit purchases made by their customers

purchase return A reduction in an amount owed to a supplier as a result of returned goods

Q

quick asset A current asset (cash, a cash equivalent, a short-term investment, and the net amount of current notes or accounts receivable) that can be spent or deposited in a very short period of time

quick ratio A measure of an entity's liquidity; calculated as quick assets (cash and cash equivalents, short-term investments, and net current receivables) divided by current liabilities

R

ratio analysis An analytical technique that involves studying the relationship between two (or more) financial statement items

relevant range An organization's normal annual operating range of activity

replacement cost The current cost required to buy an asset similar to one that is already in use

responsibility center An organizational subunit under the control of a designated manager

retail inventory method A periodic inventory method that requires information to be kept on the retail prices of the goods purchased and a cost-to-retail percentage to be determined to estimate the cost of ending inventory; provides better internal control than most periodic systems because the retail value of goods that should be on hand at year-end is known

retained earnings The total profits generated by a company and not distributed to stockholders

return on equity A key measure of a corporation's profitability; calculated by dividing net income, less preferred stock dividends, by average common stockholders' equity

return on investment A ratio that indicates the income generated by an organization or organizational subunit relative to the asset base used to produce that income; calculated as income divided by asset investment

revenue recognition rule An accounting rule requiring revenues to be both realized (or realizable) and earned before they are recognized (recorded)

revenue An increase in assets or decrease in liabilities resulting from an entity's profit-oriented activities

reverse stock split A decrease in the number of shares of a company's stock accompanied by a proportionate increase in the stock's par value

rolling budget A budget that consistently plans for the upcoming 12-month period; when one budget month (quarter) ends, a new month (quarter) is added

S

sales allowance A price reduction granted to customers to persuade them to keep damaged or defective merchandise

sales discount A reduction in price offered to customers to entice them to pay their account balances on a timely basis

sales price variance The revenue earned (favorable) or lost (unfavorable) because of the difference between the actual selling price for goods (services) and the budgeted selling price for goods (services) multiplied by the number of units sold

sales return A refund paid to or a reduction of the amount owed by customers who return damaged, defective, or unwanted merchandise

sales volume variance The revenue earned (favorable) or lost (unfavorable) because of the difference between the actual volume of goods (services) sold and the budgeted volume of goods (services) multiplied by the budgeted selling price

salvage value The estimated value of an asset at the end of its useful life

secured bond A bond collateralized by specific assets of the issuing company; sometimes referred to as a mortgage bond

Sarbanes-Oxley Act of 2002 (SOX) A U.S. law enacted in response to several major corporate scandals; also known as the Public Company Accounting Reform and Investor Protection Act of 2002; establishes new or enhanced standards for all U.S. public company boards of directors, managers, and public accounting firms

Securities and Exchange Commission (SEC) A U.S. federal agency that regulates the sale and subsequent trading of securities by publicly owned companies; also oversees the financial reporting and accounting practices of those companies

sole proprietorship An unincorporated business owned by one individual

source document Any supporting item that identifies the key features or parameters of business transactions; examples include invoices, sales slips, legal contracts, and purchase orders

specific identification method An inventory costing method in which the actual per unit cost for each inventory item is used to establish the cost basis of ending inventory

standard cost system An inventory valuation method that uses budgeted norms for material, labor, and overhead to develop product cost

standard cost A budgeted cost to manufacture one unit of product or perform a single service

standard quantity allowed A measure of quantity that translates the actual output into the standard input quantity that should have been used to produce that output

standard A norm or average

stated interest rate The rate of interest paid to bondholders based on a bond's face value; also known as the face, contract, or coupon interest rate

statement of cash flows A financial statement that accounts for the net change in a business's cash balance during a period; summarizes the cash receipts and disbursements from a business's operating, investing, and financing activities

statement of stockholders' equity A financial statement reconciling the dollar amounts of a corporation's stockholders' equity components at the beginning and end of an accounting period

stock dividend A proportionate distribution of a corporation's own stock to its stockholders

stock option A right to buy a company's stock at a future date at a guaranteed price

stock split An increase in the number of shares of a company's stock accompanied by a proportionate reduction in the stock's par value

stockholder An owner of a corporation

straight-line method A depreciation method that allocates an equal amount of depreciation expense to each year of an asset's estimated useful life

subsidiary A company that has more than 50 percent of its stock owned by another company (the parent)

T

T-account An account typically used for illustrative or analytical purposes whose name is derived from its shape; such accounts are not part of any formal accounting system

temporary account An account whose period-ending balance is transferred or closed to Retained Earnings in a corporation or to an owner capital account in a sole proprietorship or partnership

temporary difference A difference between an entity's taxable income and pretax accounting income that arises from applying different accounting methods for tax and financial accounting purposes

term of a note The time from the date a promissory note is signed, not counting the signing date, to the date the note matures

time value of money concept The idea that a dollar received (or paid) currently is worth more than dollar received (or paid) in the future because the current dollar can be invested to earn interest

times interest earned ratio A financial ratio used to evaluate a firm's ability to make interest payments on its long-term debt; calculated as (net income, interest expense, and income taxes expense) divided by interest expense

trademark A distinctive name, symbol, or logo used to identify a specific business entity or one of its products

transfer price An internal charge that allows a producing department to "sell" goods or services to another internal department; generally no actual funds are distributed between the departments and these amounts are eliminated in the preparation of external financial statements; allow a cost center to become a profit center

Treasury bill (T-bill) A short-term promissory note issued by a government; is considered a basically risk-free investment instrument

treasury stock Common or preferred stock that has been issued by a corporation and then reacquired by that corporation; is often held for future distribution to corporate executives (or other internal parties) under stock option plans

trend analysis The study of percentage changes in financial statement items over a period of time

trial balance A two-column (debit and credit) listing of a business's general ledger account balances

U

underapplied overhead The result of applying less overhead (through the use of a predetermined rate) to Work in Process Inventory than the actual amount of overhead incurred

unearned revenue An amount that has been received in cash by the business but for which the business has not yet provided the product or service that will cause the earnings process to be complete

unit of measurement concept The accounting principle dictating that a common unit of measurement is used to record and report transactions and other financial statement items

units-of-production method A depreciation method in which an asset's useful life is expressed in the number of units of production or use; depreciation expense for any given period is calculated as actual asset usage multiplied by the unit rate of depreciation

V

value-added activity An activity that increases a product or service's worth to a customer and for which the customer would be willing to pay

variable cost ratio The variable cost percentage of each revenue dollar; calculated as (100 percent − CM ratio), or total variable cost per unit divided by unit selling price

variable cost A cost that changes in total in direct proportion to changes in activity as long as operations are within the relevant range; a cost that remains constant on a per-unit basis with changes in activity

variance analysis The process of determining whether a variance is favorable or unfavorable and finding its underlying cause

variance A difference between actual and budgeted prices or quantities

W

working capital The difference between an entity's current assets and current liabilities

INDEX

PHOTO CREDITS